INSIDERS' GUIDE®

INSIDERS' GUIDE® TO
BALTIMORE

FOURTH EDITION

ELIZABETH A. EVITTS AND NANCY JONES-BONBREST

INSIDERS' GUIDE®

GUILFORD, CONNECTICUT
AN IMPRINT OF THE GLOBE PEQUOT PRESS

The prices and rates in this guidebook were confirmed at press time. We recommend, however, that you call establishments before traveling to obtain current information.

To buy books in quantity for corporate use or incentives, call **(800) 962–0973, ext. 4551**, or e-mail **premiums@GlobePequot.com**.

INSIDERS' GUIDE®

Copyright © 2002, 2004, 2005 Morris Book Publishing, LLC
A previous edition of this book was published by Falcon Publishing, Inc. in 1999.

Text design by LeAnna Weller Smith
Maps by XNR Productions, Inc. © Morris Book Publishing, LLC

ISSN: 1529-5893
ISBN-13: 978-0-7627-3499-3
ISBN-10: 0-7627-3499-X

Manufactured in the United States of America
Fourth Edition/Second Printing

Port of Baltimore. BALTIMORE AREA CONVENTION & VISITORS ASSOCIATION/RICHARD NOWITZ

[Top] *Baltimore's Inner Harbor.* BALTIMORE AREA CONVENTION & VISITORS ASSOCIATION/RICHARD NOWITZ
[Bottom] *Night view.* BALTIMORE AREA CONVENTION & VISITORS ASSOCIATION/RICHARD NOWITZ

Baltimore skyline. BALTIMORE AREA CONVENTION & VISITORS ASSOCIATION/RICHARD NOWITZ

Johns Hopkins Hospital. BALTIMORE AREA CONVENTION & VISITORS ASSOCIATION/RICHARD NOWITZ

Peabody Library, Mount Vernon. BALTIMORE AREA CONVENTION & VISITORS ASSOCIATION/RICHARD NOWITZ

The Washington Monument. BALTIMORE AREA CONVENTION & VISITORS ASSOCIATION/RICHARD NOWITZ

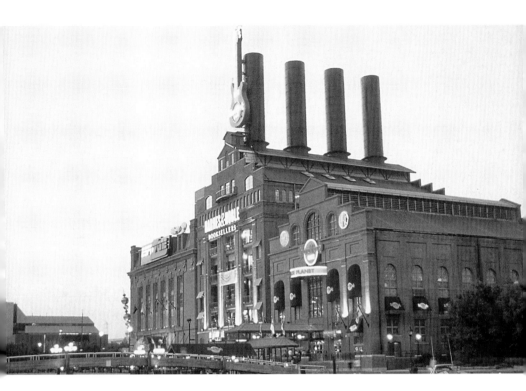

[Top] *Power Plant on the Inner Harbor.* BALTIMORE AREA CONVENTION & VISITORS ASSOCIATION/RICHARD NOWITZ
[Bottom] *Baltimore's Penn Station.* BALTIMORE AREA CONVENTION & VISITORS ASSOCIATION/RICHARD NOWITZ

Fells Point. BALTIMORE AREA CONVENTION & VISITORS ASSOCIATION/RICHARD NOWITZ

Harborplace. BALTIMORE AREA CONVENTION & VISITORS ASSOCIATION/RICHARD NOWITZ

M&T Bank Stadium. BALTIMORE AREA CONVENTION & VISITORS ASSOCIATION/RICHARD NOWITZ

Oriole Park at Camden Yards. BALTIMORE AREA CONVENTION & VISITORS ASSOCIATION/RICHARD NOWITZ

Sailing on the Inner Harbor. BALTIMORE AREA CONVENTION & VISITORS ASSOCIATION/RICHARD NOWITZ

[Top] *Docked boats on the Inner Harbor.* BALTIMORE AREA CONVENTION & VISITORS ASSOCIATION/RICHARD NOWITZ
[Bottom] *OpSail Baltimore.* BALTIMORE AREA CONVENTION & VISITORS ASSOCIATION/RICHARD NOWITZ

Fort McHenry National Monument. BALTIMORE AREA CONVENTION & VISITORS ASSOCIATION/RICHARD NOWITZ

CONTENTS

CONTENTS

Directory of Maps

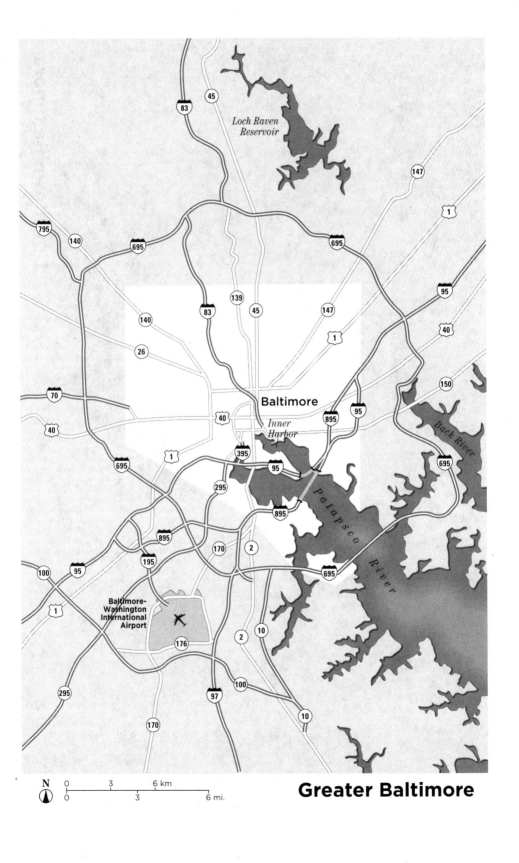

Greater Baltimore

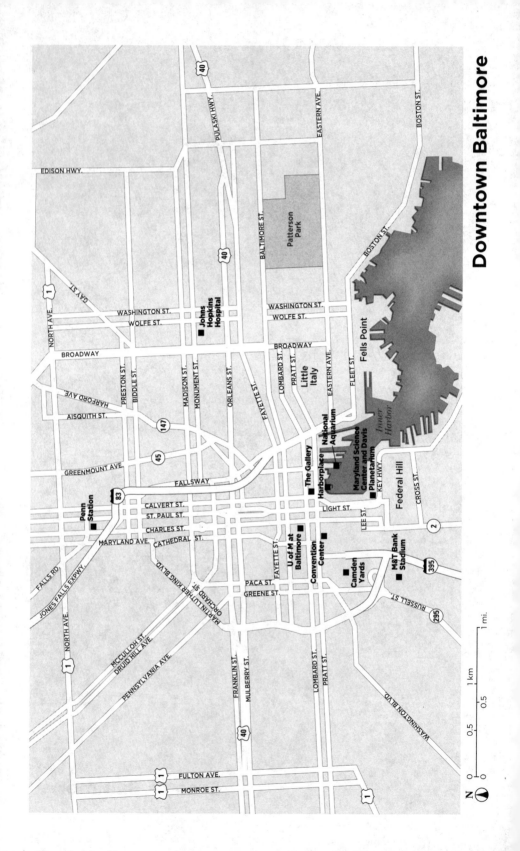

Downtown Baltimore

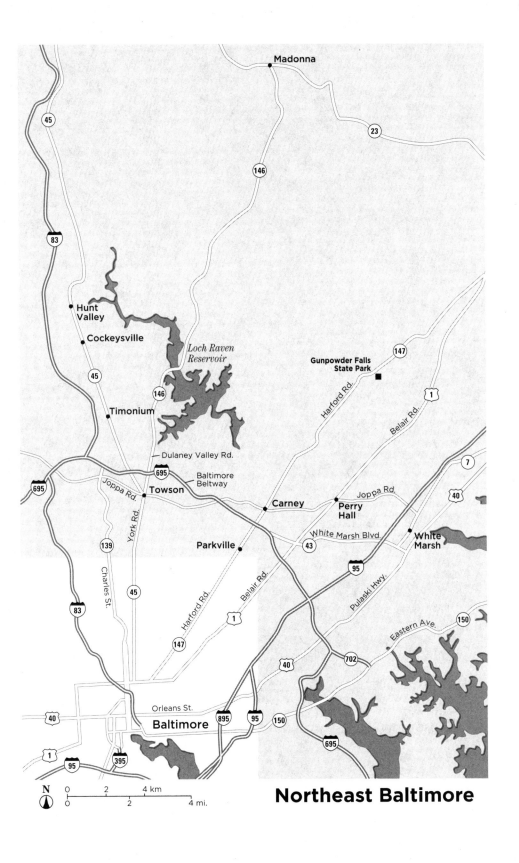

Northeast Baltimore

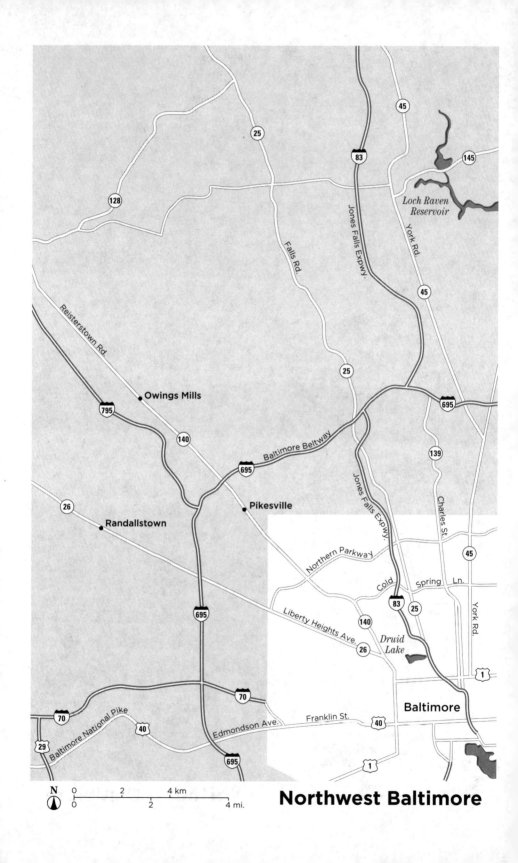

Northwest Baltimore

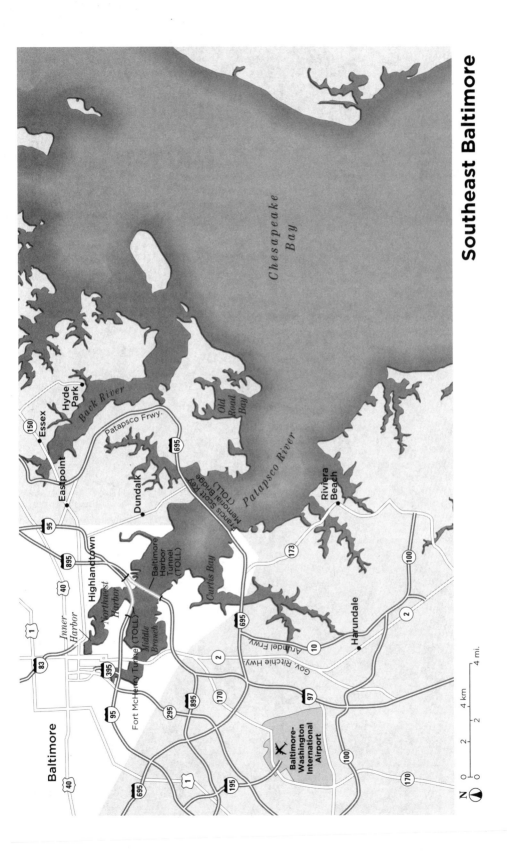

Southeast Baltimore

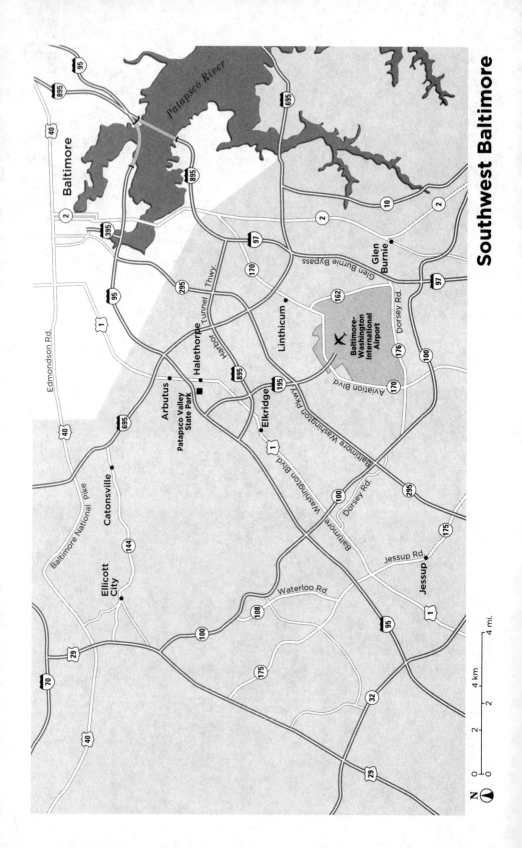

Southwest Baltimore

PREFACE

Baltimore has many faces. It is a big city that greets thousands of foreign visitors every year, but it's a small town, filled with friendly people and good neighbors.

It is a modern city, among the world leaders in medical advances. Yet, Baltimore is a city of history. From Fort McHenry to the majestic Mansard rooftops that hover over the shaded parks of Mount Vernon Square near the city's center, it is still, in many ways, the land of Lord Calvert.

We are a city of firsts. We've done more things first than any other city in the country. We had the first commercial railroad train, the first strip shopping center, the first Catholic cathedral, the first American rabbi, and hundreds of others. But we are also slow to change. Some businesses in Baltimore have been operating from the same spot for more than the 200-plus years that our city has been incorporated. Some Baltimore families live in the same houses their great-grandparents lived in.

Baltimore owns a skyline filled with metal and glass towers. Our Inner Harbor is a showplace. But, we are also a city that time forgot—home to row upon row of archaic buildings with gleaming white marble steps.

We are, for the most part, a city that is easy to get along with. But, true to our heritage, we will put our back up if threatened. We grouse among ourselves but defend each other when it's us against them.

We stay in touch with each other at crab feasts and church bazaars, at neighborhood bars and ethnic festivals. Our favorite summer treat is a snowball and please, don't confuse a snowball with a snow cone, a slushy, a Slurpee, or any other kind of icy confection. A Baltimorean invented the snowball machine, that wondrous mechanism that drops perfect, soft pebbles of ice into a cup. And whether it's smothered in chocolate syrup with marshmallow whip or root beer syrup with a scoop of vanilla ice cream, it's the only thing that can cool you right down to your toes on a hot summer day.

But if you don't like the weather, just wait a minute. It will change. We've had 86-degree Christmases and snow on Easter. We've seen hot and muggy Aprils followed by cool Julys. It can be a pain, but it's Baltimore. So we keep sweaters handy in the summer and shorts nearby in the winter. We expect it, because Baltimore's weather is like the city itself—a dichotomy. New and old. Forward thinking, yet filled with ghosts. A city of independent neighborhoods that form an eclectic conglomeration. A metabolic mix of color, ethnicity, history, and culture that enjoys its collective diversity.

We welcome you to join us. Join the fun—join the family. Join the ongoing celebration that is Baltimore.

ACKNOWLEDGMENTS

A special thank you to the city of Baltimore and its many organizations for maintaining such comprehensive and accessible information. The librarians and the staff at the Research Room of the Enoch Pratt Library are the best around, and the Downtown Partnership helped in providing valuable information. Larry Noto and the entire staff at the Baltimore Area Convention and Visitors Association deserve a medal for continually taking time out of hectic schedules to assist with images and information. Thanks to Teddy Brach at the American Visionary Arts Museum and to the Department of Transportation.

Thank you to my family for their continued support and their feedback and assistance in this project. Finally, I want to acknowledge Nancy Jones-Bonbrest, my coauthor.

—Elizabeth A. Evitts

I am foremost grateful to the many, many people who took time out of their busy schedules to talk with me and answer my often very detailed questions. To the endless public relations specialists who provided photographs, press kits, and that "inside" information—thank you. The conversations I had with these and so many other people have ensured that this book is a true reflection of the area.

My first call was to Nancy Hinds, director of communications for the Baltimore Area Convention and Visitors Association. Nancy not only supplied many crucial contact names and numbers, but also an endless number of wonderful slides that show off the great sights throughout the city of Baltimore. I am grateful also to Donnet Yatsko and Patrice Shultz at Metropolitan Regional Information Systems Inc. (MRIS) for the detailed information in the Relocation chapter and to Harriett Sagel at the Baltimore–Washington International Airport for her much appreciated help. Frank Fulton, David Buck, and others at the Maryland Mass Transit Administration, State Highway Administration, and Maryland Department of Transportation provided valuable information for the Getting Here, Getting Around chapter.

I also extend my thanks to Bert Basignani and Tim McKenna for their insights and information on the Maryland wine industry, as well as to Rory Calhoun Nagy, Boordy Vineyards, for digging up a great photograph only two days before the Wine in the Woods Festival.

Thanks to the Baltimore Office of Promotions for their generous help with contact information and to The Globe Pequot Press for offering me this assignment, which afforded me the exceptional opportunity to contribute to the city I love.

Finally, I especially thank my family—my husband, Lou, for his support and encouragement and my daughter, Sydney.

—Nancy Jones-Bonbrest

HOW TO USE THIS BOOK

The pages you are now thumbing through are a combination of things—a scrapbook of discoveries, observations, trials and errors, memories, and, probably most of all, love for the Baltimore area. If we've succeeded in what we set out to accomplish, the book should convey—and become—some or all of the same things for you.

But that requires several things from you. First, you have to use this book. It's a guide, after all. It's not meant to sit in your house while you trek through Baltimore. Take it with you, mark it up, highlight places you want to visit or things you've already seen. Put stars against the best stuff, or put Xs next to the ones you didn't like. Use it as a diary of your visit, putting notes in the margin or on the inside front and back pages. Put it to use. Keep it close by for its maps, its insights, its selections, its ability to tell you more about where you are than you might find on your own.

Second, you have to tell us if you find something you like, something you dislike, or if information contained within the pages becomes inaccurate. Our goal has been to present accurate information; if we have failed, either because of the usual changes in businesses and attractions or because we made an error of our own, tell us. We need to know so we can fix it for the next edition. You can reach us at: *Insiders' Guide,* The Globe Pequot Press, P.O. Box 480, Guilford, CT 06437, or visit our Web site (www.insiders.com).

WHICH WAY IS NORTH?

We have tried to make things easy to follow. Baltimore's city limits do not fully take into account the area we wanted this book to address, so instead we've concentrated on the Greater Baltimore area, which in most cases we have defined as that which can be contained within I-695, commonly known as the Baltimore Beltway.

We have made exceptions. They reflect a reality we cannot overcome—that people and places are not easily defined by geographic boundaries. To that end, we offer information about the area near Baltimore-Washington International Airport, which is where many tourists stay in hotels and motels, attend conferences, or visit either on their way into or out of town. We have included information about Hunt Valley, an area about 15 miles north of Baltimore with hotels and conference facilities. Similarly, we have included information about White Marsh, a growing suburb where the tourist trade seems to be growing as well.

We have broken the area into four distinct geographic areas, named by their geographic location if you were to look down on the city from above. These areas—Northeast, Northwest, Southeast, and Southwest—are not consistent with the names people give the area. Baltimoreans discuss their city in terms of neighborhoods. However, one glance at just the sample of communities covered in the Relocation chapter makes it obvious why we could not expect to craft a well-organized book broken into neighborhoods and neighboring towns too numerous to count. The maps we've provided give the best indications of what our areas include. Insiders' Tips (indicated by an 🛈), offer quick insights.

Basically, the east-west divider with which we chose to define our regions is Interstate 83 to State Highway 139 (Charles Street) from the north, extending down to State Highway 2 (Hanover Street and

Ritchie Highway) to the south. The north-south divider of our regions is State Highway 150 (Eastern Avenue) from the east until you reach U.S. Highway 40, which extends west. It isn't a perfect crossing, nor would any other one be, but it works for our purposes here.

We made another exception as a concession to the realities of our area. A significant portion of Baltimore's tourist emphasis is on the area surrounding the Inner Harbor—including Harborplace, Oriole Park at Camden Yards, M&T Bank Stadium, Little Italy, and Fells Point. We've created a Downtown district that encompasses these areas. It's a sort of hole in the middle of the four-area system explained previously. Our Downtown district's boundaries include North Avenue to the north, Edison Highway and Highland Avenue to the east, Cross Street and the northwest branch of the Patapsco River to the south, and I-395 (Martin Luther King Jr. Boulevard) to the west. For people visiting the city proper, this Downtown district offers activities, restaurants, events, and other things that are either within walking distance of each other or a short bus or taxicab ride between.

The intersection of Charles and Baltimore Streets is known as "ground zero." This is where the north/south and east/west addresses generate. Streets running north to south in the city are north streets above Baltimore Street and south streets below it. An example would be Charles Street, our east-west divider throughout the book. Heading north from Baltimore Street, it's North Charles Street; heading south, South Charles Street. Similarly, Charles Street serves as the city's east-west divider. So if you are looking for West Eager Street, you know that you need to be west of Charles Street, because if you were on the east side of Charles Street, you would be on East Eager Street.

A typical listing in this guide has the name of the business or organization on the first line and the address, telephone number, and Web site (when available) on subsequent lines. If the address includes a town or city name after it, then it is outside the official city limits of Baltimore. If no town is listed after a street address, then it is within the city limits of Baltimore, but that does not necessarily mean that the establishment is in Downtown Baltimore. For instance, the B&O Railroad Museum is listed under Southwest in the Attractions chapter. You know it's in Baltimore because its address shows it as being on West Pratt Street, with no town name after it. It's listed as Southwest because it is outside of the Downtown district we created.

OTHER HINTS ABOUT THE BOOK

Telephone Numbers

In Maryland, callers must dial the three-digit area code to make any call. This additional dialing is required because Maryland recently added a new area code to the Baltimore area. Most lines have a 410 area code; however some have the newer 443 area code. Although virtually no telephone numbers contained within this book use the new area code, we still thought it would be a good reminder to people unfamiliar with our wacky telephone calling requirements if we included the 410 area code before all telephone numbers. You have to use these new 10-digit numbers, including the three-digit area code, but if you fear being charged for it, rest easy. You will not be charged for a long-distance call unless you dial a 1 before the area code.

Highway Numbers vs. Road Names

We've included the highway numbers for most main roads, although a number of people in the area refer to roads by their more common names. This may cause problems if you ask someone where I-695 is. Most people refer to this loop around the city as the Baltimore Beltway. If you have to ask for directions, give the place you are trying to get to and the street address, whenever possible. Based on this information you should be able to find the right way, probably using common road names rather than the highway numbers. (See the Getting Here, Getting Around chapter for more information.)

Have Fun

We wish this book was available when we were finding out about Baltimore, since it would have saved us lots of time and energy over the years. But don't expect it to do everything for you. Nothing can replace your own experiences when you visit a city or town. Our hope is that we've found ways to make your stay in Baltimore more enjoyable and fun. If we've done that, then we truly have accomplished what we set out to do.

Enjoy!

AREA OVERVIEW

Baltimore is a fascinating mixture of old and new. Its buildings, its businesses, its people, and its image run the gamut from progressive to old-fashioned—sometimes all in the same block. In this chapter we provide a general overview of some of these people and places as well as tell you other chapters in which you'll find more information about these subjects.

THE PEOPLE

Baltimoreans are good neighbors. We're the kind of folks who will stop to give you directions, who'll help you find your lost cat. We might not agree with our neighbors' politics, but that won't stop us from watching their house while they are away on vacation.

We like to get together. In addition to all the citywide festivals that are held every year, neighborhood bazaars, flea markets, bingo nights, crab feasts, ham and oyster suppers, and dances abound. Even though we're a big city, we gather like small-town folks at our churches and our schools and we love to linger over dinner at our local restaurants.

We get together for group yard sales, block parties, and just talking over the backyard fence. Baltimore is not a place where people walk by with their heads down and their eyes averted, fearing to speak. We are congenial. Philosophical dissertations with a stranger while standing in line at the grocery store are not uncommon. Strangers walking up to touch a pregnant woman's distended stomach and ask when she's due are not all that out of the ordinary.

We come in all colors, shapes, and sizes. Overall, we're a good group.

THE PLACE

Perhaps one of the reasons Baltimoreans are such good neighbors is that most of us are clustered together in neighborhoods. Each major area of Baltimore (Downtown, Northeast, Northwest, Southeast, and Southwest) is broken down into neighborhoods. Very few of these neighborhoods were intentionally laid out, so geographic boundaries sometimes overlap. Yet, each neighborhood exudes a distinct character that is often defined by both its historic origin and its population.

The general ethnic mix of Baltimore and its neighborhoods continues to change, but many of the neighborhoods retain their original flavor and, in some cases, the descendants of their original resident populations. Just the names of the local places of business will sometimes tell you what the main industry of the original community was or what its ethnic origin is.

Places such as Little Italy, Little Lithuania, and Greektown are the easiest to figure out. There are also Butcher's Hill, Brewer's Hill, and Pigtown. No misunderstandings there either. Many of the neighborhoods in Baltimore were culled from the estates of prominent citizens. Homewood, Guilford, Bolton Hill, Mount Clare, Mondawmin, Walbrook, and many others carry the names of their original estates. (See the Relocation chapter for more information.)

Cities and towns in Baltimore County to the north, east, and west of Baltimore City as well as Howard and Anne Arundel Counties to the southeast and southwest, respectively, took their names directly from the people who originally settled the land. That's why we have Jonestown, Towsontown (now just Towson), Reisterstown, Ellicott City, Cockeysville, Catonsville, and Dickeyville, to name only a few.

Selected Baltimore Firsts

In 1800 Alexander Brown opened the first investment banking house in America in Baltimore. The original building, which miraculously survived the Great Baltimore Fire, still stands at the southwest corner of Baltimore and Calver Streets. The company, Alex. Brown & Sons, is also still going strong.

In 1803 Thomas More invented the first icebox refrigerator.

Samuel Morse inaugurated the first commercial telegram service here in 1844—which was appropriate, since the first telegraph line in America was erected here that same year.

—*Excerpted from* Baltimore—America's City of Firsts, *a pamphlet published by Baltimore Bicentennial Celebration, Inc.*

Some neighborhoods sprang up because of some industry that drew workers. Fells Point in Downtown was established in 1730 by shipbuilder William Fell and his family and became the hub of shipbuilding (and privateering) in Baltimore during the Revolution (see the History chapter). The streets he named and the area he laid out are still here, populated with local crafters, great little shops, and lovers of old things. (See the Antiques and Collectibles chapter.) Baltimore has many neighborhoods that were once mill towns. Hampden, in Northwest Baltimore, is one of those, as are all the neighborhoods that cluster around the Jones Falls Valley. The valley was once lined with mills that were powered by the swiftly running waters of the Jones Falls.

Baltimore does have a few neighborhoods, however, that were specifically designed as residential tracts. Peabody Heights, established in the 1890s and renamed Charles Village in the mid-1970s, is one of these areas. You can see the original tracts in the different housing styles that were constructed by each builder: porch fronts in the 2800 block of Maryland Avenue and bowed fronts in the 2600 block; five-story, 20-foot-wide houses on Charles Street; two-story, 13-foot-wide houses on Howard Street. There were houses for every income and every size

family in the original Peabody Heights, and Charles Village continues today as one of Baltimore's most eclectic areas.

Interestingly, Baltimore also boasts the first neighborhood ever designed specifically as a suburb. Walbrook was laid out in 1870 but did not have a long suburban life span—it was annexed by the city in 1888, as was Hampden.

One truth, then, about Baltimore is woven throughout the city and its neighborhoods: It is an area of history, and it is because of that history that much of Baltimore was built in the first place.

BIG BUSINESS

Baltimore's location prompted the growth of Baltimore's business interests. Because we boast the best protected harbor in the world and, at the same time, are central to the Eastern seaboard (as close to New York and Massachusetts as we are to Norfolk and the Carolinas), Baltimore was an obvious choice for businesses that needed to touch both North and South and reach West.

The cotton mills that made Baltimore the largest supplier of southern cotton duck canvas in the entire world were a natural. Baltimore, an industrialized city with plenty of water for power, was just a hop, skip, and

---

If you're moving to Baltimore, you must exchange your valid out-of-state driver's license and your car registration for their Maryland counterparts within 30 days. Call MVA at (800) 950-1682 for how to go about it or be prepared to pay the fines.

---

a short rail commute to the raw cotton suppliers of the South. As for customers, they were right here, as long as most ships that came to port were under sail.

It was this ability to get products to market just about anywhere in the United States that made Baltimore boom, and much of its current economy still revolves around the transportation industry. The port has a huge economic influence, contributing $1.4 billion a year and 126,700 direct and indirect jobs. Railroads, warehousing, and distribution are once again a rapidly growing sector of business in Baltimore, and Baltimore–Washington International Airport has become one of the busiest airports in the country.

Baltimore also has retained a solid manufacturing base. General Motors, Black and Decker, and Bethlehem Steel all have facilities in Baltimore. We also claim a growing number of high-tech, defense industry manufacturers, perhaps, in part, due to our proximity to the nation's capital. Being near Washington, D.C., also spurs some of the smaller businesses in Baltimore, particularly those related to real estate and tourism. A great many people who come to visit Washington also make the short trip north to Baltimore, and many residents of the Washington area come here regularly to shop at the Inner Harbor, see the sights, and attend sporting events. Some former residents of D.C. have settled in Baltimore because of the relatively short commute by car or train (about 40 minutes) and because the real estate is cheaper and the quality of life higher.

The growing business focus in Baltimore, however, is on service industries. Education, medicine, international banking

and investment, international trade, real estate, and tourism are all big business in Baltimore.

Maryland rates as the best-educated workforce in the country due largely to the many hospitals and research universities in town. World-renowned colleges and research universities like Johns Hopkins and the University of Maryland are home to some 45 top federal research labs, and our state houses the highest percentage of professional and technical workers, the second highest number of doctoral scientists, and the third highest concentration of doctoral engineers. As a result, Maryland receives 10 percent of national research and development monies.

Once a state known primarily for its blue collar and its blue crabs, Maryland is now home to a burgeoning high-tech and biotech industry. Unlike other states that primarily support Internet companies, Maryland has laid the groundwork for broad technology growth. Some of the most exciting research in the areas of genetics and biotechnology is taking place right in Baltimore's backyard. Maryland is home to 300 of the most vital, fastest-growing bio-science firms in the world, including Celera Genomics, Gene Logic, Human Genome Sciences, and Guilford Pharmaceuticals. Baltimore serves as the backbone to the state's high-tech rebirth. Visionaries, like local developers at Strueuer Bros. Eccles & Rouse, Inc., are reinventing old warehouse space by transforming the large, underdeveloped sites into wired workplaces. Deserted factories—like the American Can Company on the waterfront in Canton—now attract savvy business and retail clients with high-tech office space upstairs and high-end shopping and dining on the ground floor.

Baltimore has a comprehensive banking sector that began with the first mortgage banking house in the United States, Alex. Brown & Sons. Alex. Brown, which recently merged with Deutsche Bank, owns one of the largest market research staffs in its industry. Baltimore is also home to such financial industry giants as T. Rowe

Price and United States Fidelity and Guarantee Company.

THE COST OF LIVING

As cities go, Baltimore is not an expensive one. The real estate boom that skyrocketed rents and housing costs in most major cities certainly affected the housing costs locally, but Baltimore is significantly less expensive than neighboring cities like Washington and Philadelphia. The average home cost in Baltimore in 2002, according to the Metropolitan Regional Information Systems, Inc. (MRIS), was $91,208, which is up 20 percent since 2000. Housing runs the gamut from the exorbitant to the modest. A few years ago you could scoop up a fixer-upper in Canton for the low fifties; now those rehabbed beauties are selling for $200,000. There are still bargains to be found in the city, both for renting and buying (See the Relocation chapter for more information.)

Daily expenses like groceries and eating out are very reasonable. Groceries for a family of four will cost about $120 if that family buys brand names. Eating out is easy with a laundry list of chains and a high volume of outstanding locally owned cafes and restaurants. (See the Restaurant chapter for dining out options). Clothing and amenities can also be found at reasonable prices. We have all the big national stores, but one of Baltimore's best attributes is its plethora of little shops and specialty markets. There are neighborhood shops with bargains on everything from T-shirts to furniture. Some of our second-hand stores offer designer and vintage clothing for a steal (see the Shopping and Antiques and Collectibles chapters for specifics).

When it comes to making a living, Maryland has one of the country's lowest poverty rates and ranks among the top states in median household and per capita personal income. Staying on the job is easier, too, when you have some of the best child care in the country. Maryland was rated in the top ten states for quality of child care by *Working Mother* magazine in August of 1999.

While jobs are on the rise, crime is on the decline. Baltimore earned a bad reputation for its high number of drug-related homicides in the mid-1990s, but those

Economic Interests

Maryland is the center of the Boston-Atlanta Corridor on the Atlantic seaboard and borders on Washington, D.C., the nation's capital. Among the 50 states, Maryland ranks 42nd in size and 18th in population. Its per capita income is the fifth highest in the United States. Of Maryland's population age 25 and over, nearly 1/3 hold a bachelor's degree or higher, which is the third highest percentage among the states. Professional and technical workers constitute 25 percent of the state's work force, the highest concentration among states in the nation. In Baltimore there is increasing interest in recycling waterfront industrial buildings to house technology firms, as part of Baltimore's new "Digital Harbor." The Can Company in Canton, for example, is an old manufacturing plant transformed into a mixed-use space that couples high-end retail and restaurants with digitally wired office space for high-tech companies.

—Excerpted from the State Department of Business and Economic Development Web site, www.choose maryland.com.

How to Speak like a Native

If you've come to Baltimore expecting to be able to speak the language, you may have a more difficult time than you expected. Our location causes some problems. Because we are in the middle of the Eastern seaboard, just below that pesky Mason-Dixon Line, when it comes to our culture and our language, we take some of our cues from the South and some from the North.

Whereas in some areas of the country, all cola drinks are called Cokes or Pepsis even if they're Diet Rite, in Baltimore, we call a spade a spade. If you want a Pepsi-Cola, you must order "Pepsi," and a "Coke" is a Coca-Cola. And don't ask for a pop, unless you don't care what you get. We call anything that fizzes a "soda." If you ask for an orange pop, you're likely to get frozen orange ice on a stick!

There are some generic names that you might misconstrue as a simple mispronunciation. "Zinc" is one such word. "Sinks" were originally made of zinc. So when we put our dishes away at the end of a meal, we put them in the "zinc." (We are not mispronouncing "sink.") If you're used to having your hamburger or sandwich on a bun, ask your waitress for a "roll." If you want a sweet roll with your morning's breakfast, ask what type of "buns" are available.

If you want a tissue, ask for a "Kleenex." If you want to put some brown-bag leftovers away, you'll be putting them in the "Frigidair," even if it's a refrigerator made by Hotpoint.

In the summer, we don't barbecue, we "cook out." We live in rowhouses, or rowhomes, not town houses.

If you're hungry for a hoagie, you can find them in a few places, but if you want the Baltimore version, you'll need to go in search of a "sub" shop. "Sub" is the short version of "submarine sandwich," our name for hoagie.

On the other hand, if you want directions to the nearest sub shop, you may encounter a language barrier that is built of more than just the words you use. In Baltimore, we have our own language of sorts. We call it Bawlmerese. No one we know of has documented the origins of the language, though it shares similarities with a dialect spoken in Philadelphia and with England's Cockney. Bawlmerese is spoken mostly on the eastern, northeastern, and southern sides of Baltimore. You will also hear it in valley communities that were once teeming with cotton mills. Though most of the mills are now closed, many descendants of the original settlers remain, and they speak Bawlmerese.

The o's are broad, unless spoken before a consonant, and the t's often come out as d's, as in "wudder." (Wudder, by the way, is the clear, cool liquid that often rains on us. We spell it water.) Sometimes the t's get lost altogether, or syllables are simply left out, as in "Bawlmer," the town in which we live.

L's are often swallowed, and words tend to run together as if there were no space between them. "B'lair" is one of those. It is how we locals pronounce Bel Air, a nearby town in Harford County, and also a road in Bawlmer.

Some words become so Bawlmerized they are hardly recognizable. Take "styrofoam." In these parts it's pronounced, and sometimes even spelled, "skyraphone." On a cold winter night, smoke goes up our "chimbly." When school's out, we like to go "down-e o'shun" to "Ocean City, Murlin" (that would be Maryland), or "Rehoebet

Beach, Delwaware." "The shure," on the other hand, is much closer. If someone you know in Baltimore is going "down-e shure" for the weekend, they're probably only going as far as Middle Fiver, about 25 minutes away. All shure places are on the Chesapeake Bay and the rivers that flow into it.

Baltimoreans go down to ("down-e") lots of places besides the shure and the oshun, even when they're north, east, or west. We often go down to the corner store: or down to a friend's house. Actual direction is of no consequence.

Bawlmerese plays havoc with pronoun references and adjectives as well as direction. Don't faint if you hear a native say that "Me and him went to see dem Birds last night." "Dem Birds" are also known as "dem O's" or "dem Orals"—our baseball team. In fact, a common greeting from a Baltimorean after a winning baseball game is "How about dem O's?" ("A great game!" would be an appropriate response.)

If you want to go to an Orioles game, don't ask the way to Oriole Park. Few people will know what you're talking about. You see, we had an argument over what to call our new stadium. The powers-that-be wanted to call it Oriole Park, the citizenry wanted to call it Camden Yards. So a compromise was reached, and the stadium's formal name is Oriole Park at Camden Yards. Baltimoreans, however, don't care what the formal name is. We call it "Camden Yards" or, more simply, "the Yards."

We're very stubborn like that. Although our airport was long ago renamed Baltimore–Washington International Airport, or BWI, the native Baltimorean will often call it "Friendship." Friendship Airport was the original name.

Oh, and don't be surprised or insulted if someone calls you "hon." The waitresses do it. A woman on the street whom you ask directions from might do it. We mean nothing by it—in fact, it's a term of inclusion. We are a friendly people, and we want you to feel at home . . . hon.

If you're settling here, you can expect the local children to call you Miss Susan (if your name is Susan, that is). Children would never call someone Mr. Smith—too formal—but if he was Paul Smith, they would call him Mr. Paul. It is a show of respect. In fact, Baltimoreans are generally respectful and polite. Of course, the occasional obscenity is screamed from a car window when we're stuck in baseball traffic, but, generally, we are a please-and-thank-you kind of crowd.

If someone holds the door for you, "thank you" and a smile are expected. If you don't give it, don't be surprised if you hear a surly "you're welcome" as the door closes behind you. If you're driving in Baltimore and someone offers you his or her right of way, raise your hand as a thank-you as you pass. It's expected.

Thanks are often given to the store clerk who helps you or the antiques dealer who lets you look around the store. We thank our bus drivers and cabbies when they let us out at our stops, and often the response is not "you're welcome" or another "thank you," but "have a good one . . . ." "One" is the day, the afternoon, or the evening.

And you will, we hope. Have a good one, that is. Hopefully, knowing a little bit about the native tongue will help you get settled in. To help, we've listed a few other words from the Bawlmer lexicon below. Enjoy Bawlmer, hon!

At Mealtimes

boilt aigs: Of course, you can also have them scrammled.

orng jewz: Orng jewz is great with boilt or scrammled aigs.

toess: Smothered in budder and jelwy is always best.

sammich: My favorite is ham and cheese, but you might prefer rosbeef or cormbeef, or maybe even sofcrab.

baffroome: Somewhere you might need to go before meals to wursh, or at least wrench, your hands.

asspern: Take two if you're feeling the effects of a two-martini lunch.

Everyday Items

dest: Where you write letters home.

arn: To keep your clothes pressed.

buwra: Where you put your pressed clothes.

dowl: They used to be on phones, but we don't use dowl phones much anymore.

Around Town

Drood'ul Park: Where the animals in the zoo are.

Li'l Edolwy: A very nice place for dinner. Where lots of Eye-talyans live.

Cammer: You'll need it if you want to take pitchers of the balt iggle at the zoo.

John Hopkins: The native abbreviation for Johns Hopkins, but don't you leave off the s.

Abnew: Like a street, only an abnew. Also, the main street in a neighborhood, as in "I'm goin' down to the abnew to meet mah frens."

Payment: The hard surface of a street or abnew.

Ool: Make sure you have a least two quarts in your car's engine before you get out on the payment.

Quair: Visit one of our churches on Sunday, and you might get to hear one.

Public Services

Far N'gin: The farmun ride in them when they go to put out fars.

Poe-leece: We have foot poe-leece as well as mounted poe-leeces.

beegeen'ee: BG&E—the people to call if your lights go out. Although some Baltimoreans call it the gas kumpknee. (BG&E recently changed its name to BGE, but that's done little to change the pronunciation around town.)

If you want to know more about Bawlmerese, there have been actual books written about it! Consult one of our many local libraries or bookstores.

---

numbers have decreased somewhat. Baltimore's mayor and police force are dedicated to reducing crime on our city streets and their efforts can be seen in the numbers—the homicide rate dropped below 500 in 2000 for the first time in years. Although Baltimore can feel like a small town, it is a city and it does have its share of muggers and panhandlers. There is no need to fear the city, but a level of awareness is required to successfully navigate Downtown. Common sense tells us not to leave items in our cars that might attract a burglar and to keep purses and shopping bags close when walking the streets.

CLIMATE

Being centered on the Eastern seaboard, we tend to get the tail end of cold fronts coming down from the north, followed by the top end of warm fronts coming up from Georgia. Every now and then we are affected by hurricanes, and small tornadoes occasionally touch down.

The fronts that typically drop feet-deep snow on Minnesota and the Midwest usually drop the rest of it in the Appalachian Mountains. Hence, Baltimore does not get very much snow from the west, unless a cold front meets moisture coming from the south. Then we can get foot after foot of very wet snow. There is sometimes significant snow or rain from the northeast. Nor'easters, as they're called, come rarely, but when they hit, they do so with a vengeance.

Besides the occasional messy travel conditions, the only real problem caused by Baltimore's weather is what to wear. Take one particular moment in time, in September. One morning temperatures started out in the 60s—normal for fall, but then, September is not quite fall until late in the month. By the end of the day, temperatures were in the 90s as a warm front moved through. The next day started out hot; then a thunderstorm brought a cool breeze.

You will hear a lot of Baltimoreans say, "It's not the heat, it's the humidity," and they would be correct. If it's 90 in Baltimore and the humidity is 30 percent, then it feels about 85. If it's 90 in Baltimore and the humidity is 95 percent—which is possible—then it feels about 120. The only places where it can be hotter than Baltimore when Baltimore is HOT is a steam bath or an oven.

The cobblestone circle around the Washington Monument on Charles Street has a regular traffic pattern: Cars simply split to either side of the monument rather than drive around the circle. But in suburban Towson, the busy traffic circle on York Road in the heart of town has a circuitous traffic flow.

We also take note of the windchill index in winter, which can make temperatures seem much colder. Normally (and we use that term loosely here), winter weather usually hits in late December and continues through early February. Daytime highs are normally in the upper 30s and overnight lows are in the low 20s to upper teens. In the spring and fall, temperatures tend toward the upper 50s and 60s, with lows in the mid-40s. Summer has highs generally in the low to mid-80s range, but there is always a week or so where temperatures are 95 or higher.

Baltimore also has what is often referred to as "Indian summer." The term describes periods of warm weather following the first freeze; however, Baltimoreans tend to use the term to refer to any warm period that occurs after we've had some cold, freeze or no.

When summer is at its sultriest, expect your hair to curl and your shirt to stick. Wear earmuffs and mittens in the winter, because the north wind doth blow. But always know that a beautiful day in Baltimore is just around the corner. When the weather is just right, Baltimore can be the most beautiful place in the world—hot sun, cool, flower-scented breezes, and clear blue sky. The birds sing, the crickets chirp, and just about all is right with the world.

Vital Statistics

Mayor: Martin O'Malley

Governor: Robert Ehrlich

Outlying counties: Baltimore County, Harford County, Howard County, Montgomery County, Anne Arundel County

Populations:
    City: 638,614
    State: 5,458,137

Nickname: Charm City (most common), Monument City, Mob City

Average temperatures:
    July: High 88° F, Low 72° F
    January: High 41° F, Low 28° F

Average rain: 41 inches
    Snow: 20 inches
    Sun: 120 days

Major universities: University of Maryland System, Johns Hopkins University, Towson University, Loyola College, Goucher College, Morgan State University

Major area employers: Port of Baltimore; Johns Hopkins Institutions; The University of Maryland, Baltimore; General Motors; Deutsche Bank Alex. Brown; St. Paul Companies

Major airport: Baltimore–Washington International Airport

Military bases: Aberdeen Proving Grounds, Fort Detrick, Fort Meade, Patuxent River Naval Air Station, United States Naval Academy, Andrews Air Force Base, United States Coast Guard Yard at Curtis Bay

Alcohol laws: DWI limit .08; DUI limit is .07; must be 21 years old to purchase or consume alcohol; bars open until 2:00 A.M.; liquor stores closed on Sunday, but bars can be open and packaged goods may be bought from bars on Sunday.

Daily newspapers: *The Baltimore Sun, Daily Record*

Sales tax: 5 percent state sales tax, 11.5 percent tax on car rentals

Major interstates: Interstate routes such as I-68, I-95, I-70, I-695 are marked with a blue and red interstate shield-shaped sign.
    United States routes such as U.S. 1, U.S. 15, U.S. 40, U.S. 113, U.S. 301, and U.S. 219 are marked with a white U.S. shield-shaped sign.
    Maryland State highways such as MD 2, MD 45, MD 140, and MD 404 are marked with a white Maryland rectangular sign.
    The Baltimore Beltway (I-695) is 51.59 center line miles.

Public transportation: Maryland Mass Transit Authority (410-539-5000, 800-543-9809, www.mtamaryland.com)—Light Rail, Baltimore Metro Subway, Maryland Rail Commuter Service (MARC) Train, Maryland Mass Transit Authority Buses

Driving and Traffic Safety Laws (as provided by the Maryland State Highway Administration): Maryland law limits the extent to which speed limits may be raised or lowered.

The most notable restrictions are those that prohibit any speed limit greater than 65 miles per hour and any limit above 55 miles per hour anywhere except on interstate highways or other expressways.

Every child under four years old, regardless of weight, and every child weighing 40 pounds or less, regardless of age, must be secured in a U.S. DOT–approved child safety seat. Children and young people up to 16 years of age must be secured in seat belts or child safety seats, regardless of their seating positions. It is strongly recommended that all children ride secured in the rear seat. Drivers and front-seat passengers regardless of their ages, are required to wear seat belts. It is strongly recommended that all occupants wear seat belts.

Motorcycle operators and passengers are required to wear U.S. DOT–approved helmets. Operators must wear eye protection as well.

Stay alert and give driving your full attention.

Show courtesy to other drivers, pedestrians, and cyclists.

Comply with our traffic laws and heed all traffic signs, signals, and markings.

Avoid driving aggressively.

Vehicles must stop for school buses when the bus's red flashers are on (except when the bus is on the opposite side of a highway divided by a barrier or median strip).

After stopping and yielding to pedestrians and other vehicles, a right turn or left turn from a one-way street to another one-way street may be made on a red signal, except where prohibited by a sign.

Maryland has a mandatory adult seat-belt law that covers the driver and the front-seat passenger next to the door, if the passenger is at least 16 years of age. Maryland's law allows primary enforcement, i.e., police may stop a vehicle and issue citations to violators solely for violating the seat-belt law. Both the driver and an adult passenger may receive tickets for not wearing seat belts.

Chamber of Commerce and Visitors Bureaus:

Maryland Office of Tourism Development, 217 East Redwood, 9th Floor, Baltimore 21202; (800) 719-5900; www.mdisfun.org

Annapolis and Anne Arundel County Conference & Visitor Bureau, 26 West Street, Annapolis 21401; (410) 280-0445; www.visit-annapolis.org

Baltimore Area Convention and Visitors Association, 100 Light Street, 12th Floor, Baltimore 21202; (410) 649-7000 or (800) 343-3468; www.baltimore.org

Baltimore City Chamber of Commerce, 3 West Baltimore Street, Baltimore 21201; (410) 837-7101

Baltimore Office of Promotion, 7 East Redwood Street, Suite 500, Baltimore 21202; (410) 752-8632; www.baltimore events.org

Calvert County Department of Economic Development, 175 Main Street, #202, Prince Frederick 20678; (800) 331-9771; www.co.cal.md.us/cced

Carroll County Visitor Center, 210 East Main Street, Westminster 21157; (800) 272-1933; www.carr.org/tourism

Dorchester County Tourism, 2 Rose Hill Place, Cambridge 21613; (410) 228-1000, (800) 522-TOUR; www.tourdorchester.org

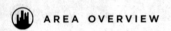

Garrett County & Deep Creek Lake Chamber of Commerce, 15 Visitors Center Drive, McHenry 21541; (301) 387-4386; www.garrettchamber.com

Harford County Tourism Council, 3 West Bel Air Avenue, Aberdeen 21001; (410) 575-7278 or (800) 597-2649; www.harfordmd.com

Howard County Tourism Council, 8267 Main Street, P.O. Box 9, Ellicott City 21041; (410) 313-1900 or (800) 288-8747; www.visithowardcounty.com

Kent County Office of Tourism, 400 High Street, Chestertown 21620; (410) 778-0416; www.kentcounty.com

Ocean City Convention & Visitors Bureau, 4001 Coastal Highway, Ocean City 21842; (410) 289-8311 or (800) OC-OCEAN; www.ococean.com

St Mary's County Division of Tourism, P.O. Box 653, Leonardtown 20650; (800) 327-9023; www.co.saint-marys.md.us

Washington County Convention & Visitors Bureau, 16 Public Square, Hagerstown 21740; (301) 791-3246; www.maryland memories.org

Time and temperature phone number: (410) 662-9225

GETTING HERE, GETTING AROUND

B altimore serves as a hub for every-thing from Amtrak trains to Grey-hound buses, regional commuter rail lines to national and international airlines. To meet the growing needs of these travelers, getting here and getting around the area can be simple and cheap or expensive and complicated. The choice is yours. Happy traveling.

GETTING HERE
By Air

Baltimore–Washington International Airport
End of Interstate 195 East, Linthicum
(410) 859-7111, (800) I-FLY-BWI
www.bwiairport.com
Baltimore–Washington International Airport (BWI) is located in Linthicum, about 9 miles from Baltimore and 32 miles from Washington, D.C. The airport sits just minutes off Interstate 95, the major north-south East Coast highway. BWI is the fastest growing airport in the Baltimore–Washington region and among the fastest growing airports in the nation. Operated by the Maryland Aviation Administration of the Maryland Department of Transportation, BWI covers an expanse of 3,596 acres, with 1.4 million square feet of passenger terminals. Passenger terminals are separated into five concourses (four domestic and one international) with 64 jet gates and 18 gates dedicated to commuter aircraft. Thirty-one commercial airlines service BWI, with an average of 648 domestic and 22 international flights departing daily. Some 52,000 passengers use the airport each day, and more than 19 million people traveled through BWI in

2002. The additional security measures at the airport often translate into very long lines. Security checkpoints can add a significant wait to your travel time, so it makes sense to get to the airport at least two hours before flight departure.

Southwest is the fastest growing air carrier at BWI and represents more than 44 percent of consumer travel through the airport. US Airways, American, Delta, and United make up the majority of the rest of the domestic air travel. On average, there are 64 nonstop domestic destinations leaving out of BWI. Eight airlines provide international scheduled service, including Aer Lingus, Air Canada, Air Jamaica, Air Tran, British Airways, Ghana Airways, Icelandair, and USA 3000. Some of the regularly scheduled nonstop international destinations include Dublin, Cancun, London, Reykjavik, Toronto, and the Caribbean.

BWI's excellent rail connections make the airport a great choice for passengers traveling throughout the Baltimore–Washington, D.C., area and beyond. Amtrak, Maryland Rail Commuter (MARC), and the Light Rail all serve the airport (see By Rail later in the chapter).

BWI is currently in the midst of a $1.8 billion expansion that began in April 2001. The five-year project will increase parking by 12,000 spaces, add new concourses, and improve access to terminals. The extensive construction in and around BWI can mean additional delays, so plan to arrive early for departing flights.

The airport features all the creature comforts that weary travelers seek, from restaurants and bars to observation decks, local cultural displays, and sitting areas. A master list of all departures and arrivals is available on the second floor at the center of the airport, near the large escalators. If you want to know which gate to go to, try there first. The wings each have names that start with A, B, C, and so on in alphabetical sequence from south to north (or right to left) as you look directly at the airport structure. The A and B wings are on the side you enter by car or bus. The center area is wing C; wings D, E, and the International Pier are to the north (or left, as you look from the parking structure).

GETTING TO THE AIRPORT

Access to the airport is convenient from I-95 using I-195, a feeder road designed to connect that major north-south highway with the airport.

The Light Rail system offers transportation to and from the airport for a fee of up to $1.60 one way. The Light Rail will take you to Downtown Baltimore or as far north as Hunt Valley (about an hour and 40 minutes away). Tickets are available at the Light Rail terminal on the south side of the airport terminal. Call (410) 539-5000 for more details.

 When driving within a 5-mile radius of BWI, tune in to 1040 AM for current roadway conditions and take note of variable message signs.

ONCE AT THE AIRPORT

BWI has a two-story terminal, with check-ins on the second floor and pickups on the first level. Park on the third or fourth level of the four-story parking garage if you're departing, and have the folks greeting you park on the first level of the garage if you are being picked up. This saves a lot of energy, especially if you pack heavy (and who doesn't?).

The loading and unloading locations directly in front of each airline's check-in area are convenient spots for dropping someone off. If someone will be waiting for you to pick up your baggage on the first level upon arrival, it's a good idea to send them around the half-mile loop outside the parking garage a couple of times. Don't even think of parking or having others park in the loop near the terminals; increased security at the airport means no cars are allowed to stop here.

Duty-free shops, gift counters, magazine stands, and candy stores are open during the day and early evening in the central terminal area, between gates B and C, and between gates C and D. Restaurants, coffee shops, bars, and several fast-food options also serve travelers in these corridors. There are arcade machines, fax phones, and a courtesy phone to contact taxicabs and hotel shuttles in these corridors. Large bathroom facilities with baby changing stations are also available. If you have kids, the observation deck is the perfect place for a good view of incoming and outgoing flights, and there's a scale model airplane that kids can climb on (see the Kidstuff chapter for more information).

RENTAL CARS AT BWI

If you are renting a car, you need to go to the baggage claim area, where rental car check-in sites are lined up. When you leave the airport, your rental car will be on the ground floor of the terminus. Rental cars are to be returned to the surface parking lot located directly in front of the entrance to the airport's terminal garage. When approaching the airport on I-195, take exit 1A (Aviation Boulevard), turn onto Elm Road, and proceed past the Maryland Department of Transportation headquarters. Follow signs to the Rental Car Return Area on the left. Some of the rental car providers include Avis, (800) 831-2847; Budget, (410) 859-0850; Dollar, (800) 800-4000; Enterprise, (800) 325-8007; Hertz, (410) 850-7400; and National, (410) 859-1136. If you are calling to reserve a car from out of town, use the company number in your local telephone directory. Rates range from $30 to $80 a day, depending on the size and make of the car, the options you choose, and how long you are planning to rent.

AIRPORT SECURITY

Security has tightened at all U.S. airports, and BWI is no exception. The U.S. Transportation Security Administration has transferred the screening of selected passengers from the aircraft boarding areas to the security checkpoints at airports across the country. This can translate into long lines and delays, so plan on arriving at least two hours before your flight. Additionally, all passengers are now required to have their boarding passes before going through the security screening areas.

E-ticket receipts, itineraries, and vouchers are no longer valid. Boarding passes can be obtained at the ticket counters when you enter the airport or at curbside check-in. You can also use the airline self-check-in kiosks. In addition to a boarding pass, remember to bring valid government-issued photo identification, such as a driver's license or passport.

By Roadway

INTERSTATES AND HIGHWAYS

I-695, known locally as the Baltimore Beltway, forms a circle outside the city limits. No matter where you get on, you will end up in the same place in about an hour's driving time. (We don't recommend this, unless you are really, really bored.) The road varies in width from two lanes in each direction on the east side to five lanes in the Northeast quadrant, where rush-hour traffic leaving the Social Security Administration in southwestern Baltimore County fills the roads beginning about 3:30 P.M. If you get on I-695 on the east side of the roadway, you'll have to drop $2.00 to cross the Francis Scott Key Bridge over the Patapsco River.

I-83, the Jones Falls Expressway, heads south into the city from Pennsylvania, but its path is confusing. From the Pennsylvania line to I-695 (the Baltimore Beltway), about 30 miles, it's a straight shot, but at the Beltway southbound traffic has to get

Confused about the Inner Loop and Outer Loop of the Baltimore Beltway? It's simple. The Inner Loop is closest to the city, with exit numbers going in ascending order, while the Outer Loop is outside the Inner Loop and has exit numbers going in descending order.

onto the Beltway for one exit before veering right, then left onto I-83 again. Once back on I-83, southbound traffic will find itself dropped right near Little Italy, leaving a convenient trip of about 4 blocks west to reach the Inner Harbor. The northern section of the highway becomes icy in extremely cold weather; the southern portion in the city can be slow going during rush hour and when it rains.

I-95 runs north to Maine and south to Florida, passing on the east side of Baltimore. During rush hour, traffic bottles up at the entrances to the Baltimore Beltway. The highway goes through the Fort McHenry Tunnel, one of the two tunnels that carry motorists beneath the Patapsco River toward the Inner Harbor area. The tunnel costs $2.00 for cars and provides an easy connection to I-395, aka Martin Luther King Jr. Boulevard.

State Highway 295, the Baltimore–Washington Parkway, is an old, four-lane connector between Baltimore and Washington, D.C. Beautifully lined with trees (rather than the standard concrete, soundproof walls), the highway can be a good alternate route for travel between the two cities. Heading north, the highway passes the Capital Beltway (I-495 in Washington), I-195 (which takes you to BWI Airport), and I-695 (the Baltimore Beltway) before dropping into the city near Oriole Park at Camden Yards, M&T Bank Stadium, and the Baltimore Convention Center. A right turn on Conway Street leads you to the Inner Harbor. Heading south into Washington, the highway leads to New York Avenue, which can take you to the Capitol area. Past New York Avenue, Highway 295

Selected Baltimore Firsts

Edward Warren, reported to have been only 13 years old at the time, made the first American hot-air balloon ascension in 1784.

Even in 1806, our proximity to Washington had its benefits! It was in that year that the first federally financed road opened in Baltimore. Of course, that proximity and that road didn't seem so great when the British tried to land during the War of 1812!

The first horse-drawn streetcar line opened in Fells Point in 1859.

Not to be outdone, even by ourselves, the Baltimore Union Passenger Railway Company, the first commercial electric streetcar line in the western hemisphere, began service in Baltimore in 1885.

Baltimore ushered in the modern era when the first drive-in gas station opened for business in 1917. Baltimore got a treat in 1920 when Hubert Latham made the first nonstop airplane flight over a city. He circled Baltimore's skyline 22 times.

The first coal-burning, steam locomotive, the Tom Thumb—a stagecoach on wheels—was built here in 1830 by B&O as well as the first electric locomotive, built in 1894. The elevated electric railway to run it on was erected in 1893.

The first passenger train and the first commercial carrier left from Baltimore in 1830 and 1827, respectively.

The first train to operate at 30 miles per hour got on the B&O tracks in 1830.

The first train to have a center aisle boarded passengers in 1831, and the first air-conditioned train in the world, B&O's Columbian, left Baltimore in 1931.

We also lay claim to the first city railroad station, the President Street Station, which opened in 1853.

—Excerpted from Baltimore—America's City of Firsts, a pamphlet published by Baltimore Bicentennial Celebration, Inc.

---

turns into I-295 and takes motorists toward Richmond, Virginia. If you use this highway, watch out for police officers in the medians behind the trees. The speed limits are strictly enforced.

I-395, aka Martin Luther King Jr. Boulevard, carries motorists from I-95 into Downtown Baltimore near the baseball and football stadiums and the convention center. During morning rush hour the road into the city is bottlenecked; in the afternoon, the lanes carrying motorists out of the city are filled. Also, if heading out of the city on this road, keep right to head north, following signs for northbound I-95 and New York. Heading south toward Washington requires motorists to stay to the left to feed into southbound I-95.

I-795, aka the Northwest Expressway, heads from Reisterstown in northwest Baltimore County to the Baltimore Beltway (I-695). It serves as a major feeder route to and from bedroom communities in Owings Mills and Reisterstown and connects, via State Highway 140, to Westminster, a community about 40 miles northwest of Baltimore.

I-895 is a bypass for I-95, offering motorists a second tunnel under the Patapsco River near the Inner Harbor. The Harbor Tunnel Thruway, the older of the two tunnels beneath the river, costs $1.00 to go through and connects to the Baltimore Beltway. It also provides access to I-97, which leads to Annapolis, the state capital, about 25 miles southeast of the city.

U.S. 40 is a major east-west highway running through Baltimore. As the highway runs through the city, at times it takes on the names Pulaski Highway and Orleans Street. However, the U.S. 40 signs are clearly marked. It's a good alternate route to I-95 and I-895 that doesn't require a toll—you don't have to cross the Patapsco River. Instead, you'll catch lots and lots of traffic lights. Still, it's a good route for seeing different parts of the city.

I-70 comes into the Baltimore Beltway as the major route for traffic coming in from Pittsburgh or other points west. It does not reach the city limits.

By Bus

Baltimore Travel Plaza
6523 O'Donnell Street
(410) 633-6389

Lots of free parking and bright, clean, inviting facilities are the lure of the Baltimore Travel Plaza, conveniently located off I-895 and I-95 in Northeast Baltimore. If you are planning to take a Trailways or Peter Pan bus heading to New York City, Atlantic City, or a variety of other locations up and down the East Coast and beyond, then this is the place to catch it in the Baltimore area.

Like the Greyhound terminal on Fayette Street near Baltimore's Inner Harbor, the Baltimore Travel Plaza also offers access to Greyhound buses, traveling to New York City more than 10 times a day and to points farther north, south, and west. In addition, a number of tour buses heading to points all over the Mid-Atlantic, especially Atlantic City, Pennsylvania Dutch Country, and western Maryland, also offer pickups and drop-offs at the Travel Plaza, which also sports more than 100 hotel rooms for travelers looking for a night's rest.

The plaza offers clean and open counters for purchasing tickets, plenty of wood tables and chairs for waiting for the bus, and a variety of time-killing ideas. Sbarro's,

a pizza place; KFC; the Tradewinds Restaurant, a moderately priced buffet and sit-down restaurant; and Buckhorn's, a steak and potato and so much more restaurant across the street, provide the eats. Vending machines and a small shop feature magazines, newspapers, snacks, and touristy wares, such as T-shirts, Orioles caps, and Maryland mugs. There is also an array of video games for idling moments waiting for the loudspeaker's call for your bus.

It's about a 15-minute taxicab ride from the Travel Plaza to the Inner Harbor area. The plaza is also accessible by city bus.

Greyhound Lines
210 West Fayette Street
(410) 752-1393, (800) 231-2222
www.greyhound.com

The weakest link in appearance in Baltimore's public transportation systems, the Greyhound bus station still provides thousands of travelers with valuable and reliable service to myriad points at all hours of the day. Ocean City, Atlantic City, New York City, Atlanta, Miami, Boston, Indianapolis, and Chicago are all served from this station. Customers enter on Fayette Street, buy tickets to the right of the small building, and exit to buses waiting out back. It's dark, cramped, and loud, making the potential for missteps or unplanned adventures great. The station, about 10 blocks west of the Inner Harbor, is not a great place in which to wile away hours as there are barely enough plastic chairs for the occupants of one bus, much less the five or six buses that can be loading and unloading at any given hour. Parking can be challenging, but there are garages 1 block away on Cathedral or Fayette Streets. As far as creature comforts, the bus station shows its age. Vending machines accept coins and dollar bills for candy bars, sodas, coffee, and aspirin. Newspapers are available at a small kiosk or at machines outside on Fayette Street.

Tickets purchased two weeks or more in advance can be reserved with a credit card; tickets purchased within two weeks of departure must be obtained from the ticket window, but advance purchases are not required because Greyhound does not work on a reservation system.

By Train

Amtrak
Penn Station, 1525 North Charles Street
(410) 291–4261, (800) USA–RAIL
www.amtrak.com
Penn Station is a marvel, with beautiful light-wood benches with high backs waiting for weary travelers to sit on for a minute or a day. A major terminal between New York and Washington, Penn Station attracts a great many business travelers heading to those cities on the Metroliner. Travelers can also take advantage of the Acela Express, Amtrak's high-speed train that travels between Boston and Washington, D.C. The station also manages to draw people looking to head farther north, and south to Florida. Located conveniently on Charles Street and just off I–83 (the Jones Falls Expressway), the station's biggest challenge used to be parking for those picking up or dropping off passengers. However, a new parking garage has answered many a train traveler's prayers. During normal business hours, you can find a store selling juices, candy, and magazines and a small sandwich counter.

By Water

Eastern Baltimore County's rivers and the Inner Harbor provide good boat access to the area, and a number of local marinas

offer daily, weekly, and monthly mooring rates. See the On the Water chapter for more information.

GETTING AROUND
By Car

Compared with other major East Coast cities, Baltimore's road system is in pretty good shape. Unlike its neighbor to the south, Washington, where roads seem to defy any logic, Baltimore's highway and road system is pretty easy to understand, and (believe it or not) readily available maps give fairly good descriptions of what you might encounter. One of the few challenges facing motorists is finding roads that go in the direction you want to travel; many streets run one way through the city, leaving visitors and the uninitiated perplexed.

Here's a simple approach to the one-way system: If the road you want to be on is going the opposite direction, head one street farther, make either a right or left turn (depending on the location of the road you're seeking), then another right or left as soon as possible. Before long you should see the road you want. It's that easy. As you get farther from downtown, the roads become less complicated. Unlike some East Coast locales, Baltimore's roads are well marked in most cases. Major highways and interstates heading in all directions are clearly posted with highway signs.

Remember, many of the people in our area have encountered the same confusion you might be running into. Therefore, don't be afraid to ask for directions or help. We tend to be friendly when approached the right way. When asking for directions, try to be (no pun intended) direct: Ask how to get from point A to point B. As in most big cities, rush hours and lunch hours can make traffic devilish, to say the least. When you want to be somewhere, the best route often varies with the time of day and the weather conditions.

 During weekdays, WBAL 1090 AM has traffic reports at 11-minute intervals from 6:11 through 9:00 A.M. and from 3:44 to 6:00 P.M. Major traffic tie-ups are also reported during the station's hourly news reports.

Major north-south roadways include Belair Road, Harford Road, and Charles Street, and east-west roadways include Northern Parkway, North Avenue, and Frederick Road. Watch out for Hillen Road, which seems to pop up everywhere you look. It, along with many of the city's less traveled roads, come and go, as if someone erased a few blocks then drew it back in. It's confusing, but it gives you a feeling of pride when you overcome it.

Most people who drive in the Baltimore area follow the rules. We use our directional signals, we try to follow speed limits, and we appreciate people who don't indicate their lack of preparation, planning, or understanding of our roads. In other words, ask, ask, ask before you get lost, lost, lost.

Ice, sleet, and snow, any and all of which can occur on winter nights, can be a problem on Baltimore roadways. Even though a number of schools and businesses close at the first sign of snow, those of us who have to or want to drive in inclement weather can often make a mess of things. This isn't the territory where chains are needed, but you do need common sense.

Part of the problem is that we don't often get enough snow for plowing; instead, local crews apply lots of sand and salt. It melts the snow and ice into a brown slush that often refreezes the following evening if temperatures again drop below freezing. Compounding matters is that many motorists don't respect the cardinal rule for driving in winter weather: Moving slow is fine in the snow. On the bright side, we can be grateful that these days usually only come a couple of times a month, normally from December to March, and most major highways are well cared for, even in the worst weather. Mass transit, which seems to operate remarkably well in these conditions, can be a safe, efficient, and prudent option. Remember, forewarned is forearmed.

If you're listening to a traffic report in Baltimore, the "JFX" is the Jones Falls Expressway (or I-83); the Harbor Tunnel Thruway is on I-895; and the Fort McHenry Tunnel is on I-95. The "MLK" is Martin Luther King Jr. Boulevard (I-395), and the Northwest Expressway is I-795.

RULES OF THE ROAD

There are several driving rules you need to observe in the state of Maryland.

• Seat belts are mandatory for all front-seat passengers. Police officers will pull over motorists and issue tickets to those who violate the law. Children younger than four or weighing less than 40 pounds must be kept in a child safety seat.

• Right turns are permitted when the traffic light is red, except where posted otherwise. Left turns on red lights, when going from one one-way road to another one-way road, are also allowed, except where signs say "All Turns Prohibited" or "No Turn On Red."

• Speed limits are strictly enforced, using all means available, including VASCAR radar (which usually is not picked up by radar detectors), speed guns, and aerial surveillance. On highways, state troopers, operating olive-and-brown cars, make their fair share of speeding arrests, especially on holiday weekends and at busy travel times. Radar detectors are allowed.

The maximum speed limit in Maryland is 65 mph, but this speed is only allowed on major highways leading away from urban areas. Watch for speed limit signs. In rural areas where speed limits are not posted, motorists can travel at 50 mph; in urban areas, the unposted speed limit is 30 mph.

• Motorists must stop for all school buses with their stop signs out or flashing red lights and can be ticketed for violating the law based on the observation of the bus driver.

Baltimore's Horsepower

Mounted police are a magnificent sight; particularly when they are in pursuit. The larger than average horses with helmeted officer astride thunder through the city. Through lines of stalled cars, down narrow alleys or sidewalks, their on-the-hoof raw power is, to say the least, awe inspiring.

Their value in a pursuit is not only in the terror they can engender when riding full-tilt but also in their versatility. Rubber horseshoes allow for a comfortable run on city streets, but the horses can leave the streets if necessary to gallop across and through places where motorized vehicles can't go.

Baltimore's mounted police unit was formed in 1888, making it the oldest in the United States. The unit became necessary when Baltimore annexed adjacent county lands, almost doubling its size. Baltimore's police force up until then had been foot patrolmen, but these patrols simply could not cover the vast, new areas.

Permanent stables for the horses were built in 1899 at what is now the Northern District Police Station at 3858 Kesick Road in Hampden; the original stables and courtyard take up the entire block behind the cabled Victorian brick building.

The horses were moved from that location in 1923 and are currently housed at 401 Holliday Street, a few blocks north of City Hall. Call Public Affairs, (410) 396-2012, to arrange a tour. There is no charge and no minimum number of people required.

The officers of the Mounted Police Unit volunteer for this duty and come from all areas of the city's police department. They must have at least three years of patrol experience before they can be considered. Once trained for the unit, each officer becomes responsible for his assigned mount, who is actually considered a fellow officer, right down to being assigned a badge number. The horses work an eight-hour day and get a 30-minute lunch break and a 15-minute break every hour.

In 1888 there were only 10 officers in the unit. Since then, the mounted police unit has grown or diminished over the years, depending on the city's needs and who's in control of overseeing them. Not long ago the unit was 23 men and horses on neighborhood patrol. Their criminal arrest record was one of the highest in the city, and it won them a unit citation. Their numbers have since dropped, and they are now used more for downtown traffic control and in a ceremonial capacity. This diminished role allows the mounted patrols to stop and answer questions visitors have about the city or the mounted police. These goodwill on-the-hoof ambassadors are part of the city's pride and a direct link to our pastoral heritage.

By Taxi

Baltimore boasts an array of options for people without wheels. For $1.60, plus $1.25 a mile, you can get just about any-where with local cabbies who speak the language, know their way around, and are willing to share some personality and sightseeing suggestions with you. Many cab companies charge an extra dollar for radio-dispatched calls. If you find yourself needing to get somewhere in the Down-town area, it's probably more cost-effective and more efficient to simply hail a cab. Most tourist destinations and major hotels as well as shopping areas and the train station have cabbies waiting nearby.

The following companies provide cab service.

BALTIMORE CITY

Arrow Cab, (410) 261-0000
Diamond Cab, (410) 947-3333
Royal Cab, (410) 327-0330
Yellow Cab, (410) 727-6237

BALTIMORE COUNTY

Arrow Cab, (410) 338-0000

Atwater Cab (based in White Marsh),
(410) 682-2100

County Cab,
(410) 284-3330, (410) 484-4111

Jimmy's Cab (based in Towson),
(410) 296-7200

Valley Cab (based in Pikesville),
(410) 486-4000

BALTIMORE-WASHINGTON INTERNATIONAL AIRPORT/ANNE ARUNDEL COUNTY

Baltimore Airport Shuttle
(410) 821-5387
www.baltimoreairportshuttle.com

The Airport Shuttle
(410) 381-2772
www.theairportshuttle.com

Associated Cabs
(410) 766-1234

Airport Sedan
(410) 768-4444

Hotel Shuttles

Most of Baltimore's major hotels operate shuttle buses to take passengers to the airport, train station, bus station, and other points of interest. It's best to check in advance about whether the place where you are staying provides this free or discounted service.

By Bus

Mass Transit Administration Buses
(410) 539-5000, (866) RIDE-MTA
www.mtamaryland.com
The MTA operates 51 local and express bus lines throughout the Baltimore area, making it one of the best systems of its kind on the East Coast. Practically all parts of Baltimore and most stretches of Baltimore County, Anne Arundel County, and Howard County are accessible by bus.

For many Baltimoreans, the bus is their transportation to work, to play, to sports events, to the theater, to just about every-thing. Most north-south and east-west roads into and out of the city are serviced by at least one bus line. If you're confused

Planning to use public transportation often during a certain day or month? An all-day pass allowing unlimited travel on the buses, Light Rail, and Metro subway is $3.50. They're available at any stop. Buy a Transit Link Card (TLC) by adding $50 to your MARC monthly pass and get a month of unlimited travel on the MARC, Baltimore Metro, buses, and Light Rail as well as Washington's sub-way system. That's a lot of miles for your money.

by the schedule, the routes, or some other aspect of travel on the white and blue buses, ask the first bus driver who stops or call the previously listed number.

Customers pay when they board the bus, and exact change is mandatory. You're going to be putting your money into a machine that gobbles up extra change without a thought for returning the extra coins. Plan ahead. Really. Fares are $1.60 for a one-way pass or $3.50 for an all-day pass.

Keep your eye out for your stop and press the yellow strip running above the windows of the bus to notify the operator of your stop. Drivers don't call out stops unless you request it, so either ask someone to remind you when your stop is coming or stay alert. Smoking, eating, drinking, and playing radios without earphones are all prohibited on MTA buses.

Bus routes are marked with small signs (white with blue trim) on the right side of roadways. Route numbers are on the signs. Schedules are available at most hotels, tourist attractions, and visitor centers. The MTA will also mail one to you.

By Rail

It's only fitting that the city that was home to the first railroad places a major emphasis on rail travel. In the last decade, Baltimore's old rails have been put to significant use by the area's growing Light Rail and MARC (Maryland Rail Commuter) systems. Baltimore also is a frequent stopping point for Amtrak trains.

MARC
(800) 325-RAIL
A total of 81 Maryland Rail Commuter trains operate on three lines running throughout the Baltimore–Washington corridor, eight Maryland counties, and northeastern West Virginia. In all, MARC services an average of 23,445 commuters a day.

For Baltimore, the Camden Line runs between Baltimore and Washington's Union Station (a major hub for transportation in all directions). The Camden Line stops near the Camden Station at Oriole Park at Camden Yards. In all, there are nine stops between Baltimore and Washington, D.C.

MARC's Penn Line starts about 50 miles north of the Inner Harbor in Perryville, off I-95 near the Susquehanna River in Cecil County, and continues south to Penn Station and on to Washington. Ten stops are along the way.

No matter which line you use, ample free parking is available at the stops, making it an affordable way to reach the city. Ride passes are available at the stops; prices vary depending on your point of origin and destination. A one-way fare from Penn Station in Baltimore to BWI Airport is $4.00, while the one-way fee to go from Camden Station to Washington's Union Station is $7.00. Unlimited weekly tickets and unlimited monthly tickets are available.

Central Light Rail Line
(410) 539-5000, (866) RIDE-MTA ext. 2
Baltimore's Central Light Rail Line operates from Hunt Valley, about 25 miles from the Inner Harbor, through the Downtown area near Oriole Park at Camden Yards and on to Cromwell Station/Glen Burnie, a small community about 10 miles south of the Inner Harbor in Anne Arundel County. This system is 30 miles long and serves 32 stops between Hunt Valley and Penn Station to the north. In late 1997, Light Rail service to BWI was added, but the time it takes to get from Timonium to the airport, about 90 minutes, is somewhat disconcerting given that by car it takes about 30 minutes to make the 25-mile trip. A stop at Penn Station, where passengers can pick up Amtrak service, was also opened, making the Light Rail much more useful for out-of-town visitors. The line runs about every 17 minutes during normal hours and every eight minutes during rush hour.

Hours of operation are from 4:00 A.M. to 1:30 A.M. Monday through Friday, 5:00 A.M. to 1:30 A.M. Saturday, and 10:00 A.M. to 9:00 P.M. Sunday. The line also operates special service for baseball and football games (see the Spectator Sports chapter).

Tickets cost $1.60 for one-way trips. If you are planning on riding more than twice a day or need to connect with their other MTA services, buy a day pass for $3.50. It includes unlimited travel that day on Light Rail, regular bus, or Metro Subway. Tickets can be obtained from machines at all stops. Tickets must be purchased before boarding the trains.

Metro Subway
(410) 539-5000, (866) RIDE-MTA ext. 2
Baltimore's Metro provides service between Johns Hopkins Medical Campus to the east and Owings Mills in southwestern Baltimore County. The 15.5-mile subway system has 14 stations scattered east-to-west across the city. It takes about 25 minutes to reach the Downtown area from Owings Mills. Parking at most stops is free, and the parking at Owings Mills is close to a large mall, Owings Mills Town Center, that has more than 100 stores (see the Shopping chapter). If you want to head to the city for a day of sightseeing, the subway from Owings Mills is a fun, clean, and affordable way to go. It's also a great way to get to Johns Hopkins Hospital, which can be a tough place to find parking.

Ride passes are available (exact change only) at machines at each stop, and the cost is $1.60 for a one-way fare, or $3.50 for an all-day pass. Subway cars run about every eight minutes during rush hour, every 10 minutes during the day, and every 15 minutes in the evening and on Saturday. The subway operates from 5:00 A.M. to 12:30 A.M. Monday through Friday and from 6:00 A.M. to 12:30 A.M. on Saturday. No service is available on Sunday. Old Court and State Center Stations close at 8:00 P.M. daily.

By Water

Seeing Baltimore's harbor area from the water provides insights into its industries and history. Several companies provide

MARC trains now provide Quiet Cars for commuters in which cell phones, laptops, radios, and children are not allowed.

tourists with fun and entertaining ways to go from place to place by water; however, availability depends on the season, the weather, and whether tourist groups have made prior reservations. All services depart from the Inner Harbor. (See the On the Water chapter for more information about traveling Baltimore's waterways.)

Clipper City
(410) 539-6277
www.sailingship.com
Two-hour cruises on the bay are available every day from April to October at noon, 3:00 P.M., and 6:00 P.M. Adults pay $12.00, children 10 and younger pay $4.00. Sunday brunch cruises are $30 per person, and reservations must be made in advance.

Harbor Cruises
(410) 727-3113
www.harborcruises.com
Daily lunch, dinner, and moonlight cruises of the harbor are offered by this company. Lunch cruises cost $30 per person, dinner cruises range in price from $46 to $65 per person, and moonlight cruises cost $27 a person. Reservations are required. Passengers must be 21 years old to board.

Harbor Sightseeing Shuttle

If you've got a couple of hours to kill, the shuttle offers a great view of the city as well as access to shopping and historical sites and cultural spots in Canton and Fells Point. You'll get the same water view of Fort McHenry that the British and Francis Scott Key had. Don't forget that an evening trip on the shuttle in summer is enchanting and romantic—a great change of pace that provides a terrific view of the city's skyline.

Ed Kane's Water Taxi
(410) 563-3901
www.thewatertaxi.com
This service visits 12 stops in the Inner Harbor, Fells Point, Canton, and Fort McHenry. An all-day ticket providing unlimited use costs $6.00 for adults and $3.00 for children 10 and younger. The pontoon boats have covers and bench seating.

HISTORY 🏛

H ere in Baltimore, we like to think of ourselves as being on the Chesapeake Bay, but, in truth, we live on the Patapsco River. We're probably better off for it because the Patapsco provides us with many benefits.

Although it is removed from the Atlantic Ocean by about 150 miles, the Patapsco River is a tidal river. And even though the ebb and flow of the ocean can be seen in the Inner Harbor, the 5 miles of river between Baltimore and the bay insulate us from most of the major wave cycles and storms that move up the East Coast. The river has also discouraged attacks by sea.

In addition to protection, the Patapsco provides a connection. It ties Baltimore to trade in Europe, South America, and most everywhere else. That connection served as a lifeline and economic dynamo for the city as it grew from a settlement to a town to a city and emerged as an industrial powerhouse helping meet the needs of a growing nation.

DISCOVERING "FROTH"

Captain John Smith probably only had a small sense of the bounty he discovered in 1608 while exploring the Chesapeake Bay. He described in his journal the area he had found: "Thirtie leagues Northward is a river not inhabited, yet navigable." The river, one of four major waterways that flow into the Chesapeake Bay, was given its Indian name, Patapsco, which many believe meant "backwater" or "tidewater covered with froth." (More than three centuries later, a froth of a different kind, that produced by National Bohemian beer, "Natty Bo" to locals, would garner the attention of beer drinkers.)

What Smith found was vast, relatively flat, open land that the Susquehannock tribe had used for hunting. The Susque-hannocks would venture down from northern Maryland on what would a century later become Charles Street in Baltimore. As impossible as it seems now, bears were abundant then. Over time, the bear proved to be less of an opponent to the Susque-hannocks than smallpox and tuberculosis, new diseases brought to America by early colonists at the end of the seventeenth century. By 1700 only a few hundred surviving Indians lived in any part of Maryland.

DAVID (NOT DAVY) JONES SETTLES

In 1632 proprietor George Calvert, the first Lord of Baltimore, was granted the land north of the Chesapeake Bay. Although Calvert was a Roman Catholic, Calvert-led Baltimore County was tolerant of the Protestants and Quakers who began moving into the area. In 1649 Maryland passed the Toleration Act, allowing any religion to be practiced in the colony.

The first local government of the area, Baltimore County, was established in 1659. The county provided settlers with what they and their ancestors had come from England for—economic opportunity in a place where they could freely practice their chosen religion. Settlers soon began taking sites along the water. In the mid-1600s, they settled near where Fort McHenry now stands and along Harford Road in the northeastern section of Baltimore, near Harford Run.

In 1661 one of Baltimore's first settlers, David Jones, moved onto 380 acres along a stream that would later be named Jones Falls in his honor. Today the Jones Falls Expressway, a six-lane highway running parallel to that stream, also refers to Jones, when it is not being called by its nickname, "the JFX."

WATER AND WHEELS

Activity on and around the waterfront began to grow. One of the first settlements, Whetstone Point, where Fort McHenry now stands, was named a port of entry by act of legislature in 1706. Five years later, the first mill for the area was built along the Jones Falls by Jonathan Hanson.

Transportation was primarily by water, though some roads had been cut in the woods. In 1704 a new law required trees to be cut down so the main road could be widened to 20 feet and, probably more important, marked. Since it was long before travel guides like this one, slash marks charted the course. There was one vertical slash on trees beside the road leading to the church; there were three horizontal lines (one higher than two others close together) on roads heading to the county courthouse.

Soon settlers began making iron for England and growing wheat for the British colonies in the West Indies. The Jones Falls and two other rivers, Herring Run and Gwynns Falls, provided the water power for the iron furnaces and the mills that turned wheat into flour.

LOTS FOR SALE

With an economy in place, workers needed housing. In 1729, 60 acres of land in what is now Downtown Baltimore were approved for division into one-acre lots. Buyers would have to pay the owners, Daniel and Charles Carroll, either 40

Fort McHenry, the five bastioned, pentagonal shaped fort, takes its name from Dr. James McHenry (1753–1816), who served as a medical officer with Gen. George Washington during the Revolutionary War. He later served on the Continental Congress and as secretary of war for presidents Washington and Adams between 1796 and 1801.

shillings an acre or tobacco at the rate of one penny per pound. Philip Jones, a county surveyor, laid out the land. Three roadways, Calvert, Forest (now Charles), and Long (later Market and now Baltimore) Streets, were created. Nine narrow alleys ran between the three streets, and the lots were numbered and divided.

Land buyers agreed to either build a house of at least 400 square feet within 18 months or forfeit the land. The first 18 buyers, all of whom made purchases on the first day the land was available, bought land close to the Patapsco; Charles Carroll selected a lot at the corner of Calvert Street and the harbor basin on January 14, 1730. The surveyor Philip Jones, who selected second, picked land at the foot of Charles Street near the waterfront.

The growing port on the Patapsco became the outlet for sending wheat from fields in western Maryland and Pennsylvania to England and the Caribbean islands. But economic success bred frustration. Merchants chafed at British taxes and commercial policies. As intolerance for British interference continued to grow, Baltimore found its place in the political world of the colonies.

After representatives of the 13 colonies signed the Declaration of Independence in Philadelphia on July 4, 1776, Baltimore soon became a temporary national capital. Leaders feared a possible attack by British troops, so they fled from Philadelphia to Baltimore, where they convened in a newly built tavern named Congress Hall. For 68 days, from December 20, 1776, through February 27, 1777, the delegates handled big and small matters of state in Congress Hall. Delegates granted George Washington powers to pursue war, and they ordered that pigs and geese stay off Baltimore's unpaved streets.

HOME FOR PESKY PRIVATEERS

Baltimore's economy boomed during the Revolutionary War. Shipyards in Fells

Point, named after the wharf's creator, William Fell, produced warships. Privateers from Baltimore, eager to make a buck by sinking British ships or seizing their assets, filled the waters of the Patapsco River and Chesapeake Bay. Between 1776 and the end of the Revolution, about 250 private ship owners armed themselves and were granted government commissions (called "letters of marque and reprisal") that empowered them to seize enemy vessels—and their assets—on planned attacks or in pursuit of trade. Everyone tied to these seizing ships—the sailors, owners, and financial backers—took their share of the booty from these missions.

During and after the war, Baltimore continued to be a commercial hotspot, benefiting greatly from the on-again, off-again trade wars between England and France. Local leaders decided to pursue status as a city. The commissioner who had been appointed to rule Baltimore County was picked in Annapolis, and merchants and businessmen wanted greater control of their own destinies.

Eventually, it happened. On December 31, 1796, the city of Baltimore was born. As the nineteenth century began, Baltimore's population swelled. Doubling by 1810 to 27,000 people, Baltimore passed Boston to become America's third-largest city, trailing only Philadelphia and New York.

"A NEST OF PIRATES"

In 1812 Baltimore again would find itself in the middle of a war with England, and again it would prove to be a financial boon. President James Madison's declaration of war on Great Britain was a problem for the U.S. fleet, which numbered 17 ships. Privateers, whose success in the Revolutionary War had provided good training and income more than 30 years earlier, helped increase the U.S. fleet's numbers. Still, at about 1,000 ships, the British fleet significantly outnumbered America's. During the war, the 126 privateers led the water attack, either seizing

or sinking more than 550 British ships. Frustrated by this successful tactic, the British war leaders called Baltimore "a nest of pirates" and "the great depository of the hostile spirit of the United States against England."

As successful as the privateers were, British troops, led by Admiral Sir George Cockburn, ruled the Chesapeake Bay in the summer of 1814. By the dog days of August, British forces sailed up the Patuxent River on their way to Washington. On August 24, 1814, Baltimoreans could see the smoke on the horizon as the British burned Washington's Capitol, the White House, and other public buildings 40 miles away. In Baltimore residents took the smoke as a signal that they would be next. Under the leadership of Mayor General Samuel Smith, a veteran of the Revolution and a popular politician, the city quickly prepared for an attack.

With Smith's guidance, the newly created militia fortified Fort McHenry, a strategic location guarding the city and its harbor from invasion up the Patapsco River. The 16,000 men, 90 percent of whom were untrained citizens, were ready for battle, though they had practically no realistic chance of winning. On September 12, about 4,700 British troops took the shore on the west side of North Point, a section of the Patapsco River about 8 miles southeast of the fort, as they prepared to take over the city. The Battle of North Point lasted for more than two hours, as the hometown militia held off the British by land. The next day the city shook as British troops bombarded Fort McHenry for many hours.

Francis Scott Key, a lawyer who grew up in Baltimore, watched the bombardment from 8 miles away, on the deck of a boat where truce negotiations were in progress. Fearing the worst, with dawn emerging through fog and rain, Key trained a small spyglass on the fort and saw the tattered, 30-foot-by-42-foot American flag. The emotion of the moment stirred him to write a poem, "The Star-Spangled Banner," on the back of a

CLOSE-UP
Important Dates in Maryland History

10,000 B.C.—First humans arrived by this date in the land that would become Maryland.

1498—John Cabot sailed along Eastern Shore off present-day Worcester County.

1608—Capt. John Smith explored Chesapeake Bay.

1620—Earliest appearance in Maryland of European objects in archaeological context.

1632—June 20, Maryland Charter granted to Cecilius Calvert, Second Lord Baltimore, by Charles I, King of Great Britain and Ireland. The colony was named Maryland for Queen Henrietta Maria (1609–1669), wife of Charles I (1600–1649).

1633—Nov. 22, English settlers on *Ark* and *Dove* set sail from Cowes, England, for Maryland.

1634–1644—Leonard Calvert, governor.

1659–1660—January 12. Baltimore County known to have been established by this date, when a writ was issued to county sheriff.

1663—Augustine Herrman, first naturalized citizen of Maryland.

1689–1690—Maryland Revolution of 1689. Protestant Associators overthrow proprietary officers.

1727—September, *Maryland Gazette,* first newspaper in the Chesapeake, published by William Parks at Annapolis (until 1734).

1729—Baltimore Town established by charter.

1744—June 30, Native American chiefs of the Six Nations relinquished by treaty all claims to land in colony. Assembly purchased last Indian land claims in Maryland.

1766—Sons of Liberty organized in Baltimore County.

1769—Maryland merchants adopted policy of nonimportation of British goods.

1772—March 28, Cornerstone laid for new State House in Annapolis.

1776—July 4, Declaration of Independence adopted in Philadelphia. Engrossed copy signed by Marylanders William Paca, Charles Carroll of Carrollton, Thomas Stone, and Samuel Chase.

1776—July 6, Maryland Convention declared independence from Great Britain.

1777—February 5, First General Assembly elected under State Constitution of 1776 met at Annapolis.

1777—March 21, Inauguration of Thomas Johnson, first governor elected by General Assembly.

1781—March 1, Maryland ratified the Articles of Confederation.

1784—December 30, St. John's College established at Annapolis. General Assembly designated it, with Washington College, as University of Maryland.

1787—September 17, U.S. Constitution signed by Marylanders Daniel Carroll, James McHenry, and Daniel of St. Thomas Jenifer, at Philadelphia.

1788—April 28, Maryland Convention ratified U.S. Constitution, making Maryland the seventh state to do so. Convention adjourned without recommending amendments.

1789—December 19, Maryland ratified federal Bill of Rights, first 10 amendments to U.S. Constitution.

1791—December 19, Maryland ceded land for federal District of Columbia.

1799—Construction began on Fort McHenry, Baltimore.

1814—September 12, British repelled by local militia at Battle of North Point.

1814—September 13, Bombardment of Fort McHenry inspired Francis Scott Key to write "The Star-Spangled Banner."

1827—February 28, Baltimore and Ohio Railroad chartered.

1829—Oblate Sisters of Providence opened school for black children, Baltimore.

1830—Baltimore & Ohio Railroad Station at Mount Clare, first in United States.

1832—In aftermath of Nat Turner rebellion in Virginia, Maryland laws enacted to restrict free blacks.

1837—May 17, *Baltimore Sun* began publication under Arunah S. Abell.

1838—Frederick Douglass escaped from slavery in Baltimore.

1845—Lloyd Street Synagogue constructed in Baltimore, first Maryland synagogue, a Robert Cary Long, Jr., design.

1845—Frederick Douglass published narrative of his life in slavery.

1845—October 10, U.S. Naval Academy founded at Annapolis, when Department of the Navy established officers' training school at Fort Severn, Annapolis.

1849—Harriet Tubman escaped slavery in Dorchester County.

1859—October 16, John Brown launched raid from Maryland on federal arsenal in Harper's Ferry, West Virginia.

1861—April, James Ryder Randall wrote "Maryland, My Maryland."

1861—April 19, Sixth Massachusetts Union Regiment attacked by Baltimore mob.

1861—April 22, Federal troops occupied Annapolis.

1861—June 13, Congressional elections returned Unionist delegation.

1862—May 23, Marylanders opposed one another at Battle of Front Royal.

1862—September 17, Battle of Antietam (or Sharpsburg), 4,800 dead, 18,000 wounded.

1863—late June through early July, Lee's army passed through Washington County en route to Gettysburg and in retreat.

1864—November 1, Maryland slaves emancipated by State Constitution of 1864.

1865—Chesapeake Marine Railway and Dry Dock Company, first black-owned business in state, established by Isaac Myers.

1865—April, John Wilkes Booth assassinated President Lincoln, escaped through Prince George's and Charles Counties.

1870—Maryland Jockey Club sponsored racing at Pimlico track.

1872—General Assembly mandated separate but equal white and black schools.

1876—October 3, The Johns Hopkins University opened in Baltimore.

1885—Baltimore-Union Passenger Railway Company, first commercial electric street railway in country.

1887—Pennsylvania Steel (Maryland Steel, 1891) built blast furnace at Sparrows Point.

1888—October, Maryland flag of Calvert and Crossland colors flown at monument dedication ceremonies, Gettysburg.

1892—*The AFROAmerican* founded by John H. Murphy, Sr.

1894—Baltimore Orioles won their first professional baseball championship.

1899—Building program began at Naval Academy, Ernest Flagg architect.

1904—Maryland Woman Suffrage Association led by Emma J. Maddox Funck.

1904—February 7–8, Baltimore fire, 70 blocks in heart of business district devastated.

1910—August 30, First statewide primary election in Maryland.

1913—Baltimore Chapter, National Association for the Advancement of Colored People (NAACP), formed, second oldest in country.

1914—Babe Ruth pitched for International League Orioles.

1916—February, Baltimore Symphony Orchestra organized under Gustav Strube.

1917—Aberdeen Proving Ground, first testing center of U.S. Army, established.

1920—November 2, Women voted for first time in Maryland.

1931—March 3, "The Star-Spangled Banner" adopted as national anthem.

1935—University of Maryland School of Law opened to blacks after NAACP lawyer Thurgood Marshall brought suit.

1941—April–September, Bethlehem-Fairfield Shipyard produced first Liberty Ship, *Patrick Henry*.

1941—December 7, USS *Maryland* among naval ships attacked at Pearl Harbor.

1946—First photograph of Earth from space is produced at Johns Hopkins Applied Physics Laboratory.

1950—June 24, Friendship International Airport, (now BWI), began operation.

1952—July 31, Chesapeake Bay Bridge opened.

1954—University of Maryland integrated, first state university below Mason-Dixon Line to do so.

1954—First black elected to House of Delegates, from Baltimore.

1954—May, Thurgood Marshall and NAACP won Brown v. Board decision.

1967—Baltimore's Thurgood Marshall is named the first African American to serve on the United States Supreme Court.

1968—Riots follow the assassination of Martin Luther King.

1970—Colts win third Super Bowl.

1977—The 28-story World Trade Center, designed by renowned architect I.M. Pei, opens on the Inner Harbor and is the world's tallest pentagonal building.

1982—Cal Ripken's Oriole career begins.

1983—Orioles win third World Series.

1984—Robert Irsay moves Colts to Indianapolis in the middle of the night.

1987—Dr. Ben Carson, director of pediatric neurosurgery at Johns Hopkins Medical Institutions in Baltimore, leads a medical team that separates West German conjoined twins.

1992—Oriole Park at Camden Yards opens.

1996—Former Cleveland Browns become Baltimore Ravens.

2001—Ravens win the Super Bowl.

sheet of letter paper. This original document is now housed at the Maryland Historical Society. (See the Attractions chapter for more information on the Maryland Historical Society.) It was Key's brother-in-law who suggested it be set to music. It was played first in Baltimore. The song later became the national anthem, but at the time served as a reminder of the militia's unlikely success in defeating a far superior British force. Baltimore's successful defense, coupled with British losses in battles in upstate New York, helped to force the British to accept the Treaty of Ghent, signed on Christmas Eve in 1814.

BUILDING THE B&O

With another war behind them, Baltimore's leaders set out to make the city every bit as historical and cultural as the European cities of their ancestry. Some of the results of this effort remain today. Among them are the Roman Catholic Basilica of the Assumption on Maryland Avenue, the first cathedral of American Catholicism; and the Battle Monument. The city also erected the first monument to honor George Washington, known—simply enough—as the Washington Monument. Baltimore soon became known as "Monument City."

In the late 1820s, word of construction of the Chesapeake & Ohio Canal—the first of its kind—running through Georgetown, south of Washington, D.C., challenged Baltimoreans. Fearing a devastating effect on commerce, Baltimorean Charles Carroll, grandson of the Charles Carroll who obtained the 60 acres of land in Baltimore in 1729 and who at age 91 was the last surviving signer of the Declaration of Independence, began building the Baltimore & Ohio (B&O) Railroad. In 1853 the railroad finally reached its goal: the Ohio River at Wheeling, West Virginia. Besides speeding the movement of goods to the port in Baltimore for shipping, the railroad was responsible for bringing thousands of immigrants to the city, where they hoped to reestablish communities for their ethnic groups in a historically tolerant area. The rapidly growing area afforded them the opportunity to work on railroad and construction projects so they could earn a living. Some of the B&O railroad's tracks are still visible through the pavement in places on Key Highway and other sections of the city, although efforts lately have been made to pave over them for good.

Driven by economic hardships and political upheaval, immigrants streamed to the United States in increasing numbers in the 1830s, '40s, and '50s, and Baltimore received a large number of them, mostly German and Irish.

Baltimore grew from near obscurity at the time of the Revolution to become America's third-largest city by 1850.

NORTH VS. SOUTH

With its location just south of the Mason-Dixon Line, the surveyed line between Pennsylvania and Maryland and the line separating North from South, Baltimore would find itself in a difficult position as the rumblings of Civil War became a reality. The city's commercial ties were increasingly to the North—ties that could significantly affect its commerce; its emotional ties were to the South, where many relatives of Baltimore and Maryland residents had moved to seek greater prosperity on land that was more open. Slavery had been part of Maryland's agricultural history, especially with its major cash crop—tobacco. Opposition to slavery grew as more merchants became successful in endeavors not requiring slaves for labor. By 1860 Baltimore, the city, would be home to more freed blacks than any other city in the state; of the 84,000 freed slaves, more than 25,000 stayed in Baltimore.

Despite efforts to ensure balance, in early 1861 Baltimore would again be the focus of a war. In fact, the first bloodshed of the Civil War occurred in the city. When 1,200 members of the Sixth Massachusetts Infantry passed through the city on their way to Washington to answer Lincoln's call for troops on April 19, 1861, a large group of Southern sympathizers attacked them. After a hail of insults, cobblestones, and pistol shots, the infantry returned fire, creating a riot and ending the lives of four soldiers and 12 Baltimoreans. After the incident, James Ryder Randall, a Marylander living in Louisiana, wrote a poem, "My

Maryland," describing his outrage at the "gore that fleck'd the streets of Baltimore" during the riots. Set to a German tune, it soon became Maryland's state song.

On May 13, less than a month after the riots, federal troops occupied Federal Hill, aiming their weapons at Baltimore's downtown. Other federal troops bringing weapons, barricades, and fear soon followed, making Baltimore an occupied city. Troops on both sides of the war came from Baltimore, and monuments and other reminders of the war reflect that dual role for the city.

RANDOM ACTS OF KINDNESS

After the Civil War, long before the phrase "random acts of kindness" became popular, several successful Baltimore businessmen demonstrated a new, private type of philanthropy. George Peabody, who came to Baltimore from Massachusetts in 1814, amassed his first million during the next 20 years, then moved to London to further his fortune. He gave $1.5 million to the city to establish the Peabody Conservatory of Music and Library, built on Mount Vernon Place between 1866 and 1878.

Peabody's donation impressed Johns Hopkins, a friend who had earned his money first as a wholesale commodities dealer, then as a financier and an early investor in the B&O Railroad. In 1867 Hopkins gave most of his $7 million estate for the creation of a university and hospital bearing his name—a fitting gift for a man who never married and whose own formal education ended when he was 12 years old. (For more on Johns Hopkins University, see the Education chapter.)

Enoch Pratt, a merchant and banker who would become one of the nation's leading hardware dealers, donated $833,000 in city bonds toward construction of an enormous free library bearing his name. He sensed that the Peabody Library, though impressive, was not large enough for the growing city and its increasingly affluent population. In 1886 Enoch Pratt Free Library opened with its shelves stacked with 28,000 books. Today it holds one of the best collections of books, music, periodicals, and other printed materials in the country.

During this era the magnificent Victorian City Hall was built, topped with a giant cast-iron dome, visible today (as then) from miles away. The building, designed by George Frederick, did something practically unheard of today—it came in 10 percent under its $2.27 million budget.

Coinciding with the enhancement of appearances was an incredible population increase. More than 60,000 immigrants arrived at Baltimore Harbor from the 1870s to 1900, creating new enclaves in the city. To the east was a Polish enclave, and to the west near the harbor sprouted up an Italian enclave, appropriately named Little Italy. It remains today as one of the best areas to go for an authentic Italian meal. Jews from Russia also found their way to Baltimore, where established Jewish communities helped them overcome the fear of persecution. Baltimore became a true community of neighborhoods, each having a distinctive style, flavor, and feel that carries over through today. (See the Relocation chapter.)

THE GREAT FIRE OF 1904

Heading into a new century, nothing appeared able to stop Baltimore's growth. But disaster loomed. Just before 11:00 A.M. on Sunday, February 7, 1904, an automatic alarm signaled fire at a six-story brick building containing dry goods at Hopkins Place and German (now Redwood) Street. Soon, other alarms were howling, flames were billowing, and strong winds in the cold, blustery day were carrying flames to the northwest. The fire quickly spread, and those same winds challenged firefighters trying desperately to extinguish the blaze.

The fire was so intense that dynamite was used to block its spread. People in Washington could see the fire's glow on the horizon. Contained more than 30 hours after it started, the fire caused an estimated $150 million in damage but, amazingly, no deaths. More than 70 blocks of prime Downtown space was destroyed, and 15,000 buildings and 2,500 businesses were ruined. The clothes manufacturing district, an area containing wharves from Light Street to the Jones Falls and 20 banks, was left in ruins.

People in the city quickly set about rebuilding, and eight years after the fire, Baltimore played host to the contentious Democratic National Convention of 1912. It was held at the Fifth Regiment Armory. After 46 ballots, future President Woodrow Wilson, who received his Ph.D. from Johns Hopkins University, prevailed. His selection by the Democrats would be confirmed in the November election.

YET ANOTHER WAR

A few years later, the city would again play a crucial role in a war. Protected from the open seas, Baltimore provided a safe harbor, impenetrable by the feared enemy submarines that lurked out in the Atlantic Ocean. It also provided a critical link to rail lines heading west and water access to Europe.

When the United States entered World War I in 1917, many Baltimoreans enlisted in the Navy, while others were enlisted in 24-hour-a-day operations to manufacture military uniforms, a task the city had performed effectively during the Spanish-American War. By the end of World War I, more than 55,000 Baltimoreans had enlisted to help with the war effort.

By the time peace came in 1918, Baltimore had undergone a major transformation into an industrial center. Leaders also had seen the need for the city to become larger—in 1918 they annexed 62 square miles of largely undeveloped land, some in Anne Arundel County and Baltimore County. The city had grown to 92 square miles. The new suburbs would see new homes popping up everywhere in the 1920s. More than 6,000 homes a year were being built, doubling the previous record. To the north of established row house communities in Mount Vernon Place and Bolton Hill would come the new developments of Guilford, Homeland, Roland Park, and Peabody Heights (now Charles Village). Farther north, into Baltimore County, came the estates of Greenspring, Worthington, and Dulaney Valleys, areas that, today as then, remain as residential areas.

SWEET TIMES

Fueling the economy was new business. American Sugar Company built a modern refinery in Baltimore County along the Patapsco River, opposite what would become the Inner Harbor, during the second decade of the century. The site remains today, although the company's name, emblazoned in large neon letters, is now Domino. McCormick, the spice manufacturer, and Black and Decker followed suit.

During the advent of air travel during the 1920s and 1930s, Baltimore housed one of the major airplane manufacturers, Glenn L. Martin Company, based in Cleveland. The factory, which was situated on Middle River just outside the city, built thousands of major aircraft and brought the need for new homes to house workers. Shoreline communities, many of which remain today, sprouted everywhere around the facility, and the factory's runways still serve as an airport for small planes and the Maryland National Guard.

On many of those new residents' doorsteps was the *Baltimore Evening Sun*, featuring the work of H. L. Mencken, a curmudgeon born in 1880 in a row house on Hollins Street in Southwest Baltimore.

Arguably the most important journalist of his era, Mencken made sport of most everything he saw wrong with the world. One thing he liked was his hometown: "If the true purpose of living is to be born in comfort, to live happily and to die at peace, the average Baltimorean is infinitely better off than the average New Yorker."

THE CRASH HITS BALTIMORE

In New York the stock market crashed in October 1929, sending the country into the long and painful Great Depression. The toll on Baltimore would be great, but it was lessened slightly by the work of the Public Works Administration in Maryland. The organization spearheaded efforts to expand and improve the city's water supply through projects such as the construction of Prettyboy Reservoir in Baltimore County. The city continues to get most of its water from county reservoirs (Prettyboy and Loch Raven) along with the Big Inch, a water line created in the early 1960s running from the Susquehanna River, 40 miles north of the city, parallel to I-95. Even with the Public Works Administration projects, about 100,000 Baltimoreans— about one in seven people—had no income during the Depression era.

Fortunately, many of the people who had purchased new homes in the Baltimore area prior to the crash had taken five-year mortgages, so even though they had no income, they were not forced onto the streets. A sign of the times came in September 1931, when the $85 million, 32-story Baltimore Trust Company building was closed. Still, in the face of growing concern, the Baltimore Association of Commerce said in the early 1930s, "Industry as a whole is in good shape." The city's diverse economy kept it better off than most cities, but by Christmas 1933, one in six families in the city was on relief.

Love would soon take Baltimore's thoughts away from the Depression and put the city at the center of the world's attention. On December 10, 1936, England's King Edward VIII renounced his throne (to the surprise of all of England), so he could be with Bessie Wallis Warfield Simpson, a twice-divorced Baltimore woman the king had fallen in love with. She became the Duchess of Windsor and a spectacle of public attention whenever she and the duke visited her hometown.

SUPPLYING WW II

In September 1939, when World War II began in Europe, Baltimore was providing much of the materials for battle. Overseas orders for Japanese ships were coming in to Bethlehem Steel, and Glenn L. Martin Co. was busy building airplanes. Another $5.5 billion in federal war contracts were soon heading to the city by the bay.

Before long, the Great Depression was forgotten. The 47,000 workers at Bethlehem Steel built 500 Victory and Liberty ships and, along the way, cut the assembly time from 110 to 52 days using automobile assembly line techniques. By 1943 Glenn L. Martin Co. was employing 37,000 people, and another 77,000 people were involved in shipbuilding in the city.

The growing work force increased the city's population by an estimated 134,000, with another 28,000 families moving into new homes on the outskirts of the city. Baltimore's population eclipsed 1.5 million.

PEACETIME PURSUITS

In the 1950s the state spent $10 million on new schools and devoted $3 million to the construction of Friendship Airport (now Baltimore–Washington International Airport), about 15 miles south of Baltimore and 20 miles north of Washington. Mass transportation and cars enabled suburbanites to get to their jobs in the city— moving to the more open county and beyond became feasible. Brick homes were being built by the hundreds. (If you don't have an idea when a certain house was built, odds are good that if you guess the 1950s, you'll be right.)

With the flight to the outskirts, city housing was decaying, and business leaders had to do something. They created the first housing court, a body empowered to crack down on the numerous housing violations that were ruining the city's appearance. Under Mayor Thomas J. D'Alesandro Jr., the new "Baltimore Plan" received praise and acclaim for its forward-looking approach. Beyond housing, the plan led to the improvement of bus routes and the construction of a new convention center in the city (now the Baltimore Arena), where entertainment, sporting events, and other activities could be held. A new plan for 33 acres in the center of the city called for the creation of Charles Center, a commercial and retail center on Charles Street, 3 blocks north of the Inner Harbor.

All was not about big business and urban issues in the 1950s. Several drive-in theaters opened, including the Bengies, still operating on Highway 150 in Essex. And in 1954 the Baltimore Orioles appeared on the scene, having moved from St. Louis, where they had been called the Browns. (Oddly enough, more than 40 years later the Cleveland Browns football team would move to Baltimore and become the Baltimore Ravens, succeeding the Colts, who left Baltimore for Indianapolis in 1984.) The Orioles played their home games at Memorial Stadium, a ballpark built in the northeastern part of the city as a large memorial to lost wartime soldiers. The Colts, with Johnny Unitas at the helm, also used the field for their incredible brand of play.

RACIAL STRIDES AND MISSTEPS

The exodus to the suburbs by middle-income whites in Baltimore and other big cities created racial tensions. Not since the Civil War had the nation's population been so divided, both emotionally and physi-

In its early years Baltimore was so rough it was dubbed "Mob Town."

cally. But even though it was south of the Mason-Dixon Line, Baltimore was more racially integrated than most cities. In September 1952, two years before the Supreme Court's landmark ruling outlawing racial discrimination in public schools, the Baltimore City School Board voted to allow 12 black students to enroll in the city's Polytechnic Institute, a citywide college-prep engineering school. This act proved to be the start of desegregation in Baltimore.

Living in this environment was Baltimorean Clarence Mitchell Jr., chief Washington lobbyist for the National Association for the Advancement of Colored People and a persuasive leader in the passage of the civil rights acts of the late 1950s and early 1960s. He is honored as the namesake of Baltimore's City Courthouse. Despite its advanced stance on desegregation, the city became a home to rioting in April 1968, when Dr. Martin Luther King Jr. was assassinated.

AN URBAN RENAISSANCE

In September 1970 the first City Fair was held at Charles Center and the Inner Harbor in an effort to heal the city's wounds and bring people back together. Just two years after rioting, representatives of almost all of Baltimore's neighborhoods gathered under tents to share their heritages; more than 300,000 people attended. For many of these people, a trip to the city for something other than work was rare, if not unheard of, due to the lingering fear of racial clashes. In the following years the city played host to summers filled with ethnic festivals. To this day such events are common, spotlighting the food, music, arts, and other entertainment of diverse cultures, ranging from the Estonians to the Hispanics.

In 1971 Baltimoreans elected William Donald Schaefer mayor. Although the movement had actually started with several leaders before him, Schaefer quickly became the embodiment of Baltimore's urban renaissance. In 1973 a homesteading program began, allowing people to buy city-owned houses for $1.00 as long as they agreed to refurbish them. The program was an immediate success, leading to the restoration and renovation of more than 500 old homes. Some of the best examples are the 100-year-old homes in the Otterbein, Ridgely's Delight, and Reservoir Hill neighborhoods. (See the Relocation chapter for more information.)

Commercial improvements were also in the works. In time for the nation's bicentennial, the Maryland Science Center opened in a $10 million, four-story building on the Inner Harbor. In July 1976 the city held a giant fireworks display, where the rockets' red glare fell on eight beautiful "tall ships" visiting from faraway ports. In February 1977 the city launched its own goodwill ambassador vessel, the $467,000, 90-foot *Pride of Baltimore,* a replica of the clipper ships that had been popular on the area's waters more than a century earlier. Several years later, the ship sank into the Atlantic, taking with it several sailors. But the *Pride of Baltimore II* followed, a more steady clipper ship replica that has sailed to all parts of the world.

In 1978 Baltimore voters approved the construction of Harborplace, a 3.1-acre complex of shops, restaurants, and food stalls to be constructed at the center of the Inner Harbor. Built for $10 million by the Rouse Company, Harborplace's opening in July 1980 was the crowning glory of the urban revitalization effort: a tourist attraction that would bring locals and visitors to the city's Downtown area in droves for years to come.

Propelled by the city's newfound $625 million-a-year tourist industry, a new convention center opened just ahead of Harborplace in August 1979, and the 500-room, 13-story Hyatt Regency opened in 1980. With the Hyatt boasting that company's second-highest occupancy rate (92.3 percent) in its first year, other hotels soon followed. The Stouffer, Sheraton, and Harbor Courts were soon taking reservations from people hungry to visit a city that had been profiled in *National Geographic, Time, Newsweek,* and a host of travel articles in national and international newspapers. An enduring image of Mayor Schaefer, wearing an old-style striped bathing suit and sporting a yellow rubber duck, jumping into a tank at the National Aquarium, brought the city even more positive publicity.

BUILDING ON SUCCESS

Schaefer's own success led him to the state house, where he served as governor from 1986 to 1994. During his tenure as governor, he further fortified the city, leading trade missions to the Far East and other areas to woo businesses. His administration pushed for the construction of Oriole Park at Camden Yards, a new stadium for the Baltimore Orioles, that was within walking distance of the Inner Harbor. Camden Yards, as it is now referred to by most people, opened to sellout crowds in 1992 and played host to baseball's All-Star Game in 1993 and the American League Championship in 1997. A companion football stadium, now called M&T Bank Stadium, was built for the Baltimore Ravens and opened in the fall of 1998 across the parking lot from the baseball-only park.

Schaefer and other leaders could not stop the May 1986 end of the *News American,* an afternoon newspaper that appealed to the area's blue-collar workforce. Less than a decade later, the last edition of the *Evening Sun,* the city's other afternoon newspaper, published by TimesMirror Co., which also publishes the morning edition of *The Sun,* would come, leaving the city with one daily (see the Media chapter for more information).

In another medium, Baltimore would find growing success and visibility. Movies such as *Diner, Bedroom Window, Tin Men,* and *The Accidental Tourist* were shot in

Baltimore, many made by local filmmaker Barry Levinson. In 1992 Levinson used his hometown as the setting for a television project—the dramatic series *Homicide: Life on the Streets.* The show garnered critical acclaim for its gritty portrayal of Baltimore's finest, using location shoots throughout the city and especially in Fells Point.

With Schaefer's departure for the governorship in Annapolis, the reins for Baltimore's municipal leadership were taken by mayors from the city's minority population. Clarence "Du" Burns took over as mayor when Schaefer became governor and served the last 11 months of Schaeffer's term. Burns was succeeded by fellow African American Kurt L. Schmoke, a Rhodes scholar from Yale and former prosecutor for the city, who served as Baltimore's mayor for 12 years.

THE FACE OF THE FUTURE

Baltimore ushered in a new mayor in 2000, Martin O'Malley. A young, vivacious city leader, O'Malley pledged to reduce crime and raise pride in the city. In his freshman year, the murder rate in the city declined and the police force worked hard to make strides against inner city drug use. While the ills of urban centers can be daunting, O'Malley has remained a spirited leader.

Like so many urban centers, Baltimore suffered a loss of its manufacturing and corporate base as the economy shifted in the last millennium. While traditional sources of employment waned, new prospects emerged, and service sector employment, biotechnology, IT, and other tech-based employment opportunities grew. Baltimore has a low unemployment

Baltimore's Mayor Martin O'Malley is a true renaissance man—in addition to running the city and raising a family, the mayor plays some mean licks on his guitar with his Irish band O'Malley's March. You can catch his band around town at Irish bars and city events.

rate. New developments such as the Digital Harbor have created high-tech hubs for burgeoning businesses, while financial companies such as Legg Mason and T. Rowe Price, and major hospitals and universities remain solid employers.

Development in general is bustling throughout the city. Our West Side is seeing a massive overhaul, while the Inner Harbor continues to spread east along the water with new hotels, businesses, and housing. The national trend of young professionals and empty nesters moving back into cities can definitely be seen in Baltimore. It would seem our Downtown is primed for another renaissance. The city has already seen an influx of luxury high-rises Downtown, and empty office and corporate buildings are finding new life as resident buildings, bringing a whole new life to the heart of the city. Some of these new residents are D.C. transplants who realize they can buy a gracious city home for a quarter of what they would pay in our nation's capital. They are scooping up properties in Baltimore and using the MARC rail system to commute to work in D.C. The center of Baltimore increased its resident population by 50 percent in just five years, and the growth spurt does not look like it will slow anytime soon.

RELOCATION

Once upon a time . . . Baltimore City was a little pocket of industry and commerce nestled near the Patapsco River and surrounded by vast estates. Slowly but unerringly such estates were gobbled up, one by one, to create little towns and eventually larger neighborhood areas. The largest spurts of growth occurred after the Civil War, just after the turn of the last century, and in concert with World Wars I and II. By the 1950s most of the inner and midtown areas of the city had been filled in. Outside those areas, however, were still rolling green hills, horse farms, homemade ice cream, and country general stores. Those pockets can still be found, even though, in the intervening years, suburban cities and towns have reached out toward each other, paving and building in the spaces between. Out Falls Road, headed for Greenspring and Worthington Valleys, the city quickly becomes the country. Once past Joppa Road on north Harford Road, for a few miles before you reach the suburbs of Bel Air, there are cows grazing in fields, old frame houses, and waving fields of wheat. And in the suburban areas south and east of the city, the smell of salty water and the cry of the sea gulls are ever-present.

If you're moving to Baltimore, relocating to this city is easy. There are many services set up to help newcomers get acclimated. Live Baltimore Home Center is an independent, nonprofit organization founded in 1997 to promote the benefits of city living. It produces an extensive relocation kit with up-to-date information including the latest homebuying incentives. You can order a catalog for $15 by contacting **Live Baltimore Home Center** at 343 North Charles Street, 1st Floor, (410) 637-3750. You can also visit the Web site, www.live baltimore.com, which offers a comprehensive list of neighborhoods, home values, real estate contact information, and more.

In this chapter we focus on greater Baltimore and the different neighborhoods you can choose from. We also look at how these environs are evolving. Some of our regional magazines publish extensive articles about city neighborhoods and the outlying suburbs. In 2003 for example, *Baltimore* magazine produced a piece called "Rating the 'Burbs," a look at the housing markets, amenities, and relocation opportunities of five Maryland counties. You can request back issues of *Baltimore* magazine by calling the editorial office at (410) 752–4200.

Generally, even the poorest among us often have active neighborhood associations that organize street fairs in summer and neighborhood block watches all year round. Neighbors watch after latchkey children or babysit for those who have to work. Often, that neighbor is also a relative, because in many of Baltimore's neighborhoods, relatives live nearby. But whether your neighbors are real family or extended family, the sense of family is strong, possibly because our sense of history and the way we are connected to it is so much a part of our daily lives.

Newcomers to the area often talk about Baltimore's quality of life, about what a pleasant, easy place it is to live. One transplant we spoke with noted that he had lived all over the world and in all the major cities in this country, and after 17 years in Baltimore, it would "take a bomb" to blow him out of here. Natives feel the same way. A new friend who lives in Federal Hill is a great case in point. The original members of her family landed in Baltimore in the late 1700s to work in the shipbuilding industry. Since then, generation after generation has stayed on, and the current family boasts three generations of Baltimore firefighters and a Baltimore policeman. These kinds of families are the glue that holds Baltimore's neighborhoods together.

The great thing is that, unlike some small towns where distrust among the natives runs high toward newcomers, Baltimore tends to open its arms. We are always happy to have newcomers embrace the city and its way of life.

Most neighborhoods still have town squares or parks where neighborhood events are held. And, of course, there's always the corner bar that serves the function of a European pub, a place to get together with neighbors and relax. Often, there are also corner stores, where people meet as well as shop. In the counties, people gather for special events at the neighborhood mall or shopping centers.

Both in the city and the counties, schools and churches are important neighborhood fixtures, with solid outreach into the community. They are the institutions we look to to provide day care, after-school care, and places for bazaars, dances, and meetings.

Within the city limits, we try to "buy neighborhood." If there's a good drugstore on the corner, we don't go to one 3 blocks away, and if there's a good bakery 3 blocks away, we don't drive a mile to find another. This may account for the continuing success of our neighborhood grocery stores and restaurants. We often refer to even the chain stores by their neighborhood name. One doesn't just shop at the Giant, one shops at the Giant Rotunda or the Giant York Road. One doesn't run down to the Eddie's but to the Roland Park Eddie's or the Mount Vernon Eddie's.

Some neighborhoods are eclectic, both in culture and population. Some neighborhoods were created by one ethnic group for that ethnic group, and the rest of us are just visitors. Some neighborhoods are blue collar, some white collar, some hippie, some yuppie.

Baltimore is the City of Neighborhoods. All you need to do is find the right one for you. In that regard, this chapter contains capsulized views of some of Baltimore's more sought-after or more historic areas as well as some of the neighborhoods that are trying to join one of those categories. There are a minimum of 280 neighborhoods within the city's limits alone; we simply cannot mention them all.

There are some great little neighborhoods contained within other larger, more well-known neighborhoods. We may not mention them either, even though some would be well worth mentioning if we had all the space in the world. A good example is Evergreen, a lovely enclave of small, single homes built for the railroad workers beside the B&O tracks that used to run through there. Its three streets sit smackdab in the middle of Roland Park. You will find Roland Park in this chapter; you will not find Evergreen.

We've tried to note both the positives and the negatives of living in certain areas. Also, we've mentioned the range of housing prices and general condition of living in an area. At the same time, we would mention here that in big cities, areas sometimes change block by block. One block is great . . . the next block, well . . . not so much. So, realize that the subsequent descriptions are general. If you want to know more, you'll just have to go and see for yourself.

For those neighborhoods beyond the city line but in the catchment area of greater Baltimore, we've tried to do the same. We're mentioning large areas in the suburbs, however, not the individual developments and settlements, not the tiny towns that are, no doubt, wonderful but are contained within a larger, more easily recognized area.

With that in mind, we apologize to those we've left out and hope we've done justice to those we've included.

BALTIMORE HOUSING 101

Before you take a look at the neighborhoods themselves, we thought it might be a good idea to introduce you to what it takes to buy housing in Baltimore—some of the restrictions, some of the perks, some of the history.

Dollar Houses

In the early to mid-1970s, Baltimore City was beginning a renaissance. Because of the increase in housing prices elsewhere, younger professionals had begun taking another look at city neighborhoods, mostly in the midtown areas. Charles Village, for instance, got its name then (changed from Peabody Heights). It was done strictly for publicity purposes and was the brainchild of one Grace Darin, a Charles Village resident and writer. This name change and an active civic league that spent hours at zoning and other meetings pleading the neighborhood's causes stopped, for a time, the encroachment of businesses and associations into its residential area and, in the process, renovated thousands of homes. In the inner city areas, however, decay continued.

William Donald Schaefer, our mayor at the time, was a no-nonsense kind of guy. If it needed to be done, he found a way. It was a time of creative solutions, and one of these became known as the Dollar House Project.

The project was based on a simple concept: If you made it cheap enough, people would take a chance. "Cheap enough" turned out to be one single dollar. So many people wanted to take the chance on those inner city neighborhoods that each targeted block of houses ended up having to be sold by lottery.

The people who were interested would tour the targeted block or blocks of houses. Then they would submit their name for the house they were interested in. Usually, there was more than one name in the proverbial hat, so drawings were held. The winner was not only given the house for a dollar but also guaranteed a low-interest renovation loan from the city.

 The U.S. Census has searchable databases online with home values and population demographics for most cities in Maryland. Visit www.factfinder.census.gov.

The Dollar House Project succeeded in renovating not just blocks of houses, but whole neighborhoods in the inner city, most of which have retained not only their beauty but also their monetary value.

Renovator and Homeowner Tax Incentives

Although the Dollar House Project is no more, Baltimore City continues to provide tax incentives to those who will renovate and homeowners who maintain or improve their properties. In January 1995, certain incentives hit the books for the first time.

The 4 Percent Assessment Tax Credit Program is an incentive for those who improve their properties, because value reassessment often follows improvement. The fact that one is charged for improvement by a reassessment is typical of most property tax laws, whether in Baltimore or elsewhere. However, in Baltimore the new tax credit program seeks to minimize the effect of such reassessment by placing a 4 percent cap on increases. The general state cap is 10 percent. So, if you owned a single-family house in Baltimore City and your assessment was raised from $50,000 to $60,000 in one year, the taxable assessment would only be allowed to increase 4 percent instead of the actual 20 percent increase noted.

The Rehabilitated Vacant Dwellings Tax Credit Program provides direct encouragement to people who reclaim a vacant property. In the first year, the credit is 100 percent, meaning no increase in taxes after renovation; in the second year, the credit is 80 percent; the third year, 60 percent; the fourth year, 40 percent; and the fifth year, 20 percent. This is a real boon for anyone but especially for those folks who are at the edge of their finances trying to pay both mortgage and renovation loans.

The Home Improvement Tax Credit Program provides the same credits noted previously for those who are already homeowners in Baltimore but have feared doing major home improvements because of an inability to pay increased taxes after reassessment. This may not sound like a reasonable fear, but many original renovators in neighborhoods like Charles Village were forced out when they did such a great job of renovating their properties that property values took a sharp turn upward, and taxes increased accordingly, in some cases as much as 300 percent in the first year. The 100 percent tax credit in the first year after assessment would have meant a lot.

The Newly Constructed Dwelling Tax Credit Program in Baltimore City is the only program of its type in the state. You wouldn't think that there are too many new houses being built within the city line, but there is a fair amount of construction, and the city would like more. To encourage new construction, the city offers a 50 percent tax credit in the first year after the building is occupied to 20 percent in the fifth year.

Historic Designations

Many areas in Baltimore City and some areas in surrounding counties bear a historic designation. It is important to know what the designation is and what restrictions are put on your property because of it. Maryland Historic designations have different restrictions than National Historic District designations. Both require things like the facade of the building being kept in historic shape, i.e., it must look as if it is still the year that it was built. This would mean no awnings, no changes of window size, no turning double doors into single doors, and so on. On the positive side, however, it also means that a developer can't come into your neighborhood and tear down the row of homes next to you and build a high-rise.

Covenants

In both Baltimore City and surrounding counties, many neighborhoods bear covenants. For instance, all of the city communities noted as having been built by the Roland Park Company do. Covenants are strict rules about how your property can be used and what can be done to it in the way of renovation, add-ons, and sometimes even the colors it can be painted. When you are looking at property in a self-contained neighborhood, ask if there is a covenant before you fall in love with it. If there is, ask for a copy of the covenant to make sure you can live with the restrictions. You don't want to come to the settlement table not knowing what you're in for.

Real Estate Prices

Housing prices in Baltimore City were very low in the 1970s. It was the prices that brought people back in droves to renovate and rehabilitate Baltimore. Because of the renovation, housing prices soared over the next 10 years and probably would have gone higher if not for the double-digit interest rates of the 1980s. Since interest rates have dropped, property in Baltimore has sold well, but prices have neither increased nor decreased dramatically. A good example: A three-bedroom, Cape Cod home in the neighborhood of Evergreen was for sale in 1976 for $14,000. In 1981 that same house—with no improvements—sold for $58,000. In 1985 the property was again for sale . . . for more than $100,000. Today, it would probably sell in the $150,000 range. So if you buy a house in Baltimore today in a stable neighborhood, you will pay close to top of the market prices for that area, although prices in Baltimore City are still excellent bargains when compared with the suburbs. Deals can still be found on estate sales or in areas that are less stable and

Community Development Corporations

Maryland Center for Community Development, (410) 752-6223 or (800) 949-6223, www.mccd.org, a nonprofit homeownership referral hotline and resource center

HCD Home Ownership Institute (for Baltimore City), (410) 396-3124, a home buyers information line

Housing Assistance Corporation, (410) 233-1649, information line

St. Ambrose Housing Aid Center (for Baltimore City), 321 East 25th Street, (410) 235-5770

Baltimore Urban League (Baltimore City), 512 Orchard Street, (410) 523-8087, www.bul.org

Adopt-A-House Development Corporation (Coldstream-Homestead-Montebello communities), 1527 Gorsuch Avenue, (410) 235-6721

Belair-Edison Housing Service (Belair-Edison community), 3412 Belair Road, (410) 485-8422, www.belair-edison.org

East Baltimore Midway Community Development Corporation, 802 East North Avenue, (410) 243-0660

HarBel Housing Partnership Program, 5807 Harford Road, (410) 444-9152

Howard County Office of Housing and Community Development, 6751 Columbia Gateway Drive, (410) 313-6318, www.co.ho.md.us

Greater Baltimore Community Housing Resource Board, (410) 453-9500 or (800) 895-6302, www.gbchrb.org, housing information

still trying to make it. Taxes tend to be higher on these properties, and some are selling for the same price as a three-bedroom townhouse in the suburbs. In this chapter, the prices we have quoted are averages from 2002.

Ground Rents

Ground rents are something unique to older cities. Renting the land was a way for people who owned land on which houses were built to retain an income from the land—a sort of cash-only feudal arrangement. The builder/resident owned his house, but he paid rent on the land on which it stood. Many of Baltimore City's properties still have ground rents. They

are not expensive, usually in the $40-a-year range, but you can also usually buy the ground at settlement for a few extra thousand dollars. Wherever you see a home advertised as "in fee," that means that there is no ground rent. If it is not "in fee," it may have one.

Closing Costs for Homebuyers

Closing costs on housing in Maryland generally are a major expense. There are filing fees, bank fees, and property taxes to pay, among other things. In Baltimore City, however, a new program that allows semi-annual property tax payments can reduce closing costs, so don't forget to request that option. There is also a program usually referred to as a SELP loan. The acronym stands for Settlement Expense Loan Program, and what it basically does is lend you the money to pay your settlement costs, which then are figured into your mortgage and paid off over the life of your mortgage.

ORGANIZING THE CITY OF NEIGHBORHOODS

For your convenience, as we have in most of this book, we've broken the territory within the city's limits into Downtown, Northeast, Northwest, Southeast, and Southwest. Because of the large numbers of neighborhoods in the Downtown area, however, for the sake of this chapter only, we've also broken Downtown into Northeast, Northwest, Southeast, and Southwest. Also, the area that we have labeled as Downtown Baltimore includes some areas that others would label Southwest, South, and Southeast Baltimore. We have included these areas in our Downtown because they are within walking distance of the Inner Harbor, which is our central focus for the Downtown area. In the categories of Northeast, Northwest, Southeast, and Southwest, we have divided these regions into Within the City and Over the County Line in an effort to further clarify where these areas are located.

Special thanks to the folks at the Metropolitan Regional Information System Inc. for providing much of the information on average sales prices for the more than 40 neighborhoods outlined in this chapter. For more information on MRIS, visit www.mris.com or to search for homes online, visit www.homesdata.com.

NORTHEAST DOWNTOWN

Baltimore's elegant past, its turn-of-the-twentieth-century boom days, are well characterized in one neighborhood, **Mount Vernon/Belvedere,** which straddles the east-west boundary of Charles Street, running east to Guilford Avenue, west to essentially Howard Street, and north to the train tracks below Mount Royal Avenue.

Originally part of the estate of John Eager Howard, it was given up to development in the 1850s. Those first residents were the cream of Baltimore society and philanthropy, and today, Mount Vernon/Belvedere is the hub of Baltimore's cultural activity. Within its confines are the Peabody Conservatory of Music, the Walters Art Gallery, Center Stage Theatre, the Lyric Opera House, and the Joseph Meyerhoff Symphony Hall. It is the home of the Washington Monument, some of the most fabulous church buildings ever erected, and some of Baltimore's better restaurants, both old and new. Many of Baltimore's exclusive clubs are on Mount Vernon Square; the Women's Club and the Engineer's Club come to mind most often.

The neighborhood is tightly knit, serving both as gathering place and home to artists, actors, and students as well as the center of the gay community in Baltimore. Apartments and homes are fairly priced, with average home sales at $122,000. Understand, however, that the average house on the main streets of Charles, Calvert, and Cathedral is 25 feet wide and four to five stories high, not counting the basement, and most of them have 15- to 20-foot interior ceilings. You could put a typical suburban town house, including front and backyard, within the third floor of many of these buildings and still have

---

If you'd like a booklet that points out some of Baltimore City's new and renovated housing and gives you all you need to know about price, closing, and monthly payments, you can call Baltimore's Department of Housing and Community Development, (410) 396-5000, and ask for the booklet Baltimore's Best Buys.

CLOSE-UP
Mount Vernon Cultural District

Mount Vernon is one of Baltimore's richest neighborhoods, boasting some of the best architecture, culture, housing, food, and fun in the downtown area. The center of Mount Vernon is the Washington Monument on Charles Street, one of the most recognizable structures in the city. The 178-foot Doric column that supports a statue of George Washington can be seen from many spots around town. American author Herman Melville once wrote, "Great Washington stands aloft on his towering mainmast in Baltimore, and like one of Hercules' pillars, his column marks that point of human grandeur beyond which few mortals will go."

Baltimore's statue is our country's first monument to George Washington, pre-dating the one in Washington, D.C. by 55 years. The base of the monument offers an exhibit detailing the construction of the neoclassic sculpture begun in 1815 by Robert Mills, who also designed its D.C. cousin. Guests may wind their way up the dizzying 228 steps to the top of the monument for a bird's-eye view of the city (although you can get better views of the city from the top of the World Trade Center in the Inner Harbor or from the lounge and bar on the 13th floor of the Belvedere on Chase Street). Conservation sometimes prohibits visitors from climbing the column, but the exhibit on the ground floor usually remains open.

Around the statue is Mount Vernon Square, a primarily nineteenth-century neighborhood founded by Baltimore's elite. When the monument was first constructed, Mount Vernon lay far north of the burgeoning city, but by 1840 the city expanded to encompass the neighborhood. The townhouses that border the Washington Monument range from Greek Revival to Italian Renaissance and Gothic Revival, with the oldest house in the square standing at 8 West Mount Vernon Place. These homes were the place to live in the 1800s, and urban revival has put them back in high demand. There are only four buildings built after 1900 in the square. A series of landscaped parks punctuated by sculptures and fountains add to the charm of this urban setting.

room to walk around it. Hence, $450 a month for an apartment in Mount Vernon buys you plenty of space.

Oliver/Eastern Terrace is south of North Avenue, north of Biddle Street, and bounded by Broadway and Ensor Street on the east and west, respectively. Built on land that originally was known as the Green Mount Estate, owned by the Oliver family, one of its most notable attractions is the Greenmount Cemetery, dedicated in 1839, where both the Poe and Booth family plots lie. Most of the row homes in the area were constructed in the 1880s and 1890s and were owned by German and Irish merchants and industrialists. During World Wars I and II, the density of the neighborhood increased as the city nearly burst to overflowing with people who came primarily from the South to work in Baltimore's defense plants. Later came the flight to the suburbs in the 1950s and '60s, and the neighborhood saw further decline. Since the 1970s, however, the neighbor-

The circle of cobblestone and the adjoining parks that surround the Washington Monument are the site of many annual festivals and parades. Each winter the city kicks off the holiday by decorating the shaft of the monument with strands of twinkling lights. Each May the Flower Mart ushers in spring and every September the Book Festival takes over the square with books, music, and visits from famous authors.

Within 3 blocks of the monument you will find the Maryland Historical Society, the Contemporary Museum, the Walters Art Museum, the Enoch Pratt Free Libraries, and the Peabody Institute. You will also find commercial galleries, fine food, cafes, and unique shops. In recent years many cultural organizations and businesses in the neighborhood gelled to create the Mount Vernon Cultural District (MVCD), whose goal is to cooperatively improve the physical amenities in the area and to help spread the word about the many cultural, historic, and social attractions. The organization touts that Mount Vernon is "one neighborhood with 100 things to do," and with more than one million people visiting Mount Vernon in 2000, it appears that word

has spread. The MVCD is a good stepping off point for a tour of the Mount Vernon area. Its Web site has a map with links to member organizations at www.mvcd.org.

The MVCD is housed in the same building as the Downtown Partnership, a nonprofit corporation dedicated to making Downtown Baltimore a great place to invest, work, live, and play. You may want to pop into the Downtown Partnership, located at 217 North Charles Street, for brochures, general information, and friendly advice from the informed reception staff. "It's easy to fall in love with Downtown Baltimore," explains the Partnership's Web site. "Few downtowns have as true a Little Italy as does Baltimore, or fresh seafood markets such as those found in Fells Point, Market Center, and Federal Hill, or cultural institutions, restaurants, and retail establishments as in Mount Vernon." The Downtown Partnership also offers a safety escort service for people working late or playing late who want someone to walk them to their car or hotel. The service, available within the 106-block area that comprises the core of Downtown, can be reached by calling (410) 244-1030.

hood has been fighting its way back. Oliver/Eastern Terrace has seen some of its worst sections razed in recent years to be replaced by more modern row houses.

Now primarily an African-American working-class neighborhood, Oliver/Eastern Terrace has well-regarded parochial schools and active neighborhood churches. Oliver/Eastern Terrace homes average $40,000.

NORTHWEST DOWNTOWN

One of the poorest areas in Baltimore City, with a population of more than 10,000 people, **Sandtown** is a classic story of urban decay. A recent publication about Sandtown noted 50 percent of its households earn less than $11,000 a year, and 44 percent of its adult residents are unemployed or underemployed. School performance standards are low; crime is high, as are drug use and HIV/AIDS infection. However, Sandtown is undergoing a metamorphosis. Residents have decided to stay and fix it. The challenge would be astounding, even if it were just a government project; but what makes Sandtown's challenge truly memorable is the fact that its residents sparked the beginnings of the neighborhood's rehabilitation, and they work for it every day at the grassroots level. Since 1990, when a partnership was formed between the city, the residents, and The Enterprise Foundation, that spark has begun to glow. By 1996, the more than 100 block clubs organized to fight crime had helped reduce crime by 20 percent. More than 3,000 housing units have been built or renovated; parks, festivals, and new community services have become part of the Sandtown transformation. New recruits to Sandtown's cause are being enlisted every day, and as they themselves note, Sandtown is becoming a "national model for positive change." Homes in the neighborhood can be bought for as little as $5,500, with top prices falling in at about $45,000.

Seton Hill is an area of about 7 square blocks tucked above Franklin Street between Orchard and Eutaw Streets. On the National Register as a Historic District, Seton Hill took its name from Mother Elizabeth Anne Seton, now a saint, who opened the first boarding school for Catholic girls on the site. Another religious first occurred in Seton Hill when Mother Mary Lange, an African-American Catholic who is being championed for sainthood, founded the Oblate Sisters of Providence there in 1829. This mostly renovated neighborhood of some 300 homes grew up between 1800 and 1850 around St. Mary's Seminary, the first Catholic seminary in the United States, founded in 1791. The focal point of the neighborhood is now St. Mary's Park, where until 1975 the Seminary still stood, and where the Seminary Chapel—the earliest example of neo-Gothic design in the United States—still stands. One of the most interesting facts about the houses that front right at the sidewalk along busy streets is that many of them share common, landscaped garden space in the back. Though charming from the front, the difference between front and back can be as startling as when Dorothy stepped out into Munchkinland.

The average price of a single-family home in the area is $78,000.

Bolton Hill is bounded on the north by North Avenue, on the west by Eutaw Place, on the east by Mount Royal Avenue, and on the south by the Fifth Regiment Armory, where the original Bolton estate once stood. Development was begun in the 1850s at Eutaw Place by a member of the Tiffany family. After the Civil War development spread east and professional and merchant class families moved in, as did a fair number of displaced Southerners. Robert E. Lee's aide-de-camp, Charles Marshall, moved to Bolton Hill at that time. Other former residents include Ottmar Mergenthaler, who invented the Linotype in 1885, and writers Christopher Morley, Gertrude Stein, Edith Hamilton, and F. Scott Fitzgerald. One of the few neighborhoods that maintained its population and its homeownership through the postwar flight to the suburbs, Bolton Hill today offers an eclectic mix of population and lifestyle within the ambience of old-world elegance. Houses range in price, with the average going for $207,000.

In 1977 **Madison Park** became Baltimore's seventh Historic District and its first African-American historic district. On the west side of Bolton Hill just below North Avenue, Madison Park was built from 1876 to 1894 by Baltimore's gentile elite. Subsequently taken over by the well-to-do Jewish population, then settled after World War I by professionals, Madison Park is still primarily an upper-middle income, professional neighborhood. Home prices average $162,000.

SOUTHEAST DOWNTOWN

Just east of the Inner Harbor is **Little Italy,** one of Baltimore's oldest and best-known neighborhoods. Bounded on the north by

The Enterprise Foundation

The Rouse Company that Jim Rouse created has been a fixture in Maryland for more than 30 years. A major developer in Maryland generally, the Rouse Company has been responsible for some of Baltimore's more impressive development, including Harborplace, which serves as the centerpiece for Baltimore's Inner Harbor Development. The Enterprise Foundation (www.enterprise foundation.org), a nonprofit housing and community development organization begun in 1982 by Jim and Patty Rouse, supports an entirely different kind of development—the development of neighborhoods. They call the process "Neighborhood Transformation." Its goal is to literally transform neighborhoods from urban decay into safe, livable, cohesive communities.

Foundation funds go to support public housing redevelopment, assisted-living programs for low-income seniors, inner city child-care facilities, neighborhood planning, job creation, neighborhood safety programs, and more.

As of 2001, Enterprise had raised and invested more than $3.5 billion in grants, loans, and equity to the process of neighborhood transformation. The funds have leveraged an additional $4 billion in public and private financing.

Though begun in Baltimore, The Enterprise Foundation is not being stingy with with its expertise. Projects as far away as Texas have had the benefit of The Enterprise Foundation's direct intervention. Its outreach extends to just about anywhere people need help and right now that includes scores of networking organizations in 41 states.

Through an online site, Enterprise OnLine, the foundation shares practical how-to and model program information with other nonprofit organizations who seek to do the same nationwide.

A measure of its success is the fact that since its inception in 1982, the foundation and its affiliates have helped create some 144,000 homes for low-income people. They have placed more than 38,000 people in jobs and have created $4.4 billion in loans, equity, and grants. The Enterprise Foundation now has a national network of more than 2,400 organizations in 860 locations.

Pratt Street, on the west by President Street, on the east by Central Avenue, and on the south by the Harbor itself, Little Italy covers only 12 square blocks. Settled in the 1840s by Italian immigrants in search of work on the railroad, it is renowned for its cozy Italian restaurants and its continuing observation of the Italian way of life. This solidly Catholic community is very active in church, school, and neighborhood happenings. Its residents are family focused, and often three generations live in the small houses (most only 10 feet by 13 feet and two rooms deep). A little piece of Little Italy will run anywhere from $65,000 to $160,000.

Although an inner city neighborhood, Little Italy is safe. It is also incredibly clean, thanks to the neighbors and business owners who come out each morning with broom and hose. You'll find plenty of form-stone and white marble steps in Little Italy, as well as window boxes that drip with colorful flowers from spring through fall. The advantages of living in Little Italy include the short walking distance to Downtown, being right on the water, and, of course, the food.

Contiguous to Little Italy is **Fells Point.** Established in 1730 by William Fell as a shipyard, Fells Point the town was actually laid out in 1773 by William's son, Edward Fell, for the families and artisans who worked at the yard. The names of its streets are decidedly British, such as Shakespeare Street and Thames Street. (Thames is pronounced as spelled, by the way.) Because of its ideal location near a deep, protected harbor as well as, at that time, a seemingly unlimited supply of hardwood, Fells Point quickly became the main colonial shipbuilding center. The first two ships in the American Navy, the *Wasp* and the *Hornet*, were commissioned at Fells Point in 1783. The Fells Point Market, one of three original Baltimore markets, was built on land donated to the town by William Fell and still stands in its original location. Most of the small, brick row houses date back to those revolutionary days and have been highly coveted by renovators since the late 1970s, when the neighborhood was saved from demolition for a highway.

Prices can be high for the amount of house you get, but the ambience is worth it. And in today's housing market, prices actually fall in the low to normal range, between $40,000 for smaller, unrenovated properties on the area's borders to well over $200,000 for renovated properties in Fells Point's center. The average Fells Point home now sells for $184,000.

However, Fells Point is not just a bedroom community; it is a center of activity. During the day the area teams with shop-

pers who are interested in antiques and unusual craft items. Community theater, family restaurants, and bars with live music make parking hard to find in the evening, but since the water taxi can take you right to the foot of Broadway in Fells Point from the Inner Harbor, tourists really needn't worry.

On the other hand, if you're thinking of settling there, Fells Point has covered the parking problem by having two-hour parking limits for visitors on its mostly residential side streets. Residents park by permit.

The neighborhood is as eclectic as its history has painted it. The very wealthy, the middle class, the working stiff, and the homeless all live in Fells Point.

Originally part of Jonestown, settled in 1661 by David Jones, **Oldtown** is east of the Jones Falls and north of Fells Point and Little Italy. The neighborhood was originally settled by German and Irish immigrants.

Many of the original row houses in Oldtown were built prior to the Civil War. The area is now primarily an African-American community, a great many of whose ancestors crowded into Baltimore after the Civil War and during World Wars I and II, when defense work was plentiful in the area. In fact the first housing projects were built in the area to house defense workers.

Much recent renovation, demolition, and new building in the area, however, is due to the continuing influence of the Oldtown Plan, an urban renewal plan that was developed by the city and the community in 1968. This stimulated some renovation interest in the area and one of its jewels, **Stirling Street.** Originally scheduled for demolition, this block of 150-year-old row houses became instead Baltimore's first Dollar House Project of the mid-1970s. (See Dollar Houses earlier in this chapter.)

Above Little Italy and Fells Point and south of Orleans Street is a large area known as **Washington Hill.** Near the center of the community is Church Hospital, sometimes called Church Home by natives, where Edgar Allan Poe died after he was found drunk and beaten in a waterfront

---

When you find yourself at the foot of Broadway in Fells Point, look east. You will see the old Recreation Pier, which you may recognize as the outside set for the police station on Homicide, *the former NBC detective show filmed in Baltimore and produced by one of Baltimore's own, Barry Levinson.*

---

dive. The neighborhood is more currently noteworthy for the extensive renovation in its neighborhood that sparked Artisan's Row, an area within the community of stained-glass craftsmen, frame restorers and gilders, stone workers, woodworkers, and more.

Prices for restored homes in the area range from $40,000 to $150,000 with an average price of $95,000.

Still Downtown, southeast of Charles Street but across the Inner Harbor, is **Federal Hill.** The Federal Hill neighborhood is named for the promontory that has the distinction of being the tip of land Captain John Smith first sighted in 1606 as well as the area from which British ships were sighted during the War of 1812 and the site of a Union fort during the Civil War. It is said that from the observatory tower that once stood on the site ships could be seen 35 miles into the bay.

The area was first settled by factory workers, dock workers, watermen, and trainmen. It caught fire as a renovation neighborhood during the 1970s, when Inner Harbor development began and renovation fever was sweeping the city.

Federal Hill begins on the south side of the Inner Harbor at Key Highway and extends south to Cross Street. Most of its houses are row homes, usually two stories but some three and four. The larger houses are said to have been built for the supervisors and foremen, and sometimes owners and merchants, who originally settled the area. There is also some highly unusual housing there. When the old Southern High School building was closed, for instance, the neighborhood didn't want it razed. It was instead turned into condominiums that used the original halls and contours of the building wherever possible. The result can be a resident who lives in an area that used to be an entrance hall. These apartments boast cathedral ceilings, fan light windows, sunken living spaces, and lofts.

Like Fells Point, Federal Hill is not just homes. Many of the old corner stores have been turned into corner shops, antiques,

and otherwise. There are many nice restaurants and there is Cross Street Market (see the Shopping chapter for more information). Like many inner city neighborhoods, the streets are narrow, so if you're not used to parallel parking with only inches to spare, we suggest you make your first visit to Federal Hill a sunny day's stroll.

Federal Hill holds an eclectic mix of old-time residents as well as blue-collar and professional people. Properties may still be found in the area for $50,000, with large, upscale, renovated properties going for well over $450,000. The average price of a Federal Hill home is about $243,000.

SOUTHWEST DOWNTOWN

West of Federal Hill and the Inner Harbor is the small enclave of **Otterbein,** within which you will find the Old Otterbein Church, the oldest continuing congregation in the city and the site of the first Methodist congregation in the United States, begun in 1771.

Originally settled by German, Greek, Polish, and other immigrants from Eastern Europe, the neighborhood continues to be a vital, eclectic area. Otterbein was another area saved during the 1970s by the Dollar House Project; hence, most of its houses, though archaic on the outside, are thoroughly modern on the inside (see Dollar Houses earlier in this chapter). The neighborhood also has brick sidewalks, cobblestone alleyways, and its own swim club for those hot summer days.

Prices can be high: Although the houses themselves were bought for a dollar, the renovations weren't. Renovated homes in Otterbein go for well over $250,000, with the average price range at about $270,000. If you like being where the action is—and walking distance from Camden Yards—Otterbein is just the place.

Pigtown is generally considered to be the area that borders Carroll Park on the south, along Washington Boulevard, and it is usually included as part of South or Southwest Baltimore. It falls, however, in

Getting to Know Baltimore Architecture

Throughout this book, we often refer to Baltimore's architecture because it is a reflection of the city's history and the city's place in history. As a character in the TV show *Homicide* noted, Baltimore is "drowning in history," and it is Baltimore's architecture that allows citizens and visitors alike to immerse themselves in the pool.

In a way, Baltimore is a working museum. Down every street where people live and work are architectural examples from almost every historical period that harmonize across Baltimore's landscape. Yet, even those of us who are used to the give and take of old and new are sometimes astounded by the contrasts.

The 50-story skyscraper that towers over, but somehow doesn't overshadow, a three-story, iron facade. The country mansion that is no longer in the country but surrounded by black macadam roads and the roar of traffic. As we go about our twenty-first-century lives, it's sometimes hard to remember that in Baltimore almost every brick and cobblestone bears some historic significance from the three centuries that came before.

Baltimore's original cityscape was created by architectural names like Latrobe, Cassell, and Pope. The people who hired them were the Peabodys, the Pratts, and the Hopkinses—city benefactors, philanthropists, businessmen.

Sadly, many of Baltimore's exciting and architecturally significant buildings have been excised from the cityscape over the years by 1960s urban renewal and the current city government's "fix it up or we'll tear it drawn" mentality. But, luckily, much of the work of Baltimore's builders remains to be appreciated.

If you are interested in visiting specific architectural sites such as the B&O Railroad Roundhouse, the Carroll Mansion, Evergreen House, Homewood House or some of the architectural sites used as examples below, their exact whereabouts can be found in the Attractions chapter. In this brief Close-up, we're hoping to provide only some general information about architectural styles so that as you ride around town, you'll be able to tell what's what.

—Thanks to Mary Ellen Hayward and John Dilts for information about Baltimore's architecture and to John and his coauthor John Dorsey for A Guide to Baltimore Architecture, *3rd edition (Tidewater Publishers, Centreville, Maryland, 1997). Thanks also to John C. Poppeliers, et al., for their book,* What Style Is It? A Guide to American Architecture *(John Wiley & Sons, Inc., New York, 1995), which was consulted frequently while compiling this information.*

The Colonial Style and Georgian Revival
Anyone who has ever been to or seen pictures of restored buildings at Williamsburg, Virginia, has a good idea of what the colonial period wrought architecturally. Also known as English Georgian, the colonial style is characterized by white columned porticos, peaked roofs, red brick, and dormer windows that were multipaned. Good examples of colonial-style buildings still visible in Baltimore include Mount Clare Mansion, Old Otterbein Church, and Captain John Steele House.

The desire to build in the colonial style ended with the Revolution, as old English trends fell by the wayside and new American trends stepped in to take their places. By the end of the nineteenth century, however, builders who sought to lend an old-world dignity and grace to their buildings revived the style. In fact, homes with a Georgian flavor continued to be built on through the twentieth century and, even now, you will find homes being erected that have two-story-high pillars under a peaked roof portico, multipaned windows, and red-brick walls.

You can tell the nineteenth century from eighteenth because later buildings tend to have exaggerated certain elements. Pillars are larger, taller; moldings are deeper and more multilayered. Also, we've noticed that eighteenth-century brick appears to be thinner top to bottom and smaller overall; newer red brick appears thicker and larger. It may, in fact, be that there is simply more mortar between the bricks in newer houses, but, for whatever reason, the observation remains.

The Federal and Jeffersonian Styles

The Federal style has much of the colonial in it, but scaled back. A more delicate rendition, one might say. Columns are narrower, their caps simpler with no more than one level of decoration. The Jeffersonian style, which was a simplification externally even on the Federal, often does not have any decoration at all. Rooflines are dotted with hound's-tooth molding or are without adornment. Dormers may be curved instead of peaked, and if peaked the pitch is not very steep. Windows have fewer panes. Overall, lines are simpler, coming as they do from a time when function was prized above frivolity.

Doors may have fan windows above and side windows as well. Interior ceilings of this style have simple relief decorations, such as carved roses or ceiling moldings. Round rooms and domes were also popular, as were flat, fluted decorative pillars.

An example of a Federal building in Baltimore is Homewood House, the restoration of which was completed by Johns Hopkins University on whose campus it sits and after which its Homewood campus was named.

Though the Federal period dates from 1776 to about 1795, the Federal style is well used in Baltimore over the past two centuries, particularly in the porchfront row homes in neighborhoods such as Charles Village that were built between 1909 and 1923, approximately. A takeoff on the Federal style may also be found in the row homes built as recently as the 1940s through the 1960s in neighborhoods such as Northwood, where red-brick houses sport white, peaked trim, multipaned windows, and flat, fluted pillars molding the main entranceways.

Classical Revival

At the turn of the nineteenth century, there was a return to the classical styles of Greece and Rome. Whereas a Federal-style portico might have, at most, four columns, the classically styled portico might have eight, and in place of a simple column cap, there might be swirls or copious foliage. The thinner one-story columns of the Federal style gave way to two-story-high, giant fluted columns. Rooflines include domed towers and central rotundas.

One of the most famous examples of Classical Revival architecture in Baltimore is the Basilica of the Assumption, which was designed by Benjamin Henry Latrobe, who also designed the U.S. Capitol in Washington, D.C. Later examples that adhere to this style are also visible in Baltimore, however. The War Memorial across from Baltimore's City Hall is noted as one of them, although it has some Art Deco elements as well.

Gothic Revival

To think of Gothic is to think of times when myth held the reins of terror in Europe. One tends to envision sorcerers and witch burnings. The original Gothic style was heavy, almost cumbersome, in its uses of tower and gargoyle, gray stone and ironwork. Gothic Revival of the late eighteenth and early nineteenth centuries uses these elements but to a much lesser degree. No columns or porticos grace the fronts of Gothic Revival buildings, only simple steps. Rooflines are punctuated with steep, peaked caps over doorways and windows. This was the beginning of bay and oriel windows with pointed caps or crenelated stone tops, which reflected the corner watchtowers of a castle.

A straightforward example of such style is the main gate at Greenmount Cemetery, which was designed by Robert Cary Long Jr., who also designed five Gothic churches in Baltimore as well as buildings reflecting other architectural styles.

Antebellum

Antebellum architecture in Baltimore was driven by one main economic engine, the railroad. By the time the B&O Railroad reached the fertile Ohio Valley in 1652, Baltimore was finding many uses for products such as iron ore dug from the Appalachians and returned to the city by rail. Iron was already big industry in Baltimore before the Civil War, and one of the forward-thinking items it produced was prefabricated ironworks. Facades for buildings, circular staircases, railings, window grills, balconies, and the like became part and parcel of the buildings of that time. The value of iron for such use was that it could be molded like plaster, yet it was stronger and more impervious to the elements than wood, brick, or stone.

One of the most astounding interior uses of iron prefabrication in Baltimore is the five-tiered interior of the George Peabody Library, built in 1857 and designed by Edmund George Lind. The facade of the main gallery of the City Life Museums on President Street is also all iron, as is the City Hall dome, which was designed and built here in Baltimore by Wendel Bollman.

Victorian Styles

After the Civil War and through the turn of the twentieth century, Baltimore was in its heyday. The railroad and the industries that had blossomed from it ruled the cityscape. Money was being made hand over fist in a time when there were no income taxes, no zoning laws, and still plenty of land to go around. It was, therefore, a time of building.

From the 1850s Gothic and Classical styles had given way to French and Italian Renaissance stylings, and you will find a great many examples of this type of architecture in Baltimore. The features include such items as broad verandas, formal gardens, and mansard roofs. Houses from this period are often made of wood, with shingle. The mansard roofs are decorated with gingerbread trim that looks like rows of thick lace. Towers, bowed walls, and bay windows add to the look, although the Italian Renaissance styles tend to be more square, with roofs pitched lower.

During the Victorian times, however, these styles and others were drawn together into an eclectic mix that picked up pieces from all styles that had gone before and brought them together into a mix that is sometimes called Second Empire style. Mansard roofs are deeper, including dormer windows or sometimes narrow, multicapped columns and balconies. Porches, porticos, and verandas are in evidence, and the overall feeling is busy because of so many visual forms being brought together in one place. The effect is, however, grand and imposing. One sure sign of Victoriana is a capped widow's walk, which you will see on many Baltimore buildings and in other port towns. The widow's walk is a cupola, either closed or open, on the roof of the building, where, reportedly, the wives of captains and sailors paced and waited for sight of their husband's ship to enter the harbor.

Examples of Victorian architecture are found in Roland Park, Lutherville, and other country neighborhoods of the time. More formal examples are easily seen at Mount Vernon Place and the Belvedere at Chase and Charles Streets.

Art Deco

As the 1920s roared into town, Baltimore, like most big East Coast cities, was ready to become thoroughly modern. Victorian evolved into what is called Nouveau. Nouveau was really an interior and fashion style more than a building style, but buildings that were rendered during this period tend toward smoother lines overall, with larger visuals and more glass, while still reflecting the gingerbread and visual clutter of the Victorian era.

By 1925, builders were ready for the cleaner, less cluttered appearance. The style is called modern decorative, Art Deco, or simply Deco. Deco style cuts off all corners . . . literally. A typical Deco building has rounded edges. If design was rendered in brick, designers tended to use yellow instead of red, and the bricks were larger. Other building choices included smooth stone or stucco. There was a lot of chrome and a lot of glass, including glass block, and interiors tended to be rendered in lighter woods such as oak and ash rather than cherry or mahogany.

Whereas Victorian and nouveau glass renderings tended to be intricate and three-dimensional like a Tiffany lampshade, Deco was rendered boldly and often two-dimensionally—three petals above a single stem etched into a blue glass mirror. You can, in fact, see that actual item over the water fountain inside of the decidedly Deco Senator Theater, which is across the street from the definitely Deco department store building that now houses a Pier One, a health club, and a Blockbuster. But an absolute favorite expression of Art Deco in Baltimore is the interior of Werner's Restaurant on Redwood Street, where the blond wood booths are still edged in chrome and surrounded by mirrored columns.

A Word About Formstone . . .

As you move through Baltimore, you will see a great many buildings—particularly marble-stepped, two-story, nineteenth-century row houses—covered with a substance that you may not be able to identify. It looks like multicolored stone from far away, but when you get up close it seems to be some kind of formed stucco.

The substance is called formstone, and it is not original to any of the buildings to which it adheres. It can be removed, blasted, and chipped away to uncover the original brick, and we are seeing more and more of this today.

We believe that formstone was originally sold as a way to waterproof and insulate homes. This supposition makes sense, for without formstone, an old brick house that was having leakage problems would have to repoint all the brick, an expensive process, and to insulate would require losing floor space by adding depth to interior walls, which, when your living room is only 10 feet by 13 feet, hardly seems practical.

our catchment area for Downtown, and so we note it here.

Pigtown was originally named "Kuh Viertel," German for "Cow Quarter." Historically home to stockyards and slaughterhouses, it was originally populated by Irish and German immigrants and, later, black freemen, who worked in the slaughterhouses and at Alexander Russell's brickworks. Its major claim to national fame, however, is that Babe Ruth was born and lived there the first few years of his life.

Unlike the Babe, who was sent away from Pigtown before he was 10 years old, most of the residents there can trace their families' histories back three or four generations right there in those few square blocks. There are no slaughterhouses anymore, but there are plenty of white marble steps, plenty of formstone fronts, and some pretty good buys in housing, both renovated and unrenovated. If you're looking for a bargain in the $10,000 to $40,000 range, then Pigtown is your answer.

Ridgely's Delight began as the combination of two properties. In 1732 Charles Ridgely married Rebecca Howard, daughter of General John Eager Howard. As dowry, he received a large estate that buttressed a smaller property owned by him. Upon his marriage, he combined the two into one grand plantation, Ridgely's . Delight. Now, easy to find since it's directly opposite the west side of Camden Yards, the neighborhood forms a perfect triangle of land, bounded on the east by Russell Street, the north by Pratt Street, and the west by Fremont Street. By some calculations it is within the borders of Pigtown.

Another area where many of the historic row homes were reclaimed by the Dollar House Project (see previous section in this chapter), Ridgely's Delight is

touched by all the main architectural styles used in Baltimore's homes. The earliest homes date back to the Federal period, around 1804. These are the smaller, two-story homes. The larger homes that were built later, mostly to house doctors from the University of Maryland Hospital nearby, are Victorian, Edwardian, and Georgian Revival, with the bulk of the homes being built between 1840 and 1860. When sold by lottery for $1.00, many of these homes had only two side walls and a crumbling facade. Millions of dollars and more than 20 years later, Ridgely's Delight is populated with middle- and upper-middle-income professionals who enjoy the proximity to the Inner Harbor, the downtown business district, and the MARC commuter train. Renovated properties fall in the $50,000 to $150,000 range, with an average price of $113,000. Ridgely's Delight is a Baltimore City Historic District and is posted on the National Register of Historic Places.

A little south and west, encircling Ridgely's Delight to our western Downtown boundary, are Barre Circle, Scott Circle, Washington Village, Mount Clare, and Union Square. All have undergone extensive renovation and continue to upgrade, renovate, and, generally, keep the areas moving forward—not that they aren't already in a pretty good place. **Barre Circle,** for instance, which is an area of fewer than 120 homes nestled between the 1000 block of West Barre Street, the 800 block of Lombard Street, the 700 block of McHenry Street, and the 700 block of Otterbein Street, boasts prices of their renovated 1840 row houses from the mid-$90,000s to $140,000 range, with an average price of $99,488. Many of them have large backyards and gardens, and there are two large green commons for the enjoyment of all the neighbors. The houses tend to get bigger and fancier as you head west, and **Union Square** at the western border has similar prices, although in recent years they have leveled off. The area is racially and economically diverse, with active community organizations.

---

i *Need a new fridge? Energy efficient models—available from most major manufacturers—are tax exempt in Maryland, making a high-end purchase a cost saving prospect.*

NORTHEAST
Within the City

Across North Avenue from Oliver/Eastern Terrace, diagonal to Greenmount Cemetery, at the edge of our northern boundary, is **East Baltimore Midway.** Bordered by Harford Road on the east and Hargrove Street on the west, it stretches north to 25th Street, east of Charles Village. Housing here is mainly row houses, with only St. Ann's Avenue having individual homes. Most of the houses date back to the turn of the twentieth century and are two- and three-story brick. A predominantly African-American community of approximately 6,000 households, the neighborhood boasts long-term residents and has 43 percent homeownership. There are also two recreation centers in the area and two small parks. The bane of the neighborhood is the increasing vacant properties, many of which have been simply abandoned by absentee landlords who decided that they didn't want to spend the time and money dealing with lead-paint problems. The positive side of this, of course, is that some of these properties can be picked up for a song. Off the beaten track, but surrounded by it, residents of East Baltimore Midway are only three minutes by car from center city and only 10 minutes by bus. They are within walking distance of Penn Station, where they can pick up trains or Light Rail, and there are four main bus lines available to residents.

North of 25th Street, west of Harford Road across from the golf course, south of 32nd Street and Harford Road as it wraps around the community, and east of Loch Raven Boulevard is the community known as **Coldstream-Homestead-Montebello.** The area is technically three separate communities, but some time back they banded together. The area was initially developed at the turn of the century, although there is housing there that was built as recently as 1989. There are a fair number of apartment complexes in the area, but most of the homes are traditional two-story row homes, many of brown and yellow brick. There are also some freestanding homes.

Housing prices differ for each part of the community. In Coldstream, which is the area closer to 25th Street, houses tend to sell in the mid-$30,000s to $40,000 range. In Homestead, which is toward the western boundary, prices move into the low to mid-$40,000s. In Montebello, which is in the north near Montebello Lake, where houses get larger and there are more individual homes, prices move into the mid-$50,000s. The average price for the area is $40,000. Primarily a middle-income, African-American community, the neighborhood had 55 percent homeownership in 1991. Insiders say the area is trying to increase that figure, while working on creating a better mix of community-related commercial establishments.

Contiguous to the southeast side of Clifton Park golf course is the area known as **Belair–Edison.** The Brehms Brewery once claimed 624 acres there, and an Insider notes that underground tunnels have been found under the community where the brewery once stored its brew. The neighborhood grew up between 1930 and 1960 and is primarily row after row of the typical, two-story, brick row homes from those times, although there are some duplexes and individual homes here and there. The neighborhood boasts 14 churches and four parochial schools. An eclectic area of working people, homes are priced in the high $30,000 to mid-$70,000 range, with an average of $54,000.

A shoemaker's shop, a corn husk depot, a blacksmith, a wheelwright, and three small stone houses made up the original 1840s town that eventually became **Waverly.** The area where they stood is still a part of Waverly's business district, which extends from its southern border of 28th Street/Exeter Hall Avenue to within a few blocks of its northern border of 39th Street. The western border is Greenmount Avenue, contiguous to the eastern edge of Charles Village; its eastern borders are Loch Raven

Boulevard below 33rd Street and Ellerslie Avenue above it. The homes are a mixture of early 1920s row houses, stately Victorians, and both older and newer country shingle. It was, after all, a country town when it was annexed by Baltimore in 1888. More than a century later, its side streets still have that suburban, small-town feeling. An eclectic community of mostly lower-middle- to middle-class working people, it offers some excellent housing opportunities, with larger Victorian individual homes in the low $50,000s and an average price of $47,000.

The area north and east of Memorial Stadium on 33rd Street is named **Ednor Gardens/Lakeside.** Originally part of the 500-acre Montebello estate, the area matured in the late 1920s through the 1950s. The original row houses are the Tudor-style homes; the later postwar homes are the traditional red-brick, two-story porch fronts. There are also some individual homes and large duplexes that sit closer to, and on, 33rd Street across from City College.

Mayfield begins just north of Erdman Avenue, on the other side of the public golf course from Montebello. It runs north from there to Chesterfield Avenue, which is the boundary to Herring Run Park, west to Montebello Lake and east to Crossland Avenue. It was developed just after the turn of the last century and is a quiet, pleasant tree-lined area of single homes, duplexes, and row houses. The residential areas are safe, and most of the residents have been there a long time. There's a mixed group of white-collar and blue-collar professionals. There are mostly individual homes—some large enough to be considered mansions—with some smaller row homes right on Chesterfield Avenue. Individual homes sell in the $120,000 range; row houses average around $75,000, with an overall average of $118,000.

Lauraville is west of Harford Road, south of Echodale Avenue, and north of Herring Run Park. One of its particularly nice features is that it backs up to woods on its west side, giving it privacy that other neighborhoods with major roads running through them don't have. Its larger Victorian houses have been sought by renovators since the late 1970s and are still considered a bargain, although the prices have risen about 300 percent since then. Prices for Lauraville homes run from $55,000 to $130,000, with an average of $86,000.

Originally known as North Lauraville, **Hamilton** encloses the area west of Walther Boulevard and east of Perring Parkway, which extends northward from Echodale Avenue to the county line, where it runs into Parkville and Overlea. Hamilton is primarily a working-class neighborhood, with a solid community spirit and a history that dates back to its days as a farming community. Its houses are mainly of the clapboard, shingle variety of individual homes—the kind that look small from the outside but are big on the inside. Yards are generous and properties well kept.

Prices for single homes can run into the low $100,000s, with semidetached and row houses (of which there are some) hovering in the $70,000s. The overall average price for a home in Hamilton is $85,000.

Original Northwood is just across The Alameda from Ednor Gardens/Lakeside, in a triangle of land bounded on the east and south by Loch Raven Boulevard, which wraps around it, and on the north by Argonne Drive, although the houses on the north side of Argonne are also considered as being in Original Northwood. Developed in the 1920s by the Roland Park Company, the same developers who gave us Roland Park, Homeland, and Guilford, Original Northwood is a combination of individual, semidetached, and row houses. Like those neighborhoods, Original Northwood is adrift in foliage. Tall old trees, gardens, and any number of beautiful plantings line its few streets. Its row houses are of particular interest because they are not the traditional brick lineup that you see in most Baltimore neighborhoods, both older and younger. The rows were intentionally given an uneven face and a Tudor style. Similar homes are found only in Roland Park. They

Selected Baltimore Firsts

In 1816 Rembrandt Peale introduced the first building to be lighted by gas in Baltimore.

In 1828 Columbus O'Donnell and the Canton Company chartered the first planned industrial and residential community in Fells Point.

Bogardus and Hopping designed the first known cast-iron building in the world at South and Baltimore Streets; it burned in 1851.

In 1896 Frederick Olmsted, the famed landscape architect, designed the first strip shopping center to serve the country community; he also designed Roland Park.

John H. B. Latrobe invented the first stove for use in indoor heating. Known as the Latrobe Stove, or the Baltimore heater, the first one was installed here in Baltimore in 1846.

In 1937 Albert Knight of Formstone Company received the first patent for formstone. Formstone is the faux stone of different colors that has been plastered to the brick fronts of many Baltimore row houses. (Albert Knight was a good salesman!)

—*Excerpted from* Baltimore—America's City of Firsts, *a pamphlet published by Baltimore Bicentennial Celebration, Inc.*

look small from the outside, but are in fact quite roomy inside. Though not a historic neighborhood, Original Northwood does have a covenant that governs how its houses may be painted and changed on the outside.

Prices in the neighborhood range from about $70,000 for row homes and semi-detached houses to about $200,000 for the individual homes. The average price in Original Northwood is $118,000.

Northwood is a pre- and post–World War II neighborhood of mostly brick row houses built to house the growing families of the 1950s. Originally a neighborhood with a predominance of Irish, Germans, and Italians, Northwood has grown into an eclectic neighborhood that is a prime location for teachers and students of nearby Morgan State University. The neighborhood is bound by Argonne Drive on the south, Woodbourne Avenue on the north, on the west by Hillen Road, and on the east by The Alameda. Although most of the houses look the same from the outside, some are larger than others and many end-of-groups

have fireplaces. Another green area, with large trees, 20-to-30-foot front lawns, and fenced backyards, Northwood is a great family area. Houses sell in the $70,000 to $95,000 range. The neighborhood also claims one of the largest apartment complexes within the city's limits, the Northwood Apartments.

Above Northwood is a large area called **Perring Loch** that sits in the V between Hillen Road on the west and Perring Parkway on the east. Row houses of the 1950s are prevalent in this area, but they are considerably smaller overall than those in Northwood. Residents are particularly proud of the community's diversity, old and young, white and black, factory worker and professional. The average home sells for $72,000.

Just below the county line, down to Lake Avenue and west of York Road and east of Bellona Avenue, is the neighborhood of **Cedarcroft,** an area of longtime residents, quiet streets, and large, overhanging trees. An eclectic area featuring shopping and Baltimore's only remaining big-screen neighborhood theater, The Senator, and a short commute from Downtown or Towson, Cedarcroft blends convenience and comfort. Built in the 1950s, the area has a much wider choice of housing than many strictly row house neighborhoods of the same era. There are row houses in the area but also duplexes (two independently standing side-by-side row houses). Individual homes in the Cape Cod, Victorian, and colonial styles can also be found. Prices range from around $70,000 to more than $250,000.

Contiguous to Cedarcroft and Govans on the west, confined by Charles Street on the east, the county line on the north, and Homeland Avenue on the south are 391 acres of land that originally constituted the estate of David Maulden Perine known as **Homeland.** It continued as a working estate until 1922, when it was bought by the Roland Park Company for development. Most of the homes are individual and range in style from stone Tudor to brick Early American, although there are some modern ranch-style houses and large row homes as well. Streets are tree-lined, with wide expanses of green lawns and flowering shrubbery. Some of the original details from the estate still remain, such as the ponds along Springlake Way. (Baltimore's winters have been too mild in most recent years for a hard freeze, but we can remember throwing ice skates over our shoulders and heading out of our neighborhoods for the trek to Homeland and these man-made ponds that became our ice rinks.) Much of the public landscaping done by the Olmsted Brothers of Boston also remains and is tended with loving hands. Homeland is one of the most popular areas in Baltimore for the high-income professionals, because it is so close to the city and Towson, close to shopping and schools, both public and private, while saving for itself the feeling of a country estate. Housing prices now average $347,000.

Govans is named for its first owner, William Govane, a wealthy importer and shipping magnate who was granted the land by the last Lord Calvert. The growth of the community was spurred when the York Turnpike (York Road) was completed in 1786. Industrialists like W. Abell and philanthropists such as the Pratt family once settled there on country estates. With ready access, industry eventually began to locate there, and over the next hundred years the town grew steadily. Govans is now considered the area that sits above Cold Spring Lane, west of The Alameda and east of York Road. On the north, the boundary is sketchy, as it runs into the Belvedere area. Govans prides itself on a heterogeneous population. The housing is just as diverse. Large Victorians, small country frames, 1940s bungalows, and 1920s rows all can be found in Govans. The average price of a Govans home is $50,000.

South of Cold Spring Lane to University Parkway, west of St. Paul Street, and east of Greenmount Avenue (York Road) lies **Guilford,** one of the most astoundingly beautiful communities in Baltimore. Another one of the Roland Park Company's development projects, the community was designed by Frederick Law Olmsted Jr., and its first lots were offered for sale in 1913. The lots were not so much simple building areas but land enough to be claimed as small estates. Six of the nine acres that constitute Sherwood Gardens, for instance, were originally part of the Sherwood Estate. And we're ever so glad for it. Baltimoreans flock to Sherwood Gardens every spring to walk among the 100,000 tulips, 10,000 pansies, and walls of azaleas planted there. But a simple walk through the community can have the same effect. Its 700 magnificent individual homes run the gamut from castle to chalet, but every one is a gem. Prices depend on the size of the home and land, but the average is $446,000.

Okenshaw is a tiny enclave of large, two-story row houses at the foot of Guilford, to the west of Waverly and north of Charles Village. We mention it because it is such a pleasant little pocket, only about 5 blocks in all, but filled with neighbors who know each other well and still do such things as have holiday cookie swaps. Tree-shaded and well-landscaped houses can sell in the $80,000 to mid-$100,000 range.

On the edge of Guilford facing onto Greenmount Avenue/York Road, both north and south of 39th Street is an area known as **York Courts.** Prices here are much lower because the houses face the busy York Road corridor. They are unique, however, in that the row houses, rather than being in a line along the street as is true with most row house blocks in Baltimore, face onto a large, green, landscaped common.

Over the County Line

From Charles Street on the west, Loch Raven Boulevard to the east, and from the city line to the south to slightly above the Beltway on the north lies a gigantic area that is considered **Towson** (pronounced TOU-sun not TOW-zon). It started out as a small town, whose center was, and for the most part still is, at the convergence of York Road, Dulaney Valley Road, and Joppa Road (which was originally an old Indian trail). Today Towson is the county seat of Baltimore County. Within its boundaries are probably as many neighborhoods as are found within the city's limits. The ones closer to the city line developed mostly from summer estates held by city dwellers; farther out was farmland, and Towson's neighborhoods were in many ways developed a farm at a time. Most of the solid, older neighborhoods in Towson and around the county generally started out as simple suburban housing developments from the 1930s onward. They've grown, however, into unique enclaves that share a point of view and a way of life.

South of Towson's center, below Towson University and running up to the city line are the communities of **Rogers Forge, Stoneleigh, Idlewylde,** and **Anneslie.** They are among the most popular neighborhoods for city transplants because they offer quick access to Baltimore, while bestowing on the transplant lower taxes, better schools, and safer streets. Their histories began as the summer retreats of Beulah Land, owned by Joshua Regester; Anneslie Villa, the Birckhear Estate; and Stoneleigh, the Brown Estate. The communities grew when the streetcar and road building made them more accessible.

The houses in the area run the gamut from original frame farmhouses to 1950s rows. There are modern split levels, ranchers, and Cape Cods, and there is still the occasional free building lot.

North of Towson's center, past the humongous Towson Town Center shopping mall on its northeast corner, is the intersection of Goucher Boulevard and Providence Road. To the north of the intersection is an area called **Campus Hills,** where 119 acres of farmland were claimed for 369 brick, predominantly split-level, moderately priced houses in 1955. There were seven different models to choose from, with sizes up to five bedrooms and three baths. The neighborhood was much coveted at the time, being, as it was, totally modern. It is still a popular area because it has a well-landscaped setting with individual homes, but it is walking distance to virtually every major shopping area in Towson. Campus Hills homes average $170,000.

Around the corner from Campus Hills, so to speak, to the east is **Loch Raven Village.** Very much a clone of Northwood, which is just a few miles south down Loch Raven Boulevard, Loch Raven Village boasts much larger homes, although still in the style of the postwar, two-story brick porch front.

Above the Beltway, where Charles Street ends—making this community just about dead north of Baltimore—is **Lutherville.** Lutherville is only about 1 square mile, but it holds some restored Victorian gems. Large lots, big porches, bowed windows and walls, and dormers galore mark these homes as desired. Lutherville is a pleasant Victorian village right smack dab in the middle of everything. Its properties are priced from $125,000 to $995,000, with an average of $189,500.

Above the Beltway, between York Road and Dulaney Valley Road, is the community of Hampton—not to be confused with Hampden. Hampton is particularly notable because it surrounds the Hampton Mansion, built in 1790 by the Ridgely Family and donated to the National Park Service in 1947. Hampton was developed beginning in 1949. The homes are large, with landscaped yards, woods, and streams, and have prices to match, but their convenience to the Beltway, and thus Downtown, and to Towson's center make it an ideal location. Average price is $248,000.

North of Hampton, Towson ends, although it doesn't seem to, at least on York Road. The endless strip malls, fast-food restaurants, and apartment complexes continue into **Timonium,** known for its race track and its fairgrounds where the Maryland State Fair is held every year. Above Timonium is the old town of **Cockeysville,** which is much built up, but where the vestiges of the old town center still remain in the form of antiques and specialty shops. Above Cockeysville is an area known as **Hunt Valley** that was, in fact, a valley through which the elite used to sound the horn, hit the saddle, and take off across hill and dale. A very new area, it is nevertheless very popular because of its proximity to Towson and downtown. By Beltway and I-83 North, Hunt Valley is a brief 20-minute ride from Downtown. Light Rail also now goes to Hunt Valley Mall.

Above Hunt Valley is still mostly country with a few new developments. We will not go there; but if you'd like a lovely ride, you should.

East of Loch Raven Boulevard, west and south of the Beltway as it circles around, and north of the city line are the areas of Hillendale, Parkville, and Overlea. There are many smaller neighborhoods and developments within these areas, but these are the names given generally to the area that begins east of Towson and wraps around the city line to the east. Hillendale is directly adjacent to Towson and continues the feel of Loch Raven Village, showing large row house developments as well as single homes from the late 1940s and '50s, although much of the area at Loch Raven Boulevard and Taylor Avenue was farmland and woods into the early 1960s. Memories are vivid of piling on the #3 bus and heading north from Northwood up Loch Raven Boulevard, all dressed for riding in jeans and leather boots. A large apartment complex was built on that horse farm in the mid-'60s, much to our disappointment, but south down Hillen Road, there is still an excellent golf course and a well-used skating rink.

Parkville is contiguous to Hillendale on the east and north of the city neighborhood of Hamilton. Parkville has always seemed like an extension of Hamilton, its neat little Cape Cod houses all tucked side by side among green lawns and large trees. And **Overlea** holds more of the same but also lays claim to Overlea Hall, which is still the site of many wedding receptions and high school dances. Houses in Overlea average about $140,000. They are mainly working-class neighborhoods and are still filled with the kind of folk who are happy to roll up their sleeves and help at the neighborhood church bazaar, the Girl Scout cookie drive, or the Little League game.

Right at the edge of the Beltway and beyond it are the very popular residential areas of **Carney, Perry Hall, Fullerton,** and **White Marsh.** Perry Hall, Fullerton, and Carney were all small towns that fanned out over the years, filling in farmland, to meet one another. Other towns around the area—Rosedale, Rossville, Poplar, and White Marsh—grew up around train stops.

White Marsh is particularly interesting, however, because although the shopping mall is less than 20 years old and much of the housing that surrounds it dates back only to that time, the original community stood on land owned by Charles Ridgely, who named the area when he claimed it just after the American Revolution. Local historians say Ridgely named it White

Marsh because of the white glare of the sun on the sands of the marsh. Although you'll find the occasional country farmhouse, the White Marsh area is filled mostly with new housing. Tract housing, condos, and apartment complexes from the small and simple to the grand and gracious are found there with prices from about $82,000 to $330,000 with an average price of $140,000.

NORTHWEST

Within the City

In 1896, 50 acres of land above the city line and then contiguous to some of the grander estates were bought for development. Blocks of land were turned over by the developer to individual builders who constructed exteriors and then finished the interiors to suit the buyers. Called "tract housing" now and a standard sales technique in suburban developments, **Charles Village,** as it is now known, is thought to be the first community to employ such tactics. Because of it, however, original interior details of Charles Village homes may be grand or sparse depending upon how much the original owner could afford or what he considered important. Some have simple woodwork and ceilings, only to have intricate parquet floors and marble fireplace mantels. Some have entrance halls framed by the classic Baltimore arches, intricate ceiling detail, and hand-inlaid designs in woodwork, only to show underfoot a simple, tongue-in-groove pine floor. Houses also come in all shapes and sizes. There are individual, rather country-looking homes in the 2600 block of St. Paul Street. Around the corner on 26th Street are two-story, 10-foot-wide bow fronts, known as Pastel Row, because of their pastel facades. On Calvert Street are large, three-story porch fronts; on Charles Street across from the Baltimore Museum of Art, four-story, 20-foot-wide individual behemoths and apartment buildings. Once you cross Charles, the houses become smaller again, with Howard Street homes measuring typically 13 feet wide, 45 feet deep, with only 9-foot ceilings (as opposed to the typical 15-foot ceilings of Charles Street homes).

It may be the Village's eclectic housing that accounts for its eclectic population, or it may be the fact that Charles Village is right in the middle of everything—near the Johns Hopkins Homewood campus, all major bus routes to Downtown, two minutes by car to the Jones Falls Expressway, and seven minutes (not in rush hour) from

Zoning

Don't forget to call the Zoning Commission in whatever area you want to settle down in, have an office in, or do business in. You may think that because you are a done-by-computer business that has no clients visit and has no need to hang out a shingle that you need not worry about zoning. And, you may not. New regulations are being written all the time in all divisions. So it's better to be sure.

Baltimore City Zoning Commission, (410) 396-4301, www.ci.baltimore.md.us

Baltimore County Zoning Commission, (410) 887-3391, www.co.ba.md.us

Howard County Planning and Zoning, (410) 313-2393, www.co.ho.md.us

Anne Arundel Zoning Enforcement, (410) 222-7446, www.aacounty.org

Downtown. The neighborhood actually straddles the line of our east and west boundary of Charles Street, with its borders running to Greenmount Avenue on the east (thereby taking in parts of Waverly within its boundaries), Howard Street on its west, 21st Street to the south, and 33rd Street to the north. The area below 25th Street is often referred to as South Charles Village and on the east side also encompasses some of the neighborhood known as Harwood. Generally, it is a neighborhood of all colors and ethnic persuasions, primarily professionals. A great many writers, designers, artists, weavers, social workers, lawyers, and professors live in the Village. Real estate prices range from the $40,000s for smaller, unrenovated properties to $125,000 and more for larger, renovated homes. The average sales price is $135,000.

North and west of Charles Village is **Roland Park.** The neighborhood was the first development of the Roland Park Company and one of the first planned communities in the United States. It's home to the first strip shopping center in the country, designated with a historic marker. The development was built as summer housing for those who lived and worked in the city. It was typical of the times that during the summer months, those who could afford to took family out to the suburbs out of the pollution and the inner city heat and humidity. In Roland Park, the large shingle houses, with their wide wraparound porches and ceiling-to-floor windows, were built with air circulation in mind. The whole area is inundated with shade trees, and it is amazing the difference in summer's heat when one emerges from their canopy. Commonly called "affluent" Roland Park when referred to in the city's papers, the neighborhood is in fact a very middle-class area. Its new residents are young professionals with growing families, and its older residents are seniors living on pensions— many of whom came here themselves as young people. The wonderful thing about Roland Park is that little of its visage has changed. There are, however, pockets of

new housing in Roland Park, mostly suburban-like town house condominiums, but they are behind walls of trees and do not change the overall look of the neighborhood. From the first, there has been a very active community organization, the Roland Park Civic League, and the community remains strong and cohesive. The few row houses in the neighborhood sell in the $150,000 range, with the average home in the area going for $364,000.

East of Roland Park on University Parkway, west of Charles Street, south and east of 39th Street, is another little pocket of homes named **Tuscany-Canterbury.** Densely populated because of the five large apartment complexes that are within its borders, Tuscany-Canterbury also offers large, two-story row houses, tree-lined streets, and the quiet confidence of a stable, safe area. Prices average $257,000.

Hampden/Woodberry is one of the towns that grew up around the grist mills, cotton mills, and foundries of the Jones Falls Valley. The land was originally owned by a family named Ensor, and descendants of the original owners are said to still live in the community. The first cotton mill, Druid Mill, opened in 1865, followed by Mount Vernon Mills, Clipper Mill, and Woodberry Mills. Although idle now, many of the mills have been refurbished in recent years and are used for other purposes such as offices and shops. There is still industry in the Valley, and many of Hampden's citizens still work there.

About 15 years ago, the city rediscovered Hampden. South of Roland Park, north of Charles Village, and east of the Johns Hopkins Homewood campus, it had sat all those years pretty much as it had for a century, a small enclave of, for the most part, two-story, stoop-front and porch-front homes inhabited by generations of hardworking, blue-collar people. A self-sustaining community within the city limits, it kept to itself. But, by the late 1970s, people who wanted to buy in the city could no longer afford housing in the nearby renovation areas, and they began to look for other midtown areas that satisfied their commuting and housing needs, at a price they could afford. At the time, perfectly livable houses could be bought in Hampden for around $15,000; ones that needed renovation could be bought for $5,000. Prices still hover in the bargain range, with an average of $61,000, except in the premium areas of Stone Hill and Brick Hill. Stone Hill consists of only 46 houses, built 160 years ago for some of the original mill workers. The houses are primarily gray fieldstone duplexes, separated by narrow alleyways. Brick Hill is a semicircle of three-story brick homes built on a hill directly opposite Stone Hill. Between Brick Hill and Stone Hill was Mount Vernon Mill #2, now The Mill Center, a complex of offices and crafts studios. Above these was the home of David Carroll, who owned Mount Vernon Mills and was both builder and benefactor of Stone Hill and Brick Hill. Houses on Stone Hill sell for an average price in the low $100,000 range. Brick Hill homes tend to be a little less.

South of Hampden and contiguous to Charles Village west of Howard Street is the community of **Remington.** Another mill town area, which dates back to 1789, Remington grew with the railroad when the mainline of the B&O was laid. Remington had streetcar service by 1885, and by the turn of the last century, three separate lines ran through the neighborhood, connecting it east, west, north, and south. Most of the brick row houses were built around that time. There are some duplex homes and some larger porch-front row houses here and there, but most houses are 10 feet wide and two rooms deep, abutted to the sidewalk. A relatively eclectic community racially, it is still home to primarily lower income groups. Homes have an average sales price of $67,000.

Medfield, a neighborhood of middle-class working people, sits north and west of Hampden but contiguous to it. The neighborhood is a mixture of row homes and individual homes, most of which were built after World War II. Home prices range $55,000 to $145,000, with an average of $83,000. Most of the community sits on

the highest hill around and one of the few that rises above the smog of the Jones Falls Valley. This smog is caused mainly by the continuous traffic on the Jones Falls Expressway. It is easily visible—some would say "palpable"—on a hot, muggy Baltimore day. But if you live in Medfield, you need only look down on it.

Mount Washington sits essentially at the north end of the Jones Falls Valley at the confluence of Western Run and the Jones Falls. It grew up around the Washington Cotton Manufacturing Company, which built a mill there in 1810. The mill itself has recently been rehabbed for alternate uses, one of which is a Fresh Fields grocery store. Also near the mill is a swim club with one of the largest pools you'll ever see—it's as if someone put three Olympic-size pools side by side—and in a separate building is a well-used skating rink. The town of Mount Washington sits above this area and has a small town center that has craft shops and some very nice restaurants, the Mt. Washington Tavern being one of our favorites. Mount Washington's older single homes are built above and around its center, climbing up the sides of the hills that lead out of the valley. Some of the more interesting ones are actually set into the side of a hill. Mount Washington does have a fair number of more modern apartment complexes outside of this original area. Prices for this country setting are in the $70,000 to $350,000 range, with an average of $220,000.

The land on which **Mount Royal Terrace** and **Reservoir Hill** stand—above the Jones Falls Valley but much farther back toward Downtown than Mount Washington—was originally owned by Jonathan Hansen, a Pennsylvania Quaker. It was called Mount Royal because it stood on one of Baltimore's highest hills. In 1720 Hansen acquired 340 acres that extended all the way down to the area just north of the harbor. In 1730 the Maryland Colonial Assembly acquired from Hansen a little 60-acre tract near the harbor and called it Baltimore Town. In 1789 Dr. Solomon Birckhead bought part of it and, on it, built a mansion that he called Mount Royal Mansion, Hansen's original name for the property. Unlike many areas where the mansions have been razed to make way for other buildings, Dr. Birckhead's mansion has been converted to alternative uses over the years. By 1862 land had been sold to the city to create Druid Hill Park, which is still essentially as it was in those days, with the added benefit of being the home of the Baltimore Zoo.

More than 100 years later, the neighborhoods of Mount Royal Terrace and Reservoir Hill are confined on the west by McCulloh Street, on the east by the Jones Falls Expressway, between the park on the north to North Avenue on the south—although Mount Royal Terrace extends beyond, down Mount Royal Avenue to the Maryland Institute of Art. These neighborhoods suffered all the effects of abandonment, subdivision, and poverty known to most of the city over time and faced rebirth during Baltimore's 1970s renaissance. In fact, they were a prime target, because at the time only 12 houses in Reservoir Hill were valued at more than $20,000, yet the area owns some of the most beautiful and unique architecture in the city. Some of the original mansion houses and swank apartment complexes from the turn of the twentieth century still stand, and a plethora of three- and four-story brownstones, with windows bayed and walls bowed. Stone porches, cupolas, and tile fronts can be found there. Today, the area still teeters on the edge between elegance and poverty, with some blocks restored to their former glory and some boarded up, waiting for a savior. Homes and potential homes sell in the $60,000 to $180,000 range with an average of $80,000.

Within the confines of Reservoir Hill but worthy of its own space because of its separate historic designation, **Upper Eutaw/Madison** covers the 2300, 2400, and 2500 blocks of Madison Avenue and Eutaw Place. A recent publication of the Upper Eutaw/Madison Neighborhood Association described the area as "eclectic,

elegant, and exciting, but not expensive." We think that says it pretty well. Prices for restored homes in the area fall between $110,000 to $350,000, depending mostly on size. There are unrestored but still livable houses selling for around $85,000. An Insider assured us, however, that there are still some vacant properties that might be bought for less.

Ashburton has tree-lined streets and magnificent individual houses, south of Wabash Avenue and north of Liberty Heights Avenue, that many of Baltimore's most prosperous African Americans have called home since the late 1950s. Only 10 minutes to Downtown from the Metro at Mondawmin Shopping Center and less than that by car, the setting recalls the large suburban estates that once surrounded the city. Smaller, unrenovated homes may still be found in Ashburton for as little as $21,000, with large properties selling for up to $300,000. A typical Ashburton house sells for $91,000.

North of Wabash Avenue and the graceful homes of Ashburton, northwest of Druid Hill Park, sits a large neighborhood of some 50,000 residents on a wedge of land bounded on the other side by Greenspring Avenue and on the west by Northern Parkway. **Park Heights** has had its problems over the years, primarily with crime, but a new program that is providing police officers to walk a beat again in the neighborhood is said to be making a difference. Regardless of its problems, however, Park Heights is one of the few neighborhoods that is not in the central city that receives thousands of visitors every year. They come for one thing—the Preakness, Baltimore's finest horse-racing event, which takes place at Pimlico Race Course, located on the Park Heights northern border. During racing season and particularly on Preakness Day, some neighbors turn their yards into parking lots, charging $10 and more to park for the day. Properties in Park Heights may be purchased for $25,000 up to $200,000.

Edmondson Village covers a 2.25-square-mile area in west Baltimore.

It Includes at least a dozen smaller neighborhoods—such as Ten Hills, Uplands, West Hills, and Rognel Heights—within its borders. Born like much of Baltimore from the estates that once claimed the land, the area began to grow with increased access and transportation. Edmondson Avenue was built in 1910, the streetcar came through a few years later, and neighborhoods began to spring up along its routes. In 1947 the first regional commercial development, Edmondson Village Shopping Center, was erected in and designed in the style of Colonial Williamsburg. The homes there range from the simple, brown-shingled cottage variety to large, Georgian mansions. There are a fair number of 1950s-type row houses and apartment complexes in the area. It is a primarily African American area of mostly lower- to middle-income residents. Edmondson Village homes sell in the $45,000 to $80,000 range.

Walbrook is south of Gwynn's Falls Parkway, east of Gwynn's Falls Park, west of the Western Maryland Railroad tracks, and just north of North Avenue. Named after an estate that belonged to Galloway Cheston in 1853, Walbrook's actual development began in 1870, and it claims the distinction of being Baltimore's first true suburb. Walbrook grew up neither because of a mill (though there was a mill nearby) nor because of the railroad (though the railroad tracks came through). Walbrook grew up around the Highland Park Hotel, which opened in 1874 after being built at a cost of some $400,000. It closed just two years later. Still, it was Walbrook's central focus in its day. Since then, Walbrook's center has been Walbrook Junction, a small town center where main streets cross. The area has some modern apartment complexes and shopping centers, but its quaint Victorian homes and diminutive junction create the feeling of country suburb. Homes in Walbrook average $30,000 to $55,000.

Harlem Park, the area between Lafayette Avenue, Monroe Street, Franklin Street, and Fremont Avenue, was subdivided in 1886 after being annexed by the city of Baltimore. The three-story brick row homes built there at the turn of the twentieth century still stand, and some retain their wood-grained mantels, stained-glass windows, high ceilings, and carved molding. You'll also find simple stone houses that were originally built for the servants of the great houses. Harlem Park was one of the first neighborhoods to catch renovation fever, with more than 2,000 buildings restored by the late 1970s. Today, Harlem Park homes are still bargains, with average home sales priced in the $26,000 to $60,000 range.

Lafayette Square was first just that—a square of green lawn and landscaped shrubbery. It was acquired by the city in 1856 and was used as a bivouac area by Union troops during the Civil War. No houses were built around it until about 1876, although three churches and the first teacher's college in Maryland had already located at that site. Today, it shares the same problems of many city neighborhoods but counts itself lucky to be an eclectic community with a multitude of glorious nineteenth-century architecture at reasonable prices. In fact, Lafayette Square offers what many would consider bargain rates, with properties selling for an average price of $72,500.

West Arlington began in 1890 in an effort to create a "model suburban town." By 1896 there were 30 houses and a church, but fewer than 10 years later, the neighborhood claimed 1,000 people. Development continued, though more slowly, into the 1950s. Hence, the area represents many housing styles, large and small, freestanding and row, Victorian and modern. Over the years, the community has sought to preserve its original mandate—to maintain its suburban atmosphere. Home prices reflect that effort, with an average sales price of $104,000.

Windsor Hills was another area that grew because of water to turn mill wheels. The original grist mill was built in 1770 by seven brothers who had left Switzerland to find their fortunes in the colonies. By 1800, the area had become a center for industry. By the end of the nineteenth century, it was being considered for redevelopment as a summer resort community for Baltimore's industrial elite.

Like many of the western communities that began as suburbs, much of Windsor Hills' suburban character remains today. The community is tucked between Leakin Park, the largest natural park in the country within the limits of a city, and the Gwynn's Falls, Windsor Mill Road, and Forest Park Avenue. Homes in Windsor Hills sell for an average price of $80,000.

One of the few almost totally unspoiled mill communities is the neighborhood of **Dickeyville.** Just 120 homes and the old Ashland Mill make up this neighborhood that faces Pickwick Road. It looks like something out of a book, with the kinds of pictures that allow you to peek through a gnarled tree at a white stone cottage. Perhaps one of the reasons that it stayed so true to its beginnings so long was that the mill operated there until 1967, when renovation fever was just around the corner. The mill reopened as Dickeyville Mill for a time during the 1970s and '80s, as artists' studios and shops, one of the first mills in Baltimore to open to a converted use. Both the mill and the village are on the National Register of Historic Places. Dickeyville home prices average $197,000.

Over the County Line

West of Towson, across Charles Street, are the very popular communities of Ruxton and Riderwood. They are often mentioned in one breath as Ruxton/Riderwood, but their characters are very different. Although both are popular because of their location—close to Towson, Downtown, and many private schools—**Ruxton** is very countrified. Among its wooded lots sit some of the loveliest Victorian homes around. Other homes are currently being built—some are small homes with small lots; others, big homes with large lots.

There are colonials from the 1920s, ranch homes from the 1960s, and just about everything in between. There is a sense of status that goes with living in Ruxton—a sense of success. The neighborhood is eclectic, primarily upper-middle class professionals, and real estate prices in the neighborhood average well over $400,000.

Riderwood was mostly developed in the 1960s. Most of its homes are ranch-style or split levels, with some simple bungalows and larger traditional colonials here and there. Individual communities within Riderwood are true developments in which the roads only go in and around the community, nowhere else. The lovely homes in the area sell for an average of $322,000.

Pikesville, Owings Mills, and Reisterstown are the main communities that form the **Reisterstown Road Corridor.** That is to say they are the main stops along Reisterstown Road, which juts out from the city to the northwest from Mount Washington. **Pikesville** is the accepted center of the Jewish community in Baltimore. You'll find interesting shops and great corned beef. One of this community's best-known places is Fields, which grew from Fields Pharmacy into a shop that now handles mainly cosmetics. The lunch counter where many a vanilla Coke was served is now a little more upscale. In fact, all of Pikesville is a little more upscale. The old town remains, but it's been built up and upon wherever space has permitted. Housing options run from the row variety to spacious ranch homes and elegant, older high-rises.

As you cross over the Beltway on the way to Owings Mills, you pass through an area known mostly as Woodhome, then into McDonogh Township, named for McDonogh School, which was begun after the Civil War as a school for boys orphaned by the war. In just the last 15 to 20 years, this whole area has been built up from farmland. It's dripping with new suburban town house communities, single-house developments, shopping centers, and business centers. Development continues across McDonogh Road to Liberty Road, where the area becomes **Randallstown.** Prices are high, but worth it for the easy access to Greenspring Valley, which is a much nicer ride to the city than going down busy, overflowing Reisterstown Road.

Owings Mills is another sleepy area that has grown to a busy center over the last few years. Until the early 1970s, it seemed too far away from Baltimore to pay attention to, but a little theater in the round, Painters' Mill Theatre, brought it into the limelight around that time. The area grew steadily, then burst into major growth when the Owings Mills Corporate Campus and the Owings Mills Town Center—a large, posh shopping mall—were built. Residences in the area include town houses, single-family houses, and apartments.

Reisterstown used to be a day trip from Baltimore, a Sunday of antiquing. It is still an antiques center, but it has been built up all the way to the Carroll County line with housing developments. Even so, the town itself remains pretty much as it has been for the last 40 years.

In both Owings Mills and Reisterstown, you can find anything from a small country home to a large country estate, both of which will probably be surrounded by development housing. There are myriad apartment and condo complexes in this area, as well as developments of town houses and large individual homes. Prices for a single-family home average in the low $200,000 range and more, although some select properties may be purchased for less.

SOUTHEAST
Within the City

Patterson Park is a 155-acre park and the centerpiece for 18 Baltimore neighborhoods as well as the general name often given to the area that immediately surrounds it. (A few of those 18 neighborhoods are mentioned subsequently.) A publication of Southeast Development Corporation noted prices as little as $20,000 for small, unrenovated row

houses, though new condominiums near the water can go for as much as $1 million. The median price falls somewhere in the $80,000 range, but needless to say, such prices guarantee housing for virtually every income level, making it one of the most eclectic and stable communities in Baltimore.

West of Patterson Park, below Baltimore Street but above Fells Point, is the area known as **Butchers Hill.** The neighborhood was originally named Loudenslager Hill for Jacob Loudenslager, who operated both an inn and butchery near the corner of Baltimore Street and Patterson Park Avenue in 1810. Dozens of butchers eventually moved into the area because of its easy access to Broadway (Market Street), hence Broadway Market. The area developed separately from Baltimore itself, with the bulk of its row house development occurring after the Civil War and through the turn of the twentieth century. By the time the last butcher closed up shop in 1925, the area was still largely occupied by German and Jewish residents. Like much of Baltimore, the 1950s and '60s saw a major downturn in fortune, and the 1970s saw an eclectic population interested in the area's history and beauty. Today, Butchers Hill maintains much of its 1970s population of renovators and innovators. It is a neighborhood united, and one that is becoming more popular. Butchers Hill homes sell for an average of $155,000.

On one of the highest points around Baltimore's harbor, above Canton and Fells Point and contiguous to the east corner of Patterson Park, is Highlandtown, which essentially includes the neighborhoods of Brewers Hill and Greektown. Highlandtown was once the site of the Union's Fort Marshall. Abandoned in 1866, after the Civil War, the area's development was begun by an Irish immigrant named Thomas McGuiness, with investment from the Philadelphia Land Company. McGuiness laid out streets, planted trees, and built one house—his own. For years he was the only resident, but as industry developed, others—mainly German brewers—joined him. The area was renowned for its taverns and beer gardens. By 1918 the area was still booming, and Baltimore City just couldn't resist the temptation to once again enlarge its city limits and its industrial base by annexing it in that year. By the 1920s a few slaughterhouses and meat-packing plants had located in Highlandtown, and with B&O's rail yards in Canton, employment for residents was not a problem. Highlandtown continued through the war years as a thriving blue-collar community. Unlike many of the neighborhoods that lost residents in the rush to the suburbs during the postwar years, Highlandtown has remained the same, with generation after generation staying on. It is a clean, safe area where the houses in the main are small row homes, with traditional white marble steps and flat fronts with corniced rooflines. Homes are selling for an average price of $68,000.

Canton is the waterfront area south and west of Highlandtown and east of Fells Point. Its small workman's houses, warehouses, and other industrial buildings have been transformed over the last 20 or so years into some of the most expensive and exclusive real estate in Baltimore. The original land was purchased by an Irish sea captain named O'Donnell in 1785 with money he made selling tea, silk, and satin that he'd picked up in Canton, China. (Although named for that Chinese city, Baltimore's Canton is pronounced CAN-tin, not CAN-tawn.) By the mid-1800s O'Donnell still held the land, but built on it was a thriving industrial complex that included the B&O rail yards, the first charcoal ironworks, a copper-smelting plant, a cotton mill, a distillery, two shipyards, and, later in the century, a series of small oil refineries. Whereas the world wars decimated some areas, Canton's industry continued strong, and the blue-collar neighborhood primarily of Welsh, Germans, Poles, and Irish grew in population. By the 1970s, however, much of the industry had moved away, warehouses and factories lay abandoned, and it looked as if Canton might be headed for truly hard times. Then, as luck would have it, renovation fervor hit the city. Planners

considered warehouse loft apartments, boat slips, and the wonderful advantages to living on the water. Today, Canton is a thriving area, architecturally and ethnically diverse, filled with innovative housing and upper-income professionals as well as traditional housing and blue-collar workers. Renovated homes can go in the $200,000 range, while unrenovated homes go for much less. The average Canton home price is about $165,000.

The point of land that divides Baltimore's Inner Harbor from the Patapsco River's Middle Branch, just south and east of Federal Hill, is known as **Locust Point.** Surrounding Fort McHenry, the neighborhood is composed mostly of small, brick row houses with traditional white marble steps. Originally inhabited by dockworkers, workmen in the shipbuilding and water-related trades, Locust Point is another area where people tend to stay. Some families boast six generations at the Point, many in the same house as it passed down from one generation to the next. The ethnic mix includes Germans, Irish, Poles, Bohemians, Hungarians, Austrians, Swedes, Norwegians, Russians, Scots, and Welsh. This is not odd when you consider that in 1706 Locust Point was made the official port of entry for Baltimore. Immigrants got off the boat and simply stayed where they landed. Like a small town unto itself, Locust Point has a strong sense of community focused on church and family. If you'd like to become a part of it, you might want to get to know someone in the neighborhood. Many of Locust Point's houses are sold by word of mouth. Homes in the area range from $40,000 to $235,000, with an average of $130,000.

Over the County Line

Essex/Middle River is tucked between Back River and Middle River, south of U.S. 40. Riding east on Eastern Avenue through Little Italy, Fells Point, Butchers Hill, and Highlandtown, you'll be in Essex once you've crossed Back River. Inundated at every opportunity by rivers, streams, and creeks, Essex began primarily as a watermen's community. Industry grew during the war years, and during the 1950s and '60s Essex was known mostly as a place to escape the city's summer heat. During those years many people in Baltimore bought cottages in Essex and Middle River. Used mostly on weekends, these cottages were known as the "shore" places; and, even now, many people from the city and northern suburbs spend their weekends at these shores. Even more people, however, live permanently in these areas, working at the factories nearby or still plying the waters for their livelihoods. Many older homes are small, clapboard cottages that sit quietly by tree-shaded inlets. There are also old and new row house developments and apartment and condominium complexes. Essex/Middle River homes run the gamut in price from $45,000 to more than $300,000 for waterfront property.

Dundalk, named after the Irish city, is primarily a blue-collar, industrial area. Fairly large, it encompasses most of the land east of Dundalk Avenue to Old North Point Road and all the way to Bear Creek to the south. The whole area is crisscrossed by creeks and inlets, and many houses sport boats as part of their permanent backyard equipment. The individual houses are mostly clapboards, built in the war years to house defense workers. There are also row houses that date back to the same era as well as some newer row house and apartment developments. Individual homes sell in the mid-$80,000 range, with prices increasing as you get closer to the water. Waterfront properties sell in the $200,000 range and above. But there are still bargains.

SOUTHWEST
Within the City

Cherry Hill sits on land that juts into mouth of the Middle Branch River where it

meets the Patapsco. It is bounded on the south by Patapsco Avenue and on the west, essentially, by railroad tracks. A large park takes up almost one-third of the neighborhood on its east side, running the full length of the neighborhood's boundary along the Patapsco. Cherry Hill Park has softball, football, and soccer fields, basketball courts, and both indoor and outdoor swimming pools. On the northern boundary, Middle Branch Park and Harbor Hospital Center hem in the neighborhood. Originally a small planned community for veterans returning from World War II, by 1945 Cherry Hill Homes had 1,600 rental units and was growing. By the 1970s, Cherry Hill had more than 22,000 residents and some serious crime problems, but residents have worked hard to mitigate them. Cherry Hill still has individual home bargains for about $47,000.

Across the Patapsco River from Cherry Hill and the south Baltimore areas contiguous to the Inner Harbor is Brooklyn. It is that spit of land that looks like Baltimore's chin when you view the city's outline. With water on three sides and the Anne Arundel County line at its back, Brooklyn began as Curtis' Neck, the estate of Paul Kinsey, who took title to 200 acres of land there in 1663. For 200 years it was primarily a farming and fishing community, with access to market just a quick sail across the Patapsco to Fells Point. It had also had some claim to fame as a summer resort for Baltimoreans by the mid-1800s but became more of a part of the city in 1856, when a bridge was constructed that linked it directly to South Baltimore. By 1878 rail lines also extended to the area, spurring construction of shipping facilities for coal and iron ore. By 1892 there was also streetcar service to Brooklyn, and industry rushed to locate there. By the time the century turned, the area had everything from smelting furnaces to oyster packing plants mostly right on the water's edge at Curtis Bay. With industry came workers who needed a place to live. The community of Brooklyn grew up around the industry and continues as a blue-collar working community. Houses tend to cluster around the west side of the point. Property prices can vary, but average $48,000.

Transportation and ease of access have always been, and continue to be, the grist from which communities are made. So it was with **Irvington.** When the Frederick Turnpike was permanently carved out to link Baltimore Town and Frederick Town in the late 1700s, communities began to spring up along the road. The site of Irvington had been settled before that, however, by one Thomas Coale, a Quaker. His 450-acre estate, Maiden's Choice, dated back to 1673. By the time the Civil War had ended, some two centuries later, the area was populated enough to support Mount Saint Joseph's College, which opened in 1873 and is still an active parochial high school. (See the Education chapter.) One of Irvington's well-known landmarks is Loudon Park Cemetery, created in 1853 on the original site of Maiden's Choice. In 1861 the federal government carved out a section for a federal cemetery where 2,300 Union and 275 Confederate soldiers were laid to rest. Irvington, named for Irving Ditty, one of the first builders in the area, today is an eclectic community that still boasts many of the original Victorian masterpieces built before the turn of the twentieth century. It also offers multifamily housing, brick-and-frame duplexes, and row houses. Housing lots are, on average, fairly large, and the whole area is very green. Giant trees overhang houses ranging in price from $30,000 to about $105,000.

Over the County Line

If you head out Frederick Road, west of the city, the first main area you will come upon is **Catonsville.** Catonsville's center at Ingleside/Bloomsbury Avenues and Frederick Road looks very much as it did a century ago, although spreading out from that center are convenience stores, gas stations, and fast-food places. Still, Catonsville seems to be able to maintain its charm. Down its side streets are grand homes that reflect the Victorian country estates and simple Cape Cod homes that were built in the 1940s. It has maintained a reputation as a good place to raise a family and is peopled with all colors and backgrounds. Right in Catonsville's back pocket, as it were, are Catonsville Community College, the University of Maryland, Baltimore County, and large expanses of Patapsco Valley State Park, which borders the Patapsco River, the county line between Baltimore County and Howard County. Catonsville home prices run from $70,000 to $370,000.

Just over the Howard County line is **Ellicott City,** a brief 20 minutes from northwest Baltimore, and it is a treasure. Or, should we say, it's filled with treasures. Ellicott City is the antiques and collectible shopper's paradise (see our Antiques and Collectibles chapter), but the city itself is a postcard. It sits at the level of the Patapsco, which is hardly more than a wide stream there. All the buildings are made of brick and stone and rise up the hill from the river. This center looks much as it did in the middle of the nineteenth century, but in recent years because of its proximity to Columbia, Maryland, much of the open land around the city has been developed, and there are all manner of modern suburban town houses, single-family homes, and apartments available. But the houses that are truly prized are the ones that are within the old community. Property prices in Ellicott City average $120,000 to more than $500,000.

More south of the city, south and east of Catonsville, just above where the wandering Patapsco separates Baltimore County from Anne Arundel County, you will find **Arbutus** and **Halethorpe.** These areas, like most of the county, began as farmland and estates but grew when road and rail came to their communities. Halethorpe, which originated with a train stop, boasts some century-old Victorians among its housing stock. Some of the estate homes in Arbutus and Halethorpe still stand, but most of the land around them was filled in mainly after World War

II. Lynnewood, the first planned development in the area, grew up in 1954. Its housing may be slightly unique for Baltimore in that its split-level and ranch houses were built on concrete slabs with no basements, similar to a typical house in California. (Most Baltimore row houses from the period are famous for their knotty-pine panelled basements.) Arbutus and Halethorpe are made up of single-family, freestanding homes. The twist is that in the 1960s many of them had one floor converted into an apartment. Hence, a great many homeowners have an apartment that they rent out on a continual basis. Most of the homes sit on average suburban lots with shrubbery and greenery, although one Insider noted that if you want giant oak trees, **Relay,** just to its west, is really the place to go. Relay also boasts a Victorian community hardly touched by the twentieth century. Prices for housing in Arbutus run in the $110,000 to $140,000 range; in Halethorpe and Relay, $180,000 and up.

LIVING IN THE BIG B . . .

Now that you have a handle on where you'd like to bed down, the questions become: "Apartment, condo, co-op, row house, or individual home?" and "Should you rent, purchase, or share?" Most of these housing opportunities are available in all areas in greater Baltimore, albeit at differing price levels and with differing housing stock. The organizations below can help you determine what you can afford and where you can get the most for your money, and the real estate companies, of course, can help you directly rent or purchase the property you want.

Apartments

In every area mentioned previously in this chapter, there are apartments. In Downtown you'll find traditional apartments cut from row houses or new and relatively new high-rise apartments, but you'll also find apartments in alternative-use buildings. Alternative-use buildings are those edifices that started their lives as a warehouse or a school but now function as apartments. In the counties garden apartments and apartment/town houses are more the order of the day, although in some areas such as Pikesville, there are many high-rise buildings—the kind where the doorman meets you. Some of these are condominiums, but there are still many elegant apartment complexes.

In racks as you leave most grocery stores or at places where travelers frequent such as hotels and the train station, you'll see published guides that list apartments for rent or sale in the area. These are good for contact information for the larger apartment complexes, but if you'd like to touch base with a person who can tell you generally what's available in the particular area, the organizations below will be able to help you.

Apartment Assistant.net
www.apartmentassistant.net
ApartmentAssistant.net combines a high-tech approach to apartment locating along with personalized knowledge of the individual apartment and condo communities. The site offers city-specific information that includes contact information for necessities like the telephone, cable, and water companies.

Apartment Solutions
(888) 994-7368
www.apartmentsolutions.com
Apartment Solutions focuses on providing comprehensive apartment solutions services in Pennsylvania, New Jersey, Delaware, Virginia, Maryland, and Washington, D.C. Apartment Solutions has more than 1.4 million apartment units and over 4,000 owners and property managers participating in its system.

Relocation Central
(800) 480-3733
www.relocationcentral.com
Relocation Central is a service organiza-

Renter's Resources

Baltimore has many renting options, and it doesn't have the pressure-cooker issues of major metropolises like New York and Boston. It's not unreasonable to find a listing, see a place, and rent it on a handshake. Most places do require a one-year lease and a security deposit. Like every city Baltimore has its share of dubious landlords, the ones who take advantage of newcomers and their need to find a place fast. Tenant-landlord information resources are available and are worth consulting before signing any agreement. Baltimore Neighborhoods, Inc. provides a counseling hotline at (410) 243-6007.

•   Landlords also frequently require their tenants to carry renters' insurance. You can usually procure insurance through your auto insurance company and tack it on to your car premiums for a minimal monthly cost. If you do not own a car, try companies like American Skyline Insurance, 14 Light Street, Suite 200, (800) 711-4452.

tion that helps locate available apartments. There are more than 170,000 apartments in its database.

**Southern Management
Apartment Locators
(800) 999-7368
www.southernmanagement.com**
Apartment Locators is one of the oldest locator services in the Baltimore area. It has more than 65 apartment complexes in the Baltimore area.

Management Companies

Management companies may own the properties that they manage, or they may simply manage properties for others. Some do both. There are a great many management companies in Baltimore; we've only mentioned a few here.

**Bridge Street Corporate Housing
(410) 296-0900 (locally) or
(800) 278-7338 (nationally)
www.bridgestreet.com**
Recently merged with a national and international firm, BridgeStreet has been in business for around two decades in the Baltimore area. The service provided deals in temporary housing, primarily for business travelers and corporate executives who are relocating. If you're just coming to town, expect to stay but need time to canvass neighborhoods and decide where you'd like to live, you might want to try out a place by renting temporarily. If the train carrying your furniture from California got derailed, if your settlement's been delayed, if you've just been transferred, or if you're simply on an extended vacation and would like a base from which to take day trips all around the Mid-Atlantic area, then BridgeStreet can provide fully furnished apartments and/or individual homes by the night, the week, the month, or the year. A lot of businesses use BridgeStreet, but it also works with individuals. It has housing stock in such neighborhoods as Fells Point, Federal Hill, and other Inner Harbor areas as well as in Baltimore, Howard, and Anne Arundel Counties. Prices range from $55 to $200 a day, depending on the property, its location, and a 30-day minimum. Prices per day do vary, depending on length of stay, with shorter stays costing more per day

and longer stays costing less. Rentals are fully equipped, right down to the towels, dishes, and the first few rolls of toilet paper. Cleaning services are available.

The Hubble Company
38 East 25th Street
(410) 889-6900

The Hubble Company is a family-owned business that was begun in 1919 by the father of the current owner, John Hubble. For a long time, the company also handled private homes sales, but its main business now is commercial real estate and apartment rentals. Most of the properties it manages are in the Charles Village neighborhood. Many of its buildings are restored row houses that have been divided into four to six apartment units. The average rental for a one-bedroom apartment is $350 to $375 per month; a two-bedroom unit goes for about $525; and three-bedroom apartments are around $630. A year's lease is required on most properties, all of which are rented unfurnished. The company also brokers sales of apartment buildings for those who want to live in an apartment but would like to own the building. Mr. Hubble notes that Fannie Mae mortgages may be available for four units and fewer, under certain conditions.

Houses/Condos/ Co-ops

Baltimore has many options in housing. But to really understand the market takes an expert. There are simply too many qualifiers on some properties—ground rents, covenants, historic district designations, co-op/condo fees, settlement costs, inspections, and more. There are also a great many options on some properties. You might be qualified for a low-interest rehab loan or you might be able to receive a loan for closing costs or a VA or FHA mortgage. It's better to get help with questions that you might have before

problems arise, which is why we've listed some community development corporations (see sidebar at the beginning of this chapter) that may be able to help you determine how much property you can afford and the best way to pay for it.

Real Estate Firms

Baltimore has some well-respected local and national real estate agents, and most have multiple locations. What follows is just a small sampling of those available.

Allen Realty
8314 Liberty Road
(410) 496-6700
www.allenrealty.biz

This is a small, independently owned business formed in 1996. The Realtors focus on simplifying the process of homeownership to help low to middle income families find and select the best loan programs available. They specialize in HUD homes and foreclosures.

Century 21 Associated, Baltimore
8507 Liberty Road, Randallstown
(410) 521-4400
www.c21associated.com

Century 21 is one of those national firms that comes to an area and gathers affiliates to its respective bosom. It has done quite a job in Baltimore over the last 20 years or so and currently counts 56 independently owned affiliates in Baltimore among its national number.

The Randallstown Century 21 sales office was begun by Hyman Adler as Associated Realty Company in 1955. Ted Coate, the current owner, came to work there in 1973. The firm affiliated with Century 21 in 1979. Today, the office has about 40 agents. The firm services the northwest and northeast quarters of Baltimore City and Baltimore County as well as Howard County, Carroll County, and the northern part of Anne Arundel County. The average price for a single-family home handled by the firm is $105,000.

Chase Fitzgerald & Company, Inc.
4800 Roland Avenue
(410) 366-7700

Chase Fitzgerald is a Baltimore company that traces its roots back to the Roland Park Company. The focus is in Roland Park, Guilford, and points north. It's neither a high-end or low-end real estate company, selling row houses for $170,000 and country estates for $2,500,000.

Coldwell Banker Residential Brokerage
808 South Broadway
(410) 327-2200
www.coldwellbankermove.com

With over 2,800 agents throughout the state of Maryland and 4,000 agents serving the Mid-Atlantic, Coldwell Banker has Realtors in most neighborhoods throughout Baltimore City, including Fells Point, Federal Hill, and Roland Park. The agency also covers the eastern shore and the Maryland suburbs around Washington D.C. With more than 90 offices total, Coldwell Banker provides services ranging from concierge and relocation services to mortgage and insurance advice. The firm handles a wide range of housing prices and options, and also services the bustling rental market downtown.

Fiola Blum Realtors, Inc.
110 Slade Avenue
(410) 484-4800, (800) 486-4038
www.fiolablum.com

Fiola Blum Realtors is one of Baltimore's independent realtors. It has been in business for more than 50 years and is still family-owned and -operated. The firm's 40 agents handle property primarily in the northwest and northern areas of Baltimore County, including condominiums and individual, single-family homes. Prices of its properties range from $50,000 to $1,000,000 and above. When you call, ask for Harry Blum or his wife, Phyllis.

Hill & Company
255 Village Square II, Cross Keys
(410) 435-2000
www.hillrealtors.com

Hill & Co. has been in business in the Baltimore area for more than 75 years. It has a reputation for handling only high-end properties, and you will definitely see its signs in all of Baltimore's prestigious neighborhoods, including Guilford, Homeland, Roland Park, Mount Vernon, and Bolton Hill. Jake Boone, who's been with the company for more than 10 years, says that the company's 36 agents handle lower-priced properties as well, even though he admitted the bulk of the homes sold fall in the $200,000 to $2,000,000 range. The company also handles property out the Charles Street corridor, Inner Harbor homes, and farm properties and estates in the Greenspring and Worthington Valleys.

Long & Foster, Roland Park
4800 Roland Avenue
(410) 889-9800
www.longandfoster.com

Long & Foster is one of the largest real estate companies in the area, with offices in Maryland, Virginia, and Washington, D.C. Its first office opened in Virginia, but there are currently 50 offices in the greater Baltimore region doing business in virtually every neighborhood.

The Roland Park office handles properties primarily in Roland Park, Guilford, and Hampden and considers itself "Downtown oriented," even though most of its 25 agents also do business in Baltimore County. Homes sold range in price from $90,000 to $300,000.

O'Conor, Piper & Flynn–ERA
22 West Padonia Road, Timonium
(410) 561-8800
www.opf.com

O'Conor, Piper & Flynn (OPF) is one of the largest real estate companies in the Baltimore area, with more than 1,500 agents operating in 45 offices across the states of Maryland and Pennsylvania. OPF offers residential and commercial properties and leasing and relocation services, as well as mortgage, title, and insurance options. The company also has an offshoot—OPF Coastal—that can help you rent vacation property.

Otis Warren Real Estate Services
7034 Liberty Road, Lochearn
(410) 484-6700
Otis Warren has been in the real estate
business for more than 40 years. The
company started out in rental property
management and currently offers residential and commercial real estate to its West
Baltimore neighbors. Otis Warren prides
itself on its continuing service to customers, which includes after-the-sale services as well, such as helping customers
get a lower interest rate when they refi-
nance their home mortgages. The average
price of a home sold by the company is
around $95,000, but prices range from
$30,000 to $250,000. John McFall, an
agent with the company since 1981, notes
that whatever the customer's price range,
an agent will try and find a home.

RE/MAX Realtors
22 West Road, #100, Towson
(410) 337-9300
www.remaxgreatermetro.com
RE/MAX is the largest franchised real
estate broker in the world, with more than
50,000 agents in the United States and
Canada alone—1,100 of which are in the
state of Maryland. Broker Mary Lou Kaest-
ner has been in the real estate business
since 1970. She opened her own office in
1981 and became affiliated with RE/MAX in
1994. She and her 20 full-time independent
agents list and sell properties in Baltimore
City and Baltimore, Anne Arundel, Howard,
Harford, and Carroll Counties. One of the

perks of being associated with a worldwide agency is the ability to reach people
on the other side of the globe—real people
with a name, a face, and a bio—and work
with them to help clients who are looking
to relocate or need to move people and
companies. The bulk of the company's
business, however, is home sales. Agents
handle properties in all price ranges, from
$30,000 to $2 million and more.

Yeager Realty
400 South Clinton Street
(410) 563-1111
Michael Yeager Jr., known as Mr. Mike to
his neighbors, was born and raised on
Clinton Street and has been in business in
Highlandtown for more than 40 years. The
first 30 years, he owned Yeager's Music
stores; the last 10 years he has been Yeager Realty. A small brokerage, with only
three other agents on staff, Yeager specializes in properties in Highlandtown and
its neighbors to the south—Fells Point and
Canton. Yeager notes that he knows Highlandtown homes "like the back of his
hand." He knows what problems to look
for. He knows at a glance if the plumbing's
been updated or if these classic row
homes with their hand-painted screens
and marble steps have all the housepower
they need. Yeager notes that a well-kept
property in Highlandtown still goes for a
median price of about $40,000 to
$50,000, but bargains abound. Properties
in need of renovation or rehab fall in the
$20,000 to $30,000 range.

ACCOMMODATIONS

Only a few of the elegant, old-world hotels still serve Baltimore's guests. The others that once welcomed some of the most influential people in the world to their doors gave way first to the Depression, then war, urban blight, office towers, and urban renewal. A few were saved and turned into condominiums. The Belvedere Hotel in Mount Vernon is one of those. Its apartments are modern, but the lobby, main ballroom, and the Owl Bar, where H. L. Mencken liked to come after a hard day of curmudeoning, are still much as they were at the turn of the twentieth century.

The urban renewal of the 1960s produced Charles Center and the Downtown Holiday Inn on Fayette Street. At the time the most modern and one of the tallest buildings in that area, the Holiday Inn is now dwarfed by the towers that have grown up around it in the last 40 years.

Once the Inner Harbor became the focus of Downtown events, there was a tremendous building spurt, both at the harbor itself and in the entire area near it, especially between the harbor and Camden Yards. As their business travelers have grown in number, Timonium and Towson have also added a fair number of new accommodations.

Being, as we are, on the main north-south truck routes of I-95 and U.S. Highway 1 and essentially at the beginning of western U.S. Highways 40 and 50, we've always boasted a number of motels. (Well, since the invention of the automobile, any-way . . .) Up and down these well-used roads—every few feet, it seems—there are motels. Some of them are nothing more than a few cabins; some of them are pretty posh establishments. Most of them have been excluded from our list. We have included only those few that are close to Downtown or other major business areas. As for the others, we figure you're pretty

much like us. When you're on a long drive and you get tired, you stop at the next vacancy sign.

Hotels are different. For them, we usually plan ahead. Here we've provided a sampling of these accommodations in the area, including the chains. Of course, most of the chains have more than one location. For instance, Holiday Inn still has its hotel in Downtown Baltimore, but it also has hotels at Baltimore–Washington International Airport (BWI), in Towson, in Columbia, in Glen Burnie, in Pikesville, and on Frankfort Avenue. You'll find Marriott Hotels at two locations in the Inner Harbor and also at BWI and Hunt Valley; the Sheraton has hotels at the Inner Harbor, BWI, and Towson.

All told, Baltimore has more than 75 hotels and motels in and around the immediate area. The accommodations we've presented in this chapter are in the Downtown area and around the Baltimore Beltway. Each is within easy access of the Inner Harbor or is convenient to expressways, Light Rail, subway, or bus service.

You can assume that every listed hotel is wheeelchair accessible. You can expect that you cannot have your dog with you (although there are a few that do allow pets).

Cabs make a habit of parking outside of most Downtown hotels. Buses are also convenient to most Downtown locations, as is the MARC train to Washington, the subway, and the Light Rail (see the Getting Here, Getting Around chapter). These modes of transportation are less convenient to some of the suburban locations we mention, but if a suburban location does have access, we've noted it.

If you arrive in Baltimore by car, be it a rental or your own, expect hotels in the Downtown area to charge a daily parking fee. We've noted those that do. Hotels outside the city and around the Beltway tend to offer free parking.

Many hotels now include some kind of breakfast in the price of the room. The full American breakfast often includes a choice of eggs, pancakes, waffles, hot cereals, fresh fruit, milk, juice, and coffee or tea in the hotel's on-site restaurant. If it is included, we'll tell you, but more often than not you'll be offered a continental breakfast of some combination of muffins, biscuits, toast and the like, juice, and coffee or tea. You'll also find information about recent renovations, decorations, and amenities a particular hotel offers, such as swimming pools, exercise rooms or equipment, van service, etc.

Most hotels in Baltimore also have smoking rooms, but they now constitute a smaller percentage of total rooms available. So, if you're a smoker, you'll need to make your reservations well in advance.

PRICE CODE

The room rate we've chosen to quote is the industry standard, known in the trade as the RACK rate. In cases where a hotel has seasonal rates, we've taken an average price to quote as the standard. For instance, a room that costs $129 during the hotel's off-season may cost $190 during its peak season. That hotel's price would then average out to $160. What we've provided here is meant to be only a guide for selecting an accommodation. For specific rates applied to a particular time of year, call the hotel.

$	Less than $80
$$	$80 to $125
$$$	$126 to $150
$$$$	$151 to $199
$$$$$	$200 and more

There is a room tax in Baltimore City of 12½ percent; in Baltimore County, 13 percent. Most hotels require a major credit card to guarantee a reservation; some require you to confirm. If they don't, then they have a cutoff time after which your reservation is not held.

DOWNTOWN

Admiral Fell Inn $$$$
888 South Broadway
(410) 522-7377
www.AdmiralFell.com

In the heart of historic Fells Point at the foot of Broadway is the Admiral Fell Inn. Eighty rooms are spread through eight buildings, some of which date back to the 1770s. The inn reflects that period with Federal-style decorations and furnishings throughout. It is a very classy, old-world place and often used by Baltimoreans for wedding receptions, rehearsal dinners, and the like—pretty much in any case where image and ambience are the order of the day. In 1996 the Admiral Fell underwent a complete renovation and expansion, including the building of meeting and banquet facilities on the roof—now the fifth floor.

The inn boasts three restaurants on the premises, including Hamilton's (see the Restaurants chapter). The room price includes a light continental breakfast. There is no exercise room or pool, but guests may request that exercise equipment be brought to their room, or, for an additional charge of $15, they may take advantage of the Downtown Athletic Club's facilities just about five minutes away by hotel van. (If you want exercise, however, we would recommend a good brisk walk through Fells Point's charming cobblestone streets.) A few specialty rooms run as high as $289 per night, such as the "attic room" in the oldest building. It's tucked up under the eaves, with the original hand-hewn beams gently rising to a peak. If you want a taste of Baltimore history and a short commute to the Inner Harbor, the Admiral Fell Inn is where you want to be.

Baltimore Marriott Inner Harbor $$$$-$$$$$
Pratt and Eutaw Streets
(410) 962-0202 or (800) 228-9290
www.marriott.com

The Marriott Inner Harbor and its attached

parking garage sit not quite on the harbor itself, but a block west, just across from Camden Yards. Built in 1984, this 10-story modern hotel offers 524 traditional rooms as well as 34 suites. Amenities include an on-site restaurant, gift shop, full business center, secretarial services, and safe deposit box at the front desk. The rooms come equipped with a two-line phone, speaker phone, voice mail, and the dataports. The Marriot has seasonal rates that vary accordingly. Packages are available that include breakfast.

If you'd like to stay at the Inner Harbor, but you're concerned about Downtown traffic, don't be. It only really gets crowded during rush hours (8:00 to 9:30 A.M.; 4:00 to 5:30 P.M.), or if there's a baseball or football game.

Baltimore Marriott Waterfront $$$$-$$$$$
700 Aliceanna Street
(410) 385-3000 or (800) 228-9290
www.marriott.com

The Marriott Waterfront is the newest of several hotels in Baltimore's Inner Harbor. The hotel overlooks the harbor and is within walking distance to various shops and popular restaurants including the ESPN Zone, Hard Rock Cafe, and the popular neighborhood of Little Italy. There are three restaurants, a deli, and a lounge, either in the hotel or attached. This huge hotel offers 750 guest rooms, all with harbor view. The rooms come equipped with amenities that include climate control, two-line telephone with message light, dataport, and voice mail. In-room coffee and tea, hair dryer, iron, and ironing board are also included. There is on-site parking and the hotel offers water taxi service—a truly great way to get around the harbor (see Getting Here, Getting Around chapter for information on the water taxi).

Brookshire Inner Harbor Suites Hotel $$$$-$$$$$
120 East Lombard Street
(410) 625-1300
www.harbormagic.com

The Brookshire is a small corporate hotel, with 97 guest rooms and 10 suites. Executive suites have a living room, wet bar, and separate bedroom with bath and are more expensive than the standard price; junior suites have the same except the separate wet bar. Some suites have a view of the harbor. Because the hotel is small, it does not have its own parking lot. Valet parking is provided for a fee of $25 a night. While the hotel has an exercise room you can also receive a pass to a nearby health club, which has pool, sauna, and even aerobics, for a charge of $15. In the less than two decades the hotel has been at this location, it has been renovated three times in an effort to modernize and make each suite as up to date and comfortable as possible. The Brookshire does not have seasonal rates, but it does run seasonal specials and offers special corporate rates as well as major discounts for members of the American Association for Retired Persons and AAA.

Clarion Hotel Peabody Court $$$$$
612 Cathedral Street
(410) 727-7101 or (877) 424-6423
www.choicehotels.com

Located in the heart of the Mount Vernon Cultural District, just 1 block from the Washington Monument and walking distance to all the galleries, restaurants, and shops along Charles Street, this is an elegant boutique hotel with 104 newly renovated guest rooms. Each room features heated towel warmers, glorious pillow-top mattresses, full marble bathrooms, and imported French marble-topped furniture. The in-house restaurant, aptly named George's On Mount Vernon Square, is in honor of the "Three George's" of Baltimore—George Washington, George Peabody, and George Herman ("Babe") Ruth. The hotel also offers a fitness room, and a business center with high-speed

Internet access. Valet parking is available for $20 a night and arrangements can be made for pets.

Courtyard by Marriott, Baltimore Inner Harbor $$$-$$$$
1000 Aliceanna Street
(443) 923-4000
www.marriott.com

Situated in a new development of buildings and hotels known as Inner Harbor East, this Courtyard is across the parking lot from the towering Baltimore Marriott Waterfront and a few blocks from the Inner Harbor and Fells Point. Ten guestroom floors provide 205 rooms replete with two-line phones, dataports, and cable TV. There is an indoor pool and exercise room on-site, a conveniently located garage, and a nearby Whole Foods natural food market with a great salad bar, deli, and sushi stand.

Days Inn, Inner Harbor $$$
100 Hopkins Place
(410) 576-1000
www.daysinnerharbor.com

The Days Inn is only 3 blocks west of the Inner Harbor proper, directly across from the Convention Center. It offers 250 rooms with two double beds, 42 rooms with queen-size beds, and 8 over-size rooms on its nine floors. Because the hotel is so close to Camden Yards, its busiest season is baseball season. Rental car service is available by asking the concierge. Guests are charged an additional $11 per day for parking, but the price can vary. The hotel offers an outside swimming pool, open May through September, and a fitness center. There is also a restaurant, Hopkin's Bar and Grill, on site.

Harbor Court Hotel $$$$$
550 Light Street
(410) 234-0550
www.harborcourt.com

Architecturally, the Harbor Court, with its huge, twin, red-brick towers, is one of the most striking hotels in Baltimore. The English country interior is just as phenomenal.

The grand staircase is reminiscent of ball gowns and footmen. The pickled oak paneling in the lobby was imported from England; and the 25 specialty suites sport canopy beds and marble bathrooms. The Harbor Court has 195 rooms and three restaurants. Guests may take advantage of 24-hour room service and a full-service health club, including tennis and racquetball courts, tanning salons, and massage. There's a concierge staff of three. All rooms must be guaranteed with a credit card. Package rates and corporate rates are available.

Holiday Inn Inner Harbor $$
301 West Lombard Street
(410) 685-3500
www.holiday-inn.com

The downtown Holiday Inn is two buildings containing a total of 375 rooms, with a two-level parking garage in between, and a breezeway connecting them. It was built in 1964, but a few years ago saw a $7 million renovation to all rooms, which included such everyday amenities as a voice mail system, iron and ironing boards, and gourmet coffee in every room. There is a $14 daily parking fee. The hotel is only a block from Camden Yards and a seven-minute walk from the Inner Harbor. And get set to get wet—it boasts the largest indoor pool of any hotel in Baltimore.

Hyatt Regency $$$$-$$$$$
300 Light Street
(410) 528-1234 or (800) 233-1234
www.hyatt.com

The Hyatt Regency was one of the first high-rise, luxury hotels built at the Inner Harbor. Opened in the early 1980s, its 486 rooms, including 25 suites, underwent a $7 million renovation in 1996 and 1997. In 1999 the hotel's lobby was completely renovated. The hotel's amenities are legion, ranging from the more standard concierge service to a jogging track, rooftop tennis courts, and a putting green. If you stay at the Hyatt, your feet need never touch the ground, as its skywalks can take you over the street and across to Harborplace or the Convention Center. All rooms must be guaranteed with a credit card or a one-night deposit. Parking is an additional $17 per day for self-park and $22 per day for valet.

Inn at Henderson's Wharf $$–$$$
1000 Fell Street
(410) 522-7777 or (800) 522-2088
Henderson's Wharf was built on the "point" of Fells Point. Built in 1894 for the B&O Railroad, the site is a registered National Historic Landmark. The 38-room inn takes up only the first floor of the building, with the second through sixth floors serving as private apartments, most of which must be rented for at least a year. A gated parking lot is on the property, if you need a place to park a car; there is also a full-service marina right out the front door of the inn, if you need a place to park your boat. The water taxi is nearby. Half of the rooms have a view of the water; the others overlook the inner courtyard, with its cobblestone patio and wooden tables sheltered by white umbrellas. The lobby's floors and walls are in evidence. The rooms are large and decorated in an English country style. The hotel also has a 24-hour fitness center on the premises. All reservations must be guaranteed with a credit card. Continental breakfast is included in the price of the room.

Before the city gets busy and the offices and shops open is a wonderful time to soak in the scenery. Come out on your balcony or stroll around the Inner Harbor just after sunup. You'll enjoy the fresh smell of the air, the early morning sparkle of the sun on the water, and the occasional gust that carries the scent of bread baking.

Mount Vernon Hotel $$–$$$
24 West Franklin Street
(410) 727-2000 or (800) 245-5256
www.bic.edu/mtvernon
For more than 50 years, the downtown YMCA was housed at this address. When the Comfort Inn bought it and renovated it for a hotel, it traded the Olympic pools for parking under the building. The Mount Vernon Hotel took over the site in 1994 and completely renovated the building, redecorated the lobby and in-house cafe, appropriately, in the Victorian style. It offers 133 rooms on nine floors, including single, double, and wheelchair-accessible rooms as well as loft and Jacuzzi suites. This is a basic hotel, right in the center of everything. It's across the street from the central branch of the Enoch Pratt Free Library, the Basilica of the Assumption, and the First Unitarian Church. One block north is the Walters Art Museum; 2 blocks north is Mount Vernon Square. It is a 7-block walk from Pratt Street and the Inner Harbor and is accessible on major bus lines. Parking is available on site for an extra $8.00 for your entire stay.

Pier 5 Hotel $$$$–$$$$$
711 Eastern Avenue
(410) 539-2000
www.harbormagic.com
The Pier 5 Hotel is the only hotel with an Inner Harbor location that sits right on the water. And it's right in the thick of things. Pier 6 Concert Pavilion is out the door to your right; the Hard Rock Cafe is out the door to your left; and there is one restaurant on the premises. The Inn offers 65 rooms on three floors, including seven suites. Guests can self park for $18 a day on two lots, next to and across the street from the hotel. Valet parking is available for $25 a day. The Pier 5 Hotel is smoke-free. Twenty-four-hour concierge service and room service are available. Even with all this, however the Art Deco ambience and the sound of the water lapping up against the dock are probably the best features of the Pier 5 Hotel.

Quality Inn at the Stadiums $–$$
1701 Russell Street
(410) 727-3400
www.qualityinn.com
This motel is 4 blocks south of Camden Yards, across Russell Street Bridge in an

industrial area. The motel is, however, a clean place to call home for a time, particularly if you're traveling on a budget. It offers cable TV, complimentary continental breakfast, free parking, and a swimming pool in summer. It's only about 20 feet from the on ramps to I-95 and the Baltimore–Washington Expressway.

Radisson Plaza Lord
Baltimore $$-$$$$
20 West Baltimore Street
(410) 539-8400 or (800) 333-3333
www.radisson.com

Built in 1928, the Radisson Plaza Lord Baltimore is the city's only National Historic Landmark hotel. It's located right in the heart of the city, within walking distance from many attractions. The hotel was built in Baltimore's heyday, and the historic interior reflects the grand style of the roaring '20s. Plush carpet, warm wood, brass, and a three-story lobby compliment the 424 deluxe guest rooms, including suites with full kitchens, living rooms, and whirlpools. You can upgrade to a Plaza Level room and be lavished by private concierge attention, silver service continental breakfast, and evening cocktails and hors d'oeuvres.

While the hotel reflects the past, it is anything but archaic. Modern amenities abound, including a gym, in-room fax and e-mail service, and personalized concierge attention. Rooms can range drastically in price depending on the time of year, from $60 for a double to upwards of $260 for an executive suite.

Renaissance
Harborplace Hotel $$$$-$$$$$
202 East Pratt Street
(410) 547-1200 or (800) HOTELS-1
www.renaissancehotels.com

The Renaissance Harborplace Hotel is directly opposite the Pratt Street Pavilion at Harborplace, the World Trade Center, and the National Aquarium. It has 622 rooms on 12 floors, with one of its most interesting features being the secured Club Level Floor—it's only accessible with a key. Club Level rooms include a conti-

nental breakfast and other food amenities such as hors d'oeuvres and dessert in the evening. Built in 1988, the hotel saw a complete renovation of the sleeping rooms that was finished in 1996; additional renovations were completed in 1998. A few of the hotel's amenities include an indoor pool, an exercise facility, the Windows Restaurant, and a lounge that overlooks the harbor (see the Restaurants chapter). There is a $16 daily self-parking fee and a $25 per day valet parking fee.

Sheraton Inner Harbor Hotel $$$$
300 South Charles Street
(410) 962-8300 or (866) 226-9330
www.sheraton.com

The Sheraton Inner Harbor offers 337 rooms and 20 suites in a high-rise building that is, essentially, right next door to Camden Yards. Amenities include two in-house restaurants, including the Orioles Bar and Grill (see the Nightlife chapter). An indoor pool and health club with sauna help you shed the unwanted pounds you might gain eating out. All Sheraton hotels offer discounts of up to 35 percent off their regular rates through their Sure Savers program. The special club rooms incorporate a small office space into the room that includes a fax/copier/printer. Call for information about special programs and rooms like the "Take me out to the ballgame" package that includes Orioles tickets. There is on-site parking in the Sheraton garage for $18 per day.

Wyndham
Baltimore Inner Harbor $$-$$$
101 West Fayette Street
(410) 752-1100
www.wyndham.com

The Wyndham is one of the largest hotels in Maryland, with 707 rooms on 27 floors. It is actually not on the Inner Harbor but 3 blocks north and 2 blocks west of it. It's situated directly across Cathedral Street from the Baltimore Arena and just across Hopkins Plaza from the Morris Mechanic Theatre right in the middle of Charles Center. A subway stop is just beyond the cab stand, and the hotel is only a few blocks east of the Light Rail. The Wyndham offers singles, doubles, triples, quads, junior suites, and suites. There's an exercise room on-site. Unlike some hotels that base rates on season and availability, the Wyndham's rates are based strictly on availability, which can make it an excellent choice if you're looking for a bargain. The hotel includes two award-winning steak houses, Shula's Steak House and Shula's Steak 2.

NORTHEAST

Chase Suite Hotel by Woodfin $$$
10710 Beaver Dam Road, Hunt Valley
(410) 584-7370 or (888) 433-6141
www.woodfinsuitehotels.com
The Chase Suite Hotel offers 96 suites that include one- and two-bedroom suites as well as single and double studios. All rooms come with full kitchens. Located in Hunt Valley, about 18 miles from the Inner Harbor, this hotel is convenient to the Light Rail and Timonium Fairgrounds. The Chase Suite Hotel allows pets for an additional $5.00 charge per night. The accommodation offers its guests a homey atmosphere that includes a complimentary weeknight dinner. An outdoor pool and outdoor spa are part of the hotel's amenities.

Days Hotel & Conference Center $-$$$
9615 Deereco Road, Timonium
(410) 560-1000 or (800) DAYS-INN
www.daysinn.com
Days Hotel has 145 single and double rooms on six floors, above a floor of office and meeting room space that can be combined to create a large ballroom. Built in 1989, the hotel is constantly renovating, so that all rooms are kept up to date with the latest amenities. The hotel is one of the few in the area to offer a standard long-term stay rate. If you stay longer than 30 days, you are exempt from the 13 percent tax. Days Hotel offers some common, modern in-room amenities, such as refrigerators and dataports, but it also gives visitors free local phone calls, use of on-site washers and dryers, and complimentary continental breakfast. The best convenience, however, may be that the hotel is attached to a Chili's Grill and Bar, which has an on-premises lounge and provides room service to the hotel as well as a take-out window.

Days Hotel & Conference Center is about a 20-minute drive from Downtown Baltimore via I-83.

Days Inn Baltimore East $
8801 Loch Raven Boulevard, Towson
(410) 882-0900 or (800) DAYS-INN
www.daysinn.com
This five-story, 156-room hotel offers free parking, an on-site restaurant and lounge, complimentary breakfast, and free HBO. About 20 minutes from downtown Baltimore and minutes from Towson Town Center (see the Shopping chapter), the hotel is close to shopping, movies, golf, and bowling as well as to some historic sites, such as Hampton Mansion. Also within a short distance are Towson University, Morgan State University, Goucher College, Loyola College, the College of Notre Dame, and the Johns Hopkins University.

Embassy Suites
Baltimore Hunt Valley $$$-$$$$
213 International Circle, Hunt Valley
(410) 584-1400 or (800) 362-2779
www.embassysuites.com
Embassy Suites, only a 25-minute drive or a short ride on Light Rail from the heart of Baltimore City, offers 223 two-room suites over eight stories. All suites include a living room and bedroom. Some have king-size beds; others have two double-size beds. All have pull-out sofa and offer balconies that overlook a garden atrium, complete with waterfalls and a park-like setting, right in the heart of the business complex in Hunt Valley. Breakfast, which is included in your room rate, is cooked to order. Rates vary based on availability.

Hampton Inn White Marsh $$-$$$
8225 Town Center Drive, White Marsh
(410) 931-2200
www.hampton-inn.com

White Marsh is a suburban shopping mall, surrounded by a bedroom community of the same name. But the mall has grown over the years to include an industrial park and some unique shopping opportunities. (See the Shopping and Relocation chapters for more information.) With easy access to I-95, the hotel is at least 25 minutes from the center of Baltimore City. The four-story building has 127 rooms, most featuring two double beds or a king-size bed. Amenities include an outside pool during the summer, an on-site exercise room, and access to the Bally Total Fitness center next door.

Marriott Burkshire Guest Suites & Conference Center $$
10 West Burke Avenue, Towson
(410) 324-8100 or (800) 435-5986
burkshire@towson.edu
Adjacent to Towson University, the Marriott Burkshire's 135 guest apartments were originally meant to be retirement condominiums. This means that when we say the Burkshire has fully equipped kitchens, we're not talking about a microwave and a hot plate. The living rooms are living-room size, and each apartment even comes with its own washer and dryer. There are one-, two-, and three-bedroom apartments available. There is an on-site fitness room, but all guests of the Marriott Burkshire have access at no additional charge to the sports facilities at Towson University, which includes racquetball, tennis, and wallyball courts. Long-term parking is hard to find in Towson, so the hotel's free underground parking lot is an added bonus. Discounts off already low prices are available for people who have business with the university, and Marriott reward points are honored here. Advance reservation with a credit card is suggested.

Marriott Hunt Valley Inn $$-$$$$
245 Shawan Road, Hunt Valley
(410) 785-7000 or (800) 228-9290
www.marriott.com
Marriott Hunt Valley Inn has 290 rooms, eight suites, and 22 meeting rooms. It's right in the heart of the Hunt Valley business district near McCormicks and Procter & Gamble. You'll find a restaurant, indoor and outdoor swimming pools, a health club, whirlpool, and sauna all on site. There's golfing nearby at Hunt Valley Golf Club, Longview Golf Course, and Pine Ridge Golf Course (see the Golf chapter for more information).

Red Roof Inn $-$$
111 West Timonium Road
(410) 666-0380 or (800) RED-ROOF
www.redroof.com
Red Roof Inn has recently finished an extensive renovation of all of its 137 rooms. Off-season rates have fallen in the past to as low as $55, and there is no additional charge for a pet. This is a comfortable, clean facility 20 minutes north of the city by car, 10 minutes to Towson, and close to two Light Rail stops.

Sheraton Baltimore North Hotel $$$-$$$$
903 Dulaney Valley Road, Towson
(410) 321-7400
www.sheraton.com
Right in the heart of Towson, at the intersection of Dulaney Valley Road and Goucher Boulevard, you'll find the Sheraton Baltimore, a 284-room, luxury hotel. It's location is one of its best attributes—right in Towson, only 20 minutes from the center of Baltimore, not quite a mile from the Beltway and connected by skywalk to Towson Town Center, the largest shopping mall in the area (see the Shopping chapter). However, traffic can be relentless, particularly at rush hours, so keep that in mind if you need to be somewhere at a particular time. Although bus service does go out to Towson, main access is by car.

The Sheraton is another hotel that prices according to demand, so rates can fall precipitously depending on whether it's busy or not. All reservations must be guaranteed with a credit card. Pets are allowed with a security deposit.

Among the in-room amenities are two phones, voice mail, and modem accessibility. There is also an indoor pool.

NORTHWEST

Baltimore Days Inn West—
Security Boulevard   **$–$$$**
1660 Whitehead Court
(410) 944-7400 or (800) DAYS INN
www.the.daysinn.com/Baltimore 09351
Built in 1958 and totally renovated in 1997, this two-story Days Inn offers single rooms at prices as low as $67 and suites as high as $169. Right in the thick of west Baltimore's suburban business centers, the hotel is near shopping, fitness centers, and tennis courts, and it has a pool and restaurant on-site. The hotel has special parking for RVs.

Doubletree Inn
at the Colonnade   **$$–$$$**
4 West University Parkway
(410) 235-5400
The Colonnade is a luxury high-rise condominium building, directly across form the playing fields of the Johns Hopkins University's Homewood Campus, on the southern edge of the community known as Tuscany-Canterbury. The Doubletree Inn takes up the first three floors of the building, offering 125 rooms, among which are a presidential suite and a honeymoon suite. Rates are based on availability. The award-winning Polo Grill restaurant is in the lobby, as well as the Crobin Salon, a full-service hair salon. An indoor pool sits under a glass dome facing an inner landscaped courtyard.

Hilton Pikesville   **$$–$$$$$**
1726 Reisterstown Road, Pikesville
(410) 653-1100 or (800) 774-1500
www.hilton.com
The Hilton Pikesville offers everything from single rooms to suites with full kitchens.

Rooms have the usual amenities—phones, TV, alarm clock. But this particular Hilton has some things that you won't find everywhere, such as a Budget car rental desk on site. The Hilton Pikesville offers a multilingual staff that speaks Spanish, German, Russian, French, and Italian—a true rarity among Baltimore lodgings. The Hilton Pikesville also offers an outdoor swimming pool, six lighted indoor tennis courts, and an on-premises health club with massage. Also located on the property is a hair salon, jewelry shop, travel agent, camera shop, and bank. There is also a restaurant and lounge on the premises.

Radisson Hotel at Cross Keys   **$$–$$$**
Village of Cross Keys
100 Village Square
(410) 532-6900 or (800) 333-3333
www.radisson.com
The Radisson is located in the Village of Cross Keys, a relatively modern secured development within the bounds of one of the oldest developed neighborhoods in Baltimore, Roland Park. The inn has 148 rooms on four floors. It sits at the west end of the community shopping center, which boasts some of the more exclusive shops in the area. The inn serves mainly business travelers and neighborhood guests. One of the hotel's more unique amenities is complimentary access to the Cross Keys Tennis Club. Rooms have voice mail, dataports, and coffeemakers. Complimentary scheduled shuttle service to the Baltimore Inner Harbor is available. There is also a full-service restaurant on the premises.

SOUTHEAST

Best Western Hotel &
Conference Center   **$–$$**
5625 O'Donnell Street and I-95
(410) 633-9500 or (800) 633-9511
www.bestwestern.com
Best Western has Inner Harbor access but is less expensive than most Inner Harbor hotels (about half the rate). The 175 rooms

on 12 floors have either one king-size bed, two double beds, a king-size bed with a sitting area (known as a minisuite), and a living room with separate bedroom and bath with Jacuzzi (known as a Jacuzzi suite). Recent years have seen the complete renovation of the hotel and the addition of a large ballroom on the first floor. The hotel also boasts an in-house pool, fitness center, and full-service restaurant. (**NOTE:** the Jacuzzi suite is more than $200 per night, year-round.)

Hampton Inn Glen Burnie   **$$**
6617 Ritchie Highway, Glen Burnie
(410) 761-7666
www.hampton-inn.com
Ten minutes from BWI and from Camden Yards, the Hampton Inn Glen Burnie offers 115 rooms on five floors. It is actually a part of the Governor Plaza shopping center, so it's a short walk to restaurants, shops, and Bally's Holiday Health Club, to which guests have complimentary access. One of its unique features is 9-foot ceilings, which give an additional feeling of spaciousness to the relatively large guest rooms. Dataports are in every room, and copy and fax service are available. A complimentary continental breakfast is served. Built in 1989, the inn underwent a complete renovation that was completed in 1998. All room reservations must be guaranteed with a credit card.

SOUTHWEST

Best Western Baltimore-
Washington Airport   **$-$$**
6755 Dorsey Road, Elkridge
(410) 796-3300 or (800) 780-72334
www.bestwestern.com
The Best Western on Dorsey Road offers 33 rooms in a pleasant low-rise building that lies 7 miles from the Baltimore–Washington International Airport. Children younger than 17 stay free with a full-paying adult. On the premises you'll find a fitness center and spa, indoor heated pool, whirlpool, and sauna, as well as meeting

and banquet facilities that can service affairs for up to 100 people. A welcome amenity is the free courtesy transportation to BWI.

Comfort Inn–Airport   **$$-$$$**
6921 Baltimore Annapolis Boulevard
(410) 789-9100
www.comfortinn.com
Comfort Inn offers singles (queen- or king-size beds), rooms with two double beds, a penthouse, and two executive suites, totaling 188 rooms on six floors. The Comfort Inn was completely renovated in 1996. The hotel has no seasonal rates but offers the same low rate year-round. There is a large exercise area, which includes Jacuzzi and sauna, and a video game room. Guests are treated to a full buffet breakfast. Pets are allowed with the proviso that guests notify the hotel in advance. There's a restaurant on-site.

Courtyard by Marriott Baltimore-
Washington Airport   **$$-$$$$**
1671 West Nursery Road, Linthicum
(410) 859-8855 or (800) 321-2211
www.marriott.com
This Marriott Courtyard is just a little more than 2 miles from BWI. A low-rise building with 149 rooms and 12 suites, it caters to the business traveler, as many of the airport hotels do. The positive aspect of this for tourists is that hotel rates are lower on the weekends and amenities are high. The Courtyard offers valet service, an indoor pool, and exercise room, and there is a restaurant on the premises.

Embassy Suites Hotel
Baltimore at BWI Airport   **$$$$-$$$$$**
1300 Concourse Drive, Linthicum
(410) 850-0747 or (800) 362-2779
www.embassysuites.com
Weekend prices can be almost half of the weekday rate at this eight-story, atrium-centered facility near BWI. Amenities in its 251 suites include wet bar, refrigerator, coffeemaker, and microwave. The hotel features an indoor pool, Jacuzzi, sauna, exercise room, gift shop, newsstand, and

on-site steakhouse-style restaurant. Thirteen of the suites are wheelchair accessible. Transportation is also easy here, with free hotel transportation not only to and from BWI but also to the BWI Amtrak stop, the Light Rail, and MARC train. The hotel also offers an evening complimentary reception for hotel guests and complimentary breakfast.

Marriott Residence Inn $$$-$$$$
1160 Winterson Road, Linthicum
(410) 691-0255 or (800) 228-9290
www.marriott.com

The 120 suites at the three-story Marriott Residence Inn are designed for comfort over the long term. In fact, each suite features a fully equipped kitchen; however, we doubt you'll ever have need to use it. There is no restaurant on-site, but every morning the house kitchen prepares a complimentary continental breakfast for guests. Selections on the menu vary, but you can always be assured of one hot item, such as waffles or sausage, and cold fresh fruit as well as pastries, breads, and other goodies. Evening socials feature a complimentary light dinner, which might be anything from a sandwich to the weekly guest barbecue. When you're not chowing down, you can take advantage of the outdoor pool, Sport Court, and exercise room. Rates change depending on the season, availability, and length of stay, with price breaks available at five nights, 12 nights, and 30 nights. Only 2 miles from BWI and within jogging distance of NSA and Martin Marietta, the Marriott Residence Inn is excellent as a home-away-from-home for the long-term business traveler or as a base for sightseeing in the Baltimore-Washington area. Pets are allowed for a $100 nonrefundable deposit and an extra $10 per day.

Sheraton International Hotel-
BWI Airport $$-$$$$
7032 Elm Road, Linthicum
(410) 859-3300
www.sheraton.com

The Sheraton at BWI offers 201 rooms on the grounds of the BWI Airport. Other than sheer convenience, amenities include an outdoor pool, exercise room, jogging area, and 24-hour room service, as well as an on-site restaurant. The best thing about this Sheraton location is its rates, which during low occupancy times can fall as low as $99. On-site parking is free, and rooms were recently renovated.

Turf Valley Resort &
Conference Center $$$-$$$$$
2700 Turf Valley Road, Ellicott City
(410) 465-1500 or (888) 833-8873
www.turfvalley.com

Turf Valley could be considered outside the Baltimore area, in that it is on the outside edge of the area considered Ellicott City, about 25 minutes from Downtown. We include it, however, because it offers some accommodations and amenities not available anywhere else in the area. Before the hotel was opened at the site in the mid-1980s, Turf Valley was a country club, and its three 18-hole championship golf courses are open to hotel guests. Turf Valley offers 220 hotel rooms and suites, and 40,000 square feet of meeting space. Also offered are one-, two-, and three-bedroom villas with added amenities such as Jacuzzis and fireplaces. Golf is not the only thing for guests to do. There is a complete recreation area with tennis courts, sand volleyball, basketball, and shuffleboard. A full-service European spa, two restaurants, a lounge, and both an indoor and outdoor swimming pool are here. If that's not enough, Turf Valley has over 1,000 acres of beautifully landscaped grounds to stroll through.

BED-AND-BREAKFASTS

One of your best bets to really get an insider's sense of Baltimore's neighborhoods is to stay at one of our bed-and-breakfasts.

These owner-operated rest stops, nestled within communities such as Federal Hill, Fells Point, and Mount Vernon, offer a much more intimate picture of Baltimore than is available at other accommodations. The stories that flow from the walls, the innkeepers, the other visitors, and the communities that surround these establishments will color your stay. The owners and operators are part of their communities; therefore, they can provide insights into where to eat, what to do, how to get around—things that might not be available to you in any other way.

"If you want to see Baltimore, you need to stay in one of our bed-and-breakfasts," says Paul Bragaw, an innkeeper and past president of the Maryland Association of Bed and Breakfasts.

Practically every era of Baltimore's history is represented. Waterfront houses built in Baltimore's earliest years, Victorians with all their beauty and splendor, and converted row houses, acquired during the city's ambitious effort to bring people back to the cities in the 1970s are just some of the offerings awaiting those willing to pass on the familiar chains of hotels and motels dotting the area.

Of equal appeal to many who stay at inns and bed-and-breakfasts is the slower pace. TVs give way to conversation, radios give way to reading. Quiet, contemplative time in front of a fireplace or sipping tea and relaxing with others after taking in the sights are to be expected. Mere pleasantries exchanged over a shared, family-style breakfast lead to shared insights and discussions about how home and away are similar and different. Occasionally, visitors who meet at a bed-and-breakfast become long-term friends, often returning to the site of the blossoming of a newfound relationship year after year.

PRICE CODE

Prices can range from $80 to $150, depending on whether it's a weekday or weekend, the size of the room, the location and the time of the year.

A safe average would be about $100 a night, which includes a full breakfast in the morning. Most rooms are not open to children or pets. Because many bed-and-breakfasts are often in older buildings, they usually offer poor wheelchair accessibility. Smoking is usually prohibited to satisfy nonsmoking visitors.

The price codes shown reflect the weekend rates. Rates do not include city and state taxes, which usually add about 15 percent to the bill.

$	$80 to $100
$$	$101 to $125
$$$	$126 and more

Don't expect to make reservations for a weekend from April to November just a few days in advance. Home games for the Baltimore Orioles and/or the Baltimore Ravens as well as conventions in the area draw many visitors during these months, so rooms are booked well in advance.

A sizable portion of the bed-and-breakfast trade in the Baltimore area is geared toward businesspeople who visit the area, often with their spouses or other family members. A number of people staying at bed-and-breakfasts are friends or relatives of people living nearby. And you may be surprised by the number of locals who abandon their homes for a few nights in a bed-and-breakfast. After all, just because we live here doesn't mean we're not entitled to a little pampering.

Baltimore's bed-and-breakfast industry is still in its youth. The relative newness of the market has encouraged some illegal entrepreneurial spirit, so make sure that the place where you stay meets all of the local codes. The listings that are certified by the Maryland Bed and Breakfast Association are noted. Certification ensures that members meet parking, use, occupancy, and safety requirements. Be cautious of people who have large homes and "open them up" to people on the weekends.

DOWNTOWN

Abacrombie
Food and Accommodations   **$$**
58 West Biddle Street
(410) 244-7227
www.badger-inn.com
This row house from the 1880s provides 12 rooms with distinctive features in Mount Vernon. A partner to the Mr. Mole Bed & Breakfast of Bolton Hill (see listing later in this chapter), this site is convenient to the city's cultural center for the symphony, art galleries, or theaters. The first floor features an open parlor for relaxing. Each morning, guests select from the restaurant's Dutch continental breakfast.

Single and double occupancy are available. The rooms all have private bathrooms and telephones, which were added to appeal to business travelers. Televisions, "in a major concession to the 20th century," according to the owners of the inn, are in each room. Rooms also have their own temperature controls connecting to the central air system. Smoking is not permitted. Abacrombie Food and Accommodations is a Maryland Bed and Breakfast Association member.

Ann Street B&B   **$**
804 South Ann Street
(410) 342-5883
In 1988 Baltimore's innkeeping veterans, Joanne and Andrew Mazurek, opened Ann Street B&B in a house Andrew had grown up in.

More than 20 years ago, the city condemned the site and about 70 houses in preparation for the planned extension of I-95 through the city. But community opposition sent the highway in another direction. In the mid-1980s the city offered the homes back to their last owners. The Mazureks bought the family row house and one next door. The result is a happy ending for the Mazureks and guests at their three-bedroom bed-and-breakfast. Restored to an earlier era when Andrew's ancestors lived there, the inn features double poster beds, original hardwood floors, and a country colonial charm. Each room has a private bathroom and two have fireplaces. The inn also features central air conditioning. Twelve fireplaces help to keep the place warm in the winter as guests talk, snack, visit, and read. Another favorite feature of the house is the private garden, which from spring to fall is the ideal location to relax, away from the hustle and bustle of modern life. The Mazureks tend to it daily to ensure that guests always have an inviting outdoor spot in which to visit.

Located in the heart of Fells Point, there's no limit to the dining, dancing, and imbibing possibilities near the inn. The Mazureks are active participants in the Fells Point business community, offering guests insights into special-interest restaurants and stores in the area. According to Joanne Mazurek, their goal is provide guests "not a real formal place to relax for a while."

Celie's Waterfront
Bed and Breakfast   **$$$**
1714 Thames Street
(410) 522-2323 or (800) 432-0184
www.baltimore-bed-breakfast.com
In the heart of the Fells Point waterfront, Celie's Waterfront Bed and Breakfast features open rooms, many with skylights, and lots of modern conveniences for a bed-and-breakfast. All seven rooms offer private baths, air conditioning, and a choice of king-, queen-, or single-size beds. Rooms vary in their offerings, some with fireplaces, whirlpool tubs, private balconies, and harbor views. Everyone can spy the city skyline from the rooftop deck

and visit the private gardens maintained by innkeepers Kevin and Nancy Kupec. The Courtyard Room is wheelchair accessible and has its own courtyard.

Guests will find many antiques and collectibles, fresh-cut flowers, down comforters, flannel sheets, thick terry robes, and bath sheets in all of the rooms. They'll also find TVs, refrigerators stocked with soft drinks, juices, and mineral water, and even VCRs and coffeemakers in all rooms. The most popular rooms are the Harbor Front rooms, where guests can have a king-size bed, wood-burning fireplace, wicker seating, a whirlpool tub, and three windows facing the harbor.

Although it's not close to the university, Celie's offers discounts to Johns Hopkins University "family members" during weekdays. Children older than 10 are welcome, but smoking is prohibited. Private telephone lines are in all rooms, and breakfast is a combination of fresh fruits, juices, baked breads, and cereals. Celie's is a Maryland Bed and Breakfast Association member.

1870 Guest House $-$$
21 South Stricker Street
(410) 947-4622
www.bbonline.com/md/1870guest house/

Located in a restored Italianate-style row home, the 1870 Guest House offers accommodations complete with a fully equipped private kitchen and bath. Set in Southwest Baltimore, known as SoWeBo to insiders, the house faces the 1.3-acre Union Square Park that was established in 1847. About 15 blocks away from the Inner Harbor, the 1870 Guest House is a closer walk to the B&O Railroad Museum, H. L. Mencken House Museum, and Hollins Market. The market was built in 1836 and is Baltimore's oldest market still in use.

The third floor suite features a queen bed, bath with tub and shower, AC, TV/VCR, and private phone. The kitchen is stocked with a substantial breakfast and guests may serve themselves at their leisure.

Mr. Mole Bed & Breakfast $$$
1601 Bolton Street
(410) 728-1179
www.mrmolebb.com

Amid the quiet, tree-lined streets and brick row houses of Bolton Hill is Mr. Mole Bed & Breakfast, where eighteenth- and nineteenth-century antiques fill a building busting out with a comfortable English style. Innkeeper Collin Clarke's Australian accent and the large Dutch-style breakfast add flavor to the five-bedroom bed-and-breakfast. This is the only Mobil Travel Guide four-star lodging in Baltimore.

Mr. Mole's House has a separate street-level entrance, while the Explorer Suite offers a blue and white bedroom and sitting area with prints and artifacts from all over the world. The Garden Suite has a third-floor sunroom and a large private bath. The suite is decked out in floral prints. The Print Room boasts a formal, spacious setting of gray and white for the two bedrooms and sitting area. Silhouettes, engravings, and eighteenth-century prints complete the decor.

Colored in red and green and offering a sitting area and two bedrooms, the Balmoral Suite is the inn's largest accommodation. Single and double occupancy are available.

The first floor, with its 14-foot ceilings, has a living room, breakfast room, and drawing room. Bay windows and marble fireplaces remind visitors of the 1870s, when this house was built. With its location near Baltimore's cultural district, near the symphony hall, the Lyric Opera House,

Baltimore's bed-and-breakfasts are busiest in May. The Preakness Stakes, the second leg of horse racing's Triple Crown, is the third Saturday of the month, and numerous college graduation ceremonies draw relatives and friends from near and far throughout the month. Reservations are hard to come by through September without advance planning.

various art galleries, and Antique Row, this bed-and-breakfast is perfect for those who have been to the Inner Harbor and are looking for something new to experience.

Scarborough Fair $$$
1 East Montgomery Street
(410) 837-0010
www.scarborough-fair.com

Owners Ashley and Ellen Scarborough picture their bed-and-breakfast, which opened in January 1997, as a place where people from diverse backgrounds can gather to share everything from food to conversation to tips on the area they are visiting. Ellen fell in love with the idea for an inn after reading *Pilgrim's Progress*, which tells the stories of a group of visitors who head to the seacoast and share their life stories and lessons while staying at an inn.

This house, built in 1801, was a rehabilitated office building in the 1980s and now has become a six-bedroom guesthouse, about 2 blocks from the Inner Harbor. The Scarboroughs put six months of work into converting the office building into a guest house, and their time was well spent.

All of the rooms have different color schemes, colonial- and Victorian-era antiques, and queen-size beds, with the exception of one room that offers two twin beds that convert into a king. Ellen sewed all of the window treatments and other fabric accouterments in the rooms. Each room has a private bath either adjoined to it or across the hall from it. Four of the rooms have gas fireplaces.

A full breakfast, prepared by a professional chef, is served in a 12-seat dining room. A greeting room and library, featuring a variety of books collected by the Scarboroughs, is available to travelers. Because of the inn's easy access to the Inner Harbor area, Oriole Park at Camden Yards, M&T Bank Stadium, and the Baltimore Convention Center, reservations are recommended.

The Inn at Government House $$$
1125 North Calvert Street
(410) 539-0566

Set in the historic district of Mount Ver-
non, the Inn at Government House is a terrific cross between a bed-and-breakfast and hotel. With 19 rooms, the inn is larger than most bed-and-breakfasts in the area, but no less spectacular. Rooms come with a private bath, hair dryer, ironing board, iron, TV, and refrigerator. A continental breakfast and parking is included in the price of the room. Restoration of the Government House took place from 1983 to 1985, at a total cost of $2.5 million. Once the renovation was complete, the mansion was open to the public and has since served as the official guesthouse of the City of Baltimore. The mansion offers original woodwork and stained glass, as well as a Knabe square grand piano in the Music Room. More than 150 years old, it is probably one of the very few pianos of its kind left in existence. The mansion's library shows off detailed woodwork and a rounded bay windowseat with original stained glass. In the dining room guests are invited to have breakfast at the Pothast table. The table was manufactured in Baltimore and is nearly as old as the mansion, which dates back to 1889.

SOUTHWEST

The Wayside Inn $$
4344 Columbia Road, Ellicott City
(410) 461-4636
www.waysideinnmd.com

Nestled on the outskirts of Ellicott City, a historic mill town about 8 miles outside of Baltimore's city limits, the stone farmhouse offers guests the package of history and charm in four distinctive guest rooms. Margo's Suite is a romantic two-room suite with a queen-size bed, antique painted chests, floral blue wallpaper, and eyelid windows. The second room is a quaint sitting room, and the private bath offers an antique clawfoot bathtub. Betty's Suite is a two-room suite filled with Federal period antiques and reproductions. This suite offers a queen-size pediment bed, sitting room, and private bath with tub and shower. The Banneker

Room offers a queen-size antique rice bed and coordinating dresser and nightstand. The room has its own fireplace. And there is a bath, with shower and tub, that may be shared with the Ellicott Room, across the hall. The Ellicott Room offers an artistic rendering of Main Street, Ellicott City, in the mid-1800s. The room also includes a queen-size sleigh bed, cozy settee, and wood-burning fireplace.

To recall that era, the owners have maintained stately trees, flower gardens, and a small pond, giving the location a distinctly rural feel despite its closeness to urban life. One tradition of old inns that owners David and Susan Balderson maintain is the keeping of lighted candles in each window to signal the availability of rooms and the welcoming spirit of its owners.

For antiques lovers, historic mill enthusiasts, and people looking for a place out of the mainstream, the Wayside Inn is a good bet. (See the Antiques and Collectibles chapter for more information about Ellicott City.)

NORTH

**Gramercy Mansion
Bed & Breakfast** $$$
**1400 Greenspring Valley Road,
Stevenson**
(410) 486-2405 or (800) 553-3404
www.gramercymansion.com

Nestled in the middle of the Green Spring Valley, just 20 minutes from downtown Baltimore and the Inner Harbor, the Gramercy Mansion Bed & Breakfast is a step back in time. The Tudor style mansion and estate, which dates back to 1902, is situated on 45 acres of bucolic countryside.

Built by Alexander J. Cassatt, owner of the Pennsylvania Railroad and brother of American Impressionist painter Mary Cassatt, the mansion was presented as a wedding gift to his daughter, Eliza. In the 1950s, the estate became home to the Koinonia Foundation, a predecessor of the Peace Corps. The present owners have since restored the mansion and its surrounding gardens.

This bed-and-breakfast offers eight stylish rooms. The Aphrodite Retreat is a sun-filled room with oriental carpets, French antiques, and a king-size bed. Aunt Mary's Suite has a Victorian flare with sitting room, fireplace, and extra large clawfoot tub with shower. The Ambassador's Room is furnished with elegant draperies, fireplace, and whirlpool tub with statuary shower. All rooms include TV, fresh flowers, robes, coffee, tea, soda, and full gourmet breakfast. Visitors can also take advantage of the Olympic-size pool and tennis court, stroll along a woodland trail, through the orchard, flower, or herb gardens, or visit the organic farm.

The Gramercy Mansion is a Maryland Bed and Breakfast Association member.

RESTAURANTS

Baltimore has an eclectic mix of restaurants. Although we are known primarily for our seafood—crabs, oysters, and shrimp—Baltimore's culinary scene has much more to offer than just crustaceans. Baltimore now gives neighboring metropolises like Washington and New York a run for their money when it comes to fine dining. We now boast a number of innovative and traditional restaurants that offer five-star service and exquisite menus. Located on the water near Fells Point, Chef Cindy Wolfe's Charleston has a gorgeous menu of innovative Southern cuisine and an extensive wine list. Her well-trained staff can help anyone navigate both the food and the wine menus to create the perfect dining experience. Want Italian? Try Little Italy in the heart of the city for a number of traditional, Southern Italian pasta dishes, or head up Charles Street to Sotto Sopra, where the chef de cuisine hails from Milan and the carpaccio rivals that of the best Tuscan trattoria.

There are also more casual settings for good food, places to meet after work for a cocktail and an appetizer, or after the theater for cappuccino and dessert. Downtown is now dotted with wine bars, breweries, tapas restaurants, and small cafes with creative vegetarian dishes. Baltimore is still very much a big small town, and small neighborhood joints provide some of the best surprises. Friendly service, small but interesting menus, and a selection of local beers and artwork make these smaller, off-the-beaten-path places a great Baltimore experience. At Peter's Inn in Fells Point, the restaurant occupies the first floor of a small row house and owners Bud and Karin change the menu weekly depending on what's fresh at the market. At Sobo Café in Federal Hill, locals head for the phenomenal macaroni and cheese and the chance to run into friends and neighbors.

No trip to Baltimore would be complete without a trip to one of the many local diners, where some of the servers have waited tables for 30 years. The Sip N' Bite on the waterfront in Canton, for example, serves 24 hours a day, seven days a week, except Christmas Day.

Of course there is the great seafood. From sushi to paella, Baltimore is the best place on Earth to find fresh seafood. Baltimoreans love their shellfish, and you'll see the counters of Nick's Seafood at the Cross Street Market in Federal Hill packed with locals year-round. You can belly up to the raw bar for oysters shucked on the half shell, or order one of the famous lump meat crab cakes.

With hundreds of restaurants in the area, we tried to list a diverse collection, designed to offer something for everyone. Not every restaurant in places like Little Italy or Greektown or Fells Point, where there are more than a dozen eating establishments within a few blocks of one another, could be listed. In all cases, we have favored the tried and true or those that are newer and receiving high praise from all quarters. Just because a restaurant that's your personal favorite or one that others rave about isn't listed doesn't mean it's inferior and should not be visited.

We've tried to list specialty items, those entrees or appetizers or desserts that can't be replaced on the menu because they're in constant demand. We've also listed a few of our favorites (because we couldn't resist the temptation). One category you will not find too often is the chains, those restaurants that are in every city or town serving the same food. You know what they have, how they serve it, what the seating is like. They're all around but not nearly as exciting as a locally owned restaurant.

Wherever possible, we've tried to give you a feel for what you might expect once inside the door. Just remember that things change; in the last few years, ownership has changed tremendously at many restaurants, as have menus, decor, chefs, and names. The fluid nature of the restaurant trade in Baltimore is a sign of success and innovation rather than a sign of failure.

In the listings that follow, casual means anything from jeans and a dress shirt to a shirt and tie for guys and everything from jeans and a blouse to a dress for the gals. Where it says formal, expect to wear good pants or a dress, a shirt with a collar, and in some cases a sport coat and tie. We've mentioned where coats are required of men, but you won't run across those instructions too often here.

We have also tried to clue you in on the peculiarities of the alcohol regulations, where they apply. Restaurants can have licenses to serve beer and wine and liquor, just beer and wine, or to allow people to bring in their own alcohol. Most of the smaller, non-dinner-oriented places don't serve alcohol (nor would you probably want them to). Maryland also requires that restaurants and bars have separate areas for smoking, removed from the nonsmoking section by a door, wall, or glass partition. Most of them meet the rules by making the bar a smoking area, and to accommodate those who want to smoke and eat, they offer the full menu to bar patrons. A great situation for nonsmokers, the policy can become dicey for groups including smokers and nonsmokers.

If you want to avoid crowds, watch out for dinner hours on Thursday, Friday, and Saturday as well as brunch hours, say 11:00 A.M. to 3:00 P.M., on Sunday, when the after-church crowd makes way for a group or family get-together. In the tourist areas such as the Inner Harbor, Fells Point, and Mount Vernon, the crowds can get thick at just about any time, but your patience or planning can be rewarded with some great nectar from Baltimore's gods of the kitchen.

We have also tried to keep you posted on parking, which in the city can mean pumping quarters into a meter or paying top dollar for a private lot where they have control of your keys while you are dining. If you're in the city, you can expect to pay 25 cents per 15 minutes of parking at meters on the street and an average of about $6.00 for two hours of parking at the underground or covered parking garages in the Downtown area. As you get farther away from the Downtown area, you'll find free and ample parking is more available. To make it easier, we've highlighted your best parking options wherever possible.

Wherever you park, make sure you remember the street and closest cross street. A friend of ours parked his car in the city, went to a meal, and then he—and the people who he had dropped at the restaurant's door before parking the car—couldn't find his car for more than a hour because he couldn't remember the names of the streets where it was parked. Don't laugh. It can happen, but hopefully not to you.

PRICE CODE

To further explain what to expect we have included a price code for the restaurants listed. It isn't foolproof, but we have tried to offer a good average, meaning some meals cost more and some less. But, in general, it should give you enough of a guideline to avoid sticker shock. The price code includes the cost of a dinner for two people, excluding appetizers and desserts, wine and spirits, taxes, and tips. Basically, it is the price of the entrees two people will have for the main meal served, usually dinner unless the restaurant doesn't serve dinner.

$	**$15 and less**
$$	**$16 to $30**
$$$	**$31 to $40**
$$$$	**$41 and more**

The restaurants are grouped by geographic area—Downtown, Northeast, Northwest, Southeast, and Southwest—the same geographic areas we've used in most of the other chapters. If you refer back to the beginning of the book and the area maps, you can orient yourself to where you are staying and where you wish to go to eat. If there is no town or city listed after the street address, that means the eatery is within the city limits. If a town or city follows the street address, it means you will be leaving the city. We've provided you with clues on what restaurants are near or how to get to them, so you can focus on the thing you want to do most now—EAT!

DOWNTOWN

Amicci's $$$
231 South High Street
(410) 528-1096

The High Street location opened for fine dining in Little Italy in 1991. Neighborhood people, tourists, and businesspeople rave about the pane Rotundo appetizer, a round loaf of Italian bread hollowed out and covered with garlic butter to make room for six jumbo shrimp cooked in garlic sauce. For a main course, try the ziti La Rosa, jumbo shrimp, mushrooms, and onions covered with pureed sun-dried tomatoes and garlic sauce.

The Little Italy location offers lunch and dinner seven days a week. The restaurant serves beer, wine, and cordials. Reservations are a good idea, especially on weekends or summer weeknights. Parking is available on the street, but you better have some change handy for the meters.

Attman's Delicatessen $
1019 East Lombard Street
(410) 563-2666

Like one of New York's best delis, Attman's features 10 cooks arguing and jockeying for position as they prepare deli sandwiches for the masses. Local favorites include hot corned beef, available in the three-quarter–pound variety, which is plenty for most people, or the "extra heavy," which costs an extra $2.00 for about a third-pound to a half-pound more meat. Like any self-respecting deli, this one offers a real deli pickle to go with the meal. A word of advice: Know what you

want when you get in line because there isn't usually much time for waffling.

If you plan ahead, you can hit the deli on your way out in the morning, or you can go during lunch or the dinner hour. It's open Monday through Sunday. On-street parking is available.

Bagel Works $
The Belvedere,
1023 North Charles Street
(410) 347-2790

There's no place to sit at these works, located within The Belvedere condominiums complex. But if you're looking for a wide range of bagels, you won't notice. The most basic is the New Yorker, any style in the bins with cream cheese on top, and the most unusual, the Beast, which is roast beef, Swiss cheese, onions, and horseradish. Your eyes might water, but your taste buds will rejoice. Some less adventurous sandwich options, including turkey and ham, are also available, as are the usual toppings such as butter, lox, and flavored cream cheeses. And there's always a pot of coffee on.

Bagel Works serves breakfast and lunch only and is closed on Sundays.

Bertha's $$
734 South Broadway
(410) 327-5795

If you look on the bumpers of many Baltimoreans' cars, you'll see a sticker saying, "Eat Bertha's Mussels." It's a tribute to this family-run business that opened as a bar in the Fells Point area in 1972. Since then it's grown up to have two dining rooms for casual dining. The mussels are the mainstay of the menu, steamed with a choice of eight butter-based sauces, such as garlic sauce with capers. When basil is in season, in the late summer and early fall, try the basil-pesto sauce on the mussels. Other menu items have a Caledonia heritage, with a Scottish afternoon tea served every day except Sunday.

You need to make a reservation for the teas, but otherwise, drop by when the green bumper stickers weigh heaviest on your mind. Parking is available on the streets of Fells Point.

The Bicycle $$$
1444 Light Street
(410) 234-1900

A bicycle mounted on the outside of this brightly painted rowhouse in South Baltimore announces the restaurant from the street. The caveat for this place is its small, linear interior. Tables can sometimes feel crowded (making it a poor choice for large parties), but the food and the bustle in the open kitchen make up for it. The self-described "global bistro" menu is exotic. Grilled tenderloin of pork is served on red rice, sweet-corn pancakes are topped with avocado tomatillo salsa, and corn-crusted oysters accompany a spicy remoulade. In summer months a garden patio is open for dining. The Bicycle serves dinner only, Monday through Saturday. Reservations are accepted. Parking is on the street, or you can park in the Federal Hill Garage on West Street (about $6.00) and walk the 5 blocks to the restaurant.

Blue Agave Restaurante y Tequileria $$
1032 Light Street
(410) 576-3938
www.blueagaverestaurant.com

Blue agave is the plant that produces the nectar of Mexico: tequila. And this place has its share. The bar offers tequila tastings and delicious margaritas (served on ice, only—don't offend the traditionalist owners and ask for a frozen margarita in a blender). As for the food, you won't find canned refried beans or enchiladas drowning in cheese. The menu is true classic Mexican and Southwestern cuisine, featuring slow-roasted pork and the best fish tacos in town. The house salad is a signature with delicious mix of greens, pepitos (crunchy, roasted pumpkin seeds), and jicama. Casual and fun, Blue Agave serves dinner only Thursday through Monday. Parking is on the street or in the Federal Hill Garage on West Street.

Bo Brooks Crab House $$
2701 Boston Street
(410) 558-0202
www.bobrooks.com

This is easily Baltimore's most popular home for steamed crabs. Bo Brooks's reputation brings people from near and far for a chance to sit down for a platter of crabs served on paper-covered tables. What the place lacks in atmosphere (diners drop the picked-through crab shells in buckets on the floor) it more than makes up for in the taste of the steamed crabs.

There's alcohol and some other entrees for those who don't partake, but the pickings are slim. Crabs, crabs, crabs.

Bo Brooks is open seven days a week for lunch and dinner.

The restaurant takes only a few reservations, so if you don't want to wait in the long, long lines, plan to arrive before 6:00 P.M. or after 8:00 P.M. You can call ahead to learn the prices and sizes of the crabs of the day; the best selection is from March to September, when crabs are typically in season.

Boccaccio $$$
925 Eastern Avenue
(410) 234-1322

This is one of Little Italy's priciest locales, but the service from the black-tie staff makes it worthwhile. The Italian dishes, especially the thick lasagna and the cheese ravioli, are as good as you can find in Baltimore, making the price seem that much more reasonable. The restaurant is open for lunch and dinner seven days a week, and reservations are a real good idea, especially on weekends.

Bombay Grill $$
2 East Madison Street
(410) 837-2973
www.bombaygrill.com

Bombay Grill was Baltimore's first true Indian restaurant, founded in 1987 by Tony and Ann Chemmannoor. There's a collection of vegetarian fare, including Aloo Phool Gobi, spiced potatoes cooked with fresh cauliflower, and a Veg Masala, a vegetarian dish prepared with spices usually used with meats. For couples, there is the Maharaja dinner, a six-course meal with soup, a non-vegetarian appetizer mix, a collection of seafood, meat and vegetarian entrees, rice, salad, bread, dessert, coffee, and tea. It's the perfect meal for two people who want to share their love over dinner.

Situated near the art galleries, monuments, and historic churches of Mount Vernon, the restaurant is open every day for fine dining at lunch and dinner. There's a daily luncheon buffet that's a real bargain. Reservations are recommended, and parking is available on the street.

---

i *Several restaurants validate parking. Check when you enter to see if this is the case. It doesn't hurt to ask, and it may even save you a few bucks.*

Brass Elephant $$$$
924 North Charles Street
(410) 547-8480
One of the Baltimore area's favorites since its opening in 1980 in the historic and arts-oriented Mount Vernon area, the Brass Elephant means fine dining in a restored nineteenth-century Victorian town house that's practically overrun with history and elephants (check out the elephant sconces—really!). Focused on northern Italian cuisine, the menu changes with the seasons. But you are guaranteed lots of entrees featuring lots of local, in-season produce and seafood, especially crabmeat. This is a coat-and-tie establishment for professionals and people on important nights out who have a respect and appreciation for the restored building and for a four-course meal that might take more than three hours to enjoy.

The Veal Valdostano, a favorite of the management, is a veal cutlet sautéed with butter, shallots, mushrooms, cream, white wine, and Fontina cheese. There's also a hot antipasto that's worth a try.

There's a full bar and an upstairs lounge that has a casual happy hour Monday through Friday. Free parking is available. The restaurant serves dinner seven days a week. A jacket is required.

The Brewer's Art $-$$$
1106 North Charles Street
(410) 547-6925
www.belgianbeer.com
This place straddles the line between restaurant and bar. Upstairs, a gloriously majestic nineteenth-century space has been transformed into a restaurant and lounge. The dinner menu includes elaborate entrees and classic European-style country fare featuring meats, fish, seafood, pasta, and a vegetarian offering. Downstairs is a whole other world. The cavernous, dark, smoke-filled bar is popular with art students and local hipsters, and cozy alcoves are packed with friends commiserating over pints of the house brews. The Resurrection Ale, served in a Belgian Ale mug, is a favorite, but with a nearly 8 percent alcohol content, it can catch up to you quickly. A less expensive light-fare menu is served downstairs; the seasoned, shoestring pommes frites are the best in town. Dinner is served daily, and the light fare is available as late as 11:00 P.M.

Brighton's $$$
Harbor Court Hotel, 550 Light Street
(410) 234-0550
www.harborcourt.com
One of two restaurants in the grand Harbor Court Hotel, Brighton's boasts a bistro menu and a casual atmosphere that's perfect for an impressive business meeting over a meal, but without all the pomp. Continental favorites and local favorites, especially seafood specialties like heavy crab cakes, scallops, and rockfish (a local favorite known as "striped bass" by many), are the perfect companion to the great view of the Inner Harbor. This is one of the best places to see and be seen in the city.

Reservations are recommended at all times for this restaurant, which serves breakfast, lunch, dinner, and afternoon tea. During tea, scheduled between 3:00 and

5:00 P.M., a variety of homemade pastries and dessert fare is served with several types of tea. Brighton's is open every day but doesn't serve tea or dinner on Sundays. If you plan to smoke or want to relax for a drink, try the Explorer's Lounge, right next door to the restaurant (see the Nightlife chapter). Valet parking is available, or you can park at the harbor and walk over.

Burke's Cafe and Comedy Club $$
36 Light Street
(410) 752-4189
Close enough to the Inner Harbor and its attractions but far enough away to not be perpetually crowded, Burke's Cafe offers gigantic burgers, homemade soups, sandwiches, oyster stew, and salads. A favorite for visitors, many of whom stop by after an Orioles' game, is the Burke's onion ring, a large, tasty, breathtaking, and breath-killing appetizer.

Reservations are a good idea on weekend nights or if you plan to go before an event, but otherwise you'll be seated for breakfast, lunch, or dinner pretty quickly. The bar is known for its frosty mugs of beer and soda; it's also a good place to wait for a table. Burke's is open 7:00 A.M. to 11:30 P.M. daily.

Parking is available at several parking garages within a block of the restaurant. Try the garage at the Gallery shopping area, or if it's late at night or the weekend, park on the street.

Cafe Bombay $$
114 East Lombard Street
(410) 539-2233
Operated by the same Indian couple who own the Bombay Grill (see the listing previously in this chapter), fine dining here means a variety of vegetarian favorites. Cafe Bombay is also the only restaurant in the area to serve Balti cooking, which originated in the rugged terrain of Pakistan's Baltistan region.

Within a few blocks of the Inner Harbor, the restaurant is open every day. Park-ing is available for a fee at a number of area parking lots or at metered parking spaces near the Inner Harbor. Reservations are suggested, especially on weekends.

Café Brio $
904 South Charles Street
(410) 234-0235
A coffeehouse-turned-restaurant, this bohemian cafe is tucked into a beautifully restored Federal row house in the heart of Federal Hill. The menu is heavy on the vegetarian and vegan entrees, and typical coffeehouse fare like muffins, desserts, and smoothies are available from the juice bar. A few tables clutter the sidewalk in nice weather, and you are allowed to bring your dog if you're sitting outside. This is a popular spot for everyone in the neighborhood and is very busy during peak hours—like the pre-work coffee rush hour and weekend mornings. Parking is at meters on the street. And remember, read parking signs in Federal Hill. Many of the streets offer limited parking unless you have a residential parking sticker. Open every day for breakfast, lunch, and dinner.

Charleston $$$$
1000 Lancaster Street
(410) 332-7373
Charleston is a singular dining experience. A contemporary American restaurant set in Baltimore's Inner Harbor East development, this is the place to spoil yourself with rich, decadent food, phenomenal service, and an impeccable wine list. Educated servers guide you through the wine menu, which features more than 600 vintages, while famed chef Cindy Wolfe dazzles with her fabulous menu crafted from the finest seasonal seafood, game, and fresh produce. One typical spring menu included lobster with julienne mango and tarragon-mint vinaigrette, jugtown bacon wrapped beef tenderloin with grilled Southern ratatouille, and rockfish with lump crab and tomato and arugula salad. Her signature grilled scallop BLT is a mainstay. And don't forget the cheese course.

CLOSE-UP

How to Eat Crab

When you come to Baltimore, you will, no doubt, want to try our most famous local delicacy—the Chesapeake Bay blue crab. You can try them in a variety of ways.

Crab soup is a nice choice in cooler weather. We produce an assortment of local crab soups, from a mild, creamy bisque to the traditional Maryland hot-and-tangy, thick with floating claws.

Pan-fried, backfin crab cakes are great plain, on crackers, or nestled in rolls with Maryland tomatoes and crisp lettuce, dripping with tartar sauce.

If you're the adventurous type, you can have a soft-crab sandwich. This is a whole crab—that's right, shell and all—laid between two slices of the bread of your choosing. You can eat the shell because this pan-fried pleasure is a soft-shell crab. He's shed his hard shell and would have had to grow a bit before it hardened up again. Unluckily for him, but luckily for you, we plucked him from the bottom of the Chesapeake Bay before that could happen.

If you're a little more conservative, there are multitudes of crab salads, crab imperials, and pasta and crab dishes. Somewhere in this town you can probably even find a crab burrito.

But the best way to eat crab is just to eat crabs. Smothered in Old Bay Seasoning (a product with salt and other spices made by McCormick, a local spice maker) their red shells heavy with sweet, white meat, a pile of crabs is hard to resist—although some newcomers do have a little difficulty eating food that is staring at them.

If you dare to eat crabs, you'll want to know what you're doing. So, let's

begin at the beginning. Use this chapter to pick a crab restaurant that sounds good to you. Then, set aside some time. Crabs are not fast food at any stretch of the imagination.

As you're seated, most likely you'll notice that the table is covered with newspaper, brown paper, or tail cloth. This is your clue to the first truth about eating crabs: they are messy, so dress appropriately. If you're wearing your favorite silk blouse or you're just coming from the opera, don't eat crabs. Jeans and a T-shirt will do.

You will also see a bib in front of you on the table. Wear it. Even T-shirts can only stand so much! In addition to the bib, you'll find a wooden mallet and a knife. These and your two hands are the only tools you need to pick a crab. The mallet is used for cracking the claws—which, among crab connoisseurs, are eaten either first or last: never as you go. The knife is for removing the crab's shell and air sacs (or lungs, as they're sometimes called) and for cutting apart the crab so that you can reach the meat.

Now that you're appropriately bibbed and have your tools in hand, here's how it's done.

Pull a crab from the pile and turn it over. On its white underside, you will see an outline that looks either like a tower on a hill or a Brownie's beanie. The tower configuration signifies a male crab; the beanie is a female. Take your knife, or fingernail if you'd prefer to be a totally hands-on crab picker, insert it along the edge of the outline, and lift the flap. You'll see, toward the back of the crab, a sort of indentation where the top shell is attached. Place your knife in that "v" and press down, while gripping the body of the crab with your free hand. At this point, all you need do is lift. The body of the crab will peel away from its shell.

Discard the shell, unless you want to keep it for a souvenir. (A note on that: crab shells, once cleaned and lacquered, make excellent ashtrays and candy dishes.) Now, turn the crab back over. First, take your knife and cut away the eyes and the "mouth."

Just two cuts, from the first claw to the center of the body—forming the two sides of an isosceles triangle—will do it. This may sound a bit yucky, but it's really not as bad as it sounds. Once you've cut the front part away, look at the back. At that little "v," you may see some yellow stuff. Some people like to scoop that out and eat it. (It's called mustard.) Personally, we suggest you scoop it out and discard it, but it's your call. Use your knife to scrape away the stringy, intestinal-looking material and to cut off the wedge-shaped, fleshy looking sacs that are attached to the undershell. This is not an option. Some novices think these sacs are the meat and try to eat them. DON'T. They may make you sick. What you want, the sweet meat, is inside the thin undershell upon which the sacs sit.

Once you're discarded the sacs, you're almost ready to eat. Take the crab in both hands, each hand cradling the crab's legs and firmly gripping each side of the body. With the upside of the crab still facing you, push your hands down and together, thus cracking the body in half. Now, look inside. That white stuff is what you're after. There

are a few different ways to get at it, any of which will make you look like an old hand at crab-eatin'.

Option #1: Local experts suggest that you break off the claws at this point and use your knife to cut off the "knuckles," those little knobby things where the claws are attached. You can then use your knife or your finger to pull or push the meat out.

Option #2: Access it from the inside. Break off the claws, and then cut away the thin shell that still protects the meat on the inside of the body, opposite the knuckles. Then scoop the meat out with your knife.

Option #3: The most difficult, but the most satisfying, technique is to remove the meat as you remove the claws. Rather than just breaking off the claws, detach them with a gentle twist and pull. If you do it just right, the meat will come along. If it doesn't, options #1 and #2 are still available.

Having finished this operation, you may now opt to tackle the claws, or you can set the claws aside for later and pick another crab from the pile. You have only picked and eaten about an ounce or two of meat, in—on your first try—about 25 minutes time. So, you need to keep eating. You will, however, be full before you know it. When you get to the claws, simply crack the shell with your mallet, then break it away. The claw meat is resting on a thin piece of cartilage inside. All you need to do is put your fingers near the claw joint and slide the meat off.

Good drinks with crabs are beer or soda; good side orders are slaw and corn on the cob. Enjoy!

City Cafe $$$
1001 Cathedral Street
(410) 539-4252

In addition to its American fare, focusing on pastas and traditional entrees, City Cafe offers a collection of vegetarian dishes on its ever-changing menu. There's always a vegetarian sandwich, a vegetarian pasta dish, and a vegetarian soup for customers to try. The casual dining experience includes outdoor seating at tables with umbrellas during the warmer months. Because of its location, it attracts a large neighborhood clientele from Mount Vernon who return often to try the latest creation on the menu. It's open every day.

Since 1994 the restaurant, winner of several *City Paper* Awards, has been serving breakfast, lunch, and dinner. There's also a full and smokefree bar, where you can order from the menu. Parking is available at meters, which cost money before 6:00 P.M. Reservations aren't needed for this restaurant, which can seat up to 170 people. You can call the listed number for daily lunch and dinner specials.

Da Mimmo $$
217 South High Street
(410) 727-6876

Regarded as one of the best of the Little Italy restaurants, Da Mimmo's offers a great selection of seafood and veal dishes as well as all the usual Italian specialties. Shrimp dishes are among the best, while the collection of wines to choose from is equally impressive. Don't fill up on the breads or salads, because the entrees offer super-large servings. The fine-dining atmosphere can be noisy; it just isn't a place for privacy. Open daily for lunch and dinner.

Reservations are an absolute must. There's live piano music most nights. Park on the streets of Little Italy.

Ding How $$
631 South Broadway
(410) 327-8888

Fells Point and Chinese food really don't seem like a likely match, but Ding How is apt to change your mind. In this restau-rant in this historic part of Baltimore, you can find the usual Chinese favorites as well as lots of vegetarian and local seafood specialties, including lobster, soft-shell crabs, and calamari. A favorite is the boneless orange roughy with vegetables served in a spicy sauce. The restaurant is open for lunch and dinner every day, and you can park on the streets of Fells Point pretty easily. Dress is casual.

Eichenkranz $$$$
611 South Fagley Street
(410) 563-7577
www.eichenkranz.com

Eichenkranz has been offering true German food since it opened in 1934, and while ownership has changed a few times, with the latest owners taking over in 1992, the food has remained constant. Located off Fleet Street in Fells Point, the restaurant offers four types of schnitzel—Wiener schnitzel, Jeager schnitzel, schnitzel Holstein, and the Eichenkranz schnitzel, which features veal, shredded ham, and Swiss cheese. The casual atmosphere, which tends to draw lots of couples, is enhanced by a number of pictures of Germany retained from its original owners.

The restaurant serves lunch and dinner every day. Reservations are recommended, even if you call that day, and parking is free on a lot at the restaurant. There's a smoking room and full bar, too.

Ghion Ethiopian International Restaurant $
1100 Maryland Avenue
(410) 752-3865

Blink and you could miss this tiny cafe on a corner of Maryland Avenue. The exterior is actually rather bleak and somewhat foreboding and the space inside is minuscule, with a long L-shaped bar and only a few tables for eat-in dining. So why recommend it? Because this is the kind of small, well-loved dive you hope to stumble on in your travels. The food is fantastic and the owners are so kind and accommodating, they immediately ingratiate you with a broad smile and a ready explanation of any of the traditional Ethiopian dishes on their small menu. The vegetarian sambusa, a pastry turnover filled with green lentils and a hint of jalapeño, is a must for an appetizer. Each entree is served over a traditional flatbread called injera. Close to the Meyerhoff Symphony Hall and the Lyric, this is a great place for a casual bite to eat before or after a show. Open 2:00 to 10:00 P.M. Monday through Saturday.

Hamilton's $$$
888 South Broadway
(410) 522-2195
A beautifully preserved eighteenth-century building in Fells Point plays host to this fine-dining restaurant, where modern American cuisine with a distinct Southern accent is served. Seared monkfish, veal medallions, and lamb chops are surefire winners in this restaurant that serves food as good as the history lesson the building tells.

Lunch is served on Sunday, while dinner is served Tuesday through Saturday. Parking is available on the streets of Fells Point, and during the day it's a wonderful place to do some shopping for books, clothes, trinkets, and other items. Reservations are a good idea, especially on weekends.

Hampton's $$$$
Harbor Court Hotel, 550 Light Street
(410) 234-0550
www.harborcourt.com
The companion restaurant to Brighton's (see the previous listing in this section), also in the Harbor Court Hotel, this is one of the finest restaurants in Baltimore. *Condé Nast Traveler* named it one of the two best restaurants in America. Since its opening in 1985, it has garnered a great reputation. Serving high-end French and American cuisine, the fine-dining restaurant attracts businesspeople as well as members of the medical and college communities in the city. The trio of lamb is the specialty, bringing together braised osso buco, seared loin, and a roast chop, seasoned with cilantro gremolada and a

Grand Marnier reduction and served with a sun-dried tomato and roasted garlic polenta.

A marvelous view of the Inner Harbor competes with the piano player on weekdays or the jazz group that performs on weekends. Valet parking is available, or you can hoof it from the Inner Harbor. Outside the restaurant is the Explorer's Lounge (see the Nightlife chapter), where you can smoke and grab a nightcap.

The restaurant serves dinner only Tuesday through Sunday, with a champagne brunch on Sunday between 10:30 A.M. and 2:00 P.M., featuring all the usual breakfast favorites as well as fresh carved beef and ham, several seafood dishes, soups, salad, and vegetables. It's more than two meals. As you might imagine, getting in requires lots of advanced planning on weekends—try three weeks advanced reservations for a Saturday and just slightly less for a Friday.

Helen's Garden Restaurant $$$
2908 O'Donnell Street
(410) 276-2233
www.helensgarden.com
Located in Canton Square, Helen's Garden is a cozy, intimate cafe with a great wine list and an equally wonderful menu. This is the kind of place where you can either dress casual and get away cheap with a bottle of vino for under $20, or you can show up in black-tie attire and have an elegant meal. Grilled fish entrees, like the tuna, are superb and the weekend brunch menu is well loved by locals. Reservations are recommended. Open for lunch and dinner, Tuesday through Sunday; brunch is served Saturday and Sunday.

The 2900 block of O'Donnell Street in Canton, known as "The Square," has a number of great restaurants and bars concentrated on both sides of a small grassy park. If you're not sure what you're in the mood for, come here and walk around. You're sure to find something to please.

The Helmand $$
806 North Charles Street
(410) 752-0311
www.helmand.com
There's seemingly every type of food at this Afghani restaurant that's fewer than 10 blocks north of the Inner Harbor. For a reasonable price, you can dine on ravioli filled with ground beef and topped with a creamy sauce made of split peas and yogurt. Lots of meals have yogurt in them, including the pumpkin with garlic yogurt sauce. The atmosphere is really casual for this dinner-only restaurant that's open nightly. This is a Baltimore favorite and it fills quickly.

Henninger's Tavern $$$
1812 Bank Street
(410) 342-2172
www.hennigerstavern.com
Vintage photos and an antique china closet greet visitors at this Fells Point area restaurant known for its seafood. Don't kid yourself: This is on the outskirts of Fells Point, removed by several blocks from the hubbub of the Fells Point area. No matter—pan-fried, breaded oysters and flounder stuffed with crabmeat make the trip worth it.

There's a full bar and a semiformal atmosphere. Parking is available on the street. Reservations are not taken, meaning you may spend a fair amount of time looking at the photos before being seated. To avoid the crowds, come early or late to this restaurant that serves dinner Tuesday through Saturday from 5:00 to 10:00 P.M. The bar stays open until 1:00 A.M.

Joy America Cafe $$$$
American Visionary Art Museum,
800 Key Highway
(410) 244-6500
www.avam.org
This restaurant is located at the American Visionary Art Museum. Organic foods with Southwestern, Italian, and Asian influences are what the staff calls its fare, but it's really much more. Consider this one that the staff swears has been served: tortilla

and lime-crusted chicken with chile-chocolate sauce and a poblano-potato tamale. Get the idea? The chef is a visionary, so make sure you know what you're getting before you order if you aren't the adventurous type. However, even the shy ones among you should feel free to try the wide and exotic range of desserts.

The restaurant serves lunch and dinner Tuesday through Saturday and brunch on Sunday. Parking is available on Key Highway most of the time.

Kawasaki and Kawasaki Café $$$
413 North Charles Street and
907 South Ann Street
(410) 659-7600 or (410) 327-9400
www.kawasaki-restaurant.com
You'll feel as if you've landed in Tokyo when you try the truly Japanese cooking at Kawasaki. The 12-foot sushi bar, where you can watch the preparation of sushi and sashimi, is one of the largest in the city, while the fried shrimp tempura has been bringing people back for fine dining week after week since 1985, when it opened.

The restaurant has a full bar and free parking at a garage across the street. Reservations are always necessary for dinner, but it's not a bad idea to make them for lunch. If the sushi bar offers its popular "crunch roll" on special, you should give it a try. The restaurant serves lunch Monday through Friday and dinner Monday through Saturday. A second restaurant, Kawasaki Café, now sits on the waterfront in Fells Point.

Maison Marconi $$$
106 West Saratoga Street
(410) 727-9522
Tuxedo-wearing waiters have been serving fine meals on the immaculate white tablecloths at Maison Marconi since its opening in 1920. The clientele, made up mostly of businesspeople and couples on important dates, favors the lobster Cardinale, which features large chunks of lobster covered in a sherry cream sauce, with fresh mushrooms all broiled and then placed inside a lobster shell. Make sure you save room for

dessert, because the chef always makes the chocolate sauce for the chocolate sundaes from scratch. It's a favorite guaranteed to leave a sweet spot on your palate. The restaurant features lots of other French favorites.

There's complimentary valet parking and a full bar for patrons. Reservations are needed, usually four or five days in advance, because of the proximity to the Inner Harbor and the area hotels. The restaurant is open for lunch and dinner Tuesday through Saturday.

Matsuri $$
1105 South Charles Street
(410) 752-8561

There's plenty of Japanese cuisine to go around here. Take the two-page sushi and sashimi menu. Served from a long, long bar, the options include tuna, salmon, sari clams, eels, and quail eggs. Among the favorites is the nabeyaki udon, broth-laden noodles topped with shrimp and fish cakes.

The restaurant is open for lunch Monday through Friday and dinner Monday through Saturday. Parking is available on the street or in one of the parking garages nearby. Dress is casual, and reservations are important on weekend nights, when the restaurant fills with regulars.

Minato $$$
800 North Charles Street
(410) 332-0332

In the heart of Mount Vernon, Minato offers tasty Japanese food at a reasonable price. Portions are large, especially the tempura and teriyaki. The noodle soups, ramen, soba, and udon, are also winners, served in portions that carry them from soup to meal in a few spoonfuls.

Dress is casual. The restaurant is open for lunch Monday through Friday and dinner every day, and parking is available on the street. Reservations are necessary for weekend nights.

Nacho Mama's $
2907 O'Donnell Street
(410) 675-0898

Several local museums have more than just great art, they also have award-winning restaurants. The Joy America Cafe at the American Visionary Art Museum and Gertrude's at the Baltimore Museum of Art top the list.

i

With a giant statue of Elvis greeting you at the door and walls adorned with funky local art and oddities, this festive Tex-Mex restaurant in Canton is always hopping. The hot sauces are hidden in medicine cabinets mounted on the walls above the tables, and the tortilla chips are served in hubcaps. The inexpensive menu is chock full of your basic Mexican eats, like enchiladas, quesadillas, and fajitas, while more traditional American dishes like Mama's Meatloaf and baby back ribs offer dining options for those who don't feel like going south of the border. Be prepared to wait on a weekend night for a table. Nacho Mama's serves lunch and dinner daily.

Obrycki's Crab House $$$
1727 East Pratt Street
(410) 732-6399
www.obryckis.com

Be prepared—crab houses have all the trappings of a fire hall banquet. The long tables are covered with newspaper or some other paper covering allowing diners to enjoy the crabs piece by piece. You'll be invited to sit down, you'll be given a bib, and then you'll begin foraging through a bushel of crabs for the tasty meat that draws visitors to Baltimore. Obrycki's has that memorable name that sticks with you for hours, but it's the steamed crabs and crab cakes that will draw your attention and forge Obrycki's strong reputation for being the place in Baltimore to savor the local seafood specialty.

When you're not getting your hands and face dirty with Old Bay Seasoning, you can view the pictures of early 1900s Baltimore that cover the walls. In a unique touch, the walls are painted to appear as if there's peeling plaster and exposed brick.

Between March and November, this place gets really, really busy as locals get the unmistakable hankering for steamed crabs. Reservations are a good idea at all times. It's closed in the winter, however, as there aren't any local crabs to steam. The restaurant serves lunch and dinner when it's open, and parking is available at meters on the streets nearby.

Peter's Inn $$
504 South Ann Street
(410) 675-7313
www.petersinn.com
Owners Karin and Bud Tiffany run this small restaurant on the first floor of a row house, just a few blocks north of the hustle and bustle of Fells Point. The place seats under 30 and has a long wood bar that never seems to empty of neighborhood friends chatting away over beers. Hanging out at Peter's is kind of like hanging out at home—there is a comfortable couch in the back for larger parties to sit and eat, and it seems everyone knows one another. Karin changes the menu weekly based on what's fresh in the markets and keeps the simple but exceptional offerings (usually including one soup, one appetizer, and five entrees) listed on a chalkboard at the back of the room. Every meal comes with garlic bread and mixed salad. Peter's is open for dinner only and is closed Sundays. Other important things to note: Peter's does not take reservations. It almost never offers dessert, and the bar is not separate from the dining area so it can get smoky. You may want to turn off your cell phone before coming in. Peter's is a place to get away and catch up with friends and enjoy a good meal; a ringing phone may earn you dirty looks from the locals. Park on the street or at meters.

Phillips Harborplace Restaurant $$$
301 Light Street
(410) 685-6600
Located at the Inner Harbor, Phillips Harborplace Restaurant is actually three entities in one, seating as many as 870 people. The main dining room has indoor seating with a piano bar and outdoor seating along the water. The extensive menu offers traditional Maryland-inspired seafood like spicy Maryland crab soup, steamed crabs, and Old Bay shrimp. Those who don't eat seafood will still find plenty to choose from, including steak and chicken entrees. Phillips Harborplace also houses Phillips Seafood Festival Buffet, a self-service buffet featuring seafood, chicken, soups, salads, sides, and desserts. And for those on the go, there is Phillips carry-out and seafood market, serving crab cake sandwiches, soups, and salads.

Pierpoint $$$
1822 Aliceanna Street
(410) 675-2080
www.pierpointrestaurant.com
A bistro in Fells Point that focuses on local seafood dishes, Pierpoint is best known for its smoked crab cakes, a variation on an area favorite that gives it a hickory-smoked flavor like no other. You can also try owner Nancy Longo's homemade Eastern Shore rabbit sausage, the smoked duck quesadillas, or the Moroccan lamb. Save some room for the bread pudding, served just out of the oven and topped with a praline crust. Yum!

The restaurant serves lunch Tuesday through Friday and dinner Tuesday through Sunday. Reservations are required, so call at least a day in advance. Parking is available on the street, but bring some change for the meters, which need to be fed until 6:00 P.M. most days.

Red Maple $$
930 North Charles Street
(410) 547-0149
www.930redmaple.com
A modishly sleek interior formed from teakwood, steel, and glass makes this one of the most architecturally stunning spots in the city. Opened in 2001, the modern lounge vibe fueled by the best resident and guest DJs earned the Red Maple a slot on *In Style* magazine's list of the top 60 nightspots in America. The patrons are

Baltimore Firts

In 1879 Constantine Fahlberg and Professor Ira Rensen of The Johns Hopkins University discovered saccharine, the first synthetic sweetening agent.

In 1848 William Young patented the first ice cream freezer.

In 1891 Captain Isaac E. Emerson came up with the first formula for Bromo-Seltzer. The giant, stories-high, blue replica of the Bromo bottle graced the Bromo tower building until the 1960s. The building now houses an art gallery.

In 1819 Thomas Kennett invented the first mode of preserving meats, fruits, and vegetables.

—Excerpted from Baltimore—America's City of Firsts, *a pamphlet published by Baltimore Bicentennial Celebration, Inc.*

---

as good looking as the surroundings as they imbibe the bar's exotic cocktails. Linear benches offer seating for an Asian tapas menu created by chef T. J. Lynch. Try the red duck salad in a red currant vinaigrette or the perfectly seared arctic char on Thai basil rice cakes. There is usually a cover at the door in support of the music. Once inside, there's no smoking at all, but an outdoor courtyard (home to the namesake red maple) allows smokers to light up. The attire is hip, not formal, but tennis shoes are not allowed. The kitchen closes before the lounge, but it usually stays open late on weekends. Open daily after 5:30 P.M. Reservations for dinner are recommended. Park on the street or pay to park in a surface lot for about $6.00.

Sobo Café $$
6 West Cross Street
(410) 752-1518
www.sobocafe.com

Owner Brent Ludtke opened this small cafe in Federal Hill several years ago, and it has since evolved into a busy neighborhood establishment. The bright lemon-yellow walls are decorated with local artwork, and the menu is written on a creative chalkboard over the bar. Although the menu changes weekly, the macaroni and cheese and the "meat muffins" (meat loaf shaped like a muffin) with mashed potatoes are local favorites and usually

stay. Sobo specializes in comfort food, but it also does creative vegetarian and seafood dishes very well. This is a great spot to grab a beer and watch the local activity. Sobo does not have a great AC system, so the restaurant can get hot in warm months. The dress is casual. Sobo is open daily for lunch and dinner.

Soigné $$$
554 East Fort Avenue
(410) 659-9898

Tucked in a South Baltimore neighborhood of mostly row homes, this corner restaurant is quite a surprising find. The space is small but appealing, and the menu is a rich, textured mix of Asian-European fusion. In fact, chef Edward Kim may be one of Baltimore's best kept secrets. His seafood entrees offer an inexplicable combination of spices and flavors and all are complimented by wonderfully creative side dishes. This is great food in an unpretentious environment. Parking is easy to find on the street; dinner is served Tuesday through Sunday.

Sotta Sopra $$$
405 North Charles Street
(410) 625-0534
www.sottasoprainc.com

If you're in the Mount Vernon cultural district, figure this eatery to be Little Italy North, a place where you can find some great homemade northern Italian fare. Some of the staff's favorites are the homemade gnocchi and buckwheat ravioli and fettuccine.

Sotta Sopra is open for lunch and dinner every day. Valet parking is offered on weekends; during the week metered parking is available. This place is packed for dinner, so definitely make reservations.

Spike & Charlie's Restaurant and Wine Bar $$$
1225 Cathedral Street
(410) 752-8144
www.atlanticrestaurant.com

Owners Charlie and Spike Gjerde have an eclectic eatery near Baltimore's cultural district.

The food is new American, and this is fine dining, a place to go before the show at the Lyric, the Meyerhoff, or the various theaters in the Mount Vernon area. The menu changes with the seasons, but the sourdough bread rolls are consistently great. They are sold to anxious customers when there are extras, which isn't as often as people might like. A good example of a Spike & Charlie's meal would be the horseradish encrusted salmon, which is a fillet grilled with horseradish and other spices that give it a definite kick. There's also a beef tenderloin that's served in a blue cheese soufflé with grilled mixed vegetables. Spike & Charlie's is renowned for its wine list and has been cited by *The Wine Spectator.*

You'll want to save some room for dessert. The restaurant has been repeatedly recognized by *Baltimore* magazine and *City Paper,* an alternative weekly in Baltimore, for its desserts, which include the apple Crostada, an open-faced apple tart with sautéed apples and a puff pastry.

The restaurant has a full bar and a separate smoking section. Parking is available on the street or in a nearby garage, which can cost up to $5.00. Reservations at least a week in advance, and sometimes as much as a month in advance for big theater or show nights, are necessary. The restaurant serves dinner only Tuesday through Sunday.

Spoons Coffeehouse and Roastery $
24 East Cross Street
(410) 539-6751

Spoons is a coffeehouse and restaurant that serves breakfast and lunch. The owners decorated with cozy couches as well as tables for dining, so guests can curl up with coffee and a book or sit down at a table for full service. A bookshelf offers books, magazines, newspapers, and board games. All art on the walls is local, and most of it is for sale. Breakfast is especially popular, with French toast and huevos rancheros topping the list of favorites.

Thai Arroy $
1019 Light Street
(410) 385-8587

This casual, small restaurant serves traditional Thai dishes, like red curry and Pad Thai, and it has quickly become a neighborhood staple. The food is delicious and well priced. As of publication, the restaurant did not have a liquor license, but you are welcome to bring your own beer or wine (Smitty's liquor store is two blocks away—see the Shopping chapter for details). Or try the delicious Thai iced tea, made with coconut milk. If you find the place too packed for a seat on a busy weekend night, you can always get takeout.

Thairish $
804 North Charles Street
(410) 752-5857

This authentic Thai restaurant is primarily for takeout, but there are a few seats in the small space located in the heart of Mount Vernon. The owner whips together a great Pad Thai. Thairish is open Tuesday through Friday for lunch and dinner, dinner only on Saturday and Sunday. It is closed on Monday. If you're curious about the name, the owner will tell you he chose it to honor his marriage: He is Thai and his wife is Irish.

Vespa $$$
1117–21 South Charles Street
(410) 385-0355

As the name suggests, Vespa is a small, spunky, Italian-inspired cafe and wine bar just 1 block south of the Cross Street Market in Federal Hill. For a lighter meal, try a small plate, like the crispy fried calamari with a red pepper aioli or one of the creatively garnished brick-oven pizzas. For a bigger meal, choose from one of the entrees—salmon over green lentils and fennel or tenderloin with wild mushroom risotto are two favorites. Accompany your meal with one of the wines from the primarily Italian list. If you are not familiar with Italian wines, the knowledgeable staff will happily fill you in. Desserts are not to be missed. Try the warm apple tart, or keep to the Italian theme and take the house-made tiramisu. Reservations are highly recommended for this restaurant, which is open every day for dinner. Although you will be comfortable wearing jeans, Vespa tends to attract a hip, well-dressed crowd. Park on the street or at meters.

Windows $$$$
Renaissance Harborplace Hotel
202 East Pratt Street
(410) 547-1200

Located in the Renaissance Harborplace Hotel, Windows offers exactly what the name implies along with contemporary American cuisine. From the fifth floor of the building, there are window views of the Inner Harbor as well as crab cakes, salmon, and swordfish, served every day in new and traditional ways. The tortellini and shrimp scampi stir fry is a staff favorite. Save room for dessert because they're all made in the hotel kitchen. But no matter how good the food is, the view's the thing that sticks in your mind and in your camera lens.

Reservations are absolutely necessary; you can park in the hotel parking lot or walk over from the Inner Harbor area.

Woman's Industrial Exchange $
333 North Charles Street
(410) 685-4388

Besides the fact that a scene from *Sleepless in Seattle* was filmed here and the fact that there's a craft shop upstairs, this is a great place to hit for breakfast or lunch, especially if you miss your grandmother's or mother's cooking. Women with the same qualities, both in terms of age and attitude, serve breakfast and lunch fare Monday through Friday. The chicken salad is a frequent request, along with charlotte russe. There's no need for reservations. If you're sick of hotel or restaurant food near the Inner Harbor, take the short walk, about a half mile, for a change of pace.

Ze Mean Bean Cafe $
1739 Fleet Street
(410) 675-5999

A cute and quaint little storefront eatery offers coffee, borscht, and pirogies as well as an assortment of tasty pastries and dinner entrees. The restaurant serves lunch and dinner Monday through Friday and brunch and dinner on the weekends. Jazz music is played while you eat. Expect a wait, because this Fells Point find has been discovered by many. Park in the area and window-shop your way to and from the restaurant.

NORTHEAST

Angelina's $$$
7135 Harford Road
(410) 444-5545
www.crabcake.com

Most restaurant sections start with Angelina's, not just because it's first in the alphabet, but because of this formal dining restaurant's reputation for great homemade crab cakes. What you pay for is a good deal—crab cakes made with lump crabmeat and backfin, the preferable parts of the crab, with little filler and clawmeat.

It will take you about 15 minutes to get from the Inner Harbor to Parkville, heading north on Harford Road, but it's worth the trip for Angelina's, which also offers a variety of other seafood and meat dishes.

The restaurant serves lunch and dinner every day except Monday and has a full bar. Parking is available on the street, and reservations are a good idea on weekend nights.

Bel-Loc Diner $
1700 East Joppa Road, Towson
(410) 668-2525

No matter when you get hungry, the Bel-Loc Diner is there for you, serving breakfast, lunch, and dinner whenever you want it. The diner has been an institution for years, providing a place for travelers, businesspeople, nearby residents, and everyone else who stops by to visit, eat, and relax. The menu ranges from hot roast beef and fries with gravy to meat loaf, an omelet to pancakes, served at all hours, of course. Come as you are, because the coffee is always on, and there's always a slice of pie waiting for you.

Bill Bateman's Bistro $
7800 York Road
(410) 296-2737
www.billbateman.com

Located next to Towson University, this is a popular bar and restaurant for the college crowd as well as for families. The place has a sports bar feel, so it comes as no surprise that it is known for it chicken wings and its wide selection of microbrews. The full menu is a broad offering of typical bar fare, with lots of burgers, sandwiches, and salads, as well as vegetarian options. A pool table and video games entertain restless kids, and some nights will find karaoke in the bar. Open daily for lunch and dinner; a Sunday brunch is served.

Blue Nile Ethiopian Restaurant $$
2101 North Charles Street
(410) 783-0982

Casual dining on Ethiopian favorites is the menu at the Blue Nile. No matter whether you order a beef, lamb, or chicken entree, the ingera, an authentic Ethiopian bread, is a must. It comes with every meal, and it's the most memorable part of dining at this restaurant that opened in 1997.

You'll also want to try the Ethiopian Coffee Ceremony, where a smoking pot of coffee is sent to your table following the meal. It's a sight and taste treat that's worth the wait.

There's no bar, and alcohol is not allowed. There's free parking on the street. Lunch and dinner are served every day, and reservations are necessary on Friday and Saturday night. Call that day or the day before to make sure you can get in.

Cafe Troia $$$
28 West Allegheny Avenue, Towson
(410) 337-0133
www.cafetroia.com

Here's a place for all those folks who miss their Italian mother. The food is good, the servings ample. One of the best things on the menu is the piatto misto, a roasted red pepper, a marinated eggplant, shaved prosciutto, arugula, goat cheese, and mozzarella. There's a full menu of Italian treats with fish, shrimp, chicken, veal, and steak bases. Osso buco served with a grilled polenta side order is a sure winner, recommended by the staff and owner Gino Troia. Don't go in a rush. Plan to enjoy the semiformal setting in an apartment complex in the heart of Towson, about 8 miles north of the Inner Harbor.

Park at a municipal lot or on the street for change, and plan ahead with a reservation. The restaurant serves lunch Monday through Friday and dinner seven days a week.

Jerry's Belvedere Tavern $
5928 York Road
(410) 435-8600

If you plan to take in a movie at the beautiful Senator theater (see The Arts chapter), which is about a block south of Jerry's on York Road, the food here offers the perfect match to the theater. It's your basic restaurant with a combination of Italian and American food; the favorites are a basic hamburger or cheeseburger. People come to Jerry's, about a half mile from the Baltimore City line, for everything from a big anniversary celebration to a family birthday celebration. You'll see sports fans as well as business executives dining here.

There's a full bar and a separate smoking section at this eatery that's been open so long its current owners cannot remember when it first started. You'll hear Baltimoreans refer to it as Jerry's or Jerry's Belvedere often enough to make you realize what they know—there's something powerful that draws you back again and again.

Jerry's serves breakfast, lunch, and dinner seven days a week. Parking is available behind the building. You don't need a reservation because everyone will make space for a few more to join in the fun.

Lisa's Coffee House $$
2110 North Charles Street
(410) 727-7081

Lisa has much more than a coffeehouse going. In fact, her menu itself tells a visitor that the place serves "the best Balkan region food in Baltimore" like the bitochki, spiced ground beef shaped like a meatball. The menu also includes borscht, pirogies, and more traditional American food such as clam chowder, Lisa's specialty salad, and chicken salad. Save room for a slice of pie!

Parking is available at metered spots on Charles Street within a block of the restaurant. Lisa's is open Monday through Saturday for lunch only.

The Milton Inn $$$$
14833 York Road, Sparks
(410) 771-4366
www.miltoninn.com

The Milton Inn is a bit of a drive out of the city, and technically is in Sparks, Maryland, but this staple of regional dining offers a wonderfully romantic getaway. You'll wind your way along York Road, past the developments and the minimalls to find a quaint home tucked in the pastoral landscape. Seasonal American fare (clams casino, porterhouse steaks, rockfish) is mingled with a touch of the European (like the seared foie gras), all served in an eighteenth-century farmhouse, replete with period decor and roaring fireplaces. The dress code is "business casual," which basically translates to no jeans and no shorts or collarless shirts. Open daily for dinner and weekdays for lunch.

Nichi Bei Kai $$$$
1524 York Road, Lutherville
(410) 321-7090

Dine while seated around a Japanese hibachi, where the chef will be slinging your choice of shrimp, chicken, steak, or lobster into the air. Sushi is also prepared, but with not quite as much air in the cooking process. The restaurant serves lunch Monday through Friday only and dinner every day in a semiformal atmosphere, just outside of Towson off I-83.

Paul Chen Hong Kong Restaurant $$
2426 North Charles Street
(410) 235-8744

Plan to spend some time going over the 225-item menu. If you can't find what you want, may we suggest the kung pao lamb or the scallops with garlic sauce, both of which have the right amount of sweet and spice to make them really, really nice.

The take-out-only restaurant is open seven days a week from 11:00 A.M. to 11:00 P.M.

Pete's Grille $
3130 Greenmount Avenue
(410) 467-7698

A neighborhood diner is what you'll find at Pete's Grille. It serves breakfast and lunch; Pete's breakfast is hash browns, fluffy pancakes, and waffles made from scratch—tasty, down-home cooking, just like you'd expect from a good diner.

Lunch offers more homemade family foods, such as sandwiches, a soup of the day, the usual meat loaf, and other American food.

Parking is available on Greenmount Avenue, especially since lots of the people who visit live nearby and walk over.

The Prime Rib $$$$
1101 North Calvert Street
(410) 539-1804

You have to appreciate a restaurant that puts its best foot forward in its name. Guess what's the best thing on the menu? If you don't want to try your luck at its signature dish, you can try other steak and seafood offerings. But really, the prime rib's the thing, along with the buttery mashed potatoes.

If you're looking for a dark and classy atmosphere for your fine-dining experience, then this restaurant just north of Mount Vernon is for you. Black walls, carpets with leopard prints, and a baby grand piano lighted in neon are a feast for the eyes as much as the menu is a feast for the palate.

Parking is available on area streets at meters or for free. The restaurant only offers dinner. Be advised: Without a reservation, you will not get in. Jackets are required.

Tapas Teatro $-$$
1711 North Charles Street
(410) 332-0110
Located next to the historic Charles Theater, this restaurant is the perfect spot for a meal before or after a movie. The same owners also run The Helmand in Mount Vernon, and you'll find a few of their Afghan-inspired dishes on the menu, like the eggplant with yogurt. Overall, the food is a delicious mix of Spanish and international-inspired tapas cuisine. In the warm months outdoor seating lines the street. Reservations are not taken and the place is very popular, so if you're trying to eat before a movie, leave plenty of extra time. Open Tuesday through Sunday for dinner only; parking is available in a garage across the street or at meters. The garage offers discounted rates if you see a movie at the Charles (see The Arts chapter for more details).

Valentino's $$
6627 Harford Road
(410) 254-4700
Open 24 hours a day, this restaurant has a long list of regulars who make every visit a lesson in the history, economics, and sociology of the area—if you keep your ears open. The atmosphere at the cafeteria-style booths is informal and friendly for children. The menu offers Greek specials such as spinach pizza, Italian favorites such as lasagna (vegetable and meat vari-

eties), and a full complement of foods that make this a good place for anyone at any hour. Breakfast, ranging from scrambled eggs to French toast, is offered at all hours. You can also get your hands and mouth on steaks, seafood, salads, and sandwiches as well as a few tasty cakes and pies for dessert.

No reservations are necessary and parking is available on a parking lot behind the restaurant. No alcohol is served nor are you allowed to bring any in.

NORTHWEST

The Ambassador Dining Room $$
3811 Canterbury Road
(410) 366-1484
www.ambassadordiningroom.com
This ranks as one of the best all-around dining experiences in the city. Located in the historic Homewood neighborhood in a 1930s-era apartment house, The Ambassador has a rich interior and a glass-enclosed terrace room that opens onto a gloriously landscaped city garden in the summer months. In the winter the terrace glows warm from the roaring fireplaces and the twinkling votive candles. Everything on the menu is superb, from the samosas to the chana to the traditional unleavened naan bread. White-glove service complements the delicious menu. Open daily for lunch and dinner, parking is on the street.

Cafe Hon $$
1002 West 36th Street
(410) 243-1230
www.cafehon.com
"Hon," rhyming with "gun" and short for "honey," is a term of endearment used by many Baltimoreans. This cafe, with its Hon's Much Better Than Mom's Meat Loaf and its assortment of homemade pies, is a tribute to the term and the people who use it. Located in Hampden in a more than 100-year-old building that used to house a hardware store, the cafe is decorated in vintage and antique decor, with Formica

tables and an antique chest for the liquor. A vintage pachino machine is also on display.

The casual atmosphere is perfect for families and the neighborhood folks who make this a frequent gathering spot. The cafe, which opened in 1992, serves breakfast, lunch, and dinner every day.

This is Baltimore at its truest.

Cafe Pangea $$$
4007 Falls Road
(410) 662-0500

There's something for everyone at this Roland Park establishment. Although it's only been open since 1996, the Cafe Pangea has a solid reputation for delivering an eclectic mix of American, Mediterranean, and Egyptian cuisine in a casual atmosphere. A fish of the day awaits diners, along with the blackened catfish and the curried crab, made of jumbo lump crabmeat and a light cream curry sauce. It's the best of Baltimore and the best of the Mediterranean in one dish.

In addition to the food, there are two computers that diners can use to browse the World Wide Web. The price is $4.00 for half an hour, and there is usually a wait to get online.

Beer and wine aren't allowed. Parking is available at metered spots on the street. Lunch and dinner are served every day, except Sundays in spring and fall when Cafe Pangea only offers brunch.

Gertrude's $$$
10 Art Museum Drive
(410) 889-3399
www.artbma.org

Round out your cultural experience at the Baltimore Museum of Art with a culinary experience at the in-house restaurant, Gertrude's. John Shields, nationally acclaimed cookbook author, chef, and host of his own syndicated cooking program, brings his signature Chesapeake Bay cuisine to the restaurant. The menu evolves with the seasons to reflect the fresh produce and in-season seafood of the Chesapeake region. The Waterman's Oyster Stew is a hearty concoction and the grilled Maryland rockfish fillet with a roasted red bell pepper butter sauce on a bed of seafood hash is popular with diners. The wine list is extensive with an emphasis on Californian wines, although it also offers many local wines from Maryland and Virginia. Gertrude's is open for lunch and dinner Tuesday through Friday, with brunch also offered on Saturday and Sunday, but it is closed on Monday.

Jeannier's $$$$
105 West 39th Street
(410) 889-3303

French food from a restaurant in an apartment building near Johns Hopkins University? You betcha. Try the veal citronelle or the escargots en croute, rich with garlic to offer a lingering taste sensation. There's a formal dining room as well as a lounge and glass-lined bar area. It's a classy place in a classy location, designed to attract the folks at Johns Hopkins who have the means to support a high-end restaurant. The food and the staff live up to the challenge, making it one of the area's most expensive restaurants worthy of its name and growing reputation.

Lunch is served Monday through Friday; dinner, Monday through Saturday. The restaurant is closed on Sundays, except on Easter and Mother's Day. No matter when you go, you're going to want to have reservations.

The Knish Shop $
508 Reisterstown Road, Pikesville
(410) 484-5850

A knish, an oven-browned and filled dough pocket, is the namesake and the attraction at this truly kosher deli in Pikesville. The spinach knish draws constant raves, and the potato knish is another winner. An assortment of kosher specialty sandwiches is also available. Don't miss the pickles—they have a personality all their own.

The Knish Shop is open during the day, Monday though Friday and Sunday. Closed Saturday.

McCafferty's $$
1501 Sulgrave Avenue
(410) 664-2200

Want to be a radio star? Then this might be the place for you. McCafferty's plays host to a radio sports talk show for a local station, WJFK 1300 AM, Monday nights from 7:00 to 10:00 P.M. There's also a sports memorabilia collection, with items from the Orioles, the Ravens, the Colts, and NASCAR racing as well as the 1970 Super Bowl trophy.

In addition to the sports stuff, Don McCafferty's place has good prime rib, steak, and seafood entrees. But the atmosphere of this sports bar and restaurant is the draw. The upscale casual eatery has a following of area sports fans and other professionals from the Baltimore area. There's also a smoking section. Valet parking is available.

Lunch is served Monday through Friday; dinner, seven days a week. Reservations are suggested at least one day in advance, although you can always eat at the bar, where several TV sets play the best sports events of today. A piano player performs Tuesday through Saturday in the restaurant.

Mt. Washington Tavern $$
5700 Newbury Street
(410) 367-6903
www.mtwashingtontavern.com

The building goes back more than 150 years, but in 1989 the owners decided to give it a new view. They installed a fully retractable roof in one of the five dining rooms and renamed it the Atrium Room, offering a beautiful view of several trees that have been known to drop leaves onto the tables of unsuspecting diners at this upscale casual restaurant. Indoor dining space upstairs includes the Chesapeake and Pimlico rooms, decorated in hunting and lacrosse motifs. Wherever you eat, there's a feast for the eyes as well as the stomach.

The menu offers several seafood specialties, including crab soup with large, lump crabmeat, jumbo lump crab cakes, and a separate raw bar, featuring 2-inch-long shrimp. There's also a wet-cured dinner steak where so much fat is cut off that a steak billed as 16 ounces is about as close to that size as possible after cooking.

The restaurant offers lunch and dinner every day, with a Sunday brunch from 10:30 A.M. to 3:00 P.M. Parking is available for free at the Mount Washington Metro stop, just a few feet from the entrance to the restaurant, or at a private lot next door to the restaurant. Reservations are a good idea for weekends.

Papermoon Diner $
227 West 29th Street
(410) 889-4444
www.charm.net/~diner/

Imagine a restaurant filled with old toys—cars, trains, boats, and other items collected over the years. Though this casual and eclectic restaurant opened in 1993, the toys give the impression that it's much, much older. The Web site defines the Papermoon experience: "We think that everyday life is tough enough and you need to escape it sometimes." The food is distinctly American. Most people like the omelets and burgers. A favorite is the Hampden Omelet, with three eggs, ham, Swiss cheese, and onions as well as home fries and toast on the side. Try the Hampden Burger, too. Its recipe is a secret.

You can have beer and wine, and there's a separate smoking section. Parking is available at the restaurant or on the street. Reservations aren't necessary for breakfast, lunch, or dinner, which are served every day. The restaurant is open 24 hours.

Petit Louis $$$
4800 Roland Avenue
(410) 366-9393
www.petitlouis.com

Chef Cindy Wolfe and her husband, wine expert Tony Foreman, were inspired by their extensive travels in France. The couple recreated the simple, robust cuisine of the French bistro in Roland Park. The menu boasts escargot in garlic and white wine and a rich foie gras terrine served with a crusty baguette. You can choose from small or large plates, so this is a good spot for a light meal or a five-course event. The bouillabaisse is popular with the regulars as is the thoughtful wine list and the crème caramel dessert. Parking is available in a lot in front of the restaurant. Petit Louis serves dinner nightly and lunch Tuesday through Friday. Reservations are highly recommended.

Windy Valley General Store $
2346 West Joppa Road, Greenspring
(410) 339-3900

There's no place to sit, but boy is it fun to grab it and go. If you want rotisserie chicken, big sandwiches or submarines, or a salad, you're in luck. But what really draws the raves is the ice cream, that soft-serve stuff that tastes like custard going down on a hot summer day. Wind Valley has sundaes with all the toppings and banana splits, but best of all are the milk-shakes. We've never had a bad one in all the years of visits. Thick, creamy, tasty, even malted—a treat in summer, or the rest of the year.

If you want to splurge on the high-calorie treats, you're in luck during lunch, dinner, and early evening hours seven days a week. Park in the lot next door. Windy Valley is on Joppa Road, but the best way to reach it is to zip off I-695 at exit 23 (Falls Road) and go north. You can't miss it when the crowded parking lot appears on the right just before the entrance to Greenspring Station shopping center.

SOUTHEAST

The Acropolis $$
4718 Eastern Avenue
(410) 675-3384

You'll know you're in Greektown when you walk in the door: Murals and music of Greece and families dining make this a true ethnic find for casual dining in Baltimore. For a true taste of the culture, order the shrimp oregano, featuring jumbo shrimp sautéed in white wine and served over rice, or the Giouvetsi, a baby lamb braised in olive oil and baked with orzo, with a tomato, green pepper, and onion sauce. Rockfish and red snapper are also served, and all portions are large.

Reservations are a good idea, especially on weekends. You can park on the streets near the restaurant. Lunch and dinner are served seven days a week.

Gunning's Crabhouse $$
3901 South Hanover Street, Brooklyn
(410) 354-0085

Lots of restaurants serve crab cakes, but Gunning's Crabhouse is one of the few to serve three types all the time. Using its own recipes, there's the jumbo lump, which costs the most and has the best meat; the backfin, which has smaller portions of meat; and the old-fashioned Eastern Shore recipe, which no one will explain. Each of them is worth a try, or you can dine on the oyster sandwiches or fried oysters, the crab dip, or the creamy crab soup, a favorite because of its thick and rich texture.

If you just want to eat steamed crabs, then you're in the right place. They're always available on tables with paper towels at the ready. But save room for dessert: Gunning's has homemade eclairs that measure 8 to 10 inches in length, 4 inches in width, and between one half and a one full pound. No fooling!

The restaurant has a full bar, featuring 12 brands of beer and Old Dominion root beer on tap. There's also a separate smoking section. Parking is available in a lot outside the restaurant. Lunch and dinner are served seven days a week. Reservations are necessary for dinner, and it's a good idea to call ahead to find out the price and size of the crabs for the day.

For a late night meal, try the Sip-n-Bite diner on Boston Street in Canton. It's open 24 hours a day, 364 days a year— they only close on Christmas day!

Hull Street Blues Cafe $$$
1222 Hull Street
(410) 727-7476
www.hullstreetblues.com

If you were a fan of the gritty police drama *Hill Street Blues*, you probably think this restaurant's name is spelled incorrectly. Wrong, Bobby Hill. The name comes from the street on which it sits in South Baltimore. What you will find inside is a relaxing environment for eating seafood and steaks with a true Maryland appeal. The restaurant serves lunch and dinner every day, except Sunday when lunch is replaced by brunch.

Matthew's Pizzeria $
3131 Eastern Avenue
(410) 276-8755

Okay, recommending a pizza place is like picking someone's tailor, but this is one you have to try. We heard about this place for years before finally stopping by this Highlandtown treasure.

In a cozy dining room with red and white checkered tablecloths, you feast on pizza. We recommend the traditional, meaning a deep-dish crust. The toppings range from pepperoni to pineapple (try it before you turn your nose up at it). There's other stuff on the menu, but it pales in comparison to the pizza, which is the appeal to many of the families and first dates that frequently make their way here.

Park on the street, and don't worry about your dress or the need for reservations. This is casual because everyone's committed to the goal of the mission— eating lots and lots of pizza. Lunch and dinner are served daily.

P.S.: The leftovers make a great breakfast, hot or cold.

SOUTHWEST

Candle Light Inn $$$
1835 Frederick Road, Catonsville
(410) 788-6076

Situated in a largely residential area with lots of mature trees, the Candle Light Inn catches a visitor by surprise, its candlelit windows drawing the eye in the dark of the night. Once inside, the food draws the taste buds.

Chef Marc Lombardini, part of the International Culinary Olympics in 1992 and 1994, offers American food in a casual environment. His favorites, as well as many of his visitors', are crab cakes and seafood bisque, although he won't discuss what makes them so special. Try to solve the mystery on your own.

The restaurant serves lunch and dinner seven days a week, and reservations are mandatory on holidays and a good idea on weekends. This restaurant tends to be one that draws people on special occasions. The restaurant has a large bar, and parking is available in a spacious lot next to the restaurant.

Little Havana Restaurante y Cantina $$
1325 Key Highway
(410) 837-9903
www.littlehavanas.com

Little Havana boasts one of the few outside decks with a view of the Inner Harbor. On a nice day it's hard to find a seat and the service can be slow, but it's worth the wait to enjoy a mojito and a pulled pork sandwich with black beans and rice while watching the ships sail past. The interior decor includes Cuban-inspired murals and a large oval bar. If you ever watched the Gene Hackman/Keanu Reeves film *The Replacements,* you'll recognize the place from the bar scenes in the movie. Little Havana is open every day for dinner and Friday through Saturday for brunch. A few parking spots are available out front, otherwise it's all metered on Key Highway. These meters run until 10:00 P.M., so bring quarters.

No Way Jose Cafe $$
38 East Cross Street
(410) 752-2837
There's an unmistakable scent of Tex-Mex food once you enter this restaurant, where shrimp and smoked ribs compete with pork dishes, and all are served with the mandatory side of slaw and fries. Lunch and dinner in beyond ample portions are served daily.

NIGHTLIFE ⊗

Baltimore's nightlife has always thrived, but it seems the choice of things to do has exploded in the last few years. Ten years ago, you might have had difficulty finding late-night revelry on a Wednesday night, but all that has changed. Cruise Cross Street in Federal Hill or Broadway in Fells Point on any given evening, and you're bound to find the many bars, coffee shops, and music clubs filled with neighborhood friends. Flip through the latest edition of the *City Paper,* and you'll see pages and pages of concerts, theater performances, happy hours, and DJ sessions.

Nightlife is booming in part because of the influx of young business professionals working here and renting in our city's new loft and high-rise developments. Many 30-somethings are also taking advantage of low interest rates and are scooping up affordable property in up-and-coming neighborhoods, helping fuel a renaissance in club activity. Numerous artists and musicians choose to call Baltimore home because of the reasonable cost of living and the creative vibe that exists here. Nationally recognized recording artists such as Lake Trout and the Kelley Bell Band land here when they're not touring, and they frequently grace our music venues. Even our mayor, Martin O'Malley, plays guitar in a rock band.

We are also a town of tourists, and the Inner Harbor is the mecca. Traversing Pratt and Lombard Streets on a Friday or Saturday night can be a traffic- and pedestrian-clogged hassle. But these crowds translate into packed clubs and restaurants, adding to the resurgence of Downtown nightlife. Power Plant Live!, a relatively new development within walking distance of the Inner Harbor, offers a number of nightclubs and restaurants in 1 square block. There are free outdoor concerts in the summer with popular national acts.

There is a wealth of jazz in the area, as one might expect of Billie Holiday's hometown. The city has also evolved a strong DJ culture, and the number of new clubs featuring turntables attests to the talent that exists in our quarters. These DJs have a strong pipeline to the clubs in D.C., and you'll frequently find talent from the famous 18th Street Lounge and the ESL recording label spinning here. Baltimore even merited its own sound designation; when flipping through the record stacks in places like New York City, you may run across a heading called "Baltimore breaks."

Beyond the clubs and the bars, we have a strong allegiance to literature, and you'll find national chains and local literary spots stay open late (flip through The Arts chapter for theater and fine-arts happenings). In this chapter you'll find a variety of offerings, ranging from the ideal dive bar to the high-end dance club. Most of these places exist in the city, although we have listed a few suburban hot spots. You can assume that all of the major hotels Downtown have some sort of adjacent bar for imbibing, so those have not been listed here. Neither have the chain clubs, like the Hard Rock Café, since those offer the same standard fare in every city.

Parking in Downtown basically comes in two varieties—on the street or in garages. Inner Harbor garages can run a couple of dollars an hour to $12 for the night. Outside of Downtown, most nightspots offer on-site parking, or spaces are available on nearby streets. In this chapter we've noted only when this is not the case.

IMBIBING IN BALTIMORE

Maryland's alcohol laws are somewhat tricky. Municipalities, including Baltimore City and Baltimore County, have liquor boards that issue licenses for everything from full-service bars serving beer, wine, and alcohol to beer-and-wine-only establishments to places that allow people to bring their own but not purchase it at the facility. In this chapter we've tried to explain the rules where they apply, but if nothing is listed, assume that the facility offers beer, wine, and spirits.

To purchase or possess any form of alcohol in Maryland, you must be at least 21 years old—no exceptions. Increasingly, bar, club, and liquor store operators are checking ALL patrons to make sure they meet the legal-age requirements. Since they can face closures and fines if they violate the law, these operators figure an ounce of prevention is less of a pain than the cost of lost business time or fines. As a result, be prepared to be asked to show proof of age, even if you are a few years beyond your 21st birthday. Although it's always a pain to be carded, it ensures that the laws are followed. Therefore, you should carry a picture identification card with you. We recommend that you always have your driver's license with you if you plan to indulge, because it's rare that establishments don't ask for it.

The waiters and waitresses who work at bars and restaurants serving alcohol are required to be trained to identify people who have consumed too much alcohol. They are taught to handle these patrons before they become a menace to themselves and their surroundings. They're subtle but effective in these efforts, which are statewide.

Working hand-in-hand with the state's alcohol laws are increasing efforts to stop drunk driving. State, county, city, and marine police agencies have been making more drunk-driving arrests in recent years, fueled by the public's growing outrage over drunk-driving accidents and deaths. If you are planning to drink, do not plan to drive. It's not just a gamble that could lead to an expensive ticket and from two to four points on your driving record, but a gamble with your life and the lives of innocent people. Officers in marked and

The best sources for up-to-the-minute nightlife activity are the "Live" section in the Thursday Baltimore Sun, *a pullout section on what's going on for the weekend, or the* City Paper, *which offers an extensive collection of free events and outings in the area. The* Sun *is available everywhere for 50 cents.* City Paper, *which is published on Wednesdays, is free and found in stores and on newsstands throughout the Baltimore area.*

unmarked cars often patrol areas known for their entertainment and tourism. Be warned: During holiday weekends, the intensity of patrols increases, as do drunk-driving incidents.

If you plan to drink, bring along someone who will remain sober. A growing number of clubs offer designated driver programs that enable people who pledge to remain alcohol-free to drink nonalcoholic beverages for free. Oriole Park at Camden Yards offers this program for all its home games. If you are a designated driver, ask when you enter the club if you're allowed to drink soft drinks or club soda for free.

If you've had too much to drink, hailing a taxicab or using public transportation are good options. If you need a taxicab, ask the bartender to get one for you. A number of clubs and bars have arrangements with taxicab companies that will get you where you need to be quickly and safely. Some tow truck companies also provide free towing, especially on holidays, of cars whose operators have consumed too much alcohol.

All of these programs have a simple goal: to protect people from the devastating effects of too much alcohol. Do your part by knowing when you've had enough or too much.

If you're staying in and plan on purchasing alcoholic beverages, remember that Baltimore City does not allow sales of beer, wine, or liquor in grocery or convenience stores. You will need to go to a liquor store, and most of these are closed on Sundays. Some bars offer carry-out after hours and on Sundays, but be prepared to pay top dollar or plan to drive to an adjacent county, where liquor stores frequently stay open all weekend.

DOWNTOWN

Baja Beach Club
55 Market Place
(410) 752-7188
A DJ plays Top 40 dance music every night as people fill the big dance floor and bikini-clad women in front of tubs of beer serve cold ones—beers, that is. There's just no denying the beach theme here. Want to leave your mark in Baltimore? Donate your bra to the collection hanging from the bar. It's a young crowd, and there's both a cover and a line on weekends.

Bay Cafe
2809 Boston Street
(410) 522-3377
Located on the water in Canton, the Bay Cafe serves good food (like shrimp salad), but it is really known for its libations and great environment. The beach-themed space is the ideal location for cold cocktails and blended daiquiris on a hot, humid Baltimore day. Sit on the outdoor deck and watch the sailboats and tugs cruise by. Parking is available at a lot nearby.

Bohager's
701 South Eden Street
(410) 563-7220
www.bohagers.com
A large warehouse inside, featuring two floors, tables, and a stage, and a deck with sand, palm trees, and the always-essential tiki torches outside set the stage at this Fells Point hot spot. Bohager's used to be the place to see national and local musical acts of note, but in recent years it has evolved into a debaucherous party club with thumping dance music, wet T-shirt contests, and a weekly event called the "Foam Party." The crowd is young and—while the attire is casual and flirty—the club now has a long list of dress code no-no's: no hats, no head gear, no sports apparel, no extra baggy clothes, no chains, no sleeveless shirts (for guys), and no Timberlands. Whew.

Cat's Eye Pub
1730 Thames Street
(410) 276-9866
www.catseyepub.com
This Irish pub features a collection of flags from all over the world and live music every night, ranging from bluegrass to zydeco, jazz to Irish tunes. Two bars will keep your whistle whet, and a back room with games and chess tables—yes, chess tables—will keep your mind busy. Cover charges vary.

Club Charles
1724 North Charles Street
(410) 727-8815
You might bump into filmmaker John Waters at this Baltimore pillar of nightlife. Across from the Charles Theater and the Everyman Theatre (see The Arts chapter), the dark red, Art Deco–inspired bar was listed as one of the Top Dive Bars in *Details* magazine. This is an all-inclusive kind of club where you'll find a mix of funky artists, local musicians, and suburban Dockers wearers grabbing a cocktail before catching a movie across the street. A mural with a sandstone background and red brush strokes depicts Greek mythology scenes, and the bathrooms breathe fire and brimstone art. FYI: The clocks are all set a half hour ahead.

Club Midnite
2549 North Howard Street
(410) 243-3535
You might turn into a pumpkin if you don't do it all in this wonderland of nocturnal entertainment. Downstairs is a nightclub with disco music, a light show, and a pool room. Upstairs is a casual bar featuring four more pool tables and a big-screen TV. In the main room is a large

stage with black-lit colorful drawings lining the walls. At the back is a lounge area reminiscent of your parents' basement with end tables, couches, and, yes, more pool tables. Live music is performed on some Sundays. A separate cover charge is applied to each area.

Club Orpheus
1003 East Pratt Street
(410) 276-5599
This two-level nightclub is known for industrial/Art Deco decor and techno, alternative, and progressive hits supplied by the DJ. A large screen on the first floor displays abstract images. Wednesday night is hip-hop night. Saturdays have a "fetish dance party." A cover of up to $5.00 is charged.

Club 13
The Belvedere, 1 East Chase Street
(410) 347-0881 or
(410) 783-1332 (hotline)
On the 13th floor of The Belvedere condominiums complex, a posh accommodation near the center of the Downtown Baltimore area, is the Club 13, where the sounds of live music—oldies, jazz, blues, and dance—can be heard Wednesday through Saturday. If you want to know what you'll see before you get there, call the hotline. The cover varies. Parking can cost you even more at the hotel. Street parking is sometimes available. Dress to impress if you want to fit in.

Comedy Club at Winchester's
102 Water Street
(410) 576-8558
A block north of the Inner Harbor, the Comedy Club brings in nationally known comedians for shows at 8:00 and 10:00 P.M. Saturday in the summer. Thursday night is for amateurs—try out your best stuff on stage or listen as some of the best and worst amateurs in Baltimore get behind the mike. Admission, which can range from $5.00 to $20.00, is charged, and it's usually hard to get tickets to some of the big performers' shows.

Comedy Factory Outlet
36 Light Street
(410) 752-4189
www.comedyfactoryoutlet.com
About 2 blocks from the Inner Harbor and above Burke's Restaurant (see the Restaurants chapter), the Comedy Factory Outlet brings in national and regional comedians Friday and Saturday nights. A $10.00 cover is charged, but if you're a hotel guest, show your key and it's only $5.00. We suggest you plan ahead; tickets go fast.

Fletcher's
701 South Bond Street
(410) 558-1889
www.fletchersbar.com
Fletcher's, located in Fells Point, ranks as one of the city's best small clubs for live music. A cousin to the famed 9:30 Club in D.C. features national and local bands of note in its upstairs room. Local musicians often launch theme nights here, such as the popular Johnny Cash tribute concert. Downstairs offers a comfortable bar with pool tables and couches. An updated list of concerts can be found by clicking on the guitar at the home page of the Web site.

Full Moon Saloon
1710 Aliceanna Street
(410) 276-6388
www.fullmoon-saloon.com
There can't be a much better mix than historic Fells Point and live blues every night. You can sit to watch the show or head out on the dance floor. A $5.00 cover is charged Friday and Saturday.

Hammerjacks
316 Guilford Avenue
(410) 234-0044
www.hammerjacks.com
The original Hammerjacks on South Howard Street was demolished in 1997 to make room for the football stadium, but it's been recently reincarnated at 316 Guilford Avenue. The large, warehouse-like space is known for its drink specials and its live entertainment. The cover charge

varies on whether the music is local or national.

Havana Club
600 Water Street
(410) 468-0022

Located directly above Ruth's Chris Steak House, 2 blocks north of the Baltimore Inner Harbor, this is an upscale nightclub decorated with soft leather sofas, state-of-the-art sound, and an extensive (and often expensive) wine and cigar list served from a 58-foot custom-designed bar. Dress is swanky at this Cuban-inspired place. The owners also rent the space for private events, so keep this in mind if you're looking for a sophisticated setting for your next party. You can become a member of the Havana Club and get privileges like valet parking and VIP entrance when it's crowded.

Hippopotamus
1 West Eager Street
(410) 547-0069
www.clubhippo.com

Known to the locals only as "the Hippo," this place is a three-for-one. The Eager Street Station bar, pinball, and pool tables are in the main room. A 14-foot video screen is the draw for the video dance bar, while the main dance floor has a sunken dance floor, elevated seating at tables, and topnotch sound and light systems to make the place rock and roll. The dance club and video bar are open Friday and Saturday nights, while each night brings something new in the main dance area, including dance party night on Sat-

---

If you want to find a lot of clubs in a small area, try Fells Point. Within a 4-block-square area are more than a dozen watering holes and clubs whose entertainment ranges from hard rock to jazz to acoustic hits and dance music. Most of the places charge a cover, but it's worth it if you stay for a drink or two.

---

urday, men's night on Thursdays, and Special Event Nights on Sundays. This is a gay-friendly club.

The Horse You Came In On
1626 Thames Street
(410) 327-8111
www.horsesaloon.com

This club in historic Fells Point is modeled after an English pub. Brick walls, wood floors, and a bar give way to a variety of live performances by local musicians on acoustic guitar and other instruments. There's no cover charge during the week and only $1.00 on Saturday nights.

Mick O'Shea's Irish Pub
328 North Charles Street
(410) 539-7504
www.mickosheas.com

Mick O'Shea's offers an authentic Irish pub experience with live entertainment most nights. Conveniently located a few blocks from the Inner Harbor, here's a place to hoist a few with true green-blooded Irishmen. You may even catch our mayor rocking on guitar with his band, O'Malley's March.

ONE
300 East Saratoga Street
(410) 230-0049
www.onebaltimore.com

The chicest new club in Baltimore is in an unlikely location—tucked under I-83. But this little corridor along Saratoga Street has become quite an enclave for clubs. Sonar is a block away, and Hammerjacks is around the corner. ONE is inspired by the elements, and each floor in this transformed warehouse offers an interior designed theme relating to earth, wind, air, and fire. Resident and guest DJs spin house, jungle, drum, and bass and trip-hop. ONE is open Wednesday through Sunday and the admission charge is usually $10 to $15. The dress code is called "club chic," described as fashionable and funky—no hats, shorts, or athletic wear. Reservations are accepted for the couches on the Water and Air levels.

The Ottobar
2549 North Howard Street
(410) 662-0069
www.theottobar.com

There's not much else in the way of bars around the Ottobar, but this is a destination spot for those looking for good live music. The two-story club has a bar and pool tables upstairs, and a stage for live music on the first floor. Since its inception in 1997, the Ottobar has consistently booked up to 100 local and national bands a month, primarily in the rock/punk/rap genres. The club is well known around the country, and it's not unusual to see someone sporting Ottobar's signature T-shirt with the cat and martini logo as far away as Los Angeles. While touring bands appear from all over the world, Ottobar is a strong supporter of the local music scene. In 2002 it even hosted a rock opera about a giant clam put on by local rockers, the Pourbilles. There is a paved lot with free parking behind the venue and usually plenty of street parking. The neighborhood has a questionable reputation, so remember not to leave anything in your car that might entice a break-in.

Paradox
1310 Russell Street
(410) 837-9110

Out of an industrial area warehouse near the Inner Harbor comes this tribute to a wild night. DJs spinning dance, hip-hop, rap, funk, and techno keep the dance floor in a constant state of excitement. Bleachers, a cafe, and even a basketball court are alternatives to the dance floor. There is also an outdoor area for enjoying a Baltimore summer night. Check out "The Chamber," a room for real dancers, with lighting effects playing on a dark, black background.

There's plenty of parking. A cover of up to $5.00 is charged some nights, but it's worth it just to take a look inside this converted warehouse.

Phillips Harborplace Restaurant
301 Light Street
(410) 685-6600

In addition to great seafood and a great location next to the Inner Harbor, Phillips offers some down-home, any-voice-will-do, singalong action at its piano bar. Whether you want to belt out your favorite Sinatra, Dixieland, or jazz hit, Phillips is ready to encourage you seven days a week.

Park at one of the garages near the harbor, or if you're staying at one the hotels nearby, walk on over for a drink, a snack, and some good or bad music, depending on your ear. There's no cover.

Power Plant Live!
Market Place and Water Street
(410) 727-LIVE
www.powerplantlive.com

Located at the intersection of Market Place and Water Street, just 2 blocks from the Inner Harbor, Power Plant Live! is the latest development in Downtown nightlife. To date, eight bars and five restaurants circle a large, open plaza where bands play for free on warm summer evenings. This is a great place to come early with the kids for a bite to eat. After dinner hours it gets rowdy with revelers partying at places like Bar Baltimore and Have a Nice Day Café. Valet parking is offered nightly from 5:00 P.M. to 2:00 A.M. There is the Harbor Park Garage off Lombard Street, or you can take your chances on the street.

Red Maple
930 North Charles Street
(410) 547-0149
www.930redmaple.com

A modishly sleek interior formed from teakwood, steel, and glass makes this one of the most architecturally stunning spots in the city. Opened in 2001, the modern lounge vibe fueled by the best resident and guest DJs earned the Red Maple a slot on *In Style* magazine's list of the top 60 nightspots in America. Linear benches offer seating for an Asian tapas menu or

Looking for a Baltimore happy hour experience? In the summer a narrow portion of Water Street evolves into a street party, where workers from nearby Legg Mason and Deutsche Bank crowd outdoor patios. Over in Federal Hill, the Cross Street Market offers a great happy hour in a unique setting throughout the year.

simply for people watching. Be aware that these seats are often reserved on weekends by diners, so check with the hostess before sitting during prime dinner hours. There is usually a cover at the door in support of the music. Once inside, there's no smoking at all, but an outdoor courtyard (home to the namesake red maple) allows smokers to light up. The attire is hip, not formal, but tennis shoes are not allowed. Open daily after 5:30 P.M. Reservations for dinner are recommended. Park on the street or pay to park on a surface lot for about $6.00.

Redwood Trust
200 East Redwood Street
(410) 659-9500

A $2.5 million investment transformed the former Mercantile-Safe Deposit and Trust Co. building on the corner of Calvert and Redwood Streets into an 18,000-square-foot playground for adults, a self-proclaimed "showcase of architecture, light, and sound." The first floor has a cavernous feel. In what used to be the bank's vault, a DJ spins house music while couples recline in intimate comfort on overstuffed couches. Upstairs the vibe is more raucous: Dancers bump and grind to the tunes pumped out of a $200,000 Phazon sound system, while lasers refract shards of colorful light off a giant disco ball, highlighting the spectacular Beaux-Arts ceiling. A balcony encircles the third floor, affording a bird's-eye view of the dancers below. Bartenders hustle on every level to

keep the colorful cocktails flowing. Need a break? Ladies commiserate in the restroom on the third floor where an attendant offers everything from mints to hairspray, while men sneak off to the basement to buy a cigar. If you really want privacy, open your wallet and pay $500 to $1,500 for a VIP room.

Sonar
407 East Saratoga Street
(410) 327-8333
www.sonarlounge.com

Sonar, as the name suggests, is a place for new electronic music. The lounge brings in the best local and regional DJs, who don headphones as they spin vinyl in two rooms. It was voted "Best New Club in America" in *URB* Magazine in 2002 for its hip environs and its eclectic music. Sonar also hosts special events, like a recent fashion show for top Baltimore boutiques. The bar offers a varied selection of bottled beverages, like Lindeman's lambic framboise, an acidic beer infused with raspberry. A weekly schedule of DJs and special promotions is listed online, and there is usually a cover charge Thursday through Saturday.

Spy Club
15 East Centre Street
(443) 685-4779
www.spyclubbaltimore.com

Washington, D.C., has its Spy museum; we have the Spy Club. The club occupies the second and third floors above the Midtown Yacht Club, a narrow row house in Mount Vernon. You enter through the downstairs bar and walk up a flight of stairs where spy-themed posters and artwork adorn the walls and warm, ambient lighting gives the space a cozy feel. Weekends find this bar buzzing with a pleasant mix of professionals, artists, and students from the neighborhood. There is a congenial, house-party vibe with a DJ upstairs spinning trip-hop. After 11:00 P.M., the music usually gets louder and a small dance floor attracts a small crowd.

Stagecoach Saloon & Restaurant
1003 North Charles Street
(410) 547-0107
A DJ blasts country tunes for the folks
moving to the beat on the large, hardwood dance floor. The country music runs
Monday, Wednesday, Thursday, and Saturday, while on Friday Reba and Hank give
way to serious, high-energy, nonstop
dance music. If you need another diver-
sion, there's a restaurant, lounge, and
game room. A $2.00 cover is charged on
Friday on occasion.

NORTHEAST

The Barn
9527 Harford Road, Parkville
(410) 882-6182
Local rock groups perform on weekends
at this bar with a dance floor that tends to
draw a younger crowd. The bar has lots of
baseball and football memorabilia. Park
where you can in the area, but watch out
for the NO PARKING signs. Police are on the
lookout for violators. There's a minimal
cover for live music.

Borders Books & Music
415 York Road, Towson
(410) 321-4265
bordersstores.com
In addition to the cavalcade of books, magazines, and CDs, Borders offers live entertainment from time to time at its Espresso
Cafe. There's no cover charge, but it's hard
to spend much time in this place without
buying a book, CD, or homemade dessert.
Parking is available in the Towson Commons parking garage for a few bucks.

Cafe Tattoo
4825 Belair Road
(410) 325-7427
Live progressive, blues, and jazz performances fill the stage Tuesday through Saturday and are complemented by late-
night eats and an informal atmosphere.
The cover charge depends on the entertainment offered.

Nashville's
2004 Greenspring Drive, Timonium
(410) 252-7373
Whether there's a live band spitting out
country tunes or a DJ playing the latest
hits, the large dance floor is always filled
with people enjoying the beat. Nashville's,
inside a Holiday Inn Select hotel, is decorated with Wild West memorabilia. Dance
lessons are held Tuesday and Thursday
nights, ladies night is Wednesday, and
Family Day begins at 5:00 P.M. on Sunday.
No cover is charged.

New Haven Lounge
1552 Havenwood Road
(410) 366-7416
You've found a home for the classic style
of jazz performed by Cab Calloway and
Billie Holiday, whose images are preserved
in murals along with other jazz greats.
Bartenders don tuxedos to bring drinks to
your table, while you listen to live jazz
Tuesday, Wednesday, Friday, and Saturday
or a DJ on Sunday. The cover varies with
the day at this lounge near Morgan State
University.

Parker's Tavern
1809 North Eastern Avenue
(410) 342-3468
Just about every type of popular and new
music form is played live by local musicians at Parker's Tavern. Smooth blues,
"unplugged" acoustical classic rock,
trendy progressive, and alternative stuff
get fair airings each week. There's no
cover for this good look at Baltimore area
music talent.

*The first Thursday of the month is
always a treat at the Walters Art
Museum, 600 North Charles Street. In
addition to free admission to the
museum, you can hear live jazz in the
arms and armory museum. It's the perfect way to get from an interminable
Thursday to the weekend. (For more
information, see The Arts chapter.)*

Putty Hill Station
2531 Putty Hill Avenue, Parkville
(410) 882-0500

This is a typical neighborhood sports bar that also has a DJ Friday nights and live bands on Saturday. No cover is charged, and you can park in the shopping center lot outside.

Rascals
1630 East Joppa Road, Towson
(410) 825-1570

There's live rock and popular music for a 40-and-older crowd at this lounge with three bars. The small stage and a dance floor get quite a workout. A cover is charged to patrons, many of whom come in search of love.

The Recher Theatre
512 York Road, Towson
(410) 337-7178
www.rechertheatre.com

Housed in a former movie theater, this nightclub offers about 10 pool tables, a full bar, and live music. It's an enchanting mix that draws many students from the nearby colleges. The cover charge varies with the entertainment, although pool playing in the afternoon and early evening requires no cover charge. Park in one of the municipal garages or parking lots in Towson or at Towson Town Center, a large mall just north of the site on York Road. Keep your eyes on the listings for this small club, as it sometimes attracts major touring acts.

Tracy's at the Bowman
9306 Harford Road, Parkville
(410) 665-8600

It's really an unlikely place for a comedy club, inside a formal restaurant, but Tracy's hosts quality local, regional, and national comedy acts at 9:15 P.M. Friday and 8:30 and 10:45 P.M. Saturday. Cover ranges from $9.00 to $15.00 with a two-drink minimum.

Tully's
7934 Belair Road, Overlea
(410) 665-9100

Just a few blocks outside the Baltimore Beltway's exit 32 (U.S. 1) is a great bar for eats, chats, and dancing. The dance floor is small, but the atmosphere is perfect for a relaxed evening of food, drink, dancing, and fun. Most nights a DJ runs the show, while on Tuesdays and Sundays karaoke is on tap. No cover is charged. Parking is available in the parking lot of Putty Hill Plaza.

NORTHWEST

Gordon Center for Performing Arts
3506 Gwynnbrook Avenue, Owings Mills
(410) 356-SHOW
www.gordoncenter.com

One of the newer performing arts centers in the Baltimore area, the Gordon Center offers cultural programming ranging from theatrical productions to book readings, concert presentations to recitals. The clientele tends to dress up, wearing dresses or shirts and ties, to take in the action. Some events are free, but tickets can go as high as $30.

McCafferty's
1501 Sulgrave Avenue
(410) 664-2200

Live big band and oldies music is performed by a variety of artists Thursday through Saturday. There's also a pianist who plays in the lounge. No cover is charged.

SOUTHEAST

Brewster's Saloon
303 East Furnace Branch Road,
Glen Burnie
(410) 760-5239

Glen Burnie's House of Blues is Brewster's Saloon, where live blues music is performed Friday and Saturday. The cover charge is $3.00.

Club Rumblefish
7954 Baltimore–Annapolis Boulevard, Glen Burnie
(410) 768-4477
Magically intoxicating lighting effects and a brightly colored interior make this nightclub with several bars a real treat. The bars and the dance floors are different on each level, and the lights make it perfect for dressing to the nines. During the summer, there's an outdoor deck for watching the more natural lights of night. The bar is closed Monday and Wednesday. Cover charge varies.

SOUTHWEST

Hull Street Blues Cafe
1222 Hull Street
(410) 727-7476
www.hullstreetblues.com
Hull Street has been a neighborhood saloon since 1889. The classic pub is sandwiched among blocks of row houses in South Baltimore's Locust Point, its crimson red front identifying it from the neighboring residences. A full menu of sandwiches, crabcakes, and bar snacks is served at the bar and at the few tables scattered in the back room. The famous Hull Street chili is the perfect antidote to a blustery winter day.

J. Patrick's Irish Pub
1371 Andre Street, Locust Point
(410) 244-8613
In the heart of Locust Point is a quaint little neighborhood bar where live Irish music is played Thursday through Sunday. No cover is charged, and parking is all over the roads near the bar.

The Royal
1542 Light Street
(410) 783-7776
www.theroyalbaltimore.com
Located on a primarily residential street, The Royal is a corner bar that has been transformed into a music venue for live rock, funk, and rock-a-billy bands. There is live music Tuesday through Sunday nights with varying cover charges, usually ranging from between $2.00 to $10.00. Lots of local bands play here, so you can get a real taste of Baltimore's music.

SHOPPING

Everywhere you go in Baltimore City and its environs, you will find places to shop. If you're looking for mall shopping, excellent bookstores, thrift stores, or indoor and outdoor farmers' markets, Baltimore has everything you could possibly want.

On York Road alone heading north from just below the county line and stopping at Hunt Valley, there are 14 shopping centers and two shopping malls, one of which is Towson Town Center, the largest shopping mall in the area. East of York Road within two minutes' drive of Towson Town Center between Joppa Road and Goucher Boulevard are six more shopping centers, and then they really begin to add up as you move east across Joppa—four more at Perring Parkway; three more at Belair Road. Then comes White Marsh, which has two large malls (White Marsh Town Center and The Avenue at White Marsh) plus a few smaller strip shopping centers with neighborhood services. Around the corner from White Marsh are two more large shopping areas, and around the corner from those are two more. It all gives you a grand total of 32 major shopping areas between Towson and White Marsh—a distance that can be traveled in 20 minutes.

York Road and Towson are not the only areas that are so inundated. Reisterstown Road, west of Baltimore, Eastern Avenue in East Baltimore, and many other major roads are saturated with shopping centers and malls. On Ritchie Highway as it heads for and through Glen Burnie, shopping centers and malls lie side by side, links in a chain that carry you almost to the Bay Bridge. It is said that there are only two things to do in Glen Burnie—shop and shop.

Some of the best souvenir/gift shops are in museums, and even the smallest historical locations sell something. However,

the bigger the attraction, the more varied the choice. The Baltimore Museum of Art and the Maryland Historical Society have two of our favorite gift stores, with items reflecting exhibits, Maryland history, and other more esoteric subjects. You can find great posters, novelty items, and even unique coloring books at reasonable prices. The main branch of the Enoch Pratt Free Library on Cathedral Street also has a great gift shop that is open weekdays and sells everything from elegant paper dolls to worry stones. Most Enoch Pratt branches also have a shelf of used books to sell in the 50 cents to $1.00 range.

If you're interested in outlet shopping, Baltimore can serve as a great home base while you tour outlets in Pennsylvania and on the Eastern Shore—Maryland's holy land of outlet shopping. Baltimore itself now has its own outlet megamall found at Arundel Mills (see information later in this chapter as well as the Day Trips chapter for more information on outlets.)

For bargains in antiques and collectibles, including arts and crafts, consult our Antiques and Collectibles chapter, where we list some of the shops in and around the city, and see our Day Trips chapter for destinations that require a little more travel time. If you'd rather be junkin', Baltimore's weekends are full of flea markets, particularly in the fall and spring. The local papers, such as the *Baltimore Sun* and the *City Paper,* will tell you all you need to know about flea markets, yard sales, auctions, and other spontaneous buying opportunities.

All malls and shops are smokefree in the state of Maryland. If you light up, you'll be thrown out. Parking is free at all the suburban malls, even in garaged space, but in most shopping districts, you'll find on-the-street, metered parking or, in the case of Downtown malls and districts, pay parking garages. Downtown garages usually charge a flat rate for the first hour or two and then "x" amount for every hour thereafter. Sometimes, it will be $3.00 for the first hour and $1.50 for every following hour, or it might be $1.00 for the first hour and $2.50 for every hour thereafter. In any case if you stay all day, you're going to be paying between $10 and $15 for parking. There are some special day rates if you park before 9:00 A.M. or after 5:00 P.M., but they vary. On the other hand, all of Downtown can be accessed by public transit, whether by bus, Light Rail, or subway. (See the Getting Here, Getting Around chapter for details.)

We couldn't possibly list every space with a cash register and merchandise in and around the city. Instead, we've done our best to hit the high notes—the best buys, if you will. We've organized the malls, shopping districts, farmers' markets, under-roof markets, and music stores by our geographic divisions—Downtown, Northeast, Northwest, Southeast, and Southwest. Bookstores and thrift stores are not separated by geographic region since many of these stores have locations in different regions. You will, however, find the geographic region for each location in parentheses next to the street address.

MALLS
Downtown

Harborplace
Light and Pratt Streets
(410) 332-4191
www.harborplace.com

Sometimes it seems as if Harborplace is the most talked about shopping mall in the country. (It has even been mentioned in *National Geographic*!) Businesspeople come from far and wide to look at it and see if the concept could work in their hometown. Opened in the early 1980s, Harborplace has become the focal point for Baltimore's "new downtown" at the head of the Inner Harbor and the main mover and shaker in Baltimore's harbor renaissance.

More than 10 million people a year come to peruse the 130 shops, restaurants, and eateries, many of which feature outside tables that face the Inner Harbor. Boaters can pull their vessels right up to the dock and eat lunch at their choice of waterside cafes. Or they can get carry-out and sit on their boats to watch the street performers at the Harborplace Amphitheater between the two glass pavilions.

You'll find chain restaurants, like Cheesecake Factory or the California Pizza Kitchen. You'll also find Maryland traditions such as Phillips Harborplace Restaurant. The bottom line on food at Harborplace: If you want it, they've got it—Tex-Mex, Chinese, burgers, cheesecake, seafood, and pizza. It's all there.

The shops are as diverse as the eateries. Of course, there are a few standards. For women's clothes, you'll find Ann Taylor, The White House, and August Max Woman. The Sport Shop has both men's and women's clothing. A branch of The Body Shop is also there, as is Sunglass Hut International, but the bulk of the stores at Harborplace are more esoteric.

Hats in the Belfry, for instance, has Easter-type hats and everyday casual hats for both men and women. In the Light Street Pavilion, you'll find The Discovery Channel Store, with a wide selection of unique gifts for any member of the family.

Although there are lots of places to pick up souvenirs of your trip to Baltimore, Harborplace has a shop that deals strictly in that dimension. Destination Baltimore is a national chain of souvenir stores whose main focus is souvenir sportswear, such as T-shirts and hats.

There are also shops with a Baltimore flavor, such as Maryland Bay Company, which sells items that have nautical themes, including sailing, crabs, and lighthouses, and Chesapeake Knife & Tool, which sells—you guessed it—knives and tools that are great for anglers, hunters, and amateur handymen.

We could go on for pages about all the shopping opportunities here, but suffice it to say that Harborplace gives you a lot of choice without requiring you to walk for miles and miles to get it. The pavilions are large but compact.

There is no parking at Harborplace and no free parking Downtown, unless you are extremely lucky and find that odd place on the street. If you're driving, consider The Gallery's parking, which is above Pratt Street on Calvert Street, or at one of the many meters or lots nearby. An hour's parking will cost $1.00 in quarters. Harborplace and The Gallery shops, restaurants, and eateries offer a $2.00 validation stamp for valet parking with any purchase.

The Gallery
Pratt and Calvert Streets
(410) 332-4191
www.harborplace.com
Across the street from the Pratt Street Pavilion at Harborplace is The Gallery, four stories of glass that hold some of the more exclusive shopping opportunities in the area. The Gallery boasts more than 75 nationally known shops and eateries under a central skylight that makes you feel as if you're shopping in the National Arboretum.

The shops at The Gallery are not unique; you'll know almost every name—Coach, General Nutrition Center, and Godiva Chocolatier are just a few. There are several clothing stores to choose from. Brooks Brothers has a bi-level store here, and you'll find Banana Republic and J. Crew as well.

There are designer clothes at Ann Taylor and specialty shops for both larger and smaller women—August Max Woman and Petite Sophisticate, respectively. For the smallest among us, The Gallery's Gap store has Gap Kids.

There's also a fair number of shoe stores—11, to be exact—including such well-known names as Lady Foot Locker, Nine West, and Aerosoles. You'll also find some really interesting ancillary shops such as Bath and Body Works, which carries all those bath and body lotions and sweet-smelling stuff you'll want to put on under the new outfit you just bought.

The mall has its own underground park-ing, but there are also many lots nearby if that one should be full. Access to the parking lot is from Calvert Street, which is one-way north. Head east on Pratt Street and turn left. The parking lot entrance is on your right, as is The Gallery. The Gallery Garage offers both self-park (24 hours a day) and valet parking (5:00 P.M. to midnight Monday through Friday, 11:00 A.M. to midnight Saturday and Sunday).

Northeast

Towson Town Center
825 Dulaney Valley Road, Towson
(410) 494-8800
www.towsontowncenter.com
Towson Town Center started life in the 1950s as a simple neighborhood shopping center that had a shoe store or two, a ten-cent store, a drugstore, and a few other things. Its location, down the hill from the original suburban Hutzler's department store, at that time the biggest local department store around and currently being renovated as a new mall unto itself, made it a popular destination. Over the years, as Towson and the demand for services grew, the shopping center added levels, stores, and, eventually, a roof.

Hutzler's has long since closed, but Towson Town Center has been renovated and reorganized to become a major player in the mall arena. As it stands today, it boasts Hecht's and Nordstrom's and more than 150 specialty stores. As with many of the malls, you'll find tons of clothing stores—about 40 of them. There are 20 or so stores that sell shoes, including Foot Locker, Nine West, and Aldo Shoes. The 18 kids specialty shops include toy stores such as KB with its great prices.

If you're after books, Towson Town has a major bookstore, Waldenbooks. For music, Sam Goody should be able to accommodate anyone's groove.

If you need a briefcase or a wallet, Coach has a location in the mall.

For gifty things, try the soaps and scents of Crabtree & Evelyn or the tasty treats of Godiva Chocolatier. For everything else, you'll find things from the classic offerings of the The Bombay Company to the wonderfully classless offerings of Spencer Gifts.

You can have your hair cut at Bubbles Salon; purchase jewelry at 17 different stores, from the premium items of Radcliffe Jewelers to the fun stuff at Claire's Accessories. You can rent a tux, have your nails done, have your eyes examined, even send a letter (there's a post office on the first floor!). There is—literally—something for everyone here.

And when you're tired of all this variety, you can hunker down in the large food terrace that offers food choices from yogurt and salad to steaks and Boardwalk Fries.

Towson Town is easily accessible. It's right in Towson and just a long block off the Beltway. The mall has four levels, three major parking garages, and some open parking. All parking options are free.

White Marsh Mall and
The Avenue at White Marsh
**8200 Perry Hall Boulevard, White Marsh
(410) 931-7100
www.whitemarshmall.com**

White Marsh Town Center is the name given to an area of planned development, at the center of which is a megamall with five department stores (Macy's, Hecht's, JCPenney, Sears, and Lord & Taylor) and more than 170 specialty stores.

White Marsh is only two stories high, so it spreads out over a large area. It is easy to get around in, however, because there is only one main drag lined with shops. The only shops that shoot off this corridor line the entrances to the department stores and the one main entrance from the outside.

Like many megamalls, White Marsh's main focus is clothing, with 29 specific clothing stores in addition to the five department stores. Among those are two shops for larger women, including Lane Bryant, one of five locations left in the Baltimore area.

White Marsh has more shoe stores than just about anywhere else—20 in all—

including Naturalizer, Rockport, Aldo, and Easy Spirit. The mall does have, however, its fair share of nonapparel stores.

You'll find a branch of Waldenbooks there; music-wise the mall boasts a Sam Goody, which offers a good selection of music. White Marsh Mall has the traditional sporting goods offerings, such as Foot Locker and The Athlete's Foot. There is also Driving Impressions, which has neat stuff for your car as well as neat stuff about cars.

You might enjoy Things Remembered, where you can buy a simple silver cup or a gold pen—lots of gift ideas for weddings, graduations, births, and all the important moments of remembrance in our lives— and have them engraved.

White Marsh has more than its fair share of high-level jewelers, including Gordon Jewelers, Kay Jewelers, Littman Jewelers, etc., etc., but for inexpensive, fun jewelry we suggest Claire's Accessories.

The food court at White Marsh is a special treat for kids (and moms) because of the full-size carousel at its center. The food court itself is decidedly one of the largest in any of the malls around and always crowded. It offers 20 food booths. There are also a few sit-down restaurants within the mall.

The mall is centrally located between Baltimore to the west and the city of Bel Air to the north. It has easy access to I-95 and I-695. Around the mall are strip shopping centers, industrial parks and business centers, a large hotel, eateries, a health club, and a new adjunct facility called The Avenue at White Marsh (www.theavenue atwhitemarsh.com).

The Avenue is not a mall but neither is it a strip shopping center. It is, instead, a Main Street clone, complete with brick sidewalks, low-level street lamps, and a giant marquee for its 16-screen movie house. Opened in 1997, The Avenue of White Marsh includes eight sit-down restaurants and cafes. Both White Marsh and The Avenue have free parking.

In addition to The Avenue, other stores and small strip shopping centers gather around White Marsh. Of special note is Ikea, the Scandinavian home-furnishing chain. This is its only location in the Baltimore area. Plants and planters, lamps and lampshades, mugs, glassware, dishes—everything you could possibly want for floor, shelf, or porch and most of it made with natural fibers, clays, and wood—make up the stock here. There is a snack bar on the premises as well as a restaurant that serves terrific Swedish meatballs. If you have children under 2 feet tall, you'll love the giant-sized glassed-in play area that comes complete with babysitters.

Northwest

Mondawmin Mall
1200 Mondawmin Concourse
(410) 523-1534

This mall was built more than 40 years ago on the site of Mondawmin, an estate owned by Alexander Brown, founder of the first mortgage banking company in the United States. The mall currently has 110 retailers and a variety of fast-food eateries.

You will, of course, find traditional stores such as Foot Locker and Payless for shoes. K-B toy stores has a location here, as does Lerner New York. Mondawmin is unusual among many of the malls around, however, because although it is a relatively large mall, it has no anchor department store. It is shops . . . lots and lots of shops.

Mondawmin is not lacking in clothing stores, with 24 to its credit, including Big & Tall Casual Male, Leather Man, Ashley Stewart, and Rainbow.

If it's music you're after, there are six stores, including The Wall, Record Town, and Inner City Records. Mondawmin also has a McCrory's Ten Cent Store—one of the last in the area—and food specialty stores that you won't find at other malls. There's Mondawmin Chicken and Seafood and Oriental Express, for instance, and Murry's Steaks, which is all over Baltimore in strip shopping centers but rarely in malls.

Mondawmin also boasts many personal service–oriented stores. Most suburban

malls will have one or two places to get your hair cut, and they might have one place that sells beauty supplies, but Mondawmin has three beauty salons, two barber shops, a wig store, two nail shops, and two beauty supply shops.

Outside the mall, you will also find the Motor Vehicle Administration office, an office of the Social Security Administration, and a well-used subway stop. Even with all the parking spaces that these organizations use, there's always plenty of free parking.

Owings Mills Town Center
10300 Mill Run Circle, Owings Mills
(410) 363-7000
www.owingsmillsmall.com

Owings Mills Town Center opened in 1987 to serve the affluent far west side of Baltimore and the county. With three major department stores (Hecht's, JCPenney, and Macy's) and almost 250 specialty shops, plus 20 eating places on the food court. Owings Mills is a mall of mammoth proportions. If that weren't enough, a 17-screen General Cinema theater boasts stadium-style seats and three premium screens.

Waldenbooks and Bath and Body Works are among the standard mall shops at Owings Mills. You'll also find some of the more high-end clothing shops, such as Nine West, Ann Taylor, and Casual Corner. Gap, Limited Too, and Victoria's Secret are also here. Owings Mills has one of the five Lane Bryant stores left in the area, and there are two electronics stores—Radio Shack and the Electronics Boutique, which sells computer software. Owings Mills also sports nine jewelry stores from the more exclusive shops that actually have "jeweler" in their name—Friedman's Jewelers, Littman Jewelers, Reeds Jewelers, and Zales Jewelers—to the inexpensive, fun costume jewelry shops, such as Claire's Accessories.

The food court has, among other establishments offering mainly snacks and drinks, Italian cuisine at Vaccaro's and Mamma Ilardo's Pizzeria; deli selections at Boardwalk Fries. There is also traditional fast food available at McDonald's and Chick-fil-A. For those of us who are watching our weight there's Everything Yogurt/Salad Cafe. You'll also find Bourbon Street Cafe and Ruby Tuesday's on the menu.

If you're driving, try to park near the JCPenney, which sits at the middle of the arc-shaped building. That way you won't have to walk so far to your car when you've finished shopping. Owings Mills is also served by mass transit. Light Rail does not have a stop at the mall, but there is a bus from the Owings Mills metro stop.

Reisterstown Road Plaza
6564 Reisterstown Road
(410) 358-2275
www.reistertownplaza.com

On March 14, 2001, Reisterstown Road Plaza turned 40 years old. Known simply as the Plaza, it started out as a relatively small neighborhood shopping area that has grown and grown over the years. Its most recent overall renovation was completed in 1986, when a two-story office building was added to house the headquarters for the Maryland State Lottery and two new entrance wings were built.

Quantity of stores is not the benchmark of Reisterstown Road Plaza—variety is. In the words of a Plaza Insider, it's an "ethnic-oriented center that has everything from bras to post offices." It generally caters to four basic surrounding ethnic communities: African American, Russian, Jewish, and Latin American. For instance, its grocery store has a complete Russian aisle and a full kosher aisle, and, simply put, has everything from chittlins to borscht.

The two department stores at the mall are Burlington Coat Factory and National Wholesale Liquidators; both are medium-size stores with moderately priced goods. In fact most of the mall stores offer good bargains. For women's clothing you can find Ashley Stewart, Casual Wear, Fashions $10 & Up, and Gallo Clothing. Shoe-store bargains include Payless Shoes/Payless Kids, Economy Shoes, and Shoe City. There's a discount pet goods stores at Reisterstown, Pet Valu; a RiteAid Pharmacy; and a liquor store, Mall Spirits. Several beauty supply houses

are also here—Visions Beauty Outlet, Vogue Hair Supply, and Sally's Beauty Supply. There are also salons for your hair and nail needs, as well as five stores that sell jewelry and accessories. Two furniture stores, Classic Furniture and Rent-a-Center, offer items for the home. The one bookstore, Sepia, Sand & Sable Books, can order any title you want but specializes in African-American literature.

There is plenty of free parking. If you'd rather not navigate Reisterstown Road, you can easily take the metro, which has a Plaza stop.

Southeast

Marley Station
7900 Ritchie Highway (State Highway 2)
Glen Burnie
(410) 760-8900
www.shopmarleystation.com

With more than 130 specialty stores, nine restaurants, and four department stores (JCPenney, Macy's, Hecht's, and Sears) as well as an eight-screen United Artists Cinema, Marley Station is easy to get to either by going straight down Ritchie Highway from Baltimore or heading down State Highway 100 from I-695.

Under the auspices of the slogan "The Fun's Inside," Marley Station has turned itself into a family-oriented shopping center, with lots of amenities and activities for parents and kids. From programs that present country guitarists or African dancers to breakfast with Peter Rabbit, Marley Station goes out of its way to make itself a center for community as well as shopping.

The mall is laid out on two floors essentially in the shape of a printed M, with main entrances at the center of the "letter" and major department stores at each of its four "points."

Along this route, you'll find a bookstore, Waldenbooks; more than 16 women's clothing stores; and one of only two Frederick's of Hollywood stores in the area. There are almost as many specialty gift stores as there are women's clothiers, counting in at 19. Marley Station offers 10 jewelry stores, including Edward Arthur Jewelers, Kay Jewelers, and Zales. There are six shoe stores that carry children's shoes in addition to the department stores. You'll also find The Children's Place and the Disney Store for kids' clothes.

Marley Station has food specialty places such Mrs. Field's Cookies, Pretzel Time, and Kohr Brothers Frozen Custard. (Yummm!) The mall is also rife with restaurants, both chain and fast food. Many are the popular mall fare, such as Sbarro's, with its thick-crust pizzas, and Boardwalk Fries, with some of the best fries in Baltimore, and a Taco Bell. This may not seem like a big deal to some, but to those of you who have vegetarian and meat-eating children in the same family, it can be very handy. Of course, if it's just Mom and Dad out shopping, they might want to try sitting down at Ruby Tuesday's.

Parking is free and plentiful, with more than 4,500 spots to choose from.

Southwest

Security Square Mall
6901 Security Boulevard
(410) 265-6000
www.securitysquare.com

Security Square Mall has more than 120 stores and eateries inside, and two additional restaurants—International House of Pancakes and Bennigan's—on its large parking lot. There are four main stores: Sears, Hecht's, Old Navy, and Burlington Coat Factory. Sears has an auto service center. The mall has a General Cinema theater with eight screens that has access from outside the mall.

The mall is very community-oriented, with ongoing special programs such as the Summer Theater for children, which presents a different children's production each month from June to August. But the most interesting thing about the mall is its signs.

You know how irritating it is to be heading for one store in the mall and inadvertently end up parking at the exact

opposite end from where that store is located? Well, that can't happen at Security. From the moment you enter the parking lot, there are signs that tell you which way to go. Hecht's this way; Sears Auto Center that way. Once you're in the mall, you don't have to search for a directory to figure out where you are and where you want to go. Signs point the way.

The only question you need answered, then, is which way do you want to go. The main entrance into the mall is by Hecht's, but that will drop you into the food court and a long hall that has a lot of service spots on it, such as the U.S. Post Office, Shoe Repair, Hair Cuttery, and Picture People.

The shortest way into the center of the mall is through International Furniture. From there, you can determine which way you want to head.

You'll encounter two kid's shoe stores, a large Super Kids store, and a smaller Payless Kids. There is a $10 Fashion Store, an Express, Hyatt & Co., as well as the Leather Man, which sells leather jackets and pants as well as leather bags. Suncoast Motion Picture Company, Software Etc., K-B toys, and Camelot Music are here as well.

You'll find 7 jewelry shops at the mall, including the Piercing Pagoda. There are also electronic and appliance stores, including AT&T Wireless and Radio Shack. There are other home-oriented shops in this corridor as well, such as Lamp & Furniture and Shades of Beauty. You'll also find things for your leisure hours—both B. Dalton Bookseller and Waldenbooks are here, as is Glauber's Hallmark store, which sells cards, gifts, and candy. The food court includes a Cajun Gourmet, the Taco Maker, Cinnabun, and McDonald's.

As with most suburban shopping centers, all parking is in open lots and free.

Arundel Mills
7000 Arundel Mills Circle, Hanover
(410) 540-5100
www.arundelmills.com

Arundel Mills opened in November 2000,

making it Baltimore's newest mall. The center includes a mix of one-of-a-kind manufacturer and retail outlets, specialty retailers, and category-dominant stores. In fact, more than 200 anchors and specialty retailers share the space with entertainment venues and a variety of dining options.

Simply put, the mall is huge, at 1.3 million square feet of retail space. Anchors and major tenants include Bed, Bath & Beyond, Books-A-Million, Off Broadway Shoe Warehouse, Off 5th—Saks Fifth Avenue Outlet, and Old Navy. A new addition is the popular H&M clothing chain.

It will be hard to not find what you're looking for at this megamall. For fashion there's a Banana Republic Factory Store, Eddie Bauer Outlet, Gap Outlet, United Colors of Benetton Outlet, and Ann Taylor Loft—just to name a few of the more than 40 apparel stores. Shoe stores are also easy to find and include Skechers USA, Cole Haan, Jarman, and a Nine West Outlet.

Handbags, leather, and luggage can be found at Leather Limited, Samsonite Company Store, and Wilson's Leather Outlet. Bath & Body Works, New York Perfumery Outlet, and Beauty Express offer the latest in health and beauty needs.

Jewelry and accessories can be found at 12 stores, including Reeds Jewelers Outlet, Claire's Accessories, Ultra Diamond and Gold Outlet, and Zales the Diamond Store Outlet.

Arundel Mills also offers some of the best shopping around when it comes to children's apparel, with Carters, Limited Too, Happy Kids, and Osh Kosh B'Gosh all under one roof. Home furnishings can be found at Island Rattan, Mikasa Factory Store, World Accents, and Country Clutter.

Arundel Mills prides itself on its specialty shops, which include Sun & Ski Sports, where shoppers can test the latest sports equipment on its 24-foot-high rock climbing and ice wall, in-line skating demo track, and indoor ski and snowboarding simulator. F.Y.E. For Your Entertainment is a music, video, and electronics store with a large children's department. The Bass Pro Shops Outdoor World is an outdoor enthusiast's paradise, with fishing, hunting, and athletic apparel, gear, and other outdoor accessories.

Shoppers will never go hungry at Arundel Mills, with 27 places to grab a bite, including the classics like Burger King, Sbarro's, and Starbucks Coffee as well as the specialties like DuClaw Brewing Co., Café ReMomo, and Kelly's Cajun Grill.

There is also Jillian's, an entertainment and dining complex with simulation games, Hi-Life Lanes bowling, billiards, and giant video wall. Muvico Egyptian 24 Theaters offers—you guessed it—a 24-screen, Egyptian-themed movie theater. But this theater also comes with valet parking and provides child care by licensed teachers.

Arundel Mills is located off I-95 and the Baltimore–Washington Parkway (State Highway 295), heading south from Baltimore, via State Highway 100 in Anne Arundel County. It is also just 2 miles west of the Baltimore–Washington International Airport. There is plenty of parking available.

SHOPPING DISTRICTS

Because Baltimore is a city of neighborhoods, you'll find that every neighborhood has a shopping district. Each one will usually have some typical neighborhood stuff, such as a grocery store, at least one bank, a drugstore, sometimes a dollar store, a shoe store, and a haircutting place.

We can't possibly list every shopping area in Baltimore's more than 200 neighborhoods as well as all of the suburban shopping centers. What we have striven to do is note those that people visit from all over town.

Downtown

Charles Street Shopping District
Charles Street, from Pleasant Street to Mount Royal Avenue
Farther up town, both north and south of Mount Vernon Square and the Washington

Monument, you'll find the Charles Street Shopping District. This area was at one time where all the posh shops were—the furriers, the saddleries, the exclusive menswear shops. Over the years those stores left as the neighborhood became more peopled with students and young professionals. Now the Charles Street corridor contains the hippest of the hip. From the south at Brown's Market, which is arcade shopping tucked into one of Charles Street's magnificent buildings, to Mount Royal Avenue, you'll find some of the most interesting shops and restaurants in the city.

At the south end is **Woman's Industrial Exchange,** 333 North Charles Street, (410) 685-4388. Organized in 1882 to provide an opportunity for women to make a living through their crafts rather than have to face the low-paying sweatshops of the time, the Woman's Industrial Exchange opened its doors at this location in 1887 and ever since has been filled with goodies hand-crafted by Baltimore women. If you're in the market for quilted pillows, handmade dolls, and knitted booties, this place should be at the top or your list. A full-service restaurant with home cooking and a sense of camaraderie that's hard to find anywhere else in town is open from 9:00 A.M. to 3:00 P.M. (see the Restaurants chapter).

Down the street are a number of small art galleries and boutiques. **Beadazzled,** 501 North Charles Street, (410) 837-2323, is a jewelry-maker's paradise, with hundreds of colorful beads sold in bulk. One block north is **Nouveau Contemporary Goods,** 519 North Charles Street, (410) 962-8248, a fashionable furniture store that also sells hip gifts and household accessories. On the same block you'll find **Foot Fetish,** 525 North Charles Street, (410) 962-8088, a shoe boutique specializing in high-end footwear. Across the street is **A People United,** 516 North Charles Street, (410) 727-4471, a collective that sells clothing, jewelry, and crafts from around the globe. Be sure to visit the furniture gallery in the basement. Around the corner on Centre Street is Ted's Music Shop (see Music later in this chapter).

On the other side of Mount Vernon Place, you'll run into **Donna's Coffee Bar,** 800 North Charles Street, (410) 385-0180. North of there is a block-long section that is sort of the neighborhood shopping spot, complete with drugstore and sub shop. Working your way north, you get to the University of Baltimore and the outskirts of the Maryland Institute College of Art, so the businesses and restaurants start to reflect the college environs. There are lots of vintage and second-hand stores with a rotating stock of yesterday's T-shirts and funky jewelry.

The Belvedere at 1 East Chase Street started life as a hotel but is now a condominium complex. It also has a couple of terrific restaurants, including the **Owl Bar,** (410) 347-0888, where H. L. Mencken used to hang out. In the other direction on Chase, you'll find **Architect's Bookstore,** 11½ West Chase Street, (410) 625-2585, a design and architecture–focused store run by the Baltimore Chapter of the American Institute of Architects.

The Charles Street Shopping District is 13 blocks of shopping, culture, and architectural wonders, and right in the middle of it at Mount Vernon Place is a cross-shaped park, whose centerpiece is the Washington Monument—the first monument built to honor ol' George. Mount Vernon Methodist Church, the Peabody Conservatory of Music, and The Gladding Mansion, which is now part of The Walters Art Gallery, are also nearby. There are also park benches, fountains, and marvelous shade trees to shelter the weary traveler.

All parking is on the street at meters or in lots on side streets. Our suggestion is to park at one of the side-street lots (there are two facing each other at Cathedral and Centre Streets, a block west of Charles Street), then walk Charles Street from south to north until you get tired, and take a cab or bus back to your parking lot. For more information about the cultural wonders of the area, see The Arts chapter.

Federal Hill Shopping District
Along and between Light and South Charles Streets, south of Key Highway

Federal Hill Shopping District has its center at Cross Street Market (see the listing later in this chapter), but it has been enhanced by the neighborhood's renaissance. Many of the corner stores that were once drugstores or grocery stores have been transformed into gift shops, clothing shops, and antiques and collectibles shops.

It's a great place to meander through, because it's within walking distance of Inner Harbor and attractions such as the American Visionary Art Museum (see The Arts chapter) and Federal Hill Park (see the Parks and Recreation chapter). The neighborhood also offers some of the best food around (see the Restaurants chapter).

The shops offer an interesting mix of neighborhood essentials such as dry cleaners, pharmacies, and shoe repair. There is **Smitty's Cut Rate Liquors,** 1044 South Charles Street, (410) 752-8288, and **Movie Time Video,** 1118 South Charles Street, (410) 528-8888. You can also find less traditional stores. **Gaines McHale Antiques & Home,** 836 Leadenhall Street, (410) 625-1900, offers English and French antique furniture and **Zelda Zen,** 46 East Cross Street, (410) 625-2424, specializes in beautiful gifts and jewelry.

Just inside the Federal Hill neighborhood, only 2 blocks south from the Maryland Science Center (see Attractions chapter), resides **A Cooks Table,** 717 Light Street, (410) 539-8600. This store is a delight for anyone interested in the culinary arts. Specializing in gourmet kitchenware, it offers specialty foods, bakeware, tools, and cooking classes.

Other specialty stores include **Patrick Sutton and Associates,** 1000 Light Street, (410) 783-1500, a storefront for one of Baltimore's top interior designers. You'll find exquisite touches for the sophisticated home. **Shofer's Furniture,** 930 South Charles Street, (410) 752-4212, has four levels of furniture and home accessory shopping, while **Home on the Harbor,** 1014 South Charles Street, (410) 234-1331, offers

Unless you park at a paid meter or have a residential parking sticker, most on-street parking in Federal Hill is restricted to two hours. During baseball and football games, however, parking is prohibited altogether on many streets, and you can get a steep ticket. Be sure to read parking signs carefully.

connoisseurs of mid-century modern furniture some great vintage finds by renowned designers like Arne Jacobsen and Paul McCobb.

Not far from A Cook's Table is **Light Street Cycles,** 1015 Light Street, (410) 685-2234, which has everything for the cyclist—bikes, wheels, and helmets. **Charles Tiles,** 801 Light Street, (410) 332-1500, sells ceramic tile, hand-painted and plain, for kitchens, baths, counters, tabletops, and floors. If you need a special piece of foam cut for a chair, a pillow, or a sofa, or if you'd like a dense foam mattress for your bed, **House of Foam,** 1108 Light Street, (410) 727-0982, has all that and more.

Federal Hill is one of the oldest neighborhoods in Baltimore, and many of the stores have been there just about as long. **Morstein's Jewelers,** 1114 Light Street, (410) 727-3232, celebrated its 100th anniversary in 1998. Grandfather William, a Russian immigrant, set up his first shop in East Baltimore in 1898. Sonny Morstein (pronounced More-steen), third generation of this still family-owned business, handles fine jewelry and does custom work, appraisals, and repairs.

Parking in Federal Hill is mostly on the street at meters. There is one parking ramp located just off of Cross Street between Charles Street and St. Paul.

Fells Point Shopping District
Broadway, from Eastern Avenue to Thames Street

Fells Point Shopping District grew up at the foot of Broadway around the Broadway Market (see the listing later in this chapter). This is a must-see area of old buildings, cobblestone streets, the smell of salt water, and the cry of sea gulls. Yet, it is dichotomous. Working tugboats slosh at their moorings, while after-theater toffs in tails and gowns head for a drink at the Admiral Fell Inn. Johns Hopkins Hospital staff, just off a shift, as well as sailors just off the boat, are drawn into Jimmy's Restaurant for a true Maryland breakfast.

We talk extensively about Fells Point's antiques stores in our Antiques and Collectibles chapter and its fine restaurants and nightlife in those respective chapters, but you'll also find just some good old-fashioned shopping available here.

The area started out as a village for workers in the Fell shipyards, and it is still a place where you'll find craftspeople. **Brass Works Company,** for instance, at 1641 Thames Street, (410) 327-7280, sells brass items, but its stock in trade is brass restoration. From bed frames to candlesticks to bunged-up brass railings, Brass Works will bang it out, refit it, and make it shine like new.

Fells Point has a number of small, kitschy stores offering a variety of clothing, gifts, and home accessories. At **9th Life,** 620 South Broadway, (410) 534-9999, you'll find vintage T-shirts, funky jewelry, and retro lunchboxes. Fans of punk and hardcore music shouldn't miss **Reptilian Records,** 403 South Broadway, (410) 327-6853, while the **Sound Garden,** 1616 Thames Street, (410) 563-9011, ranks as the best local music store in the city, specializing in both new and used CDs. The staff of music aficionados can also give you the inside scoop on live rock shows. Across the street at **Su Casa,** 901 South Bond Street, (410) 522-7010, you'll find funky furniture and home accessories.

Down the street is **The Big Iguana,** 1633 Thames Street, (410) 675-3231, where you'll find imported clothing. **Ten Thousand Villages,** 1621 Thames Street, (410) 342-5568, is for anyone who likes handmade goods. Ten Thousand Villages is essentially a third-world outlet. It's a nonprofit organization opened by the North

Baltimore Mennonite Church and the Society of Friends to provide an outlet for crafters in third-world countries. The shop carries jewelry from the four corners of the Earth, toys, sarongs, woodcarvings from Kenya, and pottery from Vietnam and Bangladesh. There's also a year-round Christmas section.

If you're really just in the market for a cotton T-shirt, **Gary's Sportswear and Athletic Shoes,** 531 South Broadway, (410) 276-2234, will be more up your alley. Looking for a new tablecloth or some towels for the bride-to-be? **Super Linens,** 601 South Broadway, (410) 732-7900, has a large selection.

Fells Point Shopping District is just like Fells Point, with top- and bottom-end shops throughout. You can pay a premium price or a low one. You can find the extremely esoteric or the more traditional—whatever fits your mood or your need at the moment.

Park and walk or simply take the Inner Harbor water taxi. It's a great way to spend an afternoon and still get all your shopping done.

Northeast

Old Towson Shopping District
York Road, between Towsontown
Boulevard and Joppa Road, Towson
As mentioned in the introduction to this chapter, Towson has one of the largest malls in the area, Towson Town Center (see Malls previously in this chapter), and is also the starting point of a shopping area that stretches east all the way to Perry Hall and north to Cockeysville. But Old Towson, the area north of Towsontown Boulevard to Joppa Road, is a little shopping district all to itself.

A block west of the district are the Towson Court House and business offices for financial and legal firms in Towson, which may account for the large number of eating places in this 2-block-square shopping area. For instance, within just 2 blocks on York Road, you'll find **The Orient**

Restaurant, 319 York Road, (410) 296–9000; a **Ruby Tuesday's,** 401 York Road, (410) 825–1334; and **The Melting Pot Restaurant,** 418 York Road, (410) 821–6358.

Towson Commons, a small mall whose main claims to fame are its movie theater and its bookstore, is in the 400 block of York Road. The General Cinema movie theater, **Towson Commons,** 435 York Road, (410) 825–5203, has eight movie screens. **Borders Books Shop,** 415 York Road, (410) 293–0791, was the first megabookstore in the area. This location has an excellent selection on three floors as well as a separate music section, (410) 321–4265.

All along this little corridor (and east and west of it) are interesting shops and sights to see. Your kids will enjoy **Ten Car Pile Up,** a secondhand clothing store for teens at 511 York Road, (410) 832–5246. If your family likes the outdoors, **Hudson Trail Outfitters,** 424 York Road, (410) 583–0494, has all the gear and apparel you'll need for a weekend in the woods.

East of York Road is **F. Scott Black's Dinner Theater,** 100 East Chesapeake Avenue, (410) 321–6595, which mounts five productions every year. (See The Arts chapter for more information.) West of it, tucked in among other interesting shops, is **Fader's Tobacconist,** 25 Allegheny Avenue, (410) 828–4555, one of the 10 oldest tobacconists in the country. In business since 1891 and in this Towson location for more than 35 years, Fader's carries more than 100 different types of tobacco, including Davidoff White Label Cigars, which are available in only 44 other retail locations across the United States.

The main branch of the **Baltimore County Library** is at the south end of the district.

In Towson Circle you'll find **Trader Joe's,** (410) 296–9851, a unique chain grocery store with great prices and more than 800 grocery items under their own label. **Pier 1 Imports,** (410) 296–4112, offers an interesting array of gift items, furniture, and art work. There is also a **Barnes and Noble** located here (see Book Stores later in this chapter).

Parking is on the street at meters, or you can park in two parking lots. The old Hutzler's parking lot is now part of the free parking system for Towson Town Mall. The Towson Commons parking garage costs about $5.00 for an average stay, but if you're going to the theater or to some of the shops around, that can be reduced if you get your ticket validated.

Northwest

Hampden Shopping District
36th Street, between Falls Road and Chestnut Avenue
www.hampdenmerchants.com
Seventeen years ago hardly anybody in Baltimore knew about the little community of Hampden. But it has come of age since then, and the shopping district that runs for four blocks along 36th Street between Chestnut Avenue and Falls Road has become a very popular spot. This neighborhood was the backdrop to John Waters's film *Pecker* and its quirky mix of stores and street life has earned it ink in publications ranging from *Travel & Leisure* and *The New York Times* to *Lucky* and *Budget Living.*

Starting on the west end of "The Avenue," as it is known locally, you'll find **Atomic Books,** 1100 West 36th Street, (410) 662–4444, the best place for independent and underground literary finds. Across the street, **Paper Rock Scissors,** 1111 West 36th Street, (410) 235–4420 is the state's largest privately owned venue for local and regional art.

For furniture, you'll find plenty of used and vintage stores, like **David's Gans Co.,** 914 West 36th Street, (410) 467–8159, or **Fat Elvis,** 833 West 36th Street, (410) 467–6030. Design-savvy hipsters will want to check out the latest clothing and accessories at **Shine,** 3554 Roland Avenue, (410) 366–6100.

Cafe Hon, 1002 West 36th Street, (410) 243–1230, was probably the first place that appealed to a larger audience than just the neighborhood. It started out as hardly more than a counter and a coffeepot but has become one of the favored destinations for a taste of down-home cookin' and a good cup of brew (see the Restaurants chapter for more information). The souvenir shop across the street from the Hon is **Hometown Girl,** (410) 662-4438. It has cards and gifts of the Baltimore variety. You can buy Baltimore Oriole Checkers and Anne Tyler's latest bestseller, a Cafe Hon T-shirt, or the bottled version of Hon's Dill Vinaigrette.

Heading east you'll find **Ma Petite Shoe,** 832 West 36th Street, (410) 235-3442, where extraordinary shoes and indulgent chocolates come together under one roof. There's **Mud and Metal,** 813 West 36th Street, (410) 467-8698, which offers fine crafts from local artists and other "art to live with" items. **Oh! Said Rose,** 840 West 36th Street, (410) 235-5170, has upbeat and stylish clothes, whimsical baby gifts, jewelry, and accessories. **Holy Frijoles,** 908 West 36th Street, (410) 235-2326, offers a great Mexican menu. Hampden also has **Fat Elvis,** 833 West 36th Street, (410) 467-6030, with clothes, records, and other knickknacks.

All along 36th Street, you'll find both new and old shops. **New Systems Bakery,** 921 West 36th Street, (410) 235-8852, is there, with its curved marble steps and its archaic facade, not to mention its luscious breads, cookies, and cakes. A few doors away at 927 West 36th Street is **Galvanize,** a vintage/retro clothing store. Nearby is the **Golden West Café,** 1105 West 36th Street, (410) 889-8891, with innovative breakfast, lunch, and dinner items.

Down near Chestnut Avenue you'll find four interesting shops clustered together. **Village Flower Mart,** 3601 Chestnut Avenue, (410) 235-0404; **In Watermelon Sugar,** 3555 Chestnut Avenue, (410) 662-9090; **The Coffee Mill,** 3549 Chestnut Avenue, (410) 243-1164; and the second location in Hampden for **The Turnover Shop** (see the Antiques and Collectibles chapter for more information).

Mount Washington Shopping District
Kelly Avenue on the east to Smith Avenue on the west

Farther out Falls Road past Northern Parkway in the community of Mount Washington is a defined shopping district clustered before, after, over, and under the Kelly Avenue Bridge. When Falls Road narrows as you head north and you see the furniture refinishing shop on your left and the pizza place on your right, you're there. At the light, turn left over the bridge and make an immediate right onto Kelly Avenue once you're on the other side. You'll head right into a large metered parking lot. There are some nice restaurants, bakeries, clothing shops, and other interesting stores and restaurants tucked into four short streets.

Many of the shops have to do with keeping yourself looking good, from a simple haircut to an hour-long body massage such as **Studio 1612,** 1612 Kelly Avenue, (410) 664-3800. Around the corner is **Diana's European Skin Care,** 1501 Sulgrave Avenue, (410) 367-1866; **Europa International Salon,** 5701 Newbury Street, (410) 367-1111; and **Goldilocks Hair Studio,** 5600 Smith Avenue, (410) 664-4330.

Once you've gotten beautiful (or handsome, as the case may be), you can have a great lunch in the atrium room at the **Mount Washington Tavern,** 5700 Newbury Street, (410) 367-6903, or talk sports at **McCafferty's,** 1501 Sulgrave Avenue, (410) 664-2200. See our Restaurants chapter for information about either of the two eateries.

Along Sulgrave Avenue are the little shops—those one-room, stuffed-with-stuff places that are great to poke around in to find treasures, new and old. **Something Else,** 1611 Sulgrave Avenue, (410) 542-0444, is typical of the offerings along Sulgrave. A mainstay in the community for more than 30 years, Something Else has imported clothing, jewelry, and bric-a-brac. All the clothing is made of natural fabrics, and the most popular material currently is flax, a wash-and-wear natural fabric. The store boasts Naot Shoes, a line of comfort shoes from Israel; folk art from Mexico, including tin frames and clay sculptures; and other items from Indonesia and India. Also included in the village is **Baltimore Clayworks,** 5707 Smith Avenue, (410) 578-1919, a nonprofit that promotes ceramics. Baltimore Clayworks is set in an old library building and offers classes as well as items for sale.

When you head out of this Mount Washington shopping district back over Kelly Avenue Bridge to Falls Road, a left turn will take you to the old mills that have been turned into shops and offices. Shops in the mill include a **Starbucks** coffee shop, **Framin' Place, Smith & Hawkins** for your gardening needs, **Fresh Fields** natural foods grocery store, and **Amazing Glaze** for you to practice your pottery skills. If all that shopping and pottery leaves your manicure in need of attention, visit **Giovanna Hair Skin Nail Salon,** 6071 Falls Road, (401) 367-3434. If you're not driving, however, and would like to meander through the Mount Washington shops, you can easily get there by Light Rail, which has a stop right on the edge of the shopping district.

Southeast

Canton Shopping District
Eastern Avenue to Conkling Street to the Waterfront to Chester Street

Canton is the waterfront area south and west of Highlandtown and east of Fells Point. Turn-of-the-twentieth-century, two- and three-story row houses as well as new town houses and condominiums line the streets of Canton. This area is thriving amid the renovation fever that hit the city during the 1990s. Canton is filled with both innovative new housing and upper-income professionals as well as traditional row homes with blue-collar workers whose families have lived here for generations.

The shopping options in Canton seem to only get better with time. What started out as a renovation around O'Donnell Square has spread to redeveloped indus-

Chesapeake Wine Company in Canton's Can Company offers more than just carry-out wine, beer, and liquor; they also have a small tasting bar in the back with a selection of wines and cocktails. Try one of their signature margaritas.

trial buildings along the waterfront filled with specialty shops and restaurants.

Three hair salons with trendy and upscale service include **AKA Studios,** 2823 O'Donnell Street, (410) 276-6898, **Geometrics Hair Studio,** 2904 O'Donnell Street, (410) 563-3180, and **Sima's,** 2927 O'Donnell Street, (410) 276-7462. O'Donnell Square, the 2800 and 2900 blocks of O'Donnell Street, offer not only hair salons but also fun eats that should not be missed. Just to name a few, there's **Claddagh's Pub,** 2918 O'Donnell Street, (410) 522-4220, with a great mix of Irish food, Baltimore seafood, and steaks. **Helen's Garden Restaurant,** 2908 O'Donnell Street, (410) 276-2233, and **Nacho Mama's,** 2907 O'Donnell Street, (410) 675-0898, which is a local favorite for Mexican food and margaritas. Check out the Restaurant chapter for more information.

The Can Company, (410) 558-CANC, a renovated industrial building at 2400 O'Donnell Street, offers the shopper an interesting mix of stores, studios, and restaurants. **Chesapeake Wine Company,** (410) 522-4556, offers the latest in wine and liquor, including one of the best selections of local wine, while **Touch the Earth,** (410) 522-1500, has essential oils and candles.

Highlandtown Shopping District
East Avenue on the west to Haven Street on the east, along Eastern Avenue and Conklin Street

Highlandtown is not upscale. It hasn't been renovated, rehabbed, or reformed for multiuse; however, the community has received a multimillion-dollar grant to spruce it up a bit. For now Highlandtown is still Highlandtown, which is to say it's the large, central shopping district in the middle of this row house, working-class neighborhood. It has all the shops and services you need and would like to be able to walk to.

What makes Highlandtown a well-used shopping area by the rest of the city is its penchant for formal-wear shops. In the 3000 block of Eastern Avenue, you'll find **Stella's Gifts & Bridals,** 3309 Eastern Avenue, (410) 522-7447, which takes up at least half the block and is jampacked with dresses, veils, tuxedos, and books that will help you plan your attire for formal occasions. This is the place you go when you want your shoes dyed to match your gown. The Highlandtown Shopping District also has traditional neighborhood stores like the **Walgreen Drug Store** (4020 Eastern Avenue, 410-534-8661). But Highlandtown also offers the unusual, like **D. J. Liquidation** (3825 Bank Street, 410-732-2245), which is a large discount variety store with weekly specials and a large selection of seasonal and holiday items. At 512 South Conklin Street, there's the **Restaurant Supply Store,** (410) 534-4500, with just about any item you can imagine for the restaurant or home kitchen. At the corner of Highland and Eastern Avenues is **Tuxedo Zone,** (410) 534-1000, which rents and sells anything men would need for a formal event.

Parking for the most part is on the street at meters, but since most of Highlandtown's patrons walk from home, it's usually pretty easy to find a spot. On the other hand, since Eastern Avenue is a main thoroughfare out of the city, it is often clogged with traffic.

UNDER-ROOF MARKETS

Baltimore's markets are our pride and joy. In continuous operation since the late 1700s, they provide a place to buy fresh foods, from garden lettuce to live crabs just off the boat, as well as serve as a central location for many neighborhood residents to meet and greet. The shopping is easy. The people are friendly. The prices are excellent. But what may be the most pleasant aspect of this kind of shopping is being able to control what you get and how much you take home with you.

It's a powerful feeling when the butcher asks you how you would like your fresh piece of meat cut, instead of just offering prepackaged, preweighed, dyed meats. It's wonderful to be able to have one and a half pounds of fresh cottage cheese scooped up for you, count out an odd number of chicken legs, or pick out a succulent rockfish and tell the fishmonger how you would like it filleted.

If you've never shopped in a market . . . if your life has been filled with Piggly Wiggly, Safeway, and Giant . . . indulge yourself by visiting one of the markets that follow.

A contact number has been provided for Lexington Market, but if you need more information about the other markets, call Baltimore Public Markets at (410) 276-9498. The markets listed here, except for Lexington Market, are open 7:00 A.M. to 6:00 P.M. Monday through Thursday and 6:00 A.M. to 6:00 P.M. Friday and Saturday. The Avenue Market opens at 7:00 A.M. Monday through Saturday.

Downtown

Lexington Market
400 West Lexington Street
(410) 685-6169
www.lexingtonmarket.com
Lexington Market opened in 1782 at its present location. Then known as Howard's Hill, it was part of John Eager Howard's estate and donated by him for the purpose of creating a market. By the 1850s, when Baltimore was the second largest city in the United States, more than 50,000 people shopped here on market days.

Today, the market doesn't host quite so many shoppers day to day as it did in 1850, but for the more than 200 years of its existence, it has served Baltimoreans as a central location to find just about anything. Lexington Market takes up 2 square blocks and has more than 130 dealers of both fresh produce and prepared foods.

You can buy just-off-the-boat fish and crabs, farm vegetables such as tomatoes and corn, homemade bread, candy, or lunch. There are plenty of places to eat, but favorites include anywhere that offers the traditional Polish hot dog with sauerkraut and mustard.

The tale is told that in 1859, Oliver Wendell Holmes visited the market and afterward named Baltimore "The Gastronomic Capital of the Universe." Suffice it to say that if you know what you want to eat, you will find it at the market.

Lexington Market is open Monday through Saturday 8:30 A.M. to 6:00 P.M. Feel free to take public transportation—both Light Rail and buses have market stops—or drive. There are more than 4,000 parking spaces under roof. Parking is by the hour—$2.00 for the first hour and $1.00 for every additional hour.

Outside the market are licensed street vendors. They have clothing, jewelry, balloons, souvenirs, and other items of interest and are part of the old-world aura of shopping at Lexington Market.

Broadway Market
Broadway and Fleet Street

Broadway Market is not the oldest market in Baltimore, but it is in the oldest market building, dating back to 1785. In fact, there are two buildings to the market, both of which sit in the middle of Broadway in Fells Point, the northern building facing Fleet and the southern building facing Aliceanna Street.

The north building has nine vendors and the south building six, but Broadway Market still manages to have a little bit of everything. The north building hosts a produce vendor, a fresh-fish vendor, a butcher, and Joy's Quality Bakery, where among the heart-stopping selections is the most amazing raspberry crumb cake that you will ever have the opportunity to let melt in your mouth. The south building holds restaurants and delicatessens. You can get a terrific veggie rollup or a big, hulking burger—whatever tempts your taste buds.

Cross Street Market
Cross Street between Light and Charles
www.southbaltimore.com/shop/cross
.mkt.html

Cross Street Market is in the middle of the Federal Hill Shopping District, just south of the Inner Harbor. It's the neighborhood market for Federal Hill and surrounding South Baltimore as well as visitors to those areas. Cross Street Market's 28 vendors sell everything from Utz potato chips to imported wines and cheeses. You'll also find a candy store, a donut shop, a natural food store, and a tobacconist. Cross Street is a great place to go for barbecued chicken or to partake in the bounty of a raw oyster bar. Don't miss out on the fun at Nick's Inner Harbor Seafood. This local hot spot hosts one of the most unique happy hours in Federal Hill. Nick's offers a large selection of seafood, including steamed and raw clams and oysters, steamed shrimp, and crab soup as well as a large selection of beer and wine. Located at the west end of Cross Street Market, Nick's stays open until 8:00 P.M. Wednesday and Thursday and until 11:00 P.M. on Friday and Saturday, and is open from 11:00 A.M. to 7:00 P.M. on Sunday.

Northeast Market
2101 East Monument Street

Northeast Market is near Johns Hopkins Hospital. It houses 35 vendors that offer fresh foods such as fresh chicken and meats, baked goods, and the like, as well as places to sit and eat. From the extensive salad bar at Something Fresh to Japanese selections at Surf & Wok, you can find pretty much anything your tastes desire.

Northwest

Avenue Market
1701 Pennsylvania Avenue

The Avenue Market opened in 1999 as a showcase market for the African-American community. Conveniently located next to

> **When shopping in one of Baltimore's indoor markets, remember to bring cash. Many of the produce and seafood stands do not accept credit cards.**

the Upton subway station, the Avenue Market has 18 vendors offering meats, produce, seafood, and baked goods. The vendors range from a Blimpie franchise offering fresh subs and sandwiches to Community Produce, offering a large selection of delectable fruits and vegetables.

Southwest

Hollins Market
26 South Arlington Avenue
Hollins Market is near Union Square, where H. L. Mencken lived. He was a regular at the market, as are Union Square neighbors today. Hollins offers 18 vendors of meats, produce, poultry, seafood, and baked goods. There are also three lunch counters and Custom Salads, which is pretty much self-explanatory.

FARMERS' MARKETS

In addition to our under-roof markets, the Baltimore area also has some farmers' markets that open at the same place and time every week.

Downtown

Downtown Farmers' Market
Jones Falls Expressway, at Holiday and Saratoga Streets
On Sunday mornings from June until mid-December, the Downtown Farmers' Market opens at 8:00 A.M. under the cover of the Jones Falls Expressway at Holiday and Saratoga Streets, just about at the expressway's end. It is a massive affair,

attended by thousands every week. Parking is easy, since there's metered parking under the expressway. You can also park on the street.

Northeast

Waverly Farmers' Market
32nd Street Market
32nd and Barclay Streets
Every Saturday morning, June through November, the metered parking lot at 32nd and Barclay Streets becomes the site of the 32nd Street Market. Hours are 7:00 A.M. to noon or until the goods are gone. About 30 vendors offer tailgate sales of fresh farm produce, homemade baked goods, and other goodies. The French bakery is a frequent stop—its chocolate croissants are the perfect treat to nibble on as you stroll among the booths. Or perhaps you'd prefer a grilled mushroom sandwich, made with fresh mushrooms of your choice. About $10 will buy you a shopping bag full of good food, but keep a few dollars for the street performers. You'll often hear blues riffs on a guitar or the haunting sound of Irish pipes.

Parking is on the street, but it's often crowded. Be prepared to go around the block a few times.

Towson Farmers' Market
Allegheny Avenue, between York Road and Washington Avenue, Towson
(410) 825-1144
Every Thursday from the last Thursday in June through the month of October, Towson blocks off Allegheny Avenue between York Road and Washington Avenue for a farmers' market. Between 11:00 A.M. and 3:00 P.M. you'll find vendors selling luncheon foods as well as more than 30 booths filled with fresh farm produce.

Park at Towson Commons and walk up a block to the market. (See the Old Towson Shopping District previously in this chapter.)

MUSIC

In almost every mall, you'll find places that sell new music. But there are stores around town that offer some special buying opportunities, such as old 45s for sale and places where you can trade as well as buy. Musicians will be interested in the shops we've listed below that offer instruments and sheet music as well as the knowledgeable advice that needs to accompany that kind of stock.

Downtown

An die Musik
409 North Charles Street
(410) 385-2638
www.andiemusik.com

Located in the Mount Vernon Shopping District, this store derived its name from a Franz Schubert composition from the early seventeenth century. It figures, then, that An die Musik specializes in classical, opera, jazz, and world music. Every member of the staff is an expert, and they welcome customer queries about obscure recordings.

Flashback
728 South Broadway
(410) 276-5086

Flashback buys, sells, and sometimes trades LPs. You will not find old 45s, and don't bother trucking in your ancient 78s. But if you've got long-playing vinyl—rock, blues, jazz, soul, or reggae—or if you're in the market for the same, then Flashback is your kind of place. Albums start at about $3.00, and the average price is between $3.00 and $10.00. The shop also sells some collectibles, videos, books, posters, and show souvenirs, such as programs. Parking is on the street.

Kentrikon Music Store
4704 Eastern Avenue
(410) 675-4100

Kentrikon means "center" in Greek, and Kentrikon Music Store has certainly been at the center of the Greek community since 1954, handling only Greek music, videos, books, and gifts. The music selections cover modern Greek selections and the pop music for the last 40 years, as well as folk. You can sample some of the music without even going down to the shop by tuning into Kentrikon's Greek radio program on WBMD (750 AM) at 3:30 P.M. Saturday and 4:30 P.M. Sunday. Parking is on the street.

Reptilian Records and Comics
403 South Broadway
(410) 327-6853
www.reptilianrecords.com

Reptilian was opened in 1989 to fill a void in the city's music offerings—there wasn't any one place to find a broad range of the thrashing sounds that hard rockers crave. Reptilian has since earned a reputation for its broad selection of punk, hardcore, noise, emo, grind, garage, and indie rock. You won't find mainstream label stuff here.

Sound Garden
1616 Thames Street
(410) 563-9011
www.cdjoint.com

Located in the heart of Fells Point, Sound Garden is the best independently owned record store in the city. Sound Garden carries an exhaustive selection of all styles of music, including new and used CDs, cassettes, vinyl, videos, imports, books, magazines, stickers, shirts, and more. There are over 250,000 CDs, 10,000 imports, and 10 listening areas, where you can hear before your purchase.

Ted's Musician Shop
11 East Centre Street
(410) 685-4198

Appropriately across the street from the Peabody Conservatory of Music, Ted's has been the place to go to either rent or buy (or rent-to-buy) new and used instruments for more than 35 years. Ted's has every kind of instrument under the sun, and most of them hang from the rafters. From ancient African drums to electronic keyboards, Ted's pretty much has it all. The shop is closed on Sunday.

Northeast

Music & Arts Center
1940 York Road, Timonium
(410) 453-0811
www.musicarts.com

Just south of Timonium Road is Music & Arts Center, which has or can order almost any piece of sheet music you want. The entire stock is on computer, so the salesperson can tell you whether what you want is on the shelf or not in a matter of moments. The fairly large collection includes classical, jazz, and rock. The store has a large selection of acoustic and electric guitars as well as horns. Instruction is also available.

Record & Tape Traders
734-736 Dulaney Valley Court, Towson, (410) 825-9450

7551 Ritchie Highway, Glen Burnie, (410) 760-4242

3003 North Charles Street (Midtown), (410) 662-96

10435 Reisterstown Road, Reisterstown (Northwest), (410) 654-0711

1547 Merritt Boulevard, Dundalk (Southeast), (410) 282-4362

806 Frederick Road, Catonsville (Southwest), (410) 788-6767

Record & Tape Traders is a large, well-known shop with 10 locations around Baltimore. We've listed a few of the closer locations. The Towson shop is the biggest location with the largest selection, but no matter which Record & Tape Traders you're near, know that its mandate is to buy and sell CDs, tapes, DVDs, and LPs. CDs and tapes come in both new and used varieties. LPs are both new and used and offer selections from all genres. The store prides itself on having the hard-to-find items, including out-of-print CDs and

a fair number of imports. Rock music is the biggest focus, but the store also carries jazz, country, Big Band, and music cut by local Baltimore artists, as well as ancillary rock items such as magazines, jewelry, posters, and T-shirts. Some records are priced as low as 50 cents; rarer albums can go as high as $30. New CDs are priced $10 and up, with used CDs priced $5.99 and up.

Northwest

Jazz House West
6035 Liberty Road, Woodlawn
(410) 265-6060

Since 1976 Jazz House West has been finding those hard-to-find jazz albums that you're just dying to add to your collection. Names such as Billy Harper, Booker Ervin, and Doug Cam are available at Jazz House, which buys, sells, and trades CDs and vinyl. It has a huge selection of vinyl and one of the best special order sections in the area. Albums sell from 50 cents, with an average price being around $5.00; CDs range from $7.00 to $14.00. In addition to jazz, the shop also sells rhythm-and-blues selections and African-American collectibles. Jazz House is open Thursday and Friday 11:00 A.M. to 7:00 P.M. and Saturday 11:00 A.M. to 5:00 P.M.

Recordmasters
The Rotunda, 711 West 40th Street
(410) 366-1250

When this Baltimorean-owned company began in 1973, it was chock-full of records, both 45s and LPs. As it grew, it became known for having a truly eclectic selection. People came from all over to see if they could find this record or that record among the store's stock. If no one else in town had it, Recordmasters did. When videos became all the rage, it began renting videos, and its video section still carries some of the most esoteric, who-knew-that-was-on-tape kinds of movies as well as the latest hits. Record-masters was also among the first stores in the area to carry CDs, then DVDs, and now those selections have completely elbowed out vinyl. Alas, Recordmasters has no records, but it is still the place to buy, sell, or trade musical selections of CDs and tapes. There is also a satellite store at the Shops at Kenilworth in Towson.

Shubert Music
518 Reisterstown Road, Pikesville
(410) 653-3196
In 1954 Herbert Froehlich started Shubert Music by offering piano tuning and repair. He still does that. His son, Myron, runs the shop, which carries all kinds of band instruments, guitars, and accessories that can be bought or rented. Shubert also offers lessons. The store's mainstay is sheet music—racks and racks of popular, classical, and jazz selections as well as instructional books. If you're looking for it, Shubert Music probably has it; if not, Myron will be happy to special-order it and mail it out to you. The store is closed Saturday and Sunday. It is in a little strip shopping center that offers free lot parking, both in front of and behind the store.

Southeast

Alan's Roadhouse Oldies
5200 Ritchie Highway (State Highway 2), Brooklyn
(410) 789-3142
www.roadhouseoldies.com
Baltimore loves rock 'n' roll. And Alan Lee, the radio personality who announces the longest-running oldies radio program in Baltimore on WQSR (105.7 FM), may be said to love it more than most. When he's not playing it, he's selling it here at Alan's Roadhouse Oldies. Alan carries music from the '50s, '60s, and '70s on 45s, LPs, cassettes, and CDs. Although he sells both new and used vinyl, a lot of old hits are available newly pressed, which means that Blue Suede Shoes is going to sound just

as it did when Elvis cut it. The standard cost of a 45 is $2.98, but rare collector's items may run into the hundreds of dollars. The shop issues a catalog of all the best-selling 45s and CDs Alan handles. If you decide to stop by, call first, as days and hours open vary depending on Alan's schedule.

Southwest

Appalachian Bluegrass Shoppe
643 Frederick Road, Catonsville
(410) 744-1144
www.appalachianbluegrass.com
Appalachian Bluegrass specializes in acoustic instruments and is a great place to buy stringed instruments and have them repaired. The store also has sheet music and instructional tapes and booklets as well as Irish flutes and hand drums. It's closed Sunday.

Bill's Music House, Inc.
743 Frederick Road, Catonsville
(410) 747-1900
www.billsmusic.com
Bill's specializes in school band instruments that you can rent, lease, or buy, but you can also find drums, guitars, and pianos. It's a large shop jammed with stuff that's new and used. You can also trade in used instruments or get them repaired. Lessons are also offered.

BOOKSTORES

All the bookstores mentioned here mostly sell new books. For antiquarian bookstores, see the Antiques and Collectibles chapter. And don't forget every mall has at least one bookstore to browse through.

Atomic Books
1100 West 36th Street (Northwest)
(410) 662-4444
www.atomicbooks.com
The tag line for this small, independently

owned store is, "literary finds for mutated minds." Located on "The Avenue" in Hampden, Atomic has survived the influx of chain megabookstores by serving up a unique selection of literary works. Owners Benn and Rachel supply the city's literati with shelves of hard-to-find indie and micropress books and obscure magazines, as well as a solid selection from mainstream writers. Atomic also carries a small selection of CDs, many produced by local musicians who frequently pop by the store to visit.

Barnes & Noble Booksellers
4300 Montgomery Road,

Ellicott City (Southwest)
(410) 203-9001

8123 Honeygo Boulevard, White Marsh (Northeast) (410) 933-9670

1 East Joppa Road, Towson (Northeast) (410) 296-7021

601 East Pratt Street (Downtown) (410) 385-1709
www.barnesandnoble.com
Barnes & Noble stores stock an impressive selection of book titles and provides access to more than one million titles. If a book is not in stock at one of the local stores, the staff can usually get it in a matter of days. Barnes & Noble offers books from more than 50,000 publisher imprints with an emphasis on small, independent publishers and university presses. Barnes & Noble also offers a wonderful children's section with the latest puzzles, games, and educational resources, as well as the classic reading favorites. The newsstand includes more than 250 magazines and newspapers from around the world.

Borders Books & Music
415 York Road, Towson (Northeast) (410) 296-0791

6151 Columbia Crossing Circle, Columbia (Southwest) (410) 290-0062
www.borders.com
Borders features a vast inventory of books, music, and videos. The selection is

second to none, and the friendly atmosphere makes shopping for books even more enjoyable. The store regularly hosts in-store appearances by authors, musicians, and artists. Borders' knowledgeable staff can help you find whatever title you might be looking for. There is also a casual espresso cafe to make the shopping experience even more pleasurable.

Gordon's Booksellers
The Rotunda, 711 West 40th Street (Northwest) (410) 889-2100

The Shops at Kenilworth,
800 Kenilworth Drive,
Towson (Northeast) (410) 296-3500

2139 Timonium Shopping Center,
York Road (Northeast) (410) 308-1900
Gordon's is a locally owned bookstore that thrives on being able to provide the basics. This is no-frills shopping, but you'll always be able to pick up the newest best-seller at the Rotunda location, which also has a good-size children's department, featuring everything from a simple counting book to the next in the series of Nancy Drew or Babysitters Club books your preteen is searching for. The other two locations are where Gordon's sells overstocked and out-of-print books at the discounted price of 70 percent off.

Greetings & Readings
Loch Raven Plaza, 809 Taylor Avenue,
Towson (Northeast)
(410) 825-4225
Greetings & Readings started out as a small bookstore and card shop in 1969. Since then it has added on and grown to take up a whole corner of the Loch Raven Plaza shopping center. It is a great place to find just about anything bookish as well as greeting cards, gifts, games, wrapping paper, and party supplies. If all these choices overwhelm you, sit down at the Espresso Cafe, which has great coffee, tea, and gourmet food and snacks, while you ponder your purchase.

Greetings & Readings is an essential location for many students—the Cliff's

Notes section is very extensive—and G&R always seems to have what you want, whether it's a Lenox dish to give as a wedding gift, a hand-drawn certificate in calligraphy, or just a good book to curl up with on a rainy day.

THRIFT STORES

One man's trash is another man's treasure it is said, and nowhere is this truth more evident than when you're scavenging for bargains at a thrift shop. Some people in Baltimore never shop anywhere but thrift stores. Their whole wardrobes are built from jackets they bought for $1.00 and jeans they bought for $2.50. Their homes are furnished with excellent finds that jumped out at them from piles of stuff in thrift stores.

Subsequently, we've listed the major thrift stores in the general area and noted their other locations around town. We have provided only a few specifics on each one because essentially a thrift store is a thrift store. At almost every one, you'll find clothing, furniture, bric-a-brac, and items such as cameras, stereos, tennis rackets, and bowling balls. What's in them depends on what treasures someone has donated that month. That is, of course, part of the fun. You can shop there today and go again tomorrow and find all kinds of new stuff.

Goodwill Industries
200 South Broadway (Downtown)
(410) 327-2211

3101 Greenmount Avenue (Northeast)
(410) 467-7505

5644 The Alameda (Northeast)
(410) 323-6638

3421 Belair Road (Northeast)
(410) 485-2211

60 North Dundalk Avenue, Dundalk
(Southeast) (410) 285-0506

11411 Reisterstown Road, Owings Mills
(Northwest) (410) 581-8960

4001 Southwestern Boulevard, Arbutus
(Southwest) (410) 247-3510
Since 1919, Goodwill Industries has collected used goods and sold them to help put members of the community back to work. In addition to employing the poor and the disabled at its stores, Goodwill funds training programs as well. Items at the stores run the gamut from the totally practical to the gee-I-wish-I-had-this—anything from an English saddle to a humidifier, from skis, bikes, and in-line skates to infant car seats, crutches, and bed frames.

The Goodwill in Owings Mills on Reisterstown Road offers an expanded inventory. The Belair Road location specializes in toys and sports.

Salvation Army
905 West 36th Street (Northwest)
(410) 243-5916

West Patapsco and Gable Avenues
(Southeast) (410) 685-8878

7856 Eastern Avenue (Southeast)
(410) 282-3997

8715 Liberty Road (Northwest)
(410) 655-93

8005 Jumpers Hole Road (Southwest)
(410) 766-4841
The Salvation Army uses its income to help Baltimore's indigents. In addition to missions, for instance, the Salvation Army funds a drug rehabilitation center. Donations can be pretty much anything, including cars, trucks, boats, and trailers. But mostly what you'll find in SA's thrift stores are secondhand clothes, toys, furniture, and knickknacks.

St. Vincent de Paul
6 North Central Avenue (Downtown)
(410) 276-7600
St. Vincent de Paul Society has only this one location in Baltimore, but it's a busy place. Six days a week the store is open to not only help you find a great bargain to purchase but also to hand out free clothes, furniture, and housewares to peo-

ple who have been victims of fire, eviction, or some other housing calamity. The Society also helps the poor with their gas and electric payments and uses the money you spend in its store to fund Camp St. Vincent during the summer months.

Value Village
3424 Eastern Avenue (Southeast)
(410) 327-5300

5013 York Road (Northeast)
(410) 433-9090

Value Village is a large thrift store chain that offers household items, toys, and such, but its main focus is clothing. Tons of it. Piles of it. Racks of it. The Eastern Avenue store, in fact, has three full floors of it! If you're looking for a new pair of jeans or a barely used pair of shoes for your two-year-old who's growing fast, this is the place to look.

The Wise Penny
5902 York Road (Northeast)
(410) 435-3244

Right next door to The Senator theater, you'll find The Wise Penny, a thrift shop owned and operated by the Junior League of Baltimore since 1970. All proceeds from the store go to support League projects in Baltimore, including such diverse projects as the Hampden Family Center and Done in a Day, which lends labor to other nonprofits when a project must be done and the organization doesn't have enough personnel to handle it. Since the shop began, it has been responsible for raising more than $1 million for the Junior League's projects. The Wise Penny operates strictly on the charity of others, including the 250 members of the League who both pledge donations and their time as salespeople.

At The Wise Penny, you'll find clothing, housewares, jewelry, books, records, and small furniture items such as tables and chairs. The shop's best thing is its sales. There's one almost every month that features special items, such as the Treasure and Trinkets sale in February. There's a Baby Sale in September and a Toy Sale in December, but the most exciting events are the biannual clearance sales that begin the first week of February and June and last until the last week of those months, at which time you can fill a bag with anything in the shop for $5.00.

ANTIQUES AND COLLECTIBLES

There are more than 700 shops across the state of Maryland dedicated to antiques and collectibles, and many of them are in the Baltimore area. Fells Point alone has more than 40 shops. Main Street in Ellicott City, only 10 miles due west of Baltimore's center, is saturated with shops selling antiques, collectibles, and crafts. Cockeysville, north of Towson, is about 20 minutes away and has a considerable number of great finds along the York Road corridor. And Reisterstown, to the city's west, has been an antiques lover's paradise for more than 30 years.

In all these locations there are junk shops, secondhand shops, consignment shops, and furniture shops. Some specialize in vintage clothing; others, vintage jukeboxes. Some shops deal strictly in collectible items, such as Looney Tunes or Coca-Cola memorabilia; others handle primarily arts and crafts collectibles.

Some shops lay out their interiors as if they were a department store window; in others the inventory is stacked pretty high but is easy to maneuver and sift through. Still others require you to search out your treasure by climbing over or digging under piles of merchandise to find what you want. Shops where everything is very neat tend to be more expensive. The busy-but-findable way of setting things out usually offers some bargains without too much effort; and the everything-thrown-in-a-pile kinds of shops can offer great bargains if you can find something you want.

Most shops are wheelchair accessible on their first floors but have no ability to transport wheelchairs between floors, since almost all of the shops, except those in the malls, are in old houses. So if you are

an antiquer on wheels, malls are your best bet. Malls also offer such amenities as public bathrooms and coffee bars or restaurants, perks the smaller shops do not. You'll most likely find them nearby but not within the shop itself.

What follows are some of the city and suburban hot spots and the major nearby malls, as well as some specialty shops that you might want to visit while you're in the neighborhood. They are listed first by area (Downtown, Northeast, Northwest, Southeast, Southwest) and then by the neighborhood or town. As with all other chapters in this book, unless designated otherwise assume these shops are in Baltimore. We do not list every shop in these areas but instead provide a kind of walking tour in which some of the shops are highlighted. Each tour begins at the suggested parking area and continues until you come back around to your car. The tour will give you a feel for the types of shops in the area and a general lay of the land.

In some cases you will find only one or two shops listed under an area title. These areas do not constitute meccas, but we didn't want you to miss these special shops. And see our Day Trips chapter for other antiquing destinations.

We've done our best to note when the shops are open. Unless we stipulate otherwise, assume a store is open seven days a week. If your heart is set on visiting a particular store, we suggest you call ahead to make sure it will be open.

If you're an antiquer, a junker, a collector, a lover of old classics or new masterpieces, then Baltimore is the place to be, and this chapter is the one you're looking for. Good hunting!

DOWNTOWN
Antique Row

Antique Row is in the 800 block of North Howard Street, south of Read Street and a few blocks west of the Maryland Historical Society. The Row has been a factor in antiques collecting for more than 100 years and is still the place to find a wide range of specialty stores offering a variety of items like sterling silver and French furniture. Because these dealers are so well known in the trade, many of them make their livings selling to other dealers and decorators, but shops are still open to the individual buyer. There are more than 20 dealers on The Row, as well as shops that specialize in ancillary services, such as restoration.

The easiest way to get to Antique Row is by Light Rail, which goes right down the middle of Howard Street. The Row is also just a short cab ride from Inner Harbor hotels. If you drive yourself, we suggest that you park on Park Avenue or Cathedral Street around Read Street or Monument Street and walk the few blocks west. There are plenty of off-Row shops on these streets that are also worth a look.

Beginning our tour at the corner of Read and Howard Streets, the first shop you'll come to is Regency Antiques.

Regency Antiques
893–895 North Howard Street
(410) 225-3455
www.regencyantiques.com
Owner Mark Klatsky stocks his store with reproductions of European handmade furniture from the seventeenth and eighteenth centuries, primarily English, Italian, and French. He also specializes in crystal chan-

---

If you are planning an antiquing trip, remember that each fall the Maryland Antiques Show and the Hunt Valley Antiques Show bring national and international dealers to Baltimore (see Annual Events for more details).

---

deliers and paintings. His store now boasts more than 200 original, signed works of art in gold leaf frames. The store is open Monday through Saturday, 10:00 A.M. to 5:00 P.M. and Sunday noon to 4:00 P.M.

L.A. Herstein and Company
877 North Howard Street
(410) 728-3856
Herstein's sells Tiffany lamps, has lamp parts, and does lamp repairs. It's one of those one-of-a-kind shops: The paint may be peeling on the sign, but it's the place to go if your Tiffany has begun to dim. The shop is open Monday, Friday, and Saturday from 10:00 A.M. to 3:45 P.M.

Cuomo's Antiques & Interiors
871 North Howard Street,
(410) 383-9195

10759 York Road, Cockeysville
(410) 628-0422
Cuomo's is known for its European furniture and fine china. It has a warehouse of sorts right on The Row at 881 North Howard Street.

Connoisseur's Connection
869 North Howard Street,
(410) 383-2624
Connoisseur's considers its antiques specialty to be continental decorative arts of the Empire period. Connoisseur's has supplied period furniture and objets d'art as set pieces for movies made in Baltimore and elsewhere. One of its more down-to-earth attributes is the layaway plan. If you see something you like, just put a down payment on it, and your treasure will be sent to the layaway room to wait in peace and contentment until you can finish paying for it. Open 11:00 A.M. to 5:00 P.M. daily.

Hamilton House Antiques
865 North Howard Street
(410) 462-5218
When asked what Hamilton House's specialty was, Pat Hamilton said, "You name it, we've bought it!" Although the collection is relatively eclectic, we liked some of

the smaller items, such as the Kirk silver salt cellars.

Thayne's Antiques
823 North Howard Street
(410) 728-7109

Thaynes is the place to go when you need to accessorize. Candlesticks, clocks, crystal, porcelains . . . if it sits on a table or hangs on a wall, Thaynes probably has it. Open daily, but call first to be sure.

Drusilla's Books
817 North Howard Street
(410) 728-7109

Drusilla has been selling books on The Row since 1981. Her most recent incarnation is in a beautifully renovated, bright, and clean space where she sells a wide range of antique books. Her specialty is children's literature, but she does have a great spectrum of rare and unusual items such as pop-up and series books. If you cannot visit the store, Drusilla's sells online through an e-mail address: drusilla@mind-spring.com. The store is open Tuesday through Saturday and by appointment.

Fells Point

Fells Point is a wonderful enclave of more than 40 antiques and specialty shops, five minutes from the Inner Harbor. There are also book shops, junk shops, and clothing shops that offer everything from handmade and imported clothing to vintage items. The ambience can't be duplicated. Brick sidewalks, cobblestone streets, and railroad and trolley tracks that lead from nowhere to no place combine with breezes off the water and the sound of sea gulls, making for a pleasant journey.

To get to Fells Point from Downtown, take Pratt Street to President Street and turn right. Just follow the traffic until you get to Broadway, the heart of Fells Point. Park anywhere you can and walk.

Most of the shops are south of Eastern Avenue and within 3 blocks on either side

of Broadway. Although they are scattered throughout the area, they seem to come in clumps—five here, eight there. (For more information about Fells Point, see the Relocation chapter.)

For our tour of Fells Point, park on the east side of Broadway on Fleet Street.

The Antique Man
1806 Fleet Street
(410) 732-0932

With 4,000 square feet jammed with a veritable treasure trove of rare items, this store is a combination antiques store and oddity museum. In one corner you may find good-quality antique furniture and Tiffany lamps, while across the room a two-headed giant mummy holds court with a full-size wooden horse. The Antique Man is open only on weekends and the hours vary, so we suggest you call ahead.

If you are planning an antiquing pilgrimage across the state, purchase a good state map and street maps as you go. ℹ️

The Bowery of Antiques & Collectibles
1736 Fleet Street
(410) 732-2778

The Bowery is the place to go if you are looking for variety. Owner David Donovan says his store "runs the gamut" with everything from Arts and Crafts furniture to children's toys and trains to Victorian lamps. The Bowery is open seven days a week.

Mystery Loves Company
1730 Fleet Street
(410) 276-6708 or (800) 538-0042

This bookstore carries only mysteries. For collectors the shop offers signed first editions of both new and older books as well as other out-of-print editions. It's a small shop with books lining the walls and piled on the floor. It's the kind of place where you will be welcomed with open arms, a friendly smile, and maybe even a cup of tea. It also has specialty gift items that relate to mysteries and will ship them any-where. The shop is closed on Monday.

Another Period in Time
1708-1710 Fleet Street
(410) 675-4776
www.anotherperiod.com
Another Period in Time has 15 dealers and boasts, "We buy, sell, and ship." Tiffany lamps, silver chalices, a whole set of ruby dinnerware, and lots of unusual bottles met us as we wandered the shop. It also has furniture, old Victrolas, and advertis-ing memorabilia. Another Period in Time is one of the largest shops of its type in Fells Point and the only one we've come across that has a discount area (on the second floor).

J&M Antiques
1706 Fleet Street
(410) 732-5339
J&M is a very small shop that specializes in jewelry—buying it, selling it, trading it, and repairing it. The store also offers rare pieces of Judaica. It is closed on Saturday.

Fells Point Antique Market
617 South Broadway
(410) 675-1726
Fells Point Antique Market is a medium-size co-op with only eight dealers but a lot of unusual and hard-to-find items. One dealer has a lot of ancient African items, such as hide drums and ceremonial masks; just down the aisle is a large sec-tion that contains mostly mannequins. The most overriding theme, however, was late 1950s/early 1960s furniture. Molded chairs as well as leatherette and wood armless waiting room furniture are in stock along with lamps and ashtrays—the kind that take up half the coffee table and come in the colors of the time, such as soft yellow and turquoise. You may also find stained glass, clothing, and jewelry. The Market is closed on Wednesday.

Federal Hill

Federal Hill is a bustling city neighbor-hood just minutes from the Inner Harbor. On a warm day it is an easy walk from the shops and attractions of the waterfront to the cobblestone streets of Federal Hill. Walk south on Light Street, turn right onto Montgomery Street, and then right onto Charles Street, which serves as the hub of the area. Charles Street is filled with tiny shops, furniture stores, art gal-leries, and restaurants. Although Federal Hill does not have a concentration of antiques stores, there are several in the neighborhood worth mentioning.

Antique Warehouse at 1300
1300 Jackson Street at Key Highway
(410) 659-0663
A few years ago, 35 antiques dealers took over a 14,000-square-foot warehouse space on Key Highway, just east of the Inner Harbor. And are we glad they did—the dealers offer a one-stop shop, with a full spectrum of antiques, including furni-ture, glass, silver, and ceramics. There is no parking lot available, so find what you can on the street. The Warehouse is closed on Monday.

Gaines McHale
836 Leadenhall Street
(410) 625-1900
www.gainesmchale.com
The gem of the downtown antiques com-munity, Gaines McHale is nationally renowned for its collection of fine French antiques. The warehouse-sized showroom is located behind the Federal Hill neigh-borhood and houses some of the best antiques in town.

NORTHEAST
Cockeysville, Maryland

Cockeysville, named for the Cockey family, is the area north of Towson and Timonium but south of Hunt Valley. The easiest way to get to Cockeysville from Baltimore City is to take I–83 north toward Timonium and York, Pennsylvania. Get off at Warren Road, then turn left at York Road. The main shopping area is on your left. Look for the small sign on the side of the building that says PARKING with an arrow pointing down. After you've parked you can either walk back up the hill to the street or just duck into the bottom floor of The Alley Shops.

The Alley Shops
10856-62 York Road
(410) 683-0421

The Alley Shops is a two-story shop with 14 dealers who show a broad base of merchandise, but there always seems to be a fair number of toys and dolls. One of the dealers on the ground floor specializes in antique camera equipment, including processors and enlargers. Items are stacked thickly in the booths, and aisles are narrow. It's closed on Monday and Tuesday.

Bill and Helen Bentley's Antiques Show Mart
10854 York Road
(410) 667-9184

Bentley's may have been the first antiques shop in Cockeysville, but we won't swear to it. There are three floors and 18 dealers with antiques and collectibles. You'll need to know what you're looking at and how much you're willing to pay to really get your money and time's worth out of this shop. Bentley's is closed on Monday and Tuesday.

Hunt Valley Antiques
10844 York Road
(410) 628-6869

This medium-size shop has two major specialties. The first is high-end fine china. There are stacks and stacks of it, both whole sets and odd pieces. If you're looking for a mate to a beautiful bone china cup and saucer your great-grandmother left you, this is where you should begin the search. The second specialty is Pot-

thast furniture. Potthast is a Baltimore furniture maker who from 1892 to the 1950s created handmade reproductions of classic pieces. The owner, Lenis Barney, authenticates all pieces, so you know you're getting the real thing. The shop is closed on Monday.

The Pack Rat
10834 York Road
(410) 683-4812

The Pack Rat is not the junk shop its name implies; in fact, it's just the opposite. The Pack Rat's owners carry, almost exclusively, what they call "traditional furniture," which is formal dining room and bedroom groups. You will find some Potthast pieces. When we were there they were showing a mint-condition formal dining table and chairs by Potthast, circa 1895. Co-owners Ric Davis and Posie Huppman do all of their own refinishing, so just about everything in the shop looks showroom new. The shop specialty is wall mirrors and fireplace equipment—screens, fenders, and tools. The Pack Rat is closed Monday and Tuesday.

Jumpin' Jim's Jukeboxes
10840 York Road
(410) 666-5575

Take a step back in time at this shop, which carries only jukeboxes and records. This Insider's favorite jukes are the Wurlitzers with the bubble lights, but you can find everything here from antiques to brand-new contemporary. Prices range from $700 to around $6,000 for the box that has everything. Owner Joe Bloodgood, who's been in this business for more than 30 years, also rents the jukes for $250 a day. He'll program it with your favorite music, from 1940s jazz and Big Band to present-day rock. And if you don't see what you want, he'll find it for you. He once found a Filben Maestro for a customer, and there were only 1,000 of them ever made. The small shop is set back a little, so look for it where the sidewalk widens and the rock 'n' roll drifts amiably through the afternoon air. The tunes keep spinnin' Wednesday, Friday, Saturday, and Sunday.

Brindley & Company Antiques
10828 York Road
(410) 666-7790

Abundant Treasures Antiques
10818 York Road
(410) 666-9797
Ruth Ann Brindley owns two shops in Cockeysville, both of which are exceptional multidealer enclaves. Abundant Treasures has abundant book dealers but overall specializes in Early American and turn-of-the-century pieces. Brindley & Company, on the other hand, specializes in more modern collectible pieces, such as 1920s wicker and 1930s bamboo, but also country and Victorian antiques. The shops are closed on Monday and Tuesday.

 Many smaller antiques stores are run by the owners. If an out-of-town show requires their attendance, or a great estate sale offers good buying opportunities, the owners may close shop for the afternoon or a few days. We highly recommend that you call ahead before visiting to make sure the hours have not been altered.

Tyrie Antique Village
11008–11010 York Road
Tyrie Antique Village is three shops together, north of the main antiques shopping area in Cockeysville. You'll need to get back in your car and head up York Road past the railroad tracks. The buildings are on your left.

The Corner Cottage, (410) 527–9535, sells primarily early American, country antiques, and bric-a-brac in a low-ceiling, multiroom building with a history. Ask owner Betsy Coakley to tell you about the building. Many of the items in the store, which is closed on Mondays and Tuesdays, are on consignment.

The Decorative Touch, (410) 757–0048, is across the alleyway in a more modern building. The owners have two specialties, Biggs furniture and hand-painted items, although you will find a fair number of collectible items as well. Biggs is another Baltimore furniture maker, and it is noted for having created the reproductions for Colonial Williamsburg. The painted furniture, depicting scenes of Baltimore and the surrounding areas, is painted by the shop's owner. The Decorative Touch is closed on Monday and Tuesday.

Amy's Stuff, (410) 785–0965, is just one small room, but it is jammed with stuff, as is the small porch that separates it from The Corner Cottage. Outside, you'll find doors, windows, and other types of reclamation items that can weather storms. Inside are cupboards, stools, tables, and cabinets as well as some tools and bric-a-brac. Everything is unfinished, but if refinishing a piece doesn't bother you, then Amy's has some great stuff. The shop is open Thursday through Sunday.

NEARBY . . .

Valley View Farms
11035 York Road
(410) 527-0700
www.valleyviewfarms.com
North of Tyrie on the right-hand side of York Road is Valley View Farms. A well-frequented roadside produce stand back in the 1950s, Valley View has grown to a giant-size place that still boasts year-round produce, but also has tons and tons of flowers and plants, everything you could possibly need for gardening, and a really good deli. A major claim to fame, however, is its Christmas Shop. Starting in

late September, Valley View's main display room lights up with more than 125 decorated trees. In the International Room, a smaller display area that opens on Labor Day and stays open until January, you can find handblown glass ornaments, nutcrackers, and outstanding manger scenes from Germany, Israel, and other European and Middle Eastern countries.

Timonium, Maryland

If you decide to trek out to Cockeysville, you might want to make a quick stop in Timonium, to visit Clearing House Ltd.

Clearing House Ltd.
200 West Padonia Road
(410) 561-4546
Clearing House Ltd. is a consignment shop, pure and simple, but it has some of the best stuff around. Be warned: It is the devil to find. Take the Padonia Road exit off I-83 North. You'll see the sign on Padonia Road, about 1 block west of York Road. But once you've turned in to where it says it is, there are two things you need to know: It is in the shopping center, but its entrance is at the back of one of the buildings. Clearing House Ltd. is open Thursday through Sunday and by appointment.

Parkville, Maryland

Parkville, east of Towson, doesn't have the numerous shops of Antique Row or Fells Point, but it does have The Dusty Attic, a must-see for any Coca-Cola enthusiast.

The Dusty Attic
9411 Harford Road
(410) 668-2343
The Dusty Attic handles only Coca-Cola memorabilia. There are Coke trays, Coke ads, Coke bottles, Coke machines, Coke anything you can possibly think of. The Attic is closed on Mondays and Tuesdays.

To get to The Dusty Attic, take I-695 to Harford Road toward Carney. The shop is on your right within a block of the exit, before you get to Joppa Road.

NORTHWEST
Hampden

If you've already read the Shopping chapter, you're familiar with the 36th Street shopping district in Hampden. The shops that follow are north of 36th Street by just a few blocks, almost to 41st Street. If you're on an antiques-and-crafts hunt, you won't want to miss them.

The Turnover Shop
3855 Roland Avenue
(410) 235-9585
The Turnover Shop has been at this location since 1943. The oldest consignment shop in Maryland, its treasures come mainly from nearby neighborhoods—not only Hampden and Roland Park, but also Homeland, Guilford, Charles Village, Remington, Woodbury, and Waverly. You'll find exceptional furniture, glassware, sterling silver, jewelry, and china. A second shop is located at 3547 Chestnut Avenue, (410) 366-2988. Both locations have two floors of goodies. The shops are closed on Sunday and Monday.

Tomlinson Craft Collection
The Rotunda, 711 West 40th Street
(410) 338-1572
Around the corner from The Turnover Shop is a neighborhood office center and shopping mall called The Rotunda. The Rotunda itself is interesting because it is a multi-use reclamation of a turn-of-the-century building that was originally the home of Maryland Casualty Company. It is named for the columned entrance rotunda that is capped with a stained-glass skylight and now houses an eating area.

On the first floor are shops, including the Tomlinson Craft Collection. The store opened in 1983 as a small framing shop that handled some limited craft items. Tomlinson no longer does framing but handles more than 150 craft artists, both local and national. Many of the pieces are one-of-a-kind, and all are unusual. Sculpture, jewelry, hats, lamps, wall hangings, blanket stands, small stools, and hand puppets can all be found among the handcrafted items at Tomlinson. Tiffany-style lamps that are created by a Baltimore artist are often in stock.

Cross Keys

Heirloom Jewels, Ltd.
The Village of Cross Keys, 5100 Falls Road
(410) 323-0100
www.heirloomjewels.com
Not far from Hampden is the Village of Cross Keys, a small shopping enclave boasting unique retail stores as well as major chains. If you are looking for that special piece of one-of-a-kind jewelry, a visit to Heirloom Jewels is a must. From Hampden, simply head north on Falls Road. Cross Keys is on your left.

Reisterstown, Maryland

Settled by German immigrants before the American Revolution, Reisterstown escaped the suburbanization of the 1950s and '60s, perhaps in part because it had already become a haven for antiques shops, and Baltimoreans enjoyed the drive out into the country.

The road to Reisterstown has since become the typical suburban sprawl all the way along. Shopping centers, housing developments, and industrial parks have replaced farms, rolling fields, and cottages by the side of the road. But the original Reisterstown is still an excellent destination for antiquers and seekers of the unique.

Only 35 minutes from Baltimore, it's easy to find by simply heading west from I-695 on Reisterstown Road. If you'd like at least a partially scenic drive, however, you

can exit I-695 (or I-83) at Falls Road and turn onto Greenspring Valley Road. Follow it through all its twists and turns through the Valley; you'll end up at Reisterstown Road. You'll know you're in Reisterstown proper when modern road signs give way to old-fashioned street lamps and brick sidewalks. Along this strip are 22 shops. Your best parking strategy is to pick a shop, park in its parking lot, and then walk.

Tina's Antiques
237 Main Street
(410) 833-9337
Tina's main focus is jewelry, including antique, modern, and modern that is made to look antique. There isn't any nickel-free jewelry, but the choice of earrings is truly staggering. You may also find small gift items. Tina's is closed Monday.

The Scratching Post
237 Main Street
(410) 833-6369
The Scratching Post, which shares space with Tina's Antiques, handles collectibles that have to do, primarily, with cats, although there are some elephants, giraffes, and bears. The shop also carries dolls and marionettes, some of which are 3 feet tall. Most of the items are handcrafted. The Scratching Post is closed on Monday.

Relics of Olde
237½ Main Street
(410) 833-3667
Relics of Olde is a small furniture shop that doesn't have a large selection but is obviously doing something right since it's been open since 1979. Chests, wicker, and a fair amount of painted country furniture are on display. Relics is open Saturday and Sunday only and by chance, so you may want to call ahead.

Ruby Slippers
215-A Main Street
(410) 833-8183
Ruby Slippers is not an antiques store, nor even collectibles as we use the word. The

business cards say crafts, but we'd say art . . . modern art. Ruby Slippers has some of the most unusual jewelry and table art anywhere, as well as unique gifts and crafts. It's closed on Monday.

The New England Carriage House
218 Main Street
(410) 833-4019

This small shop is filled with unlikely treasures, both antique and reproduction. One of its specialties is reproductions of iron toys, particularly iron mechanicals. You can find a great selection of country crafts. It's closed on Monday and Tuesday.

Derby Antiques
239 Main Street
(410) 526-6678 or (410) 848-4863

Derby specializes in ancillary furniture—cupboards, chests, and armoires, rather than sofas and tables. Roseville and Roseville clones make up a large part of the pottery section. The quality of the pieces is excellent. The shop is closed on Monday and Tuesday.

Things You Love . . .
234 Main Street
(410) 833-5019

When you first walk in, you'll be sure you're in a medium-sized shop. But after you've looked at the lovely furniture and glassware in the three front rooms, walk through the hallway. In the back is a gigantic room filled with furniture and collectibles—everything from movie posters to sleds. It's open Friday, Saturday, and Sunday only. A full coffee shop now exists in the back room, where you can recharge with a latté.

SOUTHEAST
Hanover, Maryland

Hanover is mostly known as the location of Fort Meade. Otherwise, it is a rather sleepy place about 25 minutes south of Baltimore. Access is easy from either the Baltimore–Washington Parkway (I-295) or I-95.

AAA Antiques Mall
2659 Annapolis Road
(410) 551-4101
www.kaleden.com

AAA Antiques Mall is the largest mall of its type in Maryland, with more than 400 dealers. It is actually housed in an old grocery store building at the end of a strip shopping center. If you're looking for antiques, this is a don't-miss-it destination. Each dealer booth is about 12 by 12 feet, but some of them have taken over three or four areas for their shops. We saw everything from modern McDonald's collectibles to Victorian furniture. There were trains and toys, clothing, glassware, silver flatware, and just too much other stuff to note. It took us two hours just to walk around the whole mall once.

To reach AAA, just take State Highway 175 east to Odenton off I-295. After about a mile, you're in Hanover and on your right in the shopping center is AAA. It's open every day except Christmas and Easter.

SOUTHWEST
Ellicott City, Maryland

Ellicott City's original town is a showplace. Even if it didn't have one shop, it would be worth seeing. Its old stone and brick buildings are a step back in time, untouched in many ways. However, Ellicott City does have tons of shops, including three large antiques malls. We've picked out the places that we like best, but there are also plenty of others that are worth your time. Celebrate Maryland, for instance, is all Maryland souvenirs and features crab cakes "packed for traveling." Maryland Wine Cellars stocks bottles of Maryland's finest, and all the things to go with them, such as buckets, corkscrews, and recipe books. There's an oriental rug shop on Main Street, and right across the street from it is Rugs to Riches, which has more modern rugs as well as lots of bric-a-brac.

The easiest way is to get to Ellicott City proper is to take the Beltway (I-695) to the Frederick Road exit heading toward Catonsville. Within about 10 minutes, you'll be right in the heart of Ellicott City. Once you go under the railroad bridge, turn left on Maryland Avenue. There are only a few metered parking spaces there, but you can usually find a vacant space. There are also seven other parking lots at various spots around the city. The Maryland Avenue lot is nice, though, because it is so convenient to one of the largest antiques malls in town, Antique Depot.

Antique Depot
3720 Maryland Avenue
(410) 750-2674

Antique Depot lays claim to more than 100 dealers of antiques and collectibles under one roof, and the whole place is cluttered with tons of good stuff. The first floor is wheelchair accessible and has enough room between stalls to get around. You could meander here for hours; every stall has something of value to consider. Stalls with records and comic books round out the offerings.

Discoveries
8055 Main Street
(410) 461-9600

Discoveries is a craft store. There are no antiques here, but there are one-of-a-kind artists dolls, hand-rubbed wooden bowls, handblown glass, and even some wearable art. There are new artists being showcased all the time, and a Discoveries Insider said that some real bargains can be found here on newly discovered crafts artists.

Caplan's of Ellicott City
8125 Main Street
(410) 750-7678, (877) 910-7676
www.caplans.com

Caplan's is one of the most interesting places you'll ever visit, starting with the antique sign hanging out front that says CAPLAN'S DEPARTMENT STORE. Caplan's has furniture and books and a large corner space filled with nothing but stained-glass windows and doors that have been salvaged from old houses. It specializes in mahogany furniture and estate liquidations. Caplan's also has an auction gallery at 8307 Main Street, just a little ways away in Oella, (410) 750-7676.

Taylor's Antique Mall
8197 Main Street
(410) 465-4444

Taylor's is a very large antiques mall that meanders over the whole corner at the top of the hill where Main Street meets Old Columbia Pike. Taylor's has Fiesta dinnerware reproductions, Autumn Leaf china, mahogany sideboards, and composition dolls among its stock and even more unusual items. (On the first floor, in the right-hand back corner, there are some macabre oddities—a full human skeleton and two shrunken human heads. Steer clear if you or your small children are prone to nightmares.) Taylor's is one of the few shops that asks you to check your bags when you enter the store. So, if you can't bear to part, even for a moment, with the $200 vase you just bought at another shop, consider hitting Taylor's first.

Maxine's Antiques
8116 Main Street
(410) 461-5910

Maxine's is a tiny shop, but if you're looking for jewelry or glassware, it's definitely a place you should poke into. We particularly liked a pair of pink, milk-glass candlesticks that were shaped like fish and appeared to be 1920s vintage. Maxine's is closed on Monday.

Papa's Garden
8210 Main Street
(410) 461-7272

Papa's Garden is filled with all kinds of fascinating things. Soft cotton clothing, gemstones, minerals, aroma essences, incense, wind chimes, and sterling silver jewelry are just the kinds of collectibles the earthbound scrounger is looking for. Here you can find a delicate piece of crystal hanging from a sterling silver chain or opal earrings.

Country Crafters
8080 Main Street
(410) 203-2618
This country store offers a variety of quaint furniture, floral arrangements, and crafts, but its specialty is American Girl accoutrements. If you are a collector or have a child who loves American Girl, this is the place to find the dolls and the accessories.

The Forget-Me-Not Factory
8044 Main Street
(410) 465-7355
The Forget-Me-Not Factory nourishes the inner child in all of us. It is three floors of fantasy. Fairies, mermaids, unicorns, and all manner of undersea and oversea creatures can be found here. The whole place glitters—literally—but what's best about it is that the shop is filled with practical gifts and collectibles. Items such as wrapping paper and cards, tree decorations, and wall hangings are prevalent. Toys, games, and ethereal clothing are also in evidence. It's crowded with stuff, so little ones who tend to touch everything could make shopping here a bit precarious. For kids whose fingers are not as prone to do the walking, however, it's a dream come true.

Savage, Maryland

Antique Center at Historic Savage Mill
8600 Foundry Street
(410) 880-0918
Savage Mill was built in 1822 as a textile mill. Its beautiful old buildings, which once supported a 30-foot water wheel that powered the mill, have been restored to house a giant mall with more than 225 select dealers.

Savage Mill has all the amenities, such as a cafe and meeting rooms, and excellent wheelchair access. It also has a lot of charm, with exposed brick walls, hand-rubbed wood, and high ceilings. Oddly enough, what it does not have are really exorbitant prices.

Building I, the first building completed in the renovation, houses Antique Center I,

Unique in antiquing is the town of New Market, just about one and a half hours west of Baltimore and completely given over to antiques shops and shopping. (See the Day Trips chapter for details.)

which has the most diverse group of dealers of any of the buildings. There are a fair number of dolls, crocks, glassware, and dishes and one whole glass case filled with nothing but Roseville pieces.

Building II, which is actually the first building you come to if you park in the main parking lot, has lots of early American furniture. The Sports Exchange carries nothing but sports memorabilia: Sports magazines, posters, and advertising are particularly evident.

Of particular note in Building III is The Book Guy, who handles new and used books in his relatively large shop, and The Art of Fire, which offers contemporary glassblowing.

Don't be blinded by the dealers. Take some time to admire the mill itself and the 17 acres that surround it. For instance, the last Bollman Truss semi-suspension bridge in the world still stands at Savage Mill. It was erected across the Little Patuxent River in 1860 by the B&O Railroad.

The best and easiest way to get to Savage Mill from Baltimore is to simply go south on U.S. 1—best because there are small antiques enclaves on your way, such as Historic Elkridge, and easiest because it is a straight shot out of town. No turns, no confusion. You'll see the signs on your right in about 30 minutes, right after you pass under State Highway 32. Once you turn, you'll enter the town of Savage. Almost totally restored, it boasts turn-of-the-twentieth-century country homes, some traditional brick duplex mill houses (similar to those you'll find in the mill valleys in Baltimore City), and at the end of Baltimore Street where you turn to go toward the mill, one of the most glorious mansard-roofed Victorian homes you'll ever see.

ATTRACTIONS

As one of the nation's oldest cities, Baltimore has an edge when people are looking for museums, historical sites, and attractions to visit. Many buildings from the area's early roots—churches that played a major role in developing the nation's religious tolerance and houses where famous local and national leaders lived—still exist and are open for tours. Close enough to the Inner Harbor for a quick stop for even the busiest person is the home of Mary Pickersgill, who sewed the famous U.S. flag that Francis Scott Key saw—to his relief—from the harbor after a long night of war in 1814, and the house where writer Edgar Allan Poe lived.

While historical sites abound, newer tourist attractions and cultural offerings in Charm City continue to grow. In 1998 Port Discovery, a museum for children, opened near the Inner Harbor, offering yet another way for children and adults to experience science. Port Discovery has a giant, helium-filled balloon developed by world famous balloonist Per Lindstrand. Tethered to the ground, the balloon allows guests to stand on an enclosed gondola and float 450 feet above the Inner Harbor.

More than two decades after the Inner Harbor was transformed from an old and tired industrial stretch on the waterfront into a tourist tour de force, the city continues to work hard to meet the interests and needs of an increasingly sophisticated tourist market. This trend is most evident in the Power Plant. In the early 1980s the building that once housed a power plant was transformed into a collection of six nightclubs that brought locals and visitors alike to enjoy an array of music and entertainment. The place failed when the novelty wore off. Considered often for all sorts of amusements and entertainment, the site sat vacant until August 1997, when a Hard Rock Cafe opened, its bright neon guitar project-

ing its existence throughout the Inner Harbor region. A Barnes & Noble bookstore, and the ESPNZone Restaurant were added, making the Power Plant a thriving spot for tourists and locals alike. The Power Plant exploded into the booming Power Plant Live!, which houses galleries and restaurants for daytime excursions and bars and clubs that rock late into the evening (see the Nightlife chapter).

Despite these modern developments, the area still boasts some exciting landmarks and attractions from centuries past. Lots of cities have something for everyone; Baltimore has lots of things for everyone. Interests as diverse as visiting the graves of the famous dead or viewing a submarine or diesel engine will be satisfied by the Baltimore area.

As we've done in most of the other chapters in this book, we've organized the attractions by geographic location—Downtown, Northeast, Northwest, Southeast, and Southwest. (For insight into the boundaries and general areas that these regions cover, see the How to Use This Book chapter.) In this chapter we've included homes of famous Baltimoreans, spectacular examples of architecture in the area, maritime exhibits, museums, monuments, and memorials. You'll find green spaces profiled in the Parks and Recreation chapter and art museums and galleries in The Arts chapter. Be sure to glance through the Kidstuff chapter if you have little ones in tow.

Finally, keep in mind that attractions have been known to close down, and exhibits and admission prices can change. If you're planning to visit an attraction that isn't as entrenched along the beaten path as Fort McHenry or the National Aquarium, it's worth a phone call to verify it's still open and how much it costs to visit. Note also that if no city is listed for a site, you can assume it's inside Baltimore's city limits. Sites outside the city have the town name included with the street address.

DOWNTOWN

American Dime Museum
1808 Maryland Avenue
(410) 230-0263
www.dimemuseum.com

Baltimore has a storied history of variety and novelty entertainment, and this museum captures it all. From vaudeville to burlesque, from carnival to circus, from stage and street magic to old-time medicine shows and the original "dime museums" themselves, this is a truly unique trip through classically campy Americana (filmmaker John Waters sits on the advisory board, if that gives you any indication of what to expect). Open Wednesday to Friday, noon to 3:00 P.M., and Saturday and Sunday, noon to 5:00 P.M. Admission is $5.00 for adults and $3.00 for children aged 7 to 12; "well-behaved children" 6 and younger are free.

Babe Ruth Museum
216 Emory Street
(410) 727-1539
www.baberuthmuseum.com

Although the Sultan of Swat made his name as a New York Yankee (hiss!), Babe Ruth was born in Baltimore on February 6, 1895. A museum now resides in the house where Ruth was born on 216 Emory. The house almost came under the wrecking ball in 1968 until the mayor and the Greater Baltimore Council rallied to save the historic site. Now Ruth's home is a shrine to baseball's greatest legend. Artifacts and photographs tell the story of a phenomenal life. There are also exhibits pertaining to both the Baltimore Colts and the Baltimore Orioles. The museum celebrates Ruth's birthday each year on February 6 with free admission from 11:00 A.M. to 1:00 P.M. and a champagne toast and cake. It's open daily from 10:00 A.M. to 4:00 P.M., November through March, and daily 10:00 A.M. to 5:00 P.M. April through October, with hours extended to 7:00 P.M. when the Orioles have a home game. Admission is $6.00 for adults, $4.00 for seniors, $3.00 for children ages 5 to 16, and free for those younger than 5.

Baltimore City Fire Museum
414 North Gay Street
(410) 727-2414

This 117-foot tower was built in 1853 by the Independent Fire Company so volunteers could keep watch over the city. The building, inspired by Giotto's Campanile (Bell Tower) in Florence, Italy, was an operating firehouse for Engine Company No. 6 for more than a century. Today the museum offers a look back at early firefighting in cities as well as the Great Fire of 1904, which claimed no lives but destroyed about 70 blocks of Baltimore's central business district. Free tours are offered Sunday from 1:00 to 4:00 P.M., Thursday from 9:00 A.M. to 1:00 P.M., and Fridays from 7:00 to 9:00 P.M. or by appointment.

Baltimore Civil War Museum
at President Street Station
601 President Street
(410) 385-5188
www.mdhs.org

For Civil War buffs, President Street Station, the oldest surviving large city train station in the United States, is known as the site where on April 19, 1861, Baltimore's secessionists clashed with Massachusetts volunteers heading to fight in Washington. The ensuing riot, named the Pratt Street Riot, led to the first deaths in the Civil War, placing the President Street Station in the center of Civil War lore. Relive this important historical moment and learn about the Underground Railroad and the importance of railroads during the war daily from 10:00 A.M. to 5:00 P.M. The museum is closed Thanksgiving and Christmas Days. Admission is $4.00 for adults and $3.00 for children ages 13 to 17. Group tours and rates are available with prior reservation.

Baltimore Maritime Museum
Piers 3 and 5 in the Inner Harbor
(410) 396-3453
www.baltomaritimemuseum.org

Experience history on the water on three historical ships that depict the story of American naval power from 1930 to 1986. Tour the bridge of a 337-foot-long U.S. Coast Guard cutter *Roger B. Taney* (WHEC-37), named after the Marylander who was the chief justice of the United States. It's the last warship still afloat that survived the attack on Pearl Harbor in 1941. It continued its work in the Korean and Vietnam Wars. In the drug war it seized a record 180 tons of marijuana. Pass through the narrow and submergible corridors of the U.S.S. *Torsk*, a Tench Class submarine that sank the last Japanese combatant ships of World War II, and see what it's like to work on the lightship *Chesapeake*, a 1930s floating lighthouse. Hands-on exhibits and tours offer a first-hand look at these historic seafaring vessels. The museum is open from 10:00 A.M. to 5:30 P.M. (6:30 P.M. on Friday and Saturday); winter hours are Friday to Sunday from 10:30 A.M. to 5:00 P.M. The ticket booth closes a half hour earlier than the ships. Admission is $6.00 for adults, $5.00 for seniors, $3.00 for children, and free to children younger than 6.

Baltimore Museum of Industry
1415 Key Highway
(410) 727-4808
www.thebmi.org

Located in an 1865 oyster cannery on the west side of Baltimore's Inner Harbor, this museum allows visitors to experience the industries that made the city one of the busiest ports in the nation. Learn about the long workdays at a belt-driven machine shop, garment loft, print shop, and the historic 1906 steam tugboat, the S.T. *Baltimore*. The museum is open Monday to Saturday 10:00 A.M. to 4:00 P.M. Admission is $10.00 for adults, $5.00 for students and senior citizens.

Baltimore Public Works Museum
751 Eastern Avenue
(410) 396-5565
www.ce.jhu.edu/mdcive/public.htm

Below the city streets lies a maze of pipes and drains moving our water and waste. Opened in 1982 in the historic Eastern Avenue Pumping Station at the east end of the Inner Harbor, this one-of-a-kind museum features the history of public works and the development of urban infrastructure. The highlight of the museum is the outdoor Streetscape, an interactive hands-on model where guests can walk through the maze of pipes and drains that exist below ground. Kids love the exhibits, with names like "What's Beneath the Streets?" and "The Rotten Truth About Garbage." There is also a computer room where games bring city works to life. The museum is open Wednesday through Sunday, 10:00 A.M. to 4:00 P.M. Admission is $2.50 for adults and $2.00 for seniors and children ages 6 to 17. Groups of 10 or more get a discount of $1.25 per person.

Baltimore Streetcar Museum
1901 Falls Road
(410) 547-0264
www.baltimoremd.com/streetcar

Although there are few traces of them left, streetcars played a major role in the city's transportation history. This museum, founded in 1966, traces the 104-year history, starting with the first horsecars in East Baltimore in 1859 through to the end of the streetcar era in 1963. Feel what it was like to ride a streetcar during a 1.5-mile round-trip ride aboard one of the restored streetcars. The museum offers operating layouts, displays, and a video on local streetcar history. It's open from noon to 5:00 P.M. Sunday year-round and Saturday and Sunday from June to October. Admission is $6.00 for adults and $3.00 for children ages 3 to 14 and senior citizens, with a family maximum of $24.00.

Baltimore Tattoo Museum
1534 Eastern Avenue
(410) 522-5800
www.baltotat.com

Tattoos may be back in favor with the fashionistas, but the art of body ink never went out of style in Baltimore. Both a full-service tattoo and piercing shop and a museum of classic tattoo art, this is the place to go for a lasting souvenir of your trip to Baltimore. Open noon to 8:00 P.M. Sunday to Thursday, and noon to 9:00 P.M. Friday and Saturday.

The Basilica of the Assumption
408 North Charles Street
(410) 727-3565
www.baltimorebasilica.org

The first metropolitan cathedral in the United States has been the mother church for Baltimore's Roman Catholic population since 1806. Designed by Benjamin Henry Latrobe, designer of the Capitol in Washington, the cathedral features a grand organ dating back to 1821, a high altar from 1822, and stained-glass windows installed in the 1940s. Across the street from the Enoch Pratt Free Library main branch, this example of neoclassical architecture also holds the remains of Bishop John Carroll, America's first Catholic bishop, who placed the cornerstone. Guided tours are given on Sundays at noon and by appointment. The basilica is open Monday through Friday from 7:00 A.M. to 5:00 P.M. and Saturday and Sunday from 7:00 A.M. to 6:30 P.M. Admission is free, but donations are accepted.

Brown Memorial Park Avenue Presbyterian Church
1316 Park Avenue
(410) 523-1542
www.brownmemorialparkavenue.org

Baltimore has many fine churches with stunning architecture and distinctive Louis Tiffany and John LaFarge stained-glass windows, but Brown Memorial may very well house one of the largest collections of Tiffany windows in their original setting anywhere. The 11 Tiffany windows circle a

When The Basilica of the Assumption renovated its back section, architects could not find the same Italian stone used in the original 1806 structure. If you look closely, you will see that this section of the church is actually composed of "Formstone," a concrete mixture designed to mimic the look of the original stone.

Gothic Revival interior with a magnificent vaulted dome that was recently painted a rich blue during a major restoration of the church. The two Tiffany windows in the transept are among the largest and finest stained-glass windows to ever come out of the master's studio in New York. Call for hours.

The Dr. Samuel D. Harris National Museum of Dentistry
31 South Greene Street
(410) 706-0600
www.dentalmuseum.umaryland.edu

Get ready for a brush with the world's first dental college, which opened on the campus of the University of Maryland at Baltimore in 1839. The museum building, which opened in 1904, houses collections of artifacts and educational exhibits dealing with the history and lore of teeth and dentistry.

The museum offers a look at the evolution of the toothbrush, temporary offices for a traveling dentist, and an interactive exhibition, 32 Terrific Teeth, featuring George Washington's dentures and a tooth jukebox. The museum is open Wednesday through Saturday from 10:00 A.M. to 4:00 P.M. and Sunday from 1:00 to 4:00 P.M. Admission is $4.50 for adults, $2.50 for children 7 to 18, and free for children 6 and younger.

Enoch Pratt Free Library
400 Cathedral Street
(410) 396-5430
www.epfl.net

Since 1886 this branch has served as the central library for "The City That Reads."

Among its more than 2 million volumes are extensive collections of writers Edgar Allan Poe and H. L. Mencken and a library of lyrics and music sheets for more than 100,000 songs.

The library's benefactor, Enoch Pratt, set out to educate the common man by establishing this neighborhood library system, which has served Baltimoreans for more than 100 years. All the libraries in Maryland benefit from Pratt's gift, as it lends out its extensive collection to county library systems when requested.

The library is open Monday to Wednesday from 10:00 A.M. to 8:00 P.M., Thursday from 10:00 A.M. to 5:30 P.M., Saturday from 10:00 A.M. to 5:00 P.M., and Sunday from 1:00 to 5:00 P.M. Admission is free.

Eubie Blake National Jazz Institute and Cultural Center
847 North Howard Street
(410) 225-3130
www.eubieblake.org
Honoring Eubie Blake (1883–1983), the famous ragtime piano player and musical theater composer of *Shuffle Along* and songs "I'm Just Wild About Harry" and "Memories of You," the center's museum educates and explains the legacy of jazz greats from Baltimore, including Cab Calloway, Billie Holiday, Chick Webb, and Avon Long. Monthly exhibits in the gallery highlight renowned and aspiring artists. Call for hours and admission.

George Peabody Library
17 East Mount Vernon Place
(410) 659-8179
www.library.jhu.edu/special/findit/peabody/index.html
George Peabody was a benefactor to Johns Hopkins University and is the namesake of Baltimore's Peabody Conservatory of Music. In this building owned by Johns Hopkins University are about 300,000 volumes, mostly covering the period from the sixteenth century to the early twentieth century. You'll find no books on music here; subjects include archaeology, British art and architecture, British and American history, science, and geography. The library is open to the public for reference only—none of the books can be checked out.

The building is famous for its interior architecture, including five stories of ornamental cast-iron balconies. Baltimore is the backdrop for many Hollywood films, and this library is a popular setting in several major films. Its gracious interior and exterior recently underwent a major renovation. The library is open Monday through Friday from 9:00 A.M. to 3:00 P.M. No admission is charged.

The Great Blacks in Wax Museum
1601–3 East North Avenue
(410) 563-3404
www.greatblacksinwax.org
The first and only museum of its kind, The Great Blacks in Wax Museum opened in 1983 to pay tribute to African Americans by exhibiting more than 100 lifelike statues in one place. You'll be standing next to Dr. Martin Luther King Jr., Supreme Court Justice Thurgood Marshall, Baltimore neurosurgeon Dr. Ben Carson, known for his lifesaving surgeries on infants at Johns Hopkins Hospital, and Kweisi Mfume, a former Baltimore congressman who took over the helm of the National Association for the Advancement of Colored People (NAACP). A model slave ship offers an in-depth look at the 400-year history of the slave trade, while another gives a picture of black youths' contributions to the civil rights movement. Don't miss the gift shop, where you can pick up everything from postcards to posters and tote bags.

Hours from January 15 through October 14 are 9:00 A.M. to 6:00 P.M. Tuesday through Saturday and noon to 6:00 P.M. Sunday. Hours from October 15 through January 14 are Tuesday through Saturday, 9:00 A.M. to 5:00 P.M. and Sunday noon to 5:00 P.M. Admission is $6.80 for adults, $6.30 for college students and senior citizens, $4.80 for kids ages 12 to 17 and $4.55 for children ages 2 to 11.

Greenmount Cemetery
1501 Greenmount Avenue
(410) 539-0641

Here lie many of Baltimore's greats, including Civil War generals, poet Sidney Lanier, and philanthropists Johns Hopkins, Enoch Pratt, Moses Sheppard, and William and Henry Walters. Napoleon's sister-in-law, Betsy Patterson Bonaparte, and the spymaster of the CIA, Allen W. Dulles, also share the cemetery with the infamous John Wilkes Booth. The cemetery is free to visitors and open Monday through Saturday from 9:00 A.M. to 3:45 P.M. for the grounds. Visitors can get a list and map of the 73 most visited graves from the gate office, which has the same hours as the cemetery, except Saturdays, when it closes at 11:45 A.M.

Holocaust Memorial
Corner of Water, Gay, and
Lombard Streets
(410) 752-2630

Near the Inner Harbor, this outdoor memorial and sculpture center is designed to remind visitors of the six million Jews murdered by the Nazis in Europe from 1933 to 1945. The memorial, which was expanded in 1997, is open 24 hours.

Inner Harbor Ice Rink
Rash Field at 201 Key Highway
(410) 385-0675
www.baltimoreevents.org/icerink

Open in the winter months only, this outdoor rink is located right on the harbor and lets you skate with the Baltimore skyline as a backdrop. It's within walking distance of the Maryland Science Center, the National Aquarium, and Harborplace and offers a wonderful way to cap off a day of sightseeing. The rink is usually open through early March, weather permitting. Skate rental is $3.00, and skating fees are $5.00 per person, $6.00 on weekends, $4.00 for kids 12 and under. Public skating is for a two-hour session. Special hours and prices are in effect on holidays. Staying for a while? Purchase a season pass for $99.

Jewish Museum of Maryland
15 Lloyd Street
(410) 732-6400
www.jhsm.org

The largest Jewish history museum in the United States was formed in 1960 to preserve the Lloyd Street Synagogue, built in 1845, making it the third-oldest in the country. The B'nai Israel Synagogue, built in 1876, has also been restored by the museum and now houses exhibitions, a library, archives, and collections about regional Jewish history as well as adult and children's educational programs and events. The museum is open Tuesday through Thursday and Sunday from noon to 4:00 P.M. Tours run at 1:00 and 2:30 P.M. Admission is $8.00.

Maryland Historical Society
201 West Monument Street
(410) 685-3750
www.mdhs.org

The original draft of "The Star-Spangled Banner," the world's largest collection of paintings by Charles Wilson Peale and his family, and the nation's largest collection of nineteenth-century American silver are among the attractions in this independent museum and Library of Maryland History. There's also a great collection of decorative arts and galleries with images depicting the Civil War and War of 1812. Museum hours are Wednesday through Sunday from 10:00 A.M. to 5:00 P.M. The H. Furlong Baldwin Library hours are Wednesday through Saturday from 10:00 A.M. to 4:30 P.M. Admission is free to members; $8.00 for adults; $6.00 for seniors, students (with valid ID), and children 13 to 17; and $4.00 for children 3 to 12. Admission to the library is $6.00 for adults and $4.00 for students with ID.

Maryland Science Center and
IMAX Theater
601 Light Street
(410) 685-5225
www.mdsci.org

The world of science comes alive with interactive exhibits and live demonstrations explaining light, mechanics, and sound. In addition to the hundreds of hands-on exhibits about science, the center houses the Davis Planetarium and an IMAX movie theater that features a five-story-high screen featuring films on topics ranging from the Kuwaiti oil fires to sharks to the Space Shuttle missions.

For kids, this is a must. Everything is interactive, meaning they can be touching things that other museums and science centers put behind glass. The result is happier, more educated kids (and adults who want to be kids again). It's not uncommon for people to leave saying, "I wish they had this when I was a kid!"

One of the best exhibits is the Chesapeake Bay, which offers a hands-on look at Maryland's most precious natural resources. Participants learn about the diversity of marine life and their careful interactions that are so critical to the survival and revival of the Chesapeake Bay.

Other permanent exhibitions include Energy, which allows people to use their bodies to manipulate energy or spark, crackle, spin, and glow; Science Arcade, where sight, sound, magnetism, light, and mechanics are all put to the hands-on test in this unusual arcade; Experiment, where you see up-close how scientists think and act; and Structures, which uses building blocks, paper models, and electronic games to explain how buildings stand—and fall.

Another highlight of this attraction is the Space Link, which relies heavily on The Goddard Network. Through links with the Goddard Space Flight Center outside of Washington, D.C., the Space Center offers satellite and Landsat data on Earth as well as up-close exhibits on weather forecasting and the instruments in use in space. Simply put, this exhibit puts space in your hands.

The Maryland Science Center is open Tuesday through Friday from 10:00 A.M. to 5:00 P.M., Saturday from 10:00 A.M. to 6:00 P.M., and Sunday from noon to 5:00 P.M. The IMAX Theater is open for morning and evening shows. Daytime admission for the museum only is $4.00 for everyone; for one IMAX film, $7.50 for all; and for entrance plus one IMAX film, $10.00 for all. Evening admission (after 6:00 P.M.) is $9.00 for one IMAX film and $12.50 for two for all audiences.

The Mother Seton House
600 North Paca Street
(410) 523-3443

Home of America's first native saint, the house is adjacent to the Old St. Mary's Seminary Chapel, where Elizabeth Ann Seton took her first religious vows in March 1809. Born in New York City in 1774, Mother Seton came to Baltimore in 1808. She had been a devout Episcopalian with five children when she was widowed at the age of 28. She turned to Catholicism and later opened an elementary school at the house—the first boarding school for Catholic girls—that is regarded as the basis for the nation's parochial school system. In 1809 she founded the Sisters of Charity, the first U.S. religious society. She died in 1821 and was canonized a saint in 1975.

The house and chapel are open on Saturdays and Sundays from 1:00 to 3:00 P.M. and by appointment. The house is closed on Easter, Christmas, and New Year's Days. No admission is charged.

Mount Vernon Museum of
Incandescent Lighting ·
717 Washington Place
(410) 752-8586

A local dentist's bright idea led to a museum showcasing about 8,000 of the 60,000 electric light bulbs in his personal collection. You'll even see Thomas Edison's original light bulb. The museum is open by appointment only; donations are accepted.

National Aquarium in Baltimore
Pier 3/501 East Pratt Street
(410) 576-3800
www.aqua.org

Sharks, dolphins, puffins, stingrays, poisonous dart frogs, piranhas, electric eels, and reef fish are just some of the thousands of marine creatures awaiting you here. The four corners of the globe are represented in Baltimore's Inner Harbor attraction—the frosty Icelandic coast, a misty rain forest, a coral reef, and an ocean. The aquarium has more than 14,000 animals and a dolphin show.

There's lots to see and do as you wander through the many exhibits. The Wings in the Water exhibit has stingrays that are visible from the surface and at underwater viewing windows to the pool. The stingrays represent the largest collection in the country. A highlight is when divers feed the stingrays underwater each day. Insightful narrations explaining what is going on in the tank are available above water at all times.

The highlight of any visit to the aquarium is the South American rain forest on the top level of the aquarium under a towering glass pyramid. Tropical birds fly about as poisonous dart frogs hop around; those fearful creatures, the piranhas, swim about as tamarin monkeys swing and hang in the trees. In 2000 the aquarium added a simulated Amazon River bed replete with pygmy marmosets—the world's smallest monkeys.

The aquarium also plays host to several changing exhibits that in the past have included giant collections of jellyfish and venomous snakes.

Pizza Hut pizzas and other snacks are available near The Aqua Shop, the aquarium's gift shop. The Aquarium is Maryland's number one tourist attraction, meaning it can get crowded. Hours vary by season and are complicated, so it would be best to call or check the Web site for details. The staff recommends you beat the crowds by visiting on weekdays after 3:00 P.M. when you can stay as late as 7:00 P.M., after many of the guests have left for the day. Be sure to arrive before the ticket counter closes at 5:00 P.M. On weekends, arrive between 10:00 and 11:00 A.M. to stay ahead of the crowd. Be prepared for the new security measures in place; all bags are subject to search upon entry. The building closes two hours after the last entry time so latecomers still have two hours to enjoy the sights. Admission is $17.50 for adults, $14.50 for seniors 60 and older, and $9.50 for children ages 3 to 11. Children under 3 are free.

The Inner Harbor's indoor attractions, the Maryland Science Center, Harborplace, and the National Aquarium in Baltimore, fill quickly when the weather is poor. The Baltimore Zoo and Fort McHenry are good places to go if a few raindrops won't bother you.

Nine North Front Street
9 North Front Street
(410) 837-5424
In Baltimore's Shot Tower Park, this three-story brick house is the only surviving member of a group of homes built for merchants, artisans, and gentlemen in the 1790s. Thorowgood Smith lived in the house when he became the second mayor of Baltimore. The Women's Civic League, which rescued it from demolition and restored it, now keeps its headquarters in the house, which features a colonial kitchen and an art gallery. The house is open Tuesday through Friday from 9:30 A.M. to 2:30 P.M. and by appointment Saturday and Sunday. Admission is free.

Old Otterbein United Methodist Church
112 West Conway Street
(410) 685-4703
In a city with lots of century-old churches, Baltimore's oldest church is the home to exhibits showing the role in founding United Bretheren in Christ, the first all-new American religious denomination. It is also the last standing church in the city where Bishop Francis Asbury preached. The church is open Saturdays April through October from 10:00 A.M. to 4:00 P.M. Admission is free. With its proximity to Oriole Park at Camden Yards, the church now sells peanuts before baseball games.

Old St. Paul's Church
Charles and Saratoga Streets
(410) 685-3404
oldstpauls.ang-md.us
The mother church of the Episcopal church in Baltimore since 1856, Old St. Paul's was designed in the basilica style by Richard

Upjohn. Tiffany windows and inlaid mosaic work capture the eyes, while ringing church bells capture the ears. The bells were part of a carillon given to the church by residents of Baltimore. The church is open on weekdays from 11:00 A.M. to 1:00 P.M. and Sunday from 8:30 A.M. to 12:30 P.M. Admission is free, but donations are welcome.

Pride of Baltimore II
Inner Harbor
(410) 539-1151
www.pride2.org

When it's in port, the replica of an 1812 clipper ship offers great insight into the nineteenth-century–style Baltimore clipper ships that plied the waters of the Chesapeake throughout the century. The *Pride II* has sailed all over the world, extending a dose of Baltimore charm and history wherever it docks. It's usually at sea more than half of the year. Hours vary for tours, which are conducted by the paid and volunteer staff that man it during journeys. No admission is charged. Call in advance to see when the boat is in dock.

Robert Long House and Gardens
812 South Ann Street
(410) 675-6750
www.preservationsociety.com

Robert Long was an early eighteenth-century merchant who built what is now the city's oldest urban residence, in 1765. Long's house in Fells Point has been restored to its original appearance so that visitors can learn about the life of a city merchant. Among the highlights are its proximity to the docks, the simple furnishings, and the intriguing design of its gardens. Tours of the house are available daily. Admission is $3.00, children under 7 are admitted free. Call for hours.

St. Jude Shrine
512 West Saratoga Street
(410) 685-6026
www.stjudeshrine.org

Shortly after World War II began, the shrine became the center of St. Jude devotions. People from all over the United States keep in touch with the center through the mail, while people from Baltimore and beyond require there to be four novena services each Wednesday. Every year, thousands of people enroll themselves and their living and dead loved ones in the League of St. Jude. Perpetual novena services are held Wednesdays at 7:45 A.M., noon, 5:45, and 7:45 P.M., while Sunday Masses are celebrated at 8:00, 9:00, and 11:30 A.M., with Sunday novena after the latter two masses. No admission is charged.

The Star-Spangled Banner Flag House
844 East Pratt Street
(410) 837-1793
www.flaghouse.org

Mary Pickersgill sewed by hand the 30-foot-by-42-foot flag that flew over Fort McHenry during the British bombardment in 1814. Built in 1793, this house was her home during her adult years. The adjacent museum commemorates the War of 1812 and features an audiovisual program about Pickersgill's life and her role in the war. The house is open Tuesday through Saturday from 10:00 A.M. to 4:00 P.M. Admission is $6.00 for adults, $5.00 for seniors, and $4.00 for students.

Top of the World
Observation Level
World Trade Center
401 East Pratt Street
(410) 837-8439
www.baltimoreevents.org/topworld

The 27th floor of the World Trade Center in Baltimore offers a stunning 360-degree view of Baltimore's skyline. Stationed binoculars and photo maps enhance the experience, offering a detailed look at the Inner Harbor, the surrounding city, and the lapping waters of the Chesapeake Bay. Guides offer anecdotes about Baltimore's history and happenings. The Top of the World Observation Level is open September through May from 10:00 A.M. to 6:00 P.M., Wednesday through Sunday. From Memorial Day to Labor Day, the observation level is open seven days a week from 10:00 A.M. to 9:00 P.M.

Admission is $4.00 for adults, $3.00 for seniors, and $2.00 for children aged 3 to 16. Special rates apply during events. New security measures are in place, and visitors are subject to a manual search of purses, briefcases, packages, and backpacks. For your convenience, the Trade Center staff suggests that you leave nonessential items at home or in your hotel.

USS *Constellation*
Pier 1
301 East Pratt Street
(410) 539-1797
www.constellation.org
Docked at the Inner Harbor, this majestic 1,400-ton, 179-foot sailing sloop is the only surviving Civil War–era naval vessel and all-sail warship. Built in 1854 by the Navy, the *Constellation* has a colorful history of active duty. The ship was dry-docked for a time and given a complete historic restoration. It's been put back into the water and is open every day except Thanksgiving, Christmas, and New Year's Days. A ship's store sells memorabilia. Open daily May to October 14 from 10:00 A.M. to 6:00 P.M. and October 15 to April 30, 10:00 A.M. to 4:00 P.M. Admission is $6.50 for adults, $5.00 for seniors, and $3.50 for children over age 6.

Washington Monument
Mount Vernon Place
(410) 396-1049
The view from the top of the first architectural monument to honor George Washington is worth the climb—228 steps (but who's counting?). Beyond being able to say you did it, the sights from atop the monument are breathtaking. The climb costs $1.00, but the ground-floor museum, explaining the history and construction of the monument, begun in 1815, is free. The monument is open Tuesday through Sunday from 10:00 A.M. to 4:00 P.M..

Westminster Hall and Burying Grounds
500 West Fayette Street
(410) 706-2072
Established in 1786, this cemetery is the final resting place of writer Edgar Allan Poe, among others. The cemetery, open Monday through Friday from 8:00 A.M. to dusk, is free, while the catacombs, open only by reservation, cost $4.00 for adults and $2.00 for children 12 and younger and seniors.

Many attractions and museums offer discounts on regular admission. AAA members, for example, get a break on entrance fees at the Mount Clare Museum House, while the National Park Service at Fort McHenry accepts passes such as the National Park Pass and the Golden Age Pass. Remember to ask about special discounts—it may save you a few bucks!

NORTHEAST

Baltimore County Historical Society
9811 Van Buren Lane, Cockeysville
(410) 666-1878
www.baltohistsoc.org
In an old almshouse, where the poor and destitute were housed before public welfare programs, is the county's Historical Society headquarters, including a library that provides information about county residents and history. The library is open to the public. Six of the original rooms of the 1872 house have been furnished to reflect life in Baltimore County during the nineteenth century, including the Parkton General Store and Post Office, a Victorian grandmother's house, and farmhouse. The museum is open Thursdays from 10:00 A.M. to 3:00 P.M.; admission is $3.00. The library is open Monday through Saturday from 10:00 A.M. to 4:00 P.M. and the second and fourth Saturday from 10:00 A.M. to 3:00 P.M. Hours vary, so call ahead.

Evergreen House
4545 North Charles Street
(410) 516-0341
Listed on the National Register of Historic Places, this Italianate home on 26 wooded

and landscaped acres was owned by Baltimore's Garrett family from 1878 to 1942. John W. Garrett was the president of the Baltimore & Ohio Railroad, and this house was purchased for his son, T. Harrison Garrett. The mansion, the carriage house, and the gardens have been returned to their original settings. The Garretts' collections of more than 5,000 pieces, including post-Impressionist paintings, rare books, Japanese netsuke and inro, Tiffany glass, and Baltimore's only private room featuring colorful Russian designs, offer a wide array of art and history in one place. The house, which is closed on major holidays, is open from 10:00 A.M. to 4:00 P.M. Monday through Friday and 1:00 to 4:00 P.M. Saturday and Sunday. The last hourly tour begins at 3:00 P.M. Admission is $6.00 for adults, $5.00 for senior citizens, and $3.00 for children 13 to 17 years old.

Fire Museum of Maryland
1301 York Road, Lutherville
(410) 321-7500
www.firemuseummd.org
Learn how fires are fought, including the Great Fire of 1904 in Baltimore, at this extensive collection of fire equipment and vehicles, spanning the years of pumpers to hook-and-ladder trucks to today's sophisticated and advanced technology. Open on Saturday March through December and Tuesday through Saturday June through August from 11:00 A.M. to 4:00 P.M. Admission is $6.00 for adults, $4.00 for children ages 2 to 12, and $5.00 for seniors and firefighters.

Hampton National Historic Site
535 Hampton Lane, Towson
(410) 823-1309
www.nps.gov/hamp
This 40-room Georgian mansion, built by Capt. Charles Ridgely just after the Revolutionary War, has original furnishings and is surrounded by gardens and 26 outbuildings, including original slave quarters. Owned by the same family for 160 years, the house is a great stop for people who love old houses, antiques, and early American history. Operated by the National Park Service, this 63-acre site is open from 9:00 A.M. to 5:00 P.M. daily, except Thanksgiving, Christmas, and New Year's Days. Entry to the grounds is free, but tours are $5.00 for adults, $2.00 for seniors, and free for children younger than 12.

Jerusalem Mill/Jericho Covered Bridge
2813 Jerusalem Road, off U.S. Highway 1, Kingsville
(410) 877-3560
Part of Gunpowder Falls State Park, a 16,000-acre park in northern Baltimore County, the mill was built on the Gunpowder River in 1772. The renovated second floor serves as headquarters for the park, while the first floor features historical artifacts, paintings, photographs, old stone, and the old mill. The museum is open Saturday and Sunday from 1:00 to 4:00 P.M. for free. Don't miss the Jericho Covered Bridge, a long single-span bridge over the Gunpowder River that is open to traffic.

Sherwood Gardens
Between Stratford, Highfield, Underwood, and Greenway Streets
(410) 323-7982
About 80,000 tulip bulbs are planted each year, along with a variety of other spring-flowering bulbs that illuminate this park with color and beauty. The display is most spectacular in late April and early May. A small park in the neighborhood of Guilford, Sherwood Gardens has on-street parking nearby, and the site is perfect for quiet meditation, a picnic, or reading a book. Bring a blanket to sit on. The gardens are open dawn to dusk, with no admission charge.

NORTHWEST

Baltimore Conservatory and Botanic Gardens
Druid Hill Park, 12 Druid Park Drive
(410) 396-0180
The Baltimore Conservatory and Botanic Gardens is located in the historic Druid Hill

Park, where 1.5 acres erupt in colorful flower gardens. A Victorian Palm House (circa 1888) and three display green-houses are under renovation. During the renovation/expansion project, the Palm House and the display greenhouses are closed, but the outdoor gardens remain open to the public from dawn to dusk.

The Baltimore Zoo
Druid Hill Park, 1 Druid Park Lake Drive
(410) 366-5466
www.baltimorezoo.org

Rated the top children's zoo in the nation by *The Zoo Book,* the Baltimore Zoo's eight-acre property is home to more than 2,000 animals representing life on seven continents. Go to Africa and visit Makasi, the zoo's new okapi, a rare and unusual cousin of the giraffe, then travel north to Alaska where the zoo made headlines for the addition of a confiscated female polar bear, named Alaska. Watch her swim with her new pal, the male bear Magnet.

While many zoos keep you far away from the action, The Baltimore Zoo is designed for the young at heart. Most exhibits are open enough to allow even the youngest and shortest kid to see in, while many of the habitats, including those for the lions, tigers, and bears, put you close enough to catch one of the animal's sneezes. In a few hours, you can easily see a wide range of mammals, reptiles, and birds, all from a safe yet close viewpoint.

Hours are 10:00 A.M. to 4:00 P.M. daily, except Christmas and one Friday in June, when a big fundraiser is held. Admission is $12.00 for adults, $10.00 for senior citizens, $8.00 for children 2 to 11, while children younger than 2 are admitted free. Discount coupons may be found on the Web site. Parking is free. (See the Kidstuff chapter.)

Cylburn Arboretum
4915 Greenspring Avenue
(410) 367-2217
www.cylburnassociation.org

It's hard to believe that these 207 acres of beautiful formal and woodland gardens and trails outside the historic Cylburn

mansion house are in Baltimore City. Operated by the city Department of Recreation and Parks after being started by Baltimore businessman Jesse Tyson, the mansion offers a horticultural refer-ence library and a bird and nature museum. The grounds are open daily dawn to dusk, while the mansion is open weekdays from 7:30 A.M. to 3:30 P.M. The museum, library, and gift shop, operated by the Cylburn Arboretum Association, are open Tuesday and Thursday from 1:00 to 3:00 P.M. Tours of the house and green-house are $2.00.

Homewood House Museum
3400 North Charles Street
(410) 516-5589
www.jhu.edu/~hwdhouse

One of Baltimore's oldest buildings, Homewood House and its 122-acre farm was the residence of Charles Carroll Jr., a member of the important Carroll family (see our History chapter for information about the Carrolls). The house, built in 1801 for $40,000 with the finest materials and workers, is one of the best examples of Federal architecture of the early nine-teenth century. Carroll received the money to build the five-part house as a wedding gift from his father, Charles Carroll, a signer of the Declaration of Independence. In 1987, after 12 years of research, archae-ological excavation, and restoration, the museum opened as part of Johns Hopkins University. The house, which is closed on major holidays, and the beautiful gardens are open Tuesday through Saturday 11:00 A.M. to 4:00 P.M., Sunday noon to 4:00 P.M. The last tour begins at 3:00 P.M. Admission is $6.00 for adults, $5.00 for senior citi-zens, and $3.00 for children 5 and older. AAA members get $1.00 off.

Soldiers Delight Natural
Environmental Area
5100 Deer Park Road
(410) 922-3044

About 25 miles northwest of Baltimore's Inner Harbor, this 1,900-acre park contains 39 rare, threatened, or endangered plant species as well as rare insects, rocks, and minerals. The only source for the fringed gentian, a fall-blooming wildflower, the natural park features the largest area of serpentine barrens, green mineral or rock composed of hydrous magnesium silicate, on the East Coast. A nature center provides information about serpentine barrens and how the property was used in the past. The park also has trails for touring. It's open from 8:00 A.M. to dusk daily. There's no admission fee.

SOUTHEAST

Ballestone Manor
1935 Back River Neck Road, Essex
(410) 887-0217
Guides dressed in period clothing lead visitors through this manor house built in 1780 overlooking Back River. Furnishings reflect the Federal and Victorian styles. In September only, tours are available from 2:00 to 5:00 P.M. by appointment. A donation of $3.00 for adults and 50 cents for children younger than 12 is requested.

Battle Acre Monument
3219 Old North Point Road, Dundalk
(410) 583-7313
This monument commemorates the Fifth Regiment's defensive position against an attack by the British in 1814. It was here that a ragtag group of soldiers fought a better prepared and larger British military force. The monument is open 24 hours.

Fort McHenry National Monument and Historic Shrine
End of East Fort Avenue
(410) 962-4290
www.nps.gov/fomc/
This place gives "The Star-Spangled Banner" its meaning. A 15-minute slide presentation on Francis Scott Key's penning of the song during the War of 1812, while watching from the water as the city was bombarded, is a stirring reminder of our past. The presentation closes with the playing of the anthem and the unveiling

of the "flag [that] was still there." Although the fort never came under attack, it had the cannons, the barracks, the jailhouse for prisoners, and armaments for battle, which you can walk among while touring the park. Its position at the point of the harbor leading into Baltimore's port made it a strategic military site. Today it's a beautiful place to walk and see ships heading in from or out to the Chesapeake Bay. Don't forget a jacket because the wind can be strong. The park is open every day, except Christmas and New Year's, from 8:00 A.M. to 5:00 P.M., with extended summer hours. Admission to the historic fort is $5.00 for adults and free for children younger than 16. The park also accepts various national park passes.

SOUTHWEST

The B&O Railroad Museum
901 West Pratt Street
(410) 752-2490
www.borail.org
The B&O Railroad Museum houses the largest railroad collection in the Western Hemisphere, but tragedy struck during the blizzard of 2003. In the early morning hours on Monday, February 17, 2003, the iron structure of the 1884 Roundhouse, a signature gold-and-glass dome on the Baltimore skyline, collapsed under the weight of heavy snow. While no injuries occurred, significant historic artifacts were lost to the damage, and the museum is currently closed. Curators and staff are working with structural engineers to rebuild. Call in advance to inquire about reopening, which is scheduled for November 13, 2004.

Catonsville Historical Society
1824 Frederick Road, Catonsville
(410) 744-3034
www.catonsvillehistory.org
The Townsend House has eighteenth- and nineteenth-century antiques as well as local historical exhibits and genealogical resources. Open the first three Sundays of

each month from 2:00 to 4:00 P.M. or by appointment. Admission is $2.00.

Historical Electronics Museum
1745 West Nursery Road, Linthicum
(410) 765-0230
www.hem-usa.org
This is a specialized museum with seven small galleries exhibiting the history of electronic technology. The vast displays of equipment put a particular emphasis on radar, countermeasures, and communications. Visitors can see the lunar TV camera that transmitted Neil Armstrong's first steps on the moon, and the German Enigma, which encoded messages in World War II. Open Monday through Friday 9:00 A.M. to 3:00 P.M., Saturday 10:00 A.M. to 2:00 P.M. Admission is free.

Mount Clare Museum House
1500 Washington Boulevard
(410) 837-3262
www.mountclare.org
Furnishings of the eighteenth and nineteenth centuries belonging to Charles Carroll, a barrister credited with writing Maryland's Declaration of Independence, and his wife, Margaret Tilghman, fill Baltimore's only pre–Revolutionary War mansion. Located in beautiful Carroll Park, the house offers a great example of Georgian architecture in Maryland. Open Tuesday through Saturday from 10:00 A.M. to 4:00 P.M. The

house is closed on major holidays. Admission is $6.00 for adults, $5.00 for senior citizens, $4.00 for students 18 and under.

Poe House and Museum
203 North Amity Street
(410) 396-7932
This is Baltimore's smallest museum, but it offers a big punch. One of America's most famous poets, Edgar Allan Poe, who also wrote short stories and criticism, lived in the house from 1832 to 1835. The museum features Poe memorabilia, exhibits, and a video presentation highlighting Poe's life and career. Period furniture gives visitors a sense of the time in which the poet wrote such great works as "The Raven" and "The Fall of the House of Usher." Don't miss the nearby Westminster Hall, where he was buried after his death at age 40 in 1849 (see the listing previously in this chapter). The museum also hosts the annual World's Biggest Poe's Birthday Celebration in January (see the Annual Events chapter). The museum is located on a very narrow, one-way street that can become very slick (or freeze) after a snowfall. It's best to park on neighboring streets during the winter. The museum is open Wednesday through Saturday from noon to 3:45 P.M. Admission for adults is $2.00, and for children younger than 12, it's $1.00. Hours can vary, so always call in advance.

KIDSTUFF

Whether your kids go crazy over planes, trains, or ponies, or get revved up over go-carts, science experiments, or baseball, you'll find someplace for them to expend their energies in Charm City. A multitude of exhibits, activities, programs, and historical sites offer the younger set a mindful of things to consider and be fascinated by. And though the focus of this chapter is stuff for kids, we're sure that kids at heart will be equally entertained at these attractions.

To make sure your excursions are more fun than fretful, remind your children to stay close. Some exhibits and activities can get really crowded, and a short distance between Mom and Dad can seem like miles in a sea of unfamiliar faces. Show your kids the entrance or information center when entering an attraction and remind them to go there if they lose track of you. (You know how parents tend to wander off.)

We've divided the following activities by geographic location. These attractions are traditional favorites with kids, but be sure to look to other chapters, such as Attractions and Parks and Recreation, for more outings to share with the little and not-so-little ones. You may also want to pick up a free copy of *Baltimore's Child,* a monthly publication with information about services, resources, and events for parents and children in the Baltimore metropolitan area. Copies are distributed free throughout the city, and most libraries carry them.

DOWNTOWN

Baltimore Children's Theatre
Locations vary
(443) 864-1470
www.baltimoretheatre.org
A cast of professional adult actors and talented children from the theater's conser-

vatory put on shows at different venues throughout the city and the suburbs, primarily the Chesapeake Arts Center Studio Theater (see The Arts chapter). The 2003–2004 season included classics like *Dr. Doolittle* and *Wizard of Oz.* The theater also provides acting classes for kids at the Westchester Community Center in Oella, Maryland. The shows are $8.00 in advance or $10.00 at door. Call or check the Web site for schedules.

Enoch Pratt Free Library
400 Cathedral Street
(410) 396-5430
www.pratt.lib.md.us
The Pratt programs for children feature movies, crafts, and read-aloud sessions conducted by librarians at the main branch and at smaller branches throughout the city. The programs offer kids a welcome intellectual respite, especially if the day turns inclement. It's best to call ahead if you're looking for a kids' program, but if you're really desperate, the kids will find plenty of books with which to wile away the hours in the library's children's section. Programs are free and open to all.

The library's hours are 10:00 A.M. to 8:00 P.M. Monday through Wednesday, 10:00 A.M. to 5:00 P.M. Thursday through Saturday, and 1:00 to 5:00 P.M. Sunday. During the summer hours often change. The central branch can offer information about other branches' hours and programs for children. On-street metered parking is usually available within a few blocks of the main branch on Cathedral Street. (See the Attractions chapter for more information about the library.)

M&T Bank Stadium
1101 Russell Street
(410) 230-8000
www.baltimoreravens.com
A Ravens football game is not the only

attraction at M&T Bank Stadium. For children and the young at heart, a tour through this amazing stadium is entertainment enough. The almost 69,000-seat stadium has more than one million hand-laid bricks throughout its innovative design. Tours are offered every Saturday from 10:00 A.M. to 2:00 P.M., every hour on the hour. However, tours are not available Saturdays of an event or the day before an event, so call ahead. Group tours for 20 or more are also available during the week. The cost of a tour is $5.00 for adults and $4.00 for kids under 12 with all proceeds going to the Ravens Foundation for Families. Highlights of the tour include the many sights you would never get to see on a game day. The tour takes you to the press level, the club level, and suite level, into the Ravens locker room, and for a close-up of the field.

Maryland Science Center
601 Light Street
(410) 685-5225
www.mdsci.org

The Chesapeake Bay, such a vital part of Maryland's life, is the focus of a lot of the science center's exhibits and displays. Kids can also learn how energy is created or explore Earth from satellite pictures in the Space Center. Visitors can step into the shoes of paleontologists and unearth dinosaur fossils in a simulated dig pit experience at Dino Digs. Actual dinosaur tracks (discovered in Maryland) and real dinosaur fossils offer a glimpse back to the time when dinosaurs ruled the planet. The demonstration stage offers live pre- · sentations packed with facts during regularly scheduled science demonstrations.

There is also a 4,000-square-foot hands-on exhibit featuring discoveries from the Hubble Space Telescope and other Maryland-based space science resources. It offers more than 20 original hands-on activities, 12 narrated "video-labels", two full motion, large screen projected videos, two "worlds-first" three-dimensional models of stellar nebula, and over 120 high-resolution images from the Hubble Space Telescope.

Located on the south side of the Inner Harbor and convenient to mass transit and Downtown visitors, the science center offers something to hold every kid's interest as well as many, many hands-on experiments for children as young as three. A visit to the Davis Planetarium will have the kids praying for nightfall so they can look for what they saw inside. The IMAX Theater, which costs extra, lets movie-goers immerse themselves in the action because the screens extend beyond the viewer's range of peripheral vision and treat visitors to a visual odyssey they can't experience elsewhere. The IMAX at the Science Center recently added 3-D capability that puts viewers in the action.

Hours are Tuesday through Friday from 10:00 A.M. to 5:00 P.M., Saturday from 10:00 A.M. to 6:00 P.M., and Sunday from noon to 5:00 P.M. The IMAX Theater is open after hours for evening shows. Admission for the museum only is $4.00 for everyone. IMAX prices are $7.50 for one daytime film; after 6:00 P.M., $9.00 for one film or $12.50 for two films.

Place a slip of paper or a business card in the pockets of each of your children's clothes so that if they get lost the authorities can contact you or will at least know whom to look for.

National Aquarium in Baltimore
Pier 3/501 East Pratt Street
(410) 576-3800
www.aqua.org

Walk into the world of the briny deep at Baltimore's National Aquarium. Five levels exhibit several habitats, ranging from tidal marshes along the coast of Maryland to the dense tropical foliage of a South American rain forest.

Level 1 features stingrays and small sharks in a 265,000-gallon pool. On Level 2, Mountains to the Sea, you can trace the water cycle from a freshwater pond in the mountains of western Maryland through the Tidal Marsh, into the Coastal Beach, and out into the waters of the Atlantic shelf. Visitors to Level 3 are shocked by the voltage created by an electric eel and entangled by the magnificence of a giant Pacific octopus. Patient people in this gallery are rewarded by the sight of tiny jawfish that live in small burrows that they dig.

On Level 4 visitors can see one of the aquarium's newest permanent exhibits which recreates a section of the blackwater Amazon River tributary and the forest that it seasonally floods. Along a 57-foot long acrylic wall, visitors can see schools of tropical fish, giant river turtles, dwarf caimans, caiman lizards, and a giant anaconda. Level 4 also offers the Atlantic Coral Reef, where visitors are surrounded by a rainbow—hundreds of vividly colored tropical fish.

Level 5 offers the Tropical Rain Forest, where careful observers can view colorful birds, golden lion tamarins (monkeys), red-bellied piranhas, and lizards. Other treats at the aquarium include a 1,300-seat aquarium that hosts daily dolphin shows.

A food court and The Aqua Shop, the aquarium's gift shop, round out the offerings here. For more information about the aquarium, including hours and admission prices, see the Attractions chapter.

Oriole Park at Camden Yards
333 West Camden Street
(410) 547-6234
www.theorioles.com

A baseball game is only part of the attraction of Oriole Park at Camden Yards, but unfortunately the beloved O's only play 81 home games from April to October each year. For most kids a 75-minute guided tour of the stadium is equally exciting. This railroad center–turned–ballpark is a mere 12 minutes west by foot from the Inner Harbor and only 2 blocks from the birthplace of baseball's most legendary hero, George Herman "Babe" Ruth (see the Attractions chapter for more on the Babe Ruth Museum). During the tour kids get to sit behind the dugout and at the helm of the control room while getting the behind-the-scenes scoop on the facility, the team,

and the history of this classic stadium. Tour schedules vary, but public tours usually are conducted daily from February 15 to December 23, except on days of afternoon home games. Private tours can be arranged. You can purchase tickets in advance or on the day of a tour from the ticket office in the ballpark warehouse adjacent to gate H. Tickets are $5.00 for adults and $4.00 for children under 12 and seniors. Parking is free during the weekends when the team is away. There is lot parking available during the week for $5.00. It's best to call ahead for details.

Port Discovery
35 Market Place
(410) 727-8120
www.portdiscovery.org

Since opening its doors on December 29, 1998, Port Discovery, the kid-powered museum, is one of the ultimate experiences in fun and learning for children and their families in the Baltimore area. Designed in collaboration with Walt Disney Imagineering and a team of educators, Port Discovery takes education and entertainment to a new level and brings a new vision to the idea of a children's museum. Located in the historic Fishmarket Building, Port Discovery is one of the largest children's museums in the country. On Meet and Greet Street free fun and entertainment, including live performances and special exhibits, is offered. In Kidsworks, children can crawl, jump, slide, swing, and swoosh through a three-story urban treehouse. MPT Studioworks allows kids to watch TV and find out how it works. There is also a learning library designed to enhance the museum experience. Port Discovery is open Monday through Saturday 10:00 A.M. to 5:00 P.M. and Sunday noon to 5:00 P.M. Admission is $11.00 for adults, $10.00 for seniors, $8.50 for children 3 to 12, and free for children under 3.

The museum recently added an outdoor attraction, the HiFlyer Balloon, located adjacent to Port Discovery at the Market Place Metro Subway stop at the intersection of Baltimore and President Streets. The balloon offers up to three rides an hour, each ride lasting about 15 minutes. Helium gently floats the tethered balloon and gondola 450 feet into the air, giving visitors a real bird's-eye view of the city. The balloon runs in the summer months on Monday to Wednesday from 11:30 A.M. to 8:00 P.M., Thursday to Saturday from 11:30 A.M. to 10:00 P.M., and Sunday from noon to 5:00 P.M. Admission is separate from the museum. Day tickets are $8.50 for kids (aged 3 to 12) and $12.00 for adults; after 8:00 P.M., that price jumps to $15.00. The HiFlyer has discounted tickets for groups of 20 or more, and tickets can be purchased at the Port Discovery box office. The gondola is wheelchair accessible.

Washington Monument
Mount Vernon Place
(410) 396-0929

Here's a guaranteed way to wear down those overactive kids. The first monument built to honor the nation's first president is 178 feet tall. The monument has 228 steps to climb, and your kids will love the challenge and the payoff—a view of the city from atop the structure, completed in 1829 after 14 years of work. Tour the base of the monument and see "The Making of the Monument," an exhibit chronicling the history of the monument and Mount Vernon Place. Don't even think about taking kids who won't make it all the way up because it's a long climb for adults, especially with a kid in your arms or on your back; strollers are an absolute no-no. Hearty climbers can give it a try for a $1.00 donation (a small price to pay to use up some of your children's energies) from Wednesday to Sunday from 10:00 A.M. to 4:00 P.M. and on the first Thursday of the month from 10:00 A.M. to 8:00 P.M.

NORTHEAST

Anita C. Leight Estuary Center
700 Otter Point Road, Edgewood
(410) 612-1688
www.otterpointcreek.com

Indoor exhibits designed to teach children about the Chesapeake Bay, the world's largest estuary, include an indoor turtle pond and habitats for reptiles, amphibians, and fish. The Anita C. Leight Estuary Center is the research and education facility of the Chesapeake Bay National Estuarine Research Reserve. It is part of a national reserve system established by Congress in 1972 to protect estuarine areas as natural field laboratories for long-term research and monitoring. Programs include Critter Dinners, where children can learn about turtles, snakes, and fish that live at Otter Point Creek. It also offers a chance to see the captive critters eat.

The reserve also has a pontoon boat that offers an exciting way to explore the waters of Otter Point Creek. Anyone with a minimum weight of 30 pounds is invited on Spring boat rides for a small fee. There are also canoe trips available to explore the marsh. Check out the Web site or call ahead to find out program times and availability.

The facility is about 30 miles north of Baltimore City, off U.S. 40 in Edgewood (exit 77). It's a 40-minute drive but worth the travel time for kids and adults. The center is open Saturday from 10:00 A.M. to 5:00 P.M. and Sunday from noon to 5:00 P.M. No admission is charged.

Baltimore County Public Library
320 York Road, Towson
(410) 887-6100
www.bcplonline.org

The main branch in Towson and the other 14 branches throughout the county provide programs several times a week that target children's interests and books. It's best to contact the main branch to get information about events at the branch closest to you. There is usually no charge, although increasingly libraries have been asking for reservations to control the number of kids participating. Programs include read-alouds, sing-alongs, and activities tied to holiday events. Hours vary from branch to branch, but most children's programs are in the morning or early afternoon.

The free monthly magazine for families, Baltimore's Child, offers tips and suggestions on how to fill hours with entertaining and educational activities. It's available at bookstores, convenience stores, and other locations in the Baltimore area.

Checkered Flag Go-Kart Racing
10907 Pulaski Highway, White Marsh
(410) 335-6393
www.gokartrack.com
Two go-cart courses (one fast and one slow) keep the kids behind the wheel and on the track. Five cars make their way around each track in a four-minute ride that costs $4.00. Bumping or crashing are not allowed. Snacks and a barbecue beef pit provide food and drinks for hungry and thirsty racers. The best time to go is early in the day. The tracks are open from 10:00 A.M. to 11:00 P.M. on weekdays from May to September and until midnight on weekends during those months. From October to January and in March and April, the hours are noon to 8:00 P.M. daily.

Irvine Nature Center
8400 Greenspring Avenue, Stevenson
(410) 484-2413
www.explorenature.org
The Irvine Nature Center, located just north of the city, is the place to take children for a real exploration of the outdoors. Children, families, and adults are invited to explore Maryland Piedmont habitat at the nature center. Irvine features a self-guided nature trail, demonstration gardens to attract wildlife, a natural history museum, live animal exhibits, hands-on exhibits, and a special children's corner. There are also programs, lectures, special events, and other activities. A nature store offers specialty books on gardening, birds, and ecology for all ages, birdfeeders, science kits, binoculars, and selected children's toys. Hours at Irvine are 9:00 A.M. to 4:00 P.M. Monday through Saturday and noon to 4:00 P.M. on Sunday. The trails, museum, and gift shop are free to the public, but guests are encouraged to consider a donation to the center. Programs and special events may have a fee. Call ahead of time for information on the various programs.

Sports
10 Halesworth Road, Cockeysville
(410) 666-2227
For many a Baltimorean, this indoor facility about 8 miles north of Baltimore on I-83 bridges the time between summers with batting cages, miniature golf, machines that simulate boxing and basketball, and all the latest arcade games, as well as many of the favorites of yesteryear. It's madness and mayhem, but everyone is sure to have a good time because there really is at least one game that will entertain everyone. The batting cages pitch baseballs and softballs at Little League (slow), high school league (medium), minor league (fast), and major league (very fast) speeds. Bats and the mandatory batting helmets are provided, and batters get 20 balls for $2.00. Miniature golf costs $4.50 for children under 12 and $5.00 for adults. Arcade games generally cost 50 cents. On weekend nights there may be a wait for the batting cages, miniature golf, and some of the more popular arcade games. The wait might try the patience of younger children, so be prepared. There is also a state-of-the-art rock climbing wall that costs $5.00 for two climbs, and a three-level play area for children that costs $4.00 for unlimited play. There is no admission fee and hours vary, so call ahead. Parking and food, mostly snacks, are available on-site.

Tack 'n Trot
Greenspring Avenue, Lutherville
(410) 526-6641
John and Frances Marryman offer 10-minute pony rides to children for a fee of $5.00 a child. They also offer pony lessons for $25. Their farm, about 3 miles north of Towson, has animals for petting. Tack 'n

Trot operates by appointment seven days a week, so call ahead.

NORTHWEST

The Baltimore Zoo
Druid Hill Park, 1 Druid Park Lake Drive
(410) 366-LION
www.baltimorezoo.org
The third-oldest zoo in the nation has more than 2,250 birds, reptiles, and mammals. Programs such as Keeper Encounters, EdZOOcation classes, behind-the-scenes tours, and zoo camps teach children about endangered wildlife, their habitats, and life cycles. The programs change from day to day, so it's best to call for specific details. The exhibits and cages housing the animals have low sight lines designed to allow kids of all ages to check out the action. The reptile house is a favorite, while the African Safari section offers an insight into life on another continent and is inhabited by elephants, chimpanzees, giraffes, and lions. The Children's Zoo focuses on animals that call Maryland home—from the hills and caves of the western part of the state to the waters and marshes of the Chesapeake Bay. The Children's Zoo, rated number one in the country, also includes hands-on Kid-Zone, where children can hop across lily pads, perch in an oriole's nest, and jump over a frog.

On hot summer days, shaded areas can be at a premium. Benches are available throughout the zoo, and almost every stretch is designed for stroller-pushing families. Refreshments, including beverages, pizza, hot dogs, and snacks, are available at several locations. There's also a carousel in the Village Green section. But don't spend too much time with the fiberglass menagerie. The real McCoys are much more entertaining.

The zoo is open daily, except on Christmas Day and one Friday in June for an annual fundraising event, from 10:00 A.M. to 4:00 P.M. On weekends from May through October, it's open until 6:30 P.M. Adults pay $12.00, while children ages 2 to 11 pay $8.00, and seniors 62 and older pay $10.00. Children younger than 2 are admitted free. On the first Saturday of each month, children younger than 16 get in for free between 10:00 A.M. and noon.

Had enough of the rumbles and roars? Druid Hill Park, a marvelous spot for letting the kids run free, surrounds the zoo. Open areas around a large, fenced-in lake are perfect for everything from a quick game of ball to flying a kite or flying a radio-controlled airplane. The park is free and open daily. (See the Parks and Recreation chapter for more about Druid Hill Park.)

ExploraWorld
6570 Dobbin Road, Columbia
(410) 772-1540
www.exploraworldcolumbia.com
ExploraWorld offers children a hands-on innovative form of entertainment. It includes 25 exhibits and 24,000 square feet of activity area where children can dress up as the King or Queen of their Medieval Castle, become a firefighter with the help of a real fire truck, and even watch themselves sing and dance on an enormous TV screen. There is also a play grocery store, newsroom, doctor's and dentist's office, Puppet Theater, play classroom, nursery rhyme room, and bubble lab. The exhibits are separated with low walls so you can keep track of your little ones. Hours of operation are Sunday 11:30 A.M. to 6:00 P.M., Monday through Thursday 9:30 A.M. to 5:30 P.M., Friday 9:30 A.M. to 6:00 P.M., and Saturday 9:30 A.M. to 7:00 P.M. Admission is $2.00 for adults, $7.95 for children aged 2 and up, $3.95 for children 1 to 2, and children under 12 months are free.

Northwest Family Sports Center Ice Rink
5731 Cottonworth Avenue
(410) 433-2307
This year-round ice-skating rink provides everything from private, group, and family lessons to pickup hockey games to figure skating and speed skating instruction. For those who just want to try an all-skate,

there is plenty of time, mostly on weekends and holidays, for that. Refreshments are available, and parking is on-site. Admission is $6.00 per person, with an additional $2.00 charged for skate rental. Hours vary, with two-hour blocks open for free skating several times a day. Generally the rink is open daily 10:00 A.M. to 10:00 P.M.

SOUTHEAST

Fort McHenry National Monument and Historic Shrine
End of East Fort Avenue
(410) 962-4290
www.nps.gov/fomc
Forget all the history and exhibits inside detailing the writing of "The Star-Span-gled Banner" by Francis Scott Key. Hold-ing cells for prisoners, living quarters within the fort, and cannons lining the perimeter of the facility hold the most interest for young visitors here. Weapons and munitions sit ready for review, while a walkway outside the perimeter of the fort serves as a great vantage point for spot-ting ships coming into the Inner Harbor. Bring along your binoculars.

There is a free, 15-minute informational film shown every 20 minutes from 9:00 A.M. to 4:00 P.M. The entrance fee to the park is $5.00 for adults and free for chil-dren under 16. Bring a jacket—the winds coming up the Patapsco River make it about 15 degrees colder than expected. Also, keep an eye on your brood. Though kids often think the munitions resemble playground equipment, climbing on them is not allowed. Fort McHenry is open from 8:00 A.M. to 5:00 P.M. daily, except Christ-mas and New Year's Days. On-site parking is free and within close walking distance of the fort and indoor exhibits. (See the Attractions chapter for the historical pre-sentations at Fort McHenry.)

SOUTHWEST

The B&O Railroad Museum
901 West Pratt Street
(410) 752-2490
www.borail.org
The history of trains, beginning with the first use in Baltimore more than a century ago, could seem bland on the surface. But at the B&O Railroad Museum, where visi-tors can walk among and board these big, beautiful machines, history comes alive and mesmerizes all those within earshot of a train whistle. The museum suffered during the blizzard of 2003, when the iron struc-ture of the B&O's famed Roundhouse—a signature gold and glass dome on the Balti-more skyline—collapsed under the weight of heavy snow. Damage to the museum and its treasured artifacts means the museum is closed until further notice. Cura-tors and staff are working with structural engineers to rebuild. Call or visit the Web site to inquire about the reopening, which is scheduled for mid-November 2004.

BWI Airport Observation Gallery
I-195, Linthicum
(410) 859-7111
www.bwiairport.com
Everyone knows how intoxicating an air-port can be—the sights, the sounds, the power, the takeoffs, the landings. The Bal-timore–Washington International Airport has an observation lounge between Wings B and C for kids of all ages to enjoy the scenes of a busy airport. In addition to large windows for viewing the action out-side, there's a mockup of an airplane, a baggage train, and a gas truck for kids to climb through and practice their flying and driving skills. On the second floor is an aviation exhibit that includes sections of a real airplane. You can't crawl into the cockpit, but you can look through the glass and push buttons to light up specific cockpit lights. It's the closest kids can get to an airplane without shelling out big bucks for a seat on the next flight out. Parking is the only cost, with the airport garage charging no fee for the first half

hour and $2.00 per half hour afterward. Just remember to keep the kids close by because airport activity is fast and furious, and the opportunity for kids to veer away from parents is often great.

The airport is at the end of I-195. (See the Getting Here, Getting Around chapter for information about adult pursuits at BWI.)

Cider Mill Farm
5012 Landing Road, Elkridge
(410) 788-9595

Several ponies are hitched to a machine, providing a living carousel for kids to ride on the weekends only. At a cost of $2.00 per child, you cannot go wrong with this ride. The farm is about 10 miles south of Baltimore off I-95. Take exit 2. Seven days a week in spring and fall only, Cider Mill Farm is open April through June and September through December from 10:00 A.M. to 6:00 P.M.

Thomas A. Dixon Jr. Airport Observation Area
Dorsey Road, Linthicum
(410) 859-7111
www.bwiairport.com

Near Baltimore–Washington International Airport, off I-97 at exit 15, is an outdoor parking area for observing airplane take-offs and landings. Located to the south of one of the airport's busiest runways, the parking area provides kids of all ages with an up-close view of planes in motion. The planes fly about 200 feet over the site. You'll also find a playground area. During the summer months, stop there to enjoy hot dogs, snowballs—a shaved ice and fla-vor mixture that truly quenches anyone's thirst on a hot, humid day—and other refreshments. The area is part of a 12½-mile scenic trail that encircles the airport property. Watch all you want—there's no admission fee.

ANNUAL EVENTS

Baltimore is a happening place. From family backyard crab feasts to Artscape, our yearly arts and crafts fair that draws crowds of more than one million, we have fun wherever and whenever we can.

These events and festivals are just some of those that occur every year in the Baltimore community. We cannot list them all. In any given week, there are thousands of things to do in the Baltimore area. Our most widely distributed free paper, *City Paper*, devotes about one-quarter of its pages every week to what to do in Baltimore. *Baltimore* magazine does likewise on a monthly basis.

In addition to print publications, three Web sites offer up-to-the-minute information about area events and attractions; the Baltimore Office of Promotion serves as our city's party planners, and it maintains a comprehensive calendar of Baltimore events at www.baltimoreevents.org. The Maryland Office of Tourism has a statewide calendar that highlights activities throughout Maryland at www.mdisfun.org. Finally, the Baltimore Area Convention and Visitors Association keeps a list of happenings at www.baltimore.org.

Each listing that follows tries to answer the questions what, where, when, why, and how, but in an attempt to cut out the extraneous or repetitive information, there are a few things you'll want to know up front. Most festival and event locations are user friendly; therefore, they are wheelchair accessible and bathrooms of some sort are on-site. If an event does not have a bathroom, we'll tell you. Otherwise, assume it does. We'll tell you if an event is free or list the admission fees. Prices often go up from year to year, so if price is a determining factor as to whether or not you'll attend an event, call the contact number provided to get the most recent fees.

Parking Downtown can cost as little as $1.50 an hour to about $22.00 a day. The closer you get to the Inner Harbor, the more expensive the parking. So, if you have no aversion to walking a few blocks, parking a few blocks north will save you some bucks. Coming early will also save you money. In most harbor lots, checking in before 9:00 A.M. will net you almost 50 percent in savings; if you're parking all day, that's $11.00 versus $22.00.

For specific dates of annual festivals and information on other events, concerts, and celebrations in Baltimore, consult the Media chapter for where to find publications that carry these up-to-the-minute details. Or contact the following organizations: the Baltimore Area Convention and Visitors Association, 100 Light Street, 12th Floor, (410) 837–4636 or (800) 282–6632; Baltimore Office of Promotion, 200 West Lombard Street, (410) 752–8632; and Maryland Office of Tourism, 217 East Redwood Street, (800) 719–5900 or (800) MDISFUN.

JANUARY

Baltimore's New Year's Day
Children's Fireworks
7 East Redwood Street
(410) 752–8632
www.bop.org
For those youngsters who could not keep their eyes open for the fireworks at midnight, Baltimore puts on an encore presentation with a mini-fireworks display choreographed to children's music. The show begins at sundown (usually 6:00 P.M.). Come early and strap on your ice skates for a twirl under the glorious Baltimore skyline at the Inner Harbor Ice Rink located at Rash Field on Key Highway (see the Attractions chapter) within walking distance from the Maryland Science Center.

Edgar Allan Poe Birthday Celebration
Westminster Hall,
Fayette and Green Streets
(410) 396-7932
www.poecelebration.tripod.com
Throughout the entire weekend closest to Poe's January 19th birthday, Poe House sponsors a celebration in honor of the life and works of Edgar Allan Poe. Events vary from year to year but include such goodies as theatrical presentations of Poe's stories, musical renditions of his poems, a bagpipe tribute and a graveside toast—after dark, of course. More than 1,000 people attend the celebration, which begins Friday evening with repeat performances Saturday evening and Sunday afternoon. Prices vary, but tend to run in the $18 to $25 range, with evening events usually commanding a higher price. Parking is on the street or in a nearby garage.

Reverend Dr. Martin Luther King Jr. Birthday Celebration Parade
Parade route follows Martin Luther King Jr. Boulevard, between Eutaw and Russell Streets
(410) 752-8632
www.bop.org
Baltimoreans love a good parade, and this is no exception. The city takes to the streets of Downtown to celebrate the birth of civil rights leader Reverend Martin Luther King Jr. Many of Baltimore's own living legends participate in the parade, including past civil rights activists and prominent community and political figures. Floats, marching bands, choirs, and dancers add to the festive commemoration. This is a free event.

Fishing Expo and Boat Show
Maryland State Fairgrounds
2200 York Road, Timonium
(410) 838-8687
www.fishingexpo.com
Maryland is a state crisscrossed with lakes, rivers, and streams, and our proximity to the bay and the ocean make angling and water sports a major pastime. It makes sense, then, that the East Coast's largest

fishing expo is held here each year in mid-January. Bass, saltwater, and fly-fishing retailers sell their goods while boat companies and fishing supply manufacturers display their latest toys. Seminars and demonstrations help reel in the crowds, and patrons can try their hand at pulling in a live trout. Discount coupons for admission are frequently offered on the Web site. Prices are $8.00 for adults and $4.00 for ages 10 to 14; children under 10 admitted free. Parking is free.

Horse World Expo
Maryland State Fairgrounds
2200 York Road, Timonium
(301) 916-0852
www.horseworldexpo.com
Marylanders love the field as much as the stream, and our state boasts an impressive history of steeplechase and horse races. This event, usually held mid-January, is a must for horse lovers. Hundreds of vendors boast a plethora of horse products and services for every breed of horse and every discipline of riding. A parade of breeds, educational seminars, and demonstrations are scheduled throughout the three-day event. Admission is $8.00 for adults and $4.00 for children 10 to 14; children under ten are admitted free. Admission prices may go up so it's worth calling in advance to confirm. All activities are indoors and heated. Parking is free.

Fridays After Five National Aquarium,
Pier 3/501 East Pratt Street
(410) 576-3800
www.aqua.com
The National Aquarium is one of the many treasures not to be missed at Baltimore's Inner Harbor, and now you can visit the denizens of the deep for a discounted price. For several years, on Fridays after 5:00 P.M. from mid-September to early March, the aquarium opens its doors to patrons for more than half off the regular admission price. Because of the event's popularity, tickets are sold in timed blocks. This means you can enjoy the miracles of the sea without getting crushed by over-

whelming crowds, but it may also mean you'll have some time to kill before your ticket is valid. Not to worry—the aquarium is a stone's throw from the Harbor's restaurants and shops. On Friday evenings tickets can be purchased until 8:00 P.M., and the aquarium stays open until 10:00 P.M. to accommodate visitors (see the Attractions chapter for admission). The aquarium is on a pier at the harbor so there is no adjacent parking. Parking is available at Inner Harbor parking garages, nearby metered lots, or on the street. A semicircle drive off of Pratt Street allows you to drop off individuals who prefer not to walk from the parking lots.

Baltimore is divided into north and south by Baltimore Street and east and west by Charles Street. The first block in any direction from those streets is what's known as the unit block. The 100 block is actually the second block away from those streets, so 10 East Baltimore Street is in the unit block east of Charles Street—the first block—and 101 East Baltimore Street is in the second block.

FEBRUARY

Black Heritage Art Show
Baltimore Convention Center
1 West Pratt Street, Baltimore
(410) 521-0660
www.aavaa.org
February is Black History Month, and there is no better way to celebrate than with a weekend of cultural activities and the nation's best African-American visual artists. The second weekend of the month, the African American Visual Arts Association brings together visual and performing artists, lecturers, jazz and gospel singers, and poets for a showcase of contemporary arts and crafts. This is a rare opportunity to meet internationally and nationally acclaimed African-American artists and to

purchase their work. Admission is free. There are no food vendors at this event, so do not come on an empty stomach! The Baltimore Convention Center does not have parking on-site, but several garages, like the one at Camden Yards, offer nearby parking for $5.00 per hour.

Hunt Valley Antiques Show
Holiday Inn Select
(410) 366-1980, ext. 253
www.fcsmd.org
Looking for that special something to make your house a home? For more than 30 years, the Hunt Valley Antiques Show has offered an exquisite lineup of the country's most reputable antiques dealers. Fifty-plus merchants sell a mix of items such as furniture, Oriental rugs, jewelry, and ceramics. These antiques are rare, and the prices reflect the quality of the goods. Those interested in learning more about the fine art of collecting may wish to participate in one of the many lectures or guided show tours. Tours are free with general admission, while lectures are $50. A $12 general admission fee includes a show catalogue with dealer biographies and informative articles. Parking is free and there are several restaurants on-site for a sit-down meal or a quick snack. Current event details—like great raffles, auction prizes, and dates—are highlighted on the Web site.

The ACC Craft Fair of Baltimore
Baltimore Convention Center
1 West Pratt Street
(410) 583-5401
www.craftcouncil.org
For more than 20 years, The American Craft Council fair has provided crafters space to exhibit their work. The more than 800 crafters you'll see have to go through an arduous judging process to be allowed to exhibit. Artists come from all over the country—Baltimore included. Unlike some judged shows, where the artist can send a representative to man his booth, at the ACC Fair, the artist/crafter must attend the event; and all of the items must be

handmade in the United States. Crafts include ceramics, glass, wood, metal, jewelry, fiber, and leather. Although the American Craft Council hosts these fairs in six other cities across the country, each one invites different artisans. So, if you've attended one in Atlanta, you haven't necessarily seen it all. The ACC Craft Fair is usually held over a weekend in late February but sometimes meanders into early March, so call for exact dates. Admission is $12 for adults, and there is a two-day pass that can be purchased for $18. Kids younger than 12 get in free. The Convention Center has no parking on-site, but parking is available at Camden Yards just across the street for $5.00 per hour.

Travel Expo
Baltimore Convention Center
1 West Pratt Street
(410) 332-6470
www.sunspot.net/travelexpo

This mammoth consumer travel show takes place the last weekend in February or the first weekend in March and attracts an average of 12,000 people over two days. More than 70 exhibitors representing the U.S. and most international countries stand ready to help you realize your ultimate holiday getaway. Savvy travelers should be able to strike exceptional deals. Local entertainment—like a popular steel drum band—adds to the flavor of the show. The Convention Center's in-house caterer provides basic concession food for an additional cost. Admission is $5.00 for individuals and $10.00 for a family of four; children under 12 are admitted free. Parking is available at a lot on Camden Street for $5.00.

Fridays After Five National Aquarium
Pier 3/501 East Pratt Street
(410) 576-3800
www.aqua.org

Come and party with the fishes every Friday night from mid-September through early March. Special guest appearances each week in honor of Black History Month. See the January entry for more information.

MARCH

Monster Jam
First Mariner Arena
201 West Baltimore Street
(410) 347-2020
www.baltimorearena.com

The U.S. Hot Rod Association brings its famous monster trucks to the Baltimore Arena for a weekend of explosive automotive antics. Souped-up trucks, like the popular Gravedigger, catapult over cars and obstacles in the dirt pit of the arena. Novelty vendors offer fun souvenirs, and on-site concession stands serve up snackfood and beverages. The Monster Jam is usually held in early March, but scheduling demands can move the event to late February. Advance tickets are $16.00 for adults and $8.00 for kids 12 and younger. Event-day prices are $20.00 and $10.00, respectively. A parking garage is attached to the Arena. Pre-event traffic can make negotiating the one-way streets around the arena tricky, so plan to get Downtown early to park.

Maryland Spring Craft Show and Maryland Home and Flower Show
Maryland State Fairgrounds, 2200 York Road, Timonium
(410) 863-1180
www.mdhomeandgarden.com

Every year the Home and Flower Show has a theme. "Historic Maryland" was the 2003 theme. Held over two weekends toward the middle of March, it's a gigantic show, with more than 500 exhibits of professionally landscaped gardens and home products. There are two sides to the fairgrounds—one is completely outdoor landscaping, for which prizes are given, the other is crafts and home improvement items. Free seminars on gardening and home crafts are offered, and there's a huge plant sale. There's also lots of good food and garden benches to rest on. The entrance fee for adults is $9.00 (seniors are $8.00), and for kids age 6 to 12, it's $2.50. Children younger than 6 are admitted free. There's no charge to park at the fairgrounds. Pick up coupons on the Web site.

Spring is horse season in Maryland, with a race just about every weekend. The tailgate drink of choice at the Hunt Cup is the South Side (equal part South Side mix, dark rum, and club soda) while at the Preakness the favorite is the Black-Eyed Susan (bourbon and lemonade). But if you want to look like a true native, imbibe a "Natty Boh, hon" (National Bohemian beer).

St. Patrick's Day Parade and 5-K Run
Downtown city streets
(410) 750-8617
www.irishparade.net
The Sunday closest to the annual Irish holiday includes a parade and a 5-K Shamrock Run through Downtown. The parade forms in Mount Vernon at the Washington Monument and steps off around 2:00 P.M., heading South on Charles Street. Thirty Irish organizations, 20 marching bands, pipe and drum corps, and politicians wind their way through the city heading east on Pratt Street and disbanding at Market Place. The 5-K race follows the parade route and starts at 1:35 P.M. Pre-registration is required for the race and costs $20 before March 1, $25 after March 1, or $30 the day of the race. Watching the parade and the race is free. Some years a brunch is held before the parade; in the past it was held at the Camden Club in Camden Yards for an additional fee. Rain or shine.

Contemporary Print Fair
Baltimore Museum of Art
10 Art Museum Drive
(410) 396-6345
www.artbma.org
For over a decade the Print & Drawing Society of the Baltimore Museum of Art (BMA) has coordinated one of the only fairs dedicated to the sale of contemporary prints, drawings, photographs, and other works on paper. Twenty distinguished national art dealers offer a wide range of museum-quality images at this biennial one-day event, which takes place on a Sunday in mid-March in even numbered years. Admission to the fair also affords you access to the BMA's extraordinary collection, so plan on spending the day at the museum (see the BMA listing in The Arts chapter). And since it takes place on Sunday, you should plan to partake in the spectacular brunch menu at the museum's in-house restaurant, Gertrude's, featuring the best in Chesapeake Bay and Southern cuisine (reservations are recommended). Admission to the show is $5.00 for BMA members, $8.00 for students and seniors, and $10.00 for nonmembers. The museum has two free parking lots and the adjacent Johns Hopkins University frequently opens its lots to museum guests on Sundays.

The Greenberg Train Show
Maryland State Fairgrounds
2200 York Road, Timonium
(410) 795-7447
www.greenbergshows.com
Three times a year Baltimore is treated to intricate displays of model trains. This hobby-specific show is ideal for families looking for a fun outing as well as the expert model train fanatic looking for the latest addition for a serious collection. At least 100 exhibitors offer a one-stop shop for trains, parts and accessories, and decals. "Meet the Masters" clinics provide practical advice from experts about starting, maintaining, and developing your very own train collection and building your own model railroad. Complex model railroad displays are one of the event's more popular attractions, and a few hands-on layouts even let the kids run the action. On-site food vendors offer snacks and beverages. Greenberg's is a traveling show that goes up and down the East Coast, but it does hold three shows locally. This first one is in mid-March, the second show happens during the summer months, and the third usually takes place in early December. Parking is free. Admission is $6.00 for adults and $2.00 for children ages 6 through 12. Admission usually goes up each year, so call or visit the Web site

for the most recent information.

The Great American Train Show has agreed in principal to purchase Greenberg's Train Shows, the nation's second-largest train show company, from Kalmbach Publishing Co., the nation's largest model train magazine publisher. This may change the frequency of events, so please be sure to check ahead.

Smith College Book Sale
Towson Armory, 307 Washington Avenue, Towson
(410) 821-6241

The Smith College Club of Baltimore, founded in 1917, has been holding its Smith College Book Sale in late March or early April for more than 40 years to raise money for scholarships to help local girls attend Smith. All year long, when sorting and cleaning, we pile up any books and records we can no longer use and trot them over to the Smith College Club. The sale is a great motivator to clean off shelves. Items are reasonably priced all weekend, but be advised that on Sunday all books and records are half-price noon to 5:00 P.M., after which the sale closes for an hour. It re-opens at 6:00 P.M., and from then until closing, it's all you can carry in your arms for $2.00! There is no food served, but drink vending machines are available.

On Friday the sale opens at 10:00 A.M., but to get in the door that first hour (when your pickings are greatest), the price is $5.00. At 11:00 A.M., the doors open for free, and the sale has no entrance fee from that point on. Saturday hours are 10:00 A.M. to 6:00 P.M., and Sunday the sale opens at noon. Parking is available on the street or at public parking garages nearby. No credit cards or checks are accepted.

Fridays After Five National Aquarium
Pier 3/501 East Pratt Street
(410) 576-3800
www.aqua.org

Joy to the fishes in the deep blue sea . . . and everyone else who comes to enjoy

this after-work party at the Aquarium. Discounted tickets on Friday evenings from mid-September through early March. See the January entry for admission prices.

APRIL

Inner Harbor Easter Celebration
Harborplace Amphitheater
Pratt and Light Streets
(410) 752-8632
www.baltimoreevents.org

Easter Sunday, beginning around 11:00 A.M., the city sponsors a celebration at the Inner Harbor. It began simply because so many people, who wanted someplace to go after church all dressed up in their Easter finery, headed down to Harborplace. Now it's a full-fledged celebration with great food, a roving Easter Bunny, and live music until 7:00 P.M. There is no admission. Parking is at lots around the Inner Harbor.

The Baltimore Symphony Decorators' Show House
Location varies annually
(410) 783-8023
www.baltimoresymphony.org

Each year for more than a quarter of a century the Baltimore Symphony Associates have taken one of Baltimore's architecturally renowned homes and updated its interior with the help of the area's finest designers. In addition to a tour of the exquisitely redecorated manor, visitors may shop at an on-premises boutique and dine at a small tea room. To see the true transformation, you can attend the Empty House Tour two months prior to the event for $5.00. There are some restrictions to the show: Because this is a private residence, it is not wheelchair accessible. Also, no cameras are allowed and no high heels. No children under 10 are allowed, including infants.

The Show House runs from mid-April to mid-May. Admission is $12. Advance tickets can be purchased from area stores for $10. Specific information on where to purchase discounted advance tickets is made available on the symphony's Web site by February or by calling the contact number.

Johns Hopkins University Spring Fair
Homewood Campus,
Johns Hopkins University
(410) 516-7692
www.jhuspringfair.com

The Spring Fair is a three-day event planned, organized, and run exclusively by John Hopkins students, and it attracts members of the student body and the community at large. Food, music, and art vendors round out carnival rides, children's shows, and activities.

There are usually two or three musical stages featuring daytime concerts and entertainment and larger evening concerts. Admission is free, and the fair runs from noon on Friday through Sunday evening in early April. Parking lots are available on campus, but be sure to read the signs carefully—some spots are reserved for faculty and staff, even on the weekends and in the evenings. Additional parking can be found at the meters along University Parkway or on the streets in the adjacent Charles Village neighborhood.

The Maryland Hunt Cup
Glyndon, Maryland
(410) 527-9299
www.marylandhuntcup.com

The last weekend in April for more than 100 years has seen the running of the Maryland Hunt Cup. This cross-country steeplechase, which is thought by many racing Insiders to be the most difficult race of its kind in the world, is held on private land. Amateur competitors come from all over the Mid-Atlantic region as well as from places as far away as England. Tickets to the race, which are $35 to $70 per car, must be purchased in advance. Bring a picnic lunch and plan to tailgate with pitchers of South Sides (if you don't know about this Southern tradition, see our Insiders' Tip in this chapter). Call the Maryland Historical Society, (410)

685-3750, for information about its luncheon held under tent for an additional fee.

The Mayor's Billie Holiday Vocal Competition
Center Stage, Head Theater
(410) 752-8632
www.baltimorecity.gov/arts

In celebration of Baltimore's own jazz legend Billie Holiday, this is the city's search for the state's perfect set of pipes. Each singer gets to perform a rendition of a Lady Day signature song, as well as a melody of their own choosing. Admission to the show is free and open to the public, but tickets are required and available through Center Stage from 9:00 A.M. to 1:00 P.M. on the first Saturday in April and on the day of the competition (see The Arts chapter for more information on Center Stage). Only two tickets are allowed per person.

MAY

Baltimore Waterfront Festival
Inner Harbor's West Shore and
Rash Field
Key Highway
(410) 752-8632
www.baltimoreevents.org

Baltimore's waterfront comes alive in early May for a celebration of the sea. Live music and entertainment are backgrounds to an outdoor adventure area that boasts a simulated rock wall. Visitors can learn how to hoist a sail or visit an environmental village that highlights life on the Chesapeake Bay. A Chesapeake Kitchen features popular chefs whipping up delicious seafood dishes. You can also taste the nation at the international ports of call—booths that allow visitors to explore food and traditions from nations far and wide. The event runs for one weekend, Friday through Sunday, and is free. Hours are usually Friday and Saturday 7:00 to 10:00 P.M., and Sunday 4:00 to 8:00 P.M.

Maryland Film Festival
Locations vary
(410) 752-8083
www.mdfilmfest.com

This four-day festival is Maryland's own Sundance, bringing world-renowned film-makers and movies to Baltimore, usually the first weekend in May. Not that we have to look far outside our own city limits for great motion picture art; Baltimore has a ripe filmmaking scene, with talented natives like John Waters and Barry Levin-son using the city as inspiration. But the Maryland Film Festival extends its reach globally and presents more than 120 for-eign and domestic feature films and shorts. An opening night kickoff usually takes place at the historic Senator theater, one of the oldest historic film houses in the region. Films are primarily screened at the Charles Theater (see The Arts chapter for more information on both movie houses). Screenings include an introduc-tion by the director or the producer with a Q & A session after. Special lectures and presentations take place throughout the weekend. Waters and Levinson have been guest speakers in the past. Children's events are always inspirational—one year the festival presented a silent-movie ver-sion of Peter Pan accompanied by a full orchestra! Admission to one film is $10, a three-show pass is $20, and an all-access pass for the entire event is $250. Student and senior discounts may be applicable.

Towsontown Spring Festival
In and around the Old Courthouse Plaza
1 block west of York Road and
Pennsylvania Avenue
(410) 825-1144
www.towsontownspringfestival.com

This spring fair has been entertaining visi-tors and residents for more than 30 years. It's a large event (attracting 200,000 peo-ple) that always has local as well as national bands as live entertainment on various stages throughout the fairgrounds. (The "fairgrounds" are a 4-block area between Allegheny Avenue on the north

to Susquehanna Avenue on the south.) Every year features local microbreweries, more than 40 food vendors, and many arts and crafts booths. There are plenty of children's activities, including a children's stage and the Annual Towsontown Spring Festival Youth Art Show, in which young artists get to show off their best work. This free event is held the first full week-end in May. All-day parking is available for around $8.00.

The Preakness Parade and Preakness Week
East on Pratt Street to Market Place
(410) 752-8632
www.bop.org

The Preakness Parade (held the Saturday before the Preakness) begins Preakness Week, a celebration in early-to-mid-May that often includes a hot-air balloon ascension, outdoor concerts, schooner races, benefit galas, fireworks, and more, and culminates in the running of the Preakness Stakes, "the second jewel in horse racing's triple crown." (See the Spectator Sports chapter for more about the Preakness.) As always, we hope for a fast, dry track and a warm sunny day for the race. If we're lucky, we get the same for the parade. Spring is not yet in full bloom at this time of year, but the for-sythia is often out, and the hyacinth should definitely be up. So, put on a jacket, buy some cotton candy, and watch the equestrian units, the marching bands, the clowns, and the floats. Admission is free. (See the *Baltimore Sun* and other

---

Many local antiques shows are benefits for area not-for-profits. To raise addi-tional funds for their cause, event plan-ners frequently offer a preview party the day before the show officially begins. Admission to these parties can be steep, but the trade-off is the chance to buy the objects for sale before the onslaught of the public, a real boon if you are a serious collector.

---

local publications the week before the parade for lists of activities during Preakness Week or call the Preakness Celebration number, (410) 837–3030, to receive a booklet that has it all.)

The Flower Mart
Mount Vernon Square,
Monument and Charles Streets
(410) 323-0022
www.flowermart.org

For more than 80 years, The Flower Mart has been Baltimore's harbinger of spring. The Wednesday of Preakness Week Charles Street is closed off and people crowd the cobblestone streets of Mount Vernon Square for the season's first taste of crab cakes and lemon sticks (if you are not familiar with this delicacy, see our Insiders' Tip in this chapter). Visitors scour the 200 vendors for the best bedding plants, hanging flowers, and garden-themed arts and crafts. Entertainment and plant clinics run throughout the day, and a concert takes place in the evening from 6:00 to 8:00 P.M. Come and make a day of it in the Mount Vernon cultural district. Nearby you'll find the Walters Art Museum, the Maryland Historical Society, and the Peabody Conservatory of Music, to name a few, as well as a number of interesting little shops and galleries up and down Charles Street (see the Attractions, Shopping, and The Arts chapters for more details). The Flower Mart is free, and many of the museums and attractions offer a discounted admission in honor of the event.

The Preakness Stakes
Pimlico Race Course
5201 Park Heights Avenue
(410) 542-9400
www.marylandracing.com

The third Saturday in May marks the annual running of the Preakness Stakes and has for more than 125 years. Gates usually open at 8:30 A.M. for the infield, which is the area inside the track. Infield seats are popular, first because you are right at eye level with the horses; second, because seats are less expensive; and third, because it's a great all-day picnic. When you look at the infield on television, it looks as if infielders are trapped, since the races run around them; but, in fact, there is a tunnel under the track that allows you to come and go as you please, but why would you want to go? Concession stands, betting windows, and the all-important portable toilets are available for infielders. Clubhouse and grandstands seats are more expensive (from $50 to $100), but you don't have to fight the crowd to see the racing, since all seats are reserved. The clubhouse, which is under roof, is the most posh seating, and guests dress for the occasion. (If you purchase a clubhouse seat, don't go in jeans.) Racing begins at 10:30 A.M., but the Preakness goes off at around 6:05 P.M. and is the next to last race of the day. For standing-room-only, clubhouse admission is $18, and general admission is $15. Infield admission is $37 in advance or $42 on Preakness Day. Call for reserved seating prices. Parking can be difficult. Traffic backs up for miles, so give yourself plenty of time to get there if you're driving and wear your walking shoes. Sometimes you can find inexpensive parking on someone's front lawn, but you might have to walk more than a mile. Parking at the track costs $30 to $125. However, public transportation is available, including Light Rail, and often special shuttles are set up around the city.

Market Day
Cylburn Arboretum
4915 Greenspring Avenue
(410) 367-2217
www.cylburnassociation.org

For more than 20 years, the Cylburn Arboretum Association, the volunteer group that keeps the 207-acre nature reserve running smoothly, has held Market Day on the day before Mother's Day. The group's main fundraiser, Market Day is an opportunity for us to get out in the fresh spring air and look over a selection of plants for this summer's backyard or window box. Baltimore's horticulturists are out in full force with their best offerings of flowers, vegetables, and, as one Insider put it, "just about any plant you can imagine." Crafters are also in evidence with crafts constructed on a gardening theme. While you wander through the booths or down one of Cylburn's many nature trails, you will not go hungry. Common Market Day fare includes crab cakes, fried chicken, hamburgers, and hot dogs. But don't stay out among the trees too long or you'll miss the annual maypole dance. Gates open at 8:00 A.M. and the formal closing is 2:00 P.M., but visitors tend to linger. Parking is $4.00; admission is $2.00.

**The Baltimore Symphony
Decorators' Show House
Location varies annually
(410) 783-8023
www.baltimoresymphony.org**
Come see how the other half lives at this event sponsored by the Baltimore Symphony Associates. For more than two decades, the group has given one of Baltimore's homes to designers to decorate. An Empty House Tour, given before each year's decorating begins, allows you to truly appreciate the work involved in the project. See the April entry for more information.

**BALTICON: Maryland Regional
Science Fiction Convention
Wyndham Baltimore Inner Harbor Hotel
101 West Fayette Street
(410) 563-2737
www.balticon.org**
More than 200 science fiction authors, artists, musicians, aficionados, and actual scientists—of which we have plenty in Baltimore—meet to talk about what they're doing, reading, and thinking at this convention held over a weekend in late May. Tickets prices are based on how far in advance they are purchased, ranging from $37 several months from the event,

to $52 just a few weeks before the event. For more information, call the Baltimore Science Fiction Society at the listed number or write to P.O. Box 686, Baltimore, MD 21203. Beam on in if you can, and may the force be with you in your quest.

JUNE

**Maryland Rose Society, Inc.
Annual Rose Show
Cylburn Arboretum
4915 Greenspring Avenue
(410) 367-2217
www.cylburnassociation.org**
In early June Maryland's roses are in full bloom at the Annual Rose Show. Growers, both members of the Rose Society and others, come to the mansion at Cylburn to display their beauties. All registered categories of roses may be entered, and the roses are judged by a panel of experts for their perfection. Members of the Rose Society staff a booth to answer questions about growing roses, and information is available that you can take home. If nothing else, the Rose Show gives anyone who visits a gift of the scent of summer—without the bees. Parking and admission are free.

**Greek Festival
St. Nicholas Church,
520 South Ponca Street
(410) 633-5020
www.greek-fest.com**
One of Baltimore's most popular festivals, the Greek Festival is an immersion into all things Greek. Food is always a major draw at the ethnic festivals. At the Greek Festival, it's the stuffed grape leaves and the baklava you'll find us hunting down first. If you'd like to learn how to make such treats the Greek way, the festival offers cooking lessons and cooking demonstrations. To work off what you eat, there's Greek dancing. The festival is held the second weekend of the month. Admission is free.

Between 20,000 and 30,000 people descend on this small community, and

ANNUAL EVENTS

parking is difficult, because it is all on-street parking. In recent years, organizers have utilized the Downtown trolley system. Festival goers can park Downtown and hop on the trolley on Pratt Street to bring them over to the festival grounds. Call to confirm before relying on the trolley—some years it does not run.

Gay Pride Festival
Various locations
(410) 837-5445
www.baltimorepride.org/festival.htm
Toward the middle of June, the Gay, Lesbian, Bisexual, and Transgender Association of Baltimore sponsors a weekend celebration to which all are invited. On Saturday a Gay Pride Parade heads north on Charles Street, through the Mount Vernon neighborhood, and disbands at Eager Street for a rowdy block party. The festivities continue on Sunday when the gay community hosts a festival at Druid Hill Park beginning at noon. Under the trees on the grassy lawn of the park you can listen to live music, taste ethnic food, and visit more than 100 booths full of information, arts, and crafts. More than 20,000 people attend this function, making it one of the largest gay pride events on the East Coast. The festival is free.

City Sand
Harborplace Amphitheater
Pratt and Light Streets
(410) 332-4191
www.harborplace.com
Baltimoreans love to spend their summers down at the ocean frolicking in the surf, and most natives have fond memories of building sand castles on their summer vacations. Harborplace brings a taste of the ocean to Downtown when it invites teams of architects and other design professionals to build creative sand sculptures based on an annual theme. Contestants arrive early Saturday morning to construct their masterpieces using only sand, water, and a spade. The event opens to the public from noon to 4:00 P.M. and

includes food, live music, and an awards presentation. Admission is free. The structures are left standing through Sunday, when kids are invited to climb into the giant sandboxes, knock down the masterpieces, and build their own works of art. The event takes place mid-to-late June.

Latino Fest
Location varies
(410) 783-5404
www.eblo.org
The Latino Fest is a celebration of folk music, dance, arts, and crafts from all of Central and South America. Groups perform folk music of the Andes, Latin jazz, and salsa. Arts and crafts displays and demonstrations include handcrafted pottery, silver from Peru, and woolens from Ecuador and Bolivia. Sponsored by the education-based Latino Outreach, all funds raised support children's educational and cultural programs for the Latino community. There is always plenty of dancing, as well as a dance contest. So, if you consider yourself a mambo expert, put on your dancin' shoes and come on down.

The Latino Fest, which usually takes place over a weekend in late June, has been held at a couple of different locations over the years. Previously it's been held at Hopkins Plaza and Patterson Park. We suggest you call the listed number to verify the location before you head out the door. Admission is a $3.00 donation.

JULY

Baltimore's Fourth of July Celebration
Inner Harbor
(410) 752-8632
www.bop.org
The rockets' red glare—and blue and white—casts its sparkles on the water within sight of where "The Star-Spangled Banner" was penned. If you've never seen fireworks over water, push your way into the crowd for this. It's beautiful. It's as if the sea opens up and shows another world

below, exploding into magical lights. Here's a hint, however, if you decide to go. The Harborplace Amphitheater is not a building. It's the walkway between the harbor itself and the pavilions at Harborplace. The steps serve as seats, but for this show everyone stands anyway. The free show begins at 9:30 P.M. Parking can be a nightmare, so arrive early and be patient.

Baltimore Playwrights Festival
Various locations
(410) 276-2153
www.baltplayfest.org
Every summer for more than 20 years Baltimore's Downtown community theaters have hosted the Baltimore Playwrights Festival, a celebration of the best Maryland playwrights. The festival has premiered more than 160 plays since its inception, and usually highlights 10 to 12 productions a year in seven theaters around town. Plays are selected by the end of March through a rigorous judging process, and open auditions for actors are held in April. Individual ticket prices vary from theater to theater, but an advanced subscription package (six tickets for $45) can be purchased.

Artscape
West Mount Royal Avenue,
beginning south of North Avenue
(410) 752-8632
www.artscape.org
Artscape is a city-sponsored free event that was started in the mid-1980s and is now one of the country's largest public arts celebrations. Strung out along Mount Royal Avenue from The Maryland Institute College of Art, bending around in front of the Lyric Theatre and around the Meyerhoff Symphony Hall are hundreds of arts and crafts vendors and 30 food vendors. There are potters and woodworkers, glassworkers and ironworkers—just about every kind of worker you can imagine. You can buy tiny origami earrings or a 6-foot carved statue. There are paintings, drawings, and etchings. Galleries abound, as do

live theater productions and poetry readings. There's great kidstuff at the Maryland Institute, and it's different every year. (Our personal favorite was the Lego village the kids built one year. It took up three rooms when it was finished!) Through it all, local and national talent provide continuous music; 2002 saw the addition of "DJ Culture," where the best local DJs spun their vinyl vibe. Everywhere you turn, you find food from traditional pit beef to delicately flavored crepes. Since more than a million fairgoers come over these three days during the third or fourth weekend of July, parking is difficult as people jockey for spots on the street or in lots. One of the most sensible ways to get there is by Light Rail, as there is a Light Rail stop right in the middle of the "fairgrounds." It can get hot on the city streets in July, so dress appropriately.

AUGUST

The Greenberg Train Show
Maryland State Fairgrounds
2200 York Road, Timonium
(410) 795-7447
www.greenbergshows.com
Running out of ideas to entertain the kids during the last weeks of summer? Think you'll crack before you get them back into school? Take heart—and take your children to this panoramic toyland. Usually staged in early August, as well as late March and early December, Greenberg will entertain your little ones for hours on end. See the March entry for more information.

The Inner Harbor is the name given both to the actual harbor in the center of Baltimore and the area that surrounds it. The main activity center is at the head of the Inner Harbor, in and around the Harborplace shopping area at the corner of Pratt and Light Streets.

Gospel Music Crab Feast
Oregon Ridge Park, Beaver Dam Road, 1 mile south of Shawan Road, Hunt Valley
(888) 375-0080
www.crabfeast.com
The Dixie Hummingbirds once performed at this all-day, outdoor gospel event usually held in early August. Essentially a picnic with music, the fare includes hamburgers, hot dogs, pit beef, as well as crabs. Admission ranges from $35 to $69, which includes the music as well as the fabulous fare. People come from all over to attend this event, so reservations are required at least 48 hours in advance, but group discounts are available, if you want to reserve space for two busloads of folks from your church. Note: If you're not into gospel music, this same group hosts a number of different themed crab feasts throughout the city.

India Day
Center Plaza, Charles Street
(410) 337-9567
Toward the middle of August the India Forum, in conjunction with the Baltimore Office of Promotions, puts on a free festival that not only celebrates Indian heritage but also provides information about Baltimore to the community at large. Information booths concern local schools and businesses, but the main focus is the Indian culture. The smell of curry, the whirling dancers, and the sound of ankle bells fill the square. Vendors offer Indian jewelry and decorated silks. Kids will enjoy the face painting, but decorative hand-painting is also available for the older "kids," as is palmistry. The best fun is the closing ceremonies, in which all present are invited to learn and dance the Dandia Dance in celebration.

The Maryland Renaissance Festival
Crownsville, 20 minutes south of the city off State Highway 97
(800) 296-7304
www.rennfest.com
The Maryland Renaissance Festival is habit-forming. Fondly called "The Renny" by some of those addicted, its permanent Renaissance village is truly a step back in time. Many of the crafters who attend actually reside in the village for the festival's duration. Attendees often dress up in medieval costume, but if you don't have one and want one, there are booths where costumes can be rented or bought. You can see glass blown and etched, metal work, clay work, leather craftsmen, and much more. The food is very Henry VIII—whole turkey legs, french-fried sweet potatoes, soup in bread bowls. But not everything is dinner. You can also buy a fresh glass of ice-cold milk and a pile of homemade chocolate chip cookies for about a buck. Or how about a homemade apple dumpling smothered in vanilla ice cream? There's jousting, Shakespeare, magic, madrigals, and more. One of the most interesting things about the Renny is the history lessons. For every year that passes, the festival moves forward one year in history. Recently, Henry VIII took the throne.

The Renaissance Festival is held on weekends from late August to late October. Admission fees are $7.00 to $17.00. No weapons (costume or real).

Baltimore Playwrights Festival
Various locations
(410) 276-2153
The Baltimore Playwrights Festival has been a city tradition for more than 20 years. The performances are hosted by Downtown community theaters. See the July entry for more information.

Maryland State Fair
Maryland State Fairgrounds
York and Timonium Roads, Timonium
(410) 252-0200
www.marylandstatefair.com
For 11 days in late August and early September, the state of Maryland puts its best foot forward at the Maryland State Fair, and the Maryland State Fairgrounds are allowed to fulfill the purpose for which this permanent site was created. Every exhibition hall is filled with displays and

shows. Maryland's citizens from the western counties to the Eastern Shore bring their best pigs, cows, chickens, quilts, jams, pies, wine, honey—you name it—to try and win a blue ribbon. The open area is jammed with traditional three-balls-for-a-dollar kind of games where you can win a stuffed toy, a live goldfish, or a myriad of other goodies. There's even horse racing for 10 days at Timonium Racetrack.

Rides dominate the fairway and cost from 75 cents for the smaller kiddie rides to $3.25 for the more grandiose. On some special days there are bulk ride offers, where you only pay one flat fee and can ride all the rides. Parking, which is usually free at Timonium during other events, costs $2.00 during the fair. Free parking is available at a Park and Ride off Deereco Road, west of the fairgrounds. Parking is a real zoo: York Road is always jammed with cars. For the last few years more and more people are opting to take the Light Rail. In fact, Insiders at the fair note that it's becoming the biggest entrance gate.

The entrance fee is $5.00 per person, with children younger than 12 entering for free. Gates essentially open at 10:00 A.M., but some special livestock shows begin as early as 8:00 A.M. The fair closes at 10:00 P.M. every evening.

American Indian PowWow
Catonsville Community College
800 South Rolling Road, Catonsville
(410) 675-3535
www.baic.org
Baltimore has a large American Indian population. This PowWow, sponsored by the Baltimore American Indian Center (113 South Broadway in Fells Point), is the last of the year and by far the biggest. There's plenty of good food and vendor booths with leather goods, silver jewelry, and other crafts, but, by far, the most exciting sight is American Indians in full costume competing in the dance competitions that are held throughout the weekend, usually the last one in August. Traditional dances tell stories or are more ceremonial in nature, and the regalia worn has meaning

to the dancer about the aspects of his or her tribe, family, and beliefs. There is also competition in "fancy dancing," which is a more contemporary style of dance, originated by the Ponca people. Admission is generally $3.00 to $7.00, and a three-day pass is $15.00.

A lemon stick is half of a fresh lemon that has been cored and into which a peppermint stick has been inserted as a straw. When you're eating one, keep squeezing the lemon. It helps secure the peppermint stick and ensures you're sucking juice, not pulp. When the end of the stick in the lemon starts to melt, take it out, turn it over and start again.

German Festival
Carroll Park, Washington Boulevard
and Bush Street
(410) 522-4144
www.md-germans.org
This is Baltimore's oldest ethnic festival, running annually for more than 100 years. Outdoor tents house a raucous celebration of German food, beer, oompah bands, and crafts. Dance demonstrations and special exhibitions top off the three-day event, which runs from noon to 10:00 P.M. at an outdoor park just 2 miles west of the Inner Harbor. Admission is $4.00. Friday admission is free until 5:00 P.M., and children under 12 accompanied by an adult are admitted free. Parking is free, and the tented areas provide plenty of shelter from hot sun or rain bursts.

SEPTEMBER

Maryland State Fair
Maryland State Fairgrounds
York and Timonium Roads, Timonium
(410) 252-0200, ext. 226
www.marylandstatefair.com
The Maryland State Fair is a feast for the senses. Popcorn, cotton candy, and hot

dogs are a delight for both the nose and taste buds. Games of skill test the eyes and hands for coordination. And the ears revel in pipe-organ music and the laughter of hundreds of people coming together. It's 11 days of pure fun for everyone. See the August entry for more information.

Annual Plant Sale Day
Cylburn Arboretum
4915 Greenspring Avenue
(410) 367-2217
www.cylburnassociation.org
If you've wondered where to go to buy a palm tree to put in your living room or a beautiful fern for your windowbox, Cylburn Arboretum Associations Plant Sale Day is the place. All manner of exotic and native plants are for sale from local nurseries on the grounds of the arboretum. The sale is either the weekend before or the weekend after Labor Day. Both parking and admission are free.

The Irish Festival
5th Regiment Armory
Howard and Preston Streets
(410) 747-6868
www.irishfestival.com
Fill up on Irish champ (potatoes and onions) and Guinness while tapping your foot to the lively music of the Irish folk groups that perform continuously on stage. And, although you'll find the usual kinds of souvenir-type items to buy, there are also some educational opportunities, such as a lecture on twentieth-century Irish literature. The festival, held in mid-September, is sponsored by Irish Charities of Maryland, Inc. The entrance fee is $10.00 for adults, $7.00 for seniors, $5.00 for kids 12 to 17, and free for kids under 12.

Baltimore Book Festival
Mount Vernon Place
Charles and Monument Streets
(410) 752-8632
www.bop.org
The mid-Atlantic's premier celebration of the literary arts offers well-known authors, local bookstores, publishers, children's

writers, storytellers, author signings, crafts, refreshments, and entertainment. The cobblestone streets around the Washington Monument in Mount Vernon are cordoned off and filled with vendors, food, books, and crowds of people milling about. In the past the great Emeril Lagasse cooked up a storm in the kitchen tent and signed autographs. Live music and a beer garden take over one quadrant of the festival, while a Kid's Corner fills the Mount Vernon square park with plenty of activities to keep the young ones busy. The food is always good—definitely try the souvlaki from the Greek stand! The Book Festival runs in mid-September, Friday, 5:00 to 9:00 P.M. and Saturday and Sunday 11:00 A.M. to 7:00 P.M. Admission is free.

Fridays After Five National Aquarium
Pier 3/501 East Pratt Street
(410) 576-3800
www.aqua.org
Fridays. Five. Fish. Fun. What do these things have in common? YOU!—if you're smart and looking for a good, though maybe a little wet, time on a Friday evening. See the January entry for details.

The Maryland Renaissance Festival
Crownsville, 20 minutes south of the
city off State Highway 97
(800) 296-7304
www.rennfest.com
Join peasants and princes at this event held from late summer through midfall. Food, costumes, crafts, and performances are all a step back in time to a period of mighty kings, fair ladies, and noble knights. See the August entry for more information.

OCTOBER

Maryland Oktoberfest
5th Regiment Armory
Howard and Division Streets
(410) 522-4144
www.md-germans.org
The doors open at noon, and the oompahs start at 1:00 P.M. Polka until you drop or

just sit at the communal tables and drink, eat, and sing. German imports as well as sauerbraten, sauerkraut, schnitzel, and all the respective wursts are there for the gobbling. There's also a wine garden for those with more refined tastes and crafts and souvenirs for those who want to bring a little taste of Germany home with them. Oktoberfest is usually held the second weekend of the month. Admission is $5.00. Free parking in state of Maryland lots.

Chocolate Festival
Lexington Market
400 West Lexington Street
(410) 685-6169
www.lexingtonmarket.com
For three days toward the middle of October, Baltimoreans get the opportunity to experience chocolate. We may be able to pick up a candy bar any day of the week during the year, but at the Chocolate Festival, statues are carved from it. You can watch it being melted and molded and dipped or linger at the fudge-making demonstration. If you are a chocoholic, there is no better place to go to feed your addiction. It's free, unless you buy a three-pound box of something, and parking is available in the Lexington Market parking garage ($4.00 all day).

ZooBoo
The Baltimore Zoo
1 Druid Park Lake Drive
(410) 366-LION
www.baltimorezoo.org
At Halloween, Charm City turns into Boo City. Houses are rimmed in orange lights. Ghosts made from sheets and white plastic bags float from trees. Haunted houses abound. And the zoo has ZooBoo. Be sure to have your little one dress up, as there is a costume contest. Other things of interest include 25 different booths with various attractions, trick-or-treating, a Creepy Class where they can make spooky things, and the Haunted Barn for the older and braver. All kids get an activity coloring book and a Halloween bag. Entrance to

ZooBoo is the regular zoo entrance fee of $12.00 for adults and $8.00 for kids 2 to 11 and $10.00 for seniors. The entrance fee includes the Children's Zoo. The event is usually held the weekend before Halloween, rain or shine.

The Maryland Renaissance Festival
Crownsville, 20 minutes south of the
city off State Highway 97
(800) 296-7304
www.rennfest.com
Oyez! Oyez! Come one, come all to this festival of food, theater, and crafts. Enjoy archery and jousting, magic and music here weekends from late August through late October. See the August entry for details.

Fridays After Five National Aquarium
Pier 3/501 East Pratt Street
(410) 576-3800
www.aqua.org
Come party with puffins and piranhas, do the electric slide with an electric eel, or mambo with other marine creatures at this get-together that celebrates the end of the workweek. See the January entry for more information.

NOVEMBER

The Maryland Historical Society
Antiques Show
(410) 685-3750
www.mdhs.org
For more than 20 years the Maryland Historical Society, the museum and library of Maryland history, has hosted one of the region's better antiques show and sales. The highlight of this three-day event in early November is the 30-plus purveyors of fine antiques who travel from around the country and abroad to show and sell their superior merchandise in Baltimore. A preview party is held on Thursday evening for those who wish to dine in elegance and get a first glimpse of the antiques ($100 per ticket). The show opens to the general public Friday and runs through

Sunday. General admission is $8.00 for MHS members and $10.00 for nonmembers, and includes a show catalogue and admission to the museum's galleries. Special lectures and tours take place throughout the weekend, ranging in price from $30 to $50. All funds raised from the event benefit the society's educational programming.

The Raven Ball
Location varies
(410) 685-3750
www.mdhs.org

Hosted by the 1844 Committee of the Maryland Historical Society, this black-tie gala takes place mid-November. In the past it's been held at The Center Club on the top floor of the Legg Mason Building in downtown Baltimore. Parking is always provided, and you can expect to find an open bar, copious hors d'oeuvres, music, dancing, and a silent auction. Tickets are traditionally less than $100, and you can expect to be joined by about 500 other elegantly dressed individuals. This is a young and rowdy crowd, so be prepared to party!

Thanksgiving Parade
From Camden Yards to Market Place, along Pratt Street
(410) 752-8632
www.bop.org

Santa Claus and his reindeer make their first seasonal appearance, surrounded by marching bands, equestrian units, and hosts of clowns. Bundle up and bring a folding chair. It's a short route, but usually a fairly long parade. Admission is free. Held on the Saturday before Thanksgiving, the first bands usually step off at 11:00 A.M.

Fridays After Five National Aquarium
Pier 3/501 East Pratt Street
(410) 576-3800
www.aqua.org

Friday evenings from mid-September to early March the Aquarium brings Baltimoreans and marine life together during this celebration of the end of the workweek. Discounted admission prices make this a real bargain as well as a real good time. See the January entry for more details.

DECEMBER

A Monumental Occasion
Washington Monument
Mount Vernon Place
(410) 244-1030
www.bop.org

Baltimore, once dubbed Monument City for its number of, well, monuments, sets its most prominent monument aglow for the holiday season. The first Thursday in December the city hosts the official lighting of the Washington Monument—which features entertainment, fireworks, and refreshments. The event is always festive and gets the city in the mood for the holiday season. The program begins right after work on a Thursday, around 5:30 P.M. The event is held in conjunction with First Thursday, the Baltimore event where neighborhood museums and galleries open their doors to the public for an evening of free art and entertainment. So plan to make an evening of it.

The Greenberg Train Show
Maryland State Fairgrounds
2200 York Road, Timonium
(410) 795-7447
www.greenbergshows.com

Christmas is just around the corner, and Greenberg is here to fulfill all of your child's requests. From dollhouses to trains and all that falls in between, Greenberg is a must-see for the young and young at heart. See the March entry for more information.

Baltimore's New Year's Eve
Extravaganza
Various locations downtown
(410) 752-8632
www.bop.org

Baltimore rings in the New Year in a big way—and all without alcohol. This nonalcoholic celebration started a few years ago and caught fire. There's live music and countdowns at the Harborplace Amphitheater, the Inner Harbor Ice Rink, and Fells Point. A fireworks party begins at 9:00 P.M. and culminates with fireworks at midnight, as we enter the new year. All outdoor events are free. It's a grand time, particularly if it's a balmy night. But be prepared. You could need your winter woollies.

Fridays After Five National Aquarium
Pier 3/501 East Pratt Street
(410) 752–8632
www.aqua.org
Dolphins, and stingrays, and dart frogs, oh my! You're sure not in Kansas anymore. Enjoy one of Baltimore's most popular attractions at discounted prices during Fridays After Five. See the January entry for more information.

THE ARTS

altimoreans are known as a discerning audience. There was a time when no Broadway show would open in New York until its company had played in Baltimore. If Baltimore's audiences didn't like the show, then producers could be sure New York audiences wouldn't either.

Theater is still very big in Baltimore and includes some pre-Broadway entries as well as Broadway touring company offerings. Community theater offerings are diverse, and prices are low. You can often see experimental efforts or the works of new authors that you would not be privy to in a larger, more professional venue. In fact, during July and August of every year, many of the community theaters focus entirely on new scripts as they present the works of entrants in the Baltimore Playwrights Festival (see the Annual Events chapter). We've listed the major professional theaters and a few of the older or more unique community theaters and groups later in this chapter.

If you're looking for a music recital or a concert, Baltimore has many groups, some professional and some amateur, that perform on a continuing basis. Many of these do not have permanent performance venues, but if you call the contact numbers we've provided, the individual organizations will give you current performance information, including what, when, where, and how much.

Of course, there are some performance groups that do have permanent venues, such as the Peabody Conservatory of Music. Students of the Peabody mount more than 60 concerts per year, most of which are recitals and public performances. (For concert information, call the Concert Office at (410) 659-8100. For more information about the school, see the Education chapter.)

Next to theater and music, Baltimore's biggest love is probably movies. Until the early 1960s Baltimore claimed a fair-size theater in every neighborhood as well as magnificent downtown movie houses. The Stanley, The Mayfair, The Hippodrome, and The Century-Valencia were the most splendid. Baltimore was a stop on the promotional tours of all the big production houses, and local theaters played host to big movie names like Errol Flynn and the Marx Brothers. The accoutrements they boasted for such entertainers send today's lavish lifestyles into the pale. Consider, for instance, an Olympic-size swimming pool beneath the Hippodrome Theater that rumor has it was completely made of marble and designed in the style of a Greek temple. Many of the neighborhood houses and major downtown theaters are gone now, victims of urban renewal or simply ground down by urban decay. We've listed some of the more unique ones as well as a more complete listing of family theaters later in this chapter.

With all of these museums, galleries, and performances going on, how can you possibly choose between them? Well, what are you doing Thursday? The first Thursday of the month features a continuing Downtown art celebration known simply as First Thursdays. First Thursdays takes place along the Charles Street corridor, both above and below Mount Vernon Place, the acknowledged center of Baltimore art and culture. All the galleries, museums, shops, and restaurants are open late, with some providing special entertainment, either inside or out on the sidewalk. Live music is a mainstay, whether classical, jazz, or Dixieland. It's a great way to sample a lot of the city's arts offerings. For more information about First Thursdays, call the Downtown Partnership of Baltimore at (410) 244-1030.

More than walking distance from Mount Vernon Place but wanting to join in the festivities, the Baltimore Museum of

Art presents Freestyle Thursdays. The museum is not only free that day but also stays open until 9:00 P.M. to offer special activities, performances, films, tours, and lots of other good stuff. For more information about Freestyle Thursdays at the BMA, call the museum at (410) 396-6314.

VISUAL ARTS
Museums and Centers

American Visionary Art Museum
800 Key Highway
(410) 244-1900
www.avam.org
CNN called the AVAM "one of the most fantastic museums anywhere in America." The museum features artwork produced by self-taught individuals, usually with no formal training. "Visionary" art, according to the museum, "arises from an innate personal vision that revels foremost in the creative act itself. Visionary art begins by listening to the inner voices of the soul, and often may not even be thought of as 'art' by its creator." In this spiraling, four-story gallery space you will discover inspirational creations made by extraordinary people. The museum is open Tuesday through Sunday 10:00 A.M. to 6:00 P.M. Admission is $9.00 for adults and $6.00 for seniors and students.

Baltimore Museum of Art
10 Art Museum Drive
(410) 396-7100
www.artbma.org
Maryland's celebrated art museum houses a permanent collection of more than 100,000 objects, ranging from ancient mosaics to contemporary art pieces. The Cone Collection features the works of Matisse, Picasso, Cezanne, van Gogh, Gauguin, Renoir, and others from the Modernist era, while the New Wing boasts post-1945 artwork, including a gallery of major works by Andy Warhol. The John Russell Pope Building houses furniture, decorative arts, paintings, and miniature rooms, while the sculpture gardens boast works by artists such as Rodin and Cabler. Hours are Wednesday through Friday from 11:00 A.M. to 5:00 P.M. and Saturday and Sunday from 11:00 A.M. to 6:00 P.M. The museum is closed Monday, Tuesday, New Year's Day, July 4, Thanksgiving, and Christmas. Admission is $7.00 for people older than 18, while senior citizens and full-time students with valid identification pay $5.00. There's no admission on the first Thursday of the month from 5:00 to 8:00 P.M.

Contemporary Museum
100 West Centre Street
(410) 783-5720
www.contemporary.org
The Contemporary Museum is "dedicated to creating education programs and cultural experiences that reach an exceptionally wide range of constituents." Contemporary exhibitions and educational programs are on show at the gallery space on Center Street, just 1 block from the Maryland Historical Society and the Walters Art Museum. Hours are Thursday through Saturday noon to 5:00 P.M., Sunday through Wednesday by appointment.

On the first Thursday of every month, the Baltimore Museum of Art hosts FREESTYLE—a free event where guests can enjoy the exhibits as well as entertainment and light refreshments from 5:00 to 8:00 P.M.

Creative Alliance at the Patterson
3134 Eastern Avenue
(410) 276-1651
www.creativealliance.org
The Creative Alliance is a member-based nonprofit group that presents and promotes the arts throughout the city. Founded in 1995 as the Fells Point Creative Alliance, the original goal of this group was simply to be a guild for the active community of local artists. The organization soon

broadened its mission by developing performance, video, film, and music series. The Creative Alliance organizes at least six exhibitions a year as well as the popular Big Show, an open members' exhibition presented in venues throughout Fells Point. The alliance is an integral part of our community; each summer it holds Open Minds, a free art education program for children at the Enoch Pratt Free Library. The best testament to the group's growing success is the recently renovated Patterson Park Arts Center, a theater, gallery, artist studio residencies, media lab, and cafe in the former Patterson movie theater. Situated on Eastern Avenue 1 block east of Patterson Park, the Creative Alliance at the Patterson serves as an anchor for the revitalization of this historic neighborhood.

Maryland Art Place
38 Market Place
(410) 962-8565
www.mdartplace.org

Maryland Art Place is the place to see contemporary art in Baltimore. The nonprofit arts center has garnered support for local artists and has facilitated exchange between the community and the art world through thought-provoking exhibits and educational outreach programs. This is the best place to go to see the rising stars of the art world. MAP also sponsors the 14 Karat Cabaret, a place for scintillating performance art. Hours for MAP are Tuesday through Saturday from 9:00 A.M. to 5:00 P.M.

The Maryland Institute, College of Art
1300 West Mount Royal Avenue
(410) 669-9200
www.mica.edu

All around The Maryland Institute, art abounds. On the lawns, in the median strip down Mount Royal Avenue, and just about anywhere there is space to put sculpture. But, if you're after a more formal structure for viewing, the institute has four galleries that mount between 60 and 90 exhibitions a year. Three major galleries—the Decker Gallery in Mount Royal Station, the Meyerhoff Gallery in the Fox Building,

and the Pinkard Gallery in the Bunting Center—are supplemented by student galleries.

The Pinkard Gallery is at the Bunting Center at 1401 West Mount Royal Avenue, and the Decker Gallery is in Mount Royal Station at the corner of Cathedral and Dolphin Streets, right across the street from the Lyric Theater. The Mount Royal Station is a magnificent space that was once a train station for the main line of the B&O Railroad, which still runs through tunnels under the street there. The station, hence the gallery, is tucked down into a gully that in the summer serves as a natural amphitheater for live musical entertainment during Artscape (see the Annual Events chapter).

All the galleries display student and faculty art as well as other exhibits. The Thesis Gallery is especially busy during the spring semester of each year, when the exhibitions of graduate work change every week. The Pinkard Gallery is primarily dedicated to faculty works. All galleries are free and open to the public. Hours are Monday through Wednesday and Saturday, 10:00 A.M. to 5:00 P.M.; Thursday and Friday, 10:00 A.M. to 9:00 P.M.; and Sunday, noon to 5:00 P.M. (See the Education chapter for more information about The Maryland Institute.)

The Walters Art Museum
600 North Charles Street
(410) 547-9000
www.thewalters.org

The Walters collection is one of only a few worldwide to present a comprehensive history of art from the third millennium B.C. to the early twentieth century. This collection is renowned in the cultural community for its breadth of pieces, including a rare sarcophagus from second-century Rome, Fabergé eggs, rare Ming vases, and a large collection of ivories. The museum also plays host to major traveling exhibitions, such as a recent show featuring works by Edouard Manet.

The museum has undergone a major facelift in the recent years and has transformed its space in the heart of Mount Vernon into a well-planned, aesthetically thoughtful place to see its extraordinary collection. The new museum opened its doors to the public in the fall of 2001. The additions to the museum include an audio tour of the collection and a computer kiosk where visitors can view rare manuscripts. Hours are Wednesday through Sunday 10:00 A.M. to 5:00 P.M. The first Thursday of every month it is open 10:00 A.M. to 8:00 P.M. Extended hours may apply for special exhibitions. Admission is $8.00 for adults, $6.00 for seniors, $5.00 for students, and free to children under 6. Additional admission fees may be charged for special exhibits.

Commercial Galleries

DOWNTOWN

Angeline's Art Gallery
1631 Thames Street
(410) 522-7909

Angeline Culfogienis paints Baltimore scenes and pieces that concern female themes. She offers signed and numbered Baltimore prints, many scenes from around the area. Her gallery also shows and sells ceramics, sculpture, crafts, and exotic jewelry from around the world.

Art Gallery of Fells Point
1716 Thames Street
(410) 327-1272

This is a cooperative gallery of local artists. You'll find watercolors, oils, pastels, landscapes, portraits, and still-life offerings. The artists are also available for private commissions. Ann Rupert, a local sculptor, has some pieces available through the gallery, as do some local jewelry artists and potters. Several large shows each year include national and Mid-Atlantic artists as well. The gallery is generally open Tuesday through Friday from 11:00 A.M. to 5:00 P.M., and Saturday and Sunday from 10:00 A.M. to 6:00 P.M., but because the gallery is a co-op and, hence,

staffed by volunteers, hours sometimes vary. Be sure to call ahead if this is your primary destination.

C. Grimaldis Gallery
523 North Charles Street
(410) 539-1080

If you're interested in abstract art, you'll want to head to Grimaldis, which handles primarily post–World War II contemporary painting and sculpture from American artists. The gallery deals with local and national artists and sculptors, including Anthony Caro, Grace Hartigan, and Elaine De Kooning. You'll find lithographs and etchings alongside oil paintings. Individual artists are shown separately, and the featured artist changes every month. The gallery is closed on Sunday and Monday.

Craig Flinner Gallery
505 North Charles Street
(410) 727-1863
www.flinnergallery.com

Located in the Mount Vernon Cultural District, this expansive gallery specializes in original vintage posters and maps. Everything is original—you'll find posters dating from the 1890s Belle Epoque to the designs of the 1960s. Prints, lithographs, and engravings line the wall as do a number of original and intricate maps. The Flinner gallery also carries some contemporary work and a great collection of vintage food labels. Custom framing is done on the premises.

Ludwig Katzenstein
729 East Pratt Street, (410) 727-0748

Ridgely Plaza, 1774 York Road,
Lutherville, (410) 252-0748

Since 1941 Katzenstein has been providing a venue to view and purchase paintings, prints, and watercolors of local scenes by local artists. The location at Ridgely Plaza has more fox hunting and duck paintings for those who enjoy dreams of riding to hounds across the rolling valleys that span northward from Towson. Both galleries are closed on Saturday and Sunday.

Maryland Federation of Art Gallery
330 North Charles Street
(410) 685-0300
www.mdfedart.org
The MFA was established in the 1960s by a group of regional artists looking to advance professional opportunities for its members. The MFA opened its first gallery in Annapolis, and its success fueled the launch of second gallery space in 2001 in the Mount Vernon Cultural District. Both locations have continuous exhibitions featuring member artists as well as presentations and kids' programs. Anyone can visit the gallery for no charge. Artists may join the MFA for a $40 membership fee; the group also offers access to its video library for $10 a year.

Mission Media
338 North Charles Street, Second Floor
(410) 752-8950 or (800) 760-9008
www.missionmedia.net
Mission Media is part multimedia consulting firm, part music studio, and part art gallery. The second-floor gallery is small, but it hosts some of the best local and national contemporary artists and performers. Past exhibitors have included famed rock poster artist Derek Hess. Locally focused theater productions have included *Welcome to Baltimore, Hon,* a one-man parody examining Baltimore's national white-trash image. The space also hosts movie screenings and live music.

School 33 Art Center
1427 Light Street
(410) 396-4641
www.school33.org
Housed in an old schoolhouse, School 33 Art Center has fostered contemporary art in this city for more than 20 years. Administered by the Baltimore Office of Promotion and the Arts, its gallery space has mounted more than 300 shows featuring the paintings, sculpture, photography, fiber arts, and installations of well over 1,000 artists. The center's Studio Artist Program provides inexpensive studio space for working artists, while affordable, year-round classes and special weekend workshops taught by professional artists bring art to the masses. Each year the center sponsors the Open Studio Tour, which takes us around the city and allows us to peek into the magical spaces where the artists create their work. The gallery is open Tuesday to Saturday from 11:00 A.M. to 4:00 P.M.

NORTHEAST

Bendann Art Galleries
The Shops at Kenilworth,
834 Kenilworth Drive, Towson
(410) 825-0585
In 1859 Bendann opened as a simple portrait photography studio on West Baltimore Street. The gallery today, still owned and operated by the Bendann family, shows and sells fine art, including oil paintings and watercolors. The 45 regional artists represented offer items in styles from classical realism to contemporary impressionism. In addition, the gallery has historic Maryland and Baltimore prints and restores paintings. Bendann is closed on Sunday.

NORTHWEST

G Spot
2980 Falls Road
(410) 230-3737
Baltimore once was a thriving industrial city, but the shifts in economic forces have resulted in abandoned warehouse space. Many of these large, empty spaces have been taken over by artists, and the G Spot, located on the outskirts of the Hampden neighborhood, is one of the more creative and successful. The G Spot was opened in 1999 by Jill Sell, a musician, and Reuben Kroiz, a sculptor. The name derives from Kroiz's late father, Gerson Kroiz, who provided startup funds for the project. Since its inception, the commercial gallery has grown into a popular venue for live music and DJ performances, art shows, and film screenings.

Paper Rock Scissors
1111 West 36th Street
(410) 235-4420
www.paperrockscissors.com
Established in June 1998, this funky
gallery on "The Avenue" in Hampden represents over 60 artists and features
affordable art in a comfortable atmosphere. The artwork for sale runs the
gamut from painting, mixed media, col-
lage, sculpture, and ceramics to jewelry,
pastel, watercolor, handmade paper,
stained glass, textiles, and decorative furniture. Paper Rock Scissors has a separate
exhibition space in the back with a rotating cast of featured artists. These exhibits
occur approximately every six weeks and
highlight a particular theme, medium, or
individual. Opening receptions for these
shows happen on the first Thursday of the
exhibit from 5:30 to 8:30 P.M. The gallery is
open Tuesday to Saturday.

PERFORMING ARTS
Music and Dance

Baltimore Dance Theatre
Howard County Arts Council
8510 High Ridge Road, Ellicott City
(410) 997-3899
This dance company, directed by Eva
Anderson, was originally part of The
Mayor's Committee on Arts and Culture. It
incorporated as a separate entity in 1980
and since then has been performing original modern dance compositions at least
three times a year at the Baltimore
Museum of Art theater. The company is in
residence at the Howard County Arts
Council in Ellicott City, where it offers
classes to the adult public. The company
itself doesn't use students but rather is
made up of eight professional dancers.

Baltimore Opera Company
110 West Mount Royal Avenue
(410) 727-6000
www.baltimoreopera.org

Since its founding in the early 1950s, the
Baltimore Opera Company has grown from
a group of well-meaning amateurs to a
well-respected opera company. The company mounts three main productions a
year that are performed at the Lyric Opera
House. A recent season included such
standards as *Carmen* and *Il Trovatore*.

Baltimore Symphony Orchestra
Meyerhoff Symphony Hall
1212 Cathedral Street
(410) 783-8000
www.baltimoresymphony.org
The Baltimore Symphony Orchestra performs more than 200 concerts each year
at the Meyerhoff and at various locations
around the city, including an outdoor
series at Oregon Ridge Park. It also plays
a summer MusicFest at the Meyerhoff in
June. Organized in 1916, the BSO is the
only major American orchestra originally
founded as a branch of municipal government. It was supported by city funds until
1942, when it incorporated as a private
institution. A community outreach arm
mounts specialty concerts, including an
annual tribute to Martin Luther King Jr. in
January, and 30 youth concerts for more
than 50,000 kids every year. The BSO is
under the direction of Yuri Temirkanov.

Concert Artists of Baltimore
1114 St. Paul Street
(410) 625-3525
www.cabalto.org
Since 1987, founder and artistic director
Ed Polochick has organized a group of
professional chamber orchestra musicians
and vocal ensembles to present engaging,
accessible classical music programs
throughout the state. The group, which
ranges from duos to a full cast of 65 musicians, performs operettas, pops concerts,

---

*For 24-hour information about dance
events in Baltimore, Towson University
has an information line called Danceline
at (410) 830-3309.*

and classical favorites in a number of venues around town. Performances are frequently followed by informal question-and-answer sessions with the audience. Tickets for seniors and students are $5.00; adult admission is $8.00. Call for concert schedules and locations.

Handel Choir of Baltimore
3600 Clipper Mill Road
(410) 366-6544
www.charm.net/~hcob
The Handel Choir, directed by T. Herbert Dimmock, is probably best known for its rendition of Handel's masterpiece, *The Messiah*. In fact, the Handel Choir has performed this work every year since 1934. In addition, the choir performs approximately 15 other concerts during the year that include not only Handel's choral works but also those of other classical composers, such as Gabrieli and Bach. Public performances are held at local concert halls and houses of worship, with at least one concert every year at the Basilica of the Assumption. A 14-voice a cappella choir breaks off from the group every October and June to perform smaller concert pieces. Anyone may audition to become part of this nonprofit choir. Auditions are held in late summer.

Hopkins Symphony Orchestra
Shriver Hall, Johns Hopkins University
3400 North Charles Street
(410) 516-6542
The Hopkins Symphony began as a creative outlet for Johns Hopkins students in the 1980s. It has grown over the years into a true community orchestra. Only about one-third of its 90-plus performers are students at the university. The orchestra performs two subscription series at Johns Hopkins' Shriver Hall during the year. One features four major concerts with a full orchestra, and the other entitles you to attend three chamber music concerts throughout the year.

The chamber group is not the typical five or six people, but rather a large chamber orchestra of 13. The group's size allows the musicians to play such pieces as *Appalachian Spring* by Aaron Copeland. The group also provides educational concerts for Baltimore's youth and donates tickets to senior centers and schools in the Baltimore area. The orchestra holds auditions annually in the fall. General admission is $10.00.

Peabody Ragtime Ensemble
3226 Midfield Road
(410) 484-5200
www.peabodyonline.com
The Peabody Ragtime Ensemble began when its members were students at the Peabody Conservatory of Music. It has continued not just because its members put on a great show but also because they are dedicated to their stated mandate: "to preserve the roots of American jazz through research, arrangement, and performance of the vintage repertoire." The group's history includes such honors as performing with Eubie Blake, Baltimore's own ragtime legend, as well as appearing with the Baltimore Symphony Orchestra and such notables as Aaron Copeland and Hal Linden. Under the direction of Ed Goldstein, the ensemble has toured other countries and won numerous competitions and awards. Put all that aside, however, and you'd still have one great band that plays authentic ragtime, Dixieland, jazz, and 1940s swing year-round. Just give them a call to find out where, when, and how much.

Professional Theater

Arena Players
801 McCulloh Street
(410) 728-6500
Arena Players is one of the nation's oldest continuous African-American theater companies. Begun in 1953, its first production was William Soroyan's one-act drama *Hello Out There*. By 1961 the company had found its permanent home and has since continually reshaped the space to create a modern theater. A recent season of five

major productions included *Come Back Little Sheba* by William Inge, *If My Heart Could Sing: A Night With Billie Holiday,* John Henry Redwood's *No Niggers, No Jews, No Dogs,* and *Who Shot Uncle Benny* by Mildred Dumas. The company offers workshops for adults and children. It also plays host to stand-up comedy artists and sponsors poetry readings and live jazz music.

Center Stage
700 North Calvert Street
(410) 332-0033
www.centerstage.org
Center Stage is the State Theater of Maryland and has been in business for more than 30 years. The theater is in the Mount Vernon neighborhood, just 2 blocks east of Mount Vernon Square, in what was once the building for Loyola College and Preparatory School. The building was donated by the Jesuits in 1974. There are actually two theaters in the building, the Pearlstone Theater and the flexible-configuration Head Theater. Both theaters are intimate. The larger Pearlstone has only 541 seats. Sight lines are excellent, and no seat in the house is a bad one. Center Stage mounts six shows on the main stage every year—some Broadway, some classic, some more avant-garde. A recent season featured William Inge's *Picnic* and Stephen Sondheim's *Sweeney Todd.* There are also always offerings by new writers as well. Irene Lewis is the company's resident director. The main-stage season runs from October to June, but the theater is never really dark.

Children's Theater Association
100 West 22nd Street
(410) 366-6403
Children's Theater Association has been a Baltimore fixture for more than 40 years. CTA also offers three public performances every year for general audiences at the Baltimore Museum of Art theater. The season runs from September through May. Recent performances include such educational pieces as *Stay Tobacco Free* and

Teddy Roosevelt. CTA also offers acting classes to students throughout the year at its now-permanent classroom space at an old office building in South Charles Village.

Lyric Opera House
140 West Mount Royal Avenue
(410) 685-5086
www.lyricoperahouse.com
The Lyric presents all manner of theatrical and musical entertainment. One can see a Broadway road company production as well as performances by groups such as the Baltimore Opera Company. *The Nutcracker* is a Christmas tradition; but *Stomp* has also been on stage here. All told, the Lyric hosts 25 to 30 productions a year. The Lyric was built in 1894 and today seats 2,564 (1,000 orchestra, 206 boxes, and 1,358 balcony). Although its antique facade has been replaced by a more modern front and a gallery-type outer lobby, the theater remains as it was built, including perfect acoustics and excellent sight lines, even for those in the last row. The old lobby, which is now the inner lobby, has been renovated to look as it did when the theater first opened—which is to say, spectacular. The theater and its continuing history are part of Baltimore's pride.

Morris A. Mechanic Theatre
1 North Charles Street
(410) 625-4230
www.themechanic.org
The Morris Mechanic is an excellent house. Although a relatively new theater by Baltimore standards, open a little more than 30 years, it offers 1,600 comfortable seats with excellent sight lines and is another theater where we are comfortable saying there's not a bad seat. It is leased long-term by the Baltimore Center for the Performing Arts, which mounts pre-Broadway productions and national Broadway road companies essentially year-round. Subscriptions are available to four-show and six-show series, but individual tickets can be hard to come by.

The address is confusing. Although it is listed at 1 North Charles, in fact, the

entrance is on the Hopkins Plaza side, midway down the unit block of West Baltimore Street, just under the pedestrian footbridge.

Theatre Project
45 West Preston Street
(410) 752-8558
www.theatreproject.org
When you think experimental theater in Baltimore, think Theatre Project. Originally an extension of the experimental theater at Antioch College, it became its own professional entity in 1971. Theatre Project mounts 10 to 15 shows a year at its permanent location at the corner of Preston and Cathedral Streets, right across the street from Meyerhoff Symphony Hall. The season runs from September through June.

Dinner Theater

F. Scott Black's Dinner Theater
100 East Chesapeake Avenue, Towson
(410) 321-6595
The Broadway musical lives large at the oldest dinner theater in greater Baltimore. The group mounts a minimum of five productions throughout the year. *My Fair Lady* and *The Sound of Music* are standard, and the occasional musical revue is thrown in for good measure. A recent summer series featured an original musical revue called the *Nifty Fifties Review*. A teacher of theater at Essex Community College, F. Scott Black often uses local student talent for his theater's productions. Tickets, which include the show and a buffet meal with a choice of five main entrees, salad bar, and dessert, cost around $30.

Lorenzo's Timonium Dinner Theatre
9603 Deereco Road, Timonium
(410) 560-1113 or (877) 560-1113
www.timoniumdinnertheatre.com
Timonium mounts musicals and comedies for adult audiences five days a week and children's productions every Saturday.

Tickets to the show and buffet dinner range from $22.50 to $41.50. Parking is free. To get to the theater, take I-83 north to Timonium Road, then go east toward York Road. The first light is Deereco Road.

Community Theater

Axis Theatre
3600 Clipper Mill Road
(410) 243-5237
The Axis Theatre in Hampden is nearly 10 years old, but "they said" it wouldn't last a year. The two partners that began it sought to create a venue for modern, nontraditional plays and productions, and they've done just that. Its production of *The Glass Menagerie,* for instance, incorporated a multimedia approach. The group has also performed the works of such burgeoning local and national writers as Nicky Silver. The theater stays open all year; the summer offers softer fare, such as dramatic readings and shows put on by the resident teen group. The house has only 68, essentially orchestra, seats. The actual theater is only a small part of a renovated mill complex that sits right beside the Light Rail. There is also a large free parking lot.

The Baltimore Theatre Alliance
100 East 23rd Street
(410) 662-9945
www.baltimoreperforms.org
The Baltimore Theatre Alliance (BTA) is an invaluable resource to the 43 community theaters in Baltimore that are its members. BTA gives member theaters a central clearinghouse for theater information, actors, and technicians. For instance, once a year, BTA holds major auditions to which all member theaters send representatives. If you were interested in acting at the community-theater level in Baltimore, instead of auditioning for every single play at every single theater in the city, you could become one of the 250 people who audition at BTA for all the theaters. If a

theater needs a lighting tech for a particular play, it calls BTA. If you are a lighting tech who wants work at the community-theater level, you can get on the list by sending your resume to BTA.

Encore Theater
4801 Liberty Heights Avenue
(410) 466-2433

Encore began in the 1980s, when local playwright Belva Scott was looking for a venue to produce her own plays. It has grown into Community Arts Project Inc. (CAP), a nonprofit organization that not only manages the Encore Theater's original productions but also creates and coordinates educational and cultural activities. The national dance troupe from Sierra Leone has performed at Encore, as has the Morgan State University Jazz Ensemble. A yearly April offering is *A Day in Africa,* in which the audience gets an opportunity to explore native African culture. CAP also has an outreach program through which it takes productions to such venues as The Walters Art Gallery and Johns Hopkins University. Recent offerings included *Soul Staring Sam,* a play by local playwright Belva Scott, and *The Vote,* another play by Belva Scott. The theater is open Friday, Saturday, and Sunday September through June. Sometimes dinner is offered before the show. Open auditions are held for all major shows, and actors and performers are paid.

Everyman Theatre
1727 North Charles Street
(410) 752-2208
www.everymantheatre.org

Located next door to The Charles Theater (see At the Movies later in this chapter), Everyman produces high-quality professional theater in an intimate house that seats at most 180. The resident company is composed of actors who hail from both Baltimore and Washington, D.C., and they work together regularly, making their performances cohesive and engaging. The stage structure is malleable and alters depending on the needs of the particular production, making every show a unique experience.

Fells Point Corner Theater
251 South Ann Street
(410) 276-7837
www.fpct.org

Fells Point Corner offers two theaters, one up, one down. Both are small: 65 seats up, 85 seats down. The upstairs theater has stadium seating and even in the top row at the back, you can easily see the expressions on the actors' faces. Of course, sometimes this kind of intimacy makes it difficult for audience members not to feel that they're part of the action. (A former actor at the theater tells a great story about how he was in a bar scene on stage, his table downstage near the first row. His character had just lit a cigarette when an elderly lady in the first row leaned over and asked him to please put it out.)

The season runs from September to the middle of June, after which the actors go into rehearsal for two shows for the Baltimore Playwrights Festival, which is in residence at the theater. Fells Point Corner also offers acting and directing classes for adults and children. The first-floor theater is wheelchair accessible.

Spotlighters
817 St. Paul Street
(410) 752-1225
www.spotlighters.org

Spotlighters is a true community theater. There are open auditions for every play, and actors' and stagehands' backgrounds span the gamut from acting student to doctor or lawyer. Some of the actors who began here have gone on to become professional actors. A few names you may recognize include Howard Rollins, who was nominated for an Oscar for *Ragtime,* and Edwin McDonogh, who made it to Broadway in *Moon for the Misbegotten.* The theater itself has been in the basement of the Madison Apartments since October 1962, when the group severed its ties with Baltimore City's Department of Recreation and opened as an independent theater company capitalized with a whopping $600. Since then, the theater never goes dark, except for the week between Christmas and New Year's. The company mounts 12 plays a year, including two plays in July and August from the Baltimore Playwrights Festival, and, in the winter, *Scrooge, the Musical*, which it has produced every year since the early 1980s.

Vagabond Players
806 South Broadway
(410) 563-9135
www.vagabondplayers.com

The Vagabond Players are so-called because for most of its nearly 90-year existence the group had no permanent home. In 1974, however, as Baltimore's housing renaissance was just beginning, the group took over a seedy bar/hotel near the foot of Broadway in Fells Point and turned it into a theater. For 20 years, the members made do, happy just to have a place to call home in an area that has grown into one of the most popular and artistically inclined neighborhoods in the city. In 1995 the space was completely renovated. Now the Vagabond Players perform in a modern theater with 106 seats and such unheard of community-theater amenities as handicapped accessibility and a sprinkler system. Vags, as the theater is known around town, does seven shows a year during the regular season (September through July) and then joins in the Baltimore Playwrights Festival, performing one or two plays in August. If you're interested in seeing true classic theater, Vags is the place. A recent season included, among others, *The Weir* by Conor McPherson and *Don't Drink the Water* by Woody Allen. All actors and stage crews are community volunteers. Vags is only open weekends—Friday and Saturday for an 8:00 P.M. curtain and Sunday with a performance at 2:00 P.M.

AT THE MOVIES

Bengies Drive-in Theatre
3417 Eastern Boulevard, Aberdeen
(410) 687-5627
www.bengies.com

In the 1950s drive-in theaters were all the rage across the country. If you've never experienced a drive-in movie, do it while you're here. It gives a whole new meaning to the term "big-screen" (it's the largest on the East Coast, measuring 52 by 120 feet) and offers you such amenities as playgrounds for the little ones who get antsy from sitting too long. And, of course, since seating is in your own car, you can smoke, eat, drink, nurse babies, do just about anything you darn well please, and no one can say nay.

Don't think, however, that you can bring a barbecue or let your kids run wild. Bengies has some strict rules about behavior and about what food may be brought in. If you want eats, it's better to just buy them there.

Bengies is open Friday through Sunday. The box office opens at 7:15 P.M. Prices are $5.00 to $7.00 for those 12 and older, depending on whether it's a single, double, or triple feature. Children in your car who are 11 and younger are admitted free. The theater opens in the spring for shows. Call in advance to confirm showings.

The Charles Theater
1711 North Charles Street
(410) 727-3456
www.thecharles.com

This is our city's premier cinema for international and rare films. Housed in a renovated 108-year-old Beaux-Arts building, The Charles has five screens, most with stadium seating. The lobby is spacious and comfortable and it attaches to the adjacent Tapas Teatro Café (see the Restaurants chapter), which is the perfect spot for a premovie meal. Every year The Charles helps host the Maryland Film Festival and on Sundays it offers a film series called Cinema Sunday, which begins with a simple brunch of bagels, coffee, tea, and includes a speaker after the film. Doors open at 9:45 A.M. for brunch and conversation. The film begins at 10:35 A.M.

IMAX Theater
601 Light Street
(410) 685-5225
Part of the Maryland Science Center in the Inner Harbor, the IMAX Theater shows short films about nature, culture, and science on a five-story, 70-foot-wide screen that makes you feel as though you're right there in the middle of the action. Admission is $10.00, but it also gains you access to the Science Center's exhibitions (See the Attractions chapter for more details on the Maryland Science Center).

Loews White Marsh Theatre
The Avenue at White Marsh
8141 Honeygo Boulevard, White Marsh
(410) 933-9034
Across from White Marsh Mall is a shopping area called The Avenue at White Marsh. Built in 1997, The Avenue was designed to re-create a town square of old, complete with old-fashioned gas-lamp-type street lighting, brick sidewalks, and large theater marquee (see the Shopping chapter for more information about The Avenue at White Marsh). In December 1997 Loews White Marsh Theatre opened 16 screens. A gigantic complex, it features high-back rocking-chair seats and stadium-style seating in all auditoriums. But the best perk of all is free drink refills. Loews charges $6.75 for all shows before 6:00 P.M. After 6:00 P.M., adult prices go up to $8.75 weekdays and $9.00 on weekends. You can purchase tickets in advance over the phone.

The Senator
5904 York Road
(410) 435-8338
www.senator.com
For mainstream movies with ambience, you'll want to go to The Senator, which is just south of Northern Parkway on York Road. Though average size for a neighborhood theater when it was built, it now is counted among the largest in greater Baltimore, with seating for 900 and a screen about 40 feet tall. Its 1939 Art Deco ambience is intact and preserved for posterity, right down to the etched, oval, blue-glass mirror over the water fountain and marble stalls in the ladies' room. Listed on the National Register of Historic Places and named one of the best movie theaters in the country by *USA Today,* The Senator is still a first-run house. It has had the distinction of hosting the world premieres of many of the movies that have been made here in Baltimore. Outside the theater is a Baltimore-style walk of fame, where stars and producers have their names in the cement.

Admission is $8.00 for everyone. Children younger than 5 are not admitted unless the film showing is a children's movie. However, babes in arms are never admitted.

Private skyboxes, which include an Art Deco lounge and two private viewing rooms, are available for parties of 15 to 40 people at a cost of $10 a person. Call (410) 323-1989 to reserve the space.

A Theater Near You

The following list provides the location and contact numbers for major movie houses in Baltimore, which, with the exception of the Downtown houses, are located at or near suburban malls. Most of these theaters have at least two screens, and often several more.

Ticket prices usually run $6.00 to $7.50 for adults, with matinee prices and ticket prices for children and seniors hovering around $3.00 to $4.00.

DOWNTOWN
Orpheum Cinema
1724 Thames Street
(410) 732-4614

The Charles Theater
1711 North Charles Street
(410) 727-3456

NORTHEAST

Loews White Marsh Theatre
The Avenue at White Marsh
8141 Honeygo Boulevard
(410) 933-9034

The Senator
5904 York Road
(410) 435-8338

United Artists Golden Ring Mall
6400 Rossville Boulevard
(410) 574-3336

Towson Commons 8 General Cinema
York Road and Pennsylvania Avenue
(410) 825-5233

NORTHWEST

Loew's Valley Centre 9
9616 Reisterstown Road
(410) 363-4194

SOUTHEAST

Bengies Drive-In Theatre
3417 Eastern Boulevard, Aberdeen
(410) 687-5627

Eastpoint 10, 7938 Eastern Boulevard
Eastpoint, (410) 284-3100

Loews Jumpers 7, 8120 Jumpers Hole
Road (off Ritchie Highway), Glen Burnie
(410) 768-9999

United Artists Marley Station
7900 Ritchie Highway
(410) 760-3300

SOUTHWEST

Security Square 8
1717 Rolling Road
(410) 265-6911

United Artists Westview Mall
5824 Baltimore National Pike
(410) 719-9000

PARKS AND RECREATION

A great deal of attention is paid to Baltimore's developed areas, often without fair consideration of all its open space. Greater Baltimore is dotted with areas where development has intentionally been forbidden so that people can picnic, play sports, or party with nature. Virtually every community has a park, a playground, school fields, or some kind of green space that allows for getting out among trees and grass.

Maryland has been a leader in efforts to ensure that property remains available for recreation through its Program Open Space, which for more than two decades has been targeting one half of 1 percent of the sale price of all real estate to protecting and enhancing the green areas within the state. These funds have gone to establish an ambitious network of greenways—natural corridors of open space that meander along streams and rivers—so that people can peacefully coexist and commune with all things flora and fauna.

These greenways offer areas for people to hike, bike, ride horses, fish, canoe, and kayak and act as buffers between development and nature. These buffers also protect wildlife, fish, and plants from stormwater runoff and other potentially harmful effects of development. The state's goal is to create a network of more than 100 greenways, a process that is more than a third complete. Already a greenway stretch is within a half hour of where anyone lives in the area, according to the state Department of Natural Resources, which regulates the national model program. In addition to greenways, Program Open Space funds have been used to create more than 3,000 county and municipal parks and conservation areas.

The funds are also used to buy land for state parks and state forests. Maryland boasts 47 state parks and forests, areas where people can take part in activities ranging from hiking and biking to hunting and camping, swimming and boating to birding and fishing. About a third of these areas are within the Baltimore area, while other parks, operated by the city and counties and acquired using the same funds, fill the area.

Plan an extended stay with more than 2,000 campsites and 120 full-service and camper cabins to choose from. Campsites, cabins, and shelters can be reserved from May 1 through September 30 by calling (888) 432-2267 or online at www.dnr.state. md.us/. From October 1 to April 30, call the specific park for information.

In this chapter parks are categorized by region within the Baltimore area—Downtown, Northeast, Northwest, Southeast, and Southwest. Descriptions of the parks include information on playing fields, trails for hiking, biking, and skating, and playgrounds. Recreational opportunities are listed in this chapter by jurisdiction. Groups and organizations providing organized recreational opportunities, which are too, too numerous to list individually, are grouped by organizations, which usually serve as clearinghouses for information, registrations, and referrals. Your best bet is to contact the appropriate group or agency and ask that a schedule of upcoming activities be sent to you by mail. These schedules explain the breadth of activities available in your area as well as some of the offerings that might be worth a drive.

Most recreational programs have a fee, which can range up to $5.00 a session, depending on what it is and how involved it is. Because these fees change frequently from season to season and community to community, we cannot accurately include them here, except to let you know when a fee applies. Call the department or center for specific fees involved.

Waterfront activities, such as fishing and boating, are contained in the On the Water chapter. Activities and locations geared especially toward children are in the Kidstuff chapter. And for all you duffers out there looking to hit the links, we've given golf its own chapter.

Most of the parks in this chapter do not charge an admission fee and are open year-round, usually from dawn to dusk. You can assume these parameters to be true unless we note otherwise.

PARKS

Downtown

Federal Hill Park
Key Highway at Battery Avenue

Overlooking the Inner Harbor, Federal Hill isn't the area's largest park, but it certainly offers one of the best views. There's a playground, a small basketball court, and an open section for throwing a ball or a Frisbee. For a real walking workout, try climbing the steps from Key Highway to the hilltop a few times. You'll definitely feel the burn. Benches are available for a post-workout rest. Park on the street or at the harbor and walk over.

Patterson Park
Eastern and Patterson Park Avenues

Patterson Park provides a welcome respite from the demands of city life. Sports fields, an ice-skating rink, and open areas where the bothers of urban living seem to take a backseat await you when you head toward East Baltimore's crown jewel of parks. There's even a small stadium, named Utz Towardowicz after the person who gave the funds for it, that hosts big-time baseball and softball competitions. Parking is available on the streets surrounding the park.

Northeast

Cromwell Valley Park
2002 Cromwell Bridge Road, Towson
(410) 887-2503
www.co.ba.md.us

Just minutes from I-695's exit 29, this park consists of a farming area along Minefield Run that dates back to the 1700s and a small stream feeding into the Gunpowder River; it encompasses 367 acres of pasture, open fields, woods, cultivated fields, and floodplain. It was purchased in 1993 by Baltimore County.

The park plays host to concerts and other functions, but it's Mother Nature who usually takes center stage here. Among the natural actors are raptors such as the redtailed hawk, kestrel, and great horned owl, which prey on small mammals such as rabbits and deer mice. Other actors are deer, foxes, and song birds, including Baltimore orioles (a local favorite, obviously), bobolinks, meadowlarks, indigo bunting, and great blue herons.

Parking is available on-site and best accessed from I-695 at Loch Raven Boulevard (exit 29).

Double Rock Park
Texas and Glen Avenues, Parkville
(410) 887-5300

About 3 miles inside I-695's exit 32, two small baseball fields that double as fields for football and lacrosse, some trails along a stream, and a playground and picnic area are parts of this park within a quiet and serene Parkville neighborhood. The playground is small, but the seesaw, swing, and a slide with a collection of holes where children can drop sand (simple, but quite the pastime for kids) are big hits. Picnic tables and restrooms are also available. Parking is free on-site. The picnic tables are often reserved for groups on weekends and summer days, but there's plenty of grass for spreading a blanket.

Gunpowder Falls State Park
2813 Jerusalem Road, Kingsville
(410) 592-2897
www.dnr.state.md.us

One of Maryland's largest state parks takes up about 18,000 acres of Baltimore and Harford Counties, heading west to east along the Big Gunpowder and Little Gunpowder Rivers. Horseback riding, mountain biking, hiking, bird-watching, canoeing, tubing, and fishing (especially fly-fishing) are among the favorite activities of the thousands of visitors to the park. Maps of specific park areas are available at park headquarters and provide a lot of helpful information.

The best places for entry are along U.S. 1 about 8 miles north of Baltimore City, where there's a parking area right on the river, and in the Cockeysville area, off I-83, along York Road, about 12 miles north of the city near Hunt Valley. The Hammerman area in Chase, off U.S. 40 north of Baltimore City, requires admission of $2.00 a person, but in return for the fee, you get access to a beach (one of only two public beaches in the area) for swimming (Memorial Day through Labor Day) and sunning, an open picnic area, and numerous stretches of hiking trails. The Northern Central Rail Trail, also near Hunt Valley and off York Road near I-83, offers a 19-mile flat hiking and biking route, safe and serene, like no other in the area. For more information on the trail, see the Close-up in this chapter.

Herring Run Park
Belair Road at Parkside Drive
www.belair-edison.org/herring-run

Like so many other parks in Baltimore, Herring Run was established along a waterway. Herring once ran through the waters here, hence the park's name. Trash and other obstacles would have impeded their passage over the past few years, but recent efforts are pushing forward to improve the water quality and restore the herring. The park is accessible from Harford Road, Sinclair Lane, and Belair Road in Northeast Baltimore. Park benches, pic-

nic tables, open areas for playing ball or walking dogs, and trails along the run are within a few blocks of those main road intersections with the run. Parking is available on streets within the communities nearby. Beneath the Harford Road bridge near Argonne Drive is an area with lots of picnic tables and trails, a perfect getaway for a few hours. No admission is charged.

Lake Montebello
Hillen Road and Argonne Drive

A paved walking, running, and in-line skating trail goes around Lake Montebello, one of the drinking water collection lakes for the city. From dawn to dusk, people of all ages take to the street, which also has traffic running alongside it. The circular path is a great place to meet people of all sorts and sports. Parking is available on side streets.

Insta-parks at colleges and other school facilities are often overlooked for what they offer—great open spaces for running, walking, or taking in a free and enjoyable environment, especially in the evening and on weekends.

Loch Raven Reservoir
12101 Dulaney Valley Road
(410) 887-7692
www.co.ba.md.us

The Loch Raven Reservoir is a 2,400-acre watershed that provides drinking water to a large portion of Baltimore City, even though it is located in Baltimore County. No matter. Because the water must be as clean as possible, the surrounding acres are open for recreation, not development, giving people who visit the area the chance to participate in everything from hiking to biking to fishing to equestrian activities. A portion of Loch Raven Drive, from Providence Road to a parking lot about a mile to its north, is closed from 10:00 A.M. to 5:00 P.M. on Saturday and Sunday so that bikers, hikers, in-line skaters, skateboarders, and others can enjoy the park without worrying about traffic. The Loch Raven Fishing Center rents boats and offers docking on the reservoir from April through October (see the On the Water chapter for more information). Picnic tables are near the Providence Road entrance, while open stretches for flying a kite, reading a book, or communing with nature are all over the park. No refreshments are available, so bring your own. Park only in designated areas; police issue lots of tickets to folks who fail to obey the parking regulations.

Putty Hill Park
Putty Hill and Hoerner Avenues,
Parkville
(410) 887-5300
www.co.ba.md.us
One large baseball field and a spread-out playground provide a welcome respite to residents of Parkville. Just minutes from I-695's exit 31, the park is convenient to Towson, White Marsh, and other areas just north of Baltimore City. Parking is available on the street, and restrooms are on-site.

Northwest

Druid Hill Park
Druid Lake Drive near I-83
(410) 396-6106
The park, one of the largest inner-city parks in the country, surrounds the Baltimore Zoo.

In one of the greater ironies of Baltimore, the animals remain confined inside the zoo, while people are welcome to roam freely about the outer area surrounding Druid Lake. (See the Kidstuff chapter for more information about the Baltimore Zoo.)

Tennis courts and a public swimming pool are also part of the park. Although access to the lake is prohibited, the fields, trails, and hardwoods are ideal for picnicking, hiking, and bird-watching. Tables and cabanas that date back to the last century have been restored and are strategically located around the park for picnickers and

weary revelers. Druid Hill Park also offers a fantastic view of the city as it is on one of the highest promontories in the area.

Oregon Ridge Park and Nature Center
13555 Beaver Dam Road, 1 mile south of
Shawan Road, Hunt Valley
(410) 887-1815
www.oregonridge.org
Just west of I-83, Oregon Ridge Park used to have a short ski lift, long before some of the more popular skiing locales opened in Pennsylvania. Now the 1,036-acre park offers a hill for running, hiking, climbing, and hang gliding, mostly afternoons and weekends. A large playground, an amphitheater where the Baltimore Symphony Orchestra performs about a dozen shows each summer, and an indoor banquet facility round out the offerings at the main park. Hiking trails are also on-site. The park is open seven days a week from dawn to dusk. Admission is free, and parking is available outside the banquet center.

There is also a swimming beach available 10:00 A.M. to 8:00 P.M. Memorial Day through Labor Day. The park charges $6.00 for adults and $2.00 for children under 12 years of age for the swimming area.

Visitors also enjoy the Oregon Ridge Nature Center, where recreational and educational programs are offered to the public and school groups. Full-time naturalists and volunteers offer a wide range of activities for children and adults, including moonlit hikes, bird-watching trips, beekeeping demonstrations, and maple syrup making, mostly on weekends. The center is open from 9:00 A.M. to 5:00 P.M. Tuesday through Sunday.

Seminary Park
Seminary at Burton Avenues, Lutherville
(410) 887-7684
www.co.ba.md.us
Just east of I-83 north of Towson, this facility has several lighted baseball fields that also offer space for adult softball, youth football, soccer, and lacrosse. A playground with slides, suspension bridges, swings for children and infants, a

tunnel, and a sandbox is at the back of the park, far from the on-site parking lot. Restroom facilities and picnic tables are also available.

Southeast

North Point State Park
2813 Jerusalem Road, Kingsville
(410) 592-2897
www.dnr.state.md.us
This Chesapeake Bay waterfront park could be the best-kept secret in Baltimore as far as parks go. It is more than 1,300 acres located in southeastern Baltimore County and is rich in history and natural resources. The Defenders' Trail, used during the War of 1812, goes through the park. This is also the site of the former Bay Shore Amusement Park.

With more than 6 miles of shoreline, visitors to this park can find rarely used areas for biking, cross-country skiing, fishing, flatwater canoeing, and hiking. A portion of North Point State Park has been designated as a Wildlands Area. There is also one of the finest examples of tidal marsh on the Upper Chesapeake found here.

Rocky Point Beach and Park
801 Back River Neck Road, Essex
(410) 887-3873
www.co.ba.md.us
Pick your poison—a beach, five picnic areas, a historic waterfront house, a fishing and boating pier, or two boat ramps for watching the serene waters off Rocky Point, located at the confluence of the Back and Middle Rivers. A somewhat secret place with 375 acres for getting away from the heat and humidity in the summer, Rocky Point offers great views of eagles, osprey, and great blue herons. Fishing, boating, and swimming have been part of the menu at Rocky Point since 1969.

Swimming is an option at the beach from 10:00 A.M. to 6:00 P.M. every day from Memorial Day through Labor Day. Parking can get somewhat tight on hot summer weekends, but a short delay is worth what awaits you, especially when it's really hot and humid—like throughout July and August.

Southwest

Catonsville Community Park
501 North Rolling Road
Catonsville
(410) 887-0959
www.co.ba.md.us
Catonsville Community Park boasts a sand-lined volleyball court, fields for outdoor sports, and a playground featuring a tire swing and a high, high swing. Picnic tables are also available, and parking is on-site. Bathroom facilities are available.

Gwynns Falls Park/Leakin Park
Edmondson Avenue at Hilton Parkway, Franklintown
(410) 396-7931
Spread out among several miles of eastwest land along the Gwynns Falls, this park offers hiking, biking, bird-watching, sightseeing, and relaxing spaces. Formed to protect the Gwynns Falls from development all around it, the park at one point housed an amusement park, but those days are long gone. In its place are grass, trees, and other natural amenities that provide a strong contrast to the housing close by. You can access the park from a variety of sites along Edmondson Avenue. Leakin Park, a portion of the facility, offers tennis courts, a track, abundant parking, and a ropes course, which tests even the best athletes with climbing, balance, and endurance testing. The ropes course is operated by the city and several other agencies, primarily for children in summer camps and school daytrips.

Patapsco Valley State Park
8020 Baltimore National Pike, Ellicott City
(410) 461-5005
www.dnr.state.md.us
Patapsco Valley State Park is one of Maryland's largest parks and its oldest—dating

Where to Take Pets

Baltimore's Charm City moniker extends from the way it treats people to its ability to accommodate pets, especially dogs. The area offers a variety of locations for taking Fido for a run, walk, or sense of the outdoors, and all of the places are just as rewarding for the person on the other end of the leash.

Whether you treat Rex like the king, Tiffany like the queen, or Butch like the annoying house pet he really is, there's a place around town for getting out and treating your pet to a whiff of the outdoors. Here are a few things to keep in mind when you take your pet out on the town.

- All jurisdictions require that pets be leashed.
- All jurisdictions require that pets be cleaned up after, and these requirements are maintained with fines ranging from $5.00 to $15.00 for violators. More important than a possible fine is the fact that some of the places where pets are allowed to visit are relatively pristine parks and open spaces that will continue to remain so only if people protect them from litter and animal wastes. Do your part to keep the area looking pretty.
- Watch out for ticks. Small deer ticks can lie in the woods around Baltimore, so it's a good practice to check your pet after each visit—even if they've never had one before or are wearing the latest and greatest tick collar. Favorite sites for ticks on pets are the collar area (even under the collar), ears, where the legs and torso meet and on the tail. For people—yes, ticks are attracted to people, too—the best places to look are the hair, neck, legs, ankles, and other areas that tend to be warm. Light-colored clothing can make them easier to spot, and wearing a hat, long sleeves, long pants, socks, and shoes can help prevent them from finding a piece of skin to burrow into. If you see one, remove it completely with a pair of tweezers. If it's on your pet, you might also want to keep it in a sealed envelope or plastic bag just in case something happens and doctors need to check on its size at the time it was removed to determine how long it lived on your pet.

- Not everybody's dog is as friendly as yours, and not everyone is as willing to experience the ritualistic love/hate relationship between pets on first encounter. Make sure the person with a pet ahead or behind wants your dog rubbing elbows or whatever else before you allow it. It's best to keep your dog on its leash when around other people or near the water.

Unless otherwise noted, the following sites are within Baltimore City limits. No admission fee is charged at any of these locations.

In the northeast **Herring Run Park** at the intersection of Harford Road and Argonne Drive is a 4-mile-long area along the watershed for Lake Montebello. It has easy-to-follow trails and provides dogs and owners with lots of cool sights, smells, and sounds. A playground, restrooms, and parking are all on-site.

Robert E. Lee Park at Lakeside Drive and Hollins Avenue offers a place for single dogs and cats to go in search of a mate or someone to hang with for a few hours. Owners of pets also have been known to find a mate with similar interests—namely, pets—at this park along Lake Roland. Dozens and dozens of dogs roam this park or take a plunge. On a warm afternoon or on weekends, it's the place to be. Parking is available on the street.

Northeast of the city on Ebenezer Road about a mile east of U.S. Highway 40 in the White Marsh area is the Dundee Fishing Area of **Gunpowder Falls State Park.** What could be better than calm surf, white sands, and marsh grasses? You'll find all that and convenient on-site parking at this underused section of the state park. Although originally intended for anglers and boaters, it's a perfect place to take pets. Bring a towel—few canines can resist a romp in the waves.

Another section of Gunpowder Falls State Park is north of the city and on U.S. Highway 1 near Kingsville at Belair Road. About 20 minutes outside of Baltimore City, this section of the park offers pet owners a place for hiking and swimming. Along both shores of the river are narrow trails with pull-offs leading into the water. Most pet owners favor the south side, heading east, where they don't have to compete with mountain bikers, fly-fishers, and others using the area. Occasionally, a dog even pulls out a fishy treat from the trout-filled waters. Take a towel and a change of fur because it's hard to keep them out of the water. Parking is available on-site, although it can fill quickly. Hint: Don't park on the highway, because you'll get a quick and expensive ticket. Be patient and wait a few minutes—a spot will open up.

In the Northwest area **Druid Hill Park,** at the intersection of McCulloh Street and Druid Hill Avenue, sports open fields for people and pets. This area outside The Baltimore Zoo is perfect for a quiet picnic with a loved one and pet. In the back area of the park, away from the on-street parking, are trails lined with trees, but the open areas are more than large enough to accommodate even the largest and most rambunctious dogs.

Soldiers Delight Natural Environment Area is on Wards Chapel Road about 8 miles west of I-795 in Owings Mills about 8 miles outside the Baltimore city limits. Several small streams compete with pines and other trees at this largely unnoticed, open, and protected stretch of land. The trails are not well marked, adding more mystique to this area that is used by snowmobilers and equestrians. Don't forget the bag and scoop. Because it remains natural, the need to clean up after pets is even more necessary. Make sure you check your pets for needles and briars after the trip. Parking is available on Wards Chapel Road.

Oregon Ridge Park, off Beaver Dam Read in the Hunt Valley area about 12 miles north of Baltimore City, is a former short-hill skiing area that has given way to a county park, with tulip poplars stretching up high and a tall hill for walking. Below, dogs can venture across open fields while hang-gliders, kite fliers, ballplayers, and picnickers enjoy the day. Bathroom facilities and vending machines are available on-site. You'll find ample parking throughout the area.

If Your Bow-Wow Gets a Boo-Boo

In case Fido gets to feeling a little under the weather, we've included some basic information about the local emergency veterinary clinics. Here's hoping you don't need one, since there's nothing worse than a sick pet—except maybe the smell of a wet pet.

In the Northeast the **Animal Emergency Center,** (410) 252-8387, at 1711 York Road in Timonium, a community just north of Towson, has a veterinarian on-site 24 hours a day, seven days a week.

The **Harford Emergency Veterinary Service,** (410) 836-5173, is at 2105 Laurel Bush Road in Bel Air, a community about 20 miles north of Baltimore City off I-95 in Harford County. A vet is available from 5:00 P.M. to 8:00 A.M. Monday through Thursday and from 8:00 P.M. Friday to 8:00 A.M. Monday.

About 10 miles northwest of Baltimore is the **Reisterstown 24-Hour Veterinary Complex,** (410) 833-0500, at 501 East Main Street. This clinic offers a vet on-site 24 hours a day, seven days a week for emergencies.

In the Southwest corner of the area is **Emergency Veterinary Clinic,** (410) 788-7040, at 32 Mellor Avenue in Catonsville. Just outside the Baltimore Beltway (I-695), this office has a veterinarian on-site from 6:00 P.M. to 8:00 A.M. Monday through Friday and 24 hours on Saturday and Sunday.

back to 1907—offering more than 14,000 acres of open space along the Patapsco River. The park has five separate recreation areas, including the Hilton Area, off Hilton Avenue, south of Rolling Road in Ellicott City; the Hollofield Area, off U.S. 40 just east of Ellicott City; and three other areas in Baltimore, Howard, and Anne Arundel Counties.

One of the best features of Patapsco Valley is the Thomas Viaduct, the world's longest multiple-arched stone railroad bridge. Also, a visit to Bloede Dam is always a fun hike for kids and kids at heart. Or hike the McKeldin Area Trail system for an unparalleled look at the natural valley and river rapids.

Western Hills Park
1437 Rolling Road and Crosby Road,
Woodlawn
(410) 887-0962
An open area in which to run around accompanies picnic tables and playground equipment, such as slides, tunnels, ramps, and bridges at Western Hills. Parking is on-site.

RECREATION

Departments and Centers

BALTIMORE CITY

Baltimore City Recreation Centers
3001 East Drive
(410) 396-7900
www.ci.baltimore.md.us
Baltimore City operates 46 recreation centers in virtually every neighborhood within the city limits. The programs range from

ℹ️ *Most of the larger hotels in the area have relationships with fitness centers or have their own facilities so you can easily find a way to exercise, even in the worst weather.*

after-school activities, including study groups and tutorial sessions, to more recreational offerings and summer camp programs.

The recreation centers also operate programs for toddlers, children, adults, and senior citizens in recreation and therapeutic care. These programs include sports such as baseball, softball, lacrosse, tennis, table tennis, pool, swimming, football, and track and field. Indoor sports are played within the centers, either in gyms or activities rooms, in schools and on fields at schools and parks. More sedate programs, including crafts, art, painting, and dance, are also offered.

The fees for these programs vary, with most costing less than $20 for a full season in a sport. Call to receive a schedule of the activities available.

BALTIMORE COUNTY

Baltimore County Department of Recreation and Parks
38 locations
(410) 887-3864
www.co.ba.md.us
Baltimore County's Department of Recreation and Parks operates 38 separate facilities throughout the county broken into six areas. Programs are available for all ages, with a heavy emphasis on programming for children ranging from gymnastics and arts and crafts to music and sports. Some of the more popular sports are baseball, softball, floor hockey, volleyball, football, soccer, tennis, basketball, and tumbling. Fees to participate usually cost less than $20 for lessons or a season of play. Registrations are typically held at the schools, where activities are held within the gymnasiums, classrooms, and outdoor fields. Call the department for a booklet that lists what programs are offered when.

Baltimore County Police Athletic League Recreation Centers
700 East Joppa Road, Towson
(410) 887-5864
www.co.ba.md.us

The Baltimore County Police Department operates eight recreation centers, offering video games, karate, weight lifting, table tennis, tutoring, and field trips for children ages 7 to 17. Check the Web site for the listing of centers. Most programs are free of charge.

Baltimore County Y.M.C.A
600 West Chesapeake Avenue, Towson
(410) 823-8870
www.ymcamd.org
Four Y.M.C.A.s offer programs for all ages, including swimming, aerobics, tennis, weight lifting, racquetball, driver's education, dance instruction, softball, basketball, and karate. The other locations are at 1719 Sykesville Road in Westminster, (410) 848-3660; 1609 Druid Hill Avenue in Baltimore, (410) 728-1600; 4331 Montgomery Road in Ellicott City, (410) 465-4334; and 850 South Rolling Road in Catonsville, (410) 747-9622. A fee is required for some programs. Call for a schedule of activities.

ANNE ARUNDEL COUNTY

Recreation and Parks
Harry S. Truman Parkway, Annapolis
(410) 222-7300
ww.aacounty.org
A wide range of programs is administered by the county's recreation and parks department in every neighborhood. Swimming, baseball, basketball, football, lacrosse, softball, and other activities are offered for children; many of the same activities and others, including more sedentary pursuits, are offered to adults and senior citizens. Fees ranging from $2.00 to $50.00 are charged for most programs, and advanced registration is suggested. The county publishes a booklet of activities; call to get a copy.

HOWARD COUNTY

Recreation and Parks
Ellicott City
(410) 313-4700

Various recreational programs are offered by the county through neighborhood recreation councils. Sports include baseball, basketball, swimming, gymnastics, and lacrosse. There are a number of indoor programs as well. Fees, topping out at $40, are charged for most programs. Call the previously listed number for a schedule.

ACTIVITIES
Archery/Bowhunting

Baltimore Bowmen
Harford Road, north of Cub Hill Road, Parkville
www.baltimorebowmen.com
Based on a large property north of Baltimore, this group holds archery competitions, shoots, and educational programs throughout the year.

Maryland Bowhunters Society
(800) 434-0811
www.bowsite.com/mbs
The Maryland Bowhunters Society was organized to promote safe and successful bowhunting in the area. It offers information on where to hunt, when hunting is allowed, safe procedures, and other information about bowhunting in the state.

Traditional Bowhunters of Maryland
(410) 651-2259
www.members.aol.com/traditional bowmd
This group was organized to preserve and promote the ancient art of bowhunting with traditional bowhunting equipment. The group holds four shoots a year as well as the TBM Mid-Atlantic Traditional Classic, a large-scale event pitting the best bowhunters in the state against others of their ilk. The classic's date changes each year, so call for more information.

Billiards

Baltimore remains faithful to billiards, or pool as we usually call it. Area players compete as often as they can for such prizes as pride, beer money, or cash.

Not a rowdy crowd by any stretch, most of these players, whether experts or beginners, savor the challenge that comes from trying to sink balls into the pockets in the midst of friends and like-minded spectators.

Unless otherwise noted, expect to find smoking and alcohol available as well as plentiful parking outside.

American Poolplayers Association
(410) 674-POOL
www.poolplayers.com

The city that boasts two world-class pool cue makers, Joss Cues and Tim Scruggs Custom Cues, has a thriving billiards crowd. This organization offers details about events, tournaments, places to play, and get-togethers for advanced, intermediate, and novice pool players.

DOWNTOWN

Baltimore Billiards
7701 Eastern Avenue
(410) 282-7968

Fifteen tables await players here—four of them 9-footers, the rest 8-footers. Most of the players are beginners, although its location makes it attractive to out-of-towners who are in the area. More experienced players often help newcomers to improve their skills, making this a good place to meet people and play better.

In addition to pool, Baltimore Billiards provides a full bar as well as burgers, chicken sandwiches, and other food for

ℹ️ *A quick, cheap, and fun way to exercise and see the sights up-close is to take a brisk walk or run through the area where you are staying. Besides getting a good cardiovascular workout, you get a real sense of the community.*

less than $5.00. Friday and Saturday nights are busiest.

Parking is available on the street outside the club, which is open from 4:00 P.M. to 2:00 A.M. daily.

Edgar's Billiards Club
1 East Pratt Street
(410) 752-8080
www.edgarsclub.com

Less than a block from the Inner Harbor, between the Hyatt Hotel and the Baltimore Convention Center, this club is perfect for the dressed-up businessperson who needs to cut loose for a few hours. Edgar's provides patrons 16 9-foot Olhausen pool tables for play as well as a full restaurant and bar. Smoking and nonsmoking sections are available for pool players.

Edgar's is busiest after work on Thursdays and Fridays. Saturday afternoon and evenings are also busy, especially when the Orioles or Ravens are in town. Over the past few years of its operation, Edgar's has developed a strong reputation as providing all the joys of billiards in a family-friendly environment. Dress ranges from casual to just-getting-off-of-work, depending on the day and hour.

Tables can be rented for $7.00 an hour before 6:00 P.M. and $12.50 an hour afterward. The club is open from 11:00 A.M. to 2:00 A.M. daily. Parking is available, but you will have to pay an hourly rate at several of the Inner Harbor's parking garages.

NORTHEAST

Champion Billiards
Perring Plaza Shopping Center
1969 East Joppa Road at Perring Plaza, Parkville
(410) 665-7500

In what more than a decade ago was a popular Parkville nightclub, Champion today offers nine 9-foot tables in its downstairs area as well as 12 6-foot bar-size tables and three 9-foot tables in its upstairs area. Champion, part of a four location chain in Maryland and Washington, D.C., offers a pleasant, upscale environment for its patrons, who often find themselves dining or imbibing at the 10 booths or eight tables in the dining area. Smoking and non-smoking areas are available.

Champion is open every day from 11:00 A.M. to 2:00 A.M. The cost is $4.95 per person per hour, but call to get a listing of daily specials. Champion offers a lot of specials on drinks, on specific game types, such as eight-ball or nine-ball, and on food, so make sure you check them out before you hit the table.

Should you find yourself with a group where some members would prefer to shop, a strip center and a small mall are within convenient walking distance of Champion.

Kelly's Cue Club
Parkville Shopping Center,
7901 Harford Road, Parkville
(410) 661-4308

In Parkville Shopping Center, less than a mile from Champion Billiards, is Kelly's Cue Club, a smaller facility allowing players to use its six 9-foot Brunswick tables for $3.00 per person per hour before 6:00 P.M. and $3.50 after 6:00 P.M. Open from 10:00 A.M. to midnight Sunday through Thursday, and 10:00 A.M. to 1:00 A.M. on Friday and Saturday, the club is busiest on weekend nights. Most of its customers are folks who gather each week or every few days to play a little pool and get away from life for a while. Smoking is allowed, and no food or drinks are available for sale. Patrons can bring in food and nonalcoholic beverages. When Champion's is busy, Kelly's offers a good, nearby alternative.

Rec Room Billiards
512 York Road, Towson
(410) 337-7178

Located next to the Recher Theatre and the Rec Room Restaurant, Rec Room Billiards plays host to all levels of billiard players, including men and women, adults and children, and lots of college folks from Towson University and Goucher College, both less than a mile from this Towson hot spot.

The Rec Room, as most people call it, provides players with eight 9-foot tables and video games. Busy times tend to correspond to the nightclub acts the place brings in most nights.

Visitors can dine on everything from steaks and crab cakes to submarine sandwiches and pizza. Most main courses cost between $7.00 and $15.00. There's also bar food and a full-service bar. Smoking is allowed throughout the facility. Parking is available at metered spots (25 cents an hour, with no fee charged after 8:00 P.M.).

Rec Room Billiards is open from 10:00 A.M. to 2:00 A.M. every day.

Top Hat Cue Club
8809 Satyr Hill Road, Parkville
(410) 665-1906

Yet a third pool-playing option in Parkville is at Top Hat, where billiard aficionados will find 31 pool tables, including four bar-size 7-footers, two 8-footers, and one billiard table featuring no pockets. If you have to ask about the last one, you probably shouldn't even visit this home for local pool players. Everyone pays the same— $2.50 an hour to play on any table, including its 24 9-foot regulation-size tables.

Management provides free coffee to players along with a selection of sandwiches, meatballs, hot dogs, and Italian sausages. A vending machine and soda machine are also on-site. No beverages, including alcohol, can be brought into the club. Weekend nights are busiest, but a short wait (or a stroll to use the three $2.50 an hour Ping-Pong tables) will usually be all that is required to get a pool table.

The place is open from 10:00 A.M. to 2:00 A.M. Sunday through Thursday and from 10:00 A.M. to 4:00 A.M. Friday and Saturday.

SOUTHWEST

Jack and Jills
Building 11, Crain Industrial Park
512 North Crain Avenue
Glen Burnie
(410) 766-4444

The play is serious here in Glen Burnie at the 18 9-foot regulation tables and the snooker table. Featured in Playing Off the Rail, Jack and Jills never closes, even on Christmas. The "money boys" usually arrive between 5:00 and 10:00 P.M. Friday and hang around until dawn or Sunday, depending on how the games are going. Management has an open approach to its customers. Order and peace are always present inside the building, which offers sandwiches, snacks, and soft drinks. No alcohol is served or permitted inside.

Play costs $4.00 an hour for an individual and $6.50 an hour for two players.

Boardsailing

Baltimore Area Boardsailing Association
(410) 315-8481
www.windsurfbaba.org
The membership association organizes regular competitive boardsailing events with prizes at Gunpowder Falls State Park's Dundee Creek area. Membership for a year is $20.

Camping

Maryland has 47 state parks, 11 of which offer facilities for camping in cabins, on gravel or grass, or in primitive areas far from bathrooms and other conveniences. The state park system accepts campers on a first-come, first-served basis, although some exceptions apply. Contact the Maryland Association of Campgrounds, which can offer referrals and other information about facilities, at (301) 271-7012.

Patapsco Valley State Park
8020 Baltimore National Pike,
Ellicott City
(410) 461-5005
www.dnr.state.md.us.com
The closest park to Baltimore City offering camping is Patapsco Valley State Park in Ellicott City. The Hollofield Area of Patapsco Valley State Park, off U.S. 40 just east of Ellicott City, has more than 100 campsites, some with electricity, on several wooded loops. There's a pump-out station, a shower house, and a pet loop for campers. Rates range from $10 to $50, depending on your needs and the season. Spots can be reserved, and weekends become quite busy with tourists and folks wanting an affordable way to visit the Baltimore area.

Dancing

Swing Baltimore
404 Locust Drive
(877) 537-8055
www.swingbaltimore.org
Swing Baltimore is the area's only nonprofit organization dedicated to preserving swing. The mission is simple—preserve swing dance using the three approaches of education, encouragement, and entertainment. This group hosts workshops, activities, and shows. It is also a great resource for finding out the latest news when it comes to swing dance in Baltimore.

The Friday Night Swing Dance Club
8520 Drumwood Road
(410) 583-7337
www.fridaynightswing.com
The Friday Night Swing Dance Club promotes Swing, Latin, and social dancing in the greater Baltimore area. It encourages dancers of all levels to participate and has weekend dances that are regularly attended by 300 to 400 people. With more than 6,800 people on the mailing list and more than 2,100 on the e-mail list, this is one of the largest dance groups on the East Coast.

Fencing

The Chesapeake Fencing Club
201 Homeland Avenue
(410) 532-7445
Just north of the College of Notre Dame

in North Baltimore, this club offers open practice Monday nights, with supervised junior practice Monday, Thursday, and Saturday evenings for kids ages 6 to 12 years. Foil, saber, and epee lessons are conducted by Moniteur Ray Gordon by appointment and for a varying fee.

Gymnastics

Baltimore County Gymnastics
5811 Allender Road, White Marsh
(410) 335-4646
www.baltocogym.com
Instructional gymnastic classes and tumbling programs are offered to children ages 3 to 12, and cheerleading instruction is offered to high school–age girls. Rates vary, and sessions start several times a year.

Gerstung
1400 Coppermine Terrace,
Mount Washington
(410) 337-7781
www.gerstung.com
In northern Baltimore City, Gerstung offers gymnastics programs and movement education to children from 1 to 13 years of age in a large building off Falls Road near I-83. Skills classes are also presented to children aged 5 to 13. Dance classes and rock climbing are also available. Call for rates and information on special summer programs.

Gymnastics Elite
899 Airport Park Road, Glen Burnie
(410) 590-3547
Tumbling and gymnastics for children ages 18 months to 18 years are offered at

Youth recreational programs can fill quickly—especially soccer, basketball, baseball, softball, and lacrosse. So if you want the kids to play, don't delay when it's time to register.

this site south of Baltimore City, off I-695. There is also a 40-foot spring floor and 30-foot tumble mount as well as the standard vault, beam, and bars. Dance classes and toddler programs are also available.

Horseback Riding

Maryland is horse country, so horseback-riding opportunities abound. Among the starting points are the Maryland Horse Council at (410) 489-7829, www.md horsecouncil.org, and the Maryland Horse Show Association at (410) 452-5202, www.mdhsa.org.

Running

Howard County Striders
(410) 964-1998
www.striders.net
More than 1,000 runners in the Baltimore–Washington area are part of this group that holds weekly "bagel runs" at the Swim Center at Wilde Lake in Columbia, about 10 miles south of Baltimore in Howard County. The runs start at 7:00 A.M. on Saturday, and bagels are frequently part of the post-run meal. The group also organizes races throughout the region and has many other weekly runs.

GOLF

Golf in the Baltimore area is undergoing a renaissance.

Young players and older couples are hitting the links, extending the reach of a sport that has traditionally catered to middle-aged men. More people find the challenge of chasing a small, white ball around on sun-drenched fields of green a relaxing way to unwind. Other duffers are using the links for business, making deals on the greens or in their carts, and still others are seeking to follow in the footsteps of Tiger Woods.

In the quest for the green, Baltimore has for decades offered a variety of courses, including several municipal tracks that for more than 40 years have provided hackers with big challenges in urban settings. During the 1950s and early '60s, several of Baltimore's municipal courses played host to the Eastern Open, one of the Professional Golfer's Association's premier events.

Those dependable courses remain a bargain for beginners and intermediate players, while some of the publicly owned courses and a newer municipal course in Baltimore County, Greystone Golf Course, provide challenges for even the best golfers.

Don't get us wrong. Baltimore isn't Myrtle Beach, South Carolina, yet. But you can find good courses and some real bargain plays in the city and the surrounding parts of Maryland. In fact, there are good courses in practically every section of the state, especially near major roadways such as I-70 and I-68 to the west, I-95 to the north and south, and U.S. 50 to the east.

The area's weather is good for golf, though the hearty golfers play in any weather, including snow. The best seasons for teeing off are spring and fall, but winter play is not that uncommon or uncomfortable. With the average winter temperature in the 40s, and occasional days in the 50s

and even the 60s, Insiders keep a close eye on the weather forecast, hoping for a warm front that will allow more comfortable play.

At the other extreme is summer, when the three Hs—hazy, hot, and humid—can make for a long day on the links, even if you're shooting par. The best way to avoid as much of the three-H treatment as possible is to tee off before 10:00 A.M. or after 4:00 P.M., but be forewarned: During the hottest part of summer (mid-July through August), these are typically the most coveted tee times. Hot days can also scorch the grass on even the most immaculate fairways and greens; that might make the course especially good for low liners, but the humidity can actually lessen the length of a good tee shot.

Like most areas, foursomes are mandated at most courses, meaning you're probably going to be paired up with others if you don't have enough friends to fill two carts. Most courses are too crowded to allow for walking, though exceptions are noted in this chapter.

There are a few semiprivate courses available in the immediate Baltimore area. Almost every private course requires that you play with a member; there's practically no chance to buy your way onto the private course of your choice.

The listings for each course include the cost of greens fees for one player; these prices are subject to change. Prices include the cart fee except where otherwise noted; again, carts are almost always mandated. In cases where a higher fee is charged on weekends than on weekdays, an average has been given. Yardages are from the white tees (middle markers).

All courses listed have pro shops with clubs, tees, and other essential and nonessential golf equipment.

No guide can tell you as much as you will learn by playing a course, but our goal is to help you choose the right place for you to tee it up. A great Web site for information on all Maryland courses is marylandgolf.com. Fore!

Advance notice needed to reserve tee times varies from two to seven days. Make sure you do it as soon as possible, especially for Friday and weekends.

[i]

NORTHEAST

Clifton Park Golf Course
2701 St. Lo Drive
(410) 243-3500

A good course for beginning and intermediate players, this Baltimore City–owned, 5,714-yard course has no water and just a few trees. At a price of $19, it's a good bargain for people in the city, especially golfers who like to walk. The cost is the same whether you ride or walk. Giving this par 70 course an urban flavor are the several roads that run nearby (all of which are out of bounds). Golf pro Mark Paolini offers lessons, while the course provides practice greens, a restaurant, and a snack bar.

Forest Park Golf Course
2900 Hillsdale Road
(410) 448-0734

Watch out for what is the largest sand trap on the East Coast, according to the operators here. The mega-bunker on this 5815-yard course used to be a water hazard but was covered with cement and sand some years ago. The 18th hole features a par 5 double-dogleg, forcing you to avoid the slice for two successive shots; if you can't, you're in big trouble trying to make par at 71. A round costs $20. Tim Sanders offers golf lessons at the course, which features a snack bar and shower facilities.

Greystone Golf Course
2115 White Hall Road, White Hall
(410) 887-1945
www.baltimoregolfing.com

A little farther away than most other courses listed, this 6,925-yard course is worth the drive if you are looking for a challenge. To make par (72), you're going to have to successfully negotiate your ball through a 140-foot elevation change and 85 bunkers lining the fairways and surrounding the greens—average-size at about 5,000 to 6,000 square feet. It's one of the only bentgrass courses in the area.

Designed by Joe Lee, who designed the Doral's Blue Monster and Disney courses, the toughest hole is the 150-yard No. 4. Water lines the shot, with a bulkhead to the right for this distinct downhill shot. Miss it and you'll lose your ball to the water, which comes into play on about five holes on the back nine. An average round costs $55, a real bargain for a tough-playing course. After you finish your round, you can enjoy lunch or dinner in Greystone's dining room or a cold drink on the patio deck overlooking the course.

Greystone is an easy 30-minute trek from Baltimore City. To get there, head north on I-83 north past Towson to the White Hall exit, where signs point the rest of the way.

Longview Golf Course
1 Cardigan Road, Timonium
(410) 887-7735
www.baltimoregolfing.com

An ideal, short course for beginners, this 5,880-yard masterpiece opened in 1971 on top of a landfill. No signs of the previous life lurking under the surface are present—not even to the deer and foxes that are common sights for golfers on the back nine. There's practically no water and very few trees, so errant shots don't necessarily prevent a golfer from finding the green quickly on this par 70 course. A round costs $20 or less. Pro John Lazzell offers lessons. A snack bar is on-site.

Mount Vista Golf Course
11101 Bradshaw Road, Bradshaw
(410) 592-5467

Be prepared to use all your clubs and lose

a few balls at this 3,652-yard, par 72 course. Narrow, tree-lined fairways require expert skills on this executive course, which features eight par 4 holes and 10 par 3s. This jewel has a par 3 island green on No. 3 and a par 4 peninsular green on No. 6. Because the course is flat, senior players find it a good one to play; about half the users walk. A round of golf costs $24 whether you walk or ride.

Mount Pleasant Golf Course
6001 Hillen Road
(410) 254-5100
Here's your chance to play on the course where the great Arnold Palmer won his first PGA tournament, the old Eastern Open. Sam Snead also won on this 6,003-yard course, which played host to the Eastern until 1962. Designed by maintenance employees for the City of Baltimore, this par 71 municipal course pits golfers against mature trees and lots of hills, meaning few flat lies. On a breezy day, the back nine can be a duffer's nightmare. It's one of the busiest courses in the area; 85,000 rounds of golf are played each year, so reservations are necessary. A round of golf will cost you $23 if walking and $35 with a cart on weekends. Golf pro Jim Deck provides lessons. A snack bar is on-site.

If paired with people you don't know, any of the following topics are good Baltimore conversation starters: the weather, the Orioles, the Ravens, rush-hour traffic, and did we mention the weather?

Pine Ridge Golf Course
2101 Dulaney Valley Road, Lutherville
(410) 252-1408
Built in 1958, this mature, 5,954-yard course hasn't lost its luster. Located next to the Loch Raven Reservoir, the par 72 course features lots of fully grown trees, moderate hills, and more than 100 bunkers. It played host to the Eastern Open on

occasion during the 1950s and '60s and offers golfers of all skill levels a moderate challenge on a course where every hole has a dogleg. At $23 a round, it's a definite bargain. Pro Kim Hand offers lessons at the course created by Alex "Nipper" Campbell and Gus Hook. A locker room, showers, and a snack bar are available.

NORTHWEST

Diamond Ridge Golf Course and The Woodlands
2309 Ridge Road, Woodlawn
(410) 887-1349
www.baltimoregolfing.com
Diamond Ridge features two fine tracks for enthusiasts. Try the new Woodlands, so named because of the 3,000—yes, 3,000—white dogwoods lining the fairways. As one pro put it, "It's like Christmas lights all around you when those dogwoods are in bloom." Lindsay Ervin designed this 6,500-yard, par 72 course that opened in 1998. Dramatic elevation changes offer a unique hole-by-hole mix. Check out the No. 17 par 5 hole that drops into a valley for a tough second shot. The No. 1 is a 470-yard par 4 that promises to get a fair number of golfers off to a sub-par start heading to the second tee. The pro on this course is Chris Hanson.

The older, 6,300-yard, par 72 Diamond Ridge course features rolling hills and open stretches. The lush fairways and rolling terrain has made Diamond Ridge a favorite of local golfers for more than 30 years. The 10th hole takes you over the water, while other holes have you battling the trees. Frank Blind is the pro at Diamond Ridge. The courses share a clubhouse and state-of-the-art practice facility. A round costs $45 on the new course and $22 to $37 on the older course.

Francis Scott Key Golf Club
1900 River Downs Drive, Finksburg
(410) 526-2000 or (800) 518-7337
www.golfmatrix.com
Francis Scott Key Golf is one of the most

scenic and at the same time challenging courses in the Baltimore area. Designed by renowned architect Arthur Hills, the par 72 golf course offers four par 3 and four par 5. Located about 25 miles outside Baltimore, this semiprivate course welcomes public customers. This course, just less than 6,500 yards, was selected the 1995–1996 Best Course (Honorable Mention) in the Baltimore–Washington, D.C. area by *Washington Golf Monthly Magazine*. Daily fee rates can vary greatly. Based on the day of week, season, and time of day, rates can range from $22 up to $67. The director of golf on this course is Steve Reeves.

Golf Center at Reisterstown
301 Mitchell Drive, Reisterstown
(410) 833-7721

A nine-hole executive course, the Golf Center draws beginners and good golfers alike, most of whom want a quick golf fix. Playing it through twice, it's almost impossible to make par, which is set at 61 for the total 3,772 yards. The toughest holes are No. 5, which is a 150-yard water shot that looks much easier than it is, and No. 14, a 205-yard par 3 shot over a pond. The facility also features batting cages, three miniature golf courses, and a driving range to keep the kids or others busy while you hit the links. A round costs $17 with a cart, but you don't have to ride. Greens fees alone are $10. There is also a snack bar.

Waverly Woods Golf Course
2100 Warwick Way, Ellicott City
(410) 313-9182
www.waverlywoodsnet.com/lifestyle

Located just 9 miles west of the Baltimore Beltway, Waverly Woods offers a 7,000-yard championship design through farmland and beautiful wooded areas. Opened in 1998, this par 72 course was designed by world-renowned golf course architect Arthur Hills. There is a 9,000-square-foot putting green, a separate short game practice area with practice bunkers, and an eight-acre practice range complete

Dress in layers. Baltimore's weather is notoriously fickle. In summer, an umbrella isn't a bad idea. Sudden, sometimes severe, late afternoon showers and thunderstorms can hit when cold fronts meet a prevailing warm front. They usually go as quickly as they come.

with a grass teeing area of over 60,000 square feet. When the golfing is done, the course offers an outdoor patio on the clubhouse with views of the 1st, 10th, and 18th holes. The pro at Waverly Woods is David Kim, and a round of golf in the summer, including cart, costs $61 Monday through Thursday and $78 Friday through Sunday.

Willow Springs Golf Course
12960 Livestock Road, West Friendship
(410) 489-7700

Willow Springs is an 18-hole, par 62 links style golf course that is both playable for the occasional golfer and satisfying for the serious golfer. The course offers a quick play if you're on a tight schedule. Willow Springs boasts undulating greens, grass mounds, sand bunkers, and water hazards. Tee time reservations may be made up to seven days in advance. And while Willow Springs does not require reservations, it does recommend them. The facility also offers a 32 station, full-length lighted driving range, a practice sand bunker, and putting green. It will cost you $32 to play all 18 holes at Willow Springs, but call ahead for specials.

Worthington Valley Country Club
2425 Greenspring Avenue, Owings Mills
(410) 887-9890

Worthington Valley seems wide open, but this course is narrow (20 to 30 yards wide) and tree-lined. It remains one of the area's best-kept secrets, often because people assume wrongly that its name means it's a private course. This par 70, 6,145-yard course is a real challenge, designed in 1952 by its late owner James

Dukes, a local professional golfer. Set on 110 acres, this course is an easy walk, as tees and greens are set close together. Many golfers find they're in good shape until they get to the 14th hole. It's a 600-yard par 5 followed by No. 15, a 240-yard par 3, No. 16, a 440-yard par 4; and No. 17, a 450-yard par 4. A round costs $30.

SOUTHEAST

Rocky Point Golf Course
1935 Back River Neck Road, Essex
(410) 887-0215
www.baltimoregolfing.com

This 6,750-yard, par 72 course reminds some players of a British Open site. Golfers here enjoy breathtaking views of the Chesapeake Bay from several of the holes that border this body of water. When it's windy out, particularly in the fall, the course becomes really tough, especially on No. 10 and No. 11, which are right along the shoreline. Owned and operated by the Baltimore County Revenue Authority, this is a great walking course that rewards players who keep the ball in the wide fairways. Rocky Point has a front nine that is fairly open, while the back nine is fairly tight. Beginners will find the four doglegs a big challenge. A round costs $31; walkers pay $19 Saturday, Sunday, and holidays. Saturday before noon costs $35 whether walking or riding. A discount is available for seniors.

SOUTHWEST

Carroll Park Golf Course
2100 Washington Boulevard
(410) 685-8344

The only 12-hole course in the area, Carroll Park's 3,214-yard course is good for beginners and intermediate players and is a growing favorite among women. It's a good course to walk, featuring eight par 4 holes and four par 3s. The course's newest hole, the 232-yard No. 4, requires a low, down-the-middle approach to set you up for a slight right dogleg. For an afternoon golfer looking for a quick game, this course can be completed in about two hours, even when it's busy. A round costs $15; it's $7.50 for walkers.

ON THE WATER

Since settlers first encountered what is now Baltimore, a main attraction has been its waters, hundreds of big and small tributaries to the Chesapeake Bay. Beautiful rivers, gentle and serene coves, an open harbor, and streams perfect for spending time with a fishing pole or a rudder in hand—these are some of the area's most respected and protected resources for anglers, boaters, windsurfers, and personal watercraft operators.

If you're looking for a place to fly-fish, the Gunpowder River offers one of the best trout streams on the East Coast. If you're eager to practice steering a catamaran, there are few better spots than the rivers lining eastern Baltimore County. Their many coves and inlets offer calm and shallow waters that enable the novice or the most experienced skipper to practice his or her skills.

If you want tidal waters, the Chesapeake Bay and some of its larger tributaries provide what you're looking for. If you seek nontidal waters, some of the rivers flowing in eastern Baltimore County are your best bet.

In this chapter we introduce you to Baltimore's waters and their attributes, including marinas, services, charters, and rentals. You'll also find information on boating, fishing, crabbing, and other watersports in the area.

County, and Anne Arundel County as well as U.S. Coast Guard units from Curtis Bay, an area near the Inner Harbor on the Patapsco River.

The number of people boating in Maryland has been on the rise in recent years, with explosive growth in the personal watercraft category. In the wrong hands, these sleek and slick boats can mar any boating adventure. Whether using a Jet Ski or Sea-Doo or passing by one on the water, remember to keep your guard up.

And remember that people are not the only living things out there. The bay and the rivers and creeks leading into it are full of marine life that would prefer—if they had the choice—not to share the waters with plastic bags, empty beer cans, and paper cups. So, in an effort to grant the wishes of the fishes, so to speak, we Marylanders are trying to "Save the Bay." The outgrowth of this program has been to expand the protection and restoration in the last few years into the hundreds of tributaries that feed into it. As a result, we look unkindly on those who pollute its waters, whether they drop a piece of trash into Minebank Run, a small feeder stream into the larger Gunpowder River, or pump out their on-board sewage system into the bay itself. Help us to keep the bay clean, safe, and fun, because it's our only one. And the area wouldn't be nearly as nice without it.

SAFETY ON THE HIGH SEAS

With water comes responsibility, and Maryland's Natural Resources Police (a division of its Department of Natural Resources) keeps a close watch over the surrounding waters to make sure activities follow these rules and regulations. They are joined by marine police teams from Baltimore City, Baltimore County, Howard

WATERWAYS

Consider this your formal introduction to the bodies of water that surround Baltimore. Here we've outlined the activities they welcome, the sights that dot their shorelines, and the hazards you should be aware of. For more information about boating, fishing, and watersports, see those sections later in the chapter.

Numbers to Know

If you experience marine problems, contact the Maryland Natural Resources Police, (800) 419-0743, or use Channel 16 VHF on your on-board radio.

For general information from the Department of Natural Resources, call (877) 620-8DNR

Boating emergencies, channel 16 VHF (monitored by Coast Guard, city, state, and county police)
Coast Guard Search and Rescue, (410) 576-2525
Baltimore County Fire Department, 911 or (410) 887-5974
Baltimore County Police Department, 911
Maryland Natural Resources Police, (410) 260-8881 or (800) 628-9944
Local Weather, (410) 936-1212
Coast Guard Station Curtis Bay, (410) 576-2625
Coast Guard Station Stillpond, (410) 778-2201
Coast Guard Boating Safety Hotline, (800) 368-5647
Coast Guard Auxiliary Flotilla boating class, (800) 336-BOAT

The Chesapeake Bay

The origins of the world's largest estuary, the Chesapeake Bay, date back to the last Ice Age, more than 20,000 years ago, when a colder climate prevailed on Earth. Back then, sea level was more than 300 feet lower than it is today.

Now, the bay has an average depth of 21 feet, with its deepest point in the middle bay, near Bloody Point, where it drops to 174 feet. The bay's length is 195 miles, and it draws water from a 64,000-square-mile area, extending to the headwaters of the Susquehanna River, 441 miles away from its mouth in the northern bay in Otsego, New York. Water flowing from New York to Pennsylvania to Maryland makes its way to the bay. As hard as it is to believe, the bay's shoreline at 4,000 miles is longer than the shoreline of the Pacific Ocean on the West Coast. Really.

The bay's 55-foot channel makes it a favorite for shipping companies sending ore, vehicles, coal, and other materials from all over the world to the port of Baltimore as well as Hampton Roads, Virginia, which is closer to the Atlantic Ocean and Baltimore's competitor to the south.

Because of the intense amount of commercial traffic, operating recreational vessels on the bay can be more challenging than on some of the rivers. Keep in mind that the larger commercial vessels should always have the right of way because of their size, which prohibits them from being able to maneuver easily in the channel. In foul weather, give them a wider berth and heed their horn blows.

In addition to larger vessels, the bay's depth can be a hazard. Shallow waters with unpredictable shifts, especially in side creeks, can run you aground. Furthermore, dredging of channels isn't always done as often as necessary, and sometimes the depths reflected in maps can be fluid, to say the least.

Weather conditions can also challenge

boaters. Sudden changes in weather are frequent in summer, although variances occur in spring and fall, too. Although the bay tends to offer good boating weather most of the time, sudden storms can bring high winds, thunderstorms, and heavy downpours in areas where the sun was shining brightly just a few minutes prior. Keep an ear to the radio to monitor situations as they develop, and when signs of possible trouble appear, heed them quickly. Don't wait for the storm to hit—act beforehand.

If you're planning to fish for striped bass (rockfish), you'll want to be in the deeper waters of the lower bay rather than northern sections. The fish seem to favor the deeper areas, with Bloody Point being among the best sites for them. You also might want to talk to other mariners to see where they're hitting. Just watch out for the occasional lie, designed to keep you out of their special spot.

Susquehanna River and Flats

From the city of Havre de Grace, where the Concord Point Lighthouse still stands below the Conowingo Hydroelectric Plant's dam, to the head of the Chesapeake Bay are the Susquehanna Flats, an open and expansive area known for its calm waters and marvelous natural sights. American bald eagles nest on the small islands and can often be seen in the early morning hours among the power lines and trees near the flats. A keen eye is the key to seeing these symbols of America.

In the summer fish lifts carry American and hickory shad, two protected species, over the dam on their spawning tour to the Harrisburg area of Pennsylvania. Largemouth bass, feeding on the shad and other brackish water species, are prevalent in the waters of the Susquehanna throughout the year. Crabs, however, are not too prevalent in this river.

Aberdeen Proving Ground Restricted Waters

The lower Susquehanna, Gunpowder, and Bush Rivers, from Spesutie Island to the mouth of the Gunpowder River, is closed off to boaters from 7:00 A.M. to 5:00 P.M. Monday through Friday, except on national holidays. As part of Aberdeen Proving Ground, established in 1917 after the Sandy Hook, New Jersey, proving ground became inadequate, anchoring, swimming, and going on shore are prohibited. Military patrols aboard white boats with orange stripes keep stray boats from restricted spaces, where tank and munitions testing occurs on weekdays and weekends. The sound of the blasts can carry for miles over the water, often scaring those who hear it for the first time. The busiest testing days are Tuesday and Thursday. When the cloud cover is good, testing is more intense.

Sections of Aberdeen house military functions and are therefore restricted to visitors. Guests are invited to tour the United States Army Ordnance Museum, which has one of the world's leading collections of military ordnance, ranging from small arms to 240 large armored vehicles, tanks, and artillery pieces, some of the last survivors of their type. The outside includes a 25-acre tank park (see the Day Trips chapter).

Gunpowder River and Bush River

In Harford County, the Bush River is among the more quiet, supporting a variety of local boaters and many visitors from Pennsylvania, Delaware, and other areas to the north. The Bush River feeds into the Gunpowder River, and because of a low Amtrak railroad bridge, the river has a 12-foot vertical clearance, prohibiting large sailboats from entering. The Gunpowder, farther north and west, offers excellent fishing and recreation and is protected as part of the 16,000-acre Gunpowder Falls State Park. Farther east, where the water is deeper, the Gunpowder plays host to a variety of boating and aquatic recreational activities, including swimming, water-skiing, and scuba diving. The Gunpowder River channel runs at 11 feet for 2 miles, from 6 to 8 feet for 3.5 miles, and about 5 feet in a dredged section below Joppatowne. Throughout the river, fishing is excellent, with stocking of brown trout in the spring and fall bringing the species total to an astounding 150 to 200 fish per acre. With those numbers, it's hard to miss, assuming you can find a place to cast. Word of stockings brings out the masses, so head out early or during the off season, such as winter and hot summer days, for the best results. You can also find some carp and catfish among the trout.

Middle River

An active boating area near Baltimore, Middle River is home to a number of marinas, waterfront restaurants, and boatyards. The river has several creeks, including Galloway Creek, Frog Mortar Creek, Stansbury Creek, Dark Head Creek, Hopkins Creek, Sue Creek, Hog Pen Creek,

Norman's Creek, and Seneca Creek. These creeks provide quiet, calm, and protected waters where waterskiing, swimming, and personal watercraft are allowed. Crabbing and fishing are frequent activities of residents and visitors to the area. Bass, carp, and catfish are frequent visitors to these waters. On weekends and holidays, a 6-knot speed limit is enforced upstream of Galloway Point.

Back River

Back River is between Middle River and the Patapsco River, an area that used to be home to a great deal of industry and still shows signs of the industrial age. The river is home to a number of recreational anglers and boaters who moor their boats along the shorelines. Back River has a poor reputation in the area because of the Back Water Treatment Facility, which can offer a pungent aroma.

Despite this problem—far larger in reputation than in reality—the river is a peaceful getaway from the more widely used Gunpowder, Middle, and Patapsco Rivers.

A favorite place for crabbers, moving among the crab lines or the people checking them can sometimes require effort. The area supports the same bass, carp, and catfish populations as its fellow rivers to its north.

Selected Baltimore Firsts

In 1788 the *Chesapeake* was the first American vessel to raise the colors of the United States above its billowing sails.

Our Constellation was the first ship to capture an enemy ship after the Revolution in 1797.

Isaac McKim of Fells Point built the first clipper ship, the *Ann McKim*, in 1833.

The first steamship made wholly of American steel, the *DeRosset*, was registered here in 1839.

—Excerpted from Baltimore— America's City of Firsts, *a pamphlet published by Baltimore Bicentennial Celebration, Inc.*

Patapsco River

The Inner Harbor overshadows the Patapsco River by name and opportunity, but in spite of this, the river claims its own recognition. Many of the area's finer marinas are in the Inner Harbor, Fells Point, and Canton areas, where big-ticket boats dock during weekends and summer nights. Closer to the Inner Harbor are paddleboat rentals for up to $8.00 a half hour and sightseeing tours. (For more information about sightseeing tours, see the Charter Boat and Sailboating sections later in this chapter as well as the By Water section of the Getting Here, Getting Around chapter.) These vessels, including pontoon boats, water taxis, and larger boats that head to Annapolis, can make for challenging traveling, although passing by the ports and industrial complex built up along both shores is fascinating. The Francis Scott Key Bridge is another site to behold heading up the river, as is the Domino Sugar sign. Stony Creek, Bodkin Creek, home of the Curtis Bay Coast Guard yard, and Rock Creek are peaceful inlets along the river.

Don't expect to find easy docking and mooring along the Patapsco. Most people plan well in advance for the right to dock along the Inner Harbor piers or the commercial piers nearby. To expect last-minute accommodations is to underestimate the popularity of the area and the need for those with great boats to cruise the Inner Harbor on a hot summer's night. To reserve a space, contact the Baltimore Public Docking Master's office at (410) 396-3174. Larger boats should make a reservation all the time, while smaller boats should reserve spaces at either the Harbor or Canton sites a few days in advance for weekends or summer weekdays.

Farther up, the Patapsco River provides fishing opportunities in Patapsco Valley State Park, a 14,000-acre recreational area in western Baltimore County. The park offers fishing, tubing, canoeing, and other waterside activities throughout the summer months, while anglers find their way to the river throughout the year. (See our Parks and Recreation chapter for more information about Patapsco Valley State Park.) Crabbing in the Inner Harbor is relatively poor and not recommended, as the crabs have been exposed to the pollution from trash and commercial vessel activity.

Loch Raven Reservoir

This sprawling water-collection area for much of Baltimore County is on Loch Raven Drive in Towson, (410) 887-7692. It's a great spot for fishing for largemouth bass in the spring, especially in the thick bed grasses of the smaller coves, and smallmouth bass and crappie in the summer, especially toward the end of the summer when waters warm up significantly. Fishing from the shore or by boat can be rewarding and relaxing, especially to those who covet quiet and peaceful spots removed from the more urbanized area nearby.

Rowboat rentals, ranging from $3.00 an hour to $12.00 for a day, are available. (See the Parks and Recreation chapter for more information about the reservoir.)

Loch Raven Fishing Center, near Dulaney Valley Road, www.co.ba.md.us, is operated by the Baltimore County Department of Recreation and Parks. Fishing, boating, and docking are offered on a daily or seasonal basis. Rentals include rowboats, canoes, johnboats, and electric-powered boats; rates start at $14 a day. You can not have more than three people in one boat at a time. A valid driver's license is required. Anglers make up the

Tide Point, a former Proctor and Gamble Plant built in the 1920s, recently benefited from a $67 million redevelopment. Located on the harbor in South Baltimore, the office park has a lovely waterfront promenade replete with Adirondack Chairs for lounging. Grab a cup of coffee from the nearby cafe and enjoy Baltimore's working waterfront.

bulk of the rental business, but sightseers can also rent boats. Keep in mind that it can be difficult to get a boat in the afternoon when the weather is good. Call (410) 887-7692 for more information or to check on the availability of boats during the day.

The facility is open April through Labor Day from 6:00 A.M. to dusk. After Labor Day and through October, the center is closed on Tuesday and Thursday. It opens at 7:00 A.M. all other days. Gasoline-powered boats are prohibited. No boats are rented after 4:00 P.M.

BOATING

Give Baltimoreans a body of water larger than a puddle, and they'll try to sail or motor a boat over it. Especially popular are the Chesapeake Bay, the Susquehanna, Gunpowder, and Bush Rivers, and the Middle and Patapsco Rivers (see the Waterways section for more information).

What follows is a roundup of some of the marinas, ramps, and boat rental providers in the area.

Marinas

GUNPOWDER RIVER

Gunpowder Cove Marina
510 Riviera Drive, Joppatowne
(410) 679-5454
www.gunpowdercove.com
Since 1969 this marina has been providing service to the Joppatowne area, where at least half of the mariners come in for weekends. The marina on the Gunpowder River at Taylor's Creek has 294 protected slips and a mean depth of 5 feet. Electricity and showers are provided, along with marine supplies and engine and hull repairs. Gas, but no diesel, is available on-site. A convenience store and other amenities are within walking distance in Joppatowne. Transient slip rates vary.

BACK RIVER

Weaver's Marine Service
730 Riverside Drive, Essex
(410) 686-4944
www.weaversmarine.com
A full-service marina since 1945, Weaver's offers 96 slips and a variety of services to boaters. Among its amenities are gas, showers, and pump-out facilities as well as a marine supply service and marine repair and mechanic services. The marina, which is 5 miles from the Chesapeake Bay on the Back River, has a depth of up to 6 feet. Weavers offers all kinds of sales and services, including pump-outs, washing and waxing, gas dock, haul-outs, parts department, and insurance repairs.

MIDDLE RIVER

Anchor Bay Marina
202 Nanticoke Road, Essex
(410) 574-0777
On Hopkins Creek, about 2.5 miles from the mouth of Middle River, this 6-foot-to-8-foot-deep facility provides uncovered slips for up to 42-foot vessels and covered slips for yachts measuring up to 50 feet. Among the amenities are showers, restrooms, restaurants next door, and grocery stores within a few blocks of the marina. Boating services include gas and diesel fuel pumps, generators, AC and electrical service, which can be done at the slip, and parts and accessories available at the Ships Store.

Chesapeake Yachting Center
400 Wagner Lane, Essex
(410) 335-4900
www.chesapeakeyachting.com
Designed for yacht owners, this marina features a calm, sheltered harbor on Frog Mortar Creek on Middle River. With more than 200 slips, ranging from 24 feet to 70 feet long, the center caters to yacht owners and motorboat operators. It features a complete marine maintenance and repair facility as well as 24-hour, on-site staff, pump-out facilities, travel lifts, sail lofts, mast and rigging service, engine shop, and a fuel dock for gas and diesel fill-ups.

The site also offers lots of parking, with convenient access to I–695 (the Baltimore Beltway) just a few miles away.

Maryland Marina
3501 Red Rose Farm, Middle River
(410) 335–8722
This 360-slip marina along Frog Mortar Creek lives up to its slogan "Unique Among Marinas." The facility offers all the usual amenities, including electricity and water at all slips, a store, bathhouses, shower and laundry facilities, yacht care, sailboat hardware and rigging, pump-out facilities, and spaces for up to 200 boat trailers. Maryland Marina also offers a restaurant, the Wild Duck Cafe. The nightly rate for transients is $1.00 a foot, with a $22 minimum, at the 4-foot-to-6-foot draft facility. The marina also operates a new and used boat brokerage.

Porter's Seneca Marina
918 Seneca Park Road, Middle River
(410) 335–6563
www.porterssenecamarina.com
At the mouth of Seneca Creek, giving boaters direct access to the Chesapeake Bay, this 125-slip marina offers a quiet resting place, especially for families. Proclaiming itself a "family marina," Porter's offers picnicking facilities, including tables, grills, a play area, and a swimming pool. Conveniently located near Hart-Miller Island, the marina has a variety of amenities, including haul-out and winter storage, a ship's store with ice, a gas dock, mechanics, supplies, a 30-ton open-end travel lift, and a cement launching ramp. Its showers and restroom facilities are available 24 hours a day.

PATAPSCO RIVER

Baltimore Public Docking
Patapsco River at Baltimore Harbor and Canton
(410) 396–3174
The city's docks are always crowded, but the locations at the Inner Harbor and Canton can be among the best for sightseers or for those seeking to be seen. High visibility comes at a high price at this 16-foot-deep marina. Electricity and showers are available, along with ice. Other services, including grocery stores, pharmacies, shopping, and restaurants, are near each dock.

Center Dock Marina
802 South Caroline Street
(410) 685-9055, ext. 223
www.livingclassrooms.org
In the heart of Downtown Baltimore and within a mile of Little Italy, Fells Point, and the Inner Harbor area, Center Dock Marina offers 48 modern, floating slips nestled on Baltimore's only thriving wetland. The sheltered marina offers electricity and water hookups, access to water taxi service, laundry and restroom facilities, and a picnic area. The marina is located at the Living Classrooms Foundation Maritime Institute, where youth are taught about Maryland's skipjack fleet and where some of these maidens of the sea are being restored. A tour of this facility is a must for any boating fan.

Inner Harbor East Marina
801 Lancaster Street
(410) 625-1700
www.innerharboreastmarina.com
This marina offers just about everything a boater could ask for, including 200 state-of-the-art floating boat slips. Located in the heart of the Inner Harbor, this marina has a 24-hour staff, ship store, on-site parking, fuel pier, water, and electricity hook-up. There is also an on-site restaurant with observation deck. Transients are welcome.

Inner Harbor Marina of Baltimore
400 Key Highway
(410) 837-5339
www.innerharbormarina.com
The Inner Harbor Marina of Baltimore has been serving Baltimore boaters and visitors for more than 20 years. Its convenient location in the heart of Downtown makes it a great place to dock and enjoy the sites. Both overnight and day docking are available. Amenities include 24-hour security and customer service, 24-hour dock

and pump-out facility, and a 24-hour convenience and marine store. There is also a laundry facility, concierge service, and business center.

Middle Branch Marina
3101 Waterview Avenue
(410) 539-2628
www.middlebranchmarina.com
Under the Hanover Street Bridge, about 1 mile directly across the Patapsco River from the Inner Harbor, this 365-slip marina is one of the most affordable for all the amenities it provides. With a transient rate of $1 per foot and facilities for everything from a dinghy to a 60-footer, it's hard to go wrong. The 6-foot-deep, protected cove provides safety, security, and access. A security fence surrounds the place, free parking is available to all users, and it's convenient to the Light Rail system, which allows access to the airport and Baltimore's Inner Harbor area. Among the amenities are water and electricity connections to each slip, shower rooms, a full-service repair yard, and a ships store as well as a do-it-yourself service area, where tools are provided at an hourly rate. Gas and diesel service and pump-out facilities are also available.

Boat Ramps

Baltimore County operates five public boat ramps, where fees are $5.00 a day or $15.00 for the year. The sites include:
Cox's Point, (410) 887-0255, leading into the Back River from Essex
Inverness Park, (410) 887-7228, which leads into Bear Creek and Middle River in Dundalk
Merritt Point Park, (410) 887-7155, off Bullneck Creek and leading into the Patapsco River
Rocky Point, (410) 887-3780, off Back River Neck Road and leading into the bay in Essex
Turner Station, (410) 887-7228, off Broening Highway in Dundalk, leading into the Patapsco River.

Marine Services

Deckelman's Boat Yard
201 Oak Avenue, Middle River
(410) 391-6482 or (410) 850-2993
(beeper)
If your boat's in need of a tow, Deckelman's is the place to go. They're quick, efficient, and reasonably priced. They're also available 24 hours a day. They'll tow your boat where you want it to go, or they'll do the work themselves.

Tidewater Yacht Service Center
1020 Key Highway East
(410) 625-4992
www.tysc.com
If you can float it, Tidewater Yacht Service Center can fix it—at a guaranteed rate established before the work begins. At the entrance to the Inner Harbor area, near the prominent Domino Sugar sign, Tidewater specializes in cleaning and detailing, bottom painting, engine and generator repairs and sales, fiberglass and blister repair, woodworking, awlgrip refinishing, varnishing, air conditioning and refrigeration, electrical service, sail repair, and canvas installation and repair. Since 1965 the facility has provided service to boats weighing as much as 60 tons or with beams as long as 20 feet. Towing services are also available.

Sailing

Getaway Sailing
2700 Lighthouse Point
(410) 342-3110 or (888) 342-3709
www.getawaysailing.com
Getaway Sailing offers a fleet of sailboats from 22 feet to 36 feet long at the Lighthouse Point Marina, on the Patapsco River in Canton. Rentals vary depending on the size and type of boat and on how long you decide to spend sailing it—so call ahead for details. Both baredeck and skippered charters and cruises are available. Owner Dick Mead also offers afternoon and overnight cruises to the Eastern Shore. In

addition to rentals, the company provides lessons, beginning at about $100 for an eight-hour day of instruction. If you think you might be visiting often, a membership for between $800 and $3,300 a year might be more economical.

Sail Baltimore
1809 Thames Street
(410) 522-7300
www.sailbaltimore.org
Sail Baltimore is a nonprofit, community service organization located in Baltimore City and works as a great resource for boating and sailing activities in the area. It was founded as the Mayor's Official Committee on Visiting Ships to host Baltimore's first tall ship gathering in the summer of 1976 and is responsible for coordinating Baltimore's waterfront activities. Sail Baltimore also supports other maritime events, such as the Great Chesapeake Bay Schooner Race, the Fells Point Yacht Club Lighted Boat Parade, the Blessing of Baltimore's Work Boats, and OpSail Baltimore.

FISHING

Largemouth bass, smallmouth bass, and brown trout, oh my! Baltimoreans are fascinated by marine life, and we enjoy hauling it over the side of a boat just as much as visiting it at the National Aquarium. The Chesapeake Bay as well as the Susquehanna, Middle, and Patapsco Rivers are great places to drop your line. Gunpowder River is stocked with brown trout every spring and fall offering you, the cunning angler, 150 to 200 fish per acre, and Loch Raven Reservoir has its own fishing center. (See the Waterways section for more information about fishing these areas.)

Here we've provided information for obtaining a license in Maryland and highlighted some of the charter boats in the area.

Licenses

Maryland's fishing license fees depend on whether you're from the state or from outside the state. Licenses, necessary for anyone 16 or older, can be obtained from a number of sports and tackle shops around the state as well as at several regional service centers operated by the Maryland Department of Natural Resources. For more information, call (410) 260-3220 or visit www.dnr.state. md.us.

Maryland residents pay $10.50 for a nontidal license or $9.00 for a tidal license, which is applicable to fishing in the Chesapeake Bay and its tidal tributaries. Those hailing from outside Maryland pay their state's fee for a nontidal license or $14 for a tidal license.

All other licenses, stamps, and permits are the same regardless of residency. A short-term nontidal license, which is valid for five days from the date of issuance, is $7.00. A trout stamp is $5.00. A pleasure boat decal to fish, which allows fishing from a boat by all the people on board, is $40. No license is require to fish from a charter boat.

Charter Boats

Associated Bay Captains
5980 Rockhold Creek Road, Deale
(410) 269-1115
Since 1973 the Associated Bay Captains have been providing anglers with access to the Chesapeake Bay's best fishing areas. All of its captains know the places to find trout, drum, flounder, bluefish, Spanish mackerel, spot, and croakers through chumming, trolling, bottom fishing, and jigging. Boats with six or fewer passengers cost $380 for a six-hour day and $420 for an eight-hour day. For boats with 6 to 10 passengers, the cost is $650 for an eight-hour day.

Blue Goose Yacht Charter Service
2501 Boston Street
(410) 647-2583
www.blugoose.com
This charter service, based out of the Baltimore Harbor in historic Canton, specializes in diesel trawler yachts, not sailboats. The yachts come fully equipped—complete with linens, towels, and utensils. Early boarding is allowed the night before, at no additional charge, if the schedule permits. Discounts for charters lasting longer than one week and for repeat customers are offered. Blue Goose operates from late April through the end of October.

Captain Jim Charters
6002 Parker Drive, Deale
(410) 867-4944
www.captjim.com
Captain Jim Brincefield pilots the *Jil Carrie* on charter trips for anglers, sightseers, nature lovers, and groups, but his focus is on fishing trips. Carrying up to 49 passengers, the *Jil Carrie* departs from Deale, Maryland, although Brincefield will pick up passengers anywhere in the bay area. The best fishing is in the middle and lower bay, so time spent gathering passengers can take away from fishing time. Charters go year-round, with December being a good time to chase large Virginia striped bass. For one to six passengers, charters cost a total of $525 for a full day and $50 for each additional person. The price includes bait, license, and tackle, but not a tip for the mates. Check the Web site for open dates.

Chesapeake Charters, Inc.
428 Londontown Road, Edgewater
(800) 381-2727
www.bayfishing.net
From April to November, Captain Kerry Muse steers his 48-foot fiberglass *Darlene II* through the Chesapeake Bay so that anglers can catch striped bass, sea trout, flounder, perch, or other fish of the bay. The charge for up to eight people is $550 and $50 for each additional person, including weekends, which, however, are difficult to book on short notice. Half-day

and evening trips are also available. The boat can carry up to 34 passengers, but Muse suggests no more than 20 for a fishing trip. The boat leaves at 6:00 A.M. for its eight-hour trip, which begins in Deale on the Eastern Shore.

OTHER WATERSPORTS

Chesapeake Paddlers Association
P.O. Box 341, Greenbelt, MD 20768
www.cpakayaker.com
With more than 300 members from the Maryland, Delaware, and District of Columbia areas, the Chesapeake Paddlers Association offers a forum for sea kayakers who'd like to discuss techniques and common interests, improve paddling skills, and experience the beauty of the Chesapeake Bay region's waters. Membership costs $10, and while the organization has no telephone number, you can learn more about it by sending a letter to the previously listed address or by checking the Web site.

Ultimate Water Sports
Hammerman Area of Gunpowder Falls State Park
7340 Greenbank Road
(410) 335-5352
www.ultimatewatersports.com
From May to September, Owner Hal Ashman operates a wonderland for newcomers and experienced water enthusiasts in a calm and protected 2-foot- to 3-foot-deep stretch of Dundee Creek off Maxwell Point. This location boasts some of the most spectacular natural scenery and pristine beauty the bay has to offer. Ultimate Water Sports offers kayak lessons, rentals, and tours, as well as sailing lessons, sailing rentals, windsurfing lessons, and windsurfing rentals. There is also a kids' watersport camp and other group programs available.

To reach the sports center, you must pay a $2.00 state park entrance fee; frequent visitors might want to purchase a $50 Fun Pass, allowing unlimited visits to the park throughout the year.

DAY TRIPS ⊖

Maryland is called America in Miniature because every type of land configuration that exists in the United States exists to some degree in Maryland. To the west are the Allegheny Mountains; to the east, flat plains, sandy beaches, and marshlands. In the central part of the state, you'll find green valleys, grasslands, and gently rolling foothills. And we're told that somewhere in this state, we even have a rain forest.

At the approximate center of all this lies Baltimore. Three hours from Ocean City to the east, three hours from the Cumberland Gap to the west, a little more than an hour's distance from the Mason-Dixon Line to the north and the Virginia border to the south, Baltimore makes an excellent jumping-off point for day trips and weekend getaways in the Mid-Atlantic.

We've organized this chapter essentially as usual in this book, leaving out Downtown, but including Northeast, Northwest, Southeast, and Southwest. We've also added three more directions—North, South, and West. This creates a wheel-like configuration that has Baltimore as its hub and state and interstate highway routes as its spokes. Using these main spokes as the basis for your driving directions out from the city makes the directions simple.

If you'd rather not hit the highways, a typical Maryland map will show you that most of these routes coexist beside older roads that will take you to the same place and more often than not offer a more scenic drive. I-83, for instance, runs almost parallel to York Road—actually in sight of it for most of the ride. So, if you'd rather go through small towns, drive more slowly, and stop when you feel like it, these roads are a viable alternative.

All of the trips noted in this chapter can be taken in a day. Maryland is, after all, a relatively small state. It doesn't take too many hours of driving before you are out of this state and halfway through another. (It is, for instance, only a three-and-a-half-hour drive to New York City from Baltimore.) However, Maryland is wider than it is long, and in some cases one way to the proposed destination is a three-hour trip. In those cases, we've noted generally what accommodations you can expect to find, how much you can expect to pay, and what types of restaurants are available. So, if you decide at 4:00 P.M. that you don't want to drive back to your home base in Baltimore, you'll know the lay of the land. The only exceptions are rail trips, where your accommodation is on the train itself. Since rail was born in Baltimore, the Mid-Atlantic region probably has more track crisscrossing it than just about anywhere, making rail trips an exciting and unique offering of the area.

If you're thinking national parks, Maryland has plenty of them, but you'll find them listed in the Parks and Recreation and On the Water chapters. The day trips that follow take you across Maryland's roads and tracks rather than its trails and rivers.

So, buckle the kids in the back seat, pack up the cooler, and dog-ear this page. You're on your way!

NORTH

To reach points north, you'll want to use I-83, the interstate highway that begins (or ends, depending on how you look at it) at Fayette and President Streets in Baltimore City. It is I-83 that takes you quickly out of the city (except at evening rush hour) to local destinations such as Towson, Lutherville, Timonium, Cockeysville, and Hunt Valley.

North of Hunt Valley, Baltimore County becomes country. There are plenty of little towns along the way that offer their own kinds of charm. White Hall, with its country shops and roadside stands, is a simple destination if all you're after is an afternoon's drive through the countryside. Get off I-83 at Hunt Valley, head east about a mile to York Road, and turn left. It will take you through or near many little towns and lots of scenic farmland and horse country.

If you want a true northern destination, however, the first ones are not in Maryland at all but just over the Mason-Dixon Line in Pennsylvania.

York, Pennsylvania

Exit 9 off I-83 will find you in **York, Pennsylvania,** notable in history because it served as the nation's capital during the Revolution when British troops occupied Philadelphia. The Historical Society of York County, 250 East Market Street, has a museum with exhibits that depict York County from those times as well as a reproduction of the original York village square. The museum is open 10:00 A.M. to 4:00 P.M. Tuesday through Saturday. Cost is $6.00 for adults and $5.00 for children older than 12 years of age. This allows entrance into four other sites of historic interest in the area: Bonham House, the Golden Plough Tavern, General Gates House, and Bobb Log House.

You may also find the **York County Colonial Court House** of interest. This reproduction of the original courthouse has a presentation that recounts the signing of the Articles of Confederation, adopted by the Continental Congress in the original building. Call (717) 848-1587 for more information or visit www .yorkheritage.org.

NORTHEAST

Our northeast route is I-95 North, which is easily accessed by taking I-83 to I-695 East, which at that point parallels U.S.

Highway 40 East. Don't let this confuse you. The upper end of the Chesapeake Bay gets in the way of U.S. 40's progress east, so it heads more northerly for a time. Both I-95 and U.S. 40, if you keep going, can take you straight toward Newark, New Jersey, and points north; or you can head south on the other side of the bay down U.S. Highway 301 to Eastern Shore points in both Delaware and Maryland. (See Southeast later in this chapter for destinations on the Eastern Shore.)

Whether you drive up I-95 or U.S. 40, you'll find yourself fairly quickly near Aberdeen Proving Ground.

You're in the Army Now

The U.S. Army Ordnance Museum at Aberdeen Proving Ground houses a collection of weaponry tracing the development of ordnance in the twentieth century. Just the place for the weapons or army enthusiast in the family, it's a fascinating museum just 45 minutes from Baltimore City. The museum is open daily from 9:00 A.M. to 4:45 P.M. Though closed on most holidays, it is open on Armed Forces Day, Memorial Day, July 4, and Veterans Day. Admission is free. If you'd like more information, call (410) 278-3602 or visit www.ordmusfound.org.

Northeast of Aberdeen Proving Ground is the town of **Aberdeen,** which in the last decade or so has changed from a town that was a little worse for wear into a showplace of renovated Victoriana. Giant trees, mansard roofs, and the smell of the bay make it a lovely place through which to meander.

Havre de Grace

Continuing north on I-95 from Aberdeen, just before the Susquehanna River, you'll find **Havre de Grace,** the town that came in second on the list of choices for the nation's capital in 1791. Sitting right on the point of land where the Susquehanna meets the Chesapeake Bay, close to its northernmost tip, one would think that it would have given the capital a well-protected harbor. However, the founders chose well, for during the War of 1812, Havre de Grace was essentially burned to the ground by British invaders.

The town continued due in large part to the location that put it in peril. Being at the mouth of the Susquehanna made it a trading location for points north from its earliest days. From 1839 to the turn of the next century, barges drawn by mule made their way up the Tidewater Canal 45 miles to Wrightsville, Pennsylvania. The lock house at the canal's head is still extant and can be visited from 1:00 to 5:00 P.M. on weekends May through October. Call (410) 939-5780. Admission is $2.00 for adults.

Other points of interest in Havre de Grace are its historic houses and the **Concord Point Light House,** which is one of the oldest East Coast lighthouses in continuous operation. The lighthouse is open on weekends, April through October, from 1:00 to 5:00 P.M. Admission is free. Call (410) 939-9040. **The Promenade,** a wood walkway running along the Susquehanna Flats, offers visitors a view of the water between 6:00 A.M. and 10:00 P.M. daily. Don't forget to stop by the Havre de Grace Decoy Museum at 215 Giles Street, open daily 11:00 A.M. to 4:00 P.M., for a glimpse at genuine American folk art. Admission to the museum is $4.00 for adults. If you'd like more information about sightseeing opportunities in Havre de Grace, call the **Havre de Grace Tourism Commission** at (800) 851-7756, or visit the Web site at www.hdgtourism.com.

First Outlet

Back on I-95 and across the Susquehanna River, just over the bridge from Havre de Grace, you'll see signs for **Prime Outlets**

at Perryville. Prime Outlets has 45 stores, including Elisabeth, Jones New York, Bugle Boy, Osh-Kosh B'Gosh, Beauty Express, Mikasa, Book Cellar, and Nike. Prime Outlets is open Monday through Saturday 10:00 A.M. to 9:00 P.M. and Sunday 11:00 A.M. to 6:00 P.M. To find out more, call (410) 378-9399 or visit www.primeoutlets.com.

Lancaster, Pennsylvania

Lancaster County is Amish country, the land of the Pennsylvania Dutch. To reach Lancaster hang a left off I-95 onto U.S. Highway 222 toward Lancaster, the city. The signs for Rocks, Bird-in-Hand, and Intercourse aren't jokes—they're names of real towns. One wonders if there's a story in there someplace.

Keep your eyes peeled—road signs in the Amish country are not the large, green markers we are used to. They are much smaller, usually requiring drivers to slow down to read them. As much of the "traffic" along these roads is horse-drawn buggies, traveling about 2 miles an hour, you'll have plenty of time to read the signs and enjoy the sights of this beautiful, green countryside.

There are plenty of places to shop in Lancaster, including a large number of factory outlets stores. **The Rockvale Square Factory Outlet Village** has about 119 stores, making it one of the largest outlet malls in the Mid-Atlantic. You can find everything from Jones New York to Black & Decker, from Waterford Wedgewood to L'eggs. To reach it, you'll actually want to turn off U.S. 222 before you get to the city of Lancaster. A right on State Highway 372 and a left on State Highway 896 should get you there with no difficulty. The mall is open from Monday to Saturday 9:30 A.M. to 9:00 P.M. and Sunday from 10:00 A.M. to 6:00 P.M. Call (717) 293-9595 for more information, or visit www.rockvalesquare outlets.com.

On U.S. Highway 30 east of Lancaster is the **Tanger Outlet Center,** which has

Welcome Centers

If you get lost while taking in Maryland's sights or find that you need more information on where you're heading, you can call or visit a Maryland Welcome Center. In addition to the centers listed here, Maryland also has approximately 65 picnic areas, scenic overlooks, and minor rest areas available to motorists. A complete list of these facilities is located on the Maryland Official Highway Map, which is available at any welcome center or by visiting the State Department of Transportation on-line at www.marylandroads.com.

Youghiougheny Overlook Welcome Center, (301) 746-5979. Located on I-68 East, 1.5 miles east of Friendsville in Garrett County, Maryland.

Sideling Hill Interpretive Center, (301) 678-5442. Located on I-68 West, approximately 10 miles west of Hancock in Washington County, Maryland.

I-70 East and I-70 West Welcome Centers, Located at mile marker #39, Myersville, Maryland. I-70 West (301) 293-4161. I-70 East (301) 293-2526.

U.S. 15 South Welcome Center, (301) 447-2553. Located just south of the Pennsylvania state line in Frederick County, Maryland.

I-95 South and I-95 North Welcome Centers. The Southbound site serves traffic heading towards Washington D.C. and points south. (301) 490-2444. The Northbound site serves traffic heading toward the Baltimore/Annapolis area and points north. (301) 490-1333.

Crain Memorial Welcome Center, (301) 259-2500. Located approximately 2 miles north of the Potomac River on northbound U.S. 301 in Charles County, Maryland.

Bay Country Welcome Center, (410) 758-6803. Located on U.S. 301 in Queen Anne's County, Maryland, approximately 15 miles north of its junction with U.S. 50.

U.S. 13 North Welcome Center, (410) 957-2484. Located on U.S. 13, northbound, just north of the Virginia state line in Worcester County, Maryland.

In addition to the above facilities, the Maryland Transportation Authority operates two full-service facilities on the toll portion of I-95 (JFK Memorial Highway):

The Maryland House, (410) 272-0176. Located on the median of I-95 and accessible to both northbound and southbound traffic, approximately 24 miles north of Baltimore City in Harford County, Maryland. Food and fuel are available.

Chesapeake House Welcome Center, (410) 287-2313. Located 14 miles north of the Maryland House and 12 miles south of the Delaware state line.

---

more than 60 stores to its credit. Donna Karan, Etienne Aigner, J. Crew, Hugo Boss, Liz Claiborne, Polo Ralph Lauren, and a great many other designer names are there, but you can also find Noritake and Movado. The outlet is open 9:00 A.M. to 9:00 P.M. Monday through Saturday and 10:00 A.M. to 6:00 P.M. Sunday. Call (717) 392-7260 for more information, or visit www.tangeroutlet.com.

The most interesting shopping places in Dutch country, however, are the stores that allow you to buy foods and items made locally. **The Anderson Bakery Company,** for instance, specializes in pretzels. If you've ever wanted to see how pretzels are made and taste some of the end results, you're in for a real treat here. It's open Monday through Friday; call (717) 299-2321 for hours and more information.

To immerse yourself in the Amish way of life, you can visit the **Amish Farm and House** on U.S. 30. This is a working farm, so all tours are guided, but you will get an opportunity to see the inside of an 1805 Amish farmhouse, barns, and grounds. Food is also available on-site from April through October. The cost of the tour is $6.95 for adults, $6.25 for seniors, and $4.25 for children 5 to 11. Call (717) 394-6185 for more information, or visit www.amishfarmandhouse.com. The Amish Village, also on U.S. 30, has not only a house and barn but also a schoolhouse, blacksmith shop, store, and picnicking area. Admission to the village is $6.50 for adults or $2.50 for children 6 to 12. Call (717) 687-8511 or visit www.800padutch.com for more information.

If all this doesn't satisfy your interest in the Amish culture, consider taking a tour of Amish farmlands and the countryside through **Amish Country Tours.** Tours leave daily from 3121 Old Philadelphia Pike. Call (717) 768-3600 for information.

Just about 10 minutes north of the Rockvale outlet mall (mentioned previously in this section) is the little town of **Strasburg.** Hardly more than a post office and a general store, **Strasburg Railroad** has a train ride from nowhere to no place across beautiful Pennsylvania countryside, with a pleasant picnicking stop in the middle. Chartered in 1832, the Strasburg line is now just a few cars pulled by an ancient steam locomotive, but it is great fun. The entire trip takes 45 minutes, if you don't get off midway at the picnic grounds. Round-trip fare on the coach is $9.75 for adults and $4.75 for children. Open-air cars, deluxe lounge cars, first-class cars, and a dining car are also available for a slightly higher fare. Call (717) 687-7522 or visit www.strasburgrailroad.com for details.

The best way to tour Dutch country, however, is just to get in your car and go. If you would like information about other destinations, however, call the **Pennsylvania Dutch Convention and Visitors Bureau** at (800) 723-8824 or (800) PA-DUTCH or visit www.padutchcountry. com.

The Return Trip

Obviously you can follow the same routes back to Baltimore, but if you're looking for a few more areas of interest on the return trip, consider the following attractions.

Topiary Topics

If you're interested in a detour as you head back toward Baltimore from Aberdeen, turn south on U.S. 1, instead of I-95, to State 152 and hang a right. In about 20 miles, you will come to **Ladew Topiary Gardens and Manor House.** The 15 seasonal gardens spread over 22 acres are ranked among the finest topiary gardens in America. The restored manor house is what is called a telescoping house, built in sections, with the oldest section dating back almost 300 years. The house contains Harvey S. Ladew's collection of English antiques and paintings. Much of his collection concerns fox hunting and riding. The house and gardens are open mid-April through October 31 from 10:00 A.M. to 4:00 P.M. Monday through Friday, and 10:30 A.M. to 5:00 P.M. Saturday and Sunday. The last house tour leaves at 3:00 P.M. on weekdays and 4:00 P.M. on weekends. Admission to both is $13.00 for adults, $11.00 for seniors and students, and $5.00 for children younger than 12. If you are interested in touring only the gardens, the cost is $10.00, $8.00, and $2.00, respectively. Call (410) 557-9570 or visit www.ladewgardens.com for more information.

Vino!

As you head back to Baltimore from points north, barely 15 minutes above the Beltway (I-695) at the juncture of Cromwell Bridge Road and Glen Arm Road, you will find Boordy Vineyards (exit 29 off I-695). The vineyard, with its rows and rows of vines and its restored nineteenth-century barn, is quite a change from the hustle and bustle of the city and suburban surroundings.

Except for major holidays, Boordy Vineyards is open Monday through Saturday from 10:00 A.M. to 5:00 P.M., Sundays from 1:00 to 5:00 P.M., and every day from 1:00 to 4:00 P.M. for wine tasting tours. Having tasted your favorite, bottles of wine are available for sale in the winery. For more information call (410) 592-5015 or visit www.boordy.com. You can also check the Close-up later in this chapter for more information on all the Maryland vineyards.

SOUTHEAST

Our southeast route takes I-97 south off I-695 to U.S. 50. (The parallel road to I-97 is Highway 2, Ritchie Highway, but it is not a very scenic route until you get past Glen Burnie.) The first stop on this side of the Bay Bridge is Annapolis, Maryland.

A Capital Idea!

Many people think that because Baltimore is Maryland's largest city that it is the capital of the state, but that honor belongs to **Annapolis,** about 45 minutes southeast of Baltimore.

Annapolis is one of the oldest cities in both the state of Maryland and the United States. Originally called Anne Arundel Town, 100 acres was laid out for its creation in 1684, and it was chartered in 1708. In addition to being made the capital city of Maryland in 1694, it was the first peacetime capital of the United States, when in 1783 and 1784 the United States Congress

met there. In fact, they met in Maryland's State House, which has been in continuous legislative use since those times. You can tour the **State House** free of charge from 9:00 A.M. to 5:00 P.M. daily, or call (410) 260-3400 if you'd like more information. You can also take a virtual tour of the State House at www.mdarchives.state. md.us.

The city of Annapolis holds dear the flavor of those earlier days. The area that surrounds the waterfront is known as the City Dock, and the buildings that line its cobblestone streets date back to earlier times. In almost every one is an interesting shop or eatery. Actually you could just eat your way around Annapolis; there are more than 30 restaurants in the historic district alone. Strolling through Annapolis is a lovely way to spend an afternoon because Annapolis offers living history as well as an old-fashioned ambience.

Annapolis is the home of the **United States Naval Academy,** in session from August to June. Don't even think about trying to tour Annapolis during June Week—the Naval Academy's yearly pregraduation celebration. The city is always full to bursting. From June 1 to Labor Day, guided tours of the Naval Academy leave the Armel-Leftwitch Visitors Center every half hour from 9:30 A.M. to 3:00 P.M. Monday through Saturday. From September to November and April to Memorial Day, guided tours leave the center from 10:00 A.M. to 3:00 P.M. Monday through Friday, from 9:30 A.M. to 3:00 P.M. on Saturday, and from 12:30 to 3:00 P.M. on Sunday. Tours take you through the grounds, to the crypt of John Paul Jones, and let you peek into the midshipmen's living quarters at Bancroft Hall, among other things. No advance reservation is required; simply show up at the visitor center at the main gate to the Naval Academy and wait for the next tour to begin. The cost is $7.00 for adults and $5.00 for students. Children 3 and younger are admitted free. For more information on the Naval Academy, call (410) 263-6933, or visit www.nadn .navy.mil.

St. John's College, which was chartered in 1784 and whose campus boasts what is noted as the third-oldest academic building in the United States—McDowell Hall—is also in Annapolis. St. John's also has the Carroll-Barrister House. Built in 1722, it is the birthplace of Charles Carroll, who was on the committee that drafted the Maryland Declaration of Rights in 1776. An appointment to take a campus tour may be made by calling (410) 263-2371.

The Governor's mansion in Annapolis, called Government House, was built after the Civil War. Tours are by appointment only. Call (410) 974-3531 to make an appointment.

There are also various guided walking tours of the city available from Three Centuries Tours, which conducts them from and in conjunction with the Annapolis Visitor Center. There are two points of departure, one at the visitor center at 26 West Street and the other at its City Dock location. Tours focus on such attractions as colonial homes and the Naval Academy; some are thematic, such as the African American Tour, which highlights important African-American sites, including the Banneker-Douglass Museum, which is named for Benjamin Banneker and Frederick Douglass and which mounts exhibits on prominent black Marylanders. Tours, which are presented by guides in period costume, are $11.00 for adults and $6.00 for students of any age. For more information call (410) 263-5401, or visit www.annapolis-tours.com.

For a different view of the city, consider taking a water tour of Annapolis. A 40-minute cruise around the Annapolis harbor on various boats costs between $8.00 and $15.00 for adults and $4.00 to $8.00 for children younger than 12, depending on the boat. Longer cruises are also available. Visit www.watermark cruises.com or call (410) 268-7601 for information. An all-day (close to eight hours) water tour on the *Annapolitan II* not only views Annapolis sites, such as the Naval Academy, from the water but also takes you across the bay to the Chesa-

peake Bay Maritime Museum at St. Michaels. The Maritime Museum is an 18-acre site at Navy Point that looks much as a small fishing village might have looked in the nineteenth century, although buildings now serve as exhibit halls and gift shops. Exhibits are devoted to the history and life on the bay. Baygoing vessels can be found in pictures, as models and often as full-sized, in-water craft. Although you cannot tour the boats, you can tour Hooper Strait Lighthouse, which was moved to the museum for exhibition purposes and has been totally restored to look as it did when it was built in 1879. Regular admission to the museum is $9.00 for adults, $8.00 for seniors, and $4.00 for children age 6 to 17, but if you come by sea on the *Annapolitan II,* admission is included. Although St. Michaels can also be reached by land, the water access is eminently more fun, especially on a warm, sunny day. (If you come by land, however, you might want to call (410) 745-2916 for more information.) Hours are 9:00 A.M. to 4:00 P.M. daily.

The cruise stops for three hours for lunch in St. Michaels, with good reason. Not only does St. Michaels have some wonderful eats, but the town itself is also a renovated masterpiece. Many of the houses date back to the time of the American Revolution, when St. Michaels was a thriving shipbuilding area. St. Michaels current claim to fame is as a favorite port for recreational sailors. In downtown St. Michaels, you'll find specialty shops that offer antiques, clothing, and crafts. You'll want to walk around and see the sights, and then take some time to just sit quietly in the little town park and let the breezes wash over you. These all-day water tours leave Saturdays and Sundays at 10:00 A.M. from Memorial Day through early October and are also offered on Thursdays and Fridays during the summer. The cost is between $40 and $55 per adult and between $20 and $27.50 for children younger than 12 and does not include the cost of your lunch.

If you'd like to stay over, there are plenty of hotels, motels, inns, and bed-and-break-

Wine Centerpiece

No matter what direction you head when taking off on your day trip, most likely you will not be far from one of 12 Maryland vineyards spread out across the state. Coaxing visitors with tempting outdoor celebrations, the wineries are consistently releasing new wines, offering special activities and festivals, and, of course, tours and tastings.

The award-winning wineries help to showcase Maryland's prolific and growing winemaking industry.

"Spring is one of the most exciting times to visit a winery," said Association of Maryland Wineries president Bert Basignani. "Visitors can see the budding vines—the start of the winemaking process. Maryland winemakers are thrilled to share vineyards and wineries with our guests."

The Association of Maryland Wineries includes 11 wineries that produce more than 110 varieties of wines. Maryland wines consistently win prestigious national wine competitions, are served at the region's finest restaurants, and are available at several retailers throughout the United States.

Maryland wine has a rich history dating back to the mid-1600s, when then-Governor Charles Calvert, at the prompting of Lord Baltimore, planted 200 acres on the east bank of the St. Mary's River, using vines he had received from several countries in Europe. These were later supplemented by another 100 acres.

In 1768 Charles Carroll established a vineyard in Howard County that included some natural hybrids and some European varieties, but by 1800 all but the indigenous vines died.

In the early 1940s, Philip Wagner, then an editorial columnist with the *Baltimore Sun* and later editor of the *Evening Sun,* acquired as many different hybrids as he could lay hands on and planted them at his home in Riderwood. The success of his efforts signaled a turning point in the Eastern wine industry. In addition to making his own wine, he propagated the vines and sold them throughout the East Coast.

Then in 1945 Wagner opened Boordy Vineyards, Maryland's first bonded winery, producing wines made from the hybrid grapes. Most were simple, easy-to-drink wines, and it was his philosophy that the winemaker's goal should be to make inexpensive everyday wines for consumption with meals. Wagner also produced the first up-to-date winemaking text, *American Wines and How to Make Them,* which was later revised as *Grapes Into Wine* and has become a classic in the field. He also wrote *A Wine-Growers Guide,* which has remained a staple in the vineyard establishment repertoire.

During the 1940s and '50s 15 additional wineries opened, eight of which are still in business today.

In 1981 the Maryland Grape Growers Association was formed. The primary purpose of the organization at that time was to support the Maryland wine industry by encouraging commercial growers. Since then, its perspective has broadened to include many small-scale, "backyard" vineyardists, many of whom sell their produce to amateur winemakers. MGGA produces a quarterly newsletter and a vineyard establishment manual and sponsors several on-site activities during the year.

In 1984 the Association of Maryland Wineries was founded, the purpose of which is to coordinate winery activities and deal with legal and commercial issues involving the production and distribution of Maryland wines. Currently, the association is actively engaged in pursuing legislation to hasten the growth of the winemaking and grape-growing industries in the state, and is focusing on ways to promote the broader use of Maryland wines by Marylanders.

Also in 1984 the Maryland Wine Festival was held at the Union Mills Homestead in Carroll County. All Maryland wineries participated, and its success led to its establishment as an annual two-day event now held at the Carroll County Farm Museum. The local chapter of the American Wine Society sponsors amateur wine judgings, wine education seminars, and winemaking demonstrations, and the Maryland Grape Growers Association dispenses grape juice and provides grape-growing information. The festival is held in September and offers a great opportunity to sample Maryland wines.

Association of Maryland Wineries
576 North Charles Street
Baltimore, MD 21201
(800) 237-WINE
www.marylandwine.com

Basignani Winery
15722 Falls Road
Sparks, MD 21152
(410) 472-0703
www.basignani.com

Berrywine Plantations/
Linganore Winecellars
13601 Glissans Mill Road
Mount Airy, MD 21771
(410) 795-6432 or (301) 831-5889
www.linganore-wine.com

Boordy Vineyards
12820 Long Green Pike
Hydes, MD 21771
(410) 592-5015
www.boordy.com

Catoctin Winery
805 Greenbridge Road
Brookeville, MD 20833
(301) 774-2310

Cygnus Winecellars
3130 Long Lane
Manchester, MD 21102
(410) 374-6395
www.cygnuswinecellars.com

Deep Creek Cellars
177 Fazee Ridge Road
Friendsville, MD 21531
(301) 746-4349
www.deepcreekcellars.com

Elk Run Vineyards & Winery
15113 Liberty Road
Mount Airy, MD 21771
(410) 775-2513
www.elkrun.com

Fiore Winery
3026 Whiteford Road
Pylesville, MD 21132
(410) 879-4926
www.fiorewinery.com

Little Ashby Vineyards
27549 Ashby Drive
Easton, MD 21601
(410) 819-8850 or (410) 822-6027

Loew Vineyards
14001 Liberty Road (Route 26)
Mount Airy, MD 21771
(301) 831-5464
www.loewvineyards.net

Penn Oaks Winery
11 Midhurst Road
Silver Springs, MD 20910
(301) 562-8592
PennOaksWinery@aol.com

Woodhall Vineyards & Wine Cellars
17912 York Road
Parkton, MD 21120
(410) 357-8644
www.woodhallwinecellars.com

We are grateful to the Association of Maryland Wineries for supplying the contact information above and the history of winemaking in Maryland.

fasts in Annapolis. In fact, in the historic district alone, there are more than 25 licensed bed-and-breakfasts. For other accommodations, **Annapolis Accommodations/Room Finders Realty,** (800) 715-1000, www.stayannapolis.com, can help you find what you're looking for, whether it's a one-night stay or something more long-term in a hotel, inn, or bed-and-breakfast.

Across the Bay

When you leave Annapolis and head east on U.S. 50, your first great hurdle will be crossing over the Chesapeake Bay Bridge. Let's just say it's high. So high that from its center, large oil barges in the water below look like Tonka toys. On a windy day, it can be a white-knuckle drive, but normally the problem is just trying to keep your eyes on the road instead of the view.

The bridge has a per-car toll of $10.00 as you head over, but if you come back the same way within 24 hours, the toll is $4.00.

There is heavy traffic across the bridge during the summer months (Memorial Day to Labor Day), and authorities always suggest that if you're headed to the ocean to go on the off-hours. Off-hours would be times such as 10:00 A.M. Friday versus 5:30 P.M. Friday, which is peak.

Once over the bridge, you are on the western shore of the Eastern Shore, also known as the Delmarva Peninsula (for Delaware-Maryland-Virginia). You have two directions to choose from.

Bettin' on the Bay

The first possibility is to turn north up the eastern side of the Chesapeake Bay on U.S. 301, which, if you quickly hang a left at State Highway 213, will take you on a tour through quaint little towns in Queen Anne's and Kent Counties and eventually to the top of the bay, where you can pick up either U.S. 40 or I-95 to head back south to Baltimore.

A must-see along this route is **Chestertown,** which dates back to 1706, when it was a major port for its surrounding counties. A great Web site to find out more about the town is www.chestertown.com, or call the town office at (410) 778-0500. One of Chestertown's claims to fame from those early years was a "Boston" tea party, when the townspeople dumped the cargo of tea from the brigantine Geddes into the Chester River to protest the tax on tea in 1774. Every Memorial Day weekend, the town holds the **Chestertown Tea Party Festival** at which, among other things, re-enactors ceremoniously dump tea into the harbor to commemorate that day.

Chestertown is also the home of **Washington College,** founded in 1782. The college conferred an honorary doctorate degree on George Washington in 1784.

Chestertown's biggest attraction, however, is its eighteenth-century architecture. There are formal walking tours of historic houses yearly in the fall; for information call the **Historical Society of Kent County** from May through October at (410) 778-3499 or visit www.kentcounty. com/historicalsociety. Office hours are Wednesday through Friday 9:30 A.M. to 4:30 P.M. and by appointment on Tuesday. Of course you're certainly welcome to wander around town, creating your own tour. Tour guide booklets are available from the **Kent County Chamber of Commerce,** (410) 810-2968 or www.kentcham ber.org. Or just park and meander through the historic district stopping in the more than 35 little shops and restaurants along the way

On the Strait and Narrows

If you'd like to see the Atlantic Ocean and hit some great outlet stores on the way, cross the Chesapeake Bay Bridge and continue on U.S. 50 toward the "shore points" of Ocean City, Maryland, and Rehoboth Beach, Delaware.

Once you're over the bridge, you'll start seeing signs for the various outlet malls along the highway. Outlet-mall hopping makes a good day trip in itself, if you don't want to drive more than one and a half hours from Baltimore. But if you'd like to make a day of it in one place, **Chesapeake Village Outlet Center,** which includes great clothing outlets such as Levi's, Dockers, and Nine West and great places to eat such as Harris Crab House and Annie's Paramount Steak House, at Kent Narrows is a good choice. You can also take a turn around Kent Narrows itself, which has six antiques and collectibles shops, 12 additional restaurants—most of which feature steak and seafood—and many options for a day's outing, such as boat charters and boat and bike rentals. For more information, call the **Queen Anne's County Department of Business and Tourism** at (410) 604-2100 or visit www.qac.org.

Headin' Down-e Oshun

As you touch land at the end of the bridge, you are approximately two hours from Rehoboth Beach, Delaware, and two and a half hours from Ocean City, Maryland. U.S. 50 will take you toward both destinations initially, and all along U.S. 50 you'll find turnoffs for other interesting places, such as the Wye Island Natural Resource Area, St. Michaels (mentioned previously in this section), and Blackwater National Wildlife Refuge. You'll also go right through some of the larger cities on the Eastern Shore, such as Cambridge and Salisbury.

To get to **Rehoboth** (pronounced Reh-ho-beth), you'll want to stay on U.S. 50 until you see the sign for State Highway 404. (There's a left-turn lane. You can't miss it.) Then turn left at State Highway 16 and right on Delaware State Highway 1. This is the quickest way to Rehoboth and will take you through miles of flat, open country. It's a beautiful drive through farmlands and small farming towns.

At the beach don't get overconfident about water safety. The undertow can be treacherous, grabbing hold of those who have strayed too far and placing them in life-threatening situations.

Rehoboth Beach's central city is near the water, but it is relatively small, about 10 blocks along the water's edge. The rest of the city wraps around it. There are two large lakes (one north, one south) and a great many large trees for shade. Most homes, particularly near the lakes, are substantial, year-round homes in which Rehobeth's year-round citizens live.

The bulk of tourists come during the summer season and stay in the central or western areas of the city. On season or off, however, Rehoboth is primarily a family place where most people rent an entire house or an apartment for long-term stays.

There are rides, games, miniature golf courses, restaurants, and stores on the boardwalk. In the western part of the city, you'll find water parks and outlet malls—lots and lots of outlet malls with more than 150 stores among them. (You'll see these as you initially head into town if you take the route we suggest.) When you're tired of shopping, there are ferry rides and boats and bikes to rent.

But even with all these things to do, many who rent in the town itself tend to spend their evenings on the copious screened-in porches, quietly sipping a drink and playing cards or talking.

Rehoboth is a great place to relax. It's relatively quiet and a safe place for children to feel free to go places and do things without always needing a parent along as protector. While Rehoboth is a place to spend relaxing, its neighbor, Dewey Beach, is a place to let loose at its many happening restaurants and bars.

The city part of **Ocean City** is much larger than Rehoboth's, running the length of a 10-mile-long sandbar that is not even a mile wide side to side, with nary a tree. To get to Ocean City, just continue on U.S.

50 all the way to its end. Once over the short bridge and onto the island, you'll see that Ocean City has two main streets that run north and south, Baltimore Street and Philadelphia Avenue. All along each are hotels, motels, cottages, eating establishments, and shopping areas. However, with 100,000 people on the island, which happens on many a July or August weekend, both streets resemble giant parking lots.

Once you've parked your car, which you can do at the large public lots or at your domicile if you've decided to stay over, there is public transportation that includes a bus system as well as a boardwalk train. And because the land is at sea level and flat as a pancake, you can walk a lot farther than you normally would. Ten or 20 blocks in Ocean City is a cakewalk.

The boardwalk is filled with shops, eateries, and, at the south end, a recreation pier and amusement park. Deep-sea fishing is also a big draw. You can charter a boat just for you and your family or you can grab a place on one of the large public fishing boats that troll the seas. If you don't like fishing, there are also pleasure cruises available. If land activities are your thing, there are uncountable miniature golf courses and about a dozen full-size ones.

Both Rehoboth and Ocean City have events at in-town convention centers. At different times of the year, you'll find antiques shows, trade shows, and the like, many of which are held in the off-season to entice tourists to come on down. For instance, Ocean City has a big boat show in February and a Spring Fest of arts, crafts, and music during early May. In Rehoboth the Fiddler's Festival in fall is a big draw.

If you decide to stay over, there are usually vacancy signs even in season, and housing can be found on the spur of the moment. Finding a place will take more looking, however, if you're there on a Friday or a Saturday.

Your overnight options include everything from a room in a rooming house to a two-bedroom suite at a modern hotel, from a bed-and-breakfast to a house or apartment. Costs vary depending on what accommodations you choose, how close those accommodations are to the beach, whether it is the weekend, and whether it is peak season (July and August). Obviously, a peak season, weekend, on-the-beach accommodation would be the most expensive.

Nonweekend in-season hotel prices in Rehoboth begin at about $85 a night; weekend prices, at about $120 a night; and houses, $600 a week. For help in planning your visit to Rehoboth Beach, call (800) 441-1329 for a free 100-page booklet, or call **Rehoboth Beach–Dewey Beach Chapter of Commerce and Visitor Center** at (302) 227-2233 or visit www.beach-fun.com.

For more information about Ocean City, including accommodation rates and specific hotel information, call (800) OC–OCEAN to get a free 100-page vacation guide and hotel information numbers, or call the Ocean City Convention and Visitors Bureau at (410) 289-8181 or or visit www.ococean.com.

Maryland boasted a large free black population long before the Civil War, and much of Maryland's heritage is vested in our African-American ancestors who lived, fought, and died in Maryland. Baltimore Black Heritage Tours, Inc., offers tours of historic sites. Tours must be set up in advance by calling (410) 783-5469, but they can be arranged at sites all across the state.

Assateague and Chincoteague

Just before you reach Ocean City on U.S. 50, you'll see signs for **Assateague Island National Seashore,** which includes 19,000 acres on Assateague Island, and the **Chincoteague National Wildlife Refuge.** Chincoteague's wild ponies are descendants of sixteenth-century horses who swam to safety from a sinking Spanish galleon off the coast.

One of the best-known events at Chincoteague is the annual pony roundup, which takes place the last Wednesday and Thursday in July. The horses are herded across the quarter-mile channel from Chincoteague Island to Chincoteague, Virginia, where foals are auctioned off. The story of one foal who makes the journey is a classic tale called *Misty of Chincoteague* by Marguerite Henry.

The National Park Service has a visitor center at the north end of Assateague Island that is accessible from U.S. 50 and has exhibits about the history of the islands and the wildlife refuge. A lot of people who would rather not pay hotel prices at Ocean City bring camping gear and camp at the park. The park itself offers opportunities to boat, crab, clam, fish, swim, take guided walking tours, and sing around the campfire. Admission to the park via car is by a seven-day private-vehicle permit that costs $10 or, if you're going to be around awhile, you can purchase a $20 annual permit. For more information, call (410) 641-1441. For specific camping information, call (410) 641-3030 or visit www.nps.gov/asis/.

SOUTH

Our southern tour begins where our southeastern tour began by going south on I-97. However, instead of traveling I-97 all the way to Annapolis, turn right on State Highway 3, which turns into U.S. Highway 301. By the time you hit Upper Marlboro, you'll be about 45 miles south of Baltimore, 20 miles southeast of Washington, D.C., and 20 miles west of the Chesapeake Bay, near Andrews Air Force Base.

From Upper Marlboro a left turn onto State Highway 4 takes you on a course parallel to the Patuxent River toward **Cove Point Park,** a great place to get out and stretch your legs. The 15-acre facility offers ball fields, tennis courts, a tot lot for the little guys, picnic tables, and bathrooms that

are open year-round. At Cove Point, you're just about shouting distance from the Eastern Shore, for this is one of the narrowest points of the Chesapeake Bay.

Keep going down Highway 4, across the Patuxent River, and then left at State Highway 235, dogleg right on State Highway 246 to a left on State Highway 5, and you will find yourself in **St. Mary's City,** home of St. Mary's College, and the first city in Maryland, founded in 1634.

By now, you are easily two and a half hours from Baltimore, so before you see the sights, you may decide that you want to seek out accommodations for the night. There are plenty to choose from in and near St. Mary's City.

In California, east of St. Mary's, is the **Best Western,** (301) 862-4100, a 120-room motel that boasts tennis courts, HBO, and a continental breakfast at the on-site restaurant. The Patuxent Inn offers an inexpensive weekend rate, $87. (Make sure you check about discount rates for AAA and AARP members.)

Super 8 Motel in California (800-800-8000, www.super8.com) has 62 rooms and offers a complimentary continental breakfast. The weekday rate runs as low as $55. There are a few bed-and-breakfasts in the area, also, with average rates between $50 and $90 a night. The **Brome-Howard Inn** (pronounced broom-Howard) is the largest of the bed-and-breakfasts in the area. Nestled in the center of 30 acres of farmland that boasts biking and beach trails, this restored 1840 farmhouse offers five to six unique sleeping rooms, a common parlor with television, games, a piano, and a library, and two separate dining rooms, where breakfast, lunch, and dinner are served. A hot breakfast—served from 7:00 to 8:00 A.M. on weekdays and 8:00 to 9:00 A.M. on Saturday—is included in the price of your room. On Sundays guests of the inn are treated to brunch. (A continental breakfast is served at other times.) The inn is kept by Michael and Lisa Kelley; Michael prepares the cuisine not only for their overnight guests but also for the public. Both restaurants are open to the public and can accommodate catered affairs for up to 120 people indoors and up to 500 under a tent. Weekend rates range from $145 (one king-size bed, with fireplace and private bathroom) to $160 for the Quinn-Bradlee Suite, which offers a master bedroom with a sitting room and private bath. For reservations, call (301) 866-0656 or visit www.bromehowardinn.com.

There's a fair number of fast-food places and small family restaurants along Highway 5 and at towns nearby.

The most pleasant aspect of staying in St. Mary's County is that you are surrounded by water—the Patuxent River, the Potomac River, and the Chesapeake Bay—so you are rarely out of earshot of the cry of sea gulls and the gentle lullaby of water lapping the shore.

Historic St. Mary's City

Historic St. Mary's City, an 800-acre outdoor museum, is the resurrection of the original site of St. Mary's City. The museum's hours vary depending on the season. Tickets are $7.50 for adults and $3.50 for children ages 6 to 12. Visit online at www.stmaryscity.org.

First on the museum tour is the **Godiah Spray Tobacco Plantation,** depicting a seventeenth-century tobacco operation. Godiah Spray was not a real person, but the recreation of the plantation is a piece of living history. Plantation buildings include the main house, a freedman's cottage, and two tobacco-drying barns.

Woodland Indian Hamlet recreates a Native American Yaocomico (Wicomico) village of the times, complete with hollowed-out canoes and thatched huts.

Governor's Field brings to life the historic town center and includes a reproduction of the original statehouse at St. Mary's City. The archaeological digs of the home of Maryland's first governor and the **Great Brick Chapel,** built in the mid-1600s, are also in the area.

Hungry? Stop in at **Farthing's Kitchen** after you've peeked into **Farthing's Ordinary,** which is a reconstructed seventeenth-century inn in Governor's Field.

Behind the statehouse, you'll find a replica of the **Maryland Dove** floating in the calm waters of St. Mary's River. The Dove was one of the ships that brought the first settlers to Maryland, at that time only the fourth settlement in the New World.

For more information about Historic St. Mary's City, call (800) SMC-1634, or visit www.co.saint-marys.md.us.

SOUTHWEST

Our southwest road of choice is U.S. 29, which can be accessed from U.S. Highway 40 or from I-70. The drive south on U.S. 29 is slower than I-95, and it has more trucks than the Baltimore–Washington Parkway, on which trucks are not allowed. But U.S. 29 has one thing those routes don't—a straight shot from Baltimore to Silver Spring, Maryland, just outside of Washington, D.C. Once in Silver Spring, you can follow the signs to the Metro station, then park and ride the subway into our nation's capital.

If you doubt the wisdom of this idea, remember that Washington, D.C., was designed to confuse strangers to the city—originally British troops—and it serves the same function today. Unlike Baltimore, which is laid out in a simple north-south, east-west grid, D.C. has circles, squares, tunnels, and diagonal roads that will send your head spinning if you're not accustomed to them.

If you're planning a trip to the nation's capital, you might want to consult *The Insiders' Guide to Washington, D.C.,* which includes information on northern Virginia and suburban Maryland, for an overall picture of what awaits you. What follows are just a few highlights.

Our Nation's Capital

If you followed our suggestion and took the Metro's Red Line in from Silver Spring, there are two ways to get to the National Mall. The one that doesn't require you to transfer trains is to simply get off at Union Station and walk out the main station doors. You'll see Capitol Hill essentially straight ahead of you, beyond the circle. Walk around the circle and head for the base of Capitol Hill. When you get there, you'll see the Mall stretching ahead of you, and you'll be within walking distance of most of the things that you'll want to see. The Washington Monument and the United States Capitol face each other; between them is the National Museum of American History, the National Museum of Natural History, the National Gallery of Art, the National Air and Space Museum, the Arts and Industries Building, the Freer Gallery, and the National Museum of African Art. Your other Metro option is to take the Red Line to Metro Center, where you'll go downstairs to get on either the Blue Line or the Orange Line. Both lines will take you to the Smithsonian–National Mall stop. Just make sure you're taking the train heading toward the Mall, not away from it.

Within walking distance of the Mall on the north is the White House, the Tidal Basin, where the cherry blossoms bloom in spring, and the large reflecting pool that is opposite the Lincoln Memorial. South, at the Capitol end, you're within an easy walk of the U.S. Botanical Garden and the Library of Congress.

If you'd like to shop while you sightsee, Georgetown beckons. From the Smithsonian–National Mall Metro stop, take either the Blue Line or the Orange Line to Foggy Bottom–GWU; you'll be about a half mile from Georgetown. Home to Georgetown University, the neighborhood, off its main drag of Wisconsin Avenue, N.W., is still the picture-perfect vision of the eighteenth century. You can almost see the ladies in their mob caps preparing to hail down a hansom cab.

The history doesn't stop with the elegant homes, however. Georgetown also has the C&O Canal National Historic Park, Dumbarton Oaks, and Hillwood Museum.

On Wisconsin Avenue, you'll find some great shopping at both elegant and esoteric boutiques. There are also restaurants, coffee shops, and nightclubs.

Across the Potomac

Arlington National Cemetery can be reached by Metro from Georgetown by taking the Blue Line from Foggy Bottom directly to the cemetery. Arlington's 612 acres serve as the resting place for more than 175,000 American military as well as John F. Kennedy, Robert Kennedy, the Tomb of the Unknowns, and Pierre Charles L'Enfant, who designed Washington, D.C. The grounds were once part of Arlington House, a former home of Robert E. Lee that still stands here. Dedicated at the time of the Revolutionary War, Arlington is still an active cemetery.

The Blue Line of the Metro can also take you to King Street, right in the heart of Alexandria, which is also across the Potomac River in Virginia. The center city, known as Old Town, has been restored over the past 30 years. It offers lots of unique shopping possibilities, with more than 200 retail stores clustered along Washington Street and the waterfront. At Union and King Streets, you'll find a popular Old Town destination, the **Torpedo Factory Art Center** (www.torpedofactory.org or 703–838–4565), which, though originally built to manufacture torpedo casings during the World Wars, now plays host to 84 studios and six main galleries where the works of more than 160 artists are displayed. The **Alexandria Archaeology Museum** is also under the Torpedo Factory's roof. If you are interested in the truly old, the Archaeology Museum displays items from the Alexandria area that date back as far as 3000 B.C. The museum is open Tuesday through Sunday year-round. Call (703) 838-4399 for hours and more

information, or visit www.ci.alexandria.
va.us.

Down the road a piece, you may want
to take in a tour of **Mount Vernon,** George
and Martha Washington's humble home.
Acquired in 1754 by the Washingtons, they
enlarged and improved the estate that had
been in George's family for years. The main
house has been restored to its former
glory, as have more than 12 of the outbuildings and the formal gardens. Some of
the original furniture is on display, including the bed in which Washington died, his
sword, and a present from Lafayette—the
key to the Bastille. Washington is buried on
the grounds. Mount Vernon is open year
round. Admission is $11.00 for adults and
$5.00 for children 6 to 11. Call (703)
780-2000 or visit www.mountvernon.org
for more information, but be prepared to
drive. The Metro doesn't go all the way to
Mount Vernon. From Baltimore, it's about a
two-hour trip by car. Travel south on I-95
(which becomes the beltway). As you
cross the Potomac River on the Woodrow
Wilson Bridge, move to the far right lane.
Take the first exit after the bridge, marked
MOUNT VERNON. At the light, turn right onto
the George Washington Parkway. Mount
Vernon is 8 miles south, at the large traffic
circle at the end of Parkway.

WEST

Our western route out of Baltimore is I-70,
which is easily accessed from I-695, the
Beltway. I-70 heads initially into Howard
County, where the scenery is plentiful
after you pass all the nearby developments between Baltimore and Columbia.

Antiques, Antiques, Antiques

After about an hour you will see signs for
the town of **New Market.** New Market
itself is an antique, dating back as it does
to 1793. It was a trading town originally

because it sat right on the Baltimore
National Pike, which was a main road even
back then and is now U.S. 40.

Today's New Market is still a trading
place. Only today, New Market trades in
antiques and collectibles and, in fact, is
billed as the Antiques Capital of Maryland.
There are more than 35 shops on Main
Street and other ones that trickle down the
hill on side streets. It's best to park in the
large parking lots down the hill and walk.

All shops are open on weekends, with
fewer than half the shops open Wednesday through Friday. There are only 300
permanent residents in New Market. Learn
more at www.newmarketmd.com.

North Meets South

About 20 minutes farther on from New
Market is **Frederick, Maryland,** which was
occupied by both Union and Confederate
forces during the Civil War. Today's Frederick is a thriving city with a population of
more than 40,000, but it is steeped in history. It was here that Barbara Fritchie
approached Confederate forces waving
the stars and stripes and said, according
to the poet John Greenleaf Whittier,
"Shoot if you must this old gray head, but
spare my country's flag!"

Barbara Fritchie's house was restored
early in the twentieth century, and it contains many original furnishings and artifacts from the Civil War. The cost is only
$2.00 for adults and $1.50 for children
younger than 12, but call in advance, (301)
698-0630, as hours vary depending on the
day of the week and time of year.

Monocacy National Battlefield (pronounced Mah-nah-kah-see) marks the last
attempt by Southern troops to march on
Washington, D.C. The visitor center at 4801
Urbana Pike is the best place to begin a
self-tour. Call (301) 662-3515 for more
information or visit www.nps.gov/mono.

If you're a cemetery buff, you might
want to visit the graves of Mr. and Mrs.
Francis Scott Key, Barbara Fritchie, and

others at **Mount Olivet Cemetery** at the end of Market Street. It's open daily from 8:00 A.M. to dusk. Call (301) 662-1164 for more information.

Frederick has its own historic district, as do many of the towns and cities in Maryland. From April through December you can arrange to take a guided walking tour of the district. The tour costs $5.50 for adults; $4.50 for seniors, and 2.50 for children younger than 12. Call (301) 645-7001 to arrange a tour or (800) 999-3613 to receive travel brochures for the area.

History buffs will enjoy a visit to **The Historical Society of Frederick County, Inc.,** at 24 East Church Street, (301) 663-1188 or www.hsfcinfo.org. The building, constructed in the early part of the nineteenth century, housed an orphan asylum from the 1880s until the 1950s. Docents offer tours of the museum and site from 10:00 A.M. to 4:00 P.M. Monday through Saturday and 1:00 to 4:00 P.M. Sundays. Admission is $3.00.

Many of the western cities in Maryland emphasize their antiques stores and malls in an effort to draw tourists, and Frederick is no different. Frederick has more than 40 antiques shops across town, and much like Baltimore's Antique Row, Frederick has Antique Walk at South Carroll and East Patrick Streets, where a fair number of shops can be found.

If you'd like to stay over in Frederick so that you can seek out points farther west on subsequent days, there are a number of hotels and bed-and-breakfasts in the area. Fairfield Inn (301-631-2000, www.fairfield inn.com), Hampton Inn (301-698-2500, www.hamptoninn.com), and Holiday Inn (301-695-2881, www.holidayinn.com) are all available. Prices range from $79 at the Holiday Inn to a top price of $104 at the Hampton Inn for a room with two double beds.

Harpers Ferry

About 20 minutes southwest of Frederick, down U.S. Highway 340 across the Potomac River into West Virginia, you'll find **Harpers Ferry.** This historic town is part of Harpers Ferry National Historical Park. Look for signs to the park's visitor center just after you cross into West Virginia.

Much of the town of Harpers Ferry has been restored, and there are exhibits, museums, and shops throughout. Among the specific attractions you might be interested in are **John Brown's Fort at Old Arsenal Square,** which was the old brick armory firehouse where John Brown was captured. There is also a monument to John Brown near the main line of the B&O Railroad.

Wear your walking shoes and take your walking stick because Harpers Ferry rises up from the confluence of the Potomac and Shenandoah Rivers at a steep angle. Everything, save for the main corner of the town, is either up or down. You do not have to worry about parking, however, for even though there is no parking in town, there is a shuttle bus that will take you from the parking lot at the visitor center to the town.

Admission to Harpers Ferry National Historical Park, which includes the town, John Brown's Farm and Fort, other museums and exhibits, and the shuttle bus from the parking lot is $6.00 a car and is good for three days.

The park is open from 8:00 A.M. to 5:00 P.M. daily except on Thanksgiving, Christmas, and New Year's Days. Shuttle buses to the visitor center run for a half hour to 45 minutes after closing times. For information about events and exhibits, call (304) 535-6223 or visit www.nps.gov/hafe/.

The Town Belonging to Hager

About 30 minutes past Frederick on I-70, you'll run into Hagerstown, which began when Jonathan Hager laid out the town grid on his property in 1762. It is the last big town (population more than 35,000) until you reach Cumberland, another one and a half hours west.

You can visit Hager's homestead, built in 1739, by going to **Hagerstown City Park,** 110 Key Street, and linking up with a guided tour. Hager's house is unique. When he settled this land, it was high wilderness, with mountain lions and Indians and bears—oh, my! Therefore, Hager needed to protect his home and family from predators, both animal and human. He constructed a fort over two springs to assure his water supply in times of siege, and both home and storehouse are located within the fort. All are restored, and there is a museum that has artifacts from the eighteenth century. Admission is $4.00 for adults and $2.00 for children 6 to 12. For more information, call (301) 739-8393 or go to www.hagerhouse.org.

Still surrounded by farmland for the most part, Hagerstown boasts the first county library in Maryland (established 1901) and the world's first bookmobile, which carried books by wagon to more isolated farms.

It is still a quaint setting for the most part that provides many commuters to Baltimore and Washington the opportunity to enjoy small-town living while working in bigger cities. Parades and festivals are held at different times of the year, and you can find out what's happening during your visit by calling the **Washington County Convention and Visitors Bureau** at (800) 228-7829 or visiting www.marylandmemories.org.

Antietam

South of Hagerstown and west of Frederick, equidistant from both on State Highways 34/65, is **Antietam National Battlefield,** 960 acres of rolling Maryland countryside that witnessed the bloodiest day of the Civil War. On September 17, 1862, battle began between Confederate and Union troops who, at the end of the day, saw more than 23,000 men killed or wounded. More than

one visitor to the battlefield in the twentieth century remarked on seeing reenactments where, in fact, there were none. If their visions are to be believed, then it seems that the battle rages on in some other dimension. It is certainly true that both here and at Gettysburg Battlefield in Pennsylvania (see the listing later in this chapter), the sorrow and the pain that were endured are still palpable.

Antietam is of particular interest to Marylanders not just because the battle was fought on Maryland soil but also because Maryland had sons on both sides of the battle. **The Maryland Monument** is the only monument in the world to pay homage to fallen dead on both sides of a battle—eight Union regiments from Maryland and two Maryland Confederate regiments. All together, more than 54,000 Marylanders fought in the Civil War.

Open dawn to dusk, Antietam Battlefield is dotted with monuments and tablets to those who fell there, which you can stop and read more thoroughly on your drive along the 8.5-mile trail. On weekends June through October, guides in period costume are present to show how soldiers lived at camp and to demonstrate military drills. Throughout the summer months, there are also special presentations and events.

For information, call (301) 432-5124 or visit www.nps.gov/anti. A charge of $3.00 for individuals or $5.00 for a family admits you to the battlefield as well as Antietam National Cemetery and the visitor center, where you start the tour. The visitor center is open 8:30 A.M. to 6:00 P.M. Memorial Day to Labor Day and 8:30 A.M. to 5:00 P.M. the rest of the year.

The Gap

Nestled in the heart of the Appalachian Mountains, called the Alleghenies hereabouts, is the city of **Cumberland.** To get there, take I-70 until it turns into U.S. Highway 68/40/144. It's a straight shot from Hagerstown; just follow the signs.

The name and the town are descended from Fort Cumberland, which was headquarters to General Edward Braddock and the then–Lieutenant George Washington during the French and Indian War. Because of its location on the other side of Cumberland Narrows, also known as Cumberland Gap, Cumberland became the natural jumping-off place before heading farther west. It was the western terminus of the Chesapeake and Ohio Canal, the eastern terminus of the National Road (Baltimore National Pike, now U.S. 40), and during the nineteenth century its economy was fueled by the railroad. Coal was brought down from the mountains and "gold" was returned.

The city is essentially cut in half by the railroad, which runs over the mountain and down through the center of the valley in which Cumberland sits. Homes and streets are carved up and into the surrounding mountains on either side of the tracks. The most impressive side of the city and the historic district is along and around Washington Street, which is often called **Washington Hill.**

The City Hall, library, and the stately homes of the railroad's original rich line Washington Street. Everything from sprawling Victorian mansions to conservative Federal and Georgian Revival may be seen there.

Riding up Washington Street from the center of town, you'll pass the Cumberland Station, a massive railroad station that now serves as a railroad museum and place of departure for trips on the **Western Maryland Scenic Railroad** to the countryside, around Piney Mountain, through Brush Tunnel, and into Frostburg to The Old Depot. (See Frostburg later in this section for more information on The Old Depot.) Scenic rides with either diesel or steam engines pulling the train depart from the depot. There are dinner and mystery trips available as well. Depending on what you're doing and where you're going, fares range between $10 to $39 for the three-hour excursions. For information about when and where, call (800) 872-4650 or visit www.wmsr.com.

Downtown Cumberland is only about 3 blocks long, but in the last 10 years, much has been restored in the area. Cumberland is trying to become an antiquing haven, and along the western block of downtown, there's a three-story antiques mall, and two or three separate shops are scattered around town.

Because Cumberland sits at one of the narrowest areas of Maryland's western counties, West Virginia is just across a short bridge from Washington Street, literally a five-minute trip. Within minutes you'll be in the country. Pennsylvania is only about 20 minutes north on U.S. Highway 220.

If you've gotten to Cumberland, you've been on the road a minimum of three hours. After a full day of antiquing or enjoying all things Cumberland, you might decide to stay over. There are some bed-and-breakfasts around the area, but the main hotel in town is the Holiday Inn, which sits by the railroad tracks in the center of town at 100 South George Street. Rates run between $80 and $109 a night. A highrise hotel built in the 1960s, it offers 130 rooms in six stories. There is a restaurant in the hotel, but there are also some nice eateries within walking distance. For reservation information at the Holiday Inn, call (301) 724-8800, or visit www.holidayinn.com.

To find out more information about Cumberland, call the **Allegany County Visitor's Bureau** at (800) 508-4748 or visit www.mdmountainside.com.

Frostburg

Over the mountain from Cumberland is **Frostburg;** it's aptly named because when winter storms hurl themselves at western Maryland, it is Frostburg that usually catches the worst of it. It was, however, not named Frostburg because of winter's chill but because of the Frosts, who were the first family to settle the area.

Meshach Frost brought the town into being when he turned his home into the **Highland Hall Inn** in 1818. It became a stagecoach stop on the National Road.

Other industrious entrepreneurs built around Meshach's inn, and the result was Frostburg. By 1840 Frostburg had become a coal mining and railroad town.

Today's Frostburg is a small, mostly residential area that boasts **The Old Depot,** a renovated train station that now houses a restaurant and gift shop. There is also a museum in the area that surrounds The Old Depot, called Depot Park. **Thrasher Carriage Museum** exhibits nineteenth- and twentieth-century horse-drawn carriages, sleighs, carts, milk wagons—just about anything that was ever drawn by horse. The museum building itself is also of interest in that it is a renovated warehouse dating back to the nineteenth century. The museum is open Wednesday through Sunday 10:00 A.M. to 3:00 P.M. March through December; January and February by appointment only. Admission is $3.00 for adults and $1.00 for children to 18. For more information call (301) 689–3380 or visit www.thrashercarriage.com.

To find out more about what Frostburg has to offer, call the **Allegany County Visitor's Bureau** at (800) 508–4748 or visit www.mountainsidemd.com.

NORTHWEST

Our northwest route is Highway 140, otherwise known as Reisterstown Road, which is accessible from the Baltimore Beltway, I–695. At Reisterstown (see the Antiques and Collectibles chapter for more about Reisterstown), there is a fork in the road. Stay on Highway 140.

"Wess Minister"

Westminster—or Wess Minister in Bawlmerese—is only 45 minutes from Baltimore in Carroll County. A lot of the area within Westminster's confines is suburban housing developments, apartment complexes, and shopping centers. The old town, however, is still a thriving community, partly because of Western Maryland College, which is located there. The center town has some modern buildings, but it is much the way it must have looked in the eighteenth century.

Main Street has interesting shops and restaurants, such as an Irish shop and an Italian bistro, and the area has been restored to some degree, with brick sidewalks and little parks along the way that create a provincial ambience. Behind Main Street is a large parking lot with metered parking. It's pretty well situated, so that just about anywhere in town is a short jaunt away.

Westminster boasts some well-attended yearly events, such as the Deer Creek Fiddler's Convention, held the second Sunday in June and the first Sunday in August, and the Maryland Wine Festival, held in September. During the summer it is also the home of the Ravens' football training camp. All year round, however, one of Westminster's main draws for Baltimoreans, besides its historic ambience and interesting little shops, is **Baugher's** restaurant and farm orchard market.

Baugher's restaurant and market opened in 1948 as an outlet for selling Baugher's farm produce. The restaurant at 289 West Main Street extended is known for its fresh fruit pies that are available all summer long. Strawberry pie begins the season in June; pumpkin pie ends it in the fall. You can top your pie with ice cream made on the premises, or if you'd rather, top your homemade ice cream with fresh fruit. To wash it all down, you'll want to sample Baugher's sweet apple cider, which can be purchased by the gallon at the market as well as ordered in the restaurant. Baugher's restaurant is a popular place, but no reservations are required. Sunny Sundays in June often see a line waiting outside.

Baugher's farm has family activities during the summer, such as wagon rides, but it is mainly swarmed over by those who like to pick their own produce. Call the Pick-Your-Own hotline, (410) 857–0111, before you come so you'll know what fresh fruits and vegetables are available, or visit the Web site at www.baughers.com.

Speaking of farms . . . at 500 South Center Street, you can visit the **Carroll County Farm Museum.** The farmhouse, barn, and 16 outbuildings were originally the county poor farm, where homeless people were taken in until they could get back on their feet. Now renovated, the buildings portray nineteenth-century farm life, including furnishings and tools from the period and, on occasion, demonstrations of quilting, spinning, weaving, blacksmithing, and other home crafts. It is a great place to picnic any day, but there are also special events from time to time. Admission is $3.00 for adults and $2.00 for children 7 to 18. The Farm Museum is open on weekends in May, June, September, and October and Tuesday through Sunday in July and August. Hours vary. Call (410) 876-2667 for more information.

Down by the Old Mill Stream

If you are interested in the workings of nineteenth-century American industry, ride just 7 miles north of Westminster on State Highway 97 to **Union Mills,** where you will find the Union Mills Homestead and House Museum, and the Union Mills Grist Mill at 3311 Littlestown Pike.

Union Mills Homestead was built in 1797 by the Shriver families, who created the mill, a tannery, and a cannery as well as this working farm. The homestead was in the hands of the Shrivers from that time until it was made into a museum; the furnishings, utensils, tools, and other items are not just authentic to the period but are, in fact, authentic to the Shriver family.

The Grist Mill is three stories high and was built with bricks made on the property—from good old Maryland clay, no doubt—and is powered by waterwheel, as were most mills up until the middle of this century. The Union Mills Grist Mill still operates today.

The museum is open Tuesday through Sunday June through October, and weekends starting in May. Hours of operation vary. A $2.50 charge covers admission to both the homestead and mill. Children 6 to 12 pay $1.50. For hours and more information call (410) 848-2288 or visit www .tourism.carr/unionmil.htm.

On Pilgrimage

To visit the **National Shrine of St. Elizabeth Ann Seton,** travel up Highway 140 past Westminster about an hour to the town of Emmitsburg, which lies just south of the Mason-Dixon Line and is home to Mount St. Mary's College.

The shrine of our first native-born American saint is at 333 South Seton Avenue on the campus of St. Joseph's Provincial House. A museum at the shrine holds some of Mother Seton's personal items, and a chapel houses her tomb. Other restored buildings are part of the tour that lasts approximately two hours. There is no entrance fee, and, except for major holidays, the shrine is open year-round from 10:00 A.M. to 4:30 P.M. (daily from April through October and Tuesday through Sunday November through March; the shrine closes most of January and for major holidays). Call (301) 447-6606 for more information.

The **National Shrine Grotto of Lourdes,** also in Emmitsburg, is a replica of the Grotto of Lourdes, France, created in 1805 by Father John Debois. The grotto is open dawn to dusk, daily, throughout the year. There is no entrance fee. If you would like more information, call (301) 447-5318.

Gettysburg, Pennsylvania

From Emmitsburg, take State Highway 140 to State Highway 116 in Pennsylvania, to get to **Gettysburg,** best known as the site of one of the major, bloody battles of the Civil War. More than 50,000 men were killed and wounded at Gettysburg over the

battle fought July 1–3, 1863. About 5,700 acres of open fields where 160,000 Americans met to do battle are now consecrated as Gettysburg National Military Park.

The park, which virtually surrounds the town of Gettysburg, is dotted with more than 1,300 state memorials to the fallen. Markers allow you to follow the battle from the first volley to Pickett's Charge. Gettysburg National Cemetery, on the battlefield, was dedicated by President Lincoln in 1863. The speech he gave at the dedication, the Gettysburg Address, is one of the most famous speeches of American history.

The National Park Visitor Center, which is open daily from 8:00 A.M. to 5:00 P.M. except for major holidays, is a good starting point for self-guided tours. Entrance to the park is free.

In addition to the battlefield, there are other museums and historic sites concerning the battle in the area. For a complete list, call **Gettysburg Convention and Visitors Bureau** at (717) 334–2106 or visit the Web site www.gettysburg.com.

SPECTATOR SPORTS

Sports in Baltimore is a weird mix, to say the least.

Long before it became commonplace, Baltimore lost its football team, the Colts. On a snowy night in March 1984, owner Robert Irsay packed up the team's belongings in moving vans to head for a better deal and a bigger stadium in Indianapolis. Thirteen years later, certain Baltimore higher-ups wooed Cleveland's Browns to town and renamed them the Ravens (referring to the main character of a poem by Edgar Allan Poe), doing essentially the same thing to Cleveland that was done to Baltimore in the 1980s. But of course, Cleveland was able to keep its team name and colors—something that Baltimore Colts fans could only dream about. Then there's the Baltimore Arena, which was called the Baltimore Civic Center when the NBA's Bullets ruled there. The Bullets moved to Washington, D.C., and are now called the Washington Wizards. The civic center is now called an arena. It plays host to indoor soccer but not basketball or hockey because professional teams in these sports have failed here.

Yet we consider ourselves a big-league town, where home football or baseball games can significantly affect sales at the movies, restaurants, and other venues. We drop everything for a Saturday in May when the Preakness, the second leg in horse racing's Triple Crown, comes to town.

Our sports stars are still our heroes, and our teams—pro, college, and high school—are part of our families.

For many of us, Cal Ripken Jr., the Orioles infielder who played in 2,632 consecutive baseball games before ending the streak on September 20, 1998—a major league record—is a symbol of what we demand of ourselves. Through Cal we see ourselves—working hard, playing hard, having fun, getting better and better, facing adversity. It's hard to forget Cal catch-ing the final out as shortstop in the 5-0 victory over the Phillies in Philadelphia on October 16, 1983. The catch, the raised arms, the jumping up and down, the thrill of the moment. Then there's the night time stood still in baseball—September 6, 1995. All the world's sports fans watched as the banner proclaiming 2,131—the record number game—was unfurled on the warehouse past right field. In a scene seemingly out of *The Natural*, Cal took an impromptu victory lap at Camden Yards, slapping and shaking hands of the fans in the front row, as though each was a close friend.

It's hard to forget the arm of Johnny Unitas launching touchdown passes to Raymond Berry heading down the sidelines toward the closed end of the field at Memorial Stadium more than three decades ago, or when a game between the Pittsburgh Steelers and the Colts or the New York Jets and the Colts practically paralyzed the town all day Sunday.

Then there's more heartbreak. More than 50,000 fans filled Memorial Stadium in 1988 to celebrate the end of a 21-game losing streak for the Baltimore Orioles, a record that brought the city ridicule and attention from local, national, and international sports fans. When the streak ended, the fans were there, another sellout, as if they had been a part of the streak, even though it was something they would have rather forgotten.

We live and breathe with the players— they aren't just the team. They're family, people who would be welcomed with open arms at a family picnic or birthday dinner. To love an athlete is a concept that is all too often thrown around without meaning, but in Baltimore there is truth to the statement that we love our teams. They form a big part of who and what we are—to ourselves, to our friends, and to the world. When ESPN shows the score of the Ravens' game, we take heart in the team's success or failure. They are our teams, and we love them as if they were our brothers or children. So feel free to share them with us, but don't ask us to part with them. We've learned our lesson.

BASEBALL

Baltimore Orioles
Oriole Park at Camden Yards
333 West Camden Street
(410) 685-9800
www.orioles.mlb.com

When it comes to baseball, the black and orange of the Baltimore Orioles are all that matters in this city. Since 1954 the team has been giving fans something to cheer about from April through September . . . and some years even into October, when the playoffs and World Series take place.

You've probably heard about one of the team's standouts. Name's Cal Ripkin Jr. He grew up about 30 miles north of Baltimore in Aberdeen, and he has played in more consecutive games than any other player in professional baseball history. On September 20, 1998, he ended his streak that lasted 2,632 consecutive games. Of course Cal is just one of the Birds, a team that, during the 2001 season, included many fresh faces and young talent like hard-hitting Jerry Hairston who plays second base, and right fielder Chris Richard.

The Baltimore Orioles, routinely referred to as the Os or the Birds, roost in the dugout on the first-base side of the field, even though it gets the afternoon sun. So if you're looking for shots of someone on the team, it's best to get seats in the outfield or on the third-base side. If you're on the first-base side for an afternoon game or before the sun sets for a night game, take a hat, sunglasses, and suntan lotion—the sun is going to be hitting you hard.

Legendary first baseman Eddie Murray is still with the Orioles at first base, although now he serves as first-base coach. All this talent will hopefully head the Orioles back to post-season action.

In previous decades the team, powered by Hall of Famer Brooks Robinson at third base and standout pitchers such as Jim Palmer, Dave McNally, and Mike Cuellar, won in World Series appearances in 1966, 1970, and 1983.

In 2000 Mike Hargrove joined the Orioles as a manager and the team began rebuilding its lineup, adding young rookies to play alongside veterans. Albert Belle hit 23 homers before being permanently benched from a career-ending hip injury. Cal Ripken played just 83 games due to injuries of his own, which helped prompt his decision to call the next season his last. During 2001 guests and baseball players at Major League parks across the country lauded Ripken with gifts and standing ovations. He ended his stellar career in Baltimore on Saturday, October 6, 2001 in front of a sold-out hometown crowd. Cal capped off his fairy-tale career by hitting a home run in the All-Star Game and winning the MVP award. The 2002 season saw a very young Orioles team, and the club's lineup continues to grow and mature.

Oriole Park at Camden Yards

Since its opening in 1992, Oriole Park at Camden Yards' reputation has grown to the point that it is considered one of the best venues in the country (if not the absolute best) for watching baseball. Each season, fans from all over the world come to Camden Yards (locals tend to drop the Oriole Park), a 48,876-seat (including standing-room) stadium that successfully mixes the old and new. Practically every seat has a great view of the whole field.

The old B&O Railroad warehouse runs along Eutaw Street behind the right-field seats. The seven-story brick building, built around the turn of the century, is the longest warehouse building on the East Coast; it extends an amazing 1,016 feet, although it is only 51 feet wide.

At 439 feet from home plate, the warehouse is a long shot away for a batter. No player has hit the warehouse during a game, although Ken Griffey Jr., then the Seattle Mariners' star outfielder, nailed it during a home-run hitting contest the day before the 1993 All-Star Game, which was hosted by the Orioles in their year-old stadium. As you walk among the shops and offices along Eutaw Street beside the warehouse, look down and you'll see round, bronze markers where home runs have landed as players continue to tee up for the warehouse.

Inside the ballpark, the field is set 16 feet below ground level, giving the park a more intimate feel than its predecessors. Conveniently located about 6 blocks west of the Inner Harbor, on land a block from where Babe Ruth, the Bronx Bomber himself, was born and raised, the stadium integrates the skyline and feel of today's Baltimore with some of the classic features of old ballparks. Steel, rather than concrete, trusses and an arched brick facade call to mind bygone playing grounds like Ebbetts Field in Brooklyn and Shibe Park in Philadelphia. Other distinctive features, some copied at Jacobs Field in Cleveland, Turner Field in Atlanta, and the Ballpark at Arlington in Texas, include an asymmetrical playing field and low outfield walls. On every aisle is a reproduction of the logo used by the Baltimore Orioles of the 1890s, a National League team that won consecutive pennants from 1894 to 1896.

Camden Yards even welcomes rain. The field features Professional Athletic Turf, an irrigation and drainage system below the natural grass that ends rain delays about 30 minutes after the rains stop. The field can remove as much as 75,000 gallons of rainwater from the field each hour.

Recent renovations included replacing the entire playing surface and changing the field dimensions of the ballpark. Home plate was moved about 7 feet closer to the backstop, bringing fans closer to the action, providing better sight lines from hundreds of seats, reducing obstructions near the foul poles, and increasing safety for spectators behind home plate.

The foul line measurement increased from 318 feet to 320 feet in right field and from 333 feet to 337 feet in left. The center field distance increased from 400 feet to 406 feet and the deepest part of the ballpark, left center field, increased from 410 feet to 417 feet.

In addition to repositioning the foul poles, the Orioles replaced the left field foul pole with the original left field foul pole used by the Orioles at Memorial Stadium from 1954 through 1991. The Memorial Stadium foul pole is shorter (70 feet) and requires a smaller support structure that will allow more fans in the lower club and upper decks to have an unobstructed view of the field. The Orioles have used the original right field foul pole from Memorial Stadium since Camden Yards opened in 1992.

The bleacher seats in right field and center field are really good seats, although you're looking over the shoulders of the outfielders. Standing-room-only tickets, which enable spectators to watch from an outfield porch in right field or to fill seats left unoccupied, are another bargain (see the following section on Tickets). You'll also notice the 72 luxury boxes, where movers and shakers can watch the game, sip champagne, and eat from expensive platters. They're great seats and great eats when you can get them, but don't hold your breath.

The club level is the place for those who want to be treated like royalty but can't afford to own a luxury box. In these seats, just a few feet higher than the Press Box, waiters and waitresses will get your hot dogs, turkey sandwiches, or crab cakes. Another advantage of club seats: There is access to indoor facilities with air conditioning, a bar, and TV lounges.

Tickets

Tickets for Orioles games are available at the Camden Station ticket office, at the intersection of Martin Luther King Jr. Boulevard and Eutaw Street.

Getting tickets on game day is possible but can be difficult on weekends. But planning in advance is best as the stadium is often filled to capacity from June through September, even if the Os aren't fighting for a playoff spot.

Tickets can be obtained by mail by writing to Oriole Mail Order Form, 333 West Camden Street, Baltimore, MD 21201, or by calling the Orioles at (888) 848–BIRD. You can also order online through ticketmaster.com. Tickets can be charged using MasterCard or Visa and can be sent to you by mail or picked up at the "will call" window on game day (note that there might be a line and a wait). It's better to arrive early, get your tickets, then either visit the Inner Harbor or head in to watch batting practice, which is open to the public usually 90 minutes to two hours before game time.

Ticket prices range from $45.00 for club box seats to $15.00 for the bleachers and $8.00 for standing-room-only. Season and group tickets are available from the Orioles offices; call (410) 685–9800 and choose option three.

Good places to meet up with people at Oriole Park at Camden Yards include the front of Camden Station or in front of the statues outside the Eutaw Street entrance. Both are easy to find and even easier to get directions to.

Getting There and Parking

About 5,000 parking spaces were lost in 1997 when construction of the football stadium for the Baltimore Ravens began. The loss made an already bad parking situation that much worse. Don't expect to park at the stadium's lots unless you have a license plate denoting a handicap or you managed to obtain a parking pass from a season-ticket holder. Area parking garages, including the ones at Sheraton Inner Harbor and the Gallery shopping center, offer parking that ranges in price from $5.00 for a walk of up to 15 blocks to $15.00 for parking near the stadium.

Getting to the game is made easiest by using one of the variety of mass transit options. Not only do you avoid the tough drive through the city, but you also get to meet and greet like-minded fans. The stadium is only 6 blocks from the Inner Harbor.

The state's MARC commuter rail runs between Union Station in Washington and the ballpark on game days and nights. Light Rail lines also carry passengers from Hunt Valley Mall, about 15 miles north of Baltimore City, to Camden Yards. From the south, rail lines transport fans from the Baltimore–Washington International Airport and Cromwell Station in Anne Arundel County, about 20 miles away. The Light Rail, which stops at several locations between Hunt Valley Mall and the ballpark, costs $2.70 for a round-trip pass for games or $1.35 for the regular one-way fare. The entry points north and south get crowded about 90 minutes before game time, but it's still a quick and easy way to get to and from the park. Trains usually run every 17 minutes, but more trains are put in service for games.

Park 'N' Ride lots around I–695 (the Baltimore Beltway) also offer parking and bus transport to the games. This can often be an affordable and enjoyable option, usually costing between $2.50 and $6.00 for the round trip. To find more commuter information check the MTA Web site at www.mta.maryland.com.

Ballpark Rules

The following rules apply at all Orioles home games.

• No alcoholic beverages, cans, or glass can be brought into the park. Containers, including coolers and bags, are checked as spectators enter.

• Food can be brought into the stadium, meaning those peanut and pretzel vendors outside the ballpark make good money. Their prices are lower than what you'll find inside.

• All entrants must pay, except infants sitting on the same seat as parents.

• Smoking is prohibited in all areas, except

the concourses outside the playing field and seating area.

- Selling tickets for more than face value is illegal, and undercover police stings targeting offenders are not unusual.

The Os on the Air

If you can't get to the park, Orioles games are carried on television through a unique arrangement. All games appear on TV, either over the airwaves on WJZ-TV (Channel 13) or WNUV-TV (Channel 54) or on cable on Home Team Sports, a regional cable sports programming station.

Radio broadcasts are carried on WBAL (1090 AM), a 50,000-watt megastation, and in Washington on WTOP (1500 AM), another 50,000-watt giant. Between the two stations, the teams' games can be heard on a clear night as far north as Maine and as far south as Florida.

FOOTBALL

Baltimore Ravens
M&T Bank Stadium
1101 Russell Street
(410) 230–8000
www.ravenszone.net

Over the past few years Baltimore area residents have steadily developed a love for purple. The cause—the Super Bowl XXXV Champion Ravens. Since the team came from the city of Cleveland, where they had been the Browns until 1995, Baltimore embraced them and the chance to have the NFL back in Baltimore. The Ravens, a name honoring the title of the classic Edgar Allan Poe poem, wear purple, black, and gold, and area residents are sporting those colors with pride. Although the reflexive urge to call our football team anything but the Colts is hard to break, the Ravens have made it easy to fall in love with them.

After decades during which the exploits of the greats—"Golden Arm" Johnny Unitas, Raymond Berry, Lenny Moore, and Bert Jones—cemented fans' love of the team, people are starting to find new heroes to focus their football fandom on.

After several years of rebuilding, team owner Art Modell's hard work to put together a first-rate team paid off. On January 28, 2001, under supervision of Head Coach Brian Billick, the Ravens defeated the New York Giants by a score of 34–7 at Super Bowl XXXV.

During the glory years of the 1960s and '70s, Baltimore football fans were known to skip church or go to early services to allow proper time for, er, game preparation. Now, many fans are again carrying out the tradition and of course starting their own.

In 1998 a new era began for the team, as it opened a football-only stadium, built across from Oriole Park at Camden Yards in downtown Baltimore, about 6 blocks from the Inner Harbor. After closing the book on Memorial Stadium—a 60,000-seat grande dame among outdoor stadiums, used by the Colts, Ravens, and the Canadian Football League's now-defunct Baltimore Stallions (not to mention the Baltimore Orioles until 1992)—the team's move to what is now called M&T Bank Stadium has brought more of the historic charm that came with Camden Yards. The new digs provide the team, its owner, and fans with the state-of-the-art facilities considered so essential to a winning football organization these days.

M&T Bank Stadium

The 69,084-seat stadium brought new life to the team and the city's Downtown. It follows by several years the incredible success of neighboring Oriole Park at Camden Yards, and football fans will find similarities to the baseball stadium. But there are new features, including a "split" upper seating bowl designed to serve as an architectural signature while offering football fans a great view of the city's skyline.

The stadium has several unique characteristics, including a distinct upper seating level with notched corner. There are 62 over-sized restrooms located throughout the stadium. The stadium also features

Selected Baltimore Firsts

The first baseball player to be named Most Valuable Player in both the American and National Leagues was Frank Robinson of the Baltimore Orioles (1966).

Baltimore is the first city to win championships in the National Football League, the United States Football League, and the Canadian Football League. This distinction became ours when we locked up the Canadian trophy, The Grey Cup.

—Excerpted from Baltimore— America's City of Firsts, *a pamphlet published by Baltimore Bicentennial Celebration, Inc.*

close to 250 permanent points of sale for food and beverages that are complemented with several specialty food and beverage carts throughout the stadium. Extra-wide concourses and unobstructed views place this stadium in a class of its own. But perhaps the most spectacular feature are the two Smartvision boards, each measuring 25 by 100 feet and utilizing the most advanced technology, that give every visitor the feeling of being right on the field in the middle of the action. The spectacular visual effect is enhanced with a state-of-the-art sound system.

There are seven levels, including five with seating. The facade has brick arches at its base, aluminum trim at the grid lines, and a frame of concrete supported by pewter structural steel rakers. Throughout the project, dark, rich brick and mortar, manufactured in Maryland and similar in appearance to other buildings in the area, were used.

Stadium Rules

The following rules apply at all Ravens home games.

- No alcoholic beverages, cans, or glass can be brought into the stadium. Fans must be 21 years or older to purchase or consume alcoholic beverages at the stadium. This includes any parking lots designated as tailgating zones.
- Smoking is not permitted in the seating areas or restrooms. Smoking is allowed on open concourses and ramps.
- Umbrellas are not allowed in the stadium so as not to interfere with the sightlines of other guests.
- Cameras and video equipment are permitted in the stadium during Ravens' games but cannot be used to reproduce the game.
- Selling tickets for more than face value is illegal.

Tickets

Although season ticket holders control most of the seats to a Ravens game, the team does reserve about 6,000 tickets for each game to sell to the general public. These tickets generally go on sale in mid-July and can be purchased at the Ravens box office at the stadium, through Ticket-Master Phone Charge, or online at www.tickemaster.com. Ticket prices for a single seat start at $35 and go up from there. Selected group sales package plans (for 25 or more people) are also available by contacting the Ravens ticket office at (410) 261–RAVE (7283).

To purchase a season ticket in M&T Stadium, the purchase of a Permanent Seat License is required. This is a one-time purchase that transfers the rights of the seat from the team to the individual licensee. The one-time permanent seat fee is either $2,000 or $3,000. Season tickets start at $300 and can go up to $3,000 for the top club level seat.

Most Ravens games are carried on television by WJZ-TV (Channel 13), a CBS affiliate in Baltimore, when not subject to blackout rules; for home games that aren't sold out within 72 hours of game time, TV affiliates within a 75-mile radius of the stadium can't carry the game. That means local games that aren't sellouts won't even be carried in Washington, which is Redskins country anyway. Radio broadcasts of all Raven games are on WLIF (101.9 FM) and WJFK (1300 AM).

Getting There and Parking

Ravens fans will experience similar parking woes as the folks heading to one of the 81 home games played by the Orioles. Look for the Ravens bird at Downtown parking locations. There are more than 30,000 spaces in garages within walking distance of the stadium. Some to look for include the Market Center Garage at Paca and Lexington Streets, Fayette West Garage at Howard and Fayette Streets, and the Redwood Street garage at Eutaw and Baltimore Streets. These lots can charge from $5.00 to $30.00 for parking.

But mass transit is the name of the game. About 6 blocks from the Inner Harbor, the stadium offers easy access to most mass transit options. The state's MARC commuter rail runs between Union Station in Washington and the ballpark on game days and nights. Light Rail lines carry passengers from Hunt Valley Mall, about 15 miles north of Baltimore City, to Camden Yards, and from the Baltimore–Washington International Airport and Cromwell Station in Anne Arundel County, about 20 miles south of Baltimore City. The Light Rail costs $4.00 for a round-trip pass for games or $1.60 regularly one way. The entry points north and south get crowded about 90 minutes before game time but are a quick and easy way to get to and from the stadium.

HORSE RACING

Maryland's roots in horse racing go back a long, long way. In fact, the Maryland

Seabiscuit became a legend when he defeated the Triple Crown winner War Admiral in the 1938 Pimlico Special. Pictures from that race—voted the Race of the Century by Sports Illustrated—*can be seen at the Maryland Jockey Club at Pimlico.*

Jockey Club, owner and operator of Pimlico Race Course, was established in 1743—more than 30 years before the Revolutionary War! The Annapolis Subscription Plate is the second-oldest racing trophy in America.

If you head out into horse country—the open and largely undeveloped land north and northwest of Baltimore—you'll see sprawling horse farms, their long, beautifully painted white fences leading the way to tomorrow's race champions.

Baltimore is also home of the Preakness Stakes, the middle jewel of horse racing's Triple Crown. Each May, the eyes of all horseracing fans as well as all those people who get caught up in the annual quest to win the three big races turn to Pimlico, where horses and jockeys race for the crown.

Pimlico Race Course
Hayward and Winner Avenues
(410) 542-9400
www.marylandracing.com
On 140 acres in northwest Baltimore City sits a mile-long, 70-foot-wide track with a stretch distance (from the last turn to the finish line) of 1,152 feet. That means lots of excitement as the horses head for the wire.

Bettors are serviced by 750 betting windows and automated betting machines. The new grandstand holds up to 5,692 people, while the old grandstand accommodates 5,926. The clubhouse has space for 1,269 people. The stables offer accommodations for up to 800 horses, plus tack, feed, and sleeping rooms. Quarters for the male jockeys are behind the paddock, and female jockeys' quarters are located near the paddock.

CLOSE-UP

Maryland's State Sport—Jousting?!?

Ask most Baltimoreans, and they'll tell you the state sport is lacrosse, a high-speed, bone-crunching sport played by young men and women with webbed sticks. Lacrosse is huge in the northeastern United States, and Johns Hopkins University and the University of Maryland are two local powerhouses.

But the state sport (and Maryland is the only state with a designated state sport) is actually jousting, a medieval test of bravery and skill that pitted knight against knight in battle, often for the hand of a fair maiden.

In Europe between the tenth and twelfth centuries, jousting required that an armor-clad rider on horseback knock another knight from his mount using a long pole. Jousting was an occupation and the widely accepted method throughout Europe for competing knights to prove their mettle to the fair maiden of the day, while making some money for beating an able competitor.

Thankfully, riders don't square off against each other anymore. Instead, they compete in the "running at the rings," the name given to the new approach to the sport created about the time of James I of England. It was this form that Cecil Calvert, the first Lord Baltimore, brought to the colonies in the early 1700s.

Today, as in colonial times, jousting riders take three runs at the rings, which in the first round are an inch in diameter, roughly the size of a quarter. The rider steers toward three small rings with a 5- to 7-foot-long wooden pole, designed specifically for the rider. The pole must be crafted to provide perfect balance when on the rider's arm. Inserted into the end of the pole is a 2-foot lance, handmade of aluminum, stainless steel, or steel. Riders who succeed in collecting nine rings (three in

The track's live days are Wednesday and Thursday. Admission is $4.50 for the grandstand, $3.00 for the clubhouse, and $5.00 for the sports palace, an enclosed lounge where simulcasts of other races are shown, except on weekends and holidays when it's $7.00. Inside box seats (two seats in each box) in the grandstand are $2.50 a seat. Likewise, outside box seats (four seats in each box) in the grandstand are $2.50 a seat. Sports palace seats (weekends and holidays only) are $2.50 a seat. Tickets are available at the entrance on Preakness Way; MasterCard and Visa are accepted.

Getting to Pimlico is relatively easy. Take I-83 to Northern Parkway, head west about 2 miles, and the race track is on the left. Parking is all on-site, with 4,220 spaces available; except on Preakness Day, there are a total of 2,100 general parking spots available for free on Preakness Way and Rogers Avenue, 1,500 clubhouse parking spaces cost $3.00 each, and valet parking, in 620 spots, is offered at $4.00.

The Preakness

The Preakness Stakes is a big, big event. People come from around the country to each of three rounds) compete at the next level, where the rings are about the size of a nickel. A subsequent round has rings a quarter-inch in diameter, about the size of a dime.

The rings are suspended from arches 30 yards apart, with a 40-yard starting area for the horse and rider to get their timing and approach perfect. Competitors are given nine seconds to complete a regular round, eight seconds for a championship round. They are timed from when they cross a starting line 20 yards from the first ring until they gather the third ring. Taking more time than allotted eliminates the competitor, regardless of whether the rider succeeds in gathering the rings on his pole.

The winner is crowned at an elaborate closing ceremony, where the winning knight chooses the lady to be crowned "Queen of Love and Beauty." When women win, and they increasingly compete in this skill event, they choose the "King of Love and Beauty."

In keeping with the medieval tradition, riders male and female take names like Knight of One-Thousand Days or Maiden of Mísery, often using humor or their real family names as sources for their monikers. These modern-day knights have chosen brightly colored costumes of the period over the medieval armor of centuries past.

Because the rider must focus all attention on the rings, the movements of the horse must be exact. For this reason, horses typically go through at least two years of formal training with riders before entering competitions.

Few formal jousting tournaments are held, though exhibitions are often performed at county fairs and the Maryland Renaissance Festival (see the Annual Events chapter). A careful eye to the open stretches of farmland in northern Baltimore County can often reveal the telltale arches where would-be lords practice for the opportunity to be Lord of the Rings.

watch the run for the second jewel of the thoroughbred racing industry's Triple Crown. For the Preakness, Pimlico's capacity grows to 98,983, including 22,000 standing-room-only patrons and 60,000 people filling the infield, where visitors tend to see little of the race but usually leave feeling no pain. That comes the next day, if you know what we mean.

Parking is a lot more difficult to find on Preakness weekend, and it's best to get to the track early. It's also a lot more expensive, with general parking going for $30, clubhouse preferred for $50, and valet parking for $65. The infield opens at 9:00 A.M.; if you want to park near the track, that might be the latest you can afford to arrive. (See the Annual Events chapter for more information about the Preakness.)

Laurel Race Course
Race Track Road and Route 198, Laurel (410) 792-7775
www.marylandracing.com
Located on 360 acres midway between Baltimore and Washington, D.C., Laurel Race Course offers live racing on Wednesday through Sunday with post times to be

The crown adorning the winning horse in May's Preakness Stakes isn't really made of black-eyed Susans. They're daisies with centers that have been handpainted black to resemble black-eyed Susans, which don't bloom until late summer. Shhhh, it's a secret!

decided. The dirt track is a 1⅛-mile oval with a 7-furlong chute. The length of the stretch from the last turn to the finish line is an exciting 1,344 feet.

Bettors at Laurel are serviced by 350 betting windows and automated betting machines.

In 1988 Laurel Park was the site of a complete rebuilding of the racing strip at a cost of almost $2 million. The park also received a face-lift in 1985 when the Sports Palace was built with the ambience of a plush casino complemented with state-of-the-art technology featuring computerized handicapping and a video library.

The clubhouse has space for 1,216 people and the grandstand has space for 2,964 people. The stables offer accommodations for 880 horses. Jockeys' quarters are located next to the racing secretary's office across form the paddock.

Admission to the grandstand and clubhouse is $3.00 and night and simulcasting seating is free. Seats on weekdays are also free with a few exceptions. Box seats on weekends and holidays are $2.50 per seat for grandstand and clubhouse (four seats to a box).

Getting to Laurel Park is easy; it is located just 22 miles from Baltimore on Route 198. Just take I–95 south toward Washington, D.C., and get off at exit 33, Route 198, heading east and follow the signs. General parking for live racing is free, preferred is $2.00, valet is $5.00, and park and lock is $5.00 during the day and free at night. Parking for simulcasting is free, except park and lock is $2.00 and valet parking is not offered.

STEEPLECHASE SEASON

For most people April means showers and the start of warmer weather. But for many of us in Baltimore it really only means one thing—the start of steeplechase season. During the first four Saturdays in April a different steeplechase is held on four farms in northern Baltimore and Harford Counties. If you've never experienced a steeplechase, it's an exciting opportunity to view—usually up-close—a traditional point-to-point race. But remember these events are held outside, rain or shine, so be sure to wear proper attire. A few stores in close proximity to the races usually sell steeplechase tickets; a good bet is the Butler Store and Liquors (410-771-4383) at 14921 Falls Road.

The first race of the season, held the first Saturday of April, is the **Elkridge Harford,** run over Atlanta Hall Farm in Monkton. This race has served over the past 50-plus years as the testing ground for riders and horse. Its placement on the calendar and its inviting course have attracted such world renowned horses as Jay Trump and Ben Nevis II, both of whom went on to capture the English Grand National in Liverpool. This is the smallest of the races, so observers can really get in close to the action. There are six races, both timber and flat races. General admission tickets are $25 per carload. To get there, take I-695 to exit 27/Dulaney Valley Road. Cross Loch Raven Reservoir and bear left onto Jarrettsville Pike. Continue through the light at Jacksonville and go 4 miles to Pocock Road. Left on Pocock Road and follow parking signs.

On the second Saturday of April the **My Lady's Manor Steeplechase Races** are held to benefit Ladew Topiary Gardens (see our Day Trips chapter for more information). Gates open at noon and post time is 2:30 P.M. This is Harford County's largest annual sporting event, with an estimated crowd of anywhere between 2,000 and 6,000 people attending. The day includes three races, 3 miles over timber. People may bring coolers, picnics, or charcoal stoves. Because of danger to the horses, all glass containers should be deposited only in receptacles provided. General admission tickets are $30 and family parking is $35. These are both available on race day at the gate or ahead of time at local stores. You can call Ladew Topiary Gardens for more information at (410) 557–9570. To get there take I–695 to Dulaney Valley Road, north. Keep left to Jarrettsville Pike. Go to Pocock Road and follow signs.

On the third Saturday in April, the **Grand National Steeplechase** is held starting at 3:15 P.M., with gates opening at noon. This race, second in age only to the Hunt Cup, began as an outgrowth of a boys' race that was instituted in 1898. In 1900 the race, which is restricted to amateur riders, became an annual event. The Grand National has moved four times before finding its present home in Butler. The day includes three races. General admission tickets are $30 per car the day of the event and $20 per car prior to race day. Tickets can be optained by writing to: Grand National Steeplechase, P.O. Box 1, Butler, MD 21023. To get to the race, take I–83 north to Belfast Road west. Follow to Falls Road and make a right. Go less than a mile, making a left onto Butler Road. Go out Butler Road a little over a mile, until you see signs for parking.

On the fourth Saturday in April is the most popular and largest of the races, the **Maryland Hunt Cup.** This race ranks with the English Grand National as one of the two greatest steeplechase races in the world. It was originally run as a rivalry race between the Green Spring and Elkridge hunt clubs but in 1903 opened to any recognized hunt club in the United States and Canada. The race is run over Worthington Farms, a distance of 4 miles, and gates open at 1:00 P.M. Parking passes must be obtained prior to the day of the race by sending $30 and a self-addressed, stamped envelope to: The Maryland Hunt Cup Association, P.O. Box·3606, Glyndon, MD 21071. No sales are made on race day. Tickets can also be picked up at many

local stores. To get there take I–83 north to Shawan Road. Follow Shawan Road west until you see signs for parking.

INDOOR LACROSSE

Baltimore Bayhawks
Homewood Field
Johns Hopkins University
(866) 99-HAWKS
www.baltimorebayhawks.com
After the indoor lacrosse team the Baltimore Thunder left town in 1999, the lacrosse town was left without a major league lacrosse team. But that is no longer so with the addition of a new Major League Lacrosse team—the Baltimore Bayhawks.

The new league is a professional outdoor lacrosse league founded by Jake Steinfeld, chairman of Body by Jake Enterprises. Dave Morrow, a former champion lacrosse player and now CEO of Michigan-based Warrior Lacrosse Inc., and Timothy Robertson, founder of the Fox Family Channel and SFX Entertainment, are also co-owners. Formed in 1999 to capitalize on the growing demand for world-class field lacrosse, the MLL commenced season play in June 2001 with six teams located in the Northeast/Mid-Atlantic States. The Bayhawks won the Major League Lacrosse championship in 2002.

The Bayhawks are owned by Baltimore native and owner of OnAirSports.com, Gordon Boone. The team is coached by Brian Voelker, a former defenseman for and graduate of Johns Hopkins University.

The Bayhawks play on Homewood Field at the Johns Hopkins University. Although the field can accommodate 10,000, the Bayhawks are looking to sell about 3,500 season tickets, which sell for about $75. Individual tickets are $15.00 for reserved seats; general admission is $10.00 for adults, and $7.00 for kids under 12. Group discounts are available.

CLOSE-UP

Lacrosse

Marylanders love lacrosse, and Baltimore, with its concentration of colleges and universities, is the lacrosse center for the state. Drive by any prep school at 3:30 P.M., and you'll see loads of boys and girls carting their lacrosse sticks and helmets to the fields. Many graduate to play at the collegiate level, and Maryland boasts some of the top schools for NCAA lacrosse. The game is primarily a collegiate sport with nearly 25,000 men playing lacrosse at over 400 colleges and universities.

The earliest accounts of lacrosse date back to the first French missionaries and English explorers who came to the New World around 1630. The Native American tribes playing the stick and ball game intrigued explorers in the Great Lakes area, along the northeastern seaboard, and in Canada. Lacrosse was given its name by early French settlers, using the generic term for any game played with a curved stick (crosse) and a ball. There is no evidence of non–Native Americans taking up the game until the mid-nineteenth century, when English-speakers in Montreal

adopted the sport from the Mohawks. For some classic history lessons about lacrosse, you may want to pick up George Beers' book about the Mohawk playing techniques entitled *Lacrosse* (1869) or James Mooney's *American Anthropologist* (1890), which describes in detail the Eastern Cherokee game and its elaborate rituals. *American Indian Lacrosse: Little Brother of War* (1994) by Thomas Vennum Jr. offers a good contemporary look at the history of the game.

The sport of lacrosse is a combination of basketball, soccer, and hockey. Like hockey, a small semicircle called the crease protects the goalie, and offensive players cannot step inside this area (there is a sports bar and grill on York Road in Towson that honors the game with its name, "The Crease"). The cardinal rule of lacrosse is that your hands can never touch the ball. Players handle the ball with a long stick that has a net on the end. Quickness and agility are essential skills for this fast-moving sport. Players frequently sprint down the field making fast precision

INDOOR SOCCER

Baltimore Blast
Baltimore Arena
201 West Baltimore Street
(410) 732-5278
www.baltimoreblast.com
Since fall 1992 Baltimore has fielded a professional indoor soccer team, which plays at the Baltimore Arena from October through April. The game is played on a modified hockey rink covered with artificial turf.

Games average a total of about 30 points scored; six-member teams tally either one, two, or three points for goals, depending on how far from the net the shot is taken.

Professional indoor soccer is a forum for many talented college players to continue in the field. Many of the teams feature mostly American players, in contrast to the first indoor soccer league, the Major Indoor Soccer League. The Baltimore Blast was originally the name of Baltimore's franchise in the Major Indoor Soccer League. When the passes. Men's and women's lacrosse were played under virtually the same rules, with no protective equipment, until the mid-1930s. At that time, men's lacrosse began evolving to the game that exists today, one of more physical contact. Men wear helmets and padding to protect from the occasional stick jab or elbow that comes from an opposing team member.

If you've never watched live lacrosse you are missing an exciting game. The adept skill with which the men and women play the sport coupled with the advances in sports equipment makes for a fast, graceful game that is a thrill to watch. Spring weekends at Homewood Field at the Johns Hopkins University are packed with lacrosse fans cheering the men's lacrosse team. With Loyola, Towson University, and the University of Maryland competing in the same division, hometown rivalries can get fierce. Friendly jabs at opposing team's fans are common, but it's all in good fun. The lacrosse season begins in the spring, and everyone looks forward to enjoying the breezy Baltimore weather, the blue skies, and the sun-shine at an afternoon lacrosse game and the inevitable tailgates that go with it. But even the most inclement weather won't keep the diehard fans from braving the elements to watch the game.

If you don't know the rules of the game, don't worry. The uninitiated are sure to find a friendly lacrosse fan willing to share the details of the game. If you really want to do your homework and know what you're watching before you get to the game, visit the U.S. Lacrosse National Hall of Fame and Museum located on the Johns Hopkins University campus. There you can get a crash course in the history and glories of lacrosse. You'll learn that lacrosse is considered one of the quickest growing team sports in the United States today.

Collegiate lacrosse is attracting major league–sized crowds. M&T Bank Stadium in Baltimore hosted the 2003 NCAA Lacrosse Finals and Championship over Memorial Day Weekend, attracting a record breaking 108,000 people from around the country. The Finals will again be played at M&T Bank in 2004, and the games promise to attract even larger numbers of attendees.

league folded, the team joined the National Professional Soccer League as the Baltimore Spirit. Later the team again took on the name Baltimore Blast.

The Baltimore Arena shows its age in some ways but has space for 11,400 fans. Average game attendance is about 5,500, so seats are usually available. The best seats are on the lower level on the glass, as with hockey.

All home games start at 7:35 P.M. Tickets are available at the arena box office or through TicketMaster, (410) 481–SEAT. Tickets are $20 for VIP seating (which includes the lower concourse and the midfield area), $17 for mid-level seating, and $14 for seats behind the goal. All games are broadcast on WCBM (680 AM).

COLLEGE SPORTS

Baltimore is a hotbed of college sports action, where you can often find good competition at family rates. Several area teams garner national attention for their exploits. Call the numbers listed to learn more about each school's sports teams and see our Education chapter for information about these institutions.

Towson University (410-704-2000, www.towson.edu), plays its indoor sports in the Towson Center, a 5,000-seat arena, and outdoor sports at Minnegan Stadium. Although it competes in more than 15 collegiate sports, its best include lacrosse, men's basketball, baseball, and women's gymnastics, where its teams frequently are among the top in the nation.

Johns Hopkins University (410-516-7490, www.jhu.edu) plays a variety of sports but is best known for men's lacrosse, in which it frequently competes with other powerhouses such as Syracuse, Rutgers, Towson, and the universities of Maryland, Virginia, and North Carolina. The school's outdoor field features artificial turf and recently constructed concrete grandstands on both sides of the playing surface.

Morgan State University (443-885-3333, www.morgan.edu) fields teams in most college athletics. Morgan's best sports include football and basketball.

Coppin State College (410-951-3000, www.coppin.edu) fields men's and women's teams in a number of sports but is known for its top-notch men's basketball program. Under head coach Fang Mitchell, Coppin plays against some of the best teams in the nation (usually on the road, unfortunately) and every now and again scores a big upset win and a trip to the NCAA tournament.

University of Maryland, Baltimore County (410-455-1000, www.umbc.com), is part of the University of Maryland system. The ACC-affiliated Terrapins in College Park, outside Washington, gain national attention for basketball and lacrosse play. The smaller campus at UMBC, as it is called, fields good teams in basketball, including a top-notch women's basketball team, baseball, soccer, and lacrosse.

CHILD CARE 🧸

During much of the 1990s, Maryland was rated among the top 10 states in the country for quality child care by *Working Mother* magazine. Insiders at Maryland's Child Care Administration cite staff-child ratios, group size, safety requirements for family day homes, and caregiver training and availability as the main reasons for the state's high ranking.

In the greater Baltimore area, child-care facilities are available through individuals, companies, and schools, as well as through day-care centers. Even the police force has gotten into the act, with officers volunteering to coach after-school athletics at schools and youth centers around town.

Baltimore also has an extensive system of summer camps. There are city- and county-sponsored programs, but most of the more exciting camp opportunities are sponsored by the private and parochial school systems.

The state of Maryland supports free child care for those who cannot afford to pay, particularly those who have been receiving Aid to Families with Dependent Children and those who are working their way off that welfare program. In 1998 more than 21,000 children benefited statewide. In 2000 Maryland's child poverty rate dipped to 6.9 percent, the lowest in the nation, according to a U.S. Bureau of Census Survey.

Maryland was selected as one of five states to participate in the National Governor's Association Center for Best Practices Technical Assistance project, which focuses on improving financing and delivery of early childhood care and education.

According to some sources, 61 percent of Maryland's children younger than 12 whose mothers must work receive licensed child care. More than 547,225 kids statewide are in nonregulated care, i.e., care by people not licensed by the state. Many of these thousands of children are cared for by grandparents, other family members, or concerned extended family, such as neighbors. For short-term or after-school care, sitters are also used.

Part of the reason why some parents opt out of more formalized day care is cost. Even though cost of care in Maryland, overall, is considered good versus national numbers, it has, in fact, risen dramatically along with most costs in the area since the middle to late 1980s. Center-based care costs rose 39 percent from 1988 to 1996, from an average weekly cost of $91 to more than $148. The cost of family child care, that is care in the home of a licensed child-care provider, averages $11,314 per year in the city and $12,416 per year in Baltimore County.

The popularity of au pair programs nationwide speaks to the cost issue as well. With working parents looking at sacrificing about a third of their pay every week to the cost of child care, the live-in au pair looks like a good alternative. Minimal salary plus room and board gives a foreign student the opportunity to live abroad in a family environment while providing the host family virtually one-on-one child care for the children.

Nannies are another well-used alternative in the Baltimore area. Live-ins and day nannies are the norm, but there are also some circumstances in which trained, licensed nannies are available on a per-diem basis for travelers in town just for a few days. On a per-diem basis, nannies seem relatively inexpensive, charging as little as $64 for an eight-hour day. On the other hand, when parents progress from using a nanny as an occasional answer to a necessary part of life at 10 to 12 hours per day, five days a week, the cost can increase significantly ($320 to $600).

Licensed programs in Baltimore take children as young as six weeks to as old as 12 years. Though many parents believe that their 12-year-old does not need child care, in the city of Baltimore, it is illegal for any child 12 or younger to be left home alone for any amount of time, for any reason.

It would be terrific if we could simply list all the child-care facilities in the Baltimore area in this chapter, but in this case we're going to defer to child-care Insiders who can tell you a great deal more than we could, given our limitations of space. These are the organizations listed under Child-Care Location Services. They include information services as well as regulators and placement agencies.

We've also provided some information on licensing in the state and the groups that regulate those licenses because all of the agencies noted here deal only with licensed providers and certified personnel.

Licensed child-care providers have fulfilled the state's parameters for acceptable care and are ongoing, dependable sources for child care. Those parameters include regulation space allotted, access to outdoors, numbers of safety exits, child-teacher ratios, type of care, activities and equipment provided, how snack foods are kept, and myriad other things. Admittedly, licensing doesn't guarantee that the child-care provider is without flaw, but it does go a long way toward that goal.

For instance, all personnel who work at licensed child-care centers must be certified. These requirements are often minimal, but they can save lives. At the very least, workers receive training in CPR, how to handle choking emergencies, and general first aid.

If you decide to hire independent, unlicensed child-care help, be prepared to ask applicants about their training and abilities.

---

i *Don't be fooled by perfect surroundings. It's how your child is treated that counts. Ask permission for you and your child to spend a sample day at the center; if after that you like what you see and enroll your child, make surprise visits from time to time just to check that all is going well.*

Get names and phone numbers of former employers, and call those people to chat about how their kids felt about that worker. If the child-care worker is being recommended through a friend, see if he or she will let you talk with the child and see how the child feels because it is, ultimately, the kids whose feelings are important in this matter.

When hiring a child-care worker or deciding on a child-care facility, one overall item to watch out for, however, is "fit." What kind of child is your child? Is he quiet, enjoying board games, card games, and blocks? Or is she boisterous and physical, needing lots of space for climbing, dancing, and roughhousing? Does she need continual reassurance? Does he require a bit of independence? These questions and more like them will help you define what kind of child-care situation you're looking for and help the location and placement services help you find just the right opportunity for your child.

LICENSING

One of the reasons why, in the main, child care in the Baltimore area may be considered above average is the state licensing requirements. Unlike most states that only regulate multichild situations, Maryland's Child Care Administration laws cover any situation in which even one child is being cared for by someone other than a parent. Maryland's Child Care Administration's Office of Licensing inspects, reviews, and documents the activities of existing child-care facilities and personnel through 13 regional and two field offices while actively seeking to develop new child-care options for Maryland's parents. The Office of Licensing also investigates complaints.

It is extremely important when seeking child care, whether a one-day drop-in or a permanent situation, to make sure that the person or center that you are leaving your child with is licensed. Don't assume that just because there's a sign on the front door that says DAY CARE CENTER that the center is, in fact, licensed. Ask to see the license if it is not posted in plain view. Family day cares, in which a person cares for a few children in his/her own home, must possess a child-care home license.

You are not limiting your choices by insisting on licensed service. There are close to 13,100 regulated child-care facilities in the state.

Requirements to become licensed and to maintain such a license mostly cover options pertaining to the physical environment and personnel. For instance, a minimum 35 square feet of space is required for each child in the center. If you enter a center that is the size of an average living room and in it are 15 children trying to find a place to play, then this center may not be licensed or may be in violation of its license. In homes it is required to have enough open floor space so children can have active play without fear of injury.

For child-care personnel, the Office of Licensing of the Child Care Administration approves trainers, both individuals and organizations, in the child-care arena. Specialized training in core subjects such as infant care and caring for children with special health needs is available as are some curricular subjects such as art for preschoolers.

Recent information shows that a child's environment, both physical and social, has a major influence on the child's ability to learn and think. Actual brain development is hindered if the early environment is poor, and the effects of such poor environments are both long-lasting and cumulative.

If you would like to know all the licensing regulations in Maryland, you may request more information from the Child Care Administration. In greater Baltimore there are two offices of the Child Care Administration, (800) 322-6347, www.dhr. state.md.us: Baltimore City Regional Office, 2700 North Charles Street, Suite 203, (410) 554-8300; and Baltimore County Regional Office, 409 Washington Avenue, Suite LL8, Towson, (410) 583-6200. The Child Care Administration also offers a consumer education pamphlet, "Making

the Difference For Your Child." This booklet provides information on what to look for when shopping for day care, what kinds of questions to ask, and the rights and responsibility of parents.

CHILD-CARE LOCATION SERVICES

The Maryland Committee For Children
608 Water Street
(410) 752-7588
www.mdchildcare.org
The Maryland Committee For Children (MCC) was created in 1946 when, at the end of World War II, the federal government rescinded funds for day-care centers and preschools for working mothers. Rosie the Riveter may have no longer been needed by the government, but in many cases Rosie's husband didn't come home from the war, and it was up to her to put a roof over her children's heads and food on the table. The MCC was founded to help her do just that. Currently, the MCC, a private nonprofit organization, serves as a clearinghouse for information about child care—where, how, and from whom to get it—as well as a training and research organization. The committee's informational arm is the Maryland Child Care Resource Network, noted below, but you can also call the MCC for information about such things as conferences, lectures, and training, as well as to request more information.

The Maryland Child Care
Resource Network
www.mdchildcare.org/mdcfc/network/
network.html
The Network, which is managed by the Maryland Committee For Children, includes a statewide center that is based at MCC headquarters (noted previously) and at 13 regional centers in surrounding counties. The statewide center also has two local affiliates, one in the city and one in Baltimore County, both of which offer resources and referral services at no

charge. The Network also provides technical training to child-care providers. The Network helped 170,000 callers find child care for 195,708 children between 1990 and 2001. It has also trained more than 56,000 individuals interested in providing care or improving their programs.

Network's most dynamic service, however, is LOCATE. LOCATE is a computer database, created by MCC and available through the Maryland Child Care Resource Network and its resource centers. The database can address specific needs for the care of a specific child. For instance, if you have a child who has a learning disability and you live in Baltimore City and know that you can pay only $80 a week for child care, LOCATE can find appropriate care for your child within those parameters. Parents are given the name, address, and telephone numbers of up to 10 child-care providers or programs when they call for a referral. Other topics available through LOCATE include employers that have child care on-site, child care available through schools, and child care for children with special needs.

To reach a LOCATE counselor, call (410) 625–1111 for a 24-hour recorded message for the closest resource center or contact the Resource Center numbers that follow.

**Baltimore City Child Care
Resource Center
164 Ridgely Street, Suite 200
(410) 685–5150 or
(410) 539–2209 (LOCATE)
www.mdchildcare.org**
The Baltimore City Child Care Resource Center, one of the offices of MCC's Maryland Child Care Resource Network, can help you find child care through the LOCATE database. In addition, the center offers courses for parents in child growth and development, how to deal with child-care service providers, and other topics. This is also the place to call if you are interested in becoming a child-care provider or in starting your own child-care center. Office hours are 9:00 A.M. to 5:00

P.M. Monday through Friday. LOCATE hours are 9:30 A.M. to 3:30 P.M.

**Baltimore County Child Care Links
1101 North Point Boulevard, Suite 112
(410) 288–5600 (LOCATE)
www.mdchildcare.org**
Affiliated with the MCC through its LOCATE database, Children's Services can provide a listing of all licensed child-care programs in Baltimore County, which include 1,400 family providers and 400 independent and school-based centers. A LOCATE counselor is available from 9:00 A.M. to noon and 1:00 to 4:00 P.M. Monday through Friday. Because of the vast area that the office serves, however, it is sometimes difficult to get through the line. If you can't get through, call the statewide number, (410) 625–1111, and ask about listings in Baltimore County. One unique service that Children's Services offers is provided with the help of Baltimore County libraries. Rather than spending your time and theirs copying down names and addresses of providers over the phone, they will forward the list of up to 15 providers to your local library, where it will be printed out and await your pick up.

NANNIES AND AU PAIRS

Nannies and au pairs are not licensed in Maryland, but if you choose your nanny through a referral service, he or she will receive an extensive background check.

**A Choice Nanny
201 West Padonia Road, Suite 304
(410) 823–8687**
This nanny referral service that has been in the area since 1983 first interviews nanny candidates for their suitability, at which time their three most prominent child-care references are checked. If the nanny is hired by one of the member parents, the company performs an extensive background check. Nanny training is also provided to both hired nannies and those interested in receiving such training. Par-

ents interested in hiring a nanny are first interviewed for a needs assessment. Once that is complete, the parent pays a membership fee, after which the company will refer nannies for interview that it believes can fulfill the parents' needs. When a nanny is hired, parents pay an additional referral fee, usually between $500 and $1,200, depending on the parameters and salary of the job. Of course this fee is subject to change. Hourly rates are around $10 to $15 per hour.

The Nanny Network Inc.
521 East Joppa Road, Towson
(410) 321-1566

The Nanny Network is an independent nanny referral service serving Baltimore and surrounding counties. A member of the International Nanny Association, the Nanny Network refers nannies to families for in-home care on a permanent or temporary basis for one day, one month, or even overnight. It conducts a thorough background check of all nannies that includes credit and criminal conviction records in counties the nanny has resided in for the past five years. The Nanny Network even offers a three-month guarantee. There is no finder's fee unless you hire a nanny from the network. There is a one-time, nonrefundable application fee of $175 and a finder's fee that can be as low as $50 for the "night out" service to $500 for a nanny working after-school hours (for one year) and up to more than $1,500 for a live-in nanny.

Au Pair in America
(800) 928-7247
www.aupairinamerica.com

Au Pair in America is an au pair placement service under the auspices of the American Institute of Foreign Studies in Greenwich, Connecticut. It sponsors student study-abroad programs, hiring programs both here and abroad as well as other cultural and student exchange opportunities. According to Insiders at Au Pair in America, au pairs are "international visitors" who come to America for no more than 12 months to help gain a "better understanding and appreciation of American life while living with an American family and caring for their young children." The family provides room and board and a $139 weekly stipend to the au pair in return for no more than 45 hours of work per week. There is also a fee of $5,495 paid to Au Pair in America. This fee includes the au pair's travel expenses, medical, and liability insurance, and a four-day orientation. The au pair's work does not include housekeeping or other chores unless they are directly related to taking care of children. The standard au pair is not professionally trained or licensed but has child-care experience and is a young person (aged 18 to 26) who has accepted the duties associated with the care of children while he or she visits America. There is another program at AIFS called Au Pair Extraordinaire that places au pairs who have a minimum of two years of professional child-care training or two years of work experience as nannies. Call for details.

EDUCATION

Baltimore is chock-full of schools. In fact, institutions of higher learning are one of Baltimore's main draws. Such names as the Johns Hopkins University, Goucher College, Loyola College, and the University of Maryland are known worldwide for the quality of the education provided. Our private and parochial school systems are widespread as well, and our public schools offer some surprises in vocational training and the arts.

Outside of these traditional educational institutions, the Baltimore area lays claim to specialty schools that run the gamut from institutions for physically challenged children to courses that specialize in haute cuisine.

All elementary and secondary systems across the state, both public and private, have advanced courses for academics, usually known as gifted and talented or honors programs. Most systems also offer some kind of technical course or a school-to-work program. The Maryland State Department of Education requires that all students take new high school assessments. They must take these tests in order to receive a Maryland diploma, and students must be in attendance for the entire duration of the test in order to receive credit for the course.

Most schools sponsor opportunities in the arts, but there are some in which the arts are the main focus, such as the Baltimore City School for the Arts, a public high school. The Polytechnic Institute specializes in engineering, offering courses for either future engineers whose grades reflect the fact that they actually enjoy doing integral calculus or for kids who just want a college-prep environment with an emphasis in math and science. Kenwood High School Sports Science Academy is for those who want to coach as well as those who are considering a career in sports medicine.

Newcomers to the area are struck by the way Baltimore's middle-aged adults identify with their high schools more than their colleges. We remain Poly boys and Western girls essentially forever. High school affiliations create instant bonding or distrust. We carry on our historic high school rivalries long after most communities would think reasonable. Gilman vs. McDonogh, Calvert Hall vs. Loyola, Poly (Polytechnic Institute) vs. City (Baltimore City College), Dunbar vs. Lake Clifton, IND (the Institute of Notre Dame) vs. Mercy—all are historic rivalries known citywide. Such rivalries heat up the competitions and make them as exciting as watching the Orioles trounce the Yankees or the Ravens beat the Redskins! Schools in Baltimore and surrounding counties have extensive intermural competition in such areas as soccer, basketball, football, and lacrosse.

Though we love a good game, Baltimore has always placed more emphasis on academics than sports. Many of our Baltimore Firsts have been in education. The first parochial school to educate African-American children was opened here, as were the first parochial schools for girls. (See Selected Baltimore Firsts in this chapter.)

In this chapter we provide an overall picture of the public school system in Baltimore City and the counties of greater Baltimore, as well as a more intimate look at some of the popular private and specialty schools, community colleges, and four-year institutions.

Among the information presented, you will occasionally find student-teacher ratios. It is important to note that these are average figures that do not necessarily reflect exact class size. For instance, with an average ratio of 22-to-1, you may find some seminar classes for seniors that have only 10 students and a science class with 35. However, the ratios provide a general idea of class size, which is why we've included them.

Tuition for private schools varies considerably, depending on the courses taken, the eligibility for financial aid, etc., so we have not included those rates here. Generally, however, expect to pay between $2,000 and $5,000 a year for a child in elementary school and between $4,000 and $12,000 for a child in middle and high school.

All private and parochial schools have either a strict dress code or a required uniform. Many public schools, particularly elementary schools, have uniform options, and most public high schools have some rules about acceptable attire. Call the individual school to resolve questions about uniforms and costs.

When you visit a prospective school, either private or public, elementary or university, don't just go to admissions and administration. Hang around if you can and talk to faculty and students about curricula, after-school programs and activities, and the school's approach to academic and social discipline. Their enthusiasm or lack thereof gives the best insight into what the school is really like.

PUBLIC SCHOOLS

Public education in the greater Baltimore area, as in Maryland generally, is supported by our property taxes. In past years this meant that if you were in a poorer area, such as Baltimore City or a rural county, your schools did not get as many dollars for education as those in a more affluent area. In recent years, however, the state of Maryland has tried to help the counties and the city achieve economic equality to provide needed services. Recently, the per child expenditures for a school year in greater Baltimore were $7,439 in Baltimore City; $7,061 in Baltimore County; $7,427 in Howard County; and $6,536 in Anne Arundel County.

What is really helping public education reach toward excellence, however, is its growing focus on what's going on in the classroom. Maryland's systems are in the process of making area schools more accountable for the education received.

Maryland recently adopted a new set of standards for marking a school's performance, and it also issues an annual School Performance Report, which takes a comprehensive look at individual schools' success in meeting basic educational requirements. These reports are in downloadable form on the Web site, www.marylandpublicschools.org.

Baltimore Public Schools
Baltimore City Department of Education
200 East North Avenue
(410) 396-8700
www.baltimorecityschools.org

Baltimore City's schools are in the process of a rebirth. In 1997 the school system was taken over by the state. Test scores and measured skill levels are already up among the city's children, and it is expected that this trend will continue.

Baltimore City has more than 94,000 students enrolled. Among the schools these are 15 extended elementary schools, which are essentially elementary/middle schools with grades K through 8, and 20 citywide schools. Among the citywide schools are some specialty schools: the Baltimore City School for the Arts, the Polytechnic Institute, the Merganthaler Vocational Technical Center, and the Carver Vocational Technical Center, just to name a few.

Whereas the School for the Arts prepares students to play for the Baltimore Symphony or head for Broadway and Polytechnic grounds college-bound engineering students in the basics of their field, the vo-tech schools offer a focus in commercial trades as diverse as carpentry and commercial art as well as an Occupation Prep program that deals with skills such as cosmetology and drafting.

Other classes allow students to pursue a more specialized path at nonspecialty schools. The Tech Prep program permits high school students to take courses in biotechnology, business technology, electronics/computer repair technology, child care, travel and tourism, and machine tool technology in addition to their regular coursework. Tech Prep was created in conjunction with Baltimore City Community College and is meant to help a student take courses relating to a chosen career as early as the ninth grade.

ROTC and CollegeBound are also offered at the high school level. The individual school listings book, *Planning Your High School Program*, is available free from Baltimore City Schools; it can tell you which schools offer what. Contact the Department of Education at the previously listed number for a copy to be sent to you.

Staffing Baltimore's schools are more than 6,600 teachers and nearly 1,000 school-based support staff and school-based administrators, who account for more than 60 percent of the employees of the Baltimore school system. Overall, student-teacher ratios are 16 to 1. The late 1990s saw significant betterment in the Baltimore County school system. Several

national foundations, including the Bill and Melinda Gates Foundation, contributed some $20.75 million, fueling the transformation of nine large Baltimore City neighborhood high schools into smaller learning communities. The city's Master Plan II leads the way to the next 10 years, with a long-term strategy for increased student achievement and improved resources for teachers.

Communities have the go-ahead to institute programs that they feel are needed for their children, and they're acting quickly to put new elements into play for their kids. Elementary schools, for instance, have already created after-school enrichment and/or tutoring programs that extend the school day, thereby helping out with child care and also creating another avenue to improve student performance. Nearly all of Baltimore City's elementary schools have such programs, and their success is helping test results move upward—sometimes in double digits.

Selected Baltimore Firsts

John Archer was the first medical student ever to be granted a degree from an American medical school. The year was 1768.

The Baltimore College of Dental Surgery, the first dental college in the world, opened in February 1840.

The first Catholic school for African-American girls in the United States, St. Frances Academy, opened in 1828. Today a coeducational institution, the school is still in operation at 501 East Chase Street.

Eastern High School and Western High School opened in 1844. They were the first publicly supported high schools for girls in the United States.

The Baltimore Female College, the first women's teaching college in the United States, opened its doors in 1849.

It is now known as Goucher College, a premier coed liberal arts college.

Thanks to the prodding of Hugh Bond, the owner and resident of Mount Royal Mansion in the mid-1800s, Baltimore was the first city to create publicly supported schools for African- American children. This was particularly important to Baltimore because by 1865 its citizenry included the largest population of black freemen in the country.

In 1895 the first Catholic college for women in the United States, The College of Notre Dame of Maryland, opened its doors in Baltimore.

—*Excerpted from* Baltimore— America's City of Firsts, *a pamphlet published by Baltimore Bicentennial Celebration, Inc.*

Baltimore County Public Schools
6901 North Charles Street, Towson
(410) 887-5555
www.bcps.org
The Baltimore County Public School System is the 23rd-largest in the United States. It serves 107,000 school-aged children. Choices of study include many options outside traditional academic areas, from carpentry to quilting and everything in between.

The county uses in all its schools a program called Values Education and Ethical Behavior that seeks to address values and ethics issues in the curricula, to speak to their practical application. The program is not a laundry list of values and ethics, but, as the county schools' yearly report noted, a "process of inquiry to help students pose and understand . . . ethical questions and dilemmas." A relatively unusual program, it covers everything from encouraging students to be honest and compassionate to asking larger ethical questions about scientific discovery and what constitutes responsible citizenship.

Of the county's 162 schools, 25 are magnet schools. Magnet schools offer special programs that draw students from all over a particular geographic area. At the elementary levels, it is area alone that determines if your child may enter a particular magnet school. At the middle school level, entrance is determined by prior academic achievement, student interest, and geographic location. At the high school level, geographic area still plays a part in most cases, but that area is either countywide or a large general area, such as northern Baltimore County. And if for some reason the student is not in the chosen area but has the qualifications and desire for the education offered at the site, then he or she may be admitted by special permission. Magnet programs of study at the high school level include such offerings as the Landsdowne Academy of Finance, the Kenwood High School Sports Science Academy, and the Towson High School Law and Public Policy Program.

The county also has four alternative schools for students with emotional and behavioral difficulties.

Academically, Baltimore County offers a relatively competitive environment, which includes advanced placement courses and testing. Using the state standards for performance, Baltimore County matched or exceeded state standards in 97 percent of the areas measured.

Baltimore County spends $7,521 on each pupil annually, and the student-teacher ratio is 15 to 1. The average dropout rate is 3.4 percent.

Anne Arundel County Public Schools
2644 Riva Road, Annapolis
(410) 222-5000
www.aacps.org
The Anne Arundel County school system is the fifth-largest school system in Maryland and among the 50 largest systems in the United States. Anne Arundel has over 5,000 teachers teaching 75,000 students in 115 educational sites. Because of the county's size and primarily rural/suburban configuration, more than two-thirds of those students are bused to school.

The system offers a pre-K program in selected schools as well as traditional kindergarten through twelfth grade education across the board. In addition to the basics, Anne Arundel schools offer instruction in art, music, physical education, health, library media, family and consumer sciences, computers, and technology.

The county also has two centers of applied technology at which secondary students may specialize in career and technology education.

Howard County Public Schools
10910 Maryland Highway 108,
Ellicott City
(410) 313-6600
www.howard.k12.md.us
Howard County Schools continually rank as one of the top public school systems in the state. In 2003 nearly 90 percent of its high school graduates went on to higher education, with 48 out of 2,900 seniors

earning National Merit Finalist scholarships. In 2002 the average score for a Howard County high school junior on the SAT was 1,084, which is higher than the overall Maryland average and higher than the national average.

The system serves 45,000 students, but projections foresee a 20 percent increase in student population, at about 1,000 students per year. Student-teacher ratios, however, average 23 to 1. Already the largest employer in the county, Howard County Public Schools employs more than 4,000 teachers, 50 percent of whom hold master's or doctorate degrees.

PRIVATE SCHOOLS

Baltimore has an extensive system of private and parochial institutions. Subsequently we've listed the high schools and K through 12 institutions. We have not listed private or parochial elementary and middle schools, but you can usually expect to find at least one of each serving your neighborhood. And these are not just Catholic schools, but Christian schools of many denominations as well as other religion-based schools and those classed as alternative. If you need information on a parochial elementary school in your area, it is best to contact your house of worship or simply look under Schools in the Yellow Pages.

Downtown

Institute of Notre Dame (IND)
901 North Aisquith Street
(410) 522-7800
www.indofmd.org
IND is a college preparatory high school for girls run by the School Sisters of Notre Dame. The school offers three degree programs: general academic, college preparatory, and Theresian Honors. Advanced placement courses are also available. Basketball, crew, soccer, baseball, theater,

chorus, and many, many more extracurricular activities and service clubs tend to keep the girls way past their normal school hours, but there are few complaints. The school boasts a 20-to-1 student-teacher ratio for its 423 students and a competitive academic environment. In 2000, 100 percent of IND's graduates went on to additional education. IND is the only all-girls school in the country that can count two members of United States Congress among its alumnae: Senator Barbara Mikulski (class of 1954) and Representative Nancy D'Alesandro Pelosi (class of 1958). (For more information on IND, see the Close-up in this chapter.) IND has recently increased its scholarship program.

St. Frances Academy
501 East Chase Street
(410) 539-5794
www.sfacademy.org
St. Frances Academy was founded in 1828 by Mother Mary Lange, foundress of the Oblate Sisters of Providence, who is currently being considered for sainthood by the Roman Catholic Church. The building in which St. Frances is housed once served as the mother house for the Oblate Sisters as well as an orphanage and a boarding school for young women. St. Frances was the first parochial school to be created to educate African-American children and currently serves a coeducational student body of about 280 in a college preparatory curriculum in grades 9 through 12. St. Frances serves what's deemed the "disenfranchised" student, i.e., that student who has not been performing up to his or her intellectual or social potential. The school's instructional success can be measured by the fact that more than 90 percent of its graduates go on to post-secondary education. Though a historically African-American school, the school is open to students of all races and economic backgrounds. Class size averages about 25 or less.

Northeast

Archbishop Curley High School
3701 Sinclair Lane
(410) 485-5000
www.curley.loyola.edu
"Curley" is an all-male college preparatory high school with a well-developed arts program. The school opened on its 33-acre site in 1961 to serve its surrounding, then densely Catholic, neighborhoods, but it now accepts students from all over the state, some coming from as far away as northern Baltimore County, Carroll County, Harford County, and Cecil County. For a boy who is interested in math but would also like to play trumpet, Curley is made to order. The school has professional-quality orchestra, dance, and jazz bands. They rock the house! There are also newer visual arts programs for budding painters, photographers, and other artists. The school encourages parent involvement and is proud of the fact that many of its parents continue to work with and for the school long after their own boys have graduated. Current enrollment is 550. The student-teacher ratio is 14 to 1.

Calvert Hall College
8102 Lasalle Road, Towson
(410) 825-4266
www.calverthall.com
Calvert Hall College was the first Christian Brothers school in the country, established in 1845 by the first American Christian Brother who was himself barely out of seminary at 17 years old. The first year it was in operation, the school had 100 students. In operation for more than 150 years and at its 33-acre campus in Towson for about 40 years, this all-boys college preparatory school serves approximately 1,125 students today. Academically competitive, Calvert Hall also has a full complement of arts and athletics. The Activities Center, for instance, houses Calvert Hall's art studios and learning resource center as well as its swimming pool and weight training room, and Calvert Hall's marching band is as well

known as its football team. The student-teacher ratio is 15 to 1, with an average class size of 23.

The Catholic High School of Baltimore
2800 Edison Highway
(410) 732-6200
www.tchsnt2.loyola.edu
Catholic High, begun in 1939 and currently serving 400 students, is an areawide college preparatory school for girls. The school offers two primary focuses: technology and the arts. Fine-arts offerings include advanced placement opportunities in art and chorus, but the technology side boasts not only state-of-the-art equipment but also state-of-the-art teachers. Every week teachers are trained in the latest technological offerings, so that students in their turn receive, literally, up-to-the-minute knowledge. This unique competitive curriculum offers a general academic degree, a college preparatory degree, and the McAfferty Honors program, but what is most interesting about the school is its individualized approach. Courses are mixed and matched depending on the ability of the student, so that a freshman with talent in math could be placed in pre-calculus, rather than having to wade through the typical freshman math. Catholic High's student-teacher ratio is 11 to 1. As do most schools in the area, Catholic High has an active intermural athletic program. Upper school class sizes average around 21.

Loyola Blakefield
500 Chestnut Avenue, Towson
(410) 823-0601
www.blakefield.loyola.edu
Loyola was founded in tandem with Loyola College in 1852 by the Jesuit order of the Catholic Church. The college broke off from the school in 1921 and by 1934 the high school had moved to its present site at Blakefield. Today's Loyola is a competitive college preparatory middle and high school (grades 9 through 12) serving 710 boys. The school's stated mission is to "teach boys to be men for others." In that

Learning in the Midst of Ghosts and History

The Institute of Notre Dame (IND) has ghosts. A Union soldier is seen walking post in an upstairs hall. In the old dormitories, a 40-year-old candle left on a side table by its last occupant spontaneously erupts into flame. A mother trying to find the school offices gets lost and is shown the way by a soft voice that comes from the direction of a large statue of the Virgin Mary. No one else is there.

Stories like these abound at IND, and it's no wonder. The school and its building share a palpable connection with the spirits of the young women who have trod its halls. A short walk up the central staircase, its slate stairs deeply indented by more than 100 years of footsteps, will transport you to another time. Like the city of Baltimore itself, IND is infused with history.

IND's history began when Mother Theresa of Jesus Gerhardinger, who helped found the School Sisters of Notre Dame in her native Germany, crossed the Atlantic with four others intent on educating immigrant girls. The school's original mission included only German immigrants, but it very quickly reached out to serve all Catholic girls and has, for many years now, focused simply on girls without regard to race or faith. A typical class at IND is an eclectic mix: 4 percent from the city and the remainder from surrounding areas as far as an hour's drive.

When the site for the school was chosen in 1847, it was outside the city's limits, with rolling hills and ancient trees. The Baltimore & Ohio Railroad was still laying new track when the modern marvel of the telegraph had just been discovered, and the United States of America was only 60 years old.

The initial buildings for the school were little more than large cabins, which between 1852 and 1925 were changed and added on as growth

regard, the school fosters mentor/adviser relationships between the boys and their teachers and coaches and offers opportunities for retreats, service projects, and athletics in addition to a regular academic curriculum. The student-teacher ratio is 15 to 1, and about 7 percent of the teachers are Jesuit priests or scholars.

Mercy High School
1300 East Northern Parkway
(410) 433-8880
www.mercyhighschool.com
Mercy High School was built in 1960 to serve a burgeoning Northeast city population. On a campus that takes up most of the large block between Loch Raven Boulevard and The Alameda, Mercy serves 485 female students with a college preparatory curriculum. One of Mercy's offerings is the Advisor Program, in which the school has created a new relationship between adviser and student. Typically, advisers are apart from students, sitting in their offices, waiting for the students to come to them with questions. Also, typically, advisers are attached to a particular graduating class, so that one adviser

demanded, to become the block-long complex of buildings that is still used today. Although a new gymnasium was added in 1902, the buildings look much as they did at the turn of the last century. SSND sisters still reside in the original brick convent, with its stunning stained-glass windows and tongue-in-groove wainscot. And the school building is as it was, complete with underground catacombs and stables, although students are no longer allowed access to these last two.

The student dormitories, which had not been used for more than 30 years, were rehabilitated in 1996 and 1997 to become the Caroline Center, a job training center for neighborhood women in East Baltimore. But this was just IND's most recent community outreach program.

IND was one of Baltimore's many stops on the Underground Railroad, in which former slaves on their way to freedom were housed, fed, and clothed, then passed on to those who could see them to safety.

When Civil War battle raged, the catacombs beneath the school served as an infirmary, where nuns nursed both Union and Confederate soldiers back to health or, if that was not possible, buried them.

As the city grew up around it, IND surmounted city problems. The school suffered through the Great Baltimore Fire of 1904, which decimated the area all around it but left the school unscathed. It has also survived two World Wars and the Depression and was left untouched by the riots of 1968.

Through it all, safe within, have been the girls. The study is intensive; the homework, extensive. Students spend their days learning through aggressive instruction and thoughtful debate, and their evenings pouring through Faulkner. As in any school, there is time to relax, places to make friends. There are games to cheer, places to serve.

IND is not so different from many schools in Baltimore that have a long history and an ongoing mission, but the fact that it remains constant, viewing all from its unique vantage point, provides a subtle thread that ties together generations of women under one spirited umbrella of tradition and history.

---

serves 100 or more students. In Mercy's Advisor Program, an adviser is attached to only 15 or so students whom she follows through their four years at the school. She acts as homeroom contact, mentor, and sometimes mediator, but over the students' high school careers, she becomes a vested part of each girl's success. In the past Mercy's graduating seniors received close to $4.2 million in scholarships and grants, and 95 percent entered college. The student-teacher ratio is 13 to 1.

Notre Dame Preparatory School
815 Hampton Lane, Towson
(410) 825-6202

Notre Dame Prep (NDP) recently marked its 130th anniversary. Founded in 1873 by the School Sisters of Notre Dame because the Institute of Notre Dame Downtown became overcrowded, NDP opened in 1874 as the Notre Dame Collegiate Institute for Young Ladies on what was then wilderness acreage where the College of Notre Dame now stands. At its current campus on Hampton Lane, NDP offers a competitive, college preparatory curricu-

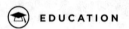

lum to more than 675 girls in grades 6 through 12. NDP boasts an active social service program, which includes the students' working with abused children at Villa Maria, spending time with patients at AIDS hospices, and working with Habitat for Humanity, among other projects. Its student-teacher ratio is 9 to 1.

Towson Catholic High School
114 Ware Avenue, Towson
(410) 427-4900
www.towsoncatholic.org
Founded in 1922, Towson Catholic is the oldest coeducational Catholic high school in greater Baltimore. Once staffed entirely by nuns, Towson Catholic is now taught entirely by lay faculty with a student-teacher ratio of 12 to 1. A small private school with only 200 students, Towson Catholic considers its size an advantage in creating a healthy environment in which young men and women can get to know one another and feel comfortable enough to actively compete with one another. Close to 98 percent of Towson Catholic's graduates go on to higher education.

Northwest

Bais Yaakov School for Girls
11111 Park Heights Avenue, Owings Mills
(410) 363-3300
Bais Yaakov School opened in 1942 to provide a comprehensive education to Jewish girls of all backgrounds. Bais Yaakov has a lower school (grades pre-K through 6) as well as an upper school (7 through 12) that teaches a competitive college preparatory curriculum. In addition, Bais Yaakov's Hebrew Department provides extensive study in Jewish history, customs, the Hebrew language, problems, ethics, and philosophy as well as study of the Torah. The school is open to all without regard to race, color, or national or ethnic origin, but it does require that the girl seeking admission be of the Jewish faith. More than 1,300 students attend

Bais Yaakov. The overall student-teacher ratio is 10 to 1.

Beth Tfiloh Community School
3300 Old Court Road
(410) 486-1905
www.btfiloh.org
Beth Tfiloh Community School opened on its 20-acre campus in west Baltimore County in 1942 with only five students in kindergarten. Currently, the school provides the only coeducational college preparatory curriculum in greater Baltimore for Jewish study in grades pre-K through 12. Because of its comprehensive course of Jewish study, the school has never had a student of another faith attend, but it does not prohibit such attendance, and it openly encourages participation of all Jewish denominations. Beth Tfiloh offers advanced placement classes and an honors track for its high school students as well as some interesting internships and study opportunities, including Senior Seminars in Israel and Poland. Enrollment is about 1,037. The student-teacher ratio is 7 to 1 with a staff of 150 teachers.

Boys Latin School of Maryland
822 West Lake Avenue
(410) 377-5192
www.boyslatinmd.com
Boys Latin School, a college preparatory day school, began in the mind of Evert Marsh Topping, a professor of long standing at Princeton University, who over time had come to believe that standard teaching methods of the time did not teach students to think and understand, and that only through understanding did children truly learn. This revolutionary idea prompted him to come to Baltimore and open his own private school in 1846. The current Boys Latin School, which straddles the city-county line just west of our east/west dividing line of Charles Street, has more than 600 boys in grades K through 12. The school's educational focus is to build on each boy's strengths and not harp on his weaknesses. The median

SAT score is 1120. The student-teacher ratio is 8 to 1.

Bryn Mawr School
109 West Melrose Avenue
(410) 323-8800
www.brynmawr.pvt.k12.md.us

Bryn Mawr was founded in 1885 on the belief that women were entitled to the same classical education that boys were receiving at the time. Bryn Mawr today has a competitive college preparatory curriculum, while still providing its girls with extensive opportunities in art, music, and athletics. Bryn Mawr has a comprehensive language department and is one of the few schools that teaches more than just Spanish and French in its middle and upper schools. Latin, Greek, German, Russian, Japanese, and Chinese are also available. Enrollment is about 796 in grades K through 12 and in a coed preschool group and day care. An eclectic group of students just around the corner from Roland Park Country and Gilman schools, Bryn Mawr coordinates some classes with both of those schools in grades 9 through 12. The student-teacher ratio averages 7 to 1.

Friends School
5114 North Charles Street
(410) 649-3200
www.friendsbalt.org

Friends School is the oldest school in Baltimore. Founded in 1784 by the Quakers, it originally stood on Aisquith Street but had many incarnations until it found its present location in 1925. Halfway between Towson and the Inner Harbor on a well-traveled stretch of road, Friends has a large campus that includes woods and stream and the use of the Roland Park swimming pool for its summer camp. The school and the camp make good use of the dance studio, fitness room, two gymnasiums, outdoor tennis courts, five playing fields, and two practice fields. Students attend Meeting on a regular basis and are encouraged in critical thinking and problem solving as well as academics. More than 1,000 students attend the school, pre-K through 12. The student-faculty ratio is 12 to 1, with 113 teachers.

Garrison Forest School
300 Garrison Forest Road, Owings Mills
(410) 363-1500
www.gfs.org

Garrison Forest was founded in 1910 as a day school for the girls of families living in Greenspring Valley, which at that time was very far away from city schools. By 1912 the school had established a boarding program, and it still offers boarding for girls in grades 8 through 12 as well as day school for girls K through 12 and a coeducational pre-K for students from age three. Approximately 612 students from all over the world, including the Pacific Rim, Latin and Central America, the Caribbean, and parts of Europe, are enrolled. The school has a new performing arts center, new lower school, and new riding and athletic facilities. Garrison Forest recently completed a campus-wide rewiring that allows students to access the school's computers from anywhere, dorm to classroom. The student-teacher ratio is 12 to 1.

Gilman School
5407 Roland Avenue
(410) 323-3800
www.gilman.edu

Gilman School, the first country day school in the United States, turned 100 years old in 1997. The school was conceived by Anne Galbraith Carey, who also founded the Women's Civic League in Baltimore and worked to help found the Girl Scouts in Maryland. At the time Carey was simply looking for a healthy educational environment in which to place her eight-year-old son that was not attached to a military or religious discipline. Approximately 970 boys attend Gilman on its 64-acre campus in Roland Park. Because of the country school concept, which seeks to educate the body as well as the mind, athletics at Gilman are almost as important as the academics. Gilman is competitive academically, as evidenced by the number of seniors moving on to top colleges and universities.

Maryvale Preparatory School for Girls
11300 Falls Road, Brooklandville
(410) 252-3366

Begun in 1945 by the Sisters of Notre Dame De Namur as a boarding school, Maryvale had only 12 students when it opened. That was OK by the sisters, however, whose mission was to set up a school that was small by design so each girl would receive a lot of individual attention. Staying true to the sisters' mission, only 290 day students are enrolled in grades 6 through 12, and the student-teacher ratio is only 8 to 1. Citing a very competitive college preparatory curriculum, Maryvale's academic focus encourages girls in mathematics and the sciences. A Science and Student Center was completed in 1997 and houses new computer and science labs. One aspect of Maryvale's curriculum is the student portfolio that every student is required to keep beginning in ninth grade. Each girl tucks into her portfolio records of her accomplishments—academic, athletic, and social. Anything that she feels proud of and wants to showcase is put in the folder. After four years, her portfolio houses her best works and is an information source when she begins filling out her college applications.

McDonogh School
8600 McDonogh Road, McDonogh
(410) 363-0600
www.mcdonogh.com

The American Civil War orphaned thousands of children and destroyed much of the South, including its schools. Philanthropist John McDonogh must have had this on his mind, for when he died, he willed money to fund a public school system in Louisiana and the McDonogh Farm School for orphaned boys in Maryland. McDonogh opened in 1873 on its 800-acre campus with a multiracial student body that worked the farm, growing vegetables, raising pigs, and milking cows. The original headmaster, Col. William Allen, who had fought with the Confederacy under Stonewall Jackson, imposed a military discipline and the military uniforms the boys wore were Confederate gray. Today, the school's original mandate to serve students in need is still very much in evidence, but the school has changed a lot in the last 30 years. Now coed, with day students as well as five-day boarders, the semimilitary atmosphere and uniform were dropped in 1971, and the farm no longer exists, save for the horse barn and riding facilities. Every McDonogh student learns to ride, and horsey amenities include riding rings and yearly horse shows. Other athletic pursuits include the more conventional football, lacrosse, tennis, golf, and swimming. Teachers, as well as students, live on campus, eat in the dining hall, and take part in campus life. The college preparatory curriculum is competitive, and virtually 100 percent of McDonogh's graduates now go on to further education. The student-teacher ratio is 15 to 1.

The Park School
2425 Old Court Road, Brooklandville
(410) 339-7070
www.parkschool.net

The Park School was founded in 1912 as a progressive school. A progressive school is one in which children are guided toward moral behavior, self-discipline, and intellectual achievement. Park is a nonsectarian, independent, coeducational day school. A 27,000-square-foot science, math, and technology center opened in 1997, and both the middle and upper schools were recently renovated to better support Park's seminar style of teaching. Approximately 875 students are enrolled in grades K through 12. The student-teacher ratio is 9 to 1.

Roland Park Country School
5204 Roland Avenue
(410) 323-5500
www.rpcs.org

Roland Park Country School (RPCS) began in 1894 as a neighborhood school

Libraries

Downtown

The Enoch Pratt Free Library is one of the oldest free public library systems in the United States. Over a span of 120 years, the Enoch Pratt has established 24 branches throughout the city and the county and has evolved a reputation as one of the finest resources in Baltimore. Book loans are just part of the services. The library offers technology centers, kids' events, and career assistance. Research rooms carry reference books with up-to-date census information and crime stats, which can be very helpful when deciding where to buy a home.

Enoch Pratt Free Library Main Branch
400 Cathedral Street
(410) 396-5430

Surrounding Counties

The Baltimore County Public Library system has 18 branches peppering the five counties surrounding the city. A full list of all branches is available on the Web site www.bcplonline.org or by calling the administrative offices at (410) 887-6100. Here are a few of the larger branches:

Towson Branch
320 York Road
(410) 887-6166

Catonsville Branch
1100 Frederick Road
(410) 887-0951

Pikesville Branch
1301 Reisterstown Road
(410) 887-1234

White Marsh
8133 Sandpiper Circle
(410) 887-5097

housed in a private home. By 1901 it had won sponsorship from the Roland Park Company and eventually became the first fully accredited independent school for girls in Baltimore City. RPCS places emphasis on both academic achievement and athletic accomplishment. It fields teams in traditional sports such as field hockey and lacrosse as well as more unusual ones for girls, such as crew. There are 708 girls in grades K through 12, who are, according to *U.S. News & World Report*, consistently admitted into the nation's 25 most selective liberal arts colleges and universities. One of its 1996 graduates made headlines when she achieved a perfect score on her SAT. The student-faculty ratio is 7 to 1.

St. Paul's School, 11152 Falls Road, Brooklandville, (410) 825-4400

St. Paul's School for Girls, 11232 Falls Road, Brooklandville, (410) 823-6323
St. Paul's School, an all-boys school, and St. Paul's School for Girls are separate schools, with separate campuses, budgets, and boards of directors. They are, however, closely associated, not only because their campuses adjoin but also because both schools share day-care, kindergarten, and lower school facilities. The coeducational day care and kindergarten, called St. Paul's Plus, is administered by the girls' school. The lower school, administered by and located at the boys' school, provides primary education for boys and girls plan-

ning to attend middle and high school (grades 5 through 12) at both St. Paul's schools.

St. Paul's School
www.stpaulsschool.org

Founded in 1849 by Old St. Paul's Church as a school for poor boys in Baltimore's downtown, the school moved to its 68-acre campus in Brooklandville in 1952. A private school that still enjoys association with Old St. Paul's, St. Paul's School offers a single-sex Episcopal education with the added benefit of coeducational classes and activities with St. Paul's for Girls at the high school level. St. Paul's welcomes students of all races, cultures, and religions, noting that its focus is to help students realize their spiritual selves and to enable them to participate in all parts of their lives. St. Paul's student body numbers 867 students in the lower, middle, and upper schools. The student-teacher ratio is 9 to 1. The campus includes the Ward Center for the Arts, a 28,000-square-foot facility for the dramatic, vocal, and fine arts, jointly operated with St. Paul's School for Girls.

St. Paul's School for Girls
www.spsfg.org

The history of St. Paul's School for Girls goes all the way back to 1799, when the Benevolent Society of the City and County of Baltimore founded a school for poor and orphan girls under the auspices of Old St. Paul's Church. After many incarnations, the current school was founded in 1959. More than 366 girls participate in a college preparatory curriculum and a strong athletic program at the 38-acre

campus. One of St. Paul's most interesting instructional features is its morning gathering called prayers, in which all students and teachers share concerns and school news. The student-teacher ratio is 9 to 1.

St. Timothy's School
**8400 Greenspring Avenue, Stevenson
(410) 486-7400
www.sttimothysschool.com**

St. Timothy's was founded in 1882. In 1974, Hannah More Academy, the oldest Episcopal girls' boarding school in the country, merged with St. Timothy's. Today, the expanded St. Timothy's offers boarding and day school from grade 9 through postgraduate studies for 122 girls on a stunning 234-acre campus in Greenspring Valley. With 70 percent of its students living on campus and a student-to-faculty ratio of 4 to 1, St. Timothy's girls receive close attention in a community atmosphere that seeks to "develop each person's ability to live thoughtfully in a community of diverse and unique individuals."

Academically, St. Tim's is competitive, with virtually 100 percent of its graduates heading for higher education. Average SAT scores hover around 1120. Not all learning is in the classroom, however. Throughout the students' tenure, the school offers off-campus experiences through a program called Connections, in which students study the political, social, economic, and cultural aspects of Baltimore, Annapolis, and Washington, D.C. And in the senior year, students perform three weeks of independent study in which they become corporate interns.

Students interested in athletics have the opportunity to compete in eight interscholastic sports, including tennis and riding. And students who tend toward the artistic have at their disposal a theater complete with costume shop, dance studio, and music practice rooms as well as the Art Barn, which boasts darkrooms and kilns.

Talmudical Academy of Baltimore
**4445 Old Court Road, Pikesville
(410) 484-6600**

Talmudical Academy is the oldest Jewish day school in the United States outside of New York. Founded in 1913, its intent was to provide young Jewish boys with an Orthodox environment in which they could receive a secular education as well as a religious one. It still serves this need. Boys in pre-K through grade 12 spend mornings in study of the Hebrew alphabet, the Bible, and other sacred Hebrew texts. In the afternoon, they pursue the reading, writing, and arithmetic part of their education. The days are long, 9:00 A.M. to 6:30 P.M., but most Jewish children in Baltimore have a similar day, attending public or private school from 8:15 A.M. to 2:30 P.M. and then heading to a specialized Hebrew school afterward.

Talmudical serves 625 students in classes of 16 to 20 students. The student-teacher ratio is 10 to 1.

Southwest

The Cardinal Gibbons School
3225 Wilkens Avenue
(410) 644-1770
www.cardinalgibbonsschool.com

The Cardinal Gibbons School was established in 1959 on the site of Babe Ruth's grammar school alma mater, St. Mary's Industrial School. Originally chosen because it provided space for athletic fields and a convent, the large campus and school serves more than 200 boys in a college preparatory program for grades 6 through 12. Gibbons students average 16 points higher than the national average on SAT scores. The student-teacher ratio is 10 to 1.

Mount Saint Joseph High School
4403 Frederick Avenue
(410) 644-3300
www.msjnet.edu

St. Joe's, as it is lovingly called, began in 1876 on the prayer of one Brother Bernadine, who asked for the intervention of Saint Joseph to help him and his Xavierian Brothers find the money to start the school. Although St. Joe's has a balanced college preparatory curriculum, the focus in its advanced placement courses is on science. The school recently added a 30,000-square-foot, state-of-the-art media and technology building to its pastoral 31-acre campus. The school serves approximately 1,100 boys and has a student-teacher ratio of 14 to 1.

Seton Keough High School
1201 South Caton Avenue
(410) 646-4444
www.setonkeough.com

Seton Keough is a hybrid that was created in 1988 when Seton High School, a midtown city high school for girls founded by the Daughters of Charity in 1865, merged with Archbishop Keough High School and moved out to its 30-acre campus where Keough had been since its founding by the School Sisters of Notre Dame in 1965. Seton Keough offers a comprehensive college preparatory program for all its girls that includes advanced placement classes as well as the Marillac Program, for students with special needs, and the Focus program, for students who enter the school achieving below their grade level in major subject areas. Close to 500 students are enrolled at Seton Keough. The student-to-faculty ratio is approximately 9 to 1.

COLLEGES AND UNIVERSITIES

College of Notre Dame of Maryland
4701 North Charles Street
(410) 435-0100
www.ndm.edu

The College of Notre Dame (CND) handed out its first baccalaureate degrees in 1896. An all-woman's college, CND began when graduates of Notre Dame Preparatory School cried out for post-secondary education. A two-year then a four-year college grew from this need, and CND still stands on the land that was originally set aside for Notre Dame Prep. CND focuses on liberal arts in its full-time, weekday program and offers 22 majors. CND also offers a Weekend College and a flexible master's degree program for men and women with full-time jobs. The college also offers a continuing education program for older women who are seeking their bachelor of arts degrees. Full-time day students on the Charles Street campus number 825, but overall enrollment is more than 3,000 in 27 major fields of study. Dormitory facilities house 440 students. The school also offers educational opportunities through community colleges in surrounding counties, including an "RN to BSN" program in Frederick County.

Goucher College
1021 Dulaney Valley Road, Towson
(410) 337-6000
www.goucher.edu

Goucher was founded in 1885 as a liberal arts college for women in midtown Baltimore. It moved to its 287-acre Towson campus in 1953 and began accepting male students in 1986. Goucher counts among its student body about 1,200 undergraduates and 700 graduate students from all over the United States and 20 foreign countries. It offers undergraduate majors in 18 departments and five interdisciplinary areas; students can also design their own majors. Internships, study abroad, and independent study and research are encouraged and in some cases required for graduation. Approximately 75 percent of Goucher's graduates pursue advanced degrees. Master's degrees in education, teaching, historic preservation, and creative nonfiction as well as a postbaccalaureate premedical program are available through Goucher.

The Johns Hopkins University
Charles and 34th Streets
(410) 516-8000
www.jhu.edu

The Johns Hopkins University (JHU) was founded in 1876 when, upon his death, Johns Hopkins willed $7 million to create it and The Johns Hopkins Hospital. Then, as now, the hospital and the university work hand in hand, so that research,

instruction, and practical application are all put together in one neat package. JHU was the first university in the United States to employ this all-encompassing method of teaching that was modeled after the European research teaching methods of the time.

Originally an all-white male facility, JHU admitted its first African-American student in 1887, but admitted women only sparingly over the years until 1970, when it officially became a coeducational facility. More than 16,000 full- and part-time students of both sexes and all colors are enrolled at its three major Mid-Atlantic campuses and campuses in China and Italy. The Homewood campus in Baltimore serves almost 5,000 of those students in its two major schools: the Krieger School of Arts and Sciences and the Whiting School of Engineering, which offer master's and doctorate degree programs as well as bachelor's degrees of both arts and science. The East Baltimore campus where the hospital is located also houses the schools of Medicine, Nursing, and Hygiene and Public Health.

Some of Hopkins' special divisions include the Paul H. Nitze School of Advanced International Studies and the Applied Physics Laboratory, and Hopkins also now runs the Peabody Institute (see the Peabody's entry under Specialty Schools later in this chapter).

A highly competitive private university, JHU has extensive community outreach. Intercollegiate sports are well attended, particularly lacrosse and football, and the annual Hopkins Fair (see the Annual Events chapter) is always crowded. JHU also boasts WJHU, a popular city-wide public radio station (see the Media chapter), and the Hopkins Symphony Orchestra (see The Arts chapter). JHU, which is the largest private employer in Baltimore, has its fingers in many pies, including building and renovating city buildings in cooperation with Habitat for Humanity on the volunteer level and through Dome Corporation, a Hopkins subsidiary, on the corporate level.

Loyola College in Maryland
4501 North Charles Street
(410) 617-2000
www.loyola.edu

Loyola College in Maryland was founded in 1852 by the Jesuit order as an all-male post-secondary institution. In 1971 it merged with St. Agnes College (an all-women's college) and became a coeducational facility. Loyola includes the College of Arts and Sciences and the Sellinger School of Business and Management, which offer undergraduate, graduate, and professional development programs. Loyola has more than 3,400 undergraduates in on-campus and study-abroad programs and 2,600 graduate students. Its eclectic student body includes students from 41 states and 48 foreign countries, 77 percent of whom live on the main campus. However, Loyola also offers classes at campuses in Columbia and Hunt Valley, Maryland, as well as Belgium, Thailand, and England. Classes are also offered through community colleges in Anne Arundel, Harford, and Cecil Counties, and graduate classes are accessible through a new site in Timonium. A competitive school, more than 58 percent of Loyola's students graduated from high school in the top fifth of their classes.

Morgan State University
1700 East Cold Spring Lane
(410) 885-3333
www.morgan.edu

Morgan State University was founded in 1867 by members of the Baltimore Methodist Episcopal Church to educate African Americans and prepare them for the Methodist clergy. Its mission quickly expanded to included educating teachers. For almost a century, Morgan functioned as a private college, but in 1968 it was accepted under the umbrella of the University System of Maryland, and with its resources became a university in 1975. Oddly, however, enrollment dwindled down to 2,000 students, until 1984 when in an effort to save itself, the school once again became independent. With current enrollments at 6,000 and a full-time faculty of 300, it has become one of the fastest growing campuses in the state. An independent state university, Morgan offers master's and doctorate programs as well as baccalaureate degrees in the arts and sciences but notes particular strengths in science and engineering, where it has seen it greatest growth. Although a historically African-American college, Morgan welcomes students of all colors, cultures, and backgrounds.

St. Mary's Seminary and University
5400 Roland Avenue
(410) 864-4000
www.stmarys.edu

This private university began in 1791 by the Society of St. Sulpice, which sought to educate students for the priesthood. The Sulpicians created St. Mary's College in 1803. Open to students of all faiths, St. Mary's College was the first college chartered in Maryland. The equivalent of a high school and community college by today's standards, it grew in importance when the Sulpicians were granted recognition as a Pontifical Theological Faculty in 1822 by Pope Pius VII and gained the ability to grant pontifical degrees. St. Mary's Seminary is one of only six seminaries in the United States that are allowed to grant such degrees. True to its ecumenical heritage, St. Mary's also offers graduate education for those not interested in ministry. The Ecumenical Institute of Theology, which opened in 1968 to persons of all faiths, continues to provide a platform for investigation and argument of religious and philosophical topics as well as award master's degrees in theology and religious education. Within its School of Theology, St. Mary's opened the Center for Continuing Formation in 1995, which hosts priests on sabbatical as well as provides learning opportunities in religion and philosophy for the general public.

The University System of Maryland

The University System of Maryland (USM) is comprised of both previously independent schools that have come under its umbrella and schools that have historically been branches or campuses of the University of Maryland. There are 13 degree-granting institutions in all enrolling some 130,000 students worldwide in 600 degree programs.

The value of the University System of Maryland for residents of Maryland falls into two categories: convenience and cost. It is convenient not only because of the many campuses and educational centers that are easily accessible within the area but also because of the worldwide academic flexibility it offers. A student in the University System, for instance, may earn credits at various campuses and have all of them count toward a degree. You could do your freshman and sophomore years at University of Maryland, Baltimore County and then transfer to Towson or UB, and your credits would go with you. You may have to take additional courses to make up requirements for a particular school or program, but you will not lose the credits already earned.

Or perhaps you'd like to move to Europe for your junior and senior years. The University of Maryland University College has campuses in Schwabisch Gmund near Heidelberg, Germany, and two campuses in Russia, at Irkutsk and Vladivostok. Perhaps you've decided on military service and would like to take advantage of one of the University College's offerings at more than 160 U.S. military bases in Europe, East Asia, and the Pacific.

Whatever your needs, academic transfer within the University System is relatively easy, and assimilation into graduate school, though not guaranteed, is often uncomplicated as a baccalaureate program in a specific discipline is direct preparation for the graduate or professional schools. For instance, a student might major in pre-med at College Park and that would prepare him or her directly for the medical professional school at the Baltimore campus.

Costwise, the University System is much, much cheaper than the private colleges in Maryland. Tuition with student fees at Johns Hopkins is currently about $28,700; at Loyola, $28,334; and at Goucher, $25,750. In-state residents at the University of Maryland, Baltimore County pay $6,500 for the same number of credit hours. This means, of course, that you could pay for four years at the University of Maryland and a few postgraduate courses besides for what it will cost to go to most private universities for a year. You can make that money go even further if you take your first two years of education at one of the local community colleges, which have transfer and scholarship programs that work with the University System and at which a full-time local student pays about $2,000. So, if you were to receive an associate's degree from Catonsville Community College and then go on to finish your bachelor's degree at UMBC, your total cost for the four years would be less than $15,000.

But students are not the only beneficiaries of the USM umbrella. For participant schools, USM offers access to the financial support of the state of Maryland, the prestige of being part of this well-respected international institution, and access to a steady stream of students seeking a good education for the least amount of money.

Listed below are those colleges and campuses that are in the greater Baltimore area. If you would like more information about the main campus in College Park, Maryland, call (301) 405-1000. For the University College at College Park or other campuses worldwide, call (301) 985-7000, or for the Baltimore City Community College Business and Continuing Education Center, call (410) 986-3200. For an overview of USM, visit the Web site at www.usmd.edu.

Coppin State College
2500 West North Avenue
(410) 383-5990
www.coppin.umd.edu
Coppin State College is a historically African-American college that was established in 1900 as a private normal school to train elementary school teachers. Coppin, which became a part of the University System in 1988, currently offers degrees and certification programs in dentistry, engineering, pharmacy, criminal justice, and social work as well as teaching. It also offers graduate degrees in the arts and sciences, including nursing and teacher education. Originally a day school, most of Coppin's 3,700 students are still daytrippers, but a new 300-bed residence hall has begun to attract students from out of state to the 50-acre campus.

Towson University
8000 York Road, Towson
(410) 704-2000
www.towson.edu
Towson University began as the State Normal School, a state-sponsored teaching school in Baltimore City. It moved to its Towson campus in 1915, and the majestic building in which it was housed is still used by the university. Since then, the school has gone through many incarnations, ending up as the present Towson University. The university grants baccalaureate degrees in 50 majors and master's degrees in 25 programs through its seven colleges: the College of Business and Economics; the College of Education; the College of Fine Arts and Communication; the College of Graduate and Extended Education; the College of Health Professions; the College of Liberal Arts; and the College of Natural and Mathematical Sciences. Enrollment numbers around 16,000 full- and part-time students. There's residential space for 3,300. The school boasts state-of-the-art facilities in radio and TV and a growing reputation in the mass-media industry. It is the second-largest university in Maryland.

University of Baltimore
1420 North Charles Street
(410) 837-4200
www.ubalt.edu
The University of Baltimore (UB) began in 1925 as a private, coeducational, two-year school of business. In 1975 it went public and became part of the Maryland system. Currently, UB offers baccalaureate study for the junior and senior years, granting bachelor's degrees in the arts and sciences as well as postgraduate degrees through the Neil Kleinman Institute for Language, Technology and Publications Design; the Robert G. Merrick School of Business; and the Yale Gordon College of Liberal Arts. It is also well known for its School of Law. UB has also been reaching out to more distant sites to centers in Harford and Howard Counties, and it also offers a virtual degree. You can get your bachelor's degree by studying with UB online from anywhere in the world. More than half of UB's 4,600 students attend evening classes. There is no campus housing for UB, whose campus is across city blocks instead of rolling hills. But sitting as it does on the edge of the Mount Vernon/Belvedere neighborhood and near Bolton Hill, there is plenty of apartment space for out-of-towners.

University of Maryland, Baltimore
737 West Lombard Street
(410) 706-3100
www.umaryland.edu
Although the University of Maryland's main campus is now in College Park, Maryland, the university actually began here in Baltimore in 1807 with the founding of the School of Medicine. Davidge Hall, a lecture hall and operating theater built in 1812 and now a National Historic Landmark, is the oldest building in the United States in continuous use for medical teaching. In 1816 a School of Law was added. In 1840 the Baltimore College of Dental Surgery, Dental School opened as the first dental college in the world. In 1841, the Maryland College of Pharmacy was begun; and in 1889, the

School of Nursing opened. The most recent addition was the School of Social Work, in 1961. This Baltimore campus of the University of Maryland focuses on professional graduate school programs. It has close to 5,400 students served by more than 1,600 faculty members. There are 42 graduate programs offered.

**University of Maryland,
Baltimore County
1000 Hillltop Circle
(410) 455-1000
www.umbc.edu**
The University of Maryland, Baltimore County (UMBC) was founded in 1966. A separate school, not just a satellite campus of the University of Maryland, College Park, UMBC has more than 10,000 undergraduate and graduate students studying in the liberal arts and sciences at its 500-acre campus. The focus is on cutting-edge science and technology as well as the visual and performing arts, but it bills itself as a "public research university." In this regard, UMBC has nine separate research institutes located on campus that include everything from the Joint Center for Earth Systems Technology, a NASA/UMBC partnership that studies the global environment, to the Center for Education Research and Development, where model science programs for Maryland schools are created. There are 11,700 undergraduates.

Community Colleges

**Baltimore City Community College
600 East Lombard Street
(410) 986-5599**

**2901 Liberty Heights Avenue
(410) 462-8000
www.bccc.edu**
Baltimore City Community College (BCCC) has two main campuses in the city. Its Downtown campus, whose center is only a few blocks from the Inner Harbor, is convenient and well used by Downtown residents and workers. Its Liberty Road campus was the original site of the school when it was known as Baltimore Junior College, and its popular radio station, WBJC, still bears the original acronym. The school, however, has come a long way since the BJC days. More than 15,000 students pursue both credit and noncredit courses in 39 associate degree career programs and eight associate degree transfer programs.

The only state-sponsored, two-year college in Maryland, BCCC enrolls more city residents than any other college in Baltimore. Such popularity may be due to the emphasis the school places on preparing people for work. BCCC has 31 certificate programs, with special emphasis on health, human services, and business, though not all of its offerings are so mundane. BCCC offers an Apparel Technology Program, which was cited by the American Textile Manufacturers Institute for its innovative curriculum design and teaching excellence.

One of BCCC's most interesting features is that its education comes with a guarantee. "If a graduate of a career program . . . does not have a full-time job within 90 days after graduation, BCCC will provide 12 additional credits of course work and other support services at no cost to the student." To the graduates' future employers, the guarantee provides that BCCC students will be "competent in their work."

To help prepare the community at large for work and the world, BCCC offers the Business and Continuing Education Center. Located at 10 South Gay Street in a renovated, historic firehouse, the center is the largest provider of literacy education in Baltimore. The center offers three main programs: Adult Basic Education, which provides opportunities for adults to hone literacy skills; General Education Development, which prepares students of all ages for the GED high school equivalency exam; and English as a Second Language, which helps prepare new immigrants to further their education and become productive citizens.

The Community Colleges of Baltimore County

There are three community colleges in Baltimore County, each of which grew up separately, responding to the needs of their respective communities. Within the last few years, however, they have been bundled under the umbrella name and administration of a new entity, The Community Colleges of Baltimore County (CCBC). Through this act of centralization, Baltimore County hopes to be able to enhance offerings while reducing overall costs through reorganization. The three original schools that now serve as CCBC's main campuses are Catonsville Community College, 800 South Rolling Road, Catonsville, (410) 455-6050; Dundalk Community College, 7200 Sollers Point Road, Dundalk, (410) 285-9802; and Essex Community College, 7201 Rossville Boulevard, Essex, (410) 780-6313. The CCBC also offers classes through neighborhood centers in Owings Mills, Hunt Valley, Towson, Parkville, and White Marsh, as well as the Occupational Training Center at the Catonsville campus.

Through all its campuses and centers, CCBC serves more than 80,000 students and offers 6,600 credit courses and 7,000 continuing education courses, including employee training courses that the county offers to employers in the area at more than 90 locations. Various certificates of completion are available for specific course offerings, but, overwhelmingly, students seek associate of arts degrees and transfer to a four-year institution.

Associate degrees are offered in more than 75 programs in the arts and sciences, business administration, computer sciences, engineering, general studies, and teacher education. Certificate programs include such options as computer graphics and visual communications, printing management technology, environmental technology, chemical dependency counseling, retail floristry, and varied allied health programs. Visit the Web site at www.ccbc.md.edu.

Schools such as Baltimore City College and Calvert Hall College are not, in fact, colleges but high schools. Established in the middle of the nineteenth century, both schools were denoted as colleges because they were degree-granting institutions.

SPECIALTY SCHOOLS

Baltimore Actors' Theatre and Conservatory
300 Dumbarton Road
(410) 337-8519
www.baltimoreactorstheatre.org

If you have a five-year-old who can really belt out a song or a 15-year-old who can make you believe he's Hamlet, then you might want to consider approaching Baltimore Actors' Theatre and Conservatory to see if your child can become one of the select few who get admitted every year. The K-12 student body at the conservatory numbers only 30, with an equal number of students pursuing a three-year baccalaureate degree and postgraduate studies. These 60 students work hand-in-hand with the resident professional performance company of 100 to produce a minimum of 12 plays per year, while pursuing a rigorous academic curriculum. High school degrees are accredited by the state of Maryland, but the baccalaureate and master's degrees offered are through Trinity College in London, although students do not study abroad.

The Baltimore Actors' Theatre and Conservatory is less expensive than many traditional private K-12 institutions and many area colleges because much of the school's expenses are paid for through performance receipts.

Baltimore International College (BIC)
17 Commerce Street
(410) 752-4710
www.bic.edu

BIC was founded in 1972 as part of Baltimore City Community College. Now a separate two-year institution, the school offers its 800 full-time students associate degrees in the School of Culinary Arts and/or the School of Business and Management. One of only four degree-granting culinary institutes in the entire country, BIC also serves more than 2,000 part-time, noncredit students with individual course offerings. Classes are all very hands-on, with cooking classes being taught in a lab situation. Also, students get the opportunity to test their food and people skills at the Cafe in the Mount Vernon Hotel, which the college both owns and operates with a student staff.

The Maryland Institute, College of Art
1300 West Mount Royal Avenue
(410) 669-9200
www.mica.edu
The Maryland Institute, selected by *U.S. News & World Report* as one of the top four visual arts colleges in the nation, was established in 1826 and has the distinction of being the oldest independent, degree-granting, fully accredited art college in the United States. The campus is made up of 16 buildings, most of which line Mount Royal Avenue from North Avenue to Park Avenue, adjacent to Mount Royal Terrace. Two of the buildings—the main building at 1300 and Mount Royal Station, a historic train station that the institute renovated for gallery and workspace—are on the National Register of Historic Places. In the winter of 2004-2005, MICA is set to open its new Brown Center, an impressive concrete and steel modern building sheathed in glass. The Brown Center will house a much-needed auditorium as well as the school's burgeoning new media studies.

But what is really most important about the institute is the education it offers its students. Undergraduate degrees are available in all major areas of artistic endeavor. All programs incorporate the use of the computer, offering state-of-the-art opportunities in design. A digital embroidery machine is available to material artists, and sculptors may now use computers to play with ideas and actually create their pieces digitally before they ever take chisel in hand.

The master's programs include six main areas of study, but the school offers two unique programs. One is the five-year, BSA/MAT program through which a student may study for five years and graduate with not only a bachelor of science degree in art, but also a master's degree in teaching. The second program is called Fine Arts in Studio for Art Educators. This program is designed for the practicing art teacher. Study is arranged so that the master's candidate may work during the teaching year, then go to class during the summers. Study is intensive, but a master's degree can be achieved in four summer sessions.

The institute also offers a plethora of options for continuing studies in everything from interior design to computer art, both for those seeking degrees and those simply wanting to learn.

Maryland School for the Blind
3501 Taylor Avenue
(410) 444-5000
www.mdschblind.org
The Maryland School for the Blind was founded in 1853. It moved from the city to its present location in 1906, because the children needed a place to run that had no obstacles. From its inception until the 1970s, the school served primarily blind and visually impaired students with a basic academic curriculum and specialized courses in Braille and orientation mobility. Daily living skills, such as personal hygiene, food preparation, and table etiquette, were also taught.

Since the 1970s when the federal government handed down a national mandate that required all states to provide education for handicapped children, the Maryland School has adapted its curriculum and services to include children that have not only visual disparities but also physical and emotional ones.

More than 300 professionals and 140 volunteers help the Maryland School's 185 students learn how to lead normal lives. Some 140 students live on campus five days a week and are supported by house parents, who live with them, and a 24-hour nursing staff on campus.

Students who are residents of Maryland pay nothing for their room, board, and tuition. Students from outside the state pay tuition and fees, but these are often picked up by their respective states that may have no facilities that fulfill the federal mandate. The Maryland School also helps public school systems develop programs within their schools for children with visual and/or physical handicaps and boasts an outreach program to an additional 200 students across Maryland. The school has also begun working with babies and toddlers in basic skills to give them a head start.

The Peabody Institute
1 East Mount Vernon Place
(410) 659-8100
www.peabody.jhu.edu

The Peabody Conservatory of Music, now the Peabody Institute of the Johns Hopkins University, was founded in 1857 with a bequest from George Peabody. It has become over the intervening years one of the premier music schools in the country. The Peabody has a preparatory division in music and dance that is open to people of all ages. The Conservatory offers high school, college, and advanced degrees in music. Close to 600 full-time and 40 part-time students are accepted into the Conservatory versus the almost 6,400 students in the preparatory school. The Peabody is performance-oriented, and its students stage almost 60 public concerts every year.

St. Elizabeth's School and
Rehabilitation Center
801 Argonne Drive
(410) 889-5054

St. Elizabeth's was started in 1961 as an outgrowth of St. Francis for Special Education, which opened in 1953. St. Elizabeth's is what is known as an Intensity 5

school, meaning that 100 percent of the student's day is spent in specialized education. Children from age 11 to 21 receive education that focuses on academics, social/emotional growth and development, and vocational skills. There is athletic competition for those who are able to participate. Recently St. Elizabeth's girls volleyball team came in third at the National Special Olympics in Minneapolis, Minnesota. A high school diploma is available through the school, as is a certificate of completion for specialized vocational curricula, which include such diverse areas as cosmetology, carpentry, and commercial cooking. Because apprenticeship and volunteer experience are a large part of the vocational focus, students often graduate with a job already in hand. This nonresident day school for the physically and emotionally handicapped has around 125 students. The student-teacher ratio is 2 to 1.

STUDENT SERVICES

Sylvan Learning Systems, Inc.
1001 Fleet Street
(888) EDUCATE
www.educate.com

Sylvan Learning Systems was founded in 1979 in Portland, Oregon, but has recently located its worldwide corporate headquarters in the Inner Harbor East. Sylvan has three divisions: Sylvan Learning Centers, Sylvan Prometric, and Caliber Learning Network.

Sylvan Learning Centers consists of approximately 950 franchised centers in the United States, 38 of which are in Baltimore. Each center provides tutoring and supplemental study in reading, writing, and mathematics for children in grades K through 12. The tutoring is focused and child-specific. Although Sylvan's teaching methods are standard across the board, what they teach each child is not. If you are interested in getting in contact with a Sylvan Learning Center near your home or school, the previously listed 800 number

will connect you with Sylvan's location center. When you call, you may find that there is a Sylvan Learning Center in your school, as Sylvan provides in-school services to some of Maryland's districts through its Contract Services Division.

Sylvan Prometric is the testing arm of the company. It offers exams to professionals who are seeking certification testing, and exams to post-secondary students who are seeking qualifying tests, such as the Graduate Record Exam. To contact Sylvan Prometric in Baltimore, call the corporate headquarters at (410) 843–8000.

Another service of Sylvan is its Caliber Learning Network, which is an online provider network for distance learning.

HEALTH CARE Ⓗ

Baltimore is dotted with great hospitals, ranging from the world-renowned Johns Hopkins Hospital in East Baltimore and University of Maryland Medical System near the Inner Harbor to smaller hospitals with increasingly impressive records and accomplishments, including Greater Baltimore Medical Center, Franklin Square Hospital, and Mercy Medical Center.

More importantly, Maryland has been a leader in caring for critically injured people since the 1970s. The Maryland Shock Trauma Center at the University of Maryland Medical Center, which involves paid and volunteer firefighters and ambulance crews, state police, and their helicopters and every hospital in the state, ensures that people who need the most serious forms of care as a result of car accidents, shootings, falls, or other injurious acts get that care quickly. The success of the system is in the number of critically injured people who live to tell the tale of their serious accident. (See the Close-up in this chapter.)

And hardly a week goes by that a doctor associated with some hospital in the Baltimore area doesn't make national or international headlines for his or her life-saving discoveries or successes in the operating room. Dr. Ben Carson, a neurosurgeon at Johns Hopkins Hospital, has saved hundreds of small children through his surgical skills and is particularly well known for separations of united twins.

Dr. Robert Gallo, a scientist and leader in the research of AIDS, opened a facility at the Institute of Human Virology at the University of Maryland School of Medicine in 1996, bringing to Baltimore a first-rate warrior against one of the era's most fatal and devastating diseases.

While advertisements and promotional materials make it seem as if there's great competition among the hospitals, a good deal of their success is in working together to help patients. Patients are routinely sent from one hospital to another for consultations, second opinions, and even surgeries. The hospitals in the area play host to thousands of patients from all over the world, who come to the area seeking the best care possible.

One thing unique to Maryland's hospital system is capitation, a system of state regulation designed to ensure that all hospitals have enough patients to be effective. Capitation also ensures proper pricing, although critics will argue that regulated pricing prevents individual hospitals from setting a rate that would encourage competition among peers. The system also forces hospitals making a profit in one year to put those revenues into capital improvements. The result is better hospitals with state-of-the-art facilities and equipment, even at smaller hospitals and those removed from the more urban areas. For a hospital to expand or contract its existing services, capitation requires the hospital to obtain permission from state regulators, meaning the area's hospitals at times can lag behind newer needs of patients. However, most of these issues are resolved in board rooms and regulators' offices, not in hospitals or at the bedside.

Beyond the traditional forms of medicine practiced in hospitals, the area has seen growth in the holistic approaches to medicine, including alternative healing methods such as acupuncture, aromatherapy, and other forms of care practiced for centuries elsewhere but only now gaining wider acceptance in this country. The best source for these services is to consult *Baltimore Resources*, a free quarterly magazine focusing on helping people find the care they need in the Baltimore area. The tabloid-size free newspaper is available at numerous health-food stores, libraries, larger bookstores, and other locations throughout the city and surrounding area.

What follows is a listing of the area's hospitals and specialty services, including psychiatric hospitals. Hospice services are also listed. Like most sections of the book, these are categorized by regions. If no city is listed, then the hospital is within the confines of Baltimore City. Hospitals outside the city limits are noted with the town, after the street address.

HOSPITALS

Downtown

Baltimore VA Medical Center
10 North Greene Street
(410) 605-7000
www.vamhcs.med.va.gov
Part of the VA Maryland Health Care System, the Baltimore VA Medical Center offers veterans some of the most state-of-the-art facilities available through the military. The 221-bed medical center is home to the world's first filmless radiology department, which allows doctors nearly instant access to patient imaging from throughout the facility.

Conveniently located near the Inner Harbor and next door to the University of Maryland Medical System, the center offers a full range of inpatient, outpatient, and research programs for veterans. The Geriatric Research, Education and Clinical Center, offering research on strokes and cardiovascular disease prevention through exercise, smoking cessation, and nutrition therapy for older veterans, is one of only 16 VA system providers of these services in the country.

When it opened in January 1993 on a site that had housed a parking lot, the center replaced the Loch Raven VA Hospital, which now functions as a rehabilitation services provider.

The center in Baltimore offers a wide range of specialties, including a state-of-the-art endoscopic suite; inpatient and outpatient mental health services; MRI, mammography, and CAT scan facilities; a home-based primary-care program; a refractory congestive heart failure program; an outpatient spinal cord injury support clinic; and a senior exercise rehabilitation facility.

The medical center offers free parking in its parking lot below the facility on Greene Street. A shuttle service taking patients to and from Perry Point and Fort Howard medical centers, separate facilities that are part of the same network of veterans services, is provided on weekdays.

Bon Secours Hospital
2000 West Baltimore Street
(410) 362-3000
www.bonsecours.org
James Cardinal Gibbons, the ninth archbishop of Baltimore, asked the Sisters of Bon Secours to come from Paris in 1881 to provide health care to the sick in their homes. Through the financial support of philanthropist George Jerkins, they opened the first Bon Secours Hospital in Baltimore in 1919. Now, with 208 beds and 973 employees, that mission has spread to include an intense community commitment, involving 10 primary-care centers around West Baltimore; the largest outpatient renal dialysis program in the city; the New Hope Treatment Center, offering drug treatment and counseling; Home, Health and Hospice, providing support as Cardinal Gibbons first envisioned it; and Operation Reach-Out, a community development program. The hospital merged in 1996 with Liberty Health System to form Bon Secours Medical System. Among Bon Secours Hospital's specialties are cardiology, podiatry, surgery, substance abuse services, and home health.

The Johns Hopkins Hospital
600 North Wolfe Street
(410) 955-5000
www.hopkinsmedicine.org
The hospital opened in 1889, and since that time its recognition and groundbreaking work have grown with the years. Established as part of philanthropist Johns Hopkins's gift to form Johns Hopkins University, the school of medicine and hospital

Important Numbers and Web Sites to Know

Police, fire, ambulance, or other emergencies, 911
(in Baltimore City, call 311 for nonemergency matters)
Maryland Natural Resources Police (maritime emergencies), (410) 260-8888,
(800) 628-9944, www.dnr.state.md.us
Poison Control, (410) 528-7701, (800) 222-1222

Departments of Mental Health and Hygiene
These numbers will lead you to people who can make referrals to specialists ranging
from community health centers to centers dealing with specific types of care.

State of Maryland, (410) 767-6783, www.mdpublichealth.org
Anne Arundel County, (410) 222-7095, www.aahealth.org
Baltimore City, (410) 837-2647, www.ci.baltimore.md.us
Baltimore County, (410) 887-2735, www.co.ba.md.us
Howard County, (410) 313-6300, www.co.ho.md.us

Other Aid Agencies
Associated Black Charities, (410) 659-0000, www.abc-md.org
Associated Catholic Charities, (410) 261-5800, www.catholiccharities-md.org
Episcopal Social Ministries, (410) 467-1264, www.esm.ang-md.org
Jewish Family Services, (410) 466-9200, www.jfs.org
Lutheran Social Services in Maryland, (410) 539-7322, www.lssnca.org

Crisis Intervention
For a larger list of contacts for crisis intervention in Maryland, visit
www.dpscs.state.md.us/vsm/
Family Crisis Center, (410) 828-6390
Grassroots Crisis Line (suicide intervention), (410) 521-3800 or (800) SUICIDE,
www.suicidehotlines.com/maryland
House of Ruth (domestic violence), (410) 889-0840; 24-hour hotline:
(410) 889-7884
Maryland Network Against Domestic Violence, (800) MD-HELPS
Maryland Youth Crisis Hotline, (800) 422-0009
Parents Anonymous, (410) 243-2322; www.familytreemd.org

Referral Sources
Maryland Psychiatric Society, (410) 625-0232, www.mdpsych.org
Maryland Psychological Association, (410) 992-4258, www.marylandpsychology.org

Substance Abuse
Al-Anon and Alateen, (410) 766-1984, www.md-al-anon.org
Alcoholics Anonymous, (410) 663-1922, www.aa.org
Narcotics Anonymous, (410) 566-4022, www.marscna.org

revolutionized American higher education, medical education, and health care by establishing an intense teaching and learning environment where doctors, teachers, and students work hand in hand. Hopkins was the first medical school to require an undergraduate degree for admission and the first to combine science learning and intensive clinical mentoring, thus creating a model for medical education that remains in use throughout the world today. Among the firsts the hospital can claim is the first major medical school in the country to admit women, the first to use rubber gloves during surgery, and the first to develop renal dialysis and CPR.

The hospital has 1,025 beds and draws seriously ill patients from all over the world who seek the cures for which Hopkins is renowned. Employing the equivalent of 6,900 full-time employees, the hospital features marvelous accommodations for those having to spend time in the hospital. Travel agents, concierges, several types of dining, and other amenities ease the tough times, and the hospital is located on the city's subway system, meaning transportation from the train station or airport doesn't require a taxicab ride. Its children's ward features games, movies, and a giant stuffed animal zoo that makes kids feel like they're not so far away from home. Among its specialties are AIDS care, anesthesiology, critical care, asthma and allergies, cancer, cardiology and cardiac surgery, dermatology, digestive disorders, emergency medicine, endocrinology, immunology and infectious diseases, kidney disorders, neurology and neurosurgery, pediatrics, pulmonary medicine, reconstructive and plastic surgery, transplant surgery, and urology.

Maryland General Hospital
827 Linden Avenue
(410) 225-8000
www.marylandgeneral.org
Founded in 1881 by a group of Baltimore doctors as a university-affiliated teaching hospital, the Baltimore Medical College, as it was called back then, became Maryland General after merging with the University of Maryland School of Medicine. In 1965 it again merged, this time with the Baltimore Eye and Ear Hospital to become the premier teaching hospital for eye, ear, nose, and throat problems. Now, the 276-bed hospital provides those same services, as well as rehabilitation, transitional care, mental health, and obstetrics and gynecological services. In 1997 the hospital opened its Obstetrical Center, which allows each mother to remain in her one, well-furnished, home-like room throughout the entire childbirthing process. The hospital's rehabilitation facility provides typical subacute services, as well as a unique brain injury program.

Mercy Medical Center
301 St. Paul Place
(410) 332-9000
www.mdmercy.com
The 285-bed hospital started as a 20-bed clinic for the poor and indigent of Baltimore. It was run by one doctor and a couple of medical students in an abandoned schoolhouse in 1867. At that time, the hospital was part of Washington University School of Medicine. In 1874 City Hospital, named for the nearby City Springs, a public fountain and park, was taken over by six Sisters of Mercy, who continued to care for the city's poor, while opening the Mercy Hospital School of Nursing in 1899. Since that time, the hospital has continued to grow into one of the area's larger hospitals, employing 2,033 people and having an operating budget of about $147 million.

In 1994 the hospital launched its Center for Women's Health and Medicine after finding that the need for specialized care for women was great. World-class gynecologic oncologist Dr. Neil Rosenshein and breast cancer surgeon Dr. Neil B. Freidman were chosen to head two of its women's programs, and in 1997, the hospital opened an innovative eating disorders clinic. In recent years the hospital has been making arrangements with a number of area businesses and government agencies to provide first-line health care to injured workers, giving it a new niche to fill in the Downtown area. The hospital provides care in internal medicine, surgery, obstetrics, pediatrics, urology, cardiology, oncology, cosmetic surgery, hospice, transitional care, and emergency medicine. The hospital also acquired the Cardinal Shehan Center/Stella Maris geriatric care facility in Towson.

University of Maryland Medical Center
22 South Green Street
(410) 328-8667
www.umm.edu
Calling itself "Maryland's other great hospital" in deference to the more widely recognized Johns Hopkins Hospital, Maryland's largest hospital serves more than 250,000 patients a year. Established in 1807, the affiliated University of Maryland School of Medicine is the nation's fifth-oldest medical school. In 1823 the medical school built the Baltimore Infirmary, which later became University Hospital. Just blocks from Camden Yards and the Inner Harbor, the hospital has 747 beds, served by 5,500 employees.

A private, nonprofit teaching hospital, the first teaching hospital in the state, the University of Maryland Medical Center often assists with referrals and the handling of difficult cases from the region's doctors and smaller hospitals. The Maryland Shock Trauma Center was the first of its kind for providing critical care to those in immediate need of medical attention, using state police helicopters and the region's ambulance systems. The Greenebaum Cancer Center opened in 1996 and serves thousands of people in the region suffering from all types of cancer. The Gudelsky Building, featuring a unique 12-story atrium to provide comfort and solace to patients and their loved ones, transcends the typical hospital environment, while rooms in the building are mostly private, many with lovely views of the Baltimore skyline. Specialties include neurosurgical care, cardiac care, and transplant surgery, as well as cutting-edge

research and surgical advancements, including pioneering work in transplants, video-assisted surgery, and the Gamma Knife, a radiological procedure that requires no surgery to destroy brain tumors and repair vascular malformations.

Northeast

Good Samaritan Hospital of Maryland
5601 Loch Raven Boulevard
(410) 532-8000
www.goodsam-md.org
Good Samaritan was founded in 1968 through a gift from Thomas O'Neill, a local merchant and philanthropist. O'Neill set the condition that all activities at the hospital conform to the Catholic Principles, as set by the U.S. National Conference of Catholic Bishops. This means that abortions and in vitro fertilizations are not performed here. Through an arrangement with Johns Hopkins School of Medicine, the hospital provides orthopedics, rehabilitation medicine, and rheumatology. It's located on a 43-acre site in northeastern Baltimore City, where its 287 beds and 1,305 employees provide care to northern Baltimore City and the greater Towson area. The Emergency Department sees more than 23,000 patients a year, and the hospital's Good Health Center offers free and low-cost preventative medical services. The hospital also offers 69 rehabilitation beds and a 24-station renal dialysis unit. Specialties include medical/surgical care, obstetrics and gynecology, pediatric care, and emergency care. Good Samaritan is one of the top ten hospitals for complex knee surgery.

Greater Baltimore Medical Center
6701 North Charles Street, Towson
(410) 828-2000
www.gbmc.org
Formed from the Presbyterian Eye, Ear and Throat Hospital, which opened in the 1880s on East Baltimore Street in the city, and the Women's Hospital of Maryland, GBMC opened on its 72-acre wooded

Selected Baltimore Firsts

The first Department of Public Health was established here in 1793.

Granville Stanley Hall established the first psychology laboratory at Johns Hopkins University in 1881.

In 1894 Dr. Williams Halsted, chief surgeon at Johns Hopkins Hospital, was the first to use rubber gloves for surgery.

In 1942 Johns Hopkins Hospital was the first to identify the polio virus.

The first intensive care unit was established at Johns Hopkins in 1955; the first shock-trauma unit, at the University of Maryland Hospital in 1961.

—*Excerpted from* Baltimore— America's City of Firsts, *a pamphlet published by Baltimore Bicentennial Celebration, Inc.*

---

campus in 1965. The 372-bed, nonprofit community hospital performs more surgeries—28,000—than any other hospital in the state. Its emergency room sees more than 20,000 patients a year, while its obstetrics wing delivers the most babies in the region. The hospital, which has been recognized nationally for its gynecological surgeries, was the first to bring laser surgery to Maryland in the mid-1970s and has continued to revolutionize the use of lasers in laparoscopic surgical techniques. The hospital has also been active in breast cancer awareness and care, providing all services—from consultation to X-rays to treatment—through its Comprehensive Breast Care Center. It's a one-stop approach to breast health. The F. Barton Harvey Institute of Human Genetics, endowed with a $1 million gift and directed by nationally known geneticist Maimon Cohen, is working to bring practical applications of genetic research, especially on the adult onset of Alzheimer's and Parkinson's diseases, to patients. Through its GBMC HealthCare program, it offers all levels of medical care, including hospice through its Hospice of Baltimore center and the Gilchrest Center.

Specialties include emergency care, obstetrics and gynecological services, cancer care, ophthalmology, otolaryngology, and laparoscopic surgery.

St. Joseph Hospital
7601 Osler Drive, Towson
(410) 337-1000
www.sjmcmd.org
Operated by the Sisters of St. Joseph, this Catholic hospital in Towson has 460 beds and employs 2,385 people. Its primary service area is Baltimore County, from Towson north to the Pennsylvania line. Specialties include cardiovascular services, open-heart surgery, obstetrics, women's services, minimally invasive surgery, and orthopedics.

Union Memorial Hospital
201 East University Parkway
(410) 554-2000
www.unionmemorial.org
The Union Protestant Infirmary was founded in 1854 to provide shelter and medical care to the sick, poor, and disabled. In 1923 its name was changed to honor the people who contributed to its founding and development. One of the first community hospitals in the nation to support graduate medical education, the hospital supports about 85 residents and fellows in areas ranging from sports medicine and orthopedics to foot surgery and obstetrics and gynecology. The hospital is nationally known for its orthopedic program. Union Memorial's more than 2,000 employees serve the people of northern

Baltimore and greater Towson. The hospital is close to Johns Hopkins University and the other colleges in the area. Specialties include mental health services, oncology, cardiac and surgery services, and women's services at the Calvert Women's Group Center.

Northwest

Kernan Hospital
2200 Kernan Drive
(410) 448-2500
www.umm.edu/kernan
Part of the University of Maryland Medical System, the 152-bed hospital began more than a century ago as a home for children with orthopedic deficits. The hospital has evolved into a site for innovative orthopedic and rehabilitation services for children and adults. Located on the border of Baltimore City and Baltimore County on a 90-acre wooded site, where founder James Kernan's original Victorian mansion still stands, the hospital, employing about 500 people, treats patients suffering from a variety of orthopedic and neurological conditions as well as sports medicine. The Maryland Centerfor Limb Lengthening, directed by Drs. Dror Paley and John Herzenberg, focuses on the cutting-edge Ilizarov technique of correcting orthopedic problems, including limb lengthening, and various congenital defects, including dwarfism.

Levindale Hebrew Geriatric Center and Hospital
2434 West Belvedere Avenue
(410) 466-8700
www.lifebridgehealth.org/Levindale
Started as the Hebrew Friendly Inn for the Old in the 1890s, the 288-bed facility is more of a hospital today. Named after Louis H. Levin, executive director of the Associated Jewish Charities from 1921 until his death in 1923, the hospital observes all Jewish laws and rituals and is strictly kosher. Now part of the Sinai Health System, of which Sinai Hospital is also a part,

Levindale has 202 nursing home beds, 50 specialty long-term stay beds, 20 psychiatric-rehab beds, and 16 comprehensive rehabilitation beds. Employing about 600 people, the hospital also provides subacute care.

Liberty Medical Center
2600 Liberty Heights Avenue
(410) 362-3000
www.bonsecours.org
Part of the Bon Secours Medical System, this 282-bed hospital is located in Northwest Baltimore. It employs approximately 725 people and provides medical, surgical, psychiatric, and gynecologic services.

Northwest Hospital Center
5401 Old Court Road, Randallstown
(410) 521-2200
www.lifebridgehealth.org/ northwesthospital
This 240-bed hospital employs about 600 doctors and serves Northwest Baltimore and the Randallstown and Pikesville areas. Specialties are minimally invasive surgery, general medical/surgical, cardiology, gynecology, and internal medicine.

Sinai Hospital
2401 West Belvedere Avenue
(410) 601-9000
www.lifebridgehealth.org/sinaihospital
Founded in 1866 as the Hebrew Hospital and Asylum, the hospital is now part of the Sinai Health System. It is Maryland's largest community hospital and the third-largest teaching hospital in the state. With 466 beds and 2,543 employees, the hospital's residency program includes doctors from Johns Hopkins University School of Medicine and other schools in Baltimore and elsewhere. Among its accomplishments are the introduction of a new procedure to heal corneal epithelial glaucoma, showing the benefits of administering magnesium to speed recovery times after open-heart surgery, development of a Minimally Invasive Direct Cardiac Artery Bypass, and the invention of Automatic Implantable Cardioverter

Defibrillator, both of which improve patient's success after heart problems. The hospital has opened a state-of-the-art Emergency Center, called ER7, which offers seven separate patient-care centers under one roof. The goal of the new center is to reduce the anxiety of patients and their families while delivering the necessary and best care possible, including concierge service, 24-hour valet parking, and 22 private waiting rooms. Sponsored by Baltimore's Jewish community, the hospital's specialties include heart services, cancer care, neurosciences, rehabilitation services, and women's and children's health care.

St. Agnes Hospital
900 Caton Avenue
(410) 368-6000
ww.stagnes.org
The first Catholic hospital in Baltimore, St. Agnes was founded by the Daughters of Charity in 1862 so they could provide nursing care to the poor. The 407-bed hospital moved to its present location, Caton Avenue at Wilkens Avenue, in 1876 and reorganized into a full-service hospital in 1906. Part of St. Agnes HealthCare, an integrated delivery system for all levels of medical care with numerous off-site centers, the hospital's 2,880 employees are part of the Maryland Health Network, which provides health services to about three million residents of Maryland and the Washington suburbs. Specialties include obstetrics, cardiology, orthopedics, and cancer services and medicine/surgery.

Southeast

Franklin Square Hospital Center
9000 Franklin Square Drive, Essex
(410) 777-7000
www.franklinsquare.org
The founding hospital in the growing MedStar Health System, this 299-bed facility is the sixth largest in Baltimore, offering subacute and acute care to eastern Baltimore County. It features one of the busiest emergency departments in central Maryland, treating more than 65,000 patients in 2000. A teaching hospital, Franklin Square has more than 750 physicians and 2,600 employees. Students at Essex Community College, located next door, receive clinical training in radiography and respiratory therapy. Its heart center is the third-largest, in terms of cases handled, in the area, while its OBTLC (Obstetrics Tender Loving Care) program, featuring home-like accommodations for birthing, makes it one of the busiest obstetrics programs in the area. The Neonatal Intensive Care Unit is the first to develop a new individualized care regimen for treatment. Its Psychology and Behavioral Medicine section handles inpatient adult, adolescent, and child psychiatric care services. Specialties include cardiology, oncology, emergency medicine, labor and delivery, and general medicine. In 2001, the hospital became the only Comprehensive Cancer Center in eastern Baltimore County.

Johns Hopkins Bayview Medical Center
4940 Eastern Avenue
(410) 550-0100
www.jhbmc.jhu.edu
Formerly known as Francis Scott Key Medical Center, this 700-bed community teaching hospital has evolved, since 1773, from an alms house to an asylum to a municipal hospital before having its ownership transferred from the city to Johns Hopkins Hospital and University in 1984. Staffed by physicians who are primarily full-time faculty at Johns Hopkins University School of Medicine, the hospital serves as a satellite to the bigger Hopkins hospital campus, although it has its own areas of specialty, too. Bayview's 2,880 employees work on a beautiful and growing 130-acre campus, featuring jogging trails and a community park-like environment. The hospital's Francis Scott Key Burn Center does amazing work for people suffering from serious burns. The hospital is home to one of Maryland's most comprehensive neonatal intensive care

units, a sleep disorder center, an areawide trauma center, and a geriatrics center.

Southwest

Harbor Hospital Center
3001 South Hanover Street
(410) 350-2563
www.harborhospital.org
Another member of the MedStar System, Harbor Hospital Center started when Dr. Harry Peterman founded the South Baltimore Eye, Ear, Nose and Throat Clinic in the industrial area of South Baltimore in 1901. Two years later, a growing population serving the industrial area, especially Bethlehem Steel shipyard, turned his clinic into a hospital that by 1918 had "an accident room" for sudden injuries, many resulting from workplace dangers. Fifty years later, in 1968, South Baltimore General Hospital moved from its home on Light Street to South Hanover Street, looking over the Patapsco River, where it continues today. Now called Harbor Hospital Center, the 376-bed, teaching hospital offers about 30 specialties, which are provided by more than 1,500 employees, many of whom are affiliated with the University of Maryland School of Medicine. Focusing on primary and secondary care, the specialties include neonatology, a chest diagnosis center, obstetrics and gynecology, pediatrics, medical/surgical, oncology, and diabetes.

North Arundel Hospital
301 Hospital Drive, Glen Burnie
(410) 787-4000
www.northarundel.org
The flagship for the North Arundel Health System, part of the University of Maryland Medical System, this 329-bed facility in southern Baltimore County employs about 1,850 people. Specialties include orthopedics, psychiatry, cardiology, and emergency medicine. A new emergency room opened in 1999, doubling the space previously available for emergency care. In

If you're heading to a hospital for the first time, call for directions to the nearest parking lot rather than driving around. People with mobility impairments can often find up-close parking by planning ahead.

1999, the emergency room saw more than 61,500 patients.

SPECIALTY FACILITIES
Downtown

Deaton Specialty Hospital and Home
611 South Charles Street
(410) 547-8500
www.umm.edu/deaton/
Part of the University of Maryland Medical System, this 380-bed facility provides specialities in wound management, traumatic brain injury, respiratory care, terminal care, clinical diatetics, and IV therapy.

Kennedy Krieger Institute
707 North Broadway
(443) 923-9400
www.kennedykrieger.org
Next door to Johns Hopkins Hospital, this facility serves more than 10,000 children annually. It specializes in the needs of children, while performing educational and research services designed to improve the lives of children. Besides providing multiple-day, home-based, and outpatient services to children suffering from disorders of the brain, either of congenital onset or acquired through injury or illness, the hospital has an internationally renowned neurogenics program that draws children from all over the world. With specialists in more than 14 disciplines, the center's scientists have identified the genes responsible for disorders including Tay-Sachs disease and adrenoleuiko dystrophy (ALD). In recent years the center has been a leader in lead-paint poisoning preven-

CLOSE-UP
Shock Trauma—"The Golden Hour"

Dr. R. Adams Cowley theorized in the 1970s that if a person suffering a serious trauma could reach specially trained doctors within one hour of suffering a life-threatening injury, the chances of survival would increase greatly.

Once he got the support of state officials, Cowley set out to create the first-of-its-kind, critical-care system. The result of his groundbreaking work is a trauma center in Baltimore bearing his name and the frequently heard sound of state police Medevac helicopters rushing patients for care. If you're near the Inner Harbor and see a large brown and yellow helicopter whizzing by, you know someone's being rushed to the R. Adams Cowley Shock Trauma Center, which is part of the University of Maryland Medical System. The Shock Trauma Center has been responsible for saving the lives of thousands of people who probably would have otherwise died of injuries sustained in car crashes, violence, and other traumas to the brain and body.

About a third of the patients treated at the Shock Trauma Center arrive by air. Fire and rescue personnel evaluate whether a helicopter ride to the Shock Trauma Center could mean the difference between life and death, but because speed is the key, rescuers often request a helicopter from the central dispatching system moments after arriving on the scene of an incident if the person appears to have been involved in any form of trauma, including head injuries, upper torso injuries, or possible paralyzing injuries.

A small percentage of the "flyouts" turn out to be unnecessary, but when it comes to saving lives, it's better to be safe than sorry. While the rescuers on the ground are removing an injured person from car or machine, the helicopter is on its way. A separate fire truck is sent to a clearing near the scene where the helicopter can land safely. Often, these landing zones are shopping center parking lots, streets, ball fields, and other open areas near the scene of an incident. The pilots of the Medevacs, many of whom served in the armed services, often land in places where it seems impossible for them to reach. Despite the risks, no pilots have ever crashed their Medevac helicopters, which are also used for aerial searches

tion and treatment as well as infant eating disorders.

Planned Parenthood of Maryland
610 North Howard Street
(410) 576–1400
www.plannedparenthoodmd.org
Planned Parenthood organizations offer affordable access to a wide range of high-quality reproductive health-care services. Medical clinics in Annapolis, Baltimore, Frederick, Owings Mills, Salisbury, and Waldor offer health care, testing, education, and counseling.

and surveillance when not being employed for medical work. The high-speed helicopters are kept in seven strategic locations across the state to minimize the time it takes the teams of two medically trained state troopers to reach the scene. The multimillion-dollar helicopters have specially equipped rear compartments allowing for stretchers, the troopers performing care, and thousands of dollars' worth of medical equipment. Rescue workers on the ground stabilize the patients before they are allowed to fly in the Medevacs, which land on the roof of University Hospital, sometimes moments after each other. Patients are met on the roof by their medical care teams and then taken quickly by elevator down two floors to the wards, where doctors and nurses complete an immediate assessment of the patient's injuries. What follows is specialized care that often takes critically injured people from the grasp of death to amazing recoveries.

About 5,508 patients per year are treated at the center, with approximately 60 percent requiring plastic or orthopedic surgery as a result of their injuries. The Shock Trauma Center operating room handled some 7,350 procedures on 1,608 patients in fiscal 1996. About 48 percent of the patients treated at the center every year have been involved in motor vehicle crashes, with about a third of the men and about a fifth of the women having tested positive for alcohol. The average blood alcohol content of those testing positive for alcohol was 0.16 in fiscal 1996, meaning the average exceeded the state's legal definition of intoxication (0.10). About 6 percent of the patients arrive as a result of violence, including half suffering gunshot wounds and 20 percent suffering stab wounds. Another 34 percent arriving at the hospital suffer from falls and recreational and industrial accidents. About three-quarters of patients are male, and about half of the patients are between the ages of 20 and 45.

Approximately 88 percent of the patients treated at the Shock Trauma Center come directly from the scene, with the remainder being sent after exceeding the capabilities of the first hospital visited.

So used to the sound of Medevacs are we in the area, that Cowley's system is often taken for granted by the very people whose lives it could one day save. His approach has been implemented all over the United States and the world, and because of it thousands of lives are saved each year.

Northeast

Sheppard Pratt Health System
6501 North Charles Street, Towson
(410) 938-3000
www.sheppardpratt.org
Moses Sheppard bequeathed his entire estate to start the Sheppard Asylum in 1862. Several years later, Enoch Pratt, who gave more than $1 million to create the free library in Baltimore bearing his name, asked that the 322-bed facility be changed to the Sheppard and Enoch Pratt Hospital after giving $1.6 million to complete the building. Today, the facility provides inpatient and outpatient behavior

health, addiction services, crisis intervention, special education schools, and employee assistance programs. Through a partnership with the University of Maryland Medical Center, the facility operates a fellowship program in child and adolescent psychiatry. Its alcohol and drug addiction services have drawn notables from all over the world who seek help at the sprawling campus in Towson in anonymity. Sheppard Pratt employs 1,500 people and has programs in 11 counties of Maryland.

Southwest

Mount Washington Pediatric Hospital
1708 West Rogers Avenue
(410) 578-8600
www.mwph.org
Founded in 1922, the 102-bed facility provides pediatric care as well as helps the children's families learn and cope. Employing about 500 people, the hospital merged with North Arundel Health System, part of the University of Maryland Medical System. The hospital's specialties include inpatient and outpatient care for infants and children with rehabilitation and special medical needs.

HOSPICE CARE

Hospice care in Baltimore is a growing industry, fueled in large part by the area's religious and familial histories. Hospice care enables people with terminal illnesses to remain in their natural settings during the final days of their lives. Instead of measures to prolong their lives with machines and technology, hospice care focuses on providing people with the medicines and services to make them as comfortable as possible. The benefits, according to proponents, are more peaceful experiences for the ill person as well as for family members and friends, who can share the final, important days of some-

one's life in the safety, protection, and security of a familiar surrounding.

Nurses, aides, and others who can ease the experience for these patients and for their families are available through the following agencies, all of which have been certified by the state and the Hospice Network of Maryland. To find out more information on hospice care in Maryland, contact the network at (410) 729-4571 or visit the Web site at www.hnmd.org.

Downtown

Bon Secours Home Health/Hospice
2000 West Baltimore Street,
(410) 837-8500

Joseph Richey Hospice Inc.
820 North Eutaw Street, (410) 523-2150

Northeast

Hospice of Baltimore
6601 North Charles Street, Towson
(443) 849-8200, www.gbmc.org

Johns Hopkins Home Hospice
2400 Broening Highway,
(410) 288-8106

Stella Maris Hospice Care Program
2300 Dulaney Valley Road, Towson
(410) 252-4500

St. Joseph Medical Center
Home Care/Hospice Program
8003 Corporate Center, (410) 931-0990

Northwest

Levindale Hebrew Geriatric
Center and Hospital
2434 West Belvedere Avenue
(410) 466-8700

VNA Hospice of Maryland
7008 Security Boulevard, Woodlawn
(410) 594-9100

Southwest

Heartland Hospice Services, Inc.
4805 Benson Avenue, (410) 247-2900

St. Agnes Home Care and Hospice
3421 Benson Avenue, (410) 368-2825

ALTERNATIVE HEALTH CARE

With a long and storied history in traditional medicine, the Baltimore area has been somewhat slow to accept alternative forms of health care. However, that is changing. New offices for holistic health providers, acupuncturists, and aromatherapists are opening all the time.

Check out the Web site www.mary landinfo.com/Medical_and_Health/ Alternative_Healthcare.

RETIREMENT

Lots of people land in Baltimore, live here for a while, and before they know it, they find it hard to imagine leaving. What grows on them is Baltimore's collection of neighborhoods. There's a feeling of home among the brick row houses, the marble steps, and roads like Hillen that begin, end, begin, end. There's a sense of familiarity that develops that is not easily purged. It's unfathomable to think of leaving an area where everyone from friends to the waitress serving them dinner at the local watering hole is familiar.

Many of Baltimore's retirees, if they aren't longtime residents of the area, once visited the city for a day, a weekend, or a week in the past, liked what they saw, and decided to retire here. Maybe they were run through the Bainbridge Naval Training Center in Cecil County while serving in the military. Maybe they were employed by a government agency such as the Social Security Administration, headquartered in Baltimore, or myriad other government agencies less than an hour south in Washington, D.C. Still other retirees are drawn to the area because of their children or grandchildren who have come to Baltimore for its colleges, its medical facilities, or its job opportunities.

Baltimore's population of people 60 and older is expanding rapidly. An estimated 15 percent of the state's five million residents have celebrated at least 60 birthdays. By 2020 the number of people blowing out at least 60 candles will make up just less than a quarter of the city's residents, following the national trend of baby boomers reaching retirement age. Even more amazing is that the fastest growing segment of this senior population is people older than 85.

This influx of older people in the area has not been lost on the developers of retirement communities and services for older people. New communities and programs are cropping up in the city and in the suburbs all the time. Where once there were few options for older people looking for a one- or two-bedroom apartment where they could live with others in their age group, now options abound—in the city, in the county surrounding the city, outside the major metropolitan area. Elevator condos, a new phenomenon designed for people who want to put their effort into activities, not getting to them, are being built increasingly in the area.

Coinciding with this increase in facilities is an ever-expanding list of activities, programs, and support services catering to older people. Everything from vouchers for transportation to a Maryland Gold Card that allows the user to obtain valuable discounts at numerous merchants in the state is available, while each jurisdiction in the state provides a "one-stop service number" for people looking for information on services and programs geared toward keeping them happy and healthy. Maryland state parks offer reduced rates to seniors, enabling them to take in the beautiful sights and sounds of nature all over the state.

Area merchants are also joining in by offering senior discounts, special senior sales, and special senior merchandise.

But don't fool yourself. This isn't Florida or Arizona—nor is it Kansas, for that matter. The area's constantly changing weather, our hazy, hot, and humid summers, and those nasty, cold, and wet winters can exacerbate everything from arthritis to asthma. But for many, good growing seasons for tomatoes and the abundance of crab cakes are reason enough to endure Mother Nature's occasional tantrums.

Even when the weather is bad, it's hard not to want to go out to take in the varied offerings of Baltimore's culture. There are matinees at the Baltimore Symphony Orchestra, at the Mechanic Theater and at

Center Stage, and the dizzying number of church, senior-center, and community group day trips to New York, Philadelphia, Atlantic City, the mountains of western Maryland, and dozens of other travel spots within the region keep older people busier than when they were working full-time.

In this chapter you'll find information on various resources, services, and senior centers in the area.

RESOURCES

Eldercare
(800) 677-1116

Calls to this toll-free number put seniors in touch with services and facilities in their area, including health care and housing options.

Home Team Program
(410) 887-2594

For seniors who want to remain in their homes but cannot be completely independent, this program offers help with friendly visits and telephone conversations, escorts to conduct personal affairs, help with shopping, chores, and maintenance, light housekeeping, and help with keeping up correspondence.

Senior Expo
(410) 887-2594
www.co.ba.md.us

This annual two-day information and resource expo sponsored by the Baltimore County Department of Aging features a wide variety of products and community services geared to make life easier for seniors and their families. More than 200 exhibitors attend this event, which takes place every October at the Timonium Fairgrounds.

Senior Information and
Assistance Program
34 Market Piace
(410) 396-1341

CARE, which stands for Baltimore City's Commission on Aging and Retirement

Education, staffs this hotline that offers referrals, assistance, and special programming information to seniors in the city. It's a good stop for people who can't find the answers to tricky questions about senior care or for those who don't know where to start their search.

Senior Information & Assistance
(410) 887-2594
www.co.ba.md.us

This should be the first place you look for answers to questions about seniors in Baltimore County. Billed as a gateway to information for seniors, their families, and caregivers, the trained staff members of the Baltimore County Department of Aging help county residents 60 and older with answers to questions, referrals and screenings. The agency operates 18 senior centers in the county. The service can also help with applications for energy assistance, homeowners/renters tax credits, and food stamps. Senior I&A also keeps a computerized directory of local senior services that can be used to access the best sources for help in your area.

Senior Digest is a large-print newspaper filled with information for seniors about local, state, and national issues of interest in Baltimore County. Issues come out eight times a year and cost $5.00 a year for a mail subscription. To subscribe, call (410) 887-3050 or go to the Web site at www.co.ba.md.us or www.senior-site.com.

Baltimore City sponsors several programs for seniors. The main number for the City Hall operator is (410) 396-3100. They can direct you to the right office.

SENIOR CENTERS

In all parts of the Baltimore area, senior centers offer activities, classes, special events, trips, guest speakers, and other programs geared toward people 55 and older. Fees range from free to a few dollars to cover the cost of supplies or a meal during a trip.

Baltimore City

The city's senior centers offer courses on computers, the Internet, financial planning, retirement savings, foreign languages, and lots of other areas of interest. The centers also sponsor trips to local and regional historical and cultural events and locations as well as visits by guest speakers and opportunities to volunteer in the community. Most centers require annual registration, costing just a few dollars, although exact amounts are set by each center.

The Baltimore City Commission on Aging (10 North Calvert Street, 410–396–4932, www.baltimorecity.gov) provides general information as well as locations of senior centers. The office can match your interest in a particular program with the senior center closest to you. Call (443) 984-2222 for housing information.

If you are looking for health screening and planning services, contact the Waxter Center for Senior Citizens at 1000 Cathedral Street, (410) 396-1324. Provided by the staff of the University of Maryland Medical System for free and reduced rates, one of the goals of this center is to ensure that older people get appropriate care for their health problems. Preventative care is always paramount.

Baltimore County

Baltimore County operates nearly 20 senior centers throughout the area. They provide training and educational programs,

May of the fine- and performing-arts organizations in the area value seniors as docents and volunteer leaders. These duties are frequently rewarded with free passes to shows and exhibits.

including courses in foreign languages, crafts, the Internet, computers, and financial planning. Senior centers also provide leads on volunteer opportunities, community events and activities, reduced-rate trips and travel, and other programs and activities of interest to people 55 and older. Several senior centers also provide fully equipped workshops with tools for use by registered members. Members have to register once a year for a small fee, but that entitles them to use the facilities and take part in the programs. Offerings vary from center to center, so it's best to call to learn what's being offered where. Call the Baltimore County Aging Department, 611 Central Avenue, Towson, (410) 887-2594, for locations of senior centers in the county.

ADULT DAY CARE

Almost Family Adult Day Care
(800) 243-2645
www.almost-family.com
Dotted throughout the Baltimore area are 10 centers that provide various services. They include door-to-door transportation, escorts to medical appointments, medical and health care, therapeutic activity programs, recreational activities, breakfast, hot lunches and snacks, and community trips.

Locations include Arbutus, (410) 242-8900; Baltimore, (410) 646-0345; Columbia, (410) 799-1228; Dundalk, (410) 282-2756; Randallstown, (410) 922-8600; Timonium, (410) 560-6717; and Towson, (410) 321-6800. Call the toll-free number to be connected to the location nearest you.

Downtown

The Hooper Center
2601 East Baltimore Street
(410) 396-8067
The Hooper Center is a city-run facility that offers adult day care to those suffering from Alzheimer's disease.

Southeast

Harbor Hospital Adult Day Care
111 Cherry Hill Road
(410) 350-8260
www.harborhospital.org
The center located at Harbor Hospital provides up to 65 participants with a wide range of programs, from meals and nursing care to activities designed to promote an active mental and physical life. Nursing care services provided include appointment scheduling, medication administration and education, exercise classes, crafts, trips, therapy, escort services, and transportation. The facility, part of Helix Health System, opened in 1996. The staff is friendly and efficient and works to provide you with the services you need.

EDUCATIONAL PROGRAMS

Arts and Aging
1300 West Mount Royal Avenue
(410) 396-4932
Sponsored by the city's Commission on Aging and Retirement Education as well as the Maryland Institute, College of Art, Arts and Aging offers classes in painting, quilting, writing, poetry, sculpture, and drama, among other topics.

Baltimore County Public Library
(410) 887-6100
www.bcplonline.org
The branches of the county library system offer programs during the day and evenings on a host of topics that may be of interest to seniors, including starting new hobbies, financial planning, and traveling on a budget. These free programs usually require advanced reservations but are free to all visitors. Programs vary from library to library.

HEALTH SERVICES

Baltimore City Health Department
(410) 396-4494
www.baltimorecity.gov

Community colleges in the area offer numerous noncredit courses for between $10 and $150, depending on the number of class meetings and the topic. The daytime courses attract lots of seniors who try their fancy at writing, art, photography, music, economics, foreign languages, bonsai, and dozens of other activities.

Geriatric evaluation services, senior planning, and other programs are available to seniors through the city's health department. The department also offers fairs and local screenings and prevention programs, including influenza vaccines each year at senior centers, schools, libraries, and shopping centers.

HealthScope
(410) 887-2594
Seniors can obtain health education, screenings, and help in managing their medicines through a variety of free seminars and programs offered all over the region.

LEGAL AID

Legal Services for Senior Citizens Program
(410) 951-7760
www.mdlab.org
If you need free legal assistance, consultations, or representation for health care issues, income maintenance, housing and utilities, protective services, unemployment benefits, or other matters, contact this service. Area lawyers provide free services to seniors in need or in risk of losing property, assets, or civil rights.

Legal Services to the Elderly
(410) 396-1322
www.baltimorebar.org
People older than 60 can be represented for free by lawyers who handle civil cases over supplemental security insurance and

Social Security matters as well as unemployment, food stamps, Medicaid/Medicare, and contract disputes. More than 3,000 lawyers take part in this program, started in 1880 by the Bar Association of Baltimore City.

Sixty Plus Wills Project
(410) 539-3112
Free assistance by qualified lawyers is provided through this project to seniors trying to draft their wills. Participating attorneys are members of the Maryland State Bar Association.

NUTRITION SERVICES

Eating Together in Baltimore City
(410) 664-0700
At senior centers throughout the city, this free service to those over 60 brings seniors together for nutritious meals and socializing. Call to register.

Meals on Wheels
(410) 558-0827
www.mealsonwheelsmd.org
If you're looking for a meal to be delivered to your door, Meals on Wheels is the ticket. Meals are provided to people in their homes five days a week through this free service.

TRANSPORTATION

CountyRide
(410) 887-2080
Low-cost transportation to doctors' appointments and to conduct other business is available to seniors regardless of what part of the county they live in. CountyRide provides door-to-door service and help to those with mobility impairments.

Elderly and Handicapped Taxi Program
(410) 664-1123
Free taxi vouchers are offered to low-income senior citizens through this program.

VOLUNTEER OPPORTUNITIES

Baltimore City Commission on Aging
10 North Calvert Street, Suite 300
(410) 396-4932
www.baltimorecity.gov
In addition to health services, senior-center locations, and a plethora of planned events, this one-stop shop for seniors in the city can help direct you to volunteer opportunities.

Retired and Senior Volunteer Program
(410) 396-8146 or
(410) 396-5253 (Baltimore City)
(410) 887-2075 (Baltimore County)
Seniors who want to offer something to their communities are matched with volunteer positions that enable them to use their previously obtained skills and experience to help others. Volunteers are also sought to help other seniors. Some seniors assist with tax preparations while others serve in schools as librarians, teachers' aides, and career counselors.

MEDIA

Baltimore's media, like the city itself, has both an international and a neighborhood focus. On the same local TV news broadcast, you're likely to hear how neighbors are taking up a collection to help a family whose home was destroyed by fire as well as coverage of the latest developments in China and the bills that were passed in Washington that day. Newspapers will run 2-inch headlines about a local high school's football victory right next to a story about the recent congressional corruption scandal.

Our port status and our location right in the center of the Eastern seaboard, spitting distance from the nation's capital, tend to make AM talk radio big in Baltimore. Music is FM radio's main focus. You can find any kind of music you like on Baltimore radio, including classical, Big Band, blues, jazz, Dixieland, country, gospel, and, of course, rock.

Baltimore has always been very big on rock 'n' roll. Back in the 1950s and '60s, we had local dance-party shows on both radio and TV. Buddy Dean and his teenage committee were the ones to watch when you got home from school every day. We watched and learned all the new dances so that at the weekend's record hop we would be in the know. (John Waters spoofed this semi-religious dedication to *The Buddy Dean Show* in his movie *Hairspray*.) Baltimore stations carried *Dance Party* and other national dance shows on radio, but the local show on Friday nights was *Lee Case and the HiFi Club*, on WCBM and sponsored by Coca-Cola. Kids could go down to the studio and be part of the show; they'd talk about local high school functions and dances and then win prizes. On Saturday nights there was always a HiFi Club record hop somewhere in town.

Print media is one of Baltimore's true passions. We have some large publishing houses, many of which are strictly book publishers and oriented toward educational or medical publishing, such as Lippincott, Williams & Wilkins, and the Johns Hopkins University Press. Agora Publishing is appreciated locally not only for the quality of its many publishing franchises but also because it embraced Baltimore's love of the past by restoring four stunning mansions in the Mount Vernon neighborhood for its headquarters. The company further ingratiated itself in the community by opening the lobbies of these buildings during neighborhood festivities such as the Flower Mart and the Baltimore Book Festival. (See the Annual Events chapter.)

Although Baltimore has only one major daily newspaper, the *Baltimore Sun,* and one main business daily, the *Daily Record,* the many free citywide weeklies and monthlies tend to make up for the loss a few years ago of the *Baltimore News American* and, more recently, the *Baltimore Evening Sun.* Baltimore also boasts newspapers that focus on specific neighborhoods, such as the *Dundalk Eagle* and the *Charles Villager,* or even a specific religion, such as the *Catholic Review.*

We also have two monthly four-color magazines that are Baltimore-centric, *Baltimore* (see the Close-up in this chapter) and *Style,* as well as some area-specific ones, such as *The Urbanite,* which chats about urban planning issues. Baltimore's active arts and culture scene is covered in two publications, *Link* and *radar.*

Subsequently we've listed some of the major players in the Baltimore media market.

NEWSPAPERS

Dailies

The Baltimore Sun
501 North Calvert Street
(410) 332-6000
www.sunspot.net
A. S. Abell originally created the *Sun* in 1837 as a penny paper to appeal to and serve Baltimore's middle class. The *Sun's* first foreign correspondent left the harbor in 1887, and its in-depth coverage of the international scene continues today with first-hand accounts from its five foreign bureaus and through the Associated Press, of which it was a founding member. The *Sun* is well known nationally for its investigative reports, and in 1997 it won particular attention for its three-part series on the continuing slave trade in Africa. Over the years the *Sun's* journalism has won 14 Pulitzer Prizes, and the company has grown into Maryland's largest news-gathering operation.

From 1920 to 1995 A. S. Abell Company also published the *Evening Sun,* which many Baltimoreans still mourn. Its focus was more community-oriented and its tone slightly more irreverent—a legacy of H. L. Mencken, Baltimore's most famous curmudgeon and founder of the *Evening Sun's* editorial page.

The *Sun,* now owned by Tribune Company, enjoys a circulation of nearly a half million for its Sunday editions. The *Sun* has a daily press run of 430,000 copies. It offers county-specific editions for Anne Arundel, Howard, Carroll, and Baltimore Counties and also recently purchased Patuxent Publishing (see the listing under Weeklies in this chapter). Weekly tabs include Thursday's "Live," a pullout that lists Baltimore happenings, while Sunday's edition has large real estate and employment sections. Additionally, the *Sun* publishes the *Daily Racing Form,* (410) 332-0129, which is a must if you've come to Baltimore to enjoy horse racing at Pimlico or Timonium.

The daily paper is 50 cents a copy; 25 cents if you buy it late in the day from a street vendor and $1.66 on Sundays. One-year subscription is $176.80.

The Daily Record
11 East Saratoga Street
(410) 752-3849
www.mddailyrecord.com
In business since 1888, the *Daily Record* delivers business and legal news to 30,000 professionals and the general public Monday through Friday. Founded by Edwin Warfield, who was the governor of Maryland in the early 1900s, the *Daily Record* continued as a family-run printing and publishing company until 1994, when Edwin Warfield IV sold the company. Not much has changed, although a Saturday publication, the *New Daily Record,* which hits the high spots of the week's events, has been added. The *Daily Record* has been in the same building for 70 years. The paper can be received through the mail by subscription ($190 per year) or bought at a newsstand for 75 cents.

Weeklies

The AFROAmerican
2519 North Charles Street
(410) 554-8200
The *AFROAmerican* has been a family-run publication for more than 100 years. The *AFRO's* first owner, John Henry Murphy Sr., was a former slave who gained his freedom with the Emancipation Proclamation of 1863. The original *AFRO* was a church paper produced by the Rev. William Alexander for members of Sharon Baptist Church. John Murphy bought the name and equipment in 1882 so that he could publish church information for the Hagerstown District of the AME Church, of which he was Sunday School Superintendent. In 1900 he joined with St. James Episcopal Church to begin publishing the *AFROAmerican Ledger.* By 1907 the paper was incorporated into the *AFROAmerican*

Selected Baltimore Firsts

The American Turf Register & Sporting Magazine, the first magazine dedicated to the subject of sports, was published here in 1829.

Ms. Dorothy Brunson became owner of WEBB-AM in Baltimore in 1979 and with that purchase became the first black woman in the United States to own a radio station.

The first telegraph line in America was completed in 1844.

—Excerpted from Baltimore— America's City of Firsts, *a pamphlet published by Baltimore Bicentennial Celebration, Inc.*

Company of Baltimore City. The paper has a distinguished history of challenging racial and political issues in its editorial pages. Today the *AFRO* enjoys a weekly circulation of 135,000 and is the best source for what's happening in the black community, both locally and nationally. Look for it every Wednesday. Newsstand price is 50 cents.

The Baltimore Business Journal
111 Market Place, Suite 720
(410) 576-1161
www.bizjournals.com/baltimore
The *Baltimore Business Journal (BBJ)* has been in business since the mid-1980s. It publishes a weekly newspaper-print mag-azine about business happenings in Balti-more as well as business guides that may be purchased separately, such as its *Book of Lists,* an indispensable guide to the top companies and their decision-makers. *BBJ* is owned by American City Business Jour-nals, which publishes similar journals for 41 other cities, including Washington, D.C.

Individual copies of the *BBJ* can be purchased for $1.25, or subscriptions are available for $85 per year.

The Baltimore Jewish Times
1040 Park Avenue, Suite 200
(410) 752-3504
www.jewishtimes.com
The *Baltimore Jewish Times* has been pub-lished every Friday since 1919. The paper

covers general national news as well as local news and issues in Baltimore's Jew-ish community, including social, political, educational, and sports topics. The paper circulates to 20,000 subscribers. It takes pride in being able to touch all members of the Jewish population from reformed to conservative. The *Jewish Times* is sold mostly by subscription ($46.15 per year). The *Jewish Times* also publishes the full-color magazines *Style* and *Chesapeake Life* and frequently offers free copies with a subscription to the newspaper.

The Catholic Review
880 Park Avenue
(443) 524-3150
www.catholicreview.org
The *Catholic Review* provides the Catholic perspective on local and national news. The most popular section is "Spotlight," which features a different regional arch-diocesan parish or school each week. The *Catholic Review* has been published by the Cathedral Foundation Press since 1913; its precursor, the *Catholic Mirror,* began in 1833. It is the largest-selling weekly news-paper in the state of Maryland, with a cir-culation of more than 72,000. Those numbers are even more remarkable given that the paper is no longer available gen-erally on the newsstand. In 1996, the *Review* went from general distribution to through-parish distribution or subscrip-tion. One distribution box remains in front

of the Basilica of the Assumption (Cathedral and Mulberry Streets), where you can pick up individual copies for 75 cents. Subscriptions are available for $35 a year, or you can request that a single copy be mailed to you for $1.75. The paper comes out every Thursday.

City Paper
812 Park Avenue
(410) 523-2300
www.citypaper.com
City Paper was started in 1977 by two students at Johns Hopkins University. Their goal was to create a liberal alternative to the mainstream papers in Baltimore, and they were very successful. Successful enough that the paper was bought by Times-Shamrock Communications in 1987. The paper is currently owned by the Scranton Times. City Paper still keeps a young voice, but it speaks honestly to the whole city and is the place Baltimoreans go to find out what's happening this week. Its calendar of events is pages and pages in length and covers everything from arts galas to movie times to yard sales. The paper prides itself on its in-depth investigative reporting and its arts coverage. There's also a really funny syndicated horoscope column, "Real Astrology," by Rob Brezsny. The paper has a circulation of 91,000 and a total readership of 300,000 and is distributed free at more than 1,800 locations in the metropolitan area. New editions come out Wednesdays; look for copies on street corners, at some corner stores, and at magazine stands. Subscriptions for home delivery are $75 per year.

Patuxent Publishing Company
10750 Little Patuxent Parkway
(410) 730-3990
www.patuxent.com
Patuxent Publishing creates area-specific newspapers in the greater Baltimore area that are delivered free right to your door once a week. The Messenger is for residents who live in the northern neighborhoods of Baltimore City, such as Roland Park, Homeland, and Guilford. Towsonians receive the Towson Times; in Owings Mills residents receive the Owings Mills Times. In all, Patuxent Publishing creates more than a dozen weeklies and in 2001, started publishing Maryland Family Magazine. These are excellent sources of information, especially if you're planning to move to a particular area. They provide in-depth cover stories, letters to the editor, crime logs, commentaries, and bulletin boards. The Enoch Pratt Library keeps back issues of these publications. Some of the papers will deliver outside their coverage areas for free or for a minimal yearly rate.

Monthlies

The Baltimore Chronicle
30 West 25th Street
(410) 243-4141
www.baltimorechronicle.com
Since 1973 this free monthly newspaper, published by Schenley Press, Inc., has had as its purpose the airing of different points of view on local as well as national issues. It pays particular attention to controversial stories that some of the bigger newspapers in town tend to overlook. All its writers are free contributors. The paper serves 27 Baltimore neighborhoods from Downtown to Towson and has a circulation of about 28,000. Look for it on store counters, or have it delivered to your home for $10 a year.

Baltimore's Child
11 Dutton Court
(410) 367-5883
www.baltimoreschild.com
Baltimore's Child is a free monthly newspaper that's been in business since the early 1980s. The paper covers topics on the diaper set as well as teens and focuses on the dissemination of practical, usable information through 55,000 monthly copies. A recent issue, for instance, had a large article that listed dance studios and dance programs in the Baltimore area. The issue also spoke to

teen spirituality and had a piece on toys. Subscriptions are available for $25.20 per year. You can find *Baltimore's Child* at newsstands, in grocery stores, street boxes, all area libraries, and other places where free papers are available.

Baltimore Gay Paper
241 West Chase Street
(410) 837-7748
www.bgp.org
Baltimore Gay Paper, part of the *Mid-Atlantic Gay Life Newspaper,* is the oldest gay paper in the region, serving the needs of this community for more than 24 years. It is published by the Gay, Lesbian, Bisexual, Transgender Community Center of Baltimore and Central Maryland, and includes breaking news, in-depth cover stories, entertainment and music information, classifieds, and regular columns written by local activists.

MAGAZINES

Baltimore
Inner Harbor East
1000 Lancaster Street, Suite 400
(410) 752-4200
www.baltimoremag.com
Started in 1907, *Baltimore* magazine is the oldest continuing city magazine in the country. It comes out monthly, and in it you'll find information that runs the gamut from who wore what at the latest charity gala to feature information about Baltimore personalities and places. A yearly subscription is $15, or you can purchase individual copies for $3.95. (For more information, see the Close-up in this chapter.)

Chesapeake Life Magazine
1040 Park Avenue, Suite 200
(443) 451-6023
www.chesapeakelifemag.com
This magazine was purchased by the *Jewish Times* and *Style* magazine in 2001, and the editorial content and graphic layout are much improved. A lifestyles magazine that focuses on food, travel, home and garden, architecture, waterfront recreation, and the arts, this is the dominant upscale magazine for the Chesapeake Bay region. It costs $4.95 an issue; a yearly subscription (six issues) is $15.00.

Link
P.O. Box 22228
(410) 327-4001
www.baltolink.org
Link is a unique arts journal on the Baltimore scene. Its tag line—"a combination of serious and eccentric writings about art and culture"—says it all. The magazine is a smart look at Baltimore arts and the art world in general, and its content straddles the line between rigorous reviews and accessible anecdotes. *Link* showcases Baltimore artists and writers in venues both in and outside town, while contextualizing the local scene on the larger stage. You can pick up *Link* in a number of area venues ($10 an issue), or you can order it online at the Web site or through Amazon.com.

Maryland Family
10750 Little Patuxent Parkway
(410) 730-3620
www.marylandfamilymagazine.com
Maryland Family, published monthly by Patuxent Publishing Company, covers topics of interest to the average young family. For instance, a recent issue had articles on theme parks and backyard cookouts, among other things. They also produce *Maryland Family's Baby Steps,* which focuses on prenatal to preschool, and were named "Best Parenting Publication" in 2002. Pick up a free copy at area grocery stores or your local doctor's office.

radar
2098 Oak Avenue
www.radarreview.org
Produced through the support of local arts organizations, *radar* is a free, pocket-

---

For bad-weather closings, listen to WBAL 1090 AM or WOSR 105.7 FM.

CLOSE-UP

Baltimore Magazine

Baltimore magazine was the first city magazine in the country. In 1991 the magazine celebrated its 90th anniversary, while the city itself was celebrating its 200th anniversary of incorporation. For almost half of Baltimore's life, *Baltimore* magazine has been chronicling the city's growth and change.

It began primarily as a business publication at a time when business in Baltimore was growing by leaps and bounds. The publication continued to change as Baltimore changed, and perhaps that's one of the main reasons it has survived all these years. In the 1950s the magazine saw itself as "square"—and weren't the '50s just the squarest? Topics tended to be about new office building dedications and . . . well . . . football. But, in the 1950s, Baltimore was football.

In the 1960s *Baltimore* magazine's life was political. By the '70s that stance had softened, but it didn't hesitate to point out Baltimore's foibles. Cover stories noted by the magazine from the early 1970s include such uplifting topics as, "The Elderly: Prisoners of Age?" (July 1972), "We Demand Our Rights: Baltimore's Homosexuals Cautiously Emerging" (April 1971) and "Black and White Together? A Discussion of Racial Attitudes" (May 1971).

By the 1980s it was keeping step with the "me generation," and was filled with articles about living well, dressing well, eating well, and, well, you get the idea.

Today *Baltimore* magazine is a little bit of all those things rolled together. In any issue you'll find pieces about Baltimore's glitterati—the balls, the concerts, and who attended and what they wore. You'll also find pieces about plain ol' Joe Smith, the carpenter who lives in Federal Hill and his point of view about

sized print publication reviewing the arts and culture in Baltimore. *Radar* comes out six times a year, and local artists and journalists write the content. The publication is new, and distribution is still a community effort. In addition to arts venues around Baltimore, distribution channels include area bookstores and the Baltimore Area Convention and Visitors' Association.

Style
1040 Park Avenue, Suite 200
www.baltimorestyle.com
Style magazine is well named. The monthly itself has glitz. It is published monthly by the *Baltimore Jewish Times* and features comprehensive articles about

living in Baltimore. In fact its subtitle is "Smart Living in Baltimore." Issues are $3.95 apiece. Yearly subscription is $15.

TELEVISION

Baltimore is considered a medium-size market with a city population of 625,000. We get all the main network channels, including Fox and Warner Brothers. Baltimore has been the launchpad for many nationally recognized talents, such as Gary Moore, Jim McKay, and Oprah Winfrey. Just as writer Anne Tyler, producer/director Barry Levinson, and writer/producer John Waters are still just being who he is and living where he lives. There are articles that cover in-depth political and social problems as well as lighthearted pieces that make sure we in Baltimore never take ourselves too seriously.

The best-selling issue every year is the "Best of Baltimore" in August. Sometime in the 1970s, the magazine decided that everyone should know where to find the best stuff, and it set out to find it. These are not arbitrary decisions. The writers go out and seek it for themselves. Much of the staff eats out all year just to decide among them what the best restaurants are. The results of their labors are profiled in such categories as best bagel, best pizza, best crab cake, etc. As you go around the city, you'll see citations on the walls of shops, lawyer's offices, neighborhood grocery stores, just every-where—that name this or that particular place as one of the Best of Baltimore.

During the year the magazine also has issues devoted in part to Baltimore's best people and services, Baltimore's 10 top hospitals, Baltimore's top singles, Baltimore's top schools, and so on.

Produced originally by Baltimore's Association of Commerce, and later the Chamber of Commerce, the magazine is now owned by Steve Geppi, a Baltimore boy whose entrepreneurial expertise took him from the level of a simple col-lector of comic books to "The Comic Book King." Geppi's Diamond Comic Distributors in Timonium is the world's largest distributor of English-language comic books, and his *Overstreet Comic Book Price Guide,* published by another publishing company he owns, Gem-stone Publishing, is said to be the uncontested bible of the comic book collector.

Serving on the boards of directors of 17 charitable organizations and a part owner of the Baltimore Orioles, Geppi is a publisher with insight into the com-munity, both now and way back when.

neighbors to us, many remember Oprah reading the news on Channel 13.

If that sounds like downhome senti-mentality, it is. Baltimore's full of sentimen-tal schtick—just watch the morning news on WJZ Channel 13, where you will see faces that have been in this town for the better part of their careers, if not their lives. And while local flavor still exists in many newsrooms, Baltimore is keeping pace with the national trend of upgraded, sophisticated broadcasting. Cable news and media mergers threaten smaller sta-tions, and many newscasts have revamped both their staff and their sets in a constant battle for viewer ratings. So far the reviews are mixed. Some welcome the fresh-faced

anchors and reporters, others mourn the loss of the local veterans they replaced. The upside to this increased competition is more news to choose from.

Local Stations

WJZ Channel 13 (CBS)
WBAL Channel 11 (NBC)
WMAR Channel 2 (ABC)
WBFF Channel 45 (FOX)
WNUV Channel 54 (WB)
WMPT Channel 22
(Maryland Public Television)
WMBP Channel 67
(Maryland Public Television)

If you want up-to-the-minute information on city politics and events, cable channel 21 provides a 24-hour focus on Baltimore. Produced by the Office of the Mayor, the station takes an in-depth look at community news through regular programming, like Cafe Baltimore, *and live press briefings by Mayor Martin O'Malley.*

Cable Services

Baltimore City and Baltimore County are served by Comcast Cable. Cable services have been getting a run for their money from the burgeoning satellite TV trend. Call Comcast Communications at (410) 649–9000.

RADIO

Baltimore still listens heavily to radio in our cars, while we work, while we hold on the telephone, while we eat. For talk, the public radio programs are available on WYPR all day, or you can do as many Baltimoreans do and tune into the personality radio on WBAL and WCBM. You'll find everything from the information-oriented guests who share their knowledge with Zoh Hieronimus (1:00 to 3:00 P.M. on WCBM) to a national feed of Rush Limbaugh's daily talk fest (noon to 3:00 P.M. on WBAL). The Mark Steiner Show on WYPR, our NPR affiliate, offers substantive conversations on local politics, culture, and lifestyle and is heard daily on 88.1 FM from noon to 2:00 P.M.

Every music station in Baltimore has a specialty. In the old days of radio, all stations did what they called "block" programming, in which each block of time was programmed separately with music, talk, game shows, or dramatic programs. Now, it's as if each station is a block of its own. We've noted the local stations under a particular category of music, and if the station's music preferences are even more specific, we've noted that in parentheses.

BIG BAND/MOR
WLG 1360 AM

CHRISTIAN
WAVA 1230 AM
WBGR 860 AM (gospel)
WCAO 600 AM
WRBS 95.1 FM

CLASSICAL
WBJC 91.5 FM

JAZZ
WEAA 88.9 FM
WYPR 88.1 FM

COUNTRY
WGRX 100.7 FM
WPOC 93.1 FM

ROCK
WHFS 99.1 FM (alternative)
WIYY 97.9 FM
WOCT 104.3 FM ('70s and '80s)
WQSR 105.7 FM ('50s, '60s and '70s)
WRNR 103.1 FM (southern fried rock and folk)
WWDC 101.1 FM (rock and alternative)
WWIN 92.5 FM (hip-hop/pop)
WWMX 106.5 FM (pop)
WXYV 102.7 FM (hip-hop/pop)

EASY LISTENING
WLIF 102.0 FM

ALL TALK
WBAL 1090 AM
WCBM 680 AM
WOL 1010 AM

TALK AND MUSIC
WYPR 88.1 FM (National Public Radio affiliate)

WORSHIP

When we think of the American colonies, we think of them as a religious haven. We often forget that, although many people emigrated to the colonies as a way to escape religious persecution in their homelands, some faced similar problems once they landed. Maryland was the first state to decree the tolerance of religion.

The decree was welcomed with a sigh of relief, and thousands of people seeking the free practice of their religions swept into the state, both from within the colonies and from other lands.

Immigrants who landed at the port of Baltimore embraced the opportunity, language, and prevailing culture of both city and country but were loath to release the religion and traditions of their ancestors. Holding on gave them security in uncertain circumstances. In many cases, building a church was one of the first things immigrants worked for as a community. Hence, historic churches color the Downtown landscape—the Lloyd Street Synagogue, the Basilica of the Assumption, Mount Vernon Methodist Church, Old Otterbein Church, and Old St. Paul's Episcopal as well as scores of other massive or intimate, stunning or simple, places of worship.

Away from Downtown, in areas that were still considered country in the 1800s, there are some fascinating "country" churches, like St. John's Church of Huntingdon in Waverly, originally built in 1846, or the chapel at the Church of the Redeemer in Charles Street, which is a Victorian masterpiece. (See the Attractions chapter for more information about visiting historic churches.)

Of course, not all of our houses of worship are old. A great many were built in the 1950s and '60s, when postwar building was at its height. We may boast the first Catholic Cathedral in the United States (the Basilica of the Assumption, see the

Attractions chapter), but we also have the Cathedral of Mary Our Queen, dedicated in 1959. We may be the cradle of Methodism in the United States, but our 290 Methodist locations show that the baby has grown up.

The fact is that, historic or modern, Gothic cathedral or one-room country chapel, Baltimore boasts more than 2,100 churches and 55 synagogues.

The Society of Friends has two large meeting houses in North Baltimore. The Church of Jesus Christ of Latter-day Saints has six churches scattered across town. Historic Baptist and African Methodist Episcopal congregations abound, and the Catholic Church is pretty much everywhere. (Don't forget we began as a Catholic state.) If you are Jehovah's Witness, Pentecostal, Mennonite, or Eastern Orthodox, you'll find places to worship here. Muslims, Buddhists, and Hindus are also among our numbers. And in almost every inner city neighborhood, there are soldiers of the Salvation Army.

If the city were cut up into square-mile portions, it would be doubtful that there would be an area that did not include at least one house of worship. Sometimes, as you ride through the city, it seems as if there is a church on every block!

Baltimore's houses of worship are very neighborhood-oriented, very community-oriented. Particularly in the ethnic neighborhoods, the life of the neighborhood revolves around the church. For instance, although there are Greek Orthodox churches in other locations, in Greektown, everyone knows St. Nicholas, whose full name is St. Nicholas Church–Greek Orthodox Community. It's where the Greek Festival is held every year, and where neighbors celebrate their culture, as well as their faith (see the Annual Events chapter).

West Baltimore has a large Jewish population. Within that area there are

 CLOSE-UP

Tiffany Windows in Baltimore

Baltimore has its share of Tiffany stained-glass windows and many can be found in their original architectural settings. At the turn of the last century, Baltimore's gentry had a strong pipeline to Louis Comfort Tiffany's New York studio. Many area churches, like St. Paul's Episcopal Church on Charles Street and First Presbyterian on Madison, requisitioned his stained glass in the early 1900s. One of Tiffany's most valued commissions was created for the private home of Elizabeth Garrett in the 1880s. That window now hangs in the Baltimore Museum of Art, while the Garrett Mansion in Mount Vernon remains one of the city's finest architectural treasures.

Early in his career, Louis Comfort Tiffany (1848–1933) was a landscape artist known as a colorist for his vibrant sweeps of vivid hues. He later turned his attention to pouring glass and—along with his contemporary John LaFarge—led a revolution in American stained-glass art. England and Europe were controlling the trade of stained glass in the 1800s, but the inferior quality of the product and the lackluster artwork spurred Tiffany and LaFarge to challenge the accepted norms. Both experimented with new techniques, ulti-mately developing "opalescent" glass, a semi-translucent material that remains unique to American glass art.

One of the best collections of Tiffany stained glass can be found at Brown Memorial Church in Bolton Hill. The church commissioned stained-glass windows at the apex of Tiffany's career and they exemplify the best of his craft. The 11 windows recently underwent an extensive restoration, capping off a $1.8 million rehab of the Gothic Revival church built in 1870. James E. Hauser of Hauser Art Glass in Minnesota per-formed the restoration on the glass. The two largest windows in the transepts, known as the Smith and Babcock Memorial windows, measure an astounding 16 feet wide by 32 feet tall. They are the largest Hauser has encoun-tered in his 50 plus years as a restorer of Tiffany glass. "This is the finest col-lection of Tiffany windows in the coun-try and quite possibly the world," Hauser argues.

Brown Memorial Presbyterian Church, located at 1316 Park Avenue, is open for tours to the general public. You can find a map to their exquisite windows on their Web site www.brown memorialparkavenue.org or by calling (410) 523–1542.

neighborhoods that are Hasidic, neighbor-hoods that are Reformed, neighborhoods that are Conservative. They wrap around, for the most part, those synagogues that cater to their needs.

In tandem, there are large areas in West Baltimore that are almost exclusively African-American. In these neighborhoods, you will find some of the largest and most socially and politically active African Methodist Episcopal churches in Baltimore.

On the other hand, there are a great many neighborhoods that are totally eclectic in race, culture, ethnicity, and religion, where populations rotate on a continuing basis. Even so, these neighborhoods tend to use their churches, synagogues, and meeting houses as centers for community functions, such as covered-dish suppers, flea markets, and community meetings. Churches in the inner city and midtown areas have big halls, big parking lots, and big chapels where many people can gather for these functions without discomfort. Worship centers also tend to be right in the middle of the community and easy to get to, as well as nonthreatening to people who might otherwise be shy of attending a large group function.

Community doesn't always mean the physical community that surrounds a church, however. It can also mean a spiritual community that is bound by some other common element besides where one lives. The Rock Church, an Evangelical church near Towson, is said to boast parishioners from as far away as northern Virginia. Quite a few Korean Methodist and Presbyterian churches dot the greater Baltimore landscape, and there are churches that serve special groups, such as the gay community.

And we do mean serve. All religious communities contribute to life in the city. There are houses of worship that have after-school care for children, those that have reading programs, health programs, and just provide a social center, particularly for the community's youth, that is safe and supervised. Even small churches like St. Vincent de Paul Church in Jonestown reach out into the community weekly. St. Vincent distributes more than 300 bags of food every week. It also sponsors a daycare center and provides cosponsorship to two East Baltimore, primarily African-American, parochial schools.

Another church-created service organization is Tri-Churches Housing, Inc. It's a 20-year-old housing development corporation that was formed in the interests of the Washington Village and Pigtown neighborhoods by three neighborhood churches, St. Jerome Roman Catholic, Dorguth

Memorial United Methodist, and St. Paul the Apostle Episcopal. (Scott Street Baptist has since joined the group.) Its ecumenical mandate is to create housing that is affordable for low and moderate income levels. In other words, members renovate. The service turns vacant housing into resident-owned housing, which makes the neighborhood safer. It also benefits the city since resident-owned housing means another taxpayer on the rolls.

One of the largest charity enterprises in the city, and the largest soup kitchen in the state, began with the simple charitable act of handing a homeless man a bologna sandwich. The pastor at the Basilica of the Assumption made it a practice to hand out sandwiches to the hungry, but by the mid-1970s, he was handing out more than 200 a day. By 1979 Catholic Charities was discussing the need for a soup kitchen nearby, and, in 1981, Our Daily Bread opened its doors. Although run by Catholic Charities, more than 6,000 volunteers from 80 churches, synagogues, groups, and businesses staff the facility, Monday through Sunday, rain, shine, snow, or cold. At last count, Our Daily Bread was serving more than 825 meals a day to Baltimore's hungry and homeless.

Such interfaith action in behalf of the community is common in Baltimore and in Maryland. We take pride not just in our tolerance, as our forefathers decreed, but also in our acceptance of one another.

RESOURCES

The following resources can provide you with specific information about houses of worship in greater Baltimore. Specific times of services are listed in the Saturday edition of the *Baltimore Sun*.

Baha'i Faith
(410) 521-0841
www.greaterbaltimorebahais.org
The Baha'i Faith has no address because there are no churches, synagogues, or meeting houses where its members wor-

 **WORSHIP**

ship or its leaders administrate. The contact number will put you in touch with the
information services for the Baltimore City
Spiritual Assembly. Meetings that discuss
community business and provide fellowship are held every 19 days, and educational firesides are held in members'
private homes in the greater Baltimore
area almost every night of the week.

Baltimore Baptist Association
8203 Harford Road
(410) 882-0000
www.bbasbc.org
The Baltimore Baptist Association (BBA)
serves as a resource for Baptist churches
in the greater Baltimore area. When you
call, you can request the name of a Baptist church in or near your neighborhood,
or you can request a church according to
more personal preferences. If you don't
care how far you have to drive to church,
but you know you want one that does a
lot of singing and a lot of community outreach, the BBA will help you find it. BBA
also offers outreach ministries to different
parts of the city, including a port ministry
that serves sailors. It also has a counseling
service for those in need, (410) 426-2359.

Baltimore Eckankar Center
2318 North Charles Street
(410) 235-0073
The Baltimore Eckankar Center offers
worship services Sundays at 11:00 A.M.
and book discussions Mondays at 7:00 P.M.
The center also serves as an informational
resource for anyone who is interested in
finding out more about Eckankar and its
religion of light and sound.

Baltimore Jewish Council
5750 Park Heights Avenue
(410) 542-4850
www.associated.org
The Baltimore Jewish Council is what you
might call a resource for resources. It has
information about congregations as well
as local and national agencies. It also
serves as the community relations and
political arm of the Jewish community.

Baltimore-Washington Conference,
United Methodist Church
7178 Columbia Gateway Drive
Columbia
(410) 309-3400 or (800) 492-2525
www.bwconf.org
The Baltimore-Washington Conference
represents 750 Methodist congregations in
Baltimore, Washington, D.C., and West Virginia. It acts as a clearinghouse for information about what those churches are
doing. It provides the location of churches
in the area through its District Office (Ext.
440), and it reports church happenings
through its newspaper, *United Methodist
Connection*. The conference also offers a
prayer line at (800) 936-6893, which during off-hours has a tape recording but
Monday through Friday from 8:30 A.M. to
4:30 P.M. has a live person at the end of the
line who will be happy to chat with you
and/or pray with you.

Catholic Center, Baltimore Archdiocese
320 Cathedral Street
(410) 547-5555
www.archbalt.org
The Catholic Center houses the administrative and service units of the Archdiocese in Baltimore. Through the previously
listed number you can reach the Office of
the Archbishop, the offices of Associated
Catholic Charities, the Department of
Catholic Education Ministries, the Department of Management Services, and the
Department of Human Resources Development. The operator will direct you to
the correct department or give you
another number to call.

A directory of Catholic churches in Baltimore is available from the *Catholic
Review*. Call (443) 524-3150 for information. The price of the directory is $25 if
you pick it up and $27 if you have it sent
to you.

Central Maryland Ecumenical Council
4 East University Parkway
(410) 467-6194
The Central Maryland Ecumenical Council
is in the business of promoting Christian

Selected Baltimore Firsts

Baltimore claims the first Methodist church in America and the first American Methodist Bishop. The Lovely Lane Meeting House, now at the corner of St. Paul and 22nd Streets, is the oldest continuously active Methodist congregation in the United States. The Reverend Francis Asbury became bishop in the same year the original Lovely Lane Meeting House was built, 1974.

The first Catholic Diocese in the United States was established here in 1789. This being the case, it seems appropriate that Baltimore also boasts the first Catholic Cathedral in the United States. The Basilica of the Assumption of the Blessed Virgin Mary—simply known around town as The Basilica—was completed in 1821. It was designed by B. H. Latrobe.

Elizabeth Seton is the first native-born American citizen to be canonized a saint. Born in 1809, she achieved sainthood in 1975.

The Oblate Sisters of Providence, the first black Catholic religious order of nuns, was founded by Mary Elizabeth Lange in 1829. She is currently being considered for sainthood.

America's first independent Unitarian Church was founded here in 1817. The first Annual Conference of the African Methodist Episcopal (AME) Church met here in 1817.

In 1834 Baltimorean William Douglas became the first black man to be ordained to the Episcopal Ministry. The first Young Men's Christian Association building was erected in Baltimore in 1859.

The Young Men's Hebrew Association, founded in 1854, erected the first Jewish Community Center. This may have been the work of the first ordained rabbi to come to the United States, Rabbi Abraham Rice, who served the Baltimore Hebrew Congregation beginning in 1840.

Henrietta Szold was the first woman to study at the Jewish Theological Seminary in America. She graduated in 1902 and went on to establish a few Baltimore firsts of her own, such as the first chapter of Hadassah.

—Excerpted from Baltimore— America's City of Firsts, *a pamphlet published by Baltimore Bicentennial Celebration, Inc.*

union. To this end, the council organizes ecumenical worship services, puts on ecumenical concerts, and helps day camps organize ecumenical services for children. In addition, the council keeps a database of more than 1,900 churches in the Central Maryland area (Baltimore City and its five surrounding counties). Churches are listed by both location and denomination, and anyone is welcome to request information.

The Ecumenical Institute of Theology
5400 Roland Avenue
(410) 864-4200
www.stmarys.edu
The Ecumenical Institute is at St. Mary's Seminary and University (see the Education chapter). It offers a platform for investigation and argument of religious and philosophical topics.

Jewish Information Service
5750 Park Heights Avenue
(410) 466-4636
The local Jewish Information Service has a list of all the synagogues in the Baltimore area, but because it is only one arm of a national information service, it can also help you locate synagogues in other parts of the country as well.

Theosophical Society in Maryland, Inc.
523 North Charles Street
(410) 727-3471
The Theosophical Society is a world organization that encourages the comparative study of religion and philosophy. A taped message notes the week's offerings as well as provides you with contact numbers for more information.

INDEX

Hull Street Blues Cafe, 116, 127
Hunt Cup, 188
Hunt Valley, 62
Hunt Valley Antiques, 155
Hunt Valley Antiques Show, 186
Hyatt Regency, 81–82

I

I-70 East and I-70 West Welcome
    Centers, 246
I-70 highway, 19
I-83 highway, 17
I-95 highway, 17
I-95 South and I-95 North Welcome
    Centers, 246
I-395 highway, 18
I-695 highway, 17
I-795 highway, 18
I-895 highway, 18–19
Idlewylde, 61
IMAX Theater, 167–68, 213
India Day, 196
IND (Institute of Notre Dame), 288, 290–91
indoor lacrosse, 275. *See also* spectator
    sports
indoor soccer, 276–77. *See also* spectator
    sports
Inn at Government House, The, 92
Inn at Henderson's Wharf, 82
Inner Harbor, 195
Inner Harbor Easter Celebration, 189
Inner Harbor East Marina, 239
Inner Harbor Ice Rink, 167
Inner Harbor Marina of Baltimore, 239–40
Institute of Notre Dame (IND), 288,
    290–91
insurance, renters, 74
interstates and highways, 17–19
Inverness Park boat ramp, 240
In Watermelon Sugar, 140
Irish Festival, The, 198
Irvine Nature Center, 180
Irvington, 72

J

J. Patrick's Irish Pub, 127
Jack and Jills, 225–26
Jazz House West, 146
jazz radio, 332
Jeannier's, 113
Jeffersonian architecture, 53

Jericho Covered Bridge, 172
Jerry's Belvedere Tavern, 110–11
Jerusalem Mill/Jericho Covered Bridge, 172
Jewish Family Services, 309
Jewish Information Service, 338
Jewish Museum of Maryland, 167
Jimmy's Cab, 23
J&M Antiques, 154
John Brown's Fort at Old Arsenal
    Square, 259
Johns Hopkins Bayview Medical Center,
    314–15
Johns Hopkins Home Hospice, 318
Johns Hopkins Hospital, The, 308–9
Johns Hopkins University, 278, 298
Johns Hopkins University Spring Fair, 190
Jones Falls Expressway, 17
jousting, 272–73
Joy America Cafe, 104, 105
Jumpin' Jim's Jukeboxes, 155–56

K

Kawasaki and Kawasaki Café, 104
Kelly's Cue Club, 225
Kennedy Krieger Institute, 315–16
Kent County Chamber of Commerce, 252
Kent County Office of Tourism, 14
Kentrikon Music Store, 145
Kernan Hospital, 313
kidstuff, 176–83
Knish Shop, The, 113

L

L.A. Herstein and Company, 152
lacrosse, 275–77. *See also* spectator sports
Ladew Topiary Gardens and Manor
    House, 247
Lafayette Square, 67
Lake Montebello, 217
Lancaster, PA, 245–47
Lancaster County, PA, 245
Latino Fest, 194
Lauraville, 58
Laurel Race Course, 273–74
Leakin Park, 219
legal aid for seniors, 323–24. *See also*
    retirement
Legal Services for Senior Citizens
    Program, 323
Legal Services to the Elderly, 323–24
lemon stick, 197

HELP US KEEP THIS GUIDE UP TO DATE

Every effort has been made by the authors and editors to make this guide as accurate and useful as possible. However, many things can change after a guide is published—phone numbers change, facilities come under new management, etc.

We would love to hear from you concerning your experiences with this guide and how you feel it could be improved and be kept up to date. While we may not be able to respond to all comments and suggestions, we'll take them to heart and we'll also make certain to share them with the authors. Please send your comments and suggestions to the following address:

> The Globe Pequot Press
> Reader Response/Editorial Department
> P. O. Box 480
> Guilford, CT 06437

Or you may e-mail us at:

> editorial@GlobePequot.com

Thanks for your input, and happy travels!

ABOUT THE AUTHORS

ELIZABETH A. EVITTS

Elizabeth A. Evitts is a screenwriter and an award-winning journalist living in Baltimore. As a contributing writer for *Baltimore* magazine, she writes about the city's vibrant arts, architecture, and media scenes. Her reporting earned top accolades from the Society of Professional Journalists in 2002 and 2003. She also contributes features on architecture, design, and the arts to *Style* and *Chesapeake Life* magazines, and her work has appeared on the Web at Slate.com.

NANCY JONES-BONBREST

Nancy Jones-Bonbrest is a native Baltimorean who grew up in Middle River, a water-oriented community in eastern Baltimore County.

As a freelance writer, her articles have appeared frequently in the *Baltimore Sun*, the *Daily Record,* and the *Country Chronicle*. Nancy also does writing consulting in the philanthropic community and has worked as a stringer for the Baltimore office of the Associated Press.

Nancy holds a bachelor's degree in journalism from the University of Maryland College Park.